Global Perspectives on Technological Innovation

A Volume in
Contemporary Perspectives on Technological Innovation,
Management, and Policy

Series Editor:
Bing Ran, *Pennsylvania State University at Harrisburg*

Contemporary Perspectives on Technological Innovation, Management, and Policy

Bing Ran, Editor

Global Perspectives on Technological Innovation (2013)
edited by Bing Ran

The Dark Side of Technological Innovation (2013)
edited by Bing Ran

Global Perspectives on Technological Innovation

Edited by

Bing Ran
Pennsylvania State University At Harrisburg

Information Age Publishing, Inc.
Charlotte, North Carolina • www.infoagepub.com

Library of Congress Cataloging-in-Publication Data

Global perspectives on technological innovation / edited by Bing Ran.
p. cm. -- (Contemporary perspectives on technological innovation, management, and policy)
ISBN 978-1-62396-058-2 (paperback) -- ISBN 978-1-62396-059-9 (hardcover) --
ISBN 978-1-62396-060-5 (ebook) 1. Technological innovations--Management.
2. Information technology--Management. 3. Business
enterprises--Technological innovations. I. Ran, Bing.
HD45.G558 2012
658.5'14--dc23

2012042006

Printed in the United States of America

CONTENTS

v

PREFACE

Bing Ran

The central theme of this book series is to explore the contemporary perspectives on managing technological innovations and related strategic policy issues. I had two objectives when editing this book: one, to be open to all potential topics that I believe need attention within the broad theme of the management of technology and innovations; and two, to promote an interdisciplinary scholarship and dialogue on the management of innovation and technological change in a global context from strategic, managerial, behavioral, and policy perspectives.

Papers selected in the first two volumes have nicely addressed these two objectives by their in-depth exploration of the four prominent sets of questions:

1. What are the current research interests and the global applications of the technological innovation?
2. What is the practicality of the research on technological innovation implementation to foster success and growth?
3. What are the sociotechnical challenges behind innovation and creativity that might outweigh the benefits?
4. What are some of the new principles/practices/perspectives on our understanding of the global technological innovation?

In these two volumes, authors from around the world have made significant attempts to address these four questions, thus I hope that readers who are interested in learning the most contemporary perspectives on the

Global Perspectives on Technological Innovation, pp. vii–ix
Copyright © 2013 by Information Age Publishing
All rights of reproduction in any form reserved.

technological innovation will be impressed, enriched, and intrigued by their analyses in each chapter.

The selection of these 29 chapters (the first volume contains 15 chapters; and the second volume contains 14 chapters) reflects truly the global nature of the research on technological innovations. Authors from Asia, North America, South America, Africa, Europe, and Australia were brought together here to discuss and exchange their perspectives on the delicacy of the technological innovation, its profound effects on management within, between, and across organizations, and the challenges and obstacles that are at risk of occurring regarding technological innovations. At least two benefits could be envisioned by this global perspective in the book. First is the practicality of the research on technological innovations for organizations around the world who must compete in a global economy and hence need to understand the fundamentally diverse perspectives regarding technological innovation; and the second is the academic curiosity for researchers who are interested in learning new perspectives, new understandings, and the counter intuitive challenges and obstacles behind technological innovation management.

The research selected in the two volumes puts heavy emphasis on how organizations can implement technological innovations into the workplace and how these apparatuses can impede or foster organizational success and growth. Scholars have explored extensively, for example, how alliance portfolios assist overcoming resource constraints in the implementation of new technological innovations; how the improper separation of work life and home life for employees when adopting new technologies brings difficulties and negative consequences; how the technology transfer is linked to the different technological forms; how business models and other related strategic components in organizations will influence the adaptation of new technological innovations; how continuous commitment towards research on technology increases the chance of both accidental and deliberate discovery of future markets; how the partnership and collaboration between organizations (especially with universities) or even within organizational units can influence innovation positively or negatively and might possibly have a spillover effect on innovational capabilities for the next generation; how intellectual property protection for open innovations is benefiting or hindering competitive advantages for different organizations; how educational institutions could utilize technological innovations to help and prepare students proactively for their professional successes; and how pressure-filled crisis management demands real-time innovation through reflective learning and open-mindedness.

This exploration reveals the great challenges behind management of technology and innovation. Almost all chapters discussed the difficulties, the obstacles, and the drawbacks of bringing in technological innovation to organizations. For example, researchers in these two volumes have studied whether the costs of implementing innovative technologies is contingent upon various organizational factors and might outweigh the benefits. Organizations in different industry sectors might not be ready to implement new technological innovations due to such issues as internal financial means or external funding support, sociodemographic factors, generational gaps, competition from other organizations, ethical and moral challenges, the old but effective technologies, the compatibilities of the technological innovation with current business models, lack of cooperation and support from universities and government programs, and too much or too few risk management, etc. As observed by researchers, innovation and technology management requires considering a constellation of many internal and external aspects to be more successful.

Some new principles, theories, and practices were also proposed in these two volumes on the global technological innovation. Readers could, to list a few as examples, taste a new framework on the integration of two popular competitive advantage perspectives, explore boundary conditions and tradeoffs for innovation collaborations, discover a new model on organizational media choice, apply the technology roadmapping in company levels, experience the newly established correlations between innovation implementation and categories of implementers' needs, conceptualize a theory on zero latency support for incident management, research an integrative model on nonacceptance of the product innovations, evaluate a framework on ethical dilemma for controversial technological innovations, analyze a distributive innovation framework that orchestrates the innovative contributions from multiple actors in the value network, verify a theory on how external factors impact perceptions of local business climate, appreciate an integrative innovation model for the adoption of innovative instructional technology in higher education, and comment a conceptual model on how structural and content factors in alliance portfolios jointly impact a firm's ability to innovate.

As the editor, I hope readers of these two volumes could enjoy these chapters by its global nature, the practicality orientation, the critical perspective, and the new theories and practices embedded in the selected research. This book would not be a possibility without the direct help from George F. Johnson, the publisher of IAP. George has been a safe net and a mentor for me in every step of editing the book. Whenever I have questions or difficulties, I know I can rely on him for guidance. Thank you George! I would also like to thank Amanda Uriarte from IAP, Frank Aguirre from IAP, and my research assistant, James Valentine, for their valuable assistance and support.

Let the journey begin here....

CHAPTER 1

COMPARING PRE- AND POST-INTERNET TECHNOLOGIES FOR THE MANAGEMENT OF THE SUPPLY CHAIN

A Technology Acceptance Model View

Damien Power

ABSTRACT

This chapter compares use of technologies used for the management of the supply chain over a 6-year period. A technology acceptance model (TAM) perspective is adopted in order to provide a basis in theory for this comparison. The data on which this chapter is based were gathered from three separate surveys conducted within the membership of GS1 (formerly EAN) Australia and CIPSA (the Chartered Institute of Purchasing and Supply Australia). The evidence from this study indicates that on average the use of Internet based technologies over the 6-year period of this study had not

Global Perspectives on Technological Innovation, pp. 1–30

1

increased substantially in the manufacturing, wholesale distribution and retail sectors. This is despite these technologies being perceived to be characteristically improved in terms of both ease of use and perceived benefits from use—both characteristics that would indicate higher levels of use and acceptance as predicted by TAM. Structural and organizational impediments to implementation, both within firms and the supply chain, were identified. The TAM model was found in this study to not predict higher usage as expected, a result attributed to the complexity of organizations, and the limitations inherent in trying to apply theories developed to predict individual actions at an organizational level.

INTRODUCTION

The potential for application of technology to the management of organizations, and in a wider sense to the management of supply chains, has been debated in both academic and practitioner literature for many years. This debate has gained renewed focus as Internet based technologies have been developed and applied to the problems of information flows between trading partners (Cagliano, 2005; Cantor & MacDonald, 2009; Foster, 2007; Johnson & Whang, 2002; Netessine, 2006). The debate came originally to prominence as a result of writings (Porter, 2001) indicating that extended use of Internet technologies will require organizations to differentiate strategies through innovative value chain design and positioning. The opposite view, however, has been taken by Tapscott (2002), stating that use of the Internet enables business model innovation through structural and cultural change.

In order to provide some clarity to this debate, this chapter examines empirical evidence of perceptions of comparative usage, costs and benefits derived from both pre- and post-Internet technology implementations using data gathered over a 6-year period. The intention is to establish (within the constraints of the samples) the degree to which pre- and post-Internet technologies differ in levels of use, perceptions of cost/benefit, and contribution to business outcomes over that period of time. The technology acceptance model (TAM) is used as theoretical lens.

DEFINITIONS

Business-To-Business E-Commerce (B2B): The exchange of products, services or information between trading partners using electronic networks. The current broader definition of e-commerce is the buying and selling of goods and services on the Internet. Traditionally B2B e-commerce was carried out using EDI via proprietary networks. Since the development of the Internet, this has become a widely accepted medium for these types of transactions. The focus is on transactions between businesses rather than between businesses and consumers.

Supply Chain: "encompasses all activities associated with the flow and transformation of goods from the raw material stage (extraction), through to the end user as well as all information flows." (Handfield & Nichols, 1999)

Supply Chain Management: "the integration of these activities through improved supply chain relationships, to achieve a sustainable competitive advantage." (Handfield & Nichols, 1999)

Advance Shipment Notification (ASN): Method of notifying (typically) retailers by electronic means of the amount and type of product shipped to a distribution centre from (typically) a manufacturer. This allows prereceipt processing to be carried out at the distribution centre enabling better planning and allocation of workloads.

EAN (now GS1) System: A system for identifying products, shipments of products, individual organizations and locations by assigning each a unique (worldwide) identifying number. This number is represented on either a barcode or an RFID chip that can be input into a computer system. Also incorporated into the system is the computer-to-computer exchange of information collected from this barcode, and other data related to the transacting and storage of these goods. The traditional means for this exchange has been through the use of Electronic Data Interchange (EDI).

EDI Gateway: Provides a network connection for EDI transmissions between trading partners. This gateway manages networking and message formats, as well as the administration of electronic trading relationships.

EDIFACT: Electronic Data Interchange for Administration, Commerce and Transport. A set of standards, directories and guidelines for the electronic interchange of structured data related to trade in goods or services, between independent computerized information systems (Anonymous, 2001).

Electronic Data Interchange (EDI): The computer-to-computer transmission of (business) data in a standard format (Anonymous, 2001).

Electronic Funds Transfer (EFT): Transfer of funds electronically between trading partners.

Evaluated Receipts Settlement (ERS): A method for automating payment to suppliers in conjunction with the use of advance shipment notices (ASNs). Typically, accounts payable would transmit (via electronic funds transfer (EFT) payment based on a formula such as: order cost x ASN quantity.

Extensible Markup Language (XML): XML is a data communication language that can specify the data and metadata relating to text documents (but not formatting information). In this sense it is more advanced and simpler to use the (say) mapping technologies, such as are used for traditional EDI. It can also be used as a means of defining data and communicating between applications.

XML/EDI: An open standard for the transmission of EDI documents via the Internet using a web-based markup language (XML).

e-Catalogs: Electronic collections of information about the products and/or services offered by an organization (Segev, Wan, & Beam, 1995). These can take many different forms, from a simple list of products and services provided by a company web page through to an intelligent catalogue able to retrieve information from multiple sources and present in a personalized format (Baron, Shaw, & Bailey, 2000)

Extranets: subset of the Internet providing a secure means for the transmission of encrypted messages allowing trading partners within supply chains to connect to each other's internal networks and share critical information at a low cost.

LITERATURE REVIEW

Cognate Theory

The theoretical lens for this study is the TAM. This theory has been most usually applied to the adoption of technology by individuals, and in particular that of personal computer use (Brown & Venkatesh, 2005; Venkatesh & Brown, 2001). The major thrust of this theory is that intention to use a technology is predicted by the combined effect of ease of use and perceived benefits, and the actual use will follow from intention to use (Davis, 1989; Huff & Munro, 1985). Although this theory has been tested empirically with supportive results in the personal adoption context there still remain doubts about whether (a), TAM has the same predictive validity in an organizational domain (Zheng et al., 2006); and (b), if the relationship between intention to use and actual use is empirically robust (Turner, Kitchenham, Brereton, Charters, & Budgen, 2010). Recent evidence suggests that the role of contingent effects such as culture and technology type also play a role (Schepers & Wetaels, 2007). The wider application of this model still remains an important field of potential research in the area of adoption of IT and related technologies by organizations (King & He, 2006). This study takes the position of looking at how both perceived ease of use, and perceived benefits from use, of supply chain enabling technologies affects actual use within organizations.

Perceived Ease of Use

Research from the US has indicated that application of Internet based technologies to facilitate better management of supply chains has increased and was being driven by "measurable goals" (Lancioni, Smith, & Schau, 2003). Comparing the results of two surveys it was found that usage of Intranets, extranets, and involvement in EDI programs had increased. Earlier studies of the adoption and diffusion of EDI (and other pre-Internet) technologies have shown, on the other hand, that use and application of these technologies had been relatively slow and more successful when implemented voluntarily rather than when imposed by a trading partner (Ramamurthy, Premkumar, & Crum, 1999; Rassameethes & Kurokawa, 2000; Raymond & Bergeron, 1996). An early study of technology uptake in the B2B context conducted by Burnell (1998) cites U.S. research findings that whilst 92% of retailers surveyed were sharing information with customers and suppliers, 79% were using fax or paper based methods. Another study conducted around the same time (again in the United States) found similarly that only 13% of purchase orders across 25 industries (493 companies) were transmitted via EDI (Carter & Hendrick, 1997). Other research in the FMCG (fast moving consumer goods) sector has shown that adoption of technologies of this type is often restricted to particular types of organizations (e.g., larger companies) (Power, 2002; Power & Simon, 2004). These results are contrasted with the finding from the Automotive sector that company size was not a significant determinant of EDI integration (Rassameethes & Kurokawa, 2000). Some also indicate that adoption of EDI technology, rather than suffering from application of Internet based alternatives, is actually increasing as XML/EDI standards become more widely accepted (Johnston & Mak, 2000; Zhang, 2006). The use of the Internet would therefore enhance current systems and technologies, rather than eliminate use of technologies such as EDI. In the early stages of transition between technological options for connecting between trading partners there was evidence, however, that firms were offering trading partners access to their internal networks via the Internet and thus avoiding transmission charges and monthly fees incurred through the use of value added networks for EDI transmission (Mohta, 1997; Segev, Porra, & Roldan, 1997; Truman, 2000). Whatever the result of this change in technological emphasis, a strong theme to emerge is that the Internet provides improved access to integration technologies for a greater number of organizations (Bao, 2005; Netessine, 2006; Rahman, 2003). Characteristic of Internet based technologies is that they are openly accessible to anyone for a generally low cost, creating a worldwide "public good." The "open" nature of this network enables potentially better business to business communication, and a more effective means by which business can be transacted between trading partners within supply chains (Garcia-Dastugue, 2003). The question remains, however, whether Internet based technologies are being used more extensively than older technologies (such as EDI using value added networks) to enable greater levels of integration. Propositions 1 and 2 are stated in order to provide a framework for testing whether this is the case. It may be that there are many companies using internet technologies, but the key issues are: (a) whether use related to promoting greater levels of integration with trading partners is greater than that of longer established technologies; and (b) whether usage is growing significantly over time.

Proposition 1: Usage of Internet based technologies for management of the supply chain will be higher than that of pre-Internet technologies

Proposition 2: Usage of Internet based technologies for management of the supply chain is increasing significantly over time

Perceived Usefulness

Cost/Benefit of Technology

Investment in information technology based solutions to enable the development of new business models has been promoted as a source of potential competitive advantage by many authors (Cagliano, 2005; Foster, 2007; Lee, Padmanabhan, & Whang, 1997a; Lee, Padmanabhan, & Whang, 1997b; Shaw, 2000; Strader, Lin, & Shaw, 1998; Tapscott, 1996; Westhead, Mortenson, Moore, & Rice, 2000; Wood, 1997). The history of investment in long established technologies (such as EDI), however, has been limited by high setup and implementation costs, and the associated perception of a high degree of difficulty (Drury & Farhoomand, 1996; Iacovou, Benbasat, & Dexter, 1995; Pfeiffer, 1992; Rassameethes & Kurokawa, 2000; Raymond & Bergeron, 1996; Senn, 1992; Suzuki & Williams, 1998). This is contrasted by early research indicating that the contribution of the cost of paperwork to the final price of a product can range from between 3.5% to 15% (Ojala & Suomi, 1992), and potential benefits of EDI implementation (other than the reduction of paperwork) can include streamlined process management, access to point of sale data, and associated visibility of demand (Lee & Clark, 1999; Lee, So, & Tang, 2000). In response to this recognized problem, it has been proposed that Internet based technologies would at a minimum provide a new platform for old technologies (Segev et al., 1997), or neutralise cost restraints and provide wide access to substantial benefits as a result (BCG, 2001; James, 2004; Karantonis, 1999; Rahman, 2003; Tapscott, 1996; Upin, Beckwith, Jennings, Chen, & Schaeffer, 2000). As discussed in relation to Propositions 1 and 2 above, the open nature of Internet standards provide access to potential sources of technological integration at substantially lower costs (Ghiassi, 2003). The feasibility of real integration is now seen to be more likely as companies have access to information that is accurate, timely and affordable (Lankford, 2004) (i.e., information is the only element within the supply chain that has become less expensive over time (Bowersox & Calantone, 1998)). This expectation was articulated best by Handfield and Nichols when they stated:

> With the emergence of the personal computer, optical fibre networks, the explosion of the Internet and the World Wide Web, the cost and availability of information resources allows easy linkages and eliminates information-related time delays in any supply chain network. (Handfield & Nichols, 1999)

It is therefore logical to suggest that there would be higher levels of optimism associated with Internet based technologies (i.e., regarding costs associated with implementation and potential benefits), and that this level of optimism would grow over time. Proposition 3 is structured to capture this notion.

> **Proposition 3:** Perception of cost vs. benefit of adoption of Internet based technologies for management of the supply chain will be more optimistic over time

Contribution of Technology to Organizational Outcomes

The direct relationship between investment in information technology and improved organizational outcomes has been the source of much recent academic debate (Frohlich, 2002; Frohlich & Westbrook, 2001; Ghose, 2007; Rosenzweig, Roth, & Dean, 2003; Vickery, Jayaram, Droge, & Calantone, 2003). Some have suggested that benefits reported as a result of such investment in internet based technologies for the management of the supply chain have been anecdotal and empirically difficult to verify (Cagliano, 2005; Van Hoek, 2001a). On the other hand, it has also been shown that benefits related to integration through extended technology use may not be easily identified as they can result in the development of entirely new business models (Muffatto & Payaro, 2004). As such, they may not be assessed as improvements (for example) in operational efficiency, but could fundamentally alter competitive criteria. In this sense, the vision of Tapscott is perhaps reflected (Tapscott, 1996, 2002) as use of the Internet enables business model innovation through structural and cultural change. It has also been shown that the relationship between integration of information technologies and firm performance may not be simple, it being subject to many potential mediating and moderating factors (Narasinhan & Kim, 2002; Rosenzweig et al., 2003; Vickery et al., 2003). There is some evidence to suggest that use of earlier technologies such as EDI, on the other hand, has focused more on promoting efficiencies than integration per se (Hill, 2000; Rassameethes & Kurokawa, 2000). In fact one study found that organizations with strong EDI links with customers, often had very weak links with suppliers (Rassameethes & Kurokawa, 2000), while another found that the requirements of customers appeared to be a prime motivator for use of this technology (Hill, 2000). On the other hand, Chan and Swatman (2000) have also identified, (through longitudinal case research), that the initial motivation for EDI adoption is likely to be cost reduction and the pursuit of internal efficiencies. However, they also found that there was a progression over time from this internal focus, to the use of technology for promotion of supplier partnerships and improved customer service. The evidence, therefore, does suggest that the characteristic differences between integration technologies pre- and post-Internet are such that it can be expected that the impact on organizational performance will be different. In general, the expectation expressed often in the literature is that Internet based integration provides a significantly improved opportunity for better performance. Benefits highlighted include increased visibility of real customer demand patterns (Coleman, Barrett, & Austrian, 2000; Ghose, 2007; Lee, Padmanabhan, & Whang, 1997), reductions in delivery lead times (James, 2004; McCormack, 1999), better information sharing leading to greater depth of relationships with trading partners (Manasco, 2000; Yao, 2008), better visibility to ascertain inventory availability (Bailey, 2005; Radjou, 2000), and the development of expertise in low cost customised manufacturing and fulfilment (Ghiassi, 2003; Westhead, Mortenson, Moore, & Rice, 2000). This expectation of improved performance deserves testing, and comparison with perceptions of contribution of pre-Internet technologies. As such, Proposition 4 below is stated suggesting that empirical testing will reveal a higher level of contribution from Internet based technologies:

Proposition 4: Contribution of Internet based technologies for management of the supply chain to organizational outcomes will be greater than that of pre-Internet technologies

METHOD

Background

The data on which this chapter is based were gathered from three separate surveys conducted within the membership of GS1 (formerly EAN) Australia, and The Chartered Institute of Purchasing and Supply Australia (CIPSA), over a 6-year period (coded Survey 1, 2, and 3 from earliest to latest). The data were collected using a traditional mail-out method comprised of two phases. The first involved the initial mail out whilst the second was targeted only at identified nonrespondents. To facilitate meaningful comparison between the three samples, respondents representing the manufacturing, wholesale distribution and retail sectors were isolated and used in the analysis. This led to the final sample size for each survey being: Survey 1 = 504 cases; Survey 2 = 254 cases; Survey 3 = 129 cases.

For the surveys conducted within the membership of GS1 (Survey 1 and Survey 2) the respondents to the survey were the "standards coordinators" nominated within each organization. As such, each respondent was the person nominated by that company as being responsible for the management of activities related to the administration of these standards (at that time known as the "EAN system"—see section above titled "Definitions") within their respective organizations. GS1 Australia is the organization that administers and controls the European Article Numbering system that is now the generally accepted worldwide bar-coding, RFID, electronic product code and product numbering standard, and has a national membership (in Australia) in excess of 15,000. The initial survey covered 3,356 companies, yielded 553 responses (response rate of 16.5%), and incorporated some variables covering the use of technologies that had been in existence for up to 30 years (bar-coding, EDI, etc.). The second survey sampled 2470 organizations, with a total of 281 usable responses being collected. This represented a response rate of 12%. The focus of this survey was on the adoption and use of Internet based technologies (XML, XML/EDI, Internet applications, extranets, etc.). The final survey conducted within the membership of CIPSA sampled 1825 purchasing professionals with 310 usable responses being received (response rate of 17%). The number of responses recorded is taken to be acceptable as they are all above 10% when a response rate below 10% is becoming more common for this type of research (Alreck & Settle, 2004). Other recent empirical studies have yielded similar or lower overall numbers and/or response rates (93 yielding a 9.5% response rate (Lee & Kincade, 2003), 50 in another study gave a 10% response rate (Yap, Chai, & Lemaire, 2005), and in another 101 responses resulted in a 6.7% response rate (Wisner & Tan, 2000)). To ensure confidence in the validity of the samples, tests for similarity between pre- and postreminder responses, or between sample demographics and national statistics, were conducted. No significant differences were found. As missing data was minimal in all three surveys mean substitution was used.

Variables and Statistical Tests Used

Demographic Items

Data from both surveys were compared on the basis of three categorical demographic variables. These covered industry sector, company size and position of the respondent in the organization (see Tables 1.1-1.3).

> **Proposition 1:** Usage of Internet based technologies for management of the supply chain will be higher than that of pre-Internet technologies

Seven variables were used (Survey 1) to identify extent of usage of long established electronic transfer technologies using EDI for the following functions at that point in time: Incoming sales orders, advanced shipment notices (ASNs), remittance advice, invoices, evaluated receipts settlement (EFT), point of sales (POS) data, purchase orders to suppliers. five point Likert scales were used with the value 1 representing "Not At All" and 5 representing "To a Very Large Extent."

Five variables from Survey 3 were also used to provide a comparison with the EDI related items from Survey 1. These items covered use of extranets, XML and XML/EDI applications, use of web-based catalogues and data sharing using the Internet. Five point Likert scales were used with the value 1 representing "Not at All" and 5 representing "To a Very Large Extent."

A further four items from Survey 3 were also used to compare usage of EDI and Internet based technologies at that time. These items covered daily use of the Internet or EDI for business to business transactions with customers and suppliers. Comparison on the basis of usage of the different technologies was carried out using the mean scores for each of the individual items.

Further data were used from Survey 2 to identify the extent to which Internet technologies were being diffused (i.e., number of users as distinct from the extent of use). The same variables identified above (seven for use of EDI in Survey 1, five for use of the Internet in Survey 2) were used in this comparison.

> **Proposition 2:** Usage of Internet based technologies for management of the supply chain is increasing significantly over time

To test for increases in use of Internet based technologies over time, nine variables common to both Surveys 2 and 3 were used. These items covered daily use of the Internet for business to business transactions with customers and suppliers, use of electronic marketplaces with suppliers and customers, use of extranets, XML and XML/EDI applications, use of web-based catalogs and data sharing using the Internet. Five point Likert scales were used with the value 1 representing "Not at All" and 5 representing "To a Very Large Extent."

> **Proposition 3:** Perception of cost vs. benefit of adoption of Internet based technologies for management of the supply chain will be more optimistic over time

Comparison on the basis of perceived cost and benefit used the same pair of variables in the three surveys. Respondents were asked to rate on a scale of 1 to 5 (1 = low, 5 = high) the potential cost and benefit of implementation of pre-Internet technologies (including EDI—Survey 1) or Internet based solutions (Surveys 2 and 3).

Comparison on the basis of usage of the different technologies was carried out using the mean scores for each of the individual items. An independent samples t-test was used to compare the statistical significance of the difference in the mean values for these items between the three survey groups ($p < .05$ being the significance cut-off value).

> **Proposition 4:** Contribution of Internet based technologies for management of the supply chain to organizational outcomes will be greater than that of pre-Internet technologies

In order to compare the contributions of Internet technologies and long established technologies such as EDI, multiple regressions were run using two pairs of independent variables from Survey 3. For Internet technologies these items covered daily use of the Internet for business to business transactions with customers and suppliers. For pre-Internet technologies these items covered daily use of EDI for business to business transactions with customers and suppliers. Five point Likert scales were used for these variables with the value 1 representing "Not at All" and 5 representing "To a Very Large Extent." The dependent variables covered firm performance assessed subjectively by respondents in the following areas: customer satisfaction, inventory control, productivity, flexibility, service quality, cycle time reduction, revenue, cost, cash flow and profit. Five point Likert scales were used for these items with the range being 1 "Poor performer" and 5 representing "Exceptional performer."

Supplementary Tests

In order to provide some explanation for the results observed, a supplementary set of tests were conducted. Independent samples (Survey 2 and Survey 3) *t*-tests were run based on responses to eleven variables relating to impediments to implementation of Internet technologies for the management of the supply chain. Five point Likert scales were used for these items with the range being 1 "Not Important" and 5 representing "Extremely Important." *T*-tests were also run comparing responses from these two surveys to three questions related to the extent to which implementation of Internet based technologies was creating pressure for change. Five point Likert scales were used with the value 1 representing "Not at All" and 5 representing "To a Very Large Extent."

DATA ANALYSIS AND FINDINGS

Comparison of Demographics

Industry Sector

In the three survey subgroups manufacturing companies formed the majority of respondents (Survey 1 = 60.7%, Survey 2 = 67.7% and Survey 3 = 81.4%), followed by wholesale distribution (Survey 1 = 34.7%, Survey 2 = 27.6% and Survey 3 = 11.6%) and retail (Survey 1 = 4.6%, Survey 2 = 4.7% and 3 = 6.6%). Table 1.1 shows these distributions.

Company Size

In both the Survey 1 and Survey 2 samples organizations employing less than 200 people accounted for the majority of responses (Survey 1 =

Table 1.1.   Comparison of Distribution of Respondents Based on Industry Sector

	Manufacturing	Wholesale /Distribution	Retail
Survey 1	306	175	23
Survey 2	172	70	12
Survey 3	105	15	9

91.4%, Survey 2 = 80.7%). In Survey 3 this group dropped to 35.6%, while organizations employing more than 200 people accounted for a greater proportion of respondents (62.7%). Table 1.2 below shows the distributions.

Position of the Respondent in the Organization

Senior Executives made up the largest number of respondents in the first two surveys (Survey 1 = 39.3%, Survey 2 = 24.2%), followed by operations managers (Survey 1 = 15.7%, Survey 2 = 15.4%), with a relatively even spread of managers from marketing, quality/customer service, financial control, and IT. In Survey 3 there was a higher proportion of operations managers than in the previous two (41.9%). The "Other" category comprised functions such as office management and administration. Table 1.3 shows these results.

Comparison of Usage between Technologies

Proposition 1: Usage of Internet based technologies for management of the supply chain will be higher than that of pre-Internet technologies

Comparison of the usage of established EDI technologies for transmitting and sharing data and documents with trading partners, with Internet

Table 1.2.   Comparison of Distribution of Respondents Based on Company Size (no. of Employees)

	<20 Employees	20-199 Employees	200 or More Employees	No Answer
Survey 1	295	166	37	6
Survey 2	120	85	47	2
Survey 3	11	35	81	2

Table 1.3.   Comparison of Distribution of Respondents Based on Position Held in the Organization

	Senior Exec.	Operations/ Logistics/ Purchasing Manager	Quality/ Customer Service Manager	Marketing Manager	Financial Controller/ Accounts	IT/ Technical Systems Manager	Other	No Answer
Survey 1	198	79	20	20	38	12	63	5
Survey 2	122	39	15	23	15	9	29	2
Survey 3	12	54	10	15	8	12	10	8

based alternatives, showed that use of Internet based technologies was on average greater in Survey 3 than for comparative EDI based technologies in Survey 1 (see Figure 1.1). Overall, reported levels of usage of both EDI and Internet based options were low, with the mean score for the seven EDI items being 1.60, and for the five Internet based methods being 1.95. When usage levels for EDI technologies were recorded for firms employing more than 200 people in Survey 1, (larger firms have been identified in previous studies as being more likely to adopt EDI based technologies (Bytheway & Braganza, 1992; Clarke, 1992; Prosser & Nickl, 1997; Raymond & Bergeron, 1996), it was found that this group recorded higher average levels of use (2.25) than were recorded for use of Internet based technologies across the full sample in Survey 3 (see Figure 1.1). This would indicate that larger firms captured in the first survey were using EDI based technologies more extensively than equivalent Internet based alternatives were being used generally in the manufacturing, wholesale distribution and retail sectors by the time Survey 3 had been conducted. It should also be noted that the sample for the third survey comprised a higher proportion of larger firms as mentioned. Low levels of EDI use are not unexpected as has been documented in the literature, and often attributed to particular characteristics of this technology, such as cost and the point to point nature of connections. It is particularly interesting, however, to note that uptake of Internet based alternatives in comparison to EDI appears to have been slow despite the expected reduced cost and generally higher levels of accessibility. This could in part be attributed to the investment current users of EDI have made over many years in this technology, and the subsequent reluctance to abandon it. The use of web-based catalogs (most popular of the Internet based options in use with a mean score of (2.30) along with data sharing generally (2.06) as the highest use areas indicate a synergy between making data available on line and sharing it with trading partners. What is surprising, however, are the particularly low scores for usage of extranets, XML based applications (i.e. for enabling integration of legacy systems), and XML/EDI for the transfer of documents. These results are shown in Figure 1.1.

The data indicate that the adoption of various Internet based alternatives for document and data transfer between trading partners were showing low absolute and comparative levels of use in the third survey. This is further highlighted when the answers to the four questions in Table 1.4 below are compared for this survey. Usage of EDI technologies is again shown to be greater than for Internet based alternatives, albeit marginally. Daily usage levels for both technologies were again shown to be low. Further confirmation comes from comparing the average usage for the five Internet based methods for firms employing more than 200 employees (i.e., in Survey 3) being only

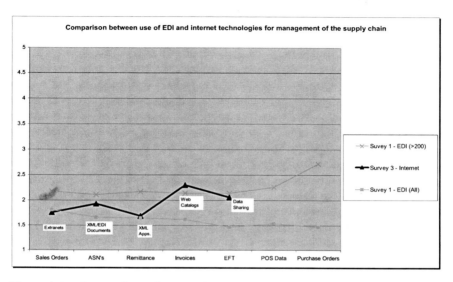

Figure 1.1.   Comparison of usage of EDI technologies (Survey 1) with internet technologies (Survey 3).

marginally greater than for the full sample at 2.03. This is also lower still than the average for usage of the EDI based alternatives in the sector employing more than 200 people (2.25) in Survey 1.

In order to augment this analysis, results were compared from a subset of cases where the respondent was known to have been involved in both Surveys 1 and 2. This created a subset of 54 cases where responses within this group were directly comparable between the two surveys. Within this group three separate categories were established to determine whether

Table 1.4.   Comparison Extent of Adoption of EDI and Internet Based Technologies: Survey 3

Survey 3	Our company is using EDI for business to business transactions with many major customers on a daily basis	Our company is using EDI for business to business transactions with many major suppliers on a daily basis	Our company is using the Internet for business to business transactions with many major customers on a daily basis	Our company is using the Internet for business to business transactions with many major suppliers on a daily basis
Mean Score— Scale 1-5	2.47	2.22	2.20	2.14

there was any discernible pattern of adoption from one survey to the next (and hence between the two types of technologies). "Active in both surveys" were respondents indicating use of both EDI and Internet based technologies in both surveys. "Active in Survey 1 but not active in Survey 2" were those respondents indicating use of EDI technologies, but not of Internet technologies. "Active in Survey 2 but not active in Survey 1" were those reporting use of Internet technologies, but not use of EDI technologies in the earlier survey. The categories, along with the number of respondents in each are detailed below in Table 1.5.

This classification indicated that 30 of these respondents (56%) reported using traditional technologies such as EDI while 47 reported use of Internet based technologies (87%). Further, 24 (44%) indicated they were using the Internet when they had reported in the earlier survey that they were not involved in using EDI based technologies. Only 7 (13%) users of EDI from the first survey reported that they had not moved on to using Internet based technologies. What these results show is that although the level of use of Internet technologies is on average comparatively low, there is evidence to suggest that these technologies were becoming more broadly diffused. Although this may appear to be a contradiction, it may not be so, as it points to a critical distinction between number of users and extent of use. In other words, although there is evidence suggesting broader diffusion of Internet technologies (i.e., more users), there is also evidence suggesting that they are not using these technologies extensively, or that in other words, use is superficial (based on data presented in Figure 1.1).

Discussion

The acceptance or rejection of Proposition 1 is problematic on the basis of this data. On the one hand use over time of Internet based technologies appears to be at lower levels than that of longer established alternatives such as EDI. On the other, however, there is some evidence that the number of users of the Internet for conducting business with

Table 1.5. Comparison of Number of Organizations That Could be Identified as Adopting One or Both of the Types of Technologies—Survey 1 and Survey 2

Active in Both Surveys	Active in Survey 1 But Not Active in Survey 2	Active in Survey 2 But Not Active in Survey 1
23 cases	7 cases	24 cases

trading partners was higher in Survey 2 than that of preceding technologies. On balance the best that can be said is that the evidence indicates more users over time of internet based alternatives, but that the extent of use within organizations as a facilitator of business activity with trading partners is still comparatively low. In other words, there is some evidence that adoption of the internet is more widespread across many organizations, but the extent of application between trading partners appears to be at a lower level than technologies the Internet has superseded. As such, the proposition is problematic and can at best be only partially accepted.

Comparison of Usage over Time

Proposition 2: Usage of Internet based technologies for management of the supply chain is increasing significantly over time

Comparison of the usage of Internet technologies for integration with trading partners over the period spanning Survey 2 to Survey 3 indicated a small increase in usage in some categories, while overall usage levels were still reported to be comparatively low. The largest shifts occurred in use of web-based catalogues and the sharing of data between trading partners generally. Some marginal increases were recorded for the use of the internet to facilitate trading partner collaboration (both customers and suppliers), use of extranets and XML based applications (see Figure 1.2).

Discussion

The evidence suggests only a marginal growth in the use of internet based technologies for the management of the supply chain within the manufacturing, wholesale distribution and retail sectors in Australia between Survey 2 and Survey 3. This small increase makes it difficult to accept the proposition that use of these technologies in these sectors is increasing significantly over time. In discussing the possible explanation of this result further relevant evidence is presented in the discussion of the results related to Propositions 3 and 4.

Perception of Cost vs. Benefit

Proposition 3: Perception of cost vs. benefit of adoption of Internet based technologies for management of the supply chain will be more optimistic over time

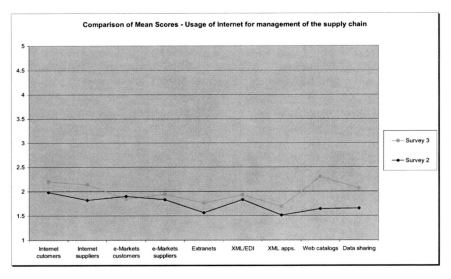

Figure 1.2.   Comparison of mean scores—change in usage of internet based technologies between Survey 2 and Survey 3.

When the results from the three surveys are compared on the basis of perception of cost incurred and benefit derived from implementation, little change in perception of cost and benefit between EDI and Internet based technologies is recorded between Survey 1 and Survey 2. Between Survey 2 and Survey 3, however, there is a significant increase in both perceived cost and benefit relating to the use of Internet based technologies. Table 1.6 below shows the difference in the mean scores and the statistical significance of the difference.

The interesting aspect of this result is that although Internet technologies are generally reported in the literature to be a lower cost alternative to the established technologies such as EDI, respondents indicate that

Table 1.6.   Comparison of Perceptions of Cost vs. Benefit
From Implementation of the Technologies
for the Three Surveys (**Denotes Significant at .01 Level)

	EDI Technologies (Survey 1)	*Internet Technologies (Survey 2)*	*Internet Technologies (Survey 3)*
Cost of implementation	2.73 (*df* 504)	2.73 (*df* 254)	3.16** (*df* 129)
Benefit from implementation	2.97 (*df* 504)	2.93 (*df* 254)	3.80** (*df* 129)

over time they perceive this not to be the case. As managers become more familiar with Internet based technologies, there appears to not only be a significant growth in recognition of their potential (i.e., benefit from implementation), but there is also a clearer appreciation of the costs associated with implementation. It is also interesting to note that the mean score for cost and benefit for the two technology categories is almost identical between Survey 1 and Survey 2. This could be interpreted to indicate little difference in the perceived trade-off between cost and benefit for either technology type. It could also over this period of time indicate (as the analysis regarding Proposition 1 also provided some supporting evidence) that this perception is related to the type of use of Internet based technologies. In the discussion of Proposition 1 it was found that there was some evidence that there were more people using these technologies in Survey 2, but that usage may have been superficial in nature. Further evidence supporting this can be found when five categories of use of Internet based technologies are compared between the first and second samples (see Figure 1.3). Although some increase in use of the Internet as part of the daily work of respondents is recorded, the increase appears to be marginal. Further, the greatest increase recorded is in the use of e-mail, whereas activities typically associated with management of the supply chain (e.g., purchasing, order fulfilment, customer service, etc.) exhibit only limited increases in use over this period of time.

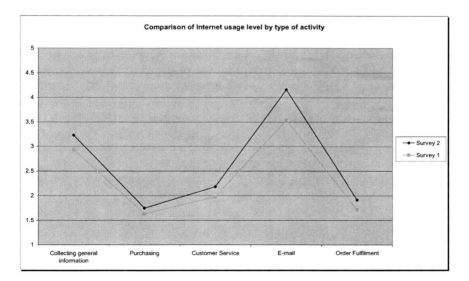

Figure 1.3.   Comparison of extent of use of the internet as part of respondents' functional role in the organization.

Discussion

The data indicate that this proposition can be only partially accepted. On the one hand the evidence suggests that respondents were more optimistic about the benefits of implementation of Internet based solutions in Survey 3, but on the other they are comparatively less optimistic about the costs associated with implementation. Internet technologies are seen to be increasing in cost to implement, but also to deliver increasing levels of benefit. In a sense this is consistent with the findings for Proposition 2 in that usage of Internet based technologies was not found to have significantly increased across a large number of supply chain management related activities between Survey 2 and Survey 3. As firms are becoming more aware of the potential of these technologies, it is apparent that they are also becoming more aware of the potential costs associated with implementation.

Contribution to Organizational Outcomes

Proposition 4: Contribution of Internet based technologies for management of the supply chain to organizational outcomes will be greater than that of pre-Internet technologies

In order to test this proposition multiple regression models were run (using Survey 3 data—see description of statistical tests used in the Method section above) with the independent variables being either extent of daily use of EDI or Internet based technologies with trading partners. The dependent variables were a range of operations and financial related performance outcomes as detailed in Table 1.7.

The comparison indicates that there are some significant differences in perception of contribution to performance of the two types of technologies. Daily use of EDI for business to business transactions with customers and suppliers was found to be having little influence on most of the performance outcomes measured other than reduction in cycle times. In this case, although the effect was significant, it was also weak. By way of contrast, the use of Internet based technologies was found to be having a significant effect on all of the operations related outcomes, albeit that the effect recorded was also weak. The only financial outcome recording a significant effect was cost reduction, and the influence of the internet based technologies here was again found to be weak.

Discussion

This proposition, as with many of those preceding, is only partially and weakly supported by the data. Some effect is recorded indicating

**Table Survey 3: Comparison of Perceptions of Contribution
to Improved Performance From Implementation
of Internet and Pre-Internet Technologies
for the Management of the Supply Chain—Values Shown
are Adjusted R^2 (*denotes significant at .05 level)**

DV - Operations	IV - EDI	IV - Internet
Customer satisfaction	.008 (df 129)	**.027***(df 129)
Inventory management	.022 (df 129)	**.024***(df 129)
Productivity	.026 (df 129)	**.035***(df 129)
Service quality	.017 (df 129)	**.023***(df 129)
Flexibility	.000 (df 129)	**.027***(df 129)
Cycle times	**.033***(df 129)	**.022***(df 129)

DV - Financial	EDI	Internet
Sales	.000 (df 129)	.005 (df 129)
Net Profit	.000 (df 129)	.001 (df 129)
Cash flow	.000 (df 129)	.003 (df 129)
Cost	.000 (df 129)	**.029***(df 129)

that, in particular, use of Internet based technologies for the management of the supply chain has a statistically significant effect on operations related outcomes. The effect recorded, however, is so weak that it is really only the consistency of the effect over the full range of operations related outcomes recorded that provides practical credibility to the proposition. The use of EDI, on the other hand, appears not to have any real impact either operationally or at the financial end of the business. In light of the findings for a number of the preceding propositions, this finding is not overly surprising. With low levels of application of these technologies for the management of the supply chain being reported it is not surprising that low levels of contribution to performance are also reported.

Supplementary Tests and Further Discussion

In summary it has been found through this study that across the three surveys conducted in the manufacturing, wholesale distribution and retail sectors in Australia:

- In Survey 3 usage of Internet based technologies for the management of the supply chain had reached levels only just equivalent to or less than those for long established pre-Internet technologies such as EDI.

- The growth in use of Internet based technologies had only marginally increased between Survey 2 and Survey 3.
- Perceptions of the potential benefits of Internet based technologies had become more optimistic, but at the same time the cost of implementation of these technologies was perceived to be increasing.
- Contribution of Internet based technologies to firm performance was found to be significant but weak for operations related outcomes. Contribution of EDI technologies was negligible.

The findings indicate that in the minds of the respondents to these surveys these technologies are slow in uptake, low in contribution to performance and increasing in cost to implement. These results run contrary to these technologies providing accessibility at low cost and capability to connect to multiple trading partners, but do have some support in the literature (Van Hoek, 2001b). In order to throw further light on the explanation for this, two comparisons were run between the Survey 2 and Survey 3 samples of responses to (a) importance of eleven impediments to adoption of Internet based technologies, and (b) three factors measuring pressure for process change as a result of implementation of these technologies. The results of these comparisons are shown in Figures 1.4 and 1.5.

In Figure 1.4 it is apparent that there had been an increase in perception of the importance of ten of the eleven impediments measured. Customer Capability was the only factor that was recorded as not having changed to any meaningful extent. Impediments such as resistance to change, legacy systems, outdated processes, rate of technological change, supplier capability and commitment of senior management had all registered substantial increases in importance based on respondents' perceptions.

In Figure 1.5 a similar trend is reported with respondents to Survey 3 indicating that implementation of internet based technologies was creating a substantial increase in pressure for change to both internal and supply chain wide processes, as well as a fundamental need to restructure the firm.

The importance of this is that it provides at least a potential explanation for the equivocal findings recorded in the testing of the four propositions. The results perhaps explain some of the reticence reported by respondents for implementation of Internet based technologies, combined with the perceived cost implications and low levels of contribution

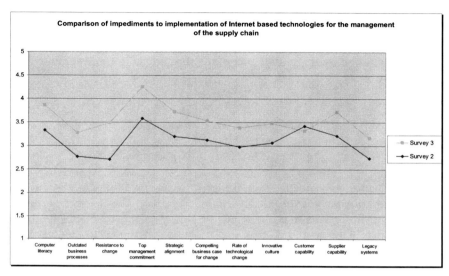

Figure 1.4.   Comparison of impediments to adoption of Internet based technologies for the management of the supply chain—Surveys 2 and 3 (all differences significant at .01 level apart from Customer Capability).

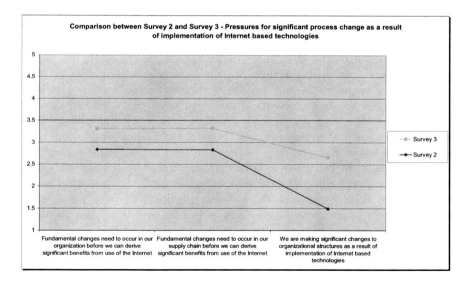

Figure 1.5.   Comparison of pressures for process change as a result of adoption of Internet based technologies for the management of the supply chain—Surveys 2 and 3.

to performance. The technologies may be low cost (comparatively), based on open standards, and offer great potential. However, it is apparent that in order to leverage the benefits, firms are faced with difficult, costly and high risk change management programs that act as impediments to further adoption.

IMPLICATIONS FOR PUBLIC POLICY

Practice

The application of Internet technologies to the problems of data availability and transfer within supply chains has been the subject of much speculation, hope and hype in terms of ability to improve supply chain performance. The results of this study provide evidence to suggest that rather than providing a low cost panacea to the problems of supply chain integration, Internet based technologies are associated with their own set of challenges that need to be overcome in order to extract maximum leverage. The testing of Proposition 1 indicates that the use of Internet based alternatives to traditional technologies such as EDI has not penetrated supply chain activity over time as deeply as could be expected. In fact, the data from this study show that in Survey 3, while more organizations were using the Internet to deal with trading partners, extent of application within these organizations was still limited, and on average on a par with EDI. In other words, while organizations can adopt Internet based alternatives (to EDI) more readily, the evidence from this study indicates they are constrained in applying them extensively to dealing with trading partners. It may be easier to connect to trading partners using the Internet, but connection does not necessarily lead to deeper application of the technological alternatives that become available. This apparent anomaly of more users (of Internet technologies) accompanied by marginal levels of use is perhaps partly related to the findings resulting from the testing of Proposition 3. In this case it was found that although Internet based technologies were perceived to offer great potential benefit (and that this perception was growing significantly over time), they were also seen to be increasing in cost of implementation. As a result, it would be plausible to suggest that organizations are attracted to using Internet based technologies to deal with trading partners (due in part to perceptions of potential benefit), but the perception of high cost acts to limit use. Reinforcement of these findings comes from the testing of Proposition 4, while at the same time providing evidence for an explanation of the constraints identified above. The comparison between the two technologies indicated that Internet based technologies made a significant, though weak, contribution across a broader range of performance out-comes. The low levels of use and perceptions of high cost are consistent with this finding.

Theory

What still remains is why technologies that are lower in cost to imple-ment (than older technologies such as EDI), based on open standards, highly accessible (i.e., perceived to be easier to implement and use than prior alternatives), and are perceived to offer great potential, are subject to what appear to be similarly impeded adoption rates to those of earlier technologies? TAM would predict that these conditions are consistent with higher levels of adoption and use. The answer is perhaps provided by the comparison of perceived impediments and forces for organiza-tional change. The evidence from the supplementary testing showed that implementation of Internet based technologies increases pressure for process change as well as restructuring of the firm and the supply chain. At the same time, in order to be able to extract the full potential benefits as a result of use of these technologies, respondents reported that funda-mental issues such as dealing with multiple legacy systems, resistance to change, trading partner capability and management commitment must be resolved. In fact, they reported that over time the importance of these factors appeared to be amplified as the potential of Internet based tech-nologies were more widely understood.

Directions for Future Research

TAM is a theory that has been most often empirically tested in the con-text of technology adoption by individuals. In the case of supply chain enabling technologies the results indicate that this theory would appear to have less predictive validity on its own given the complexities inherent in organizations. At a simple level just the fact that there are multiple stakeholders and potentially many individuals with input into the deci-sion making process would provide potential for limitation. Beyond this the drag that can be created by prior investments, the natural resistance to change, the need for costly and difficult process reconfiguration, and the need to get senior managers to buy-in all combine to create a signifi-cant constraint to adoption potentially more powerful than ease of use or even perceived benefit. This is an area of significant opportunity for future research.

Limitations of the Study

This study was based on three surveys conducted entirely within the Australian FMCG sector. As such the generalizability of the findings to other cultures, economies and industry sectors is limited.

CONCLUSION

The conclusion reached is that although the potential of Internet based technologies appears to be understood, and that there is some growth in use and application over time, more extensive use is inhibited by the concurrent need for process, systems and organizational change resulting from implementation. Internet based technologies may be on the face of it low cost and accessible, but the hidden costs of implementation reside in the pressure they produce for fundamental change. Put another way, the more powerful the technology the more pressure is created for altering business practice in order to be able to leverage that technology. The evidence is perhaps indicative of the inertia associated with change in organizations acting as a significant force counteracting the implementation of technologies offering substantial potential rewards at a comparative low cost.

ACKNOWLEDGMENT

The author would like to acknowledge the assistance of both GS1 Australia and CIPSA for providing both access to their membership, and for in kind support in administration of the surveys.

REFERENCES

Alreck, P. L., & Settle, R. B. (2004). *The survey research handbook* (3rd ed.). Boston, MA: McGraw-Hill/Irwin.

Anonymous. (2001). United Nations Directories for Electronic Data Interchange for Administration, Commerce and Transport. Retrieved from http://www.unece.org/trade/untdid/welcome.htm

Bailey, J. (2005). Internet book retailing and supply chain management: An analytical study of inventory location speculation and postponement. *Transportation Research Part E-Logistics and Transportation Review, 41*(3), 159-177.

Bao, X. (2005). The use of internet-based media in sharing product information in the global supply chain: The Canada-China case. *Canadian Journal of Information and Library Science-Revue Canadienne Des Sciences De L Information Et De Bibliotheconomie, 29*(3), 372.

Baron, J. P., Shaw, M. J., & Bailey, A. D. (2000). Web based E-catalog systems in B2B procurement. *Communications of the ACM, 43*(5), 93-100.

BCG. (2001). Organizing for e-Commerce. Retrieved from www.bcg.com/

Bowersox, D. J., & Calantone, R. J. (1998). Executive insights: Global logistics. *Journal of International Marketing, 6*(4), 83-93.

Brown, S. A., & Venkatesh, V. (2005). Model of adoption of technology in households: A baseline model test and extension incorporating household life cycle. *MIS Quarterly, 29*(3), 399-426.

Bytheway, A., & Braganza, A. (1992). Corporate information, EDI and logistics. *Logistics Information Management, 5*(4), 10-18.

Cagliano, R. (2005). E-business strategy—How companies are shaping their supply chain through the internet. *International Journal of Operations & Production Management, 25*(12), 1309-1327.

Cantor, D. E., & MacDonald, J. R. (2009). Decision-making in the supply chain: Examining problem solving approaches and information availability. *Journal of Operations Management, 27*(3), 220-232.

Carter, C. R., & Hendrick, T. E. (1997). The development of a time-based construct and its impact on departmental design and structure. *International Journal of Purchasing and Materials Management, 33*(4), 26-34.

Chan, C., & Swatman, P. M. C. (2000). From EDI to Internet commerce: The BHP Steel experience. *Internet Research-Electronic Networking Applications & Policy, 10*(1), 72-82.

Clarke, R. (1992). A contingency model of EDI's impact on industry sectors. *Journal of Strategic Information Systems, 1*(3), 143-151.

Coleman, P. V., Barrett, B., & Austrian, B. (2000). e-Logistics: The back office of the New Economy. Retrieved from http://www.bofasecurities.com/featuredresearch/content/research.asp

Davis, F. D. (1989). Perceived usefulness, perceived ease of use, and user acceptance of information technology. *MIS Quarterly, 13*(3), 319-340.

Drury, D. H., & Farhoomand, A. (1996). Innovation adoption of EDI. *Information Resources Management Journal, 9*(3), 5-13.

Foster, T. (2007). Into the depths of the I-E-I framework: using the internet to create value in supply-chain relationships. *Supply Chain Management-An International Journal, 12*(2), 96-103.

Frohlich, M. T. (2002). e-Integration in the supply chain: Barriers and performance. *Decision Sciences, 33*(4), 537-556.

Frohlich, M. T., & Westbrook, R. (2001). Arcs of integration: An international study of supply chain strategies. *Journal of Operations Management, 19*(2), 185-200.

Garcia-Dastugue, S. (2003). Internet-enabled coordination in the supply chain. *Industrial Marketing Management, 32*(3), 251-263.

Ghiassi, M. (2003). Defining the internet-based supply chain system for mass customized markets. *Computers & Industrial Engineering, 45*(1), 17-41.

Ghose, A. (2007). The impact of internet referral services on a supply chain. *Information Systems Research, 18*(3), 300-319.

Handfield, R. B., & Nichols, E. L. (1999). *Introduction to Supply Chain Management.* Upper Paddle River, NJ: Prentice-Hall.

Hill, C. A. (2000). Information technology and supply chain management: A study of the food industry. *Hospital and Material Management Quarterly, 22*(1), 53-58.

Huff, S. L., & Munro, M. C. (1985). Information technology assessment and adoption: A field study. *MIS Quarterly, 9*(4), 327-340.

Iacovou, C. L., Benbasat, I., & Dexter, A. S. (1995). Electronic Data Interchange and small organisations: Adoption and impact of technology. *MIS Quarterly, 19*(4), 465-485.

James, M. (2004). e-distribution: Internet-based management of a merchandiser supply chain. *Supply Chain Management—An International Journal, 9*(1), 7-15.

Johnson, M. E., & Whang, S. (2002). E-business and supply chain management: An overview and framework. *Production and Operations Management, 11*(4), 413-423.

Johnston, R. B., & Mak, H. C. (2000). An emerging vision of internet-enabled supply-chain electronic commerce. *International Journal of Electronic Commerce, 4*(4), 43-59.

Karantonis, A. (1999). *Web-enabled value chain management: The new paradigm.* Paper presented at the International Conference on Logistics and the Management of the Supply Chain, Sydney, Australia.

King, W. R., & He, J. (2006). A meta-analysis of the technology acceptance model. *Information & Management, 43*, 740-755.

Lancioni, R., Smith, M., & Schau, H. (2003). Strategic Internet application trends in supply chain management. *Industrial Marketing Management, 32*, 211-217.

Lankford, W. (2004). Supply chain management and the internet. *Online Information Review, 28*(4), 301-305.

Lee, H. G., & Clark, T. L. (1999). *Business value of Electronic Data Interchange: The critical role of organisational process innovations.* Paper presented at the Proceedings of the 5th International Conference of the Decision Sciences Institute, Athens, Greece.

Lee, H. L., Padmanabhan, V., & Whang, S. J. (1997a). The bullwhip effect in supply chains. *Sloan Management Review, 38*(3), 93-102.

Lee, H. L., Padmanabhan, V., & Whang, S. J. (1997b). Information distortion in a supply chain: The bullwhip effect. *Management Science, 43*(4), 546-558.

Lee, H. L., So, K. C., & Tang, C. S. (2000). The value of information sharing in a two-level supply chain. *Management Science., 46*(5), 626-643.

Lee, Y., & Kincade, D. H. (2003). US apparel manufacturers' company characteristic differences based on SCM activities. *Journal of Fashion Marketing and Management, 7*(1), 31-48.

Manasco, B. (2000). The emergence of networked markets. Retrieved from www.apqc.org/free/articles/NetMarkets.htm

McCormack, K. (1999). What really works. *IIE Solutions, 31*(8), 30-32.

Mohta, P. (1997). Conducting EDI over the Internet. *AS/400 Systems Management,* 46-48.

Muffatto, M., & Payaro, A. (2004). Integration of web-based procurement and fulfilment: A comparison of case studies. *International Journal of Information Management, 24*, 295-311.

Narasinhan, R., & Kim, S. W. (2002). Effect of supply chain integration on the relationship between diversification and performance: Evidence from Japanese and Korean firms. *Journal of Operations Management, 20*(3), 303-323.

Netessine, S. (2006). Supply chain choice on the Internet. *Management Science*, *52*(6), 844-864.

Ojala, L., & Suomi, R. (1992). EDI: An advantage or disadvantage for remotely situated countries? *International Journal of Physical Distribution and Logistics Management*, *22*(8), 35-42.

Pfeiffer, H. K. C. (1992). *The diffusion of electronic data interchange*. New York, NY: Springer-Verlag.

Porter, M. (2001, March). Strategy and the Internet. *Harvard Business Review*, 63-78.

Power, D. J. (2002). Application of established and emerging B2B e-commerce technologies: Australian empirical evidence. *Integrated Manufacturing Systems*, *13*(8), 573-585.

Power, D. J., & Simon, A. (2004). Adoption and diffusion in technology implementation: A supply chain study. *International Journal of Operations and Production Management*, *24*(6), 566-587.

Prosser, A., & Nickl, A. (1997). The impact of EDI on interorganizational integration. *International Journal of Production Economics*, *52*, 269-281.

Radjou, N. (2000). Manufacturing deconstructed. Retrieved from www.forrester.com

Rahman, Z. (2003). Internet-based supply chain management: using the internet to revolutionize your business. *International Journal of Information Management*, *23*(6), 493-505.

Ramamurthy, K., Premkumar, G., & Crum, M. R. (1999). Organizational and inter-organizational determinants of EDI diffusion and organizational performance: A causal model. *Journal of Organizational Computing and Electronic Commerce*, *9*(4), 253-285.

Rassameethes, B., & Kurokawa, S. (2000). EDI performance in the automotive supply chain. *International Journal of Technology Management*, *20*(3/4), 287-303.

Raymond, L., & Bergeron, F. (1996). EDI success in small and medium enterprises: A field study. *Journal of Organisational Computing and Electronic Commerce*, *6*(2), 161-172.

Rosenzweig, E. D., Roth, A. V., & Dean, J. W. (2003). The influence of integration strategy on competitive capabilities and business performance: An exploratory study of consumer products manufacturers. *Journal of Operations Management*, *21*(4), 437-456.

Schepers, J., & Wetaels, M. (2007). A meta-analysis of the technology acceptance model: Investigating subjective norm and moderation effects. *Information and Management*, *44*, 90-103.

Segev, A., Porra, A., & Roldan, M. (1997). Internet-based EDI strategy. *Decision Support Systems*, *21*(3), 157-170.

Segev, A., Wan, D., & Beam, C. (1995). *Designing electronic catalogs for business value: Results from the CommerceNet pilot*. Berkeley, CA: Haas School of Business, University of California.

Senn, J. A. (1992). Electronic data interchange: The elements of implementation. *Information Systems Management*, *Winter*, 45-53.

Shaw, M. J. (2000). Information-based manufacturing with the web. *International Journal of Flexible Manufacturing Systems*, *12*(2-3), 115-129.

Strader, T. J., Lin, F. R., & Shaw, M. J. (1998). Information infrastructure for electronic virtual organisation management. *Decision Support Systems, 23*(1), 75-94.

Suzuki, Y., & Williams, L. R. (1998). Analysis of EDI resistance behaviour. *Transportation Journal, 37*(4), 36-44.

Tapscott, D. (1996). *The digital economy: Promise and peril in the age of networked intelligence.* New York, NY: McGraw-Hill.

Tapscott, D. (2002). Rethinking strategy in a networked world (or why Michael Porter is wrong about the Internet). Retrieved from http://www.nplc.com/

Truman, G. (2000). Integration in electronic exchange environments. *Journal of Management Information Systems, 17*(1), 209-244.

Turner, M., Kitchenham, B., Brereton, P., Charters, S., & Budgen, D. (2010). Does the technology acceptance model predict actual use? A systematic literature review. *Information and Software Technology, 52*, 463-479.

Upin, E. B., Beckwith, M. J., Jennings, C. L., Chen, B. Y., & Schaeffer, K. B. (2000). B2B: Building technology bridges outside the four walls of the enterprise. Retrieved from www.rsco.com

Van Hoek, R. (2001a). E-supply chains—virtually nonexisting. *Supply Chain Management, 6*(1), 21-28.

Van Hoek, R. (2001b). E-supply chains—virtually nonexisting. *Supply Chain Management: An International Journal, 6*(1), 21-28.

Venkatesh, V., & Brown, S. A. (2001). A longitudinal investigation of personal computers in homes: Adoption determinants and emerging challenges. *MIS Quarterly, 25*(1), 71-102.

Vickery, S. K., Jayaram, J., Droge, C., & Calantone, R. (2003). The effects of integrative supply chain strategy on customer service and financial performance: An analysis of direct versus indirect relationships. *Journal of Operations Management, 21*(5), 523-539.

Westhead, K., Mortenson, C., Moore, J., & Rice, A. W. (2000). New economy: Forget the WEB, make way for the GRID. Retrieved from www.db.com

Wisner, J. D., & Tan, K. C. (2000). Supply chain management and its impact on purchasing. *Journal of Supply Chain Management, 36*(4), 33-42.

Wood, A. (1997). Extending the supply chain: Strengthening links with IT. *Chemical Week, 159*(25), 26.

Yao, D. (2008). Incentives to reliable order fulfillment for an internet drop-shipping supply chain. *International Journal of Production Economics, 113*(1), 324-334.

Yap, C. M., Chai, K. H., & Lemaire, P. (2005). An empirical study on functional diversity and innovation in SMEs. *Creativity & Innovation Management, 14*(2), 176-190.

Zhang, C. (2006). Secure information sharing in internet-based supply chain management systems. *Journal of Computer Information Systems, 46*(4), 18-24.

Zheng, J., Bakker, E., Knight, L., Gilhespy, H., Harland, C., & Walker, H. (2006). A strategic case for e-adoption in healthcare supply chains. *International Journal of Information Management, 26*, 290-301.

CHAPTER 2

TECHNOLOGICAL INNOVATION IN ORGANIZATIONAL NETWORKS

Designing and Implementing a Multipublisher E-Book Program in a Public University

Carolyn Wilson Green and Tracy A. Hurley

ABSTRACT

Studies of innovation in organizational networks have been conducted in a variety of research streams including innovation research, network theory and information technology innovation and diffusion research. This study explores the case of an innovative institutional e-book program developed and implemented at a small public university. Drawing from each of these research streams, the study uses three theoretical frameworks that have been proposed for understanding how innovations arise and develop in the

Global Perspectives on Technological Innovation, pp. 31–59
Copyright © 2013 by Information Age Publishing
31

context of heterogeneous organizational networks. The analysis focuses on insights offered by each of the frameworks, comparison of the frameworks' contributions to understanding the dynamics of the e-book project, and suggestions for further areas of research. Implications for public policy include establishing publicly-funded programs and incentives for the establishment of privately-funded programs that create niches for technological innovation pilot projects, promotion of heterogeneity in innovation networks in programs designed to foster technological innovation, and organizing and supporting workshops and/or virtual communities that facilitate the sharing of lessons learned by experienced innovation network orchestrators with those who are leading their first network-oriented technological innovation pilot projects.

INTRODUCTION

Although technological innovation may come through the work of a single innovator, the advances made in technological innovation are often the product of innovation processes carried out by networks of organizations and individual actors. Over the past decade, studies of innovation in organizational networks have emerged from several different research streams. These include innovation research (Dewald & Truffer, 2011; Markard, Stradelmann, & Truffer, 2009; Markard & Truffer, 2008; Suurs, Hekkert, Kieboom, & Smits, 2010), network theory (Dhanaraj & Parke, 2006; Gardet & Mothe, 2011; Mueller-Seitz, 2011; Ritala, Armila & Blomqvist, 2009; Oberg & Grundstrom, 2009;), and information technology innovation and diffusion research (Boland, Lyytinen, & Yoo, 2007; Lyytinen & Damsgaard, 2001; Tuomi, 2002; Van de Ven, 2005). Although all of these research streams are focused on understanding innovation, their approaches and level of analysis differ. The purpose of this study is to explore some of the aspects of those differences and consider how the insights gained from the three perspectives may complement each other.

Through the analysis of a case study involving the development and implementation of a multipublisher e-book program at a public university, this study explores differences in insight provided by three frameworks drawn from each of these research streams. The frameworks included in the study are Markard and Truffer's (2008) integrated multilevel framework for analyzing technological innovation systems; Dhanaraj and Parke's (2006) innovation network orchestration framework; and Boland, Lyytinen, and Yoo's (2007) wakes of innovation framework. Each focuses on innovation in organizational networks and two of the frameworks—Markard and Truffer (2008) and Boland and colleagues (2007)—focus specifically on technological innovation. The analysis concludes with a comparison of the insights emerging from each framework's perspective and a discussion of the potential value of using multiple frameworks in studying innovation in heterogeneous networks.

THEORETICAL FRAMEWORK OF THE STUDY

We analyze the e-book project from the standpoint of three theoretical frameworks that have been proposed for understanding how innovations arise in the context of heterogeneous organizational networks. The analysis focuses on insights offered by each of the frameworks, comparison of the frameworks' contributions to understanding the dynamics of the e-book project, suggestions for further areas of theory development, and implications for application to technological innovation activity.

Technological Innovation Systems

Drawing on two different perspectives found in innovation research, Markard and Truffer (2008) propose an integrated framework for analyzing innovation processes that combines elements of innovation systems concepts (Carlsson, 2006; Carlsson, Jacobsson, Holmen, & Rickne, 2002; Chang & Chen, 2004; Edquist, 1997, 2005) with a multilevel framework previously developed for analyzing technological transitions (e.g., Elzen, Geels, & Green, 2004; Geels, 2002; Raven, 2007; Rip & Kemp, 1998; Van den Ende & Kemp, 1999). Starting with the definition of innovation systems as consisting of "networks of actors and institutions that develop, diffuse, and use innovations" (Markard & Truffer, 2008, p. 597), the authors extend the definition to incorporate a sociotechnical perspective, ultimately suggesting the concept of a technological innovation system (TIS):

> A technological innovation system is a set of networks of actors and institutions that jointly interact in a specific technological field and contribute to the generation, diffusion and utilization of variants of a new technology and/or a new product. (p. 611)

Other key elements of their integrated framework are the concepts of sociotechnical regimes, niches, and landscape. The processes associated with these elements exist at three different levels—niches at the microlevel, regimes at the mesolevel, and landscape at the macrolevel of the framework.

The concept of a sociotechnical regime is drawn from technological transition research. A sociotechnical regime is presented as a set of rules "comprised in the complex of scientific knowledges, engineering practices, production process technologies, product characteristics, skills and procedures, and institutions and infrastructures that make up the totality of a technology" (Kemp, Rip, & Schot, 2001, p. 272). Incorporating Geels' (2002) definition of sociotechnical regime, Markard and Truffer add that the regime's rules and practices are shared not only by "engineers or scientists but all kinds of business people, end users, policymakers, societal interest groups, associations, etc." (2008, p. 604). The result is an "emergent, collective outcome that cannot be changed at will" (Markard & Truffer, 2008, p. 604). As such, an existing sociotechnical regime can be a source of significant resistance to innovation.

Niches exist at the level of the innovation process and serve as "protected spaces or incubation rooms" (Markard & Truffer, 2008, p. 605) that give new technologies and sociotechnical practices the opportunity to develop without the normal pressures encountered in related markets and regimes (Geels, 2005; Kemp, Schot, & Hoogma, 1998). Technological niches do not occur accidentally. They are created and supported by actors and institutions (Geels, 2005) to provide opportunity for development of technologies whose potential is as yet uncertain. Niches and regimes are similar in that they both involve communities of interacting groups and have rules that govern many of their actions, but niches are much smaller and less stable in their structure and practices. Markard and Truffer (2008) suggest that niches that demonstrate that they are potentially compatible or beneficial to a related regime may be more successful than others.

The macrolevel of the framework is the landscape, which represents the external environment in which a set of regimes and niches functions. These include general economic, political, cultural, social and technological factors that have an impact on innovation and production processes without being affected by new innovations in the short- to midterm (Markard & Truffer, 2008). The resulting integrated framework includes four major elements:

> Niches or application contexts, in which radical innovations emerge and mature; a technological innovation system, which might encompass niches and is characterized by emergent institutions and conjointly produced resources; sociotechnical regimes that represent the dominant production structure, which challenges the TIS; and a landscape with parameters that influence regimes and innovations without being influenced in turn. The environment of the TIS is composed of regimes, competing and complementary technological innovation systems and landscape level influences. (p. 613)

Orchestration of Innovation Networks

Dhanaraj and Parkhe's (2006) framework for orchestration in innovation networks draws from network theory, particularly with respect to networks characterized by low density and high centrality, to gain insight into how firms at the center of innovation networks orchestrate network activities. These "hub firms" are able to influence the activities of other actors in the network even though they have no hierarchical authority over the other network members. Dhanaraj and Parkhe propose that the influence hub firms have is due to their central position in the network (network centrality) as well as to individual firm attributes that contribute to their prominence and power (Brass & Burkhardt, 1993; Wasserman & Galaskiewicz, 1993). The hub firm uses this prominence and power to take on a leadership role in the activities carried out by members of the innovation network. Hub firms influence the network's members through key orchestration processes they perform and through their network recruiting activities as they shape the network through their choice of members.

Centrality and prominence are not sufficient to creating and extracting value from the network (Kogut, 1988). Dhanaraj and Parkhe (2006) note that they are "in essence returning to Burt's (1992) provocative insight that position alone does not create the benefit, but the entrepreneurial approach of an actor (the hub firm) to turn the position into an advantage does" (p. 666). The hub firm's success depends on carrying out particular actions that promote and encourage the network's innovation activities. These activities are (1) ensuring knowledge mobility, (2) managing innovation appropriability, and (3) fostering network stability. Ensuring knowledge mobility involves taking action to encourage and ease the flow of knowledge among network members, including identifying valuable knowledge residing at one part of the network and taking action to make that knowledge available to other members of the network (Doz, 1996; Gulati, 1999; Hansen, 1999) and using what has been learned from network members for the hub firm's own benefit (Gulati & Singh, 1998; Inkpen & Dinur, 1998; Kale, Singh, & Perlmuter, 2000; Khanna, Gulati, & Nohria, 1998).

Appropriability is defined as a property that "governs an innovator's ability to capture the profits generated by an innovation" (Teece, 1986, p. 610). Managing innovation appropriability involves the hub firm's activities aimed at ensuring that it is informed about the knowledge creation activities of network members and that partners don't try to cheat (Mowery, Oxley, & Silverman, 1996) or leak information to competing networks (Dhanaraj & Parkhe, 2006). Hub firms must "ensure that the value created is distributed equitably and is perceived as such by network members" (Dhanaraj & Parkhe, 2006, p. 662). This is achieved by fostering trust, observing procedural justice, and ensuring joint asset ownership.

The third key activity the hub firms must perform is fostering network stability. Dhanaraj and Parkhe (2006), following Weick's observations about loose coupling (Weick, 1976), note that innovation networks are loosely-coupled systems and are therefore prone to instability, particularly with the pressures that come from competition among network members (Gomes-Casseres, 1994; Kogut, 1988; Stuart, 2000; Uzzi, 1997). Thus, a hub firm's success in orchestrating the innovation network is related to its ability to foster network stability. This is a "dynamic stability (not static), which aims for a nonnegative growth rate while allowing for entry and exit of network members" (Dhanaraj & Parkhe, 2006, p. 661). A hub firm may increase the network's dynamic stability can "by enhancing reputation, lengthening the shadow of the future [linking future benefits to current actions], and by building multiplexity ... (e.g., a hub firm undertaking additional joint projects with network members or encouraging other network members to do so)" (Dhanarj & Parkhe, 2006, p. 664).

Wakes of Innovation in Project Networks

Boland and colleagues' (2007) study explores situations in which members of heterogeneous, distributed networks produce interrelated innovations, with a focal innovation spurring related innovations by other members which in turn feed back into the ongoing development of the original innovation. The theoretical framework they propose is based in a recent stream of information technology innovation research that focuses on innovation networks comprised of heterogeneous actors rather than on individual innovators (Tuomi 2002; Van de Ven, 2005). Analyzing the case of the introduction of digital 3-D representation in architecture, engineering, and construction, the study suggests that "changes in digital representation that are central to the functioning of a distributed system can engender multiple innovations in technologies, work practices, and knowledge across multiple communities, each of which is following its own distinctive tempo and trajectory" (Boland et al., 2007, p. 631). The phenomena of multiple, interacting innovations following their own tempo and trajectory are depicted as wakes of innovation, much like wakes traveling across water. In the case they analyze, the information technology (digital 3-D representation) is both the target of innovation and an engine of innovation, serving as an enabler and a mediator of interactions and knowledge creation among network members (Boland et al., 2007).

The framework developed to analyze wakes of innovation involves three main elements: path creation, intercalation, and trading zones. In contrast to the assumption of actor passivity found in the path dependence view of evolutionary economics (Arthur, 1989), path creation sees innovators as active in their efforts to explore new practices and technologies, mindfully deviating from traditional practice (Garud & Karnoe, 2001). This type of path creation activity is entrepreneurial rather than reactive. In the heterogeneous network environment analyzed in the study (Boland et al., 2007), the authors didn't discover a sole entrepreneur creating new paths, but rather multiple actors deviating mindfully from traditional practice in order to address challenges encountered in the digital 3-D project.

In order to better understand interactions among the entrepreneurial activities of various network members involved in the digital 3-D project, Boland and colleagues (2007) turned to Galison's (1997) study of the history of microphysics for the concept of an *intercalated* process of change. Intercalation, from the term *intercalate* ("to insert between or among existing elements or layers," Merriam-Webster Online (2012)), is used to explain staccato patterns in which "multiple innovations developed at different times by different members of the network are inserted into the project network" (Boland et al., 2007, p. 635).

Finally, the analysis looks at trading zones—the network's "physical and cognitive arenas" (Boland et al., 2007, p. 635) where members can share their distinct knowledge. These trading zones emerge at the permeable boundaries between member communities (Galison, 1997; Kellogg, Orlikowski, & Yates, 2006). Together, the concepts of path creation, intercalated change, and the emergence of trading zones at the permeable boundaries of the innovation network communities were found to provide a conceptual framework for explaining how and why multiple, asynchronous, interrelated innovations (wakes of innovation) emerge in heterogeneous innovation networks.

RESEARCH METHOD AND SETTING

This project concerned a single case study involving a small, public university's implementation of an institutional e-book program. Similar to Boland and colleagues (2007), we sought to examine the diverse patterns of how innovations are created and introduced throughout a network of partners and to analyze the processes and interactions that take place between and among network partners. Network partners were interviewed to form a group of single case studies with which we sought to merge theory with empirical observations (Eisenhardt, 1989; Martin &

Turner, 1986—as cited in Boland and colleagues (2007)). Our expectation was that the theoretical accounts would offer insight into the wakes of innovation created by the implementation of a university's institutional e-book program.

During this study, interviews with representatives from publishers, a digital content provider, and a printing/copying company were conducted. The objectives of these interviews were to (a) identify the ways in which the various partners developed, adopted, and implemented different or new processes, procedures, or business strategies as a function of being involved in the e-book network; (b) identify how these innovations flowed to other parts of the business operations or strategies, and how they impacted interactions with other entities outside of the e-book network; and (c) examine the behavior of network partners in a network that contained competitors.

In total, seven individuals from four network partners (two publishers, one digital content provider, one copying/printing company) were interviewed. Individuals responded in writing to a list of questions about innovations in their organizations that were directly attributable to their participation in the e-book network. Follow-up telephone interviews were also conducted with each individual who responded in order to clarify points or drill deeper into the written responses. The individuals selected for the interviews consisted of those who were responsible for their organization's interaction with the hub university. It was felt that they would have the best knowledge about how the e-book program affected operations in their organizations.

The Multipublisher E-Book Program

In August 2009, a small, public university responded to a request for proposal (RFP) for a federally-funded program that sought proposals for innovative projects that would increase students' opportunities to rent college textbooks. Based on the guidelines in the RFP, the program pursued four goals:

1. Increase student access to course-related material.
2. Substantially reduce student expenses for required course materials.
3. Engage students through the incorporation and use of electronic course content.
4. Develop and disseminate a sustainable and replicable program and program-related information.

The proposal was accepted and funded to implement a pilot e-book and electronic resources program at the university. At the heart of the proposal were three key elements: electronic textbooks rather than traditional, hard-copy textbooks; electronic textbook rental through a student fee rather than individual student purchase; and institutional agreements with major publishing companies to rent e-books and other electronic course material at discounted prices. In the early stages of the project, the university entered into e-book purchase agreements with five textbook publishing companies and an institutional agreement with a print services company that offered students a low-cost option to print their e-books on demand.

The program provided a win-win situation. Through the adoption of an electronic course material program and a design that ensured that each student would rent the material, the publishers were assured that the quantity of material rented would provide a greater financial advantage than the traditional, bookstore-based purchase models. Publishers would realize higher profits as student fees guaranteed a specified revenue base. Students would benefit by the reduced price of course material (which was targeted to be no more than 10% of tuition and fees) and by having access to required course materials from the first day of class. Faculty would benefit by having the opportunity to adopt electronic material that was likely to be more engaging to students than traditional nonelectronic materials and to be able to make textbook adoption choices without loss of academic freedom. Administrators would benefit from a system that was designed to provide a useful tool in the assessment and retention process. The program design also had the added environmental benefit of taking a green approach that minimized the use of print-based resources.

When the project started, the network included seven partners (five textbook publishers, one e-book textbook platform provider, and a print services company), the hub (the university) and 1,503 students and 75 faculty members. By the end of the fourth semester of the program, the network had grown to include 11 partners, the hub, 2,009 students and 92 faculty members.

TECHNOLOGICAL INNOVATION SYSTEMS AND THE MULTILEVEL FRAMEWORK IN THE E-BOOK PROGRAM

The primary elements of the technological innovation system and multilevel framework are the landscape, sociotechnical regime(s), niche(s) and the network of actors that form the technological innovation system itself. The technological innovation system's environment may also include complementary innovation systems that influence the activities of the network of actors (Markard & Truffer, 2008). The technological innovation system involved in the development of the e-book program involved a diverse, heterogeneous network of actors, including textbook publishers [competitors], an e-book platform vendor, a print services vendor, a Learning Management System vendor, faculty members, students, the university business office, the registrar's office, and the university bookstore. An analysis of the e-book program found evidence of and insight into each of these framework elements.

Landscape and Complementary Innovation Systems

The landscape surrounding the e-book project at its inception included a variety of technological changes and environmental forces that influenced the project's design. In 2009, the e-book market was small but beginning to gain ground. E-books represented 3.2% of the trade book market in 2009—an increase of 27% over the prior year's 1.17% market share (Publishers Report, 2011). The e-book reader market was beginning to grow as well. In November, 2007 Amazon had released its first version of the Kindle and by the time of the announcement of the grant RFP Amazon had two newer versions of the e-reader on the market—the Kindle 2 introduced in February, 2009 and the Kindle DX introduced in May, 2009 (IDG News Service, 2009a; IDG News Service, 2009b; Lawson, 2007). An August, 2009, *Publishers Weekly* article entitled "Kindle Market Share On The Rise" reported that although desktop and laptop computers were still the preferred way to read e-books, 45% of all recent e-book downloads had been to Kindle devices (Milliot, 2009). Competition was also beginning to heat up. In October, 2009, Barnes and Noble entered the market with the Nook e-reader, heralded as a Kindle killer in the October 2009 issue of *Wired* magazine (Sorrel, 2009). The complementary technological innovation systems represented by the e-book and e-reader markets provided key resources that would help shape the options available to meet the project's objectives of increased access to course materials, reduced cost, and increased student engagement in learning.

Another of the landscape features that influenced the project was the growing concern about the rising cost of higher education. An October, 2009 article in the *New York Times*, for example, reported that college tuition and fees had continued to increase over the past year (Lewin, 2009a). Citing a report issued by the College Board, the article noted that although the consumer price index had declined by 2.1% from July 2008 to July 2009, the cost of tuition and fees at public universities had increased by an average of 6.5% in the past year and by 4.4% at private colleges. The article included quotes indicating that the trend was troubling and suggested that colleges should go beyond cutting budgets to looking at restructuring in order to control costs. Along with the concern about tuition and fees, attention was also focused on the increasing cost of textbooks. In March, 2009, for example, the American Association of State Colleges and Universities issued a policy brief entitled "Cracking the Books: Policy Measures to Contain Textbook Costs" (McBain, 2009). The report cited studies published from 2004 to 2009 addressing concerns about textbook costs, among them a U.S. Government Accountability Office report which found that textbook costs had tripled over the period from 1986 to 2004. Other articles published during this period included a discussion of textbook cost containment measures included in the 2008 *Higher Education Opportunity Act* (Green, 2009) and local news stories like the September 8, 2009 *New York Daily News* article about spiraling textbook costs at the City University of New York (Gioia, 2008). Awareness of these trends and their impact on students informed the RFP issued by the federal agency and the university's interest in finding a more affordable and effective means of providing students the learning resources they needed.

Sociotechnical Regime

As noted in Kemp and colleagues (2001), a sociotechnical regime consists of the rules and practices embodied in the knowledge, technical practices, production process technologies, skills, institutions and infrastructures that make up a technology. As a regime develops, its rules and practices become the status quo—the accepted way that things are done with respect to a particular technology. The methods and practices associated with the production and distribution of books can be viewed as a sociotechnical regime. The production processes and materials used to produce and distribute books form the basic technical core and over time become embedded in a larger sociotechnical environment involving the organizations, individual actors, and infrastructures that create, transfer, and consume the resulting products. Analysis of the e-book program and its environment explored three central aspects of the sociotechnical regime associated with the textbook market—publication, adoption, and distribution.

Textbook Publication

For many years, higher education had worked under a model that was driven by the adoption and use of hardcopy textbooks. However, the growth of global markets and the availability of new technologies had begun to drive the industry in a different direction. The U.S. Government Accountability Office recognized that electronic textbooks were an emerging trend, although their success had not been as promising as originally predicted (Government Accountability Office, 2005, p. 20). Over the prior few years, however, publishers had focused on providing electronic supplemental material that had improved the amount and type of available content that directly reached Millennial-generation students. Technologically-driven and accustomed to multitasking with IPods, cell phones and the Internet, Millennials were offered electronic content such as podcasts, videos, interactive games, and simulations that provided a more engaging way to learn. Publishers were also beginning to offer textbooks in electronic form. In 2009, when the e-book project was initiated, digital textbook sales represented only 0.5% of the total textbook market, but had shown strong growth in the prior year and sales were expected to grow to 1% in 2010 and more than 18% by 2014 (Reynolds & Ioffe, 2010).

Textbook Adoption

Publishing companies and university professors have a symbiotic relationship. Instruction in most university classrooms revolves around the use of textbooks and publishing companies depend on university professors to adopt their material. Because of this symbiotic relationship, publishers contract with professors to write and update textbooks and send professors complimentary desk copies of textbooks for review. Their purpose is to convince professors to adopt specific textbooks for their courses. Student demand does not drive adoption; professors are the mediators between the students and the publishers.

Textbook Distribution

At the time that the e-book program was first proposed, purchasing textbooks was no longer the only option students had for gaining access to required course materials. Various textbook rental programs had been implemented and new entrants were joining the rental program market. In 2005, the Department of Education conducted a nationwide survey of 51 bookstores that offered a textbook rental program; 21 of the stores responded. The study found that universities estimated it would take an average of $2 million to re-create their current rental program from scratch and the average physical-space requirement of rental programs ranged from 4,000-4,500 square feet. In addition, success of the programs depended on textbook adoptions lasting approximately 3 years (Textbook Rental, 2005, p. 2), requiring multiple and costly replacement purchases of required textbooks every decade. Some of the advantages cited in the survey were cost effectiveness for students, effectiveness as a recruiting tool and the guarantee that all students would get the textbooks for their courses. Disadvantages included faculty's dislike of restrictions, particularly with respect to academic freedom; the labor-intensive nature of the programs; and the high cost of labor for a low return on investment.

At the University of Illinois-Springfield, for example, where enrollment was approximately 4,000 students, budget estimates for program start-up was $1.39 million and an annual program maintenance budget was estimated to be $750,000 (State of Illinois Board of Higher Education, 2005, p. 69). The majority of these expenses were attributable to the need for increased storage space, growing maintenance of inventory, computer systems for inventory control, and additional staff requirements. The University of Chicago estimated that a rental program would result in increasing institutional expenses by at least 12% over a traditional retail program (State of Illinois Board of Higher Education, 2005, p. 68). The reasons the Illinois Board of Higher Education cited for not implementing a textbook rental program were prohibitive start-up and maintenance costs of inventory, staffing, and administration of rental programs; the intellectual rigidity inherent in multiyear cycles of textbook use and uniform textbook assignments across multiple sections of the same course; the demands of rapidly changing resources in such areas as technology, medicine, engineering, and science; and the role of foundational textbooks in the lifelong learning process (State of Illinois Board of Higher Education, 2005, p. 70).

In August 2009, competition in the textbook rental market was growing. An August, 2009 article in the *New York Times* reported that Cengage Learning was going to begin renting textbooks to students, offering them immediate access to the first chapter of the book in e-book format and a choice of options for shipping the printed book (Lewin, 2009b). Also included in the article were accounts of rental pilot projects being initiated by Follett Higher Education Group, McGraw-Hill Education, and Barnes and Noble College Bookstores. The story also noted that, in response to rental program grants offered under the 2008 Higher Education Opportunity Act, more than 20 college bookstores had applied for grants to support the textbook rental programs.

Niches

Niches provide a protected space that give new sociotechnical practices and technologies an opportunity to develop without the usual external pressures exerted by related sociotechnical regimes and landscape forces (Markard & Truffer, 2008). The award of a federally-funded grant for the development of the e-book program and the university's authorization for the implementation of the pilot e-book program formed the basis of a niche that provided legitimation, funding, and the time needed to design the program, recruit a heterogeneous group of network partners, and implement and extend the pilot program.

Network Orchestration Activities

Network orchestration involves key activities performed by the hub firm in support of the innovation goals of the hub and the other network actors. These activities include ensuring knowledge mobility, managing innovation appropriability, and fostering network stability. The extent to which these activities were present in the e-book project is explored in the following section.

Ensuring Knowledge Mobility

The hub firm's role in ensuring knowledge mobility involves a variety of activities including improving the ease of sharing knowledge, identifying valuable knowledge held by one actor and transferring that knowledge to other actors, and using what has been learned through network activity to the benefit of the hub firm. Knowledge mobility activities were central to the hub's orchestration of the network.

Because the major network partners were competitors, sharing knowledge was not an easy task. For instance, e-book program staff had to be careful about sharing proprietary information. This made it very difficult to initiate consistent processes and procedures throughout the network of publishers which, in turn, impacted every aspect of the program. In several instances, some publishers were very proactive in working with faculty to adopt and create custom e-books. This strategy involved regularly and frequently sending sales representatives, knowledgeable about the program, to the university to visit with faculty. Even with the reduced price of the custom e-books, the price structure resulted in increased commissions to the sales reps. Other publishers in the network relied exclusively on an inside-sales strategy which left the e-book staff to inform faculty about the program and inside sales reps to assist faculty from remote locations.

As the first semester of the program approached, it became obvious that e-book staff lacked a comprehensive way of identifying adopted e-books. Faculty members were often confused between the e-book program and the bookstore. Originally, the e-book program relied on creating a spreadsheet which included an inventory of e-book adoptions and accordingly, sharing this file with respective publishers. This process became unmanageable very quickly as it was difficult to identify the most current spreadsheet; new data was being added to old versions; data was inconsistent among the spreadsheets sent to each publisher when it came back (i.e., publishers would add their own fields which the e-book staff did not need or understand).

Ideally, what was needed was a comprehensive library database that would allow individualized logins based on user so that each publisher had access to their own and only their own inventory while e-book staff had access to everything. This needed to be web-based and secured. Unfortunately, this solution was beyond the financial resources of the program. One publisher set up and suggested the use of a Googledoc spreadsheet for the sharing of information between themselves and e-book staff. This process allowed for real-time editing of data by all persons who shared the document. This was a functional solution for one publisher to the e-book program. The e-book staff set up similar Googledocs for all major publishers (those with a large inventory of titles used in the e-book program). This proved to be an adequate solution although not an ideal one. It was effective, however, in sharing critical information between network partners and the hub.

E-book staff openly negotiated with each publisher with respect to the goals of the program and the anticipated price point for e-books used in the program. While each publisher did not know the exact details of competing publisher contracts, they were all aware of the target e-book price, that is, no more than 10% of tuition and fees. Each publisher approached this in different ways. Information was not shared between publishers however, competitive leverage was used in negotiating with each publisher in an attempt to reduce the contracted price. It took about two semesters for publishers to start feeling the effect of either favorable or unfavorable decisions in their pricing structure. While they did not know specifics, they felt the impact in the increase or decrease in their market share of adoptions. Faculty quickly learned which publishers were providing more favorable pricing for e-books in their area. For instance, the pricing structure used by one publisher pushed the price of business titles way above the expected price point but allowed education titles to be offered at very favorable rates. As a result, the publisher saw its market share in business decrease dramatically. At the same time, they were almost the exclusive supplier of titles in the education department. Conversely, a second publisher with a competitive fixed price for any title in its inventory quickly captured a large percentage of the business titles. The publisher who utilized an inside-sales strategy ended up with a greatly diminished position in the network as their service could not compete with publishers who had sales representatives on the ground at the university. The publisher's sales went from approximately 25% of the market in the first semester to approximately 5% of the market in the fourth semester. Faculty began to make market-driven decisions and pitted sales representatives against each other in order to adopt more inexpensive titles for students. Faculty informally sharing knowledge with each other, with e-book staff, and with sales representatives quickly became a critical driver of sharing knowledge among network partners.

One of the important parts of the e-book program was disseminating information to students. Although students did not select the textbooks or the method of delivery, their satisfaction with the program was critical to its success. Formal attempts to provide training sessions proved ineffective as students did not attend in any great numbers. For the first semester, the university arranged multiple training sessions for students over a 2-day period. E-book platform staff members were flown in and accommodations secured. Eight 1-hour training sessions were offered at various times throughout both days and evenings. With the exception of one faculty member who brought an entire class, only 22 students attended. In the second semester, formal webinar training sessions were held in an attempt to reduce costs and provide more training sessions over multiple days. In total, 10 training sessions were provided over 7 days. While attendance was somewhat improved, it still did not achieve program objectives of informing students as only 12 students and 6 faculty members attended. Interestingly enough, network partners, who stood to gain the most from an informed student body and faculty (in terms of reduced support calls, more satisfied students, faculty who effectively utilized the product, and a generally effective e-book program so that the program would continue to be financially and programmatically viable), were not proactive in providing organized training to either students or faculty. Sales representatives provided limited training sessions to faculty during e-book adoption time but not during the implementation time period.

Beginning in the second semester, the e-book program utilized an "e-book ambassador" program to help with disseminating information to students. This program was much more successful at directly reaching students even though the program only utilized two ambassadors. One ambassador enrolled in an internship course to assist e-book staff with this program. Another ambassador was refunded his e-book course fee. Their efforts were much more effective at reaching students than formal training sessions had been. Student-to-student transfer of knowledge proved to be the most effective strategy for knowledge and skill transfer.

For the institutional printing part of the program, the original network partner was hampered by relying on their traditional business model to conceive the service demanded by the program. In other words, they developed a print-on-demand function that did not allow for adequate volume or ease of service. Communication was mostly future-oriented—focusing on how they were going to fix things going forward instead of addressing what went wrong. By the end of the second semester, the e-book program decided to change vendors for this function as additional services and more innovative ideas were proposed by one of their competitors—all at a lower price for the students.

At the root of the network, faculty and students were critical components in the sharing of knowledge with their peers and network partners. Since these two populations were the major customers that the network served, this is not surprising. While e-book staff attempted to persuade publishers about price points, the reality is they did not fully understand the effects of their decisions until they felt the effect in market share and bottom-line profits.

Managing Innovation Appropriability

Managing appropriability includes ensuring that the hub firm is informed about the knowledge management activities of network members and ensuring that value created by network activity is distributed equitably and perceived as such by network members. In contrast to for-profit networks, the hope of this nonprofit network was to spur the development of other models and encourage partners to develop additional models that would address cost and effectiveness of course material distribution. This goal is a reflection primarily of the funding source and the university administration. As such, information was widely shared not only with network members but also with other universities, other potential networks, and other potential hubs. Over the first four semesters of the program, at least six academic conference presentations were made and one journal article published which contained specific information about the program, network partners, and program evaluation. New network partners (i.e., publishers) were added as faculty members requested and publisher business models would allow. With profit and market share the guiding motivation for network members (other than the hub which had cost containment as its motivation), it quickly became evident that this program promised to significantly change industry business models, course material distribution methods, and the price students would pay for their course materials.

The value that for-profit network members realized as a function of this program was an increase in market share and profits. Value to these network members was not distributed equally among partners. As mentioned previously, publishers who established price structures which were perceived as "too high" realized significantly lower market share than their competitors within the network. The hub institution's hope was to increase the competition among publishers in order to achieve a lower price for students. It was never intended to equally distribute the value across the network. The distribution of value was targeted at students. It was important that students would feel that the program provided a better value than a more traditional model for the distribution of course materials. Evaluation surveys distributed to students over the first three semesters of the program provided a student favorability rating of more than 75% favorability rating (n = approximately 1,300 students). Nearly all students in the program considered it to be an effective cost alternative.

The success of the e-book program was extremely dependent on university faculty. Before the program started, few faculty members were aware of the price of the textbooks they were ordering for students. This information was not advertised by publishers or the bookstore. Only if a faculty member inquired at the bookstore would they know the price that students were paying for required course material. As a result of the e-book program, faculty became acutely aware of the cost of course material. On several occasions, e-book adoption requests were declined by the e-book staff because the price was too high (i.e., the selected title exceeded the target price point and there were suitable equivalent alternatives or the publisher's price was higher than the used book market price). Faculty members were asked to evaluate the need for the more expensive title and were given an option to select another publisher in order to reduce the price. Most faculty members became very conscious about prices.

Fostering Network Stability

Another of the critical roles essential to the hub firm's success is in fostering the stability of the network. The associated activities include recruiting new network members, managing the network and enhancing its reputation, getting actors to think in terms of the future benefits they would achieve as a result of network participation, and encouraging the development of multiplexity by entering into additional joint projects with network members and encouraging projects among network partners.

In the case of the e-book project, the primary reason for-profit partners joined the network was to increase profits and market share. Without exception, this was the response of each partner when asked. Secondary reasons included increasing inroads into the higher education market, initiating or testing a new business strategy, and seeing how students and faculty reacted to the new model. Partners were recruited into the network as a strategy to increase the offerings of e-books and publishers available for adoption. Some smaller publishers came and left the network as their position in the network relied exclusively on the desire of faculty to use a specific title published by a specific publisher to be used for a specific course. If the course was not offered or the faculty member changed his or her mind, that one-book publisher left the network (perhaps to reenter the network the next time that the course was offered). In several instances, a publisher left or was excluded from the network because they could not offer their e-books at a price that could compete with the used book market.

The institutional printing component of the program underwent some turbulence as one partner was replaced as the result of a competitor's offer of a better price structure and delivery model for student e-book printing. The network grew as faculty became more comfortable with the program and network partners realized that the program could be viable and profitable. Since students were dependent on faculty and their own educational goals to enter and stay in the network, students came and went as they started their tenure with the university and subsequently graduated. Faculty also joined and left the network as their employment status with the university changed. A few faculty members voluntarily discontinued their membership in the network because they did not like the program.

As the program grew, opportunities for multiplexity between the hub and several network partners increased. For instance, several publishers sought to sell the university other institutional services such as a learning management system, curriculum and course development services, and premium electronic content. In each instance, the "package" of services was promised to save the university and students money by leveraging volume of sales. At the time of the analysis of this case, the institution had not entered into any additional institutional agreements although several were under serious consideration.

WAKES OF INNOVATION IN THE E-BOOK PROGRAM

The wakes of innovation identified by Boland and colleagues (2007) are related to three main elements of network activity and relationships—path creation, intercalation, and trading zones—which together provide a lens for examining the interweaving of innovations engendered by the network's activities and fed back into the network to further the realization of the innovation project. Each of these elements was present in the activities and environment associated with the e-book project.

Path Creation

Path creation involves innovators' active efforts to explore new practices and technologies, consciously and deliberately choosing to deviate from the traditional practice in the sociotechnical systems in which they operate. Several of the e-book program's network members took on the role of path creator in embracing innovative elements of the e-book program design and extending them into other areas of their lines of business.

As negotiations between the university and textbook publishers progressed, it became obvious that publishers were feeling the heat of their current business model which relied on the publication of new editions every 2 to 3 years for many of their titles. This model led to a steady increase in the price of textbooks. Legislators and school administrators were looking for a strategy to control the price of textbooks to students. With pressure on the publishers to develop new business models that would reduce the costs to students, they were eager to work with the university's pilot e-book program to test the viability of the course-fee model. With 100% sell-through to students, publishers were assured that their copyrights were preserved as each student purchased these rights via the mandatory course fee. Although average e-book prices were less than 10% of tuition and fees—representing a significant reduction in prices of course material to students—in reality, campus bookstore reports indicated that new book purchases accounted for only a fraction of total textbook purchases. Many students purchased used textbooks on the secondary market, reducing the number of new textbooks sold.

Based on interviews, it appears that the institutional printing program was a first for the industry. Before this program, no publishers participating in the e-book program had allowed third-party printing privileges. As such, most publishers involved their legal departments in crafting contracts that were explicit about the rights conveyed to the university under this program. Nonetheless, without exception, they all ultimately agreed to allow it. Some publishers wanted a small royalty fee for this privilege; others did not. Not only was the institutional printing program new to publishers, it was also new to the printing company. Traditionally, printing and copying companies had been very cautious about the duplication of copyrighted material. Based on interviews, they had not been involved with the duplication of textbooks on an institutional scale. This project was the first in the industry.

Intercalation

The concept of intercalation is used to describe the circumstance in which innovations developed by various members of the network, often influenced by the network's collaborative innovation activities, are inserted (intercalated) into the project network as a spur to further innovation.

The e-book program involves many innovations and network partners were regularly inserting innovations into the program network. Most of the innovations were focused around new strategies and new business models. Whether it was the decision of the university to implement the institutional e-book program, publishers being willing to adopt a course-fee institutional model, the campus bookstore accepting a new definition of what a "textbook" is, publishers being willing to allow institutional printing, publishers adapting billing and invoicing procedures or a vendor developing an integrated, single sign-on solution for the Learning Management System, all network partners contributed to the many innovations which made up the e-book program.

Trading Zones

In the wakes of innovation framework, trading zones represent either physical or cognitive arenas that occur at the permeable boundaries between communities. The trading zone offers an opportunity for communication and information sharing among members of disparate communities. Because they were competitors, direct interactions between the for-profit network members were very limited. Competitors were isolated from each other with the only common link being the hub. The isolation was driven by their profit motive and the need to preserve proprietary information. Interestingly enough, there was never an instance where one network partner inquired about what other network partners were doing or about what strategies or procedures were being pursued by competitors within the network. The university's e-book staff acted as a clearing house providing the coordination needed to support network partners' activities. While information was not directly shared among partners, the university staff often suggested strategies or procedures derived from conversations with other partners. The goal was to develop best practices that could be standardized across network partners.

While internetwork communication relied almost exclusively on the hub or the customers relaying information to partners, the communication *within* organizations of the network significantly changed. Based on interview data, most partners made modifications in how they approached sales. For some organizations, this meant an organizational restructuring to include a much more focused approach toward institutional sales. One publisher indicated that the e-book program significantly changed how they operate. In addition, new products were developed to address some of the needs that were identified in the e-book program. The publisher also indicated that their participation in the e-book program had resulted in a positive impact on approximately 25 other organizations with which they currently worked. They directly attributed their ability to win several institutional contracts with other universities to their participation in the e-book pilot program and the related experience they gained with custom e-books and institutional delivery of course material.

The publishers that were interviewed all expressed a desire to expand institutional sales to include more than a single university perspective. They were all contemplating a move to attract university systems in collaborative programs. This would allow them to better align their course materials with expected state learning outcomes. One publisher highlighted the new invoicing system that has been deployed as a way to capture sales for institutional customers. Another publisher indicated that they were working on an analytics dashboard for better tracking of institutional sales.

DISCUSSION

In the analysis of the e-book project, each of the three frameworks proved to be useful in understanding aspects of the organizational network's innovation activities and interactions, not only within the network but with the larger environment in which it operated. The technological innovation system framework with its multilevel model was the most comprehensive, providing the broadest view of the innovation system (i.e., the network) and its environment—the landscape, related sociotechnical regimes and niches. With respect to the e-book project, forces in the landscape concerned with the cost of tuition and textbooks, sociotechnical regimes associated with e-book technology, e-reader technology and textbook publishing technology were all important influences in the activities and innovative practices emerging from the e-book pilot.

The network orchestration framework turned the focus from the network's environment to the structure and inner-workings of the network, which when viewed from the multilevel framework perspective would be the equivalent of its technological innovation system. In particular the orchestration framework explores the activities and influence of a hub firm in its efforts to innovate and realize value for its own benefit through the coordination of the activities of a network of actors pursuing their goals for profit or advantage. In looking at the e-book project through this lens, the central role of the hub and the orchestration activities employed to promote the project's success were delineated and highlighted as key factors that contributed to network coordination.

The wakes of innovation framework focused on the network, too, but not on a central hub firm. Although the case study used in the Boland et al. article included a central firm that performed functions consistent with the role of a hub, the framework's focus was not there but on the actions and innovation orientation of the various network members, including their mindfulness—their conscious decision to seek new paths, their independent innovation activities and their introduction of their own innovations into the network to spur and advance the innovation process. This contrast with the hub-centric focus of the orchestration framework is seen, too, in its focus on trading zones as vehicles for communication among network members as opposed to the hub firm's efforts to ensure knowledge mobility. The inclusion of intercalated innovation by multiple network members also extends the framework's analysis potential into the study of innovation diffusion through its image of wakes of innovation flowing from and into the innovation process.

We believe that each of the frameworks contributed to the understanding of the e-book project and its dynamics and that the results of the study suggest that each of the frameworks has value in gaining insight into innovation in heterogeneous organizational networks. Depending on the questions of interest in a study, elements of one or more of the frameworks could be employed to analyze various aspects of the network and its innovation and communication processes. Having a complementary set of frameworks that can be used together to examine the elements of interest at the macro-, meso- and/or microlevels of technological innovation systems provides a promising starting place for the further study of this area of innovation and innovation diffusion.

Implications for Public Policy

As noted in the discussion of the e-book case, the formation of a protected innovation development space—a niche—afforded the project with funding, time for development, and a source of legitimation that assisted in the recruitment of network members to participate in the project. The importance of niches in the development of technological innovation systems is seen in the multilevel framework presented by Markard and Truffer (2008) and in earlier work related to strategic niche management outlined in Truffer, Metzner, and Hoogma (2002). Niches may be created by public policymakers, private industry or other private organizations (Truffer et al., 2002). The authors suggest that a niche should provide an opportunity for a temporary, limited pilot project aimed at development of the technological innovation and exploration of the conditions for its successful adoption and diffusion. Public policy implications for fostering technological innovation include establishing publicly-funded programs and incentives for the establishment of privately-funded programs that create niches for technological innovation pilot projects.

The wakes of innovation framework, with its focus on intercalated innovation patterns in a heterogeneous network of actors, also provided insight into the innovation dynamics of the e-book project. The interplay of innovations introduced by the focal organization (the university implementing the e-book program) and the network members from different segments of the textbook market's sociotechnical regime illustrated the interweaving of innovation streams generated by members of a heterogeneous network and the dissemination of innovation from the focal project to the various communities represented within the network. These patterns of innovation and diffusion across diverse communities are key elements in the framework outlined in Boland and colleagues (2007). From a public policy perspective, the framework and associated case illustrations suggest that policymakers should consider the promotion of heterogeneous networks in programs designed to foster technological innovation.

Dhanaraj and Parkhe's (2006) framework for orchestration of innovation networks proposes that the hub firm's success in achieving its objectives in a network-driven innovation project depends on its success in carrying out key orchestration activities: ensuring knowledge mobility, management innovation appropriability, and fostering network stability. The analysis of the e-book project provided support for this contention. A further step that could be taken by public policymakers wishing to foster technological innovation would be to organize and support workshops and/or virtual communities that facilitate the sharing of lessons learned by experienced innovation network orchestrators with those who are leading their first network-oriented technological innovation pilot projects.

Limitations of the Study

There are several limitations to this study. First, our findings relate to a single case involving support and legitimation afforded by a federally-funded grant and cannot be generalized across all universities or actor networks. In addition, many of the network actors involved in the e-book project were direct competitors and as such, were unwilling to share information within the network. In a less competitive environment, knowledge sharing among network actors would be more likely and could enhance and improve the functionality and effectiveness of the overall network in ways not seen in this study. The network also involved a university, a nonprofit organization, as the hub. This created unique network dynamics as the hub was not interested in profits but sought instead to reduce costs. Interestingly enough, it appeared that the hub's cost-saving goal provided a unique check and balance to the profit-making goals of other network partners. Finally, this network involved partners operating in a unique industry. Although textbook publishers ultimately sell their books to students, students are not their direct customers. Students have very little input into the process of deciding which publishers and which books will be utilized in the courses they take. Faculty members, who do not purchase the textbooks but nevertheless have the responsibility of selecting the books students must pay for, are the most influential of all the network partners. As a result, publisher entry and retention in the network and the resulting interactions associated with their network activity were ultimately driven by faculty members who were largely unaware that they were performing this function.

Directions for Future Research

Avenues for future research include further comparative research involving the hub-centric communication focus of the orchestration framework and the network-centric distributed communication focus of the wakes of innovation framework, including studies that look at both patterns within the same network. A second area for research would be in comparative study of intercalated innovation in hub-centric and network-centric innovation networks. Finally, additional research might also include further studies of the dynamics of heterogeneous innovation networks composed of both nonprofit organizations and for-profit competitors.

NOTE

1.   The e-book program project was envisioned and directed by Dr. Tracy Hurley, one of the coauthors of this study.

REFERENCES

Arthur, W. B. (1989). Competing technologies, increasing returns, and lock-in by historical events. *The Economic Journal*, *89*(394), 116-131.

Boland, R. J., Lytinnen, K., & Yoo, Y. (2007). Wakes of innovation in project networks: The case of digital 3-D representations in architecture, engineering, and construction. *Organization Science*, *18*(4), 631-647.

Brass, D. J., & Burkhardt, M. E. (1993). Potential power and power use: An investigation of structure and behavior. *Academy of Management Journal*, *36*, 441-470.

Burt, R. S. (1992). *Structural holes: The social structure of competition*. Cambridge, MA: Harvard University Press.

Carlsson, B. (2006). Internationalization of innovation systems: A survey of the literature. *Research policy*, *35*(1), 56-67.

Carlsson, B., Jacobsson, S., Holmen, M., & Rickne, A. (2002). Innovation systems: analytical and methodological issues. *Research Policy, 31*(2), 233-245.

Chang, Y. C., & Chen, M. H. (2004). Comparing approaches to systems of innovation: the knowledge perspective. *Technology in Society, 26*(1), 17-37.

Dewald, U., & Truffer, B. (2011). Market formation in technological innovation systems—Diffusion of photovoltaic applications in Germany. *Industry and Innovation, 18*(3), 285-300.

Dhanaraj, C., & Parkhe, A. (2006). Orchestrating innovation networks. *Academy of Management Review, 31*(3), 659-669.

Doz, L. (1996). The evolution of cooperation in strategic alliances: Initial conditions or learning process? . *Strategic Management Journal, 17*, 55-83.

Edquist, C. (1997). Systems of innovation approaches—Their emergence and characteristics. In C. Edquist & M. McKelvey (Eds.), *Systems of innovation: Technologies, institutions and organizations* (pp. 1-35). London, England: Pinter.

Edquist, C. (2005). Systems of innovation: Perspectives and challenges. In J. Fagerberg, D. C. Mowery, & R. R. Nelson (Eds.), *The Oxford handbook of innovation* (pp. 41-63). New York, NY: Oxford University Press.

Eisenhardt, K. M. (1989). Building theories from case study research. *Academy of Management Review, 14*(4), 532-550.

Elzen, G., Geels, F. W., & Green, K. (2004). *System innovation and the transition to sustainability: Theory, evidence and policy.* Cheltenham, PA: Edgar Elgar.

Galison, P. (1997). *Image and logic: A material culture of microphysics.* Chicago, IL: The University of Chicago Press.

Gardet, E., & Mothe, C. (2011). The dynamics of coordination in innovation networks. *European Management Review, 8*, 213-229.

Garud, R., & Karnoe, P. (2001). Path creation as a process of mindful deviation. In R. Garud & P. Karnoe (Eds.), *Path dependence and creation* (pp. 1-38). New York, NY: Erlbaum.

Geels, F. W. (2002). Technological transitions as evolutionary reconfiguration processes: A multilevel perspective and a case-study. *Research Policy, 31*, 1257-1274.

Geels, F. W. (2005). The dynamics of transitions in sociotechnical systems: a multilevel analysis of the transition pathway from horse-drawn carriages to automobiles (1860-1930). *Technology Analysis & Strategic Management, 27*(3), 445-476.

Gioia, E. (2009, September 8). Textbook case of rising costs threatening CUNY affordability. *New York Daily News.* Retrieved from http://www.nydailynews.com/new-york/queens/textbook-case-rising-costs-threatening-cuny-affordability-article-1.404158

Gomes-Casseres, B. (1994). Group versus group: How alliance networks compete. *Harvard Business Review, 72*(4), 62-74.

Government Accountability Office. (2005). *College textbooks: Enhanced offerings appear to drive recent price increases.* Retrieved from http://www.gao.gov/new.items/d05806.pdf

Green, K. C. (2009). Regulating the Bookstore. Retrieved from http://www.insidehighered.com/views/2009/05/green

Gulati, R. (1999). Network location and learning: The influences of network resources and firm capabilities on alliance formation. *Strategic Management Journal, 20*, 397-420.

Gulati, R., & Singh, H. (1998). The architecture of cooperation: Managing coordination uncertainty and interdependence in strategic alliances. *Administrative Science Quarterly, 43*, 781-814.

Hansen, M. (1999). The search-transfer problem: The role of weak ties in sharing knowledge across organization subunits. *Administrative Science Quarterly, 44*, 82-111.

IDG News Service. (2009a). *Amazon unveils Kindle 2*. Retrieved from http://www.pcworld.com/article/159229/amazon_unveils_kindle_2.html

IDG News Service. (2009b). *A guided tour: Hands on with the Kindle DX*. Retrieved from http://www.pcworld.com/article/164470/a_guided_tour_hands_on_with_the_kindle_dx.html

Inkpen, A. C., & Dinur, A. (1998). Knowledge management processes and international joint ventures. *Organization Science, 7*, 211-220.

Intercalate. (n.d.). In *Merriam-Webster Dictionary online*. Retrieved from http://www.merriam-webster.com/dictionary/intercalate

Kale, P., Singh, H., & Perlmutter, H. (2000). Learning and protection of proprietary assets in strategic alliances: Building relational capital. *Strategic Management Journal, 21*, 217-237.

Kellogg, K. C., Orlikowski, W. J., & Yates, J. (2006). Life in the trading zone: Structuring coordination across boundaries in postbureaucratic organizations. *Organization Science, 17*(1), 22-44.

Kemp, R., Rip, A., & Schot, J. (2001). Constructing transition paths through the management of niches. In R. Garud & P. Karnoe (Eds.), *Path dependence and creation* (pp. 269-299). London, England: Erlbaum.

Kemp, R., Schot, J., & Hoogma, R. (1998). Regime shifts to sustainability through processes of niche formation: The approach of strategic niche management. *Technology Analysis & Strategic Management, 10*(2), 175-195.

Khanna, T., Gulati, R., & Nohria, N. (1998). The dynamics of learning alliances: Competition, cooperation, and relative scope. *Strategic Management Journal, 19*, 193-210.

Kogut, B. (1998). A study of the life cycle of joint ventures. In F. K. Contractor & P. Lorange (Eds.), *Cooperative strategies I international business* (pp. 169-186). Lexington MA: Lexington Books.

Lawson, S. (2007). Amazon Kindle finds a new use for 3G. Retrieved from http://www.pcworld.com/article/139810/amazon_kindle_finds_a_new_use_for_3g.html.

Lewin, T. (2009a, October 20). College costs keep rising, report says. *New York Times*. Retrieved from http://www.nytimes.com/2009/10/21/education/21costs.html

Lewin, T. (2009b, August 13). Textbook Publisher to Rent to College Students. *New York Times*. Retrieved from http://www.nytimes.com/2009/08/14/education/14textbook.html

Lyytinen, K., & Damsgaard, J. (2001). What's wrong with the diffusion of innovation theory: The case of a complex and networked technology. In M. A. Ardis

& B. L. Marcolin (Eds.), *Diffusing software product and process innovations* (pp. 173-190). Norwell, MA: Kluwer Academic.

Markard, J., Stadelmann, M., & Truffer, B. (2009). Prospective analysis of technological innovation systems: Identifying technological and organizational development options for biogas in Switzerland. *Research Policy, 38*(4), 655-667.

Markard, J., & Truffer, B. (2008). Technological innovation systems and the multi-level perspective: Towards an integrated framework. *Research Policy, 37*, 596-615.

Martin, P. Y., & Turner, B. A. (1986). Grounded theory and organizational research. *Journal of Applied Behavioral Science, 22*(2), 141-157.

McBain, L. (2009). Cracking the books: Policy measures to contain textbook costs. Retrieved from http://www.aascu.org/uploadedFiles/AASCU/Content/Root/PolicyAndAdvocacy/PolicyPublications/TextbooksPM-3-09(1).pdf

Milliot, J. (2009, August). Kindle market share on the rise. *Publishers Weekly.* Retrieved from http://www.publishersweekly.com/pw/by-topic/industry-news/publisher-news/article/5295-kindle-market-share-on-the-rise-.html

Mowery, D. C., Oxley, J. E., & Silverman, B. S. (1996). Strategic alliances and interfirm knowledge transfer. *Strategic Management Journal, 17*, 77-91.

Muller-Seitz, G. (2011). Leadership in interorganizational networks: A literature review and suggestions for future research. *International Journal of Management Reviews.* doi:10.1111/j.1468-2370.2011.00324.x

Oberg, C., & Grundstrom, C. (2009). Challenges and opportunities in innovative firms' network development. *International Journal of Innovation Management, 13*(4), 593-613.

Publishers report strong growth in year-to-year, year-end book sales. (2011). Retrieved from http://publishers.org/press/24/

Raven, R. (2007). Coevolution of waste and electricity regimes: multiregime dynamics in the Netherlands (1969-2003). *Energy Policy, 35*(4), 2197-2208.

Reynolds, R., & Ioffe, Y. (2010, April 19). Digital textbook sales in higher education: A 5-year projection [Web log message]. Retrieved from http://blog.xplana.com/wp-content/uploads/2010/04/DigitalTextbooks_Report_04-19-10.pdf

Rip, A., & Kemp, R. (1998). Technological Change. In S. Rayner & E. I. Malone (Eds.), *Human choice and climate change—Resources and technology* (pp. 327-399). Columbus, OH: Batelle Press.

Ritala, P., Armila, L., & Blomqvist, K. (2009). Innovation orchestration capability—Defining the organizational and individual level determinants. *International Journal of Innovation Management, 13*(4), 569-591.

Sorrel, C. (2009, October). Barnes & Noble unveils Kindle-killing, dual-screen Nook E-Reader (Updated). *Wired.* Retrieved from http://www.wired.com/gadgetlab/2009/10/barnes-nobles-kindle-killing-dual-screen-nook-e-reader-leaked/

State of Illinois Board of Higher Education. (2005). *Report on textbook rental study* (State of Illinois Board of Higher Education-10). Retrieved from http://www.ibhe.org/Board/agendas/2005/February/Item%2010.pdf

Stuart, T. E. (2000). Ambiguity and the process of knowledge transfer in strategic alliances. *Strategic Management Journal, 21*, 791-811.

Suurs, R., Hekkert, M., Kieboom, S., & Smits, R. (2010). Understanding the formative stage of technological innovation system development: The case of natural gas as an automotive fuel. *Energy Policy, 38*(1), 419-431.

Teece, D. J. (1986). Profiting from technological innovation: Implications for integration, collaboration, licensing and public policy. *Research Policy, 15*, 285-305.

Textbook Rental Study 2005. (2005). Retrieved from http://www.ed.gov/about/bdscomm/list/acsfa/txtbkpres/hershmansup1.pdf

Truffer, B., Metzner, A., & Hoogma, R. (2002). The Coupling of viewing and doing: Strategic niche management and the electrification of individual transport. *Greener Management International, 37*, 111-124.

Tuomi, L. A. (2002). *Networks of innovation: Change and meaning in the age of the internet.* New York, NY: Oxford University Press.

Uzzi, B. (1997). Social structure and competition in interfirm networks: The paradox of embeddedness. *Administrative Science Quarterly, 42*, 35-67.

Van de Ven, A. H. (2005). Running in packs to develop knowledge-intensive technologies. *MIS Quarterly, 29*(2), 368-378.

Ven den Ende, J., & Kemp, R. (1999). Technological transformations in history: How the computer regime grew out of existing computing regimes. *Research Policy, 28*(8), 833-851.

Wasserman, S., & Galaskiewicz, J. (Eds.). (1994). *Advances in social network analysis.* London, England: SAGE.

Weick, K. E. (1976). Educational organizations as loosely coupled systems. *Administrative Science Quarterly, 21*, 1-19.

CHAPTER 3

HOW DO NEW INNOVATION PARADIGMS CHALLENGE CURRENT INNOVATION POLICY PERSPECTIVES?

**Mette Praest Knudsen, Stoyan Tanev,
Tanja Bisgaard, and Merethe Stjerne Thomsen**

ABSTRACT

Successful firms today are forced to deal with new competitive realities by being globally present, innovatively resourceful and internationally competitive on multiple markets across the world. The new competitive realities challenge firms to open their innovation processes by adopting new innovation paradigms such as user-driven innovation, open innovation and value co-creation. The user-driven and open innovation paradigms have already become the subject of extensive research and are currently discussed in terms of their potential implications for policy development. The value co-creation paradigm is relatively new, but with a significant potential to also affect formulation of new innovation policy perspectives. The three paradigms are considered as examples of distributive innovation, which is based on the need of firms to orchestrate and integrate the innovative contributions from multiple actors by managing knowledge sharing processes across

Global Perspectives on Technological Innovation, pp. 61–100

entire value networks. The chapter provides a brief description and comparison of these new innovation paradigms and discusses the challenges that these paradigms imply for existing innovation policies. The innovation policy recommendations are based on insights derived from the analysis of innovation policy development in Denmark. The "triadic" approach of the new innovation paradigms suggested here will benefit the discussion of the innovation policy issues and challenges associated with the adoption of the three new paradigms in other countries than the discussed exemplary case.

INTRODUCTION

The pursuit of competitiveness through innovation has always been a key objective of national policies. Historically, innovation policies have predominantly focused on research and development (R&D) in the pursuit of high technology development for the sake of fostering competitiveness. This can be justified by the fact that, traditionally, the majority of the successful innovative companies are those that were able to develop and maintain highly competitive R&D resources and capabilities within the firm. Thus, these resources and capabilities have been considered mainly geographically localized and nationally differentiated providing the field of business and innovation management with a predominant research focus on national innovation systems, regional clusters and internal company capability development. This dominant view is being now challenged, not only by globalization, but also by some of the implications of the ongoing globalization processes. The globalization processes force even higher rates of technological change and a very different competitive dynamics forcing existing companies to reinvent the nature of their innovativeness and competitiveness. One of the potential benefits that could be harnessed from the globalization processes is the access to globally distributed resources, although they require the development of appropriate management competencies (Bogers & West, 2012). Two of the most important emerging factors contributing to the new competitive challenges are the more comprehensive, multiple actor perspective on innovation including the changing role of external actors including customers and end users in the innovation processes, as they become more knowledgeable, more active and more demanding.

This chapter claims that successful firms today are forced to consider these new competitive realities as opportunities by being globally present, innovatively resourceful and internationally competitive on multiple markets across the world. The new competitive realities challenge firms to open their innovation processes by adopting the emerging new innovation paradigms such as user-driven innovation (von Hippel, 2006; TemaNord,

2006), open innovation (Chesbrough, 2003) and value co-creation (Prahalad & Ramaswamy, 2004). The user-driven and open innovation paradigms have become the subject of extensive research in the last 5-10 years and are currently discussed in terms of their potential implications for policy development. The value co-creation paradigm is relatively new, but with a significant potential to also stimulate the ongoing policy development processes. The chapter provides a brief description and comparison of these new innovation paradigms and discusses the challenges that these paradigms imply for existing policies by analyzing the following question:

How do the different new innovation paradigms challenge the existing innovation policies?

It provides a summary of insights based on an analysis of the example of innovation policy practices in Denmark. The choice of Danish innovation policy practices is not accidental. In 2008, Denmark implemented 40 different national innovation programs by allocating about DKK 400 million emphasizing among others user-driven innovation initiatives. Since the three emerging paradigms have become globally relevant, the discussion of Danish policy development experience would be highly relevant for innovation experts from countries that are currently discussing how to address and implement proper policy initiatives emerging from the three innovation paradigms. The focus, therefore, is on exploring experiences and not so much on sharing best practices since this is a development in process. Furthermore, the chapter discusses the commonality of the three paradigms by focusing on their multiple actor perspective, the different types of contributions by the different actors involved in the value creation process, the distributed nature of the innovation management processes, and the need to orchestrate the interactions between, and the recombination of knowledge from all the relevant stakeholders. The question to be answered from a *policy perspective* can therefore be further specified as:

How can firms effectively orchestrate innovation processes originating from distributed sources, and how can innovation policies support these processes?

The chapter is organized as follows. It starts out by presenting a summary of existing innovation policies in Denmark by focusing on the tendency of moving away from a purely technological perspective on innovation and, in particular, toward the programs related to user-driven innovation. The second part of the chapter describes and discusses the commonality between the new innovation paradigms of user-driven innovation, open innovation and value co-creation. This discussion is then used as a prism for the identification of new policies that would address some of the challenges related to the new innovation paradigms. This analysis then leads to a final formulation of a number of recommendations that could be of potential interest for innovation policy development bodies.

INNOVATION POLICIES IN THE KNOWLEDGE-BASED ECONOMY: A DANISH ACCOUNT

Innovation policymaking has been part of Danish policy development practices for at least 3 decades and has been usually approached from a technological point of view. Policies were developed to enhance the adoption of new technologies as well as to ensure that new technologies invented in universities could be channelled to Danish companies as quickly as possible. However, since the turn of the millennium there has been a gradual change in what is meant by innovation policy. During the 1980s, attention was drawn toward understanding national systems of innovation, as scholars such as Freeman (1982) and Lundvall (1985) took a broader look at innovation in existing firms by going beyond the traditional understanding of technological R&D. Empirical data gathered in the United States, Japan, and Europe showed that innovations came from interactions with other firms and suppliers, or from employees on the shop floor and depended in many cases on company's organization and manufacturing processes (Freeman, 1995). But even though these changes in company innovation have been observed and acknowledged, the challenge of how institutions can support innovation has not been sufficiently addressed on a larger scale (Lundvall, 2005).

For a country to harness the potential wealth created by innovation, the fundamental economic structures must be properly functioning. Countries that manage to create sound macroeconomic policies, well functioning institutions and markets, and focus on creating an open and competitive economic environment are more successful in enabling growth and wealth creation (Organisation for Economic Co-operation and Development [OECD], Beyond the Hype, 2001). Creating wealth through innovation has been largely considered to be based on four main drivers (Nordic Innovation Monitor, 2009):

- *Information and Communication Technology*—using information and communications technologies as an enabler of innovation;
- *Human Resources*—developing highly qualified knowledge workers and capitalize on using the ability to use their creative and innovative skills;

- *Knowledge Creation*—investing in the development and utilization of new knowledge;
- *Entrepreneurship*—focusing on activities related to starting up new companies and supporting high-growth and technology-driven entrepreneurs.

While these four drivers appear to constitute a broad way of viewing innovation policy, they must all be continuously reconsidered from the point of view of their foundational principles and mechanisms. The more effective this reconsideration process is, the higher are the chances for a country to foster innovative activity and increase wealth creation.

OVERVIEW OF CURRENT INITIATIVES AND MOTIVATIONS

Innovation policy in Denmark is currently in the process of moving away from having a technology focus alone toward a broader perspective of innovation. And at the same time, it is becoming increasingly clear to policymakers that the framework conditions for a broader innovation perspective have to be different from previously formulated innovation policies (Rosted, 2003). While there is a substantial amount of funding available for technology research and development projects, the understanding of innovation as a nonnecessarily technological enterprise is only slowly gaining ground. For example, issues such as innovation processes and new forms of partnerships have already become the subject of more recent innovation policy initiatives.

The innovation policies in Denmark can be divided into eight main categories: Innovation support, technological services, innovation networks, innovation research, education and competencies, Counseling, entrepreneurship and venture capital, and international innovation programs (Figure 3.1).

Innovation policy in Denmark is implemented by five different ministries at the national level, depending on the particular focus of the policy, as well as by the five regions in Denmark. The Ministry for Science, Technology and Innovation has a focus on innovation policy and innovation research, business PhDs, innovation networks, and specific project funding in addition to existing technology initiatives. The research funding includes topics ranging from sector specific issues to more generic issues such as new innovation processes in established companies. The innovation networks aim to gather different companies as well as knowledge institutions to work together toward creating new products and services. In addition to these initiatives, the Ministry of Science, Technology and Innovation has retained specific project funding programs focusing on various

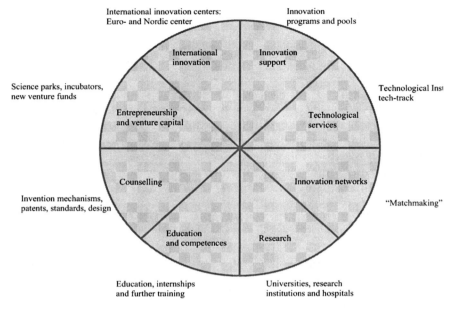

Source: Danish Agency for Science, Technology and Innovation (translated by the authors).

Figure 3.1.   Overview of Danish innovation policy.

topics such as service innovation, marketing and IT development. The Ministry of Economics and Business Affairs has a policy focus which is directly oriented toward companies and the business environment. Policies are developed to enhance entrepreneurship, facilitate company funding, provide advice on issues related to funding and running a company, as well as specific funding for innovation projects. Entrepreneurship programs have a broad focus targeting all types of entrepreneurs, while there are a few programs focusing solely on targeting the high growth companies with a clearly expressed global potential. Venture capital funding is offered by the public fund Vaekstfonden, where companies can receive loans and guaranties as well as seed capital and venture capital. Advice on how to start and run a company can be found online on various websites provided by the ministry, and in each of the five Danish regions a Vaeksthus ("Greenhouse") provides advice to entrepreneurs and enables access to relevant competences, mentors and experts within a range of business areas.

The first innovation program, with an innovation focus that was not technology based, was the Program for User Driven Innovation, offered by the Ministry of Economics and Business Affairs from 2007-2009. The yearly budget for the program was DKK 100 million (approximately 13 million Euro) and it was the first of its kind in the world. This program has now been replaced by the program "Fornyelsesfonden" (The Renewal Foundation, covering the period 2010-2012) that focuses on innovation base on research, development, and demonstration projects related to green solutions and welfare solutions. The focus of this program remains on using methods for user driven innovation in order to achieve the most innovative products and services for Danish companies. The total budget for the 3-year period is DKK 760 million (appr. 100 million Euro).

There are currently three other ministries in Denmark that are also contributing to innovation policy, albeit on a smaller scale than the Ministry for Science, Technology and Innovation and the Ministry of Economics and Business Affairs. These are the Ministry of Climate and Energy, the Danish Ministry of the Environment and the Ministry of Food, Agriculture and Fisheries (Figure 3.2). Their focus is on offering targeted innovation funding within their associated industries.

While there are signs of adaptation of the innovation policy toward a broader spectrum of the innovation focus, there is still a long way to go to formulation of a national broad-based innovation strategy in Denmark with a focus placed on encouraging the adoption of innovative solutions by existing companies. A recent example is the ABT Fond, which is a program designed to encourage companies to find solutions related to developing and improving public sector services through the implementation of labour saving technologies. The program has been allocated DKK 3 billion (appr. 400 Euro million) and will be running within the period 2009-2015. However, this important and large initiative focuses on technological solutions alone and did not include new forms of innovations.

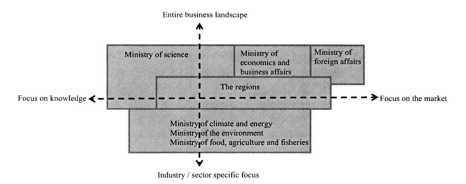

Source: Danish Agency for Science, Technology and Innovation (translated by authors).

Figure 3.2.   Division between ministries' innovation policies.

THE INTERNATIONAL AGENDA
FOR BROAD-BASED INNOVATION POLICIES

When looking beyond Denmark's borders toward others countries, it can be seen that several countries have already begun to rethink their innovation policy mix. However, no single country has yet formulated a comprehensive broad-based innovation strategy (Rosted, Kjeldsen, Bisgaard, & Napier, 2009). The OECD took up the challenge to show the way toward the development of national innovation strategies, and formulated an exemplary innovation strategy (presented in May 2010) intending to inspire policymakers to follow up on the new trends that are currently dominating the business sector and reflect these in the innovation polices. The OECD Innovation Strategy acknowledges that innovation is becoming increasingly complex necessitating the involvement of more actors than before. Innovation policies should therefore be adapted to today's environment (OECDs Innovation Strategy, 2010). Technology has always played an important role in company innovation, and it will continue to do so, but for many companies technology will cease to be the goal of R&D efforts, and rather take the role of innovation enabler (Rosted et al., 2009). There is growing relevance of technological solutions such as customer online participation platforms, user toolkits for innovation and virtual customer environments as enabler of distributed innovation processes. These solutions are in a position of changing the nature and the intensity of the interaction processes between the different members of the traditional value networks by providing the opportunity not only for a better communication between them but also for the development of common innovative visions based on shared understanding, mutual engagement and personalization. This trend carries important consequences for innovation policies.

The OECD's Innovation Strategy recommends a broad view on innovation policy including areas such as reforming the educational and training systems in order to increase the returns on public investments in innovation. Less costly initiatives such as reforming or removing regulatory barriers, including administrative regulation and tax reforms, will also spur innovation and growth at the country level. In addition, governments can become smarter about regulation and consider how innovation can be encouraged when formulating new regulatory policy. Governments can also influence the innovative activity in companies through a better use of public procurement, thereby spurring intelligent demand. Well-designed demand side policies should not be directed at individuals firms, but rather reward innovative behavior in the business community (OECD Innovation Strategy, 2010). In addition to well designed demand side policies, supply side policies are necessary to create the best conditions for firms to innovate. Supply side policy needs to move away from targeting R&D and specific technologies, toward focusing more on the networks and the environment in which innovation is created. Innovation today occurs in networks and by involving a range of stakeholders such as suppliers, partners, customers and end users. Policy should therefore be focused on the application of innovation in order to ensure a higher standard of living and create better solutions to enhance wealth creation (OECD Innovation Strategy, 2010).

The OECD has identified five areas that governments should prioritize when formulating new innovation policies:

- *Empowering people to innovate*—The educational systems need to be rethought and more focus should be placed on multidisciplinary learning and the adaption of new skills.
- *Unleashing innovation in firms*—Regulation must enhance the growth of new firms and create conditions to sustain their competitiveness.
- *Creating and applying knowledge*—Governments must ensure that the protection of knowledge and, at the same time, ensure that the conditions for sharing knowledge are available.
- *Applying innovation to address global and social challenges*—A new model for the governance of multilateral cooperation should be explored so that global challenges could be addressed collectively.
- *Improving the governance and measurement of policies for innovation*—The focus of innovation policies must be medium and long term, and policymakers need to demonstrate leadership and involve all relevant stakeholders in policymaking to develop a shared vision and make policies more effective.

While the OECD has provided an overall framework for policy development, the OECD Innovation Strategy is not a "one-size-fits-all" solution. Each country must determine its own national approach to developing an innovation strategy for the future. In the following, we suggest a particular angle that could provide the anchoring points for a Danish innovation strategy.

THE NEW INNOVATION PARADIGMS: AN OVERVIEW OF CURRENT RESEARCH TRENDS

The origin of current innovation research rests on an inward-looking model that over the past years slowly has been replaced by a more outward-looking and partly market-oriented approach (Lipsey, 2002). The inward looking model view technological change as the key driver of innovations embedded in new products and technologies. Consequently, the management of research and development was about a tight organization and management of the R&D process coupled with a strong regime for protecting the intellectual property rights. The alteration of the inward-looking model implies that the innovation process is changing from science push (technology-driven innovation) to market pull (customer- or user-driven innovation). One of the main implications of moving toward market pull is that customers, suppliers and partners become tighter connected with the innovation process by reducing the importance of technological change and increasing the relevance of other sources of innovation such as the degree of openness of the value creating networks, the functional quality of the participation platforms enabling the access to and interaction between the different stakeholders involved in the innovation processes, as wells as the need to efficiently orchestrate the distributed sourcing of the innovation outputs.

Von Hippel (1978) explains this trend as a move from a *manufacturer-active paradigm*, where the manufacturer of goods survey customer needs using market data analysis to identify emerging product needs, to the *customer-active paradigm*, where manufacturers develop much more efficient mechanisms for the identification of customer needs and generate product ideas by directly involving customers across the different stages of the innovation process (Von Hippel, 1978). This traditional understanding of the New Product Development process leaves to users the role of "passive acceptors of an innovation" (Rogers, 2003, p. 180). In the last decade a broader perspective on these interactive processes has been promoted, stressing that not only customers or users, but also a broader set of economic actors can contribute to the innovation processes of companies. These fundamental changes of the innovation models have initiated a number of developments in innovation management research leading to the formulation of at least three new (or more recent) paradigms: User-driven innovation, open innovation and value co-creation. User-driven innovation and open innovation have already been considered as examples of innovation paradigms focusing on distributed innovation processes (Bogers & West, 2012). In this chapter, value co-creation is added to form a "paradigmatic triad" that could better emphasize the policy relevance of innovation practices founded on the orchestration of distributed resources.

User-Driven Innovation

According to von Hippel (2007) economic actors are defined in terms of the way in which they expect to derive benefit from a given innovation.

Thus, "users" are firms or individual consumers that expect to benefit from using a product or a service. In contrast, "manufacturers" expect to benefit from selling a product or a service. Innovation user and innovation manufacturer are therefore two general functional relationships between innovator and innovation. The user-driven innovation paradigm focuses on actively screening and, later, involving customers and users in the innovation processes. However, currently there are no systematic theoretical investigations of how user innovations become commercial products (Baldwin, Hienerth, & von Hippel, 2006). This lack of a systematically elaborated link between user involvement and commercial products has lead to certain critical remarks concerning this innovation paradigm. Despite of this criticism, companies have increasingly recognized that involving users in innovation processes potentially can benefit both companies and users.

Denmark has been recognized as one of the leading countries in the field of user-driven innovation due to its recent national initiative on user-driven innovation. The initiative has resulted in a higher degree of awareness in the Danish industry. At the same time, the program has transformed the user-driven innovation paradigm from being just a popular slogan in the Danish industry, political life and research institutions to a more comprehensive set of tools becoming one of the sources for the potential growth of Danish economy.

There are different ways of summarizing the different approaches to user-driven innovation (Buur & Matthews, 2008; von Hippel, 2006). FORA (2010) defined a user-driven innovation framework including four main areas: user tests, user exploration, user participation and user innovation.

User Test

> User testing usually takes place toward the end of the innovation process when the company has already come up with an idea, which has been shaped into a product or a service. Potential users or customers are provided the possibility to test existing prototypes and use their experiences to provide feedback. Based on the feedback from users, the company will make minor adjustments before launching the product or service on the market. Therefore, these insights from users will usually result in small and incremental innovations. (FORA, 2010)

The user tests can be done in focus groups/"voice of customer" setting or in a more "interface testing setting" where the potential user will enter a "lab" and be asked to solve selected tasks b using the product. This can also be used more as a qualitative method to confirm market feedback before the launch of a new product. Users have previously been part of the development process when new products and services were designed but mostly as part of usability testing and implementation to align manufacture processes and user expectations. The methods of user driven innovation provide companies with new ways of understanding the needs of the user, which are difficult to communicate or articulate on their own. Here "the user" is considered to be the individual end-user, who is expected to have a direct benefit from using a specific product in contrast to manufacturers who are selling a product or service.

User Exploration

When talking about user-driven innovation many companies and organizations understand it as a set of methods used in the user exploration area (FORA, 2010). It could be also named "Design anthropology" or ethnography to emphasize the application of anthropological and ethnographical methods for a deeper study of user needs (Buur & Matthews, 2008). The user exploration area is mainly dealing with the end-users and their interaction with the product at the same time as providing a better understanding of the context of use. The main idea here is to gain insight into both the spoken and on-spoken needs of the users by engaging with the real-life interactions with products and services. It is a characteristic for these processes that they address a specific topic or an unrecognized problem, but it is not driven by a particular organization or main idea from the beginning. Instead it is the intuitive user engagement with the product or service combined with the engagement of a researcher or external observer to facilitate the identification of needs and insights for new products. It has been realized that sometimes the costs of such studies are not always justified by the degree of their innovative outcome within the companies using the method (Buur & Matthews, 2008).

User Participation

User participation happens when companies work together with users and invite them in an ideation setting with a focus on tapping on tacit knowledge to uncover unrecognized needs in typical user situations (FORA, 2010). The participation approach is taking a starting point at the end-user of the product, service or system and the focus has so far been to ensure how these user concerns were not lost in the internal development processes. This would include engineering, marketing and production issues in the company whereas different components of the more participatory innovation approach still are in its early stages (Buur & Matthews, 2008).

User Innovation

User innovation takes place when companies actively involve experts or advanced users in some of the key steps of the innovation process. In many cases users are more knowledgeable on specific areas regarding specific products or services (FORA 2010; von Hippel, 2006). They, therefore, could easily take part in the actual ideation and design development of products and services, which relate to their specific needs. Here users are actually able to innovate for themselves and not only providing a feedback to a specialized manufacturer (von Hippel, 2006).

The user innovation area includes the *lead user approach* as developed by Eric von Hippel (2001). Lead users can be found based on a systematic search using well defined criteria or within the activities of existing innovation-driven communities. They are users that are ahead of a trend and, at the same time, would have a use benefit from a given innovation. Firms invite lead users to participate in the innovation process along with representatives from the company to develop new concepts or a specific solution. The key benefit for these users is to get access and start using commercialized products that they would not be able to manufacture on their own. The company gains insights from lead users and therefore has better chances to overcome the challenges with "sticky information" (von Hippel, 1994); information that's costly to acquire, transfer, and use in a new location. It should be pointed out that there is confusion between the terms "lead user" and "lead customer." The key difference is that a lead user may not be a customer. A lead user may come from an area which is out of the marketing scope of the company. For example, an in-house software solution developed by a major bank to provide business analytics insights about its ongoing operations may become the source of a new product that could serve touristic or travel agencies in the process of their every day customer relationship management. The bank will benefit, for example, from a newly developed graphical user interface and the new functionality built into their existing software. However, they will never become a user of the newly developed product. On the other hand, a lead customer is usually one of the existing most demanding and high purchase capacity customers who is interested in the future evolution of the product idea as well as ready to invest time in its shaping seeking for a return in terms of a specific competitive advantage.

The user innovation component also includes the development of "Innovation toolkits" (Jeppesen, 2005; Piller & Walcher, 2006; von Hippel, 2001). Here the company sets up a framework where the users are empowered to create their own products with the features they request and need. Well designed innovation toolkits could be of great benefit for both user and manufacturer in sectors where the user needs are rapidly changing (von Hippel, 2001) and it's therefore more difficult for the manufacturers to keep ensuring that their products meet the actual needs of their customers. By setting up an IT based toolkit and a design space with some general constraints, the manufacture provides the users with the freedom to innovate by using the trial-and-error prototyping and by improving until satisfied after being able to evaluate the final result in their own use context. It has been found that user toolkits can be more effective than traditional manufacture-based methods (von Hippel, 2005) and, at the same time, that users using the toolkits are more willing to take part in a more consumer-to-consumer support (Jeppesen, 2005). This provides an opportunity for companies to decrease the intensity of their customer support by increasing the value in the support of their users by means of IT based user toolkits. In some areas the use of toolkits has evolved into community-based platforms where user-innovators have the possibility to combine and leverage their efforts by working with an inventory of product modules created by the community participants and thereby providing both users and manufactures with the benefit from the possibility to have an increased speed and effectiveness of the development process (von Hippel, 2006). Innovation communities have emerged within the open software area but the can also be of great importance in the development of physical products (von Hippel, 2006). The potential issue with the free-riders (people who only take from the community but do not contribute back) in this open environment is not of high importance as the innovators will get an innovation that matches their specific preferences and requirements, whereas the free-rider in most situations will get a less well suited solution (von Hippel & Krogh, 2003).

The Status of the User-Driven Innovation Paradigm

The last section has demonstrated that companies have a range of approaches to draw from when orchestrating a stronger market orientation through the involvement of users in their innovation processes.

A study focusing on Danish manufacturing companies carried out in 2008 investigated the share of companies that are familiar with the user-driven innovation concept and whether the companies were working with user-driven innovation techniques. So far the study has not been published, but other parts of the survey are used in the PhD work of Thomas Boetker Mortensen, University of Southern Denmark. The data in question was collected by Thomas Boetker Mortensen. The data was collected among manufacturing companies with at least 20 employees; 183 firms responded to the questions regarding the new paradigms equaling a response rate of 20.1%. The results indicate that 62.4% of the Danish companies are familiar with the concept, and further that 46.4% of them work with user-driven innovation. A further study also looked into the extent of familiarity and the extent of use of user-driven innovation techniques and was carried out among service and manufacturing companies with more than five employees in the Odense region (data collected in February and March 2010). 147 firms responded to the full survey equalling a response rate of 16.4%. The study showed that external partnerships are important for innovation. 30.6% of the companies utilise external partners out of which 30% collaborated directly with their customers. Further, the specific way of using user-driven innovation was investigated. 20.4% of all the companies know about user-driven innovation out of which 6% have an extensive usage of such techniques. In short, these results imply that although the paradigm is relatively well established in the academic literature and has received extensive political attention through the program for user-driven innovation in Denmark, a large share of Danish companies have not yet systematically implemented the paradigm in their innovation processes. Interestingly, this share of companies seems to increase as the size of the companies goes down, that is, smaller companies appear to be more receptive to newly emerging innovation paradigms.

Our ongoing research indicates that the user driven innovation paradigm is slowly adopting a more holistic perspective on "users" and a more refined perspective on how "technology" contributes to innovation. The newly emerging information and communication technologies challenge the traditional relationship between user and manufacturer by stimulating a stronger and real-time feedback from a more complex set of heterogeneous users across the different stages of the innovation process. One could easily see therefore how the innovation toolkit concept could move in the direction of more comprehensive participation platforms and virtual customer environments (Nambisan & Nambisan, 2008; Nambisan & Baron, 2009). This will allow for the emergence of more optimized user-driven innovation processes that will integrate a broader degree of marketing aspects and, at the same time, contribute to the emergence of specific user-driven initiatives aiming at highly relevant but hardly predictable innovation outcomes.

Open Innovation

Recent views on open innovation processes are argued to involve a wide range of actors, including firms, universities, research and technology organizations that may be public or private in nature. "Firms that commercialise external (as well as internal) ideas by deploying outside (as well as in-house) pathways to the market" have adopted the open innovation model (Chesbrough, 2003, p. 36). Using the description presented in the previous sections, one could say that in this paradigm there is a tendency to include all possible economic actors that could be potentially involved in the value creation processes. It has received a great interest from the business community, but researchers have just started to open and unravel the box of questions pertaining to the open innovation phenomena. Chesbrough and Crowther (2006, p. 229) deepen the understanding of openness by pointing out that open innovation involves flows in two directions; first "the inbound open innovation which is the practice of leveraging the discoveries of others", and second outbound open innovation where firms "look for external organizations with business models that are better suited to commercialize a given technology than the firm's own business model." Simard and West (2006, p. 222) point out that "in open innovation, some firms need to identify external knowledge and incorporate it into the firm; others seek external markets for their existing innovations."

As illustrated in Figure 3.3, firms use a range of tools to access a broad array of knowledge sources. In some situations, research partnerships, with both firms and academic institutions, are used to complement in-house R&D capabilities with specific competences. In other cases, collaboration is aiming at cost and risk sharing. Partners are selected depending on the precise objectives or problems pertaining to the firms' needs. Firms also buy licenses during the process when they identify patents corresponding to their needs. A company can also identify potentially interesting external projects and follow closely their evolution through venture capital investments. Finally, companies could engage into the acquisition of more mature firms when they consider that their competences are necessary or particularly promising.

Figure 3.3 highlights the two directions of open innovation activities. Inbound open innovation focuses on the extent of R&D collaboration (private-private and public-private), licensing in, venturing and acquisitions. Outbound open innovation may include licensing out, the provision of R&D services, spinouts and divestments.

Although the basic objective ("take advantage of resources other than your own") is not new, approaches to this objective have evolved considerably and have become more diverse, thereby shifting the balance between in-house activities and the use of external resources in response to the growing complexity and intersection of products and services within the context of growing competition. The fundamental rationale is that activation of internal capabilities is strengthened by complementing them with external inputs, and by identifying external returns for projects that no longer correspond to the firm's strategy.

When analyzing open innovation processes consideration has to be given to the collaborative architecture, while recognizing that "open" innovation often takes places in relatively closed structures. By closed structures is thought of activities that are based on restricted company-to-company agreements with the conventional commercial objectives of profitability and defensibility.

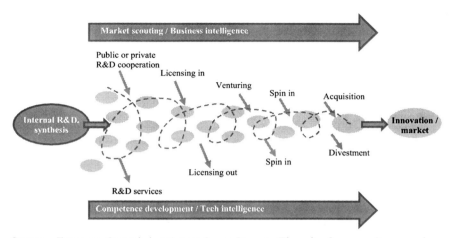

Source: European Commission Expert Group Report—The role of community research policy in the knowledge-based economy (EU Commission, 2009, p. 158).

Figure 3.3.   Open innovation integrated in the value chain.

Pisano and Verganti (2008) distinguish between the truly open collaboration that can include virtually anyone in the architecture (the participant decides to participate as seen, for example, in crowd sourcing) and closed networks, where (normally) it is a company or existing consortium that decides who to select and include in the innovative activity. The first type of network innovation, involving companies, academic research and others, has increased and central corporate laboratories have become more open to various types of cooperation of this type. Nonetheless, it is generally still the latter approach that is seen as providing the primary evidence for open innovation practices. In these more controlled open innovation practices, there can nevertheless be various types of participants.

The Status of the Open Innovation Paradigm

As was argued with the user-driven innovation paradigm, only limited evidence exists on the use of the open innovation paradigm in Danish companies. When studying a number of the policy documents (See Table 3.2 later in this chapter), then the data sources used to describe the extent of open innovation rests on data for interorganizational relationships, the degree of outsourcing of R&D and so on. In brief, these data sources are generated for describing different purposes and are generally scattered pieces of evidence. Similarly as discussed in the section on user-driven innovation, two specific studies have inquired on the use of the paradigms.

The Danish study of manufacturing companies from 2008 found that 26.2% were familiar with open innovation and only 15.4% were working to implement the open innovation paradigm. The Odense study found that only 17% of the companies have knowledge about open innovation out of which only 2.7% of the companies recorded having an extensive usage of open innovation. These results suggest that open innovation is being used to a low degree in general, and lower than user-driven innovation. The results clearly indicate that there is an opportunity for Danish policy to define strong framework conditions for its implementation.

Value Co-creation

Value co-creation is an emerging business, marketing and innovation paradigm describing how customers and end users could be involved as active participants in the design and development of personalized products, services and experiences (Etgar, 2007; Payne, Storbacka, & Frow, 2008; Prahalad & Ramaswamy, 2004). It is based on the design and development of customer participation platforms providing firms with the technological and human resources, tools and mechanisms to benefit from the engagement experiences of individuals and communities as a new basis of value creation. This active participation of customers and end users is enabled through multiple interaction channels, very often through the development of technological platforms through the Internet (Nambisan & Baron, 2009; Nambisan & Nambisan, 2008; Sawhney, Gianmario & Prandelli, 2005). The advancement of information and communications technologies enables customers to be much more active, knowledgeable, globally aware and willing to use interactive virtual environments to personalize the existing and shape new products and services. The multiple channel open interaction and dialogue between the firm and its customers, between the firm and its suppliers and partners, between the different customers, and between the customers and firms' suppliers and partners, constitute a fundamental part of the value co-creation philosophy.

As an example of value co-creation platform one could consider Expedia—an Internet-based travel reservation website driven by Expedia, Inc. which is based in the United States with localized sites for more than 18 countries including Denmark. Expedia was started by Microsoft, and then spun off as a multibillion dollar company. Expedia represent a technologically enabled participation platform providing consumers with everything they need for researching, planning, and purchasing an entire door-to-door trip anywhere in the world by providing direct access to one of the broadest selections of travel products and services across the world including airline tickets, hotel reservations, car rental, cruises, and many other in-destination services from a broad selection of partners. These partners cooperate in maintaining and evolving the platform but also compete in using it to offer their differentiated products and services. Serving many different consumer segments—from families booking a summer vacation to business people and individuals arranging a quick weekend getaway, Expedia provides travelers with the ability to research, plan, and book according to their comprehensive personalized travel needs. Travelers could arrange everything from home, through the Internet, based on the information about specific personal experiences of other travelers, or could contact directly the personnel of a hotel, airline company, a museum or restaurant to explore in more details their specific products and services. The transparency of the process and the direct access to information and resources provided by both customers and firms transform the interaction platform into an innovation hotbed enabling firms to use modern analytics capabilities in evolving and innovating the existing product and services aiming at better customer experiences. Expedia is in the process of changing the traditional meaning of a travel agency by providing travelers with the tools, resources, and mechanisms to shape their travel experiences by personally reconfiguring the existing and creating new options in a way fitting their specific plans and unique contexts.

The emergence of the value co-creation paradigm creates unprecedented opportunities for firms in dealing with the impacts of the ongoing globalization processes which include a much faster degree of technological change; the necessity to be more innovative and, therefore more competitive, by accessing and managing globally distributed resources; and the need to enhance their international competitiveness by addressing multiple markets and heterogeneous customer needs within and across different market segments (Prahalad & Krishnan, 2008). The ability of value co-creation platforms to enable the personalization of new products services challenges the operational logic of traditional marketing by moving it to a new service-dominant logic (Vargo & Lusch, 2004), which redefines the terms of existing market segmentation techniques (von Hippel, 2006) and enables firms to address a broader market with a higher degree of customer satisfaction. The new dominant logic of marketing entails a new vision of the topology and the dynamics of the entire value creation system including:

- a shift from thinking about consumers to thinking about cocreators of value;
- a shift from thinking about value chains to thinking about value networks;

- a shift from thinking about product value to thinking about network value;
- a shift from thinking about simple cooperation or competition to thinking about complex coopetition; and
- a shift from thinking about individual firm strategy to thinking about strategy in relation to the entire value ecosystem (Hearn & Pace, 2006).

Such vision promotes a new understanding of the customer centricity of the traditional value network concept which is now considered dynamically, as a people-driven web of potential value configurations that could be actualized on the basis of specific customer demands (Flint & Mentzer, 2006; Gattorna, 2009; Norman & Ramirez, 1993). The dynamic recognition and alignment to highly heterogeneous customers and customer groups requires the development of appropriate technological infrastructures that are able to seamlessly integrate contributions from globally distributed resources to real-time analytics information and flexible business processes (Prahalad & Krishnan, 2008). Technology, therefore, plays a double role in value co-creation—it could be part of the specific products and services, but more importantly, it becomes a key enabler of co-creation experiences independently of the industry sector and of the specific nature of the particular products and services, that is, it is becoming even more pervasive than before although within a completely different context.

The adoption of value co-creation practices leads to the need of "changing the very nature of engagement and relationship between the institution of management and its employees, and between them and cocreators of value—customers, stakeholders, partners or other employees" (Ramaswamy, 2008). This ongoing change affects our existing business and marketing knowledge leading to a new vision of the nature of innovation (Kristensson, Matthing, & Johansson, 2008; Prahalad & Krishnan, 2008; Tanev, Knudsen & Gerstlberger, 2009).

The Status of the Value Co-creation Paradigm

There seems to be a growing perception in both, scholars and practitioners that the ongoing interest in the value co-creation paradigm points to the emergence of a new semantic wave in business, management, marketing and innovation research. A visible degree of awareness could be also identified in Denmark but, overall, there are no systematic efforts to support research or promote practices aiming at the development of an active cocreative vision as a way for driving the innovation capacity and global competitiveness of Danish firms. Fortunately, there are some first steps in terms of policy development (Rosted et al., 2009) but more systematic work is needed to champion the adoption and study the policy implications of the value co-creation paradigm. On the purely research side there is a growing body of literature dedicated to the discussion of value co-creation frameworks, mechanisms and processes. Existing literature could be roughly divided in four main streams: (1) a more general management perspective (e.g., Etgar, 2006, 2007; Payne et al., 2008; Prahalad & Krishnan, 2008; Prahalad & Ramaswamy, 2004; Ramaswamy, 2008), 2) a service-dominant logic of marketing perspective (e.g., Cova & Salle, 2008; Lusch & Vargo, 2006), the development of virtual customer environments (Nambisan & Baron, 2009; Nambisan & Nambisan, 2008), and new product development and innovation (e.g., Nambisan & Baron 2009; Prahalad & Ramaswamy, 2004). The majority of existing research studies on value co-creation typically focus on the qualitative analysis of a small number of cases by means of deeper ethnographic description of their co-creation practices aiming at the conceptualization of the different types of the innovative contributions and interactions between end users, the firm and its value network partners (Ramaswamy, 2008). Very few studies focus on a more quantitative evaluation of the innovation outcomes of value co-creation practices, however most of the research studies point out the innovation potential of value co-creation practices (Kristensson et al., 2008; Prahalad & Krishnan, 2008; Tanev et al., 2011).

A Comparative Analysis of the Three Paradigms

Comparing the three paradigms is a challenging task since they appear to articulate different and at the same time interrelated visions about the nature of marketing and innovation. For example, user-driven innovation distinguishes itself by promoting a single firm-driven, product-centric, non transactional but participatory focus on users. However, its complementary focus on innovation toolkits and innovation communities brings it close to the value co-creation paradigm with its focus on virtual customer environments, personalized market offers, access to global resources and open dialogue between the multiple actors involved in the value creation process. The engaging platform nature of the value co-creation paradigm enables it to operate within a broader positioning across the entire innovation lifecycle starting from a purely marketing orientation to providing unique opportunities for an ecosystemic enhancement of the user-innovation potential. On the other hand, the open innovation paradigm promotes a more generic vision of the innovation landscape in the 21st century. It operates as an articulation of the key mechanisms of the interactive, inbound and outbound business and innovation process, knowledge and resource flows used by firms to engage into a more proactive pursuit of new markets and innovations.

The three paradigms have demonstrated a strong focus on bringing in external business actors, partners, customers and end users to integrate their ideas and product specific value contributions with those of the employees aiming at increasing the market potential of the next generation of innovative products and services. The involvement of the entire value chain including customers and end users contributes to the emergence of a more holistic understanding of innovation which focuses on distributed knowledge sharing processes from multiple and complementary sources instead of company owned innovation resources. One of the key consequences is the increasing role of individuals, both in the organization and in between the customers and end users, in shaping the products and services, but also the nature of the interaction processes, in a way that will enhance the value for all relevant stakeholders. This increasing role needs to be backed up with the proper sociotechnological infrastructures as its enabler. It also highlights the importance of the employees' expertise in using these sociotechnological infrastructures to bring in users, customers and other external actors into the innovation process. These processes are becoming increasingly integrated with the specialized development and business processes in the companies, as well as reaching out to the entire supply-, service-, and customer levels outside the companies as a basis for the development of product and services with a higher impact on the surrounding environment and with higher competitive edge for the companies.

The three paradigms therefore, could be characterized by the presence of a number of underlying operating principles: *first*, this is the focus on the potential role of the multiple actors involved in the value creation process; *second*, this is the acknowledgment of the different types of value contributions from these actors; *third*, this is the need to explicitly orchestrate the joint activities and distributed knowledge sharing processes between multiple actors and from distributed resources. These three underlying principles have enabled the parallel analysis of the three paradigms as different examples of distributed innovation (Bogers & West, 2012). The distributed perspective on innovation goes beyond the traditional view that the innovation process is a linear path from basic scientific discoveries, through firm R&D, and then commercialization and distribution to the customers through the market exchange and transaction mechanisms. It is based on the view that "innovation is not (purely) a vertically integrated process, but rather relies on recombining knowledge that is available outside the focal firm's boundaries, across various external stakeholders (Bogers & West, 2012, p. 5). As it was already shown, there is a growing body of ongoing research focusing on each of the three paradigms. However, there is little research focusing on their policy implications. It is our belief that the "triadic" approach suggested here will benefit the discussion of the innovation policy issues and challenges associated with the three new paradigms.

OVERVIEW OF EXISTING POLICY RECOMMENDATIONS RELATED TO THE THREE PARADIGMS

While the three paradigms are relatively new, some countries and organizations have developed policy responses that aim at enhancing and embracing the new innovation paradigms. This section provides a summary of policy recommendations proposed by the OECD, the European Union, National Endowment for Science, Technology and the Arts in the United Kingdom and the Finnish government. The goal was to describe the policy recommendations developed by all relevant organizations, however the description does not pretend to be exhaustive and needs to be continuously developed.

The user-driven innovation has historically existed for a longer time than the other two paradigms and some of the policymakers have already had the opportunity to take into account. For example, there seems to be a clear consensus on the need of improving the educational system to ensure the development of new skills, within the educational system as well as in the form of job training initiatives. There are also several organizations that recommend creating specific infrastructures that would enable companies to benefit from user-driven innovation by focusing on users and providing them opportunities to become involved in company innovation (Table 3.1).

Regarding the open innovation paradigm, there is a clear consensus regarding the rethinking of the current IPR system. However, while this is an issue relevant to all nations, it is not an issue that can be solved by one nation alone. There is a need for international cooperation for the development of a common European or international IPR system to meet the challenge of emerging open innovation activities across national borders. Enabling and encouraging networks between companies, universities and public institutions, nationally and internationally is another policy recommendation that is considered to be vital by several organizations promoting world class research and innovation. Finally, creating the optimal framework conditions encouraging firms to start up and grow is considered important from both an entrepreneurial and cluster development perspective (Table 3.2). Regarding the value co-creation paradigm, it has been difficult to find policy recommendations that specifically target this kind of emerging company behavior. Some of

Table 3.1. Overview of Policy Recommendations Related to User-Driven Innovation

Organization	Recommendations
OECD: Organization for Economic Co-operation and Development	**Empowering people to innovate** • Education and training should equip people with the foundations to learn and develop skills for innovation • Enable customers to be active participants in the innovation process • Foster entrepreneurial culture by instilling skills and attitudes needed for creative enterprises
"New nature of innovation" Report to the OECD	**Creating new knowledge** • Encourage the establishment of new multidisciplinary research, new educational institutions and effective collaboration between existing institutions • Prioritize professions involvingskills related to the social sciences and humanities • Provide services to firms and users in order to enhance user involvement in the innovation office
INNO-metrics	**Creative education** • Improve the levels of educational attainment and creative thinking in education
NESTA: National Endowment for Science, Technology and the Arts, UK	• Relax copyright rules • Allow the use of toolkits for innovation • Establish a user innovation forum for business and government to explore the implications of user-led innovation • Support user-led innovation projects • R&D tax credits should encompass user-led innovation • Develop new metrics to measure user-led innovation • Benchmark practices in the UK against its major competitors • Allow the opportunity for innovation within the procurement process by helping purchasers and suppliers to learn about the potential of user-driven innovation • Public organizations can play a more proactive role in innovation and do more to uncover consumers' ideas and hidden preferences • Innovation could be part of companies' annual reporting requirements to encourage the involvement of consumers
Ministry of Employment and the Economy, Finland	• Competence development—development of skills, multidisciplinary skills and design competences • Incentives for user-driven innovation—R&D incentives and tax incentives • Infrastructures improvements—develop IT and information systems, as well as cooperation platforms such as Living labs • Regulatory reform—reuse of public data, influence on public services by promoting partnerships and including users

84

the policies that are relevant for user driven innovation and open innovation are also highly relevant for stimulating value co-creation. However, this paradigm is quite new to have attracted the attention of policy organizations (see Table 3.3).

A DISCUSSION OF DANISH POLICIES ISSUES RELEVANT TO THE THREE INNOVATION PARADIGMS

When looking at the existing Danish policy framework, five areas that are particularly relevant in stimulating innovation within the context of the three new paradigms. Four of the areas are taken from Figure 3.1:

- Innovation support—targeted innovation programs
- Innovation networks—matchmaking between companies and in some cases knowledge institutions
- Education and competencies—the development of new skills related to innovation
- Entrepreneurship—enhancing the creation and growth of new companies

Additionally, the chapter identifies a separate highly relevant fifth area, namely IPR management.

Innovation Support

National innovation policy strategies emerge within the context of the different innovation programs that are offered by the various ministries. In 2008, about 40 different national innovation programs were implemented in Denmark, allocating about DKK 3 billion (about Euro 400 million, Table 3.4).

While there are usually multiple programs focusing on innovation, most often the dominant perspective is technological. Such dominance implies the need of broadening the innovation policy development perspective by, first, adopting a more holistic business innovation philosophy and, second, by promoting practices enabling the adoption of three emerging innovation paradigms. For example, promoting mechanisms enabling and enhancing users' participation in innovation by creating relevant infrastructures and platforms has thus far not been an area of any substantial policy focus and could become a relevant innovation policy area to target in the future.

Table 3.2. Overview of Policy Recommendations Related to Open Innovation

Organization	Recommendations
OECD: Organization for Economic Co-operation and Development	**Creating and applying knowledge** • Develop infrastructures which support innovation and frameworks which support open access to networks and competition in the market • Facilitate efficient knowledge flows and foster the development of networks and markets which enable the creation, circulation and diffusion of knowledge, along with an efficient IPR systems
"New nature of innovation" Report to the OECD	**Creating new knowledge** • Facilitate global partnerships and network activities, and loosen national restrictions on government funded research programs • Redesign the assistance to firms looking to expand internationally by helping them to focus on network and knowledge sharing activities • Enable the evolution of the IPR system to better serve the increasing importance of partnerships and collaboration **Smart regulation** • Facilitate new innovation business-led public-private partnerships bringing together companies, universities and regulatory authorities

Continued

Table 3.2. Continued

Organization	Recommendations
Vision ERA net: a European collaborative network linking leading national innovation policy agencies	**Research and technology development** • Financial incentives to stimulate R&D • High quality IPR systems • Support the emergence of standards • Support user innovation **Interaction** • Develop skills in the companies • Stimulate interaction through networks and collaborations • Enhance technology markets • Use matchmakers • Back up clusters **Entrepreneurship** • Support corporate entrepreneurship • Access to finance • Back up entrepreneurs who challenges status quo **Science** • Appropriate funding • Balanced incentives • Focus on excellence • Organized diffusion **Education** • High quality education at all levels • Entrepreneurship education
EU—Expert group report: The role of community research policy in the knowledge base economy	• Support young innovative companies beyond their start-up phase in order for them to undertake high-risk projects and pursue radical innovations • Focus support to collaborative research that emphasizes research excellence on the potential for radical innovation and the capacity to operate globally • Facilitate open innovation by implementing a community-driven patent system, reducing barriers to research mobility, reducing transaction costs in knowledge and technology exchanges
Ministry of Employment and the Economy, Finland	Enable a regulatory reform—renewal of institutional framework for IPR related to user-driven innovation and open innovation

**Table 3.3.   Overview of Policy Recommendations
Related to Value Co-creation**

Organization	Recommendations
"New nature of innovation" Report to the OECD	**Intelligent demand** • Assist in creating new types of physical and digital platforms and infrastructures where consumers, users and companies could meet and interact

Innovation Networks

Policy organizations highlight the need to foster innovation networks and partnerships among companies, as well as between companies, the public sector and other research organizations. A performance account from 2006 showed that these networks were successful in reaching these goals, and further that a high number of participating companies either developed new ideas or even products and services based on their participation in the innovation network. There are currently 23 innovation networks in Denmark that are cofinanced by the Ministry of Science, Technology and Innovation. Typically, these innovation networks are seen as part of a vision that has two main targets: i) businesses are to become more innovative, and ii) enhancing the knowledge sharing mechanism between public and private institutions. While most networks are sector specific, there are already multiple examples of networks created around the experimentation with new innovation methods. In average, the total funding received by innovation related networks has increased over the last years. However, to enhance the ongoing emergence of the three paradigms a much more structured governance of the networks should be used (Pisano & Verganti, 2008). The focus on the need of more efficient governance is a key issue across the developed world.

Education and Competencies

Most of the developed countries need to enhance their educational systems by gearing them toward the creation of new skills and competencies that could enable or enhance user and employee involvement in innovation processes. The problem is that educational systems usually fall outside of the ministries that formulate innovation policy. In addition, any potential changes in the educational system would only underline the need to formulate broader national innovation strategies cutting across and integrating the efforts of the various ministries. While there has been a stress on the need to add 'entrepreneurship' to the teaching agenda in schools and universities, little attention has been paid to preparing graduates to the newly emerging types of workplaces and innovation tasks. Fortunately, there is a visible

Table 3.4. List of Danish Innovation Programs

Pools With a Nationwide Focus	Sector or Technology Specific Pools	
Collaboration with knowledge institutions about research and innovation	• Innovation syndicate (large innovation projects) • Research coupon (mid-size innovation projects) • Knowledge coupon (small innovation projects) • Open funds (new ways of collaboration) • Danish National Advanced Technology Foundation	Energy	• Energy technology development and demonstration program • ElForsk—effective use of electricity • ForskEl—environment friendly production of electricity • ForskNG—development of gas technologies • ForskVE—development of PV cell, wave power and biogas technologies
User-driven innovation	• Program for user-driven innovation	Environment and working environment	• Technology pool for earth and ground water pollution • Grants for environmentally effective technologies • Business arrangement (environmental effort) • Danish Environmental Protection Agency for weed control research • Product development program for forestry and wood industry • Production tax foundation for Christmas trees and spruce trees • Prevention Foundation—new technology to prevent degeneration
Innovation in the public sector	• Investment in man power saving technologies • Pool for employee-driven in the public sector		
Employment of highly educated people	• Industrial PhD program • Knowledge pilots (highly educated employees)	Food	• Law of innovation (food) • Industrial development—fabrication • Industrial development—agriculture

Source: Danish Council for Technology and Innovation (translated by authors).

trend in the development of program components that developed to teach students how to work in multidisciplinary teams and obtain new skills that will enable them to be innovative employees and leaders. While there has been an expression of interest in adding "entrepreneurship" to the teaching agenda in schools and universities, little attention has been paid to preparing graduates for the emerging requirements of the new types of workplaces and tasks. In some parts of the educational system, there is an ongoing effort to teach students how to work in multidisciplinary teams and obtain new skills that will enable them to be innovative employees and leaders. One such effort is the new course taught by the Department of Anthropology at the University of Copenhagen, where there is a new Master program in anthropology and people-centred business (http://anthropology.ku.dk/studies/mscapcb/). A further example is the new product development and innovation engineering master program at the University of Southern Denmark which includes a variety of the above mentioned aspects including the training in practical entrepreneurship for technology-based companies. (http://www.sdu.dk/en/uddannelse/kandidat/product_development
_innovation)

Entrepreneurship

During the last decade, entrepreneurship has become a hot topic for policymakers worldwide. Denmark performs relatively well as compared to the U.S. in terms of the amount of new companies that have been formed. In addition, there is a growing trend related to the development and implementation of innovative business creation programs. However, there is a common weakness when it comes to both sustaining the businesses and enabling growth among start-up companies. There does not seem to be a clear understanding of the type of policies that are necessary to create innovative companies by enabling them to become globally successful by ensuring efficient job creation and stability.

IPR Issues

Creating a new system for IP and copyright rules was mentioned as one of the most relevant policy areas that could enhance the adoption of open innovation practices. While reforming the IP system is vital to enhancing the adoption of new innovation paradigms, it is not an issue to be dealt with on a purely national level. However, the entire discussion of intellectual property rights must remain high on the political agenda. Given the relevance of the topic, in the next section we will provide a discussion of the potential policy challenges associated with IPR management.

THE IPR CHALLENGE

Is the management of IPR a challenge for policy development related to the three new innovation paradigms? To answer this question, one should realize that there are two sides of the IPR "coin." *First,* one should go back to the basics by pointing out that a patent owner is granted the right to exclude others from commercially using, selling, offering and keeping in stock an invention as specified in the claim section of the patent (Junghans & Levy, 2006, p. 1). *Second,* In return for these exclusive rights, the patent owner is obliged to make the patent available to the broader audience, which is secured by the patent authorities publishing the patent documents a specific period of time after the patent application date. Thus, the fundamental rationale for granting intellectual property rights to innovators is to increase private investment in innovation. However, it is also known that there is a social welfare loss, which is caused by the owners restricting the use of their legally protected information in order to increase private profits. In other words, intellectual property rights are thought to be good for innovation and bad for competition (von Hippel, 2006, Ch. 8). Furthermore, it is important to understand that the company can protect one particular technology from being exploited by other companies through the patent application. However, it is more often becoming the case that the inventor of the technology attempts to "disguise" a real invention by "patenting around" the original invention. Already in the early 1980s when researchers really started to use patents to assess firm technology strategies, the issue of defensive patents surrounding the core patent was highlighted (Campbell, 1983, p. 142) as a key issue. Campbell also described how competitors may position offensive patents close to the defensive ones. This practice has two implications. *First,* the company can hide the invention and thereby gain a competitive advantage based on time before the competitors discover the patent, which ultimately may provide the company with additional profits and competitive benefits. *Second,* the cost of inventing around the patent carries large costs for the patent granting authorities, but also for the general knowledge generation in the society. These practices underline the particular challenge of developing an effective patenting system, and it is therefore our argument that a well-functioning international patent system is needed both in order to lower the cost of applying for protection, but also to ensure an effective protection of the invention. However, as mentioned earlier this is not a task for a single country, but should be a coordinated international effort. It is quite vital that, while opening up the innovation process, companies are encouraged to reveal proprietary knowledge to collaborators. The current trend toward a changing weight of the innovation ingredients (from technologies toward other types of innovation sources) as well as toward more open and collaborative paradigms raises the question about the development of proper IP protection systems. And this question helps to see other side of the IPR "coin," for example how the existing IP protection rules and mechanisms could be turned into a tool for the adoption of the new innovation paradigms.

The traditional view considered above emphasizes the importance of patents in excluding imitators and preserve individual incentives to invent. However, this understanding is quite restrictive and runs counter to some of the research conducted in the past few decades. Recent research indicates that one should acknowledge a dual role for patents—they can increase incentives to innovate but they can also mitigate the specific coordination difficulties linked to open innovation (Cohendet & Penin, 2011).

It is true that companies engaging into open innovation practices exchange knowledge and technologies and collaborate both formally and informally. It is therefore expected that a firm willing to develop an open innovation strategy will likely encounter challenges in locating the right partners and exchanging knowledge and technologies. The good news is that, actually, a properly developed patent system could help in solving the coordination problems. In fact, the main role of the patent system in this situation could be seen, not in its ability effectively exclude rivals, but in providing the proper ground for including all the relevant stakeholders in the innovation process (Cohendet & Penin, 2011). This ground emerges out of a fundamentally important feature of a patent—it both protects and discloses an invention. The coupling of these two properties mediates or facilitates technology transfer through the exchange of licenses on markets for ideas and technology (Cohendet & Penin, 2011; Gans & Stern, 2003) but also helps in framing collaborations, partnerships and alliances among heterogeneous organizations. It is important to point out that one of the key rationales behind the emergence of the open innovation paradigm is the fact that IP has become part of business models and patents are actually facilitating technology and knowledge trading on markets for technology. A well developed IP protection system could have a direct business impact within the context of the open innovation environment that is being tolerated by the emergence of the new innovation paradigms—it could help for a better articulation, clarification and refinement of value propositions. There are several factors that have been recently considered as determinants affecting the role and management of IPR in open innovation processes, including (Lazzarotti, Manzini, & Pellegrini, 2011):

- the characteristics of the different IP protection tools, their ability to effectively protect innovation in technological collaborations, their coherence with an open approach to innovation;

- the characteristics of the business environment in terms of industry, technological dynamics and the appropriability regime that would foster or limit the promotion of one particular IPR protection mechanisms with respect to others;
- the target group of companies in terms of size, level of competences available, organization and culture, which, again, would foster the promotion of one particular IPR protection mechanisms with respect to others;
- the specific characteristics of the innovation, especially the level of tacit versus codified knowledge embedded and the stage in the technology life cycle, which determine the effectiveness of different IPR protection mechanisms;
- the characteristics of specific collaboration types, since the number and type of partners will obviously impose or prevent the use of certain IPR protection mechanisms with respect to others; and
- the specific activity of the innovation process in which the collaboration takes place and in which the need to protect the innovation becomes critical;.

Patents represent a critical tool that supports the opening of the innovation process (Lazzarotti et al., 2011) by:

- making the company more appealing to potential technological partners and, hence, helping to attract the best partners and clients;
- ensuring some level of control over critical technologies and know-how in a way that these could be shared in partnerships; and
- ensuring that the innovation is actually new with respect to the state of the art, in order to provide a first defence line against infringement claims, that the company is actually ahead of competitors in a given technological area.

It could be argued therefore that companies do not need to fear or fight patents; they have to deal with them, and innovation policy developers have to work out the right policies that would facilitate the emergence of an IPR culture that is appropriate to the new innovation trends. The IP frontier has considerably expanded which is visibly expressed in an increased demand for IP-related intelligence and the emergence of new type of firms specializing in knowledge production. For example, markets for technology support the emergence of fabless technological firms that work upstream in the production of new technology and then transfer it to manufacturing firms which are using those technologies in their products

(Cohendet & Penin, 2011). The emergence of this new industrial trend promotes the division of labor by allowing each firm to specialize where it is most efficient and ensures that innovations are used by those that can generate the most value from them. It is just one example of the broadening of the scope of IP issues that could be potentially relevant within the context of open business environments. These issues emerge in parallel with newly emerging IP-based business models which are challenging the traditional views of doing business and which are being considered as essential for the competitiveness of entire industries, countries and regions (Radauer, 2011).

CONCLUSION AND RECOMMENDATIONS

This chapter has investigated the need for firms to orchestrate their innovation processes by integrating the innovative contributions from multiple actors and by managing distributed knowledge sharing resources. Based on these insights, the chapter described how existing innovation policies have approached the question of creating the proper framework conditions to support these processes. Based on the insights from Danish innovation and innovation policy development practices, the paper discussed five further key topics. However, even though the Danish innovation policies have taken significant steps toward creating an innovative business environment, it is only to a certain extent that the new innovation paradigms are supported sufficiently to spread and flourish to their full potential under the current innovation policies. Hence, the analysis suggested here does not focus on *best* practices but on *next* practices to seriously address how the new innovation paradigms challenge current innovation policy perspectives. Hence, the readers should consider jointly the description of existing policy, the analysis of the challenges posed by emerging innovation paradigms, and the recommendations for policymakers suggested below as inspiration for policy development in separate countries.

This section provides a summary of recommendations that would be relevant to consider for other countries, while departing in their own current policy formulations.

- The overall recommendation is to formulate a national innovation strategy.

In Europe, the main frame of reference for formulating the strategy should be the OECD approach, highlighting in particular the points of *empowering people to innovate, unleashing innovation in firms, and creating and applying knowledge*. A fundamental requirement is the integration of perspectives both on business development, technological innovation, large societal challenges (*grand challenges*), environmental issues and so forth. Therefore the strategy should be developed as a cross-disciplinary and cross-ministerial activity.

To support this strategy, the chapter further suggests a number of specific initiatives and associated measures for evaluation of the policies.

- Create new publicly funded knowledge centres investigating the extent and maturity of the adoption of the three new innovation paradigms.

As demonstrated above, Denmark is one of the most advanced countries in terms of formulating policies related to the three paradigms. However the data presented in this paper also demonstrates a significant lack of knowledge in a large base of Danish companies. The new programs should be evaluated on the basis of typical measures of research excellence such as number of publications, but also by the number and the degree of development of particular initiatives addressing the requirements for implementation in small and medium-sized enterprises (SMEs).

- Establish an understanding in companies of both, the need and the potential benefits, of adopting the new paradigms. In particular, stimulate the development of knowledge sharing mechanisms between research institutions and lead implementers of the paradigms in the business community.

These initiatives are needed to enhance the understanding of the value of the paradigms in particular for the SMEs and to grow particular initiatives suited for enhancing the knowledge base of these companies. This initiative could be evaluated by measuring the number of new products and services developed by companies and their market success, and the number of employees that receive training.

- Promote and a support a reform in the educational system targeting an enhanced cross-disciplinary education focusing on open, user-driven and participatory innovation.

One solution could be to merge different types of courses and universities, to ensure students from natural sciences, social sciences and business sciences meet and work together with small firms in addressing their real life innovation management problems. Furthermore, with an emerging trend of networked and interlinked innovation processes both resting on technological capabilities, but also on a broader range of capabilities, it is our contention that this increases the need for cross-disciplinarity and building of relational capabilities. Such combined skills should be integrated into existing programs, while recognizing that these capabilities are not deep professional skills, but rather social skills and should be developed using new pedagogical methods. This approach could be evaluated by measuring the number of cross-disciplinary courses, and the employment rate of graduates.

- Create the proper sociotechnological infrastructures and platforms that would enable small clusters of companies to meet users and innovate together.

One solution could be to set up regional Living Labs, where companies would have access to relevant information, meeting space and prototype test facilities to work with partners and lead customers in addressing particular user and development needs. Such facilities would also enable SME's to identify relevant partners for future value co-creation and innovation processes. This initiative could be evaluated by measuring the number of, for example, Living Labs projects and the number of new products and services created by the different clusters. To establish potential links for the participants in the living labs it would also be important to assess the number of users of the labs. Furthermore, valuation of emergent partnerships could be compared to other partnerships that are unrelated to the living lab activities.

A second solution could be to make exemplary platform tools available to companies in business support programs and to support the development of such platform tools for exploratory adoption and testing preferable in Danish SMEs. There are existing international examples of such participation platforms and tools that could be used as a model or inspiration for the development of similar Danish programs (http://www.coralcea.com/). The intention of the programs should follow two rationales: one of establishing the sharing of tools and the second of establishing relevant network contacts.

- Strengthen focus of innovation networks by directing structure and governance of the networks.

Although, the evaluation of current innovation networks are positive, it is our argument that, for example, closed innovation networks with stronger structure and dedicated to innovation as stressed by Pisano and Verganti (2008) potentially can foster further innovation with commercial value. This implies that the current program for innovation networks is strengthened and that the requirements toward structure and dedication are enhanced. These networks could continuously be evaluated as it is currently done.

In conclusion, this chapter highlighted the key constituents of existing innovation policies in Denmark with a particular focus on the emergence of three new innovation paradigms—user-driven innovation, open innovation and value co-creation. Danish policies have gone a long way already, but particular initiatives can be further developed and implemented in order to focus more directly on the adoption of the three innovation paradigms in particular by SMEs. However, the chapter also points out that, although focusing on broader innovation perspective and the management of distributed knowledge sharing, new policies will prove relevant and highly impactful only if they are developed within the context of a national innovation strategy. The new innovation paradigms therefore challenges existing policies to be further coordinated under the auspices of a national innovation strategy that particularly points to specific gaps and opportunities for policy initiatives. Thus, policy development for the triadic innovation paradigms starts with a national innovation strategy rather than multiple and uncoordinated initiatives.

REFERENCES

Baldwin, C., Hienerth, C., & von Hippel E. (2006). How user innovations became commercial products: A theoretical investigation and case study. *Research Policy, 35*(9), 1291-1313.

Bogers, M., & West, J. (2012), Managing distributed innovation: Strategic utilization of open and user innovation. *Creativity and Innovation Management*. doi: 10.1111/j.1467-8691.2011.00622.x

Buur, J., & Mathews, B. (2008). Participatory innovation. *International Journal of Innovation Management, 12*(3), 255-273.

Campbell, R. S. (1983). Patent trends as technological forecasting tool. *World Patent Information, 5*(3), 137-143.

Chesbrough, H. W. (2003). The era of open innovation. *MIT Sloan Management Review, 44*(3), 35-41.

Chesbrough, H. W., & Crowther A. K. (2006). Beyond high tech: Early adopters of open innovation in other industries. *R&D Management, 36*(3), 229-236.

Cohendet, P., & Penin, J. (2011). Patents to exclude vs. include: Rethinking the management of intellectual property rights in a knowledge-based economy. *Technology Innovation Management Review, December*.

Cova, B., & Salle, R. (2008). Marketing solutions in accordance with the S-D logic: Co-creating value with customer network actors. *Industrial marketing management, 37*, 270-277.

Etgar, M. (2006). Coproduction of services. In R. Lusch & S. Vargo (Eds.), *The service dominant logic of marketing*. Armonk, NY: M. E. Sharpe.

Etgar, M. (2007). A descriptive model of the consumer co-production process. *Journal of the academy of marketing science, 36*(1), 97-108.

EU Commission—Expert Group. (2009). The role of community research policy in the knowledge-based economy. Retrieved from http://ec.europa.eu/research/era/publication_en.cfm

Flint, D., & Mentzer, J. (2006). Striving for integrated value chain management given a service-dominant logic of marketing. In R. Lusch & S. Vargo (Eds.), *The service-dominant logic of marketing* (pp. 139-149), Armonk, NY: M. E. Sharpe.

FORA by Bisgaard, T., & Hoegenhaven, C. (2010). Creating new concepts, products and services with user driven innovation. *Nordic Innovation Centre Project Report, Oslo, Norway.*

Freeman, C. (1982). *The economics of industrial innovation*. London, England: Francis Pinter.

Freeman, C. (1995). The "National System of Innovation" in historical perspective. *Cambridge Journal of Economics, 19*, 5-24

Gans, J., & Stern, S. (2003) The product market and the market for "ideas:" Commercialization strategies for technology entrepreneurs. *Research Policy, 32*, 333-350.

Gattorna, J., & Friends. (2009). *People powering enterprise supply chains. Dynamic supply chain alignment—A new business model for peak performance in enterprise supply chain across all geographies*. Surrey, England: Gower.

Hearn, G., & Pace, C. (2006). Value-creating ecologies: understanding next generation business systems. *Foresight, 8*(1), 55-65.

Jeppesen, L. B. (2005). User toolkits for innovation: Customers support each other. *Journal of Product Innovation Management, 22*, 347-362.

Junghans, C., & Levy A. (2006). *Intellectual property management*. Weinheim, Germany: WILEY-VCH Verlag GmbH & Co. KGaA.

Kristensson, P., Matthing, J., & Johansson, N. (2008). Key strategies for the successful involvement of customers in the co-creation of new technology-based services. *International Journal of Service Industry Management, 19*(4), 474-491.

Lazzarotti, V., Manzini, R., & Pellegrini, L. (2011, September 9-12). *Protecting IP in the era of open innovation: An empirical study in Italy*. Paper presented at the 12th International CINet Conference—Continuous Innovation: Doing More with Less, Aarhus, Denmark.

Lipsey, R. G. (2002). Some implications of endogenous technological change for technology policies in developing countries. *Economics of Technological Change and New Technologies, 11*(4-5), 321-351.

Lundvall, B. (1985). *Product innovation and user-producer interaction*. Aalborg, Denmark: Aalborg University Press.

Lundvall, B. (2005, June). National innovation systems—Analytical concept and development tool. DRUID Tenth Anniversary Summer Conference, Copenhagen, Denmark.

Lusch, R. & Vargo, S., Eds. (2006). *The service-dominant logic of marketing*. Armonk, NY: M. E. Sharpe.

Nambisan, S., & Baron, A. (2009). Virtual customer environments: Testing a model of voluntary participation in value co-creation activities. *Journal of Product Innovation Management, 26*, 388-406.

Nambisan, S., & Nambisan, P. (2008). How to profit from a better "virtual customer environment." *MIT Sloan Management Review, 49*(3), 53-61.

Nordic Innovation Monitor. (2009). Nordic Council of Ministers. Copenhagen, Denmark.

Norman, R., & Ramirez, R. (1993). From value chain to value constellation: Designing interactive strategy. *Harvard Business Review, 71*(4), 65-77.

Organisation for Economic Co-operation and Development. (2001). *The New Economy: BEyond the Hype*. Paris, France: Author.

Organisation for Economic Co-operation and Development. (2010). *The OECD Innovation Strategy: Getting a head start on tomorrow*. Paris, France: Author.

Payne, A., Storbacka, K., & Frow, P. (2008). Managing the co-creation of value. *Journal of the Academy of Marketing Science, 36*, 83-96.

Piller, F., & Walcher, D. (2006). Toolkits for idea competitions: A novel method to integrate user in new product development. *R&D Management, 36*(3), 307-318.

Pisano, G., & Verganti R. (2008). Which kind of collaboration is right for you? *Harvard Business Review, 86*(12), 78-86.

Prahalad, C. K., & Krishnan, M. S. (2008). *The new age of innovation: Driving cocreated value through global networks*. New York, NY: McGraw Hill.

Prahalad, C. K., & Ramaswamy, V. (2004). *The future of competition—Cocreating unique value with customers*. Boston, MA: Harvard Business School Press.

Radauer, A. (2011), Cutting-edge intellectual property projects. *The Technopolitan, 7*, 5.

Ramaswamy, V. (2008). Cocreating value through customers' experiences: The Nike case. *Strategy & Leadership, 36*(5), 9-14.

Rogers, E. (2003). *Diffusion of innovations* (5th ed., p. 180), New York, NY: Free Press.

Rosted, J. (2003). *Tre former for innovation*. Copenhagen, Denmark: FORA.

Rosted, J., Kjeldsen, C., Bisgaard, T., & Napier, G. (2009). *New nature of innovation*, Copenhagen, Denmark: FORA.

Sawhney, M., Gianmario, V., & Prandelli, E. (2005). Collaborating to create: The internet as platform for customer engagement in product innovation. *Journal of Interactive Marketing, 19*(4), 4-17.

Simard, C., & West, J. (2006). Knowledge networks and the geographic locus of innovation. In H. Chesbrough, W. Vanhaverbeke, & J. West (Eds.). *Open innovation: Researching a new paradigm* (Ch. 11, pp. 220-240). Oxford, England: Oxford University Press.

Tanev, S., Bailetti, T., Allen, S., Durchev, P., Milyakov, H., & Ruskov, P. (2011). How do value co-creation activities relate to the perception of firms' innovativeness?, Special issue "Rethinking the boundaries of innovation" of the *Journal of Innovation Economics, 1*(7), 131-159.

Tanev, S., Knudsen, M., & Gerstlberger, W. (2009). Value co-creation as part of an integrative vision for innovation management. Special issue on value co-creation. *Open Source Business Review.* Retrieved from http://www.osbr.ca/ojs/index.php/osbr/article/view/1014/975

TemaNord. (2006). *Understanding user driven innovation.* Nordic Council of Ministers. Copenhagen, Denmark.

Vargo, S., & Lusch, R. (2004). Evolving to a new dominant logic of marketing. *Journal of Marketing, 68*(1), 1-17.

VISION ERA net (2009). Policies for open innovation: Theory, framework and cases. Retrieved from http://www.visioneranet.org/

von Hippel, E. (1978).Successful industrial products from customer ideas: Presentation of a new customer-active paradigm with evidence and implications. *Journal of Marketing, January,* 39-49.

von Hippel, E. (1994). Sticky information and the locus of problem solving: Implications for innovation. *Management Science, 40*(4), 429-439.

von Hippel, E. (2001). Perspective: User toolkits for innovation. *Journal of Product Innovation Management, 18,* 247-257.

von Hippel, E. (2006). *Democratizing innovation.* Cambridge, MA: MIT Press.

von Hippel, E. (2007). Horizontal innovation networks—By and for users. *Industrial and Corporate Change, 16*(2), 293-315.

von Hippel, E., & von Krogh, G. (2003). Open source software and the "private-collective" innovation model: Issues for organization science. *Organization Science, 14*(2), 208-223.

CHAPTER 4

THE ACCEPTANCE AND EXTENT OF USE OF INFORMATION TECHNOLOGY FROM THE GREEK TOURIST OFFICES

Nikolaos Pappas

ABSTRACT

There is no doubt that information technology (IT) has created new horizons and empowered tourism production globally. On the antipode, the extent of IT use defers from region to region. The nature of tourist product is based on information. Since IT gives to firms and destinations the opportunity of global coverage it becomes an increasingly important mean for products' and services' promotion and distribution. Through the consumers' interaction, the tourist offices can attract the interest and the participation of the customers, gather information according their preferences, and use them in order to produce specialized programs of communication and services. On the other hand, the use of IT has led to the increase of tourist offices' antagonism, since the opportunity on products' and services' improvement has given in all firms. Furthermore, there was a creation of a new dynamic focusing on the cost decrease of the provided products, and the better service of customers. The aim of this study is to investigate the Greek tourist offices' IT use on business to business (B2B) relations, their

Global Perspectives on Technological Innovation, pp. 101–119
Copyright © 2013 by Information Age Publishing
All rights of reproduction in any form reserved.

employees' IT training and education, and the opportunities and technical hitches created by IT use. Moreover it examines the differentiations of the expressed perceptions between the tourist offices situated in the capital of the country (Athens), and in the metropolitan city (Heraklion) of the most famous destination in Greece (island of Crete). It also analyses all the expressed perspectives toward three sociodemographic characteristics of the respondents: age, level of education, and work experience in the attempt to derive enhanced knowledge and relevancies. The study was conducted in Heraklion and Athens from June till August 2010. The respondents were the owners/managers of the examined tourist offices. In order to develop the questionnaire, the research questions from the literature review were used. The questionnaire contained 21 close ended statements using a five degree Likert scale (1: Strongly Agree, 5: Strongly Disagree). The statements focused on the effects of IT in B2B (six statements), on the employees' IT training and education (eight statements) and on the threats and opportunities created by IT use (seven statements). There were also three sociodemographic questions focused on age, level of education and work time experience in the managerial post the respondents had during the period the research was conducted. The collected data were analyzed using the Statistical Package for the Social Sciences (S.P.S.S., 16.0). In order to identify statistically significant relationships there was an analysis using t-test, and One-Way ANOVA. Furthermore, when independent variables were ordinal, Spearman's ρ correlation coefficient was used to measure the strength and the direction of the relationship. The null hypothesis for all tests was based of statistical significance at the level of 0.05. Internationally, many destinations and their tourism enterprises have to face the overcentralized administrative systems that mainly produced by the public sector. Hence the chapter's suggestions can be implemented in international level. The research indicates that the companies do not actually seem to fully take advantage of the IT beneficial impacts, and the degree of enterprising focus on traditional operative patterns. They also provide a clear understanding on the IT necessity in overcentralized states and countries, and the prospects they create in modern peripheral business. Furthermore, they highlight the necessity of IT in tourism enterprising and the dependence of tourism industry in modern operative techniques. Additionally, they give evidence on the influence of the sample's sociodemographic characteristics' change concerning the acceptance, the adaptation, the use and the enterprising evolution on IT and tourism. Conclusively, methodologies are suggested ways that IT in tourism can be more acceptable from the industry's enterprises and strengthens the overall tourism production.

INTRODUCTION

Tourism has a significant economic impact at an international, domestic, regional and local level. The tourism industry can be seen as one of the first business sectors where business functions are almost exclusively using information and communications technologies (ICT) (Garzotto et al., 2004). Information technology (IT) and ICT have played an important role in tourism development. The computerized Central Reservation Systems were among the first applications of IT globally. ICT facilitates this integration and enables customization of tourism products and services to suit the needs of individual consumers. Due to changes in tourist consumer behavior the market is becoming more segmented with each potential consumer belonging to a number of market segments simultaneously (Pease & Rowe, 2005).

Information is the new way of tourism industry's life thus the use of IT is so important. This is actually the reason for the IT's widespread and the fact that no player can escape from its impacts (Poon, 1993). IT provides the basis of vital information that makes tourism work (Sheldon, 1997). The last decades IT has greatly affected the enterprising competitiveness and the way the companies operate (Porter, 2001), while the technological development has literarily created a revolution to the economic and enterprising developmental process (Horner, 1996).

Consequently, the technologic evolution's influences on tourism industry have particularly affected the way the tourist offices have distributed their tourist products and services in the local, national, and global market (Buhalis, 2000; Poon, 1993). The nature of tourist product is based on information. Since IT gives the opportunity of global coverage it becomes an increasingly important mean for products' and services' promotion and distribution (Walle, 1996). Since the new, demanding consumer becomes a better IT user, wants more flexible and accessible products (Buhalis, 1998). Through the consumers' interaction, the tourist offices can attract the interest and the participation of the customers, gather information according their preferences, and use them in order to produce specialized programs of communication and services (Doolin, Burgess, & Cooper, 2002).

On the other hand, the use of IT has led to the increase of tourist offices' antagonism, since the opportunity on products' and services' improvement has given in all firms (Lainos, 1999). Furthermore, there was a creation of a new dynamic focusing on the cost decrease of the provided products, and the better service of customers.

The aim of this study is to investigate the Greek tourist offices' IT use on B2B relations, their employees' IT training and education, and the opportunities and threats created by IT use. Moreover it examines the differentiations of the expressed perceptions between the tourist offices situated in the capital of the country (Athens), and in the metropolitan city (Heraklion) of the most famous destination in Greece (island of Crete). It also analyses all the expressed perspectives toward three sociodemographic characteristics of the respondents: age, level of education, and work experience.

LITERATURE REVIEW

Information Technology and Tourism

As the world's largest and one of the most pervasive industries, the travel and tourism sector is as exposed as any other to the forces of change that are being brought about by ongoing developments in the ICT arena. ICT have, in fact, affected the travel and tourism industry for at least the last 50 years (SABRE, the first airline computer system was developed by IBM and American airlines in 1953), particularly in the area of automation and networking of distribution channels (LTSN, 2003).

Information technology is the nowadays way of using computers to communicate and get information throughout research, about the knowledge need to be gained. For a considerable amount of population is considered as the best way of communication. IT relates to tourism in many ways hence the only option before the advent of IT globally when people want to travel they have to walk from their residence down to the street to get the local tourist office either as outbound or inbound travellers. IT development forms an integral and crucial part of contemporary organizational strategy and plays an exceptionally important role in its success. The information intensity of tourism means that "no player in the tourism industry will be untouched by information technology" (Poon, 1993, p. 153). There is no doubt as to the benefits offered by technology—IT applications have the ability to reduce costs, enhance operational efficiency, and considerably improve service quality. On the other hand "there is, evidence to suggest room for improvement, specifically in the context of IT implementation projects involving multiple stakeholders" (Alford & Clarke, 2009, p. 580).

Since the 1980s, information communication technologies (ICTs) have been transforming national and international tourism. Developments in ICTs have undoubtedly changed and differentiated business practices and strategies as well as industry structures (Porter, 2001). The introduction of the Computer Reservation Systems in the 1970s and Global Distribution Systems in the late 1980s, followed by the development of the Internet in the late 1990s, have transformed the best operational and strategic practices in the industry dramatically (Buhalis, 2003; eBusiness W@tch, 2006), while from the beginning of the 21st century the global community has witnessed a truly transformational effect of communication technologies, something that has given scope for the development of a wide range of new tools and services that facilitate global interaction between players around the world (Buhalis, 2008).

The Use of IT in Tourist Offices

A series of researches have focused on the spread of internet among travel agencies and the perceptions of travel agents toward usage, in the new, global, different economic environment (Vrana, Zafiropoulos, & Paschalidis, 2008). Standing, Vasudaman, and Borbely (1998) did the first approach. They investigated Internet use among travel agencies and from the results of their survey it can be seen that many benefits of electronic commerce via the www are not being realized from travel agencies. Later on, Law, Law, and Wei (2001) found out that travel agents have positive attitudes toward Internet applications and they believe that they can take advantage of the Internet technology to provide value-added services for their customers. There was also an examination from Murphy and Tan (2003) dealing with the organizational use of e-mail by travel agents and concluded in poor e-mail customer services. Internet use among travel agencies in Turkey was studied by Ozturan and Roney (2004). Their research results reveal that even though there is an increase of Internet use, Turkish travel agencies use it simply as an additional mode of communication. Their websites do not possess the interactive features required for Internet marketing.

The Greek ICT market is mainly service oriented and roughly 85% of the sector is focused on telecommunications. Greece is displaying exceptional broadband penetration growth rates, driven by local-loop unbundling and the pickup of bundled telecom services in the domestic market, while it reached 1.75 million broadband lines in mid-2009, a 40% y-o-y growth, and ranks within the top 10 countries on broadband uptake in 2006 and 2007 (Invest in Greece, 2010). Information technology and communications in Greece present investors with a very dynamic area of fast growth and investment. The leading area is software development since it supports the public sector, banking and finance, tourism and manufacturing. The deregulation of the Greek telecom market has actually transformed the landscape from one of huge state monopoly to one that has dozens of new small, medium and large ICT companies active in developing and broadening ICT products and services (Lingo, 24, 2011).

The Greek tourist offices that have web pages (mainly based on consumers' information) are not many. Luckily these web pages have plenty enough visitors but they need new, more developed technologic applications such as dynamic portals offering the possibility for booking arrangements and handling financial transactions (Hotel & Restaurant Online,

2004). Moreover the Greek tourist offices are mainly based on informing their partners and clients with traditional—already tested—methods such as face to face communication, and the use of tourist offices as a mean of distribution channels for their products and services. In parallel, the amount of sales through the use of IT is relatively small. The reason of this relatively small IT use is the lack of sufficiently trained personnel on Internet use, on specialized programs and applications, on reservation systems (Central Reservation Systems, Global Distribution Systems), or even on fundamental use of personal computers (Pappas, Tsartas, Papatheodorou, & Christou 2006).

RESEARCH METHODOLOGY

Research Characteristics

The study was conducted in the cities of Athens and Heraklion from June till August 2010. The respondents were the owners / managers of the examined tourist offices. The most appropriate method considered in order to obtain primary data, was the structured personal interview. It was undertaken the technique of personal interviewing in order to reach the objectives since it is the most versatile and productive method of communication, it enables spontaneity, and also provides the skill of guiding the discussion back to the topic outlined when discussions are unfruitful (Sekaran, 2000).

Selection of Variables

The variance of the expressed opinions and the statistical significances that are formulated toward the expressed perceptions are directly connected with the individual characteristics of the sample population. Many studies, such as the researches of Collins and Tisdell (2002), Oppermann (1995), Trakolis (2001), Trethway and Mak (2005), and Walmsley and Jenkins (1993), support that the differentiations of the respondents' age create very important alternations to their perceptions. Some others support that the level of education of the sample population is considered as a crucial factor for the creation of significant differences in the expressed perspectives (Baloglu & McCleary, 1999; Stern & Krakover 1993; Teye, Sonmez, & Sirakaya, 2002). Furthermore, other studies' findings remark the importance of the work experience for the informants' decision making (Feldman & Bolino, 2000; Kunze, 2006; Paraskevas, 1999). This chapter takes under consideration all the above studies and researches, and examines the variation of perceptions toward age, level of education, and work time experience.

Questionnaire Design

In order to develop the questionnaire, the research questions from the literature review were used. The questionnaire contained 21 close ended statements using a five degree Likert scale (1 = *Strongly Agree*, 5 = *Strongly Disagree*). The statements focused on the effects of IT in B2B (six statements), on the employees' IT training and education (eight statements) and on the threats and opportunities created by IT use (seven statements). There were also three sociodemographic questions focused on age, level of education, and work time experience in the managerial post the respondents had during the period the research was conducted.

Research Sample and Data Analysis

The city of Athens is the capital of Greece with more than four million citizens, and its tourism is mainly cultural and professional. The island of Crete is the main tourism destination in Greece occupying approximately a quarter of the tourists, its tourism is mainly recreational, more than 45% of its total tourism flows are concentrated in the region of Heraklion (N.S.S.G., 2007), while the majority of tourist offices is situated in the city of Herklion. The research focused on the tourist offices in the cities of Athens and Heraklion. The sample included 100 tourist offices drawn by Hellenic Association of Tourist and Travel Agencies equally divided between both cities (50 tourist offices each). The use of stratified sampling was seen as the most appropriate way to select these firms.

The collected data were analyzed using the Statistical Package for the Social Sciences (S.P.S.S., 10.0). In order to identify statistically significant relationships there was an analysis using *t*-test, and One-Way ANOVA. Furthermore, when independent variables were ordinal, Spearman's ρ correlation coefficient was used to measure the strength and the direction of the relationship. The null hypothesis for all tests was based of statistical significance at the level of 0.05.

RESEARCH FINDINGS

Profile of the Sample

Toward age, the respondents in the Athenian tourist offices were 14 (28%) from 18 to 35 years old, 21 (42%) from 36 to 50, and 15 (30%) over 50 years old. In the city of Heraklion, 18 people (36%) were from 18 to

35, 17 (34%) were from 36 to 50, and 15 (30%) were over 50 years old. Concerning the level of education, in the Athenian tourist offices 18 (36%) respondents were primary and secondary education graduates, and 32 (64%) were tertiary education graduates, while the same proportions for Heraklion were 24 (48%) and 26 (52%) persons respectively. Toward work experience, in the tourist offices of Athens 12 (24%) respondents were having this post up to 5 years and the rest 38 ones were equally divided (19 persons, 38% each) in work experience from 6 to 10 year and over 10 years respectively. In the Heraklion tourist offices, seven respondents (14%) were having work experience up to 5 years, 21 (42%) from 6 to 10, and 22 (44%) over 10 years.

Spearman's "ρ" Analysis

In the respondents of the Athenian tourist offices Spearman's "ρ" analysis has revealed statistical significances with positive relationship toward age and work experience (Spearman's ρ: .611 / Sig.: ,000), and negative relationships toward age and education (Spearman's ρ: -.308 / Sig.: ,029), and toward education and work experience (Spearman's ρ: −.344 / Sig.: ,014). According Spearman's "ρ" analysis, the same statistical significances appear in the respondents of Heraklion. More specifically, there is positive relationship toward age and work experience (Spearman's ρ: .575 / Sig.: ,000), and negative relationships toward Age and Education (Spearman's ρ: −.367 / Sig.: .009), and toward education and work experience (Spearman's ρ: −.627 / Sig.: .000).

The above outcomes lead to the conclusion that as people get older the work experience gets more extended. In addition, the older the people become, the less educated are. Consequently, the more educated people are, the more inexperienced are. These outcomes reveal that the younger people have more opportunities to study, train and educate themselves. In order to gain senior posts to the tourism industry the younger respondents replace a part of the necessary occupational experience with a high quality of academic education.

IT and B2B

In general, the Athenian tourist offices in comparison with those in Heraklion have higher use of IT with other tourist offices, and they expect higher use of IT after 3 years. In all the other statements, the peripheral tourist offices seem to have higher involvement with IT. This can be a first indication of the IT's understanding of necessity, which is in a higher degree in the periphery than in the country's capital.

Concerning B2B statements, statistical significances appear only in the respondents of Heraklion. The first statistical significance is toward age in the statement concerning the after 3 years IT use with service providers. The overall agreements were 35, expressed by 15 respondents from 18 till 35 years old, 13 from 36 till 50, and only seven being over 50 years old. It can be said that as the respondents' age increases the less important is considered the foreseeable IT use with service providers. The other two statistical significances appear toward work experience in the statements concerning the transactions with the service providers and once more with the after 3 years IT use with service providers. In the first statement the overall agreements were five in people with up till 5 years work experience, 18 from six till 10 years, and 11 with work experience over 10 years, wile in the second statement the same proportions were seven, 16 and 12 respectively. It seems that concerning service providers, the middle work experienced group is the more favorable with the IT use not only in the present but also in the future. This strong belief within this group creates the statistical significances appeared.

The research findings reveal that the tourist offices in Athens have more agreeable proportions from those in Heraklion in the statements concerning the increase of products' quality and number and the foreseeable investments in IT training. On the antipode, the tourist offices in Heraklion have the same overall proportions with the Athenian ones dealing with the necessity of IT training and education in higher posts' personnel, while their proportions in the rest four statements are more agreeable. These results indicate that the Athenian companies focus the IT training and education directly to productivity, when the enterprises in Heraklion try to upgrade their services and products through the employees' training and education in IT use.

Concerning training and education the research findings have revealed plenty enough statements with statistical significances, especially toward age. In the tourist offices of Athens there were four statements with statistical significances toward age, while examining this independent variable in the Cretan respondents the statements with statistical significances were six. In all these statements the most agreeable proportions were between the ages of 18 and 35. It seems that the younger the population is, the more it realizes the necessity of training and education in IT use. This might be a result of IT understanding, since the younger a person is, the more frequent IT user is.

Toward level of education, statistical significances appear in two statements in the Athenian tourist offices, and two in the examined companies in Heraklion. The statistical significances in the capital's enterprises are

Table 4.1.   Provision of IT in Business to Business Operations

	IT Use With Service Providers	IT Use With Tourist Offices	Service Providers' Transactions	Cooperative T. Offices' Transactions	IT Use in 3 Years With S. Providers	IT Use in 3 Years With T. Offices
Means						
Total mean	1.67	1.98	2.83	3.75	2.18	2.97
Athens	1.74	1.90	3.38	3.94	2.22	2.60
SD	.63	.61	.85	.84	.74	.83
Heraklion	1.60	2.06	2.28	3.56	2.14	3.34
SD	.57	.51	.54	.73	.78	1.02
Athens						
Age						
18-35	1.57	1.71	3.00	3.64	2.07	2.36
36-50	1.76	1.86	3.38	4.14	2.14	2.62
Over 50	1.87	2.13	3.73	3.93	2.47	2.80
F Ratio	.80	1.83	2.87	1.51	1.25	1.03
Significance	.454	.171	.067	.232	.295	.363
Education						
Pr. & Sec.	2.00	1.94	3.83	4.28	2.17	2.61
Tertiary	1.59	1.88	3.13	3.75	2.25	2.59
T Ratio	2.27	.38	3.04	2.21	-.38	.070
Significance	.432	.891	.210	.301	.203	.977
Work Exp.						
0-5 years	1.50	1.75	3.00	3.67	2.00	2.92
6-10 years	1.63	1.95	3.47	3.89	2.42	2.37
Over 10	2.00	1.95	3.53	4.16	2.16	2.63
F Ratio	2.97	.46	1.62	1.31	1.33	1.66
Significance	.061	.634	.209	.280	.275	.201
Heraklion						
Age						
18-35	1.44	1.94	2.17	3.50	1.89	3.00
36-50	1.53	2.12	2.24	3.47	1.94	3.35
Over 50	1.87	2.13	2.47	3.73	2.67	3.73
F Ratio	2.59	.71	1.39	.60	5.83	2.21
Significance	.086	.495	.258	.555	**.005**	.121
Education						
Pr. & Sec.	1.71	2.13	2.42	3.63	2.42	3.42
Tertiary	1.50	2.00	2.15	3.50	1.88	3.27
T Ratio	1.30	.86	1.77	.60	2.53	.51
Significance	.317	.254	.222	.849	.369	.285
Work Exp.						
0-5 years	1.57	1.86	2.14	3.29	1.43	2.71
6-10 years	1.48	2.05	2.10	3.67	2.05	3.29
Over 10	1.73	2.14	2.50	3.55	2.45	3.59
F Ratio	1.05	.79	3.70	.71	5.75	2.09
Significance	.358	.458	**.032**	.498	**.006**	.135

Table 4.2.   Training and Education of Employees on IT

	IT in Lower Posts	IT in Higher Posts	Investing in IT Training	Increase Services' Quality	Increase Services' Number	Increase Products' Quality	Increase Products' Number	Invest IT (3Y) Training
Means								
Total Mean	1.56	1.54	3.39	1.62	1.51	156	170	2.64
Athens	1.66	1.54	3.74	1.82	1.70	1.48	1.54	2.10
SD	.59	.54	.88	.63	.46	.50	.50	.71
Heraklion	1.46	1.54	3.04	1.42	1.32	1.64	1.86	3.18
SD	.50	.50	.83	.50	.47	.56	.64	.75
Athens								
Age								
18-35	1.43	1.14	3.50	1.57	1.50	1.43	1.21	1.71
36-50	1.71	1.67	3.67	1.71	1.81	1.43	1.57	2.29
Over 50	1.80	1.73	4.07	2.20	1.73	1.60	1.80	2.20
F Ratio	1.61	6.45	1.69	4.76	2.01	.60	5.98	3.23
Significance	.210	**.003**	.196	**.013**	.145	.555	**.005**	**.049**
Education								
Pr. & Sec.	1.83	1.56	3.94	1.89	1.83	1.44	1.72	2.00
Tertiary	1.56	1.53	3.63	1.78	1.63	1.50	1.44	2.16
T Ratio	1.57	.15	1.24	.58	1.66	-.37	2.03	-.75
Significance	.399	.165	.087	.172	**.001**	.538	**.024**	.746
Work Exp.								
0-5 years	1.42	1.33	3.42	1.50	1.50	1.50	1.17	2.00
6-10 years	1.74	1.42	3.84	1.84	1.74	1.42	1.58	1.95
Over 10	1.74	1.79	3.84	2.00	1.79	1.53	1.74	2.32
F Ratio	1.35	3.70	1.08	2.48	1.57	.21	5.74	1.47
Significance	.269	**.032**	.348	.094	.219	.810	**.006**	.239
Heraklion								
Age								
18-35	1.17	1.22	2.83	1.22	1.28	1.33	1.39	2.83
36-50	1.59	1.71	3.06	1.41	1.35	1.65	1.94	3.12
Over 50	1.67	1.73	3.27	1.67	1.33	2.00	2.33	3.67
F Ratio	5.83	6.99	1.12	3.60	.11	7.19	13.98	6.29
Significance	**.005**	**.002**	.334	**.035**	.891	**.002**	**.000**	**.004**
Education								
Pr. & Sec.	1.46	1.71	3.25	1.58	1.33	1.79	2.00	3.17
Tertiary	1.46	1.38	2.85	1.27	1.31	1.50	1.73	3.19
T Ratio	-.02	2.38	1.75	2.31	.19	1.88	1.53	-.12
Significance	.965	.183	.376	**.048**	.706	.055	**.002**	.975
Work Exp.								
0-5 years	1.29	1.14	2.57	1.00	1.29	1.43	1.43	3.00
6-10 years	1.38	1.48	3.00	1.48	1.29	1.33	1.71	3.14
Over 10	1.59	1.73	3.23	1.50	1.36	2.00	2.14	3.27
F Ratio	1.45	4.41	1.75	3.16	.16	11.63	4.86	.39
Significance	.245	**.018**	.186	.052	.850	**.000**	**.012**	.680

in the statements concerning the increase of services' and products' number through training and education in IT use. In both statements no disagreements were expressed. In the first statement the primary and secondary education graduates strongly agreed by 16.7%, while the same proportion for tertiary education graduates was 37.5%. In the second statement the strong agreements for primary and secondary education graduates, and tertiary education graduates were 27.8% and 56.25% respectively. Dealing with the statistical significances in Heraklion, they appear in the statements concerning the increase of the quality of services, and the number of products. For once more there were no disagreements in these two statements. In the first statement 10 primary and secondary education graduates (41.7%) and 19 tertiary education graduates (73.1%) strongly agreed. In the second statement the same proportions in strong agreements were 12.5% and 42.3% respectively. These expressed perspectives indicate that the more educated a person is, the more it supports training and education in IT use. In both examined regions (Athens and Heraklion) the higher the education the respondents have, the higher their agreeable proportions seem to be in IT training and education.

Dealing with statistical significances toward work experience, there were two in the Athenian tourist offices, and three on those in Heraklion. Concerning the statistical significances produced by the respondents in Athens, they were in the statements examining the IT training and education in higher posts' personnel, and the increase of products' number. In both statements there were no expressed disagreements. In the first statement, eight respondents (66.7%) with work experience up to 5 years, 11 (57.9%) from 6 to 10, and five (26.3%) with over 10 years strongly agreed. In the second statements the same proportions in strong agreements were 10 (83.3%), 8 (42.1%), and 5 (26.3%) respondents respectively. In Heraklion the statistical significances appear in the statements dealing with the increase of products' quality and in the same two statements in Athenian respondents. In all statements with statistical significances, the proportions from the respondents in Heraklion were similar with those in Athens. All these reveal that the less experienced owners/managers feel more than the others the necessity of training and education in IT use. These tenses indicate that the less experienced a respondent is, the more he wants to cover his inexperience through IT use, and IT training and education. On the other hand, according the research findings the less experienced a respondent is, the younger is. Combining these two sociodemographic characteristics these tenses in training and education in IT use can be explained through the prism of IT frequency of use, since the older and consequently experienced respondents are not that frequent IT users.

Threats and Opportunities

Instead of the beneficial impacts the increase of IT use has crated, there was a parallel scepticism for the consequences in terms of antagonism and employment (Pappas et al., 2006). Examining the respondents' perspectives, the research findings revealed that the examined population takes both, advantages an disadvantages, under consideration. The respondents in Athens have higher degree of strong agreements only in the statement concerning the tourist offices' increase of operational capability (17 persons: 34%). In all the other statements focusing on threats and opportunities, the respondents in Heraklion seem to be more agreeable. This tense can indicate that the overall impacts of IT use are clearer and more understandable in the periphery than in the capital city, due to the existing uncertainty in an overcentralized country.

Toward age, statistical significances appear in most of the responses of the Athenian respondents, and in two examined statements in Heraklion. The statistical significances in Athens are in statements focusing on better IT training of employees, the quality improvement of products, the decrease of profits in small tourist offices, and the market domination of large tourist offices. In the first statement the strong agreements reached 50% for respondents from 18 to 35 years old, 23.8% from 36 to 50, and only 6.7% or over 50 years old. In the second statement with statistical significance, the same proportions in strong agreements were 0%, 14.3%, and 33.3% respectively. In the third statement these proportions were 28.6%, 71.4%, and 66.7% respectively. In the final statement with statistical significance toward age in Athens the proportions of strong agreements were 64.3%, 61.9%, and 20% respectively. In the respondents of Heraklion, the statements with statistical significance were dealing with the increase of tourist offices' operational capability, and the market domination of large tourist offices. In the first statement the respondents from 18 to 35 years old strongly supported this view by 33.3%, from 36 to 50 by 11.8%, and from over 50 years old by 13.3%. In the second statement the proportions of strong agreements in the above age groups were 83.3%, 70.6%, and 33.3% respectively.

In general, the younger the age group is, the more it supports the beneficial impacts of IT use. On the other hand, in both Athens and Heraklion, the globalization of tourist market and the domination of large tourist offices seems to have higher impact on the younger respondents that the older ones. According the research findings toward age, as the respondents get older they focus on the financial and qualitative aspects of IT use, when the younger ones seem to be more focused in terms of operational and training aspects, and global competitiveness issues.

Table 4.3.   Threats and Opportunities from IT Use

	Better Employees 'Training in IT	Increase of T. Offices' Operational Capability	Improve Services' Quality	Improve Products' Quality	Profits' Decrease of Small T. Off.	Market Domination of Large T. Offices	Replacement of Employees through IT
Means							
Total Mean	1.73	1.86	1.82	1.82	1.41	1.43	1.79
Athens	1.84	1.66	1.96	2.12	1.42	1.50	2.12
SD	.58	.48	.40	.72	.50	.51	.63
Heraklion	1.62	2.06	1.68	1.52	1.40	1.36	1.46
SD	.49	.68	.47	.50	.49	.48	.50
Athens							
Age							
18-35	1.50	1.50	1.86	2.50	1.71	1.36	2.00
36-50	1.81	1.71	1.95	2.10	1.29	1.38	2.33
Over 50	2.20	1.73	2.07	1.80	1.33	1.80	1.93
F Ratio	6.41	1.1	.99	3.86	3.82	4.30	2.24
Significance	**.003**	.342	.379	**.028**	**.029**	**.019**	.117
Education							
Pr. & Sec.	1.83	1.72	1.89	2.00	1.39	1.44	2.17
Tertiary	1.84	1.63	2.00	2.19	1.44	1.53	2.09
T Ratio	-.06	.69	-.94	-.88	-.33	-.58	-.39
Significance	.720	.151	.098	.563	.496	.737	.209
Work Exp.							
0-5 years	1.58	1.67	1.92	2.50	1.75	1.17	2.25
6-10 years	1.84	1.63	1.95	2.16	1.37	1.42	2.11
Over 10	2.00	1.68	2.00	1.84	1.26	1.79	2.05
F Ratio	1.95	.06	.17	3.44	4.14	7.56	.36
Significance	.155	.945	.846	**.040**	**.022**	**.001**	.698
Heraklion							
Age							
18-35	1.44	1.72	1.61	1.72	1.56	1.17	1.61
36-50	1.65	2.18	1.65	1.47	1.35	1.29	1.41
Over 50	1.80	2.33	1.80	1.33	1.27	1.67	1.33
F Ratio	2.31	4.12	.71	2.73	1.54	5.41	1.38
Significance	.111	**.022**	.496	.075	.224	**.008**	.260
Education							
Pr. & Sec.	1.67	2.21	1.75	1.50	1.42	1.54	1.46
Tertiary	1.58	1.92	1.62	1.54	1.38	1.19	1.46
T Ratio	.64	1.49	1.01	-.27	.23	2.70	-.02
Significance	.220	.800	.051	.713	.658	**.001**	.965
Work Exp.							
0-5 years	1.71	1.43	1.71	1.57	1.43	1.14	1.43
6-10 years	1.48	2.24	1.67	1.62	1.38	1.14	1.57
Over 10	1.73	2.09	1.68	1.41	1.41	1.64	1.36
F Ratio	1.60	4.23	.03	.97	.03	8.28	.93
Significance	.213	**.021**	.974	.386	.971	**.001**	.402

Statistical significance toward level of education appeared only in the respondents of Heraklion in the statement dealing with the market domination of large tourist offices. The strong agreements from primary and secondary education graduates reached 45.8%, while 21 tertiary education graduates (80.8%) strongly supported this view. The perceptions indicate that as the educational level becomes higher, the more considerable the respondents are in issues of antagonism and monopolistic practices.

Toward work experience, three statistical significances appear in the Athenian respondents focusing on the quality improvement of products, the decrease of profits in small tourist offices, and the market domination of large tourist offices. In the first statement with statistical significance there were no strong agreements from people with work experience up to 5 years, while these proportions were 10.5% to respondents with work experience from 6 to 10 years, and 31.6% with over 10 years. In the second statement the strong agreements in the above work experience groups were 25%, 63.2%, and 73.7% respectively. In the third statement these proportions were 83.3%, 57.9%, and 21% respectively. In the Heraklion tourist offices statistical significances appear in the statements concerning the operational capability increase of tourist offices, and the market domination of large tourist offices. In the first statement the strong agreements were 51.1% for respondent with work experience up to 5 years, 9.5% from 6 to 10 years, and 18.2% with over 10 years. In the second statement the strong agreements were equally 85.7% for the first two work experience groups, and 36.4% for the third one.

According work experience, the expressed perceptions reveal that more experienced the respondents were, the more they supported issues like quality improvement and financial problems of tourist offices. On the antipode, the perspective of operational capability improvement seems to be more important for the inexperienced ones. Furthermore, the findings indicate that the less the respondents are experienced, the more they take under consideration the market domination from large tourist offices. This impact might have to deal with the perspective that the more experienced ones are usually older, meaning that their remaining time of activation in the production is smaller. This actually gives them the ability not to really worry about their jobs in a long term run. Consequently the future perspective of market domination is a fact that they will not have to deal with it.

CONCLUSIONS

Even if the spread of IT use in the Greek tourist offices is a fact and necessity because of the production needs, the companies do not actually seem to fully exploit its beneficial impacts. In a relatively high degree, these enterprises are still focused to traditional ways in order to approach and serve their customers, cooperate with the partner tourist offices and tour operators, and make their business transactions. On the other hand the managers / owners of Greek tourist offices understand the IT need and they all accept that their use is going to be much higher in the forthcoming years.

The peripheral tourist offices (situated in the region of Heraklion) seem to be more dependent to IT use than those in the country's capital (Athens). This tense is actually created by the higher operational and enterprising uncertainty of the peripheral companies activated in an overcentralized state. Thus the acceptance and operational entrance of IT is higher in the tourist offices of Heraklion. Furthermore, the managers / owners in Heraklion give higher notice to potential opportunities and threats created by IT use. The only perspective dealing with threats and opportunities that the proportions of expressed perspectives were higher in the Athenian companies was the increase of companies' operational capability. This can be explained because of the differentiation on tourism product in the two examined regions, since Crete has mainly recreational packaged tourism, fully dependent on tour operators.

There are also important evidences produced by the analysis of perspectives toward the sociodemographic characteristics of the sample. Toward age, the younger the interviewed people were, the more they supported the necessity of IT use. Moreover, the younger respondents were the main supporters of more intense training and education of IT in the employees. In parallel, the younger age group seems to give more notice to forthcoming opportunities created by IT use, when the older age group is more considerable for the potential threats produced by this use. Toward level of education, the tertiary education graduates seem to be the main supporters of the extended IT use, and the necessity on training and education. On the contrary, their perceptions do not actually produce statistical significances in terms of forthcoming threats and opportunities. Toward work experience, the more inexperienced the respondents were, the more they seemed to be dependent on IT use, and consequently the more they supported the need of IT training and education.

There is no doubt that IT has stimulated radical changes in the operational and distributional activities of tourism industry. Competitive use of IT, provides information, enables financial transactions, and is proving to be a significant shaper of social and economic life (Bacchus & Molina, 2001). However "IT is not a panacea and therefore, a thorough revision of all operational and strategic managerial practices are required in order to achieve the emerging benefits" (Buhalis, 1998, p. 420). Thus in the Greek tourist offices there is the need of administrative practices' entrance aiming to empower and evolve the beneficial impacts produced by IT use.

The research findings indicate the need of IT strategic planning and development especially in the peripheral zones of Greece where the necessity of communication and interaction is much higher than in the country's capital. This can be primary accomplished through the development of electronic and enterprising presence and promotion via internet use. Tourist offices can be advertised and expand their operational activities through the interactive methods that internet provides. Secondary, the technological reformation can provide internet services and online reservations. Within this frame, the development of infrastructure and IT education will become easier and simpler mainly through the investments in cooperative tourism networks & enterprising empowerment. As a result, there can be an integration of e-tourism through the existing infrastructures and development.

The perspectives of the study population are not standardised and unchanged during time. Due to the dynamic process of tourism development, the perceptions of the respondents do not necessarily reflect the degree of tense they appear several years later (Andriotis & Vaughan, 2003). Because of this, research in the tourist offices in both Athens and Heraklion has to be repeated. This is something of a rarity in the literature, "depriving researchers of the opportunity to measure change over time" (Butler, 1993, pp. 140-141).

REFERENCES

Alford, P., & Clarke, S. (2009). Information technology and tourism a theoretical critique. *Technovation, 29*, 580-587.

Andriotis, K., & Vaughan, D. R. (2003). Urban residents' attitudes towards tourism development: The case of Crete. *Journal of Travel Research, 42*(2), 172-185.

Bacchus, L., & Molina, A. (2001). Internet-based tourism services: Business issues and trends. *Futures, 33*, 589-605.

Baloglu, S., & McCleary, K. W. (1999). US international pleasure travellers' images of four Mediterranean destinations: A comparison of visitors and nonvisitors. *Journal of Travel Research, 38*(2), 114-129.

Buhalis, D. (1998). Strategic use of information technologies in the tourism industry. *Tourism Management, 19*(5), 409-421.

Buhalis, D. (2000). Tourism and information technologies: Past, present and future. *Tourism Recreation Research, 25*(1), 41-58.

Buhalis, D. (2003). *eTourism: information technology for strategic tourism management.* London, England: Pearson, Financial Times/Prentice-Hall.

Buhalis, D., & Law, R. (2008). Progress in information technology and tourism management: 20 years on and 10 years after the Internet—The state of e-tourism research. *Tourism Management, 29*(4), 609-623.

Butler, R. W. (1993). Pre- and post-impact assessment of tourism development. In D. G. Pearce & R. W. Butler (Eds.), *Tourism research: Critiques and challenges* (pp. 135-155). London, England: Routledge.

Collins, D., & Tisdell, C. (2002). Age-related lifecycles: Purpose variations. *Annals of Tourism Research, 29*(3), 801-818.

Doolin, B., Burgess, L., & Cooper, J. (2002). Evaluating the use of the Web for tourism marketing: A case study from New Zealand. *Tourism Management, 23,* 557-561.

eBusiness W@tch. (2006). ICT and e-business in the Tourism Industry, Sector Impact Study, no. 08/2006. European Commission. Retrieved from http://www.ebusiness-watch.org/resources/tourism/SR08-2006_Tourism.pdf

Feldman, C. D., & Bolino, C. M. (2000). Skill utilisation of overseas interns: Antecedents and consequences. *Journal of International Management, 6*(1), 29-47.

Garzotto, F., Paolini, P., Speroni, M., Pröll, B., Retschitzegger, W., & Schwinger, W. (2004, August). Ubiquitous access to cultural tourism portals. *15th International Workshop on Database and Expert Systems Applications*, Zaragoza, Spain.

Horner, P. (1996). *Package holidays*. London, England: Longman

Hotel and Restaurant Online. (2004). *Information technologies improve the profitability of hospitality enterprises*. Seminar of the Academy of Tourist Research and Studies. Retrieved from http://www.marketing-net.gr/online/article.asp?returnPage=GROUP&group=3&articleid=1489

Invest in Greece. (2010, December 17). *ICT: Embracing new technologies*. Retrieved from http://www.investingreece.gov.gr/default.asp?pid=36&sectorID=39&la=1

Kunze, A. (2006). Looking again at instrumental variable estimation of wage models in the gender wage gap literature. *Research in labor economics, 20,* 373-393.

Lainos, I. (1999). *Economics of air transports in competitive environment* (2nd ed.). Athens, Greece: Stamoulis.

Law, R., Law, A., & Wei, E. (2001). The impact of the internet on travel agencies in Hong Kong. *Journal of Travel and Tourism Marketing, 11*(2/3), 105-126.

Lingo 24. (2011, November 27). *Greece: Facts and figures*. Retrieved from http://www.lingo24.com/international_business_intelligence/greece.html

LTSN. (2003). *Information and communication technologies for travel and tourism*. Learning and Teaching Support Network. London, England: Higher Education Academy.

Murphy, J., & Tan, I. (2003). Journey to nowhere? E-mail customer service by travel agents in Singapore. *Tourism Management, 24*(5), 543-550.

N.S.S.G. (2007). *Tourist arrivals on the island of Crete: Tourism per prefecture*. Athens: National Statistical Survey of Greece.

Oppermann, M. (1995). Travel life cycle. *Annals of Tourism Research, 22*(3), 535-552.

Ozturan, M., & Roney, S. (2004). Internet use among travel agencies in Turkey: An exploratory study. *Tourism Management, 25*(2), 259-266.

Pappas, N., Tsartas, P., Papatheodorou, A., & Christou, E. (2006). *Sub-action 3.2: Capabilities of information communication technologies on the production process. Promotion of competitiveness and employment in the sector of tourist offices through the adjustment of employees and businessmen in the new labour demands of tourism.* European Union's Research Program EQUAL: Always Tourism.

Paraskevas, A. (1999). Management selection practices in Greece: Are hospitality recruiters any different? *Hospitality Management, 19*, 241-259.

Pease, W., & Rowe, M. (2005, August). An overview of information technology on the tourism industry. *ITS Africa-Asia-Australasia Regional Conference*, Perth, Western Australia.

Poon, A. (1993). *Tourism, technology and competitive strategies*. Oxford, England: CAB International.

Porter, M. (2001). Strategy and the internet. *Harvard Business Review, 79*(3), 63-78.

Sekaran, U. (2000). *Research methods for business: A skill-building approach* (3rd ed.), New York, NY: John Wiley & Sons.

Sheldon, P. (1997). *Tourism information technology*. Oxford, England: CAB International.

Standing, C., Vasudaman, T., & Borbely, R.(1998). Re-engineering travel agencies with the world wide web. *Electronic Markets, 8*(4), 40-43.

Stern, E., & Krakover, S. (1993). The formation of a composite urban image. *Geographical Analysis, 25*(2), 130-146.

Teye, V., Sonmez, S., & Sirakaya, E. (2002). Residents' attitudes toward tourism development. *Annals of Tourism Research, 29*(3), 668-688.

Trakolis, D. (2001). Local peoples' perceptions of planning and management issues in Prespes lakes national park, Greece. *Journal of Environmental Management, 61*, 227-241.

Trethway, M., & Mak, D. (2005). Emerging tourism markets: Ageing and developing economies. *Journal of Air Transport Management, 12*(1), 21-27.

Vrana, V., Zafiropoulos, C., & Paschalidis, S. (2008). Attitudes towards internet use among travel agencies in Greece. *14th European Conference of Information Systems*, Goteborg, Sweden.

Walle, H. (1996). Tourism and the internet: Opportunities for direct marketing. *Journal of Travel Research, 35*(1), 72-77.

Walmsley, D. J., & Jenkins, J. M. (1993). Appraisive images of tourist areas: application of personal construct. *Australian Geographer, 24*(2), 1-13.

CHAPTER 5

OVERCOMING INNOVATION BARRIERS

Alliance Portfolio Characteristics and Technological Innovations

Manish K. Srivastava, Olga Bruyaka, and Devi R. Gnyawali

ABSTRACT

We first identify the key innovation barriers and review the literature at the intersection of alliance portfolios and innovation. Subsequently, we advance a conceptual model showing how the two key factors of alliance portfolios—structural and content—jointly impact a firm's ability to innovate. In advancing the conceptual model of how the effects of alliance portfolio content factors (resource richness and diversity) on firm innovativeness are moderated by alliance portfolio structural factors (strength of ties and partner interconnectedness), we explicate the underlying alliance portfolio mechanisms that help the firm overcome key innovation barriers in generating innovations on a sustained basis. Our theorization of how and why the structural attributes moderate the effects of the content attributes suggest that the firm needs to strategically design and change its alliance portfolio configuration to maximize innovation benefits occurring from the portfolio.

Global Perspectives on Technological Innovation, pp. 121–156

Our study contributes to both innovation and alliance network literatures and is likely to stimulate future research on the role of alliance portfolio factors in firm innovation. We also discuss the policy and managerial implications and key limitations of this study.

INTRODUCTION

In their quest for understanding the determinants of innovation, scholars have shifted their attention from examining the role of internal sources (Damanpour, 1991; Dewar & Dutton, 1986) to the role of external relational sources (Ahuja, 2000a; McGill & Santoro, 2009). Two dominant approaches have been followed in examining the role of relational resources: structural network approach (Ahuja, 2000a; Bae & Gargiulo, 2004; Burt, 1992; Powell, Koput, & Smith-Doerr, 1996; Zaheer & Bell, 2005) and dyadic alliance approach (Sampson, 2007). In the network approach, relational resources are assumed to stem from a firm's position in the network structure and the relationships themselves are viewed as resources (Burt, 1992; Powell et al., 1996). However, this approach often does not explicitly examine the resources possessed by the nodes (i.e., alliance partners) (Wellman, 1988). Scholars taking the dyadic perspective do examine the impact of resources held by individual partners but do not consider the resources of the entire set of partners of a firm (Grant & Baden-Fuller, 2004; Kale, Dyer, & Singh, 2002; Khanna, Gulati, & Nohria, 1998). More recent research (Hoffmann, 2007; Jiang, Tao, & Santoro, 2010; Lavie, 2007; Srivastava & Gnyawali, 2011; Vasudeva & Anand, 2011) combines the strengths of both approaches and suggests the importance of studying a firm's portfolio of alliances. This line of inquiry blends the holistic perspective of the network approach, that is the need to examine all the ties of a firm, and the resource- and learning-focused perspective of dyadic approach to examine resources of the partners. Following this emerging stream, we focus on both the structure and content of an alliance portfolio and examine how they together help a firm overcome innovation barriers and succeed in technological innovation.

The process of technological innovation involves creation, design, production, first use, and diffusion of a new technological product, process, or system (Damanpour, 1991; Dewar & Dutton, 1986). More broadly, innovation or innovativeness is concerned with ideas, practices, or objects that are perceived as new and introduced to a market or a community. We argue that in order to explain how a firm's network can enhance its innovativeness, it is important to first examine important barriers that inhibit a firm's innovative efforts (Mohr, 1969). Based on existing literature we discuss three critical innovation barriers: organizational rigidity, resource constraints, and uncertainty (Dogherty & Hardy, 1996; Galia & Legros, 2004; Greis, Dibner, & Bean, 1995; Mansfield & Rapoports, 1975) and develop our theory explaining how the content and structural aspects of a firm's alliance portfolio help the firm to overcome the above-mentioned barriers. Drawing from the prior literature on alliance portfolio and alliance network, we focus on two most important aspects of alliance portfolio content—resource-richness and resource diversity—and two most important aspects of portfolio structure—degree of partner interconnectedness and strength of ties. By examining how the content and structure of a firm's alliance portfolio separately and jointly influence a firm's likelihood of overcoming innovation barriers and enhancing its innovation outcomes, we fill an important gap in the literature. Our model suggests that while the contents of the alliance portfolio, in terms of both resource richness and diversity are generally important for overcoming innovation barriers, the nature and extent of benefits depend on the structure of the alliance portfolio itself.

Our alliance portfolio theory of innovation contributes to the literature in several important ways. First, our identification of innovation barriers and discussion of how they might cripple firm innovation provide a strong starting point to discern why a firm struggles in innovation. Second, our discussion of how the content and structure of a firm's alliance portfolio contribute to the reduction of barriers enhances our understanding of the *mechanisms* by which network effects are likely to occur with respect to firm innovation. While previous studies have explored the independent effects of alliance portfolio simultaneously content and structure on innovation but to our knowledge have neither examined how content and structure of a firm's alliance portfolio impact innovation nor explicated the mechanism through which such effects occur (see Phelps, 2010 for exception). We discuss the mechanisms through which alliance portfolio content factors—resource richness and diversity—help firms to overcome innovation barriers and then describe the moderating role of portfolio structural factors—partners' interconnectedness and strength of ties. Finally and more broadly, our theorization of how and why the structural factors moderate the effects of the content factors suggest that the firm needs to strategically design and change its alliance portfolio configuration to maximize innovation benefits from the portfolio. Our chapter thus contributes to both innovation and alliance network literatures and is likely to stimulate future research on the role of alliance network factors in firm innovation.

CONCEPTUAL BACKGROUND

Innovation Barriers

A barrier to innovation is any factor that influences negatively the innovation process (Piatier, 1984). The factors with a positive influence are called facilitators. Barriers to, and facilitators of, innovation are, however, related. On the one hand, facilitators may turn to barriers, or vice versa, as the firm evolves throughout its life cycle stages or as external conditions change (Koberg, Uhlenbruck, & Sarason, 1996). Barriers can be classified in a number of ways, and there are several typologies. They are usually based on the origin or source of barriers. Barriers can be internal to the firm or external (Piatier, 1984). External barriers have their origin in the external environment of the firm and the latter has little influence on such barriers, but the firm can influence internal barriers (Hadjimanolis, 1999). Based on prior literature, we identify three barriers as being the most critical: resource constraints (Mansfield & Rapoports, 1975; Mone, Mckinley, & Barker III, 1998), organizational rigidity (Ahuja & Lampert, 2001; Dogherty & Hardy, 1996) and uncertainty (Abernathy & Utterback, 1978; Kline & Rosenberg, 1986). While resource constraints and rigidity are mainly internal barriers, uncertainty stems primarily from external conditions faced by the firm. Resource constraints indicate that a firm does not have the means, uncertainty arises when a firm does not know what to do, and rigidity indicates that in spite of knowing what to do and having the means, the firm may still not be able do it because it cannot change. These barriers act like clogs in a pipe—unless the focal firm is able to overcome all key innovation barriers, its ability to innovate on a sustained basis will be very limited. Below we discuss in detail each of the three innovation barriers we chose to study in this chapter.

Resource Constraints

Resource constraints refer to the lack of both tangible and intangible assets relevant for innovation. Resources include technological knowledge and know-how, cash, equipment, and similar other factors (Barney, 1991). Resource barriers may arise when the firm lacks its technological know-how, has limited organizational resources dedicated to develop new technological capabilities, and has inadequate experience or knowledge. Resource-related barriers are also what Teece (1986) has called appropriability constraints, that is lack of complementary assets or capabilities to take full advantage of an innovation that a firm has developed or adopted. Due to lack of resources firms struggle to innovate (Ahuja & Lampert, 2001; Dougherty & Hardy, 1996; Galia & Legros, 2004; Mone et al., 1998) as sustained innovation activities necessitate continued flow of resources to innovation projects. Furthermore, path dependency, causal ambiguity, time pressure, and the lack of "prerequisites" debilitate a firm's ability to develop new resources (Cohen & Levinthal, 1990; Dierickx & Cool, 1989). Sometimes developing those resources may not be economically worthwhile when the focal firm requires them for a limited purpose. Thus, the focal firm may not have the ability or motivation to develop those resources. Organizations often find their resources thinly stretched to support continued experimentation, which is an integral part of the innovation process (Dougherty & Hardy, 1996). The resource barrier may further intensify in a dynamic environment in which firms need different types of complex resources over time to meet changing resource needs for innovation.

Organizational Rigidity

Organizational rigidity—the inability of the organization to initiate changes—is another major innovation barrier (Ahuja & Lampert, 2001; Dougherty & Hardy, 1996; Mohr, 1969). Organizational rigidity may stem from deeply ingrained mental models of the top management or the dominant coalition (Cyert & March, 1963; Hambrick & Mason, 1984), established organizational routines (Nelson & Winter, 1982), and similar factors that resist innovation and changes. Decision makers' mental models influence the way in which they perceive opportunities and act on them (Hambrick & Mason, 1984). Therefore, managers with deeply ingrained mental models may not be able to notice and value new and critical technological trends. Even if they notice some, they may not be willing to try out new things due to high costs of failure (Rosner, 1968). Organizational routines (Nelson & Winter, 1982) serve another major source of organizational rigidity. Even though routines bring benefits to a firm in terms of coordination, reliability, efficiency, and control (Nelson & Winter, 1982), the same routines become ingrained in organizational practices over time and resist changes and therefore hurt innovation (Ahuja & Lampert, 2001). Innovations are also likely to disturb the organizational truce (Nelson & Winter, 1982). While fostering innovation requires new incentive systems, people fear and resist changes in the power structure and reallocation of organizational resources (Kaplan & Henderson, 2005). The effects of organizational rigidity on innovation occur throughout the various stage of innovation (Ahuja & Lampert, 2001). In the project selection phase, for example, many lucrative projects may be rejected as they may unsettle the organizational truce or may not fit with current organizational routines. A myopic mindset may constrain managers' ability to see value in many attractive projects. During the developmental stage, some projects may be delayed and others may be abandoned if the projects are deviant from current organizational routines.

Uncertainty

Innovation entails, among other things, assessing the technological trends in the external environment, knowing what technology or product has the most potential, and developing organizational capability to pursue the innovation. Each of these things, however, involves a high degree of ambiguity (Dickson & Weaver, 1997). Given the rapidly changing environment, existence of multiple technology options, and technological convergence and divergence, it is very difficult for a single organization to deal with such ambiguities, discern a promising innovation path, and commit valuable resources for the particular innovation path (Folta, 1998; McGrath, 1997). This barrier, when combined with other barriers as discussed above, makes it extremely difficult for firms to innovate on a sustained basis. For example, the resource barrier intensifies when the focal firm enters into unfamiliar technological territories on its own. The innovation process becomes more uncertain if a focal firm lacks the technical know-how and it does not have access to the know-how to undertake an innovation project. When the market is fast changing, unfamiliar, or emerging (Chen, Reilly, & Lynn, 2005), managers find it difficult to discern the desirable properties of the product, technological attributes, and configurations and cannot predict the demand pattern (McGrath, 1997). Similarly, understanding competing technologies and their implications is an enormous challenge. When uncertainty is high in the environment and in the innovation process, organizational rigidity further intensifies (Mone et al., 1998), making it difficult to get the critical mass (key managers of the organization) to agree on a few projects and commit resources to them.

While each of the innovation barriers is critical on its own, these barriers, in combination, make it extremely difficult for a firm to pursue innovations on its own. Furthermore, the process of technological innovation has become ever more complex with innovation demanding "close coordination of adequate technical knowledge and excellent market judgment in order to satisfy economic, technological, and other types of constraints [i.e., innovation barriers—all simultaneously" (Kline & Rosenberg, 1986, p. 275). This is particularly true in the industries with complex knowledge structure and widely dispersed sources of expertise such as biotechnology, semiconductors, chemicals, telecommunications and others (e.g., Marin & Siotis, 2007; Phelps, 2010; Powell et al., 1996; Stuart, 2000). In such industries firms widely rely on strategic alliances as "the locus of innovation will be found in networks of learning, rather in individual firms" (Powell et al., 1996, p. 116). Following the existing research in management we define strategic alliances as "interfirm cooperative arrangements aimed at pursuing mutual strategic objectives" (Das & Teng, 2000, p. 77). In the following section we briefly review literature linking alliances and innovative performance and discuss a portfolio approach to innovative collaborations.

Strategic Alliances and Innovation:
An Alliance Portfolio Approach

Strategic alliances are important for the firm's accumulation of resources, learning, competence building and acquisition of capabilities (Wassmer, 2010). Existing empirical studies have shown that strategic alliances between firms increase innovation output of both mature and young firms (Baum, Calabrese, & Silverman, 2000; Powell et al., 1996; Shan, Walker, & Kogut, 1994). For example, Yli-Renko, Autio, and Sapienza (2001) showed that young technology-based firms benefit from social interactions with their key customers, and from the network ties of those customers in their product development. Similarly, Durand, Bruyaka & Mangematin (2008) found that alliances between small biotech firms and large pharmaceutical companies have a positive effect on small firms' rent generation potential (research outputs—patents and scientific articles). Alliances can also boost innovations in large companies (Ahuja, 2000a; Henderson & Cockburn, 1994; Hughes & Wareham, 2010).

A firm's alliance relationships are helpful for innovation for several reasons. First, cooperative agreements can ease a number of transactional and contractual differences (Hennart, 1988; Jarillo, 1988; Williamson, 1985) In particular, when asset specificity is intermediate, alliances are considered to be the governance mode of choice (de Man & Duysters, 2005). Second, alliances lower risk of large research projects and their costs, thus, stimulating innovation. Instead of investing in all technological opportunities, alliances make it possible for a firm to get a variety of options without fully committing to them (real options perspective on alliances, Kogut, 1991). A company may decide to pursue the most promising technologies, while abandoning less promising ones. Furthermore, costs of developing new generations of chips, aircrafts or computers may be up to billions of dollars. Only very few firms are able to finance these projects by themselves (de Man & Duysters, 2005). Third, forming an alliance with competent partners may also lead to a significant reduction in lead times. In high-tech markets where prices sometimes decline by more than 30% a year, it is obvious that the ability to bring products to the market more rapidly can offer a significant competitive advantage. An alliance-specific reason why alliances may increase innovativeness lies in the radar function of alliances (Duysters & De Man, 2003; Greis, Dibner, & Bean, 1995)—alliances enable firms to scan their environment for promising new technologies at low cost.

Firms rely on various types of alliances—both upstream and downstream—to develop innovative products and services and introduce them on the market (Powell et al., 1996; Rothaermel, Hitt, & Jobe, 2006;

Wassmer, 2010). The skills needed to bring a product to market include R&D, manufacturing, marketing distribution, and selling skills. Therefore, firms in general need to access or acquire a variety of resources and capabilities in order to insure success of their products and services. A diverse alliance portfolio composed of various types of alliances and partners is one way to achieve this goal (Bruyaka & Durand, 2012).

Our focus in this chapter is on a firm's portfolio of alliances, defined as a firm's egocentric alliance network (i.e., direct ties with partner firms and ties among those partners) (Everett & Borgatti, 2005). Alliance portfolios have aggregated properties (such as portfolio size, partner and ties diversity, and mix of tie strength) that affect performance but are not meaningful for single ties (Ozcan & Eisenhardt, 2009). Whereas the bulk of traditional alliance research has mainly focused on the formation, governance, evolution and performance of single alliances as well as the performance consequences for firms entering into alliances (Wassmer, 2010), a portfolio approach to interfirm cooperation is "concerned with trying to explain how involvement of an individual or organization in a network affects its actions and outcomes" (Provan, Fish, & Sydow, 2007, p. 483). We suggest that the portfolio approach is particularly appropriate for examining focal firm's innovation barriers and firm innovativeness for three key reasons. First, since innovation is complex and requires combination of diverse resources and capabilities, and since a firm may participate in multiple alliances (Gulati, 1999), focus on an alliance portfolio allows us to examine contributions of diverse network members to the focal firm's ability to overcome innovation barriers. While Wellman (1988) pointed out "ability—the competencies and resources at the nodes of the network [i.e., alliance partners]—occupies an ill-defined place in the current state of social theory," few systematic efforts have been made to address this issue. The alliance portfolio perspective therefore helps to more clearly understand the role of nodal factors. Second, since innovation resources are sticky and require deeper level of interaction and trust to flow, focus on direct ties in an ego network helps to more deeply and precisely examine the role of network resources on innovation. Finally, from the standpoint of network design and management, the focal firm can more easily structure and orchestrate its alliance portfolio defined as an ego network (Dhanaraj & Parkhe, 2006). The portfolio of alliances becomes more of a strategic tool to the managers. Thus, the portfolio perspective on innovativeness enables us to more deeply examine the role of network factors in a holistic yet parsimonious manner. Below we briefly review existing studies establishing the relationship between alliance portfolio characteristics and innovation.

Alliance Portfolio and Firm Innovation:
A Review of the Literature

Research on alliance portfolio characteristics is about the content and structure of a firm's alliance portfolio (Wassmer, 2010). Below we briefly review existing studies on the following key dimensions: (1) portfolio size; (2) portfolio diversity; (3) partners' interconnectedness and (4) strength of ties. Table 5.1 provides illustrative examples of empirical studies and their findings on how each dimension of alliance portfolio relates to firm innovativeness.

Alliance portfolio size refers to the number of strategic alliance agreements and partners of a focal firm. Prior research in the alliance portfolio tradition suggests a positive impact of alliance portfolio size on firm innovation output. Shan and colleagues (1994) found that biotech start-up firms' number of patents were positively impacted by the number of commercial ties those firms had, suggesting a linear relationship between portfolio size and innovation. Interestingly, Deeds and Hill (1996) did not find support for such a linear relationship between the biotech start firms' number of patents (also new products) and number of alliances in the same biotech industry, however, Deed and Hill find support for a curvilinear relationship between them. In a study of large chemical firms Ahuja (2000a) finds support for linear relationship between number of patents and portfolio size.

Alliance portfolio diversity reflects differences in a firm's alliance partners' characteristics (e.g., industry, country of origin, size, experience, etc.) (Goerzen & Beamish, 2005; Jiang et al., 2010; Vasudeva & Anand, 2011) and in a firm's alliance types (e.g., R&D, marketing, manufacturing, etc.) (Powell et al., 1996). Alliance portfolio diversity has been found to affect firms' learning and innovation. As Powell and colleagues (1996) noted "R&D ties and other types of collaborations are the admission ticket, while diversity, experience, and centrality are the main drivers of a dynamic system in which disparate firms join together in efforts to keep pace in high-speed learning races." In strategy and entrepreneurship several studies on alliance portfolio diversity showed that difference in alliance partners' characteristics and alliance types positively influences how well the firms in an alliance learn from each other. The common argument of these studies (e.g. Baum et al., 2000; Beckman & Haunschild, 2002; Powell et al., 1996; Srivastava & Gnyawali, 2011) is that partners with diverse capabilities have more to learn from each other than partners with very similar capabilities. However, there is strong evidence that increased alliance portfolio diversity does not always lead to greater learning and innovation. For example, Rothaermel and Deeds (2006), and Lane and Lubatkin (1998) argued that greater similarity in organizational

Table 5.1. Summary of Scholarly Research on Alliance Portfolio Characteristics and Firm Innovativeness

Author(s)	Dependent Variable: Type of Innovation Output	Independent Variable	Data and Sample	Impact on Innovative-ness	Comments
Portfolio Size					
Shan, Walker &Kogut, 1994	# of patents	# of alliances	85 biotech start-ups	Positive	Innovation output of start-up firms increases with their relationship with large firms
Deeds & Hill, 1996	# of new products on the market # of patents	# of alliances	132 U.S. biotech firms	Inverted U-shaped	There is an inverted U-shaped relationship between a firm's strategic alliances and the rate of new products development.
Ahuja, 2000	# of patents	# of direct partners	97 leading chemical industry firms	Positive	The effect of portfolio size on innovation decreases with increasing number of indirect ties
Soh & Roberts, 2005	# of new product awards	# of partners	49 primary vendors (networking)	Positive	Number of partners has positive impact on the likelihood of getting new product award
Portfolio Diversity					
Baum, Calabrese & Silverman, 2000	# of patents	Partners' diversity (network efficiency)	142 Canadian biotech start-ups	Positive	A startup's patenting rates increase with the efficiency of its alliance network at founding
Ruef, 2002	# of patents	Diversity of partners	766 entrepreneurial teams	Positive	Entrepreneurial teams who are embedded in heterogeneous networks are significantly more likely to attempt innovation than entrepreneurs in homogenous networks
Rothaermel & Deeds, 2004	# of products in development	# of exploration alliances	325 Canadian biotech firms	Positive	A firm's exploration alliances are significant in predicting the firm's products in development
Sampson, 2007	# of post-alliance patents	Partner's technological distance	463 R&D alliances in the telecommunications equipment industry	Inverted U-shaped	R&D alliances with moderate diversity contribute more to firm innovation than alliances with very low or very high levels of capability diversity
Srivastava & Gnyawali, 2011	# of breakthrough patents	Partners' technological diversity	180 semiconductor industry firms	Positive	The effects of portfolio diversity increases at lower rate with increasing technological diversity of firm

130

Portfolio Resource Richness

Stuart, 2000	# of patents	Partners' technological capabilities	150 firms in semiconductor industry	Positive	Firms that possessed technologically advanced alliance partners innovated at a substantially greater rate than those that did not
Hsu, 2005	Organizational innovativeness	Network resources	126 Taiwan firms in the hardware industry and 43 firms in the software industry	Positive	Network resources have a positive effect on organizational innovativeness
Srivastava & Gnyawali, 2011	# of breakthrough patents	Partners' resource quality	180 semiconductor industry firms	Positive	The effects of portfolio quality increases at lower rate with increasing technological strength of firm

Portfolio Structure: Partners' Interconnectedness

Ahuja, 2000	Innovation output	Structural holes	97 leading chemical firms	Negative	Structure holes have negative impact on innovation output.
Bell, 2005	Innovativeness	Centrality in the managerial networks	77 mutual fund companies in Canada	Negative	Centrality in managerial network has negative impact on innovation output.
Schilling & Phelps, 2007	# of patents	Combination of degree of clustering and reach	1106 firms in high-technology manufacturing	Positive	Firms embedded in alliance networks that exhibit both high clustering and high reach (short average path lengths to a wide range of firms) will have greater innovative output
Padula, 2008	# of patents	Cluster Involvement (densely connected ties) and Shortcuts (spanning bridges across clusters)	371 firms in US mobile phone industry in the 1990s	Positive	The development of a dual alliance network structure, made up of both cohesive and sparse alliances, contributes to innovation.

Portfolio Structure: Strength of Ties

Ruef, 2002	# of patents	Weak ties	766 entrepreneurial teams	Positive	Entrepreneurial teams who rely heavily on information from acquaintances are more likely to engage in what they see as innovative activity than those who rely on information from family and friends

131

properties and knowledge bases between alliance partners enhanced alliance success and innovation output. Sampson (2007) showed that moderate level of technological diversity between a firm and its alliance partners is ideal: allying firms that differ moderately from their partners gain more from their collaborative R&D than firms with either very high or low diversity. Similarly Vasudeva & Anand (2011) found that moderate level of alliance portfolio diversity contributes to optimal knowledge utilization and results in higher patent output.

Alliance portfolio resource richness reflects the collective volume and quality of resources and capabilities possessed by the focal firm's alliance partners. Intellectual capital (Nahapiet & Ghoshal, 1998), for example, knowledge and technologies of the network members, is a key part of ego network resource richness. The basic logic behind the resource richness of an alliance portfolio is that friends would be helpful only if they have the capability to do so; they may be of little help if they lack the necessary capabilities in spite of all their willingness. Several empirical studies showed importance of alliance portfolio resource richness. For example, Stuart (2000) investigated the relationship between interfirm technology alliances and firm performance. The author argued that "alliances are access relationships, and therefore that the advantages which a focal firm derives from a portfolio of strategic coalitions depend upon the resource profiles of its alliance partners" (p. 791). The results of the empirical analysis of the United States semiconductor firms confirmed positive effect of alliance partners' resourcefulness (i.e., alliance portfolio resource richness) on these firms' patent rate and sales growth. In the same context of the United States semiconductor firms, Srivastava & Gnyawali (2011) found that the quality and diversity of alliance portfolio technological resources contribute to breakthrough innovation. The benefits were found to be greater for firms with low internal strength and low internal diversity, thus "suggesting positive synergy between portfolio and internal resources for such firms" (p. 797). Vasudeva and Anand (2011) studied how fuel cell technology firms facing technological discontinuities utilize knowledge from alliance portfolios. The authors found that a medium diversity of partners' technological resources in the portfolio contributes to optimal knowledge utilization (citation-weighted patent count). Thus, too little diversity imposes a cost in the form of reduced exposure to alternatives, greater redundancy, and underutilization of a firm's latitudinal absorptive capacity (i.e., capacity to utilize unfamiliar or unrelated technological knowledge) as does too much diversity by placing an excessive burden of the firms' latitudinal absorptive capacity (p. 619).

Portfolio structure: Strength of ties. Strength of ties captures the quality of relationship between the focal firm and its partners. A strong tie implies a tie imbued with deeper interpersonnel and interorganizational relationships between the focal firm and its partners (Gilsing & Nooteboom, 2005; Krackhardt, 1992). However, in the context of alliance portfolios large number of strong ties can be a double-edged sword. On one side, an alliance portfolio of strong dyadic ties can affect a focal firm's innovative capabilities positively if they are trust-based, knowledge intensive, and reinforced through the development of social content between alliance partners, relationship-specific investments, and the deepening of mutual knowledge (Capaldo, 2007; Gilsing & Nooteboom, 2005). On the other side, they can also affect a focal firm's innovative capabilities negatively by stimulating a vicious circle in which a reduced number of contacts, decreased flexibility for collaboration with new partners, and diminishing responsiveness to new market trends reinforce each other, leading to a small, homogeneous, and closed network (Capaldo, 2007).

Portfolio structure: Partners' interconnectedness. Alliance portfolio interconnectedness refers to the degree to which a firm's alliance partners have ties with each other. Interconnectedness creates the condition in which the focal firm is able to mobilize the network resources held by the network members (Obstfeld, 2005). Research has conflicting theoretical arguments and empirical findings on the impact of portfolio partner interconnectedness. The long historical debate between Coleman's (1988) and Burt's (1992) perspectives still continues. Theoretically, Coleman argues that a dense network creates social capital that facilitates creation and sharing of resources, while Burt argues that a sparse network brings diverse information and provides controlling power. Empirically, Ahuja (2000a) finds that structural holes have a negative impact on firm innovation. Adopting a contingency approach Vanhaverbeke and colleagues (2009) find a positive impact of structural holes on the exploitative innovations and curvilinear impact on exploratory innovations.

Thus, overall, our review suggests that a large number of conceptual and empirical studies show that different alliance portfolio characteristics such as size, diversity, resource richness, strength of ties and partner interconnectedness contribute to firm innovativeness. However, important gaps exist in the literature. First, existing research rarely discusses the specific mechanisms through which the alliance portfolio characteristics influence firm innovation. Second, literature has rarely taken a holistic approach to examine the alliance portfolio characteristics and their effects. We know little about how the content and structure of alliance portfolio *together* work in determining the extent and nature of benefits to the focal firm. One of our key contentions is that considering how alliance portfolio structure shapes the ability of firms to extract benefits from the content of their alliance portfolio can further advance our understanding of how alliance portfolio factors relate to firm innovation.

CONCEPTUAL MODEL AND PROPOSITIONS

Risk and uncertainty are at the core of innovation (Teece, 1996). A superior portfolio with a diverse and unique mix or combination of resources of the partners is likely to provide the firm access to valuable and unique resources that help to cope with the uncertainty and risk and generate superior returns. When the focal firm has a holistic understanding of its entire set of relational resources, it can identify and select those resources that can help the firm address its challenges, and access, acquire and recombine the most relevant ones, and thus uniquely benefit from its entire set of partnerships and resources held by the partners (Ahuja, 2000b; Dyer & Singh, 1998; Gulati, 2007; Lavie, 2006).

In order to develop a meaningful theoretical model explaining the impact of alliance portfolio characteristics on firms' innovativeness we discuss key mechanisms through which a firm can leverage its portfolio to overcome innovation barriers. These mechanisms are associated with different alliance portfolio characteristics that we grouped in two critical sets —alliance portfolio content and alliance portfolio structure. Alliance portfolio content refers to the quality and functional characteristics of an alliance portfolio resources and is captured by the following constructs: (a) resource richness of the portfolio reflecting the potential for a firm to access its partners' resources and the context for the flow of resources (Burt, 1992; Coleman, 1988; Wellman, 1988) and (b) diversity of alliance ties and partners reflecting opportunities of choice, and superior information access (Baum et al., 2000; Beckman & Haunschild, 2002; Powell et al., 1996; Sampson, 2007). Alliance portfolio structure reflects the way alliance portfolio is organized, and includes such elements as partners' interconnectedness and strength of ties reflecting the ability of the alliance portfolio to protect the firm's competitive position and secure it from uncertainty.

Creation of a Portfolio Effect

By building on the above core ideas, we suggest three important ways in which the focal firm, its portfolio, and the elements within the portfolio interact to create the "portfolio effect" for the focal firm: (a) acquisition of portfolio resources to enrich internal resources, (b) co-development with partners by combining internal and portfolio resources, and (c) creation of interpartner synergy through the interaction among the elements of the portfolio. In the acquisition mode, a firm's internal resources get enriched when it learns from its partners, acquires relevant external resources, and combines those resources for greater advantages. While the presence of partnerships is a prerequisite, the underlying mindset in this approach does not involve working jointly with the partners, but involves accessing partners' relevant resources and acquiring them to pursue activities on its own by the focal firm. Having an alliance portfolio and access to a diverse set of resources in the portfolio provides the opportunity to search broadly, to target the most relevant and complementary resources contained in the portfolio, and to be selective in acquiring them.

In the co-development mode, the focal firm and partners can combine their complementary resources and use them for mutual gains. The focus in this mode of cooperation is on the joint value creation and involves working intimately with the partners (Dyer & Nobeoka, 2000). The locus of innovation in this mode lies in joint efforts (Powell et al., 1996), whereas the locus of innovation in the acquisition mode is internal to the focal firm. Finally, in the interpartner synergy creation mode, benefits of a particular partner's resources to the focal firm increase in the presence of other partners' resources. The synergy between partners makes the overall value created by the alliance portfolio exceed the sum of the values created by each individual alliance in the portfolio (Vassolo, Anand, & Folta, 2004). Using the different pieces of resources and recombining them, the firm will be better equipped to solve the *innovation puzzle*. This is especially critical because innovation requires emphasis on recombinatory process (Fleming, 2001). All three ways or scenarios we describe here are important in the creation of the *portfolio effect,* and they are unique and work in different ways in creating such an effect. Focus on the portfolio, as opposed to individual alliances, is critical because by using a portfolio perspective the focal firm can evaluate the elements (partners and their resources), interrelationships among the many elements (multiple partners and their resources), and have a more holistic or *gestalt* view of its partnerships and their implications. Our propositions below discuss mechanisms through which alliance portfolio content creates the portfolio effect and affects innovation barriers (i.e., resource constraints, organizational rigidity and uncertainty) and predict moderating effects of alliance portfolio structure. Figure 5.1 summarizes our theoretical model and Table 5.2 outlines key mechanisms of alliance portfolio content and structure effect on firms' innovativeness.

The Effects of Alliance Portfolio Content on Firm Innovativeness

Resource Richness

Resource richness of an alliance portfolio reflects the collective volume and quality of resources and capabilities possessed by the focal firm's alliance partners. Three underlying mechanisms work in leveraging resource richness of a firm's alliance portfolio in creating the portfolio effect.

Portfolio resource acquisition. It is nearly impossible to get all needed resources from one alliance partner. Therefore, building an alliance portfolio with additional and complementary resources may help a focal firm to create a resource stock it may use to experiment, which lies at the core of the innovation process (Thomke, 2003). As experimenting consumes significant amount of resources, having access to a larger volume of resources enables a firm to initiate and engage in more experimentation projects (Nohria & Gulati, 1996). With partners' help, the focal firm can push more of the promising experimentation projects into the development stage, scale up the prototypes, and take more of the projects already in the development stage closer to their commercial launch. As a result, fewer projects will meet their premature death due to the paucity of resources (resource constraint).

Further, collaboration with partners with strong technological capabilities will help the focal firm in handling complex technologies. When the focal firm works with several partners on cutting-edge technologies, its technological exposure as well as understanding of emerging technologies increases, which in turn enhances the firm's capability to deal with technological complexities. With the partners' knowledge and expertise, the focal firm might be able to better understand and evaluate the attractiveness of innovation projects, weed out less viable projects, and avoid unnecessary steps/missteps early in innovation process (Thomke, 2003). Working with intellectually capable partners can also reduce the number of overall failures as often projects result in failures due to technological issues. The firm can also reduce the overall development cost of successful projects by using knowledge from one project in planning and executing new projects. In sum, the firm's ability to leverage partners' technological know-how will reduce the external uncertainty for the focal firm when it experiments with highly unfamiliar technologies (Pennings & Harianto, 1992).

Co-development or value co-creation in alliance portfolio. A resourceful portfolio also equips the focal firm to develop new resources. The partners with high intellectual capital are likely to be quite innovative themselves, and therefore are willing to engage in innovative activities. By being connected with capable and motivated firms, the focal firm gets more opportunities to create new valuable resources by combing its resources with those of alliance portfolio members (Nahapiet & Ghoshal, 1998). A resourceful portfolio also creates a stimulating environment in the firm's relational neighborhood, which provides more incentives to institute learning mechanisms and knowledge sharing routines (Dyer & Singh, 1998) to enhance its internal resources. Therefore, beyond the value created in each alliance, the total value resulting from an alliance portfolio

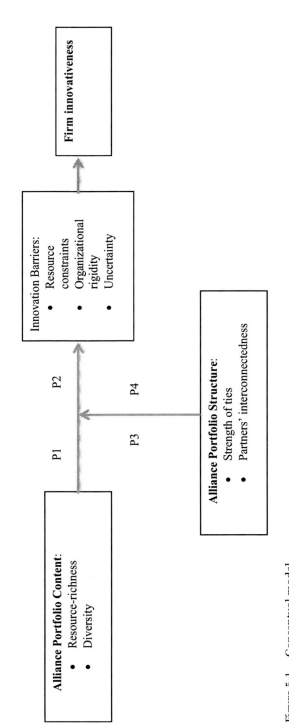

Figure 5.1. Conceptual model.

137

**Table 5.2.   Alliance Portfolio Attributes,
Underlying Mechanisms, and Effects on Innovation**

Alliance Portfolio Attributes		Mechanisms	Effects
Content	Resource richness	Accessing shared resources	Lower Resource constraint
		Positive spillover effects	Lower Organizational rigidity
		Co-development (value co-creation)	Lower Resource constraint
	Diversity	Creation of options	Lower Uncertainty
		Signaling mechanism	Lower Resource constraint
		Creativity boost	Lower Organization rigidity
Structure	Strength of Ties	Increased trust	Positive moderator at high levels of Resource-richness
		Inefficient structure	Negative moderator at low levels of Resource-richness
	Partners' Interconnectedness	Increased rigidity	Negative moderator at low level of Diversity
		Increased trust	Positive moderator at higher level of Diversity

will be greater meaning a positive portfolio effect that can benefit a firm in its innovation efforts (resource constraint).

Interpartner synergy. Extant literature suggests that collaborations present a firm with two potential routes to value, namely common and private benefits (Khanna, 1998; Khanna et al., 1998). First, common benefits are those that accrue collectively to alliance partners. These composite quasi-rents, or value generated by a firm's resources in continued association with that of another (Hill, 1990), enable firms to create value that they would be unable to accomplish individually. Private benefits refer to value generated for the firm through its alliance outside the focal collaboration, for instance, when knowledge-based spillovers from an alliance enriches a firm's stock of know-how in adjacent areas (Sarkar, Aulakh, & Madhok, 2009).

Knowledge spillovers may occur not only between alliance partners in dyads (Lavie, 2006), but also they may occur at the alliance portfolio level, where a central firm forms multiple alliances that complement one another, and can benefit both jointly and privately from each of these. As Dyer and Nobeoka (2000) found, common benefits become available at the portfolio level when a focal firm runs its alliances in an inclusive and participative way, and actively leverages relevant knowledge generated from any one alliance across the portfolio. Thus, the portfolio effect is created in this case through optimization of time, effort and money, which helps to overcome resource constraints and lower organization rigidity by favoring free exchange of ideas and resources among different projects. As the nature of resource requirements change, in order to develop new resources and capabilities, a focal firm would need to make multiple changes in its organizational routines, which at times could also disturb internal power-structure (Kaplan & Henderson, 2005). Therefore, despite necessity of making these changes, the firm faces inertia and struggles to make those changes (Kaplan & Henderson, 2005; Nelson & Winter, 1982). Alliance portfolio richness could obviate the need for developing all of those new resources and capabilities that a firm could successfully access through its alliance portfolio partners. Thus, by leveraging portfolio resources, the focal firm could overcome challenges posed by organizational rigidity barriers. Based on the discussed mechanisms of resource acquisition, co-development, and interpartner synergy, we propose:

> **Proposition 1:** The higher the resource richness in a focal firm's alliance portfolio, the higher the firm's ability to reduce its resource constraint, organizational rigidity and uncertainty barriers through increased resource acquisition, resource co-development, and interpartner synergy.

Diversity

Diversity of alliance portfolio refers to the variety in the resources, experiences, and practices of the portfolio members as well as to the diverse content of alliance ties a firm maintains with its partners. The sources of diversity may include partner firms' resources and capabilities, technological domains, geographical regions, and product/market segments. Diversity of alliance portfolio influences the likelihood of innovation by mitigating the organizational rigidity, resource constraints and uncertainty barriers to innovation. There are three key mechanisms underlying the positive impact of alliance portfolio diversity on the firms' innovativeness:

Creating options. Real options theory based on the theory of financial portfolio conceptualizes strategic alliances as real options since a pioneering study by Kogut (1991). Alliances enable the firms to learn about growth opportunities through close interaction with their partners, and thereby secure upside gains (Vassolo et al., 2004). According to this perspective, the principle of betting on heterogeneous options (risk diversification) is supposed to yield better returns as opposed to the principle of putting all eggs in the same basket. Therefore, entering into various alliances with an increasingly diverse array of partners can help a firm to overcome uncertainty and risks related to innovation projects and increase its ability to innovate. For instance, in the pharmaceutical industry (an R&D intense industry) it is known that among multiple research projects exploring different active substances, only few will end up with a commercially viable drug. In this case, diversifying a portfolio creates opportunities or options that secure the firm if one or several projects that it is involved in fail.

Signaling mechanism. Alliances are both pathways for the exchange of resources and signals that convey social status and recognition. Particularly, alliances can act as endorsements: they build public confidence in the value of an organization's products and services and thereby facilitate the firm's efforts to attract customers and other corporate partners (Stuart, 2000). The information that passes through alliances is influenced by each partner firm's position in the industry structure. Firms with access to a more diverse set of activities are better able to locate themselves in information-rich positions. Different location in a network of partnerships results in firms having divergent capabilities for benefiting from collaboration. Powell and colleagues (1996) further argue that central connectedness derived from alliance portfolio diversity shapes a firm's reputation and generates visibility, producing access to resources via benefit-rich alliance ties. Such a reputation can greatly enhance a firm's ability to attract talented new employees (star scientists), who are crucial resources in the innovation process.

Recombinatory opportunities. Diversity implies variety of information and exchanged ideas. One of the key sources of the resource barrier in the innovation process is the necessity of having a wide variety of resources and capabilities due to increasing convergence of technologies. Developing every resource and capability required for successful and sustained innovation activities may not be feasible for the firm. When a firm has diverse partners in its alliance portfolio, it can search broadly and access different types of resources and capabilities possessed by the portfolio members (Laursen & Salter, 2006). The availability of heterogeneous resources in turn equips the firm not only to think of different permutations and combinations but also provides it with the means to realize new ideas jointly with alliance partners. Thus the firm will be able to pursue innovation projects and overcome organizational rigidity because a diverse alliance portfolio offers flexibility and pushes the boundaries established by a firm's internal routines making it hard to develop new ideas and implement changes internally. Furthermore, as innovation is fundamentally about recombining existing knowledge elements in novel ways (Fleming, 2001), the more diverse the portfolio resources, the more recombinatory opportunities exist. The diversity of resources becomes particularly critical when uncertainty is high. During a period of high level of uncertainty the nature of resources needed for innovation could change very swiftly, requiring very different types of resources in a rather short period of time. A firm whose alliance portfolio is imbued with more diverse resources, therefore, can navigate through the high level of uncertainty more effectively.

Although, alliance portfolio diversity creates options, boosts firms' creativity and increases innovative opportunities through signaling mechanisms, too much diversity may have inverse effect on innovation. Increased alliance portfolio diversity can lead to a conflict of interests, increased complexity and cost of portfolio management. Specifically, increased diversity of alliance partners is associated with higher complexity of managing different alliances, which requires extensive coordination and increases demand for managerial resources (Goerzen & Beamish, 2005; Hitt, Hoskisson, & Ireland, 1994; Roth, Schweiger, & Morrison, 1991). As Sarkar and colleagues (2009) noted, "if the alliance portfolio reflects a dispersed group of partners spread widely across the value chain, then coordinating across the entire portfolio may not create the same kind of synergy as possible with a focused alliance portfolio" (p. 590). In addition, the positive effect of entering the alliances of increasingly diverse content may be bounded by a firm's capacity to absorb heterogeneous information (Shipilov, 2009). This capacity becomes critical when a firm manages alliances of diverse content and deals with partners from different operational context. Disadvantages of limited experience and cognitive capacity constraints (Fleming & Sorenson, 2001) can prevent a firm from benefiting from alliance portfolio diversity at its high level. Based on the above discussion, we propose the following:

> **Proposition 2:** As the focal firm's alliance portfolio diversity increases, the ability of the firm to overcome resource barrier, organizational rigidity and uncertainty increases due to increased range of available options and opportunities for resource recombinations. However, benefits of diversity will decline beyond a certain point due to increased conflict, complexity in portfolio management, and cognitive overload.

Moderating Effects of Alliance Portfolio Structure

In this section we consider two specific constructs—strength of ties and partners' interconnectedness—related to alliance portfolio structure and affecting the benefits a firm can receive from resource richness and diversity of its portfolio.

Strength of Ties and Resource Richness

From an alliance portfolio perspective, the relationship between tie-strength of individual alliances and the benefits that firms derive from their alliance portfolios can only be fully understood when other factors are taken into account (i.e., resource richness of an alliance portfolio). With respect to firms' innovativeness, strong ties that a firm establishes with its partners help both partners access "social, technical, and commercial competitive resources that normally require years to develop" (Baum et al., 2000). The existence of frequent interpersonal and interorganizational exchanges could contribute toward building a strong relational trust (Tsai & Ghoshal, 1998). Relational trust gets developed through mutual understanding, actions, and reactions over a period of time and is composed of trust at the interorganizational level as well as at the individual level between the employees of the focal firm and its partner firm (Gilsing & Nooteboom, 2005). The interorganizational trust and individual-level trust both reinforce each other, and one could arise because of the other as well, although presence of one does not imply presence of the other. Strong relational trust facilitates the flow of high threshold and sticky resources such as technological know-how (Krackhardt, 1992). Developing such highly valuable sticky resources entails considerable time, cost, and prior capabilities. Firms guard such resources very carefully and therefore mobilization of such resources across partnering firms requires high level of relational trust. Frequent, repeated, and multiplex exchanges and trusting relationships make it easier for the focal firm to develop partner-specific absorptive capacity and establish knowledge-sharing routines (Dyer & Singh, 1998). Established trust and routines will enable the firms to share valuable information (Koka & Prescott, 2002), and complex technologies and know-how (Rowley, Behrens, & Krackhardt, 2000), thus, contributing to lower the resource barrier to innovation and positively increasing the effect of alliance portfolio resource richness on firms' ability to innovate. However, sharing the resources between alliance partners just provides a potential to innovate, their coordinated integration is necessary to realize that potential (Tiwana & Keil, 2007). Alliance portfolios with strong ties have greater capacity to implement innovative ideas (Obstfeld, 2005). Further, strong ties enjoying mutual faith and understanding will have greater adaptation capability (Uzzi, 1996), which can lower relational uncertainty that may become particularly critical in rapidly changing environments. Rapid technological changes often impose new challenges and require alliance partners to modify the nature of their resource commitments, expectations, and obligations in order to adjust to new realities. Partners connected through strong ties view these changes not as creating a zero sum game but as providing opportunities for a win-win situation in the long run. They are less likely to play the "endgame" due to the likelihood of future interactions (Gulati & Singh, 1998). Greater ability to adjust the nature of relationship to the environmental changes, allows the focal firm to solve problems on the fly and jointly with the partners (Uzzi, 1996) and to jointly face uncertainty with lower risk of opportunistic behavior. High degree of uncertainty could provide very conducive environment for opportunistic behavior. Strong ties between firms allow them to adapt their relationship as the partnering firms need to change their level and nature of resource commitments in highly uncertain environments.

Thus, strong ties help firms to reduce organizational rigidity and uncertainty, and especially reduce resource constraint barrier to innovation: mutual trust allows them to adapt alliance relationships in the face of environmental changes, which is critical to the continued flow of resources. We suggest that strong ties have a positive effect on firms' innovativeness when alliance portfolio resource richness is high because structural trust, developed and promoted through strong ties, allows firms to extract more benefits from their relationships with alliance partners because it mitigates barriers to accessing partners' valuable resources when partner firms are likely to guard their resources as well as creates more opportunities for fruitful co-development and interpartner synergy (Ahuja, 2000a).

However, when the alliance portfolio resource richness is low, and focal firm has established a large number of strong ties, the focal firm could be trapped into relationships that bring little benefit but consume the focal firm's vital resources necessary for maintaining and managing those relationships: strong ties impose greater demands for conformity on a focal firm (Ruef, 2002), and imply considerable commitment and investment of time, energy and resources (Krackhardt, 1992; McFadyen & Cannella Jr, 2004). When the resource richness is low, large numbers of such ties create structural rigidity, which further adversely impacts the focal firm's ability to adapt.

Additionally, if the focal firm primarily relies on co-development portfolio mechanism, the firm draws rich benefits when the portfolio is high in resource richness. The focal firm can effectively co-create innovations by engaging in joint pursuit of important innovations. However, if the firm relies on the same mechanism, when the resource richness is low, there would be few co-creation opportunities as the partner firms would lack necessary resources, while due to greater reliance on the co-development mode, the extent of dependence on the portfolio partners will be high. Thus, on the one hand partners have little capability to co-create, but on the other the focal firm is highly dependent upon them in pursuit of its innovation. Therefore, the focal firm's innovation efforts are likely to suffer. However, when the portfolio resource richness is low, a focal firm primarily relying on acquisition mechanism would be at a less disadvantage, as the focal firm would be less dependent upon partner firms' resources. Additionally, the focal firm would not need to commit its valuable resources to maintain relationships that are likely to bring few benefits. However, the benefits would be much lower when the portfolio is high in resource-richness, as the partner firms would become more suspicious of the focal firm's motives, and therefore, would make extra efforts to protect their critical resources. Based on the above discussion we formulate the following proposition.

> **Proposition 3:** As the number of the focal firm's strong ties increases, it catalyzes the positive effect of the focal firm's alliance portfolio resource richness on firms' ability to overcome innovation barriers and innovate when the resource richness is high. However, tie strength has a considerable negative impact on the firm's innovativeness when the portfolio resource richness is low.

Partners' Interconnectedness and Diversity

Interdependencies in alliance portfolios are critical determinants of whether the overall value that firms derive from their alliance portfolios is greater or smaller than the sum of the values of each individual alliance in the portfolio (Wassmer, 2010). Interconnectedness indicates the degree to which a focal firm's alliance portfolio partners have ties with each other. Several studies have shown that interconnectedness brings cohesion to the alliance portfolio (Obstfeld, 2005) and builds structural trust (Rowley et al., 2000; Uzzi, 1996). In the presence of structural trust, the focal firm can rely on its partner firms to spot any deviant behavior of any particular partner. Further, interconnectedness among partners provides the focal firm with mechanisms to obtain fine-grained information about any particular potential partner from multiple sources (Dyer & Nobeoka, 2000). This information helps the firm in identifying partners with right attributes and in locating required resources. Thus, interconnectedness among partners could be helpful in mobilizing the alliance portfolio resources and further lower resource barrier to innovation.

However, the increasing interconnectedness of partners within a firm's alliance portfolio gets in contradiction with the diversity attribute of alliance portfolio. That is, when a firm is connected to highly interconnected partners, over time such partners become highly similar as they get exposed to the similar type of information and exchange resources through those multiple connections, which diminishes the benefits of diversity. Further, even though interconnectedness helps firms to choose partners with right attributes and needed resources, any conflict arising in one alliance is likely to spread to other alliances in a firm's alliance portfolio as all partners are connected. The extent of flexibility within a relationship goes down, as any

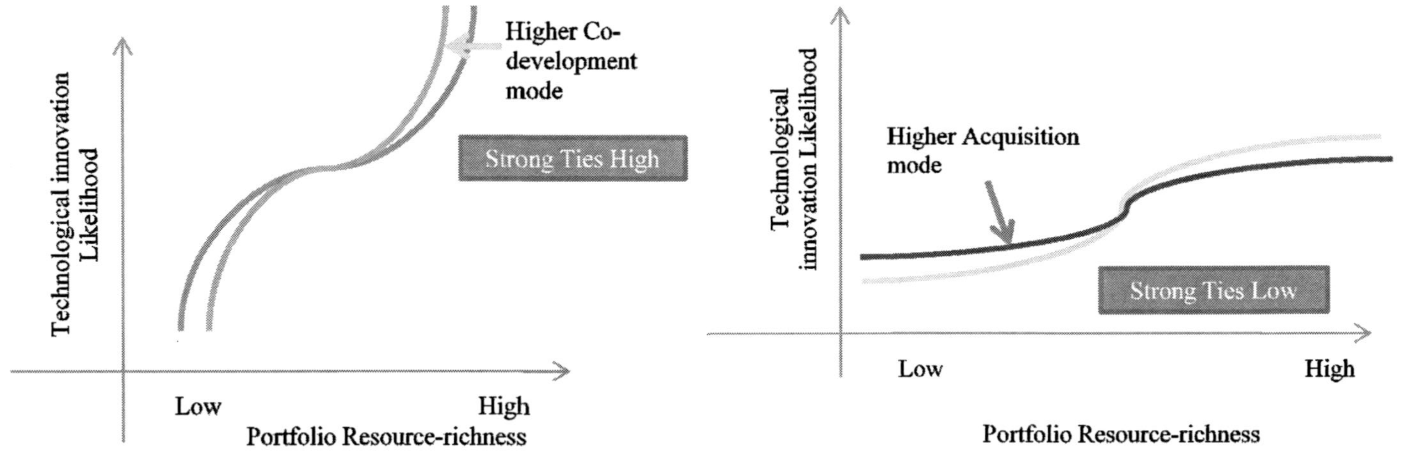

Figure 5.2.   Interaction of portfolio resource richness and strong ties.

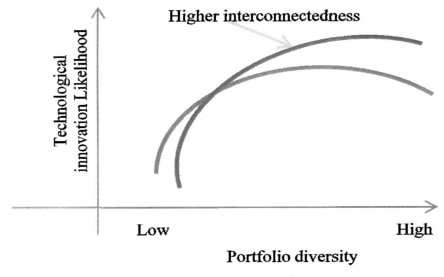

Figure 5.3.   Interaction of portfolio diversity and partners' interconnectedness.

change in it might also impact the relationship with other partners. Thus, focal firm's ability to orchestrate its alliance portfolio is adversely affected.

Overall, firms can benefit from their partner interconnectedness, however it appears to be a double-edge sword with both advantages and disadvantages. When considering jointly alliance portfolio diversity and partner interconnectedness their relationship is difficult to disentangle. As discussed in the previous section—the proposed effect of alliance portfolio diversity on firms' innovativeness is inverted U-shaped with best results achieved at moderate levels of diversity. We propose that partner interconnectedness amplifies benefits of diversity at high levels of alliance portfolio diversity, but it hinders the firms' ability to extract benefits from diversity at its lower levels.

When alliance portfolio diversity is low, a firm has reduced exposure to alternatives, gets access to redundant information and similar partners' resources and skills which does not allow much exploration necessary to develop innovative technologies and products (Lavie & Miller, 2008; Vasudeva & Anand, 2011). Alliance partners' interdependence does not help to overcome the above-mentioned barriers to innovation when alliance portfolio diversity is low. On the contrary, partner interconnectedness increases redundancy of information, which diminishes the benefits of diversity. However, when the level of alliance portfolio diversity increases, it places an excessive burden on a firm's absorptive capacity related to its ability to use unfamiliar or unrelated technological knowledge (Vasudeva & Anand, 2011), and creates issues related to difficulty of managing multiple partners with diverse goals and perspectives (Goerzen & Beamish, 2005; Sarkar et al., 2009). Interconnectedness among partner firms generates structural trust and can mitigate some of the issues arising with increased diversity (Phelps, 2010, p. 895): "Dense networks allow firms to learn about current and prospective partners through common third parties, reducing information asymmetries among firms and increasing their "knowledge-based trust" in one another."

In sum, at different levels of alliance portfolio diversity partner interconnectedness is expected to have different effect—it inhibits innovation benefits stemming from alliance portfolio diversity at its low levels and it amplifies benefits of diversity at its higher levels. Thus, we suggest the following proposition:

> **Proposition 4:** At low levels of alliance portfolio diversity, increased partners' interconnectedness reduces the benefits of diversity and contributes less to a firm's innovativeness. As the level of alliance portfolio diversity increases, increased partners' interconnectedness amplifies the benefits of alliance portfolio diversity and contributes more to the firm's innovativeness.

DISCUSSION

Contributions and Directions for Future Research

Our chapter, which is an important initial attempt to develop an alliance portfolio theory of innovation, contributes to the literature in several important ways and generates interesting possibilities for future research. First, our explication of primary innovation barriers provides a more concrete basis to examine the problems firms face in their innovation efforts. These innovation barriers, in a sense, are the missing links between network and innovation. The barriers serve as clogs in pipes and need to be explicitly addressed in order to enhance innovation. The identification of these barriers thus shifts the focus from accessing information to accessing and mobilizing other resources such as technological know-how, market knowledge, and human capital. As we have discussed, the focal firm's alliance portfolio also helps overcome resource constraints, mitigate organizational rigidity and deal with uncertainty. Our chapter provides a strong starting point to further explore innovation barriers and to develop measures to empirically examine such barriers.

Second, we explicated the underlying mechanisms of alliance portfolio effects. Specifically, we suggested three primary mechanisms through which portfolio effects occur: resource acquisition, co-development, and synergy. While it is important to develop firm capability to create the portfolio effect (Vassolo et al., 2004) through all three ways, it is likely that firms differ in their realization of these avenues for the portfolio effect. Some firms are more prone to focus on accessing and acquisition of others' knowledge and prefer to pursue innovation on their own; others could be more interested in and capable of developing intimate relationships with their partners and thrive in co-development. It is likely that firms exhibit distinct preferences for one or other portfolio mechanism due to their behavioral orientations. Future research could examine how and to what extent firms differ in their mechanisms and abilities in creating the portfolio effect and how such variation matters in various innovation outcomes. For example, it is likely that pursuit of breakthrough innovations would require exploration and recombination of unique resources held by alliance partners. Then, would the co-development mode of creating the portfolio effect be more critical than the acquisition mode in pursuit of breakthrough innovations? Examination of questions like these would significantly enhance our understanding of the mechanisms by which network resources matter for innovation.

Third, our theory illuminates the nuanced nature of alignment between the alliance portfolio's content aspects and structural aspects. Our discussion of the content captured the richness and variety of alliance portfolio resources, while the discussion of the structure illuminated the occurrence and impact of relational trust and structural trust, formation of structural rigidity, and dissipation of diversity. Our theory suggests why the simultaneous consideration of both is so critical for understanding the role of alliance portfolio on technological innovation and thus advances a contingent perspective. A firm leverages its portfolio resources more effectively when the portfolio's resource richness is high, and at the same time the firm's ties are also strong. However, the same condition becomes highly disadvantageous if the portfolio's resource richness is low. Similarly, greater interconnectedness among the portfolio members is a boon when the portfolio is high in alliance portfolio diversity, but the same becomes a liability if the portfolio is low in diversity. Further, our theory highlights the importance of firm's behavior toward its portfolio. A firm which is more reliant on co-development portfolio mechanism reaps greater reward when the portfolio richness is high and the firm has larger number of strong ties with portfolio members. However, the same firm faces considerable disadvantage in terms of innovation benefits if the portfolio is low on resource richness. While, a firm more reliant on resource-acquisition mechanism is likely to perform better when the portfolio resource richness is low, but the firm is also low on strong ties. More broadly, our theory further illustrates the necessity of alliance portfolio orchestration (Dhanaraj & Parkhe, 2006) by the focal firm keeping portfolio content, portfolio structure, and firm behavior simultaneously under consideration in order to achieve optimal fit among them. Future research could delve deeper into how these multitudes of alliance portfolio conditions and the firm's ability to orchestrate its network over time impacts innovation which is inherently a dynamic phenomenon.

Managerial and Policy Implications

Our theory also has very critical managerial implications. Managers could gain valuable insights from our conceptualization of the innovation barriers, the content and structure of the network, and the creation of the portfolio effect. Our propositions provide a useful guide for managers to shape their network conditions and make them more conducive in their innovation efforts. Managers could examine the nature of their alliance portfolio and understand whether their portfolios exhibit fit between the portfolio content and portfolio structure. Further, given the nature of their alliance portfolio content and structure the firm can adapt its behavior in order to more effectively leverage their alliance portfolio resources. From the technology policy perspective, the study suggests encouraging the firms to form variety of interfirm relationships especially in high technology sectors and reduce any policy barriers that inhibit formation of interfirm relationships so that firms can overcome myriad of innovation barriers.

Limitations

The present study has certain limitations that need to be taken into account when considering its contributions. We focused our theory development on three most common barriers to innovativeness—resource constraints, organizational rigidity and uncertainty—however, we acknowledge that many more factors impeding innovation exist that should be taken into consideration. Another limitation is a parsimonious nature of our theoretical model. In this regard, we believe further research will allow us to better understand the complexity of the interaction between alliance portfolio content and structure and their impact on the barriers to innovation.

We also recognize contextual limits of this study's propositions. Finally, there is a need to empirically test the propositions advanced in this study in different empirical contexts, which will allow us to evaluate the correctness of our predictions and their generalizability. Despite the above-mentioned limitations we believe that some of these limitations can be seen as fruitful avenues for future research.

CONCLUSION

This chapter was motivated by the need to simultaneously take a holistic approach (as opposed to individual dyads) to alliances and focus on partners' resources in understanding how alliances contribute to firm innovativeness. In filling this critical gap, we have built on the emerging literature streams that take a portfolio perspective on alliance and that explain the role of external resources on firm innovation and blended these streams in developing our conceptual model. Our conceptual development started off with a discussion of innovation barriers and showed that focus on innovation barriers helps to pinpoint the mechanisms through which alliance portfolio configuration and resources might contribute to the reduction of such barriers and subsequently enhance firm innovativeness. Our conceptualization of the role of alliance portfolios included characteristics of both the content and structure of a firm's alliance portfolio. Our propositions explicated how these characteristics separately and jointly shape the firm's ability to overcome innovation barriers.

REFERENCES

Abernathy, W. J., & Utterback, J. M. (1978). Patterns of industrial innovation. *Technology Review, 80*(7), 41-47.

Ahuja, G. (2000a). Collaboration networks, structural holes, and innovation: A longitudinal study. *Administrative Science Quarterly, 45*(3), 425-455.

Ahuja, G. (2000b). The duality of collaboration: Inducements and opportunities in the formation of interfirm linkages. *Strategic Management Journal, 21*(3), 317-343.

Ahuja, G., & Lampert, C. M. (2001). Entrepreneurship in the large corporation: A longitudinal study of how established firms create breakthrough inventions. *Strategic Management Journal, 22*(6-7), 521-543.

Bae, J. H., & Gargiulo, M. (2004). Partner substitutability, alliance network structure, and firm profitability in the telecommunications industry. *Academy of Management Journal, 47*(6), 843-859.

Barney, J. (1991). Firm resources and sustained competitive advantage. *Journal of Management, 17*(1), 99-120.

Baum, J. A. C., Calabrese, T., & Silverman, B. S. (2000). Don't go it alone: Alliance network composition and startups' performance in Canadian biotechnology. *Strategic Management Journal, 21*(3), 267-294.

Beckman, C. M., & Haunschild, P. R. (2002). Network Learning: The effects of partners' heterogeneity of experience on corporate acquisitions. *Administrative Science Quarterly, 47*, 92-124.

Bruyaka, O., & Durand, R. (2012). Sell-off or shut-down? Alliance Portfolio diversity and two types of high tech firms' exit. *Strategic Organization, 10*(1), 7-30.

Burt, R. S. (1992). *Structural holes: The social structure of competition.* Cambridge, MA: Harvard University Press.

Capaldo, A. (2007). Network structure and innovation: The leveraging of a dual network as a distinctive relational capability. *Strategic Management Journal, 28*(6), 585-608.

Chen, J. Y., Reilly, R. R., & Lynn, G. S. (2005). The impacts of speed-to-market on new product success: The moderating effects of uncertainty. *Ieee Transactions on Engineering Management, 52*(2), 199-212.

Cohen, W. M., & Levinthal, D. A. (1990). Absorptive-capacity—A new perspective on learning and innovation. *Administrative Science Quarterly, 35*(1), 128-152.

Coleman, J. S. (1988). Social capital in the creation of human capital. *American Journal of Sociology, 94,* 95-210.

Cyert, R. M., & March, J. G. (1963). *A behavioral theory of firm.* Englewood Cliffs, NJ: Prentice-Hall.

Damanpour, F. (1991). Organizational innovation—A metaanalysis of effects of determinants and moderators. *Academy of Management Journal, 34*(3), 555-590.

Das, T. K., & Teng, B. S. (2000). A resource-based theory of strategic alliances. *Journal of Management, 26*(1), 31-61.

de Man, A.-P., & Duysters, G. (2005). Collaboration and innovation: A review of the effects of mergers, acquisitions and alliances on innovation. *Technovation, 25*(12), 1377-1387.

Deeds, D. L., & Hill, C. W. L. (1996). Strategic alliances and the rate of new product development: An empirical study of entrepreneurial biotechnology firms. *Journal of Business Venturing, 11*(1), 41-55.

Dewar, R. D., & Dutton, J. E. (1986). The adoption of radical and incremental innovations: An empirical analysis. *Management Science, 32*(11), 1422-1433.

Dhanaraj, C., & Parkhe, A. (2006). Orchestrating innovation networks. *Academy of Management Review, 31*(3), 659-669.

Dickson, P. H., & Weaver, K. M. (1997). Environmental determinants and individual-level moderators of alliance use. *Academy of Management Journal, 40*(2), 404-425.

Dierickx, I., & Cool, K. (1989). Asset stock accumulation and sustainability of competitive advantage. *Management Science, 35*(12), 1504-1511.

Dougherty, D., & Hardy, C. (1996). Sustained product innovation in large, mature organizations: Overcoming innovation-to-organization problems. *Academy of Management Journal, 39*(5), 1120-1153.

Durand, R., Bruyaka, O., & Mangematin, V. (2008). Do science and money go together? The case of the French biotech industry. *Strategic Management Journal, 29*(12), 1281-1299.

Duysters, G., & De Man, A. P. (2003). Transitory alliances: An instrument for surviving turbulent industries? *R&D Management, 33*(1), 49-58.

Dyer, J. H., & Nobeoka, K. (2000). Creating and managing a high-performance knowledge-sharing network: The Toyota case. *Strategic Management Journal, 21*(3), 345-367.

Dyer, J. H., & Singh, H. (1998). The relational view: Cooperative strategy and sources of interorganizational competitive advantage. *Academy of Management Review, 23*(4), 660-679.

Everett, M., & Borgatti, S. P. (2005). Ego network betweenness. *Social Networks, 27*(1), 31-38.

Fleming, L. (2001). Recombinant uncertainty in technological search. *Management Science, 47*(1), 117-132.

Fleming, L., & Sorenson, O. (2001). Technology as a complex adaptive system: evidence from patent data. *Research Policy, 30*(7), 1019-1039.

Folta, T. B. (1998). Governance and uncertainty: The tradeoff between administrative control and commitment. *Strategic Management Journal, 19*(11), 1007-1028.

Galia, F., & Legros, D. (2004). Complementarities between obstacles to Innovation: Evidence from France. *Research Policy, 33*(8), 1185-1199.

Gilsing, V., & Nooteboom, B. (2005). Density and strength of ties in innovation networks: an analysis of multimedia and biotechnology. *European Management Review, 2*(3), 179-197.

Goerzen, A., & Beamish, P. W. (2005). The effect of alliance network diversity on multinational enterprise performance. *Strategic Management Journal, 26*(4), 333-354.

Grant, R. M., & Baden-Fuller, C. (2004). A knowledge accessing theory of strategic alliances. *Journal of Management Studies, 41*(1), 61-84.

Greis, N. P., Dibner, M. D., & Bean, A. S. (1995). External partnering as a response to innovation barriers and global competition in biotechnology. *Research Policy, 24*(4), 609-630.

Gulati, R. (1999). Network location and learning: The influence of network resources and firm capabilities on alliance formation. *Strategic Management Journal, 20*(5), 397-420.

Gulati, R. (2007). *Managing network resources: Alliances, affiliations, and other relational asset.* New York, NY: Oxford University Press.

Gulati, R., & Singh, H. (1998). The architecture of cooperation: Managing coordination costs and appropriation concerns in strategic alliances. *Administrative Science Quarterly, 43*(4), 781-814.

Hadjimanolis, A. (1999). Barriers to innovation for SMEs in a small less developed country (Cyprus). *Technovation, 19*(9), 561-570.

Hambrick, D. C., & Mason, P. A. (1984). Upper echelons: The organization as a reflection of its top managers'. *Academy of Management Review, 9*(2), 193-206.

Henderson, R., & Cockburn, I. (1994). Measuring competence—Exploring firm effects in pharmaceutical research. *Strategic Management Journal, 15*(1), 63-84.

Hennart, J. F. (1988). A transaction costs theory of equity joint ventures. *Strategic Management Journal, 9*(4), 361-374.

Hill, C. W. L. (1990). Cooperation, opportunities, and the invisible hand: Implication for transaction cost theory. *Academy of Management Review, 15*(3), 500-513.

Hitt, M. A., Hoskisson, R. E., & Ireland, R. D. (1994). A mid-range theory of the interactive effects of international and product diversification on innovation and performance. *Journal of Management, 20*(2), 297-326.

Hoffmann, W. H. (2007). Strategies for managing a portfolio of alliances. *Strategic Management Journal, 28*(8), 827.

Hughes, B., & Wareham, J. (2010). Knowledge arbitrage in global pharma: a synthetic view of absorptive capacity and open innovation. *R&D Management, 40*(3), 324-343.

Jarillo, J. (1988). On strategic networks. *Strategic Management Journal, 9*(1), 31-41.

Jiang, R. J., Tao, Q. T., & Santoro, M. D. (2010). Alliance portfolio diversity and firm performance. *Strategic Management Journal, 31*(10), 1136-1144.

Kale, P., Dyer, J. H., & Singh, H. (2002). Alliance capability, stock market response, and long-term alliance success: The role of the alliance function. *Strategic Management Journal, 23*(8), 747-767.

Kaplan, S., & Henderson, R. (2005). Inertia and incentives: Bridging organizational economics and organizational theory. *Organization Science, 16*(5), 509-521.

Khanna, T. (1998). The scope of alliances. *Organization Science, 9*(3), 340-355.

Khanna, T., Gulati, R., & Nohria, N. (1998). The dynamics of learning alliances: Competition, cooperation, and relative scope. *Strategic Management Journal, 19*(3), 193-210.

Kline, S. J., & Rosenberg, N. (1986). An overview of innovation. In R. Landau & N. Rosenberg (Eds.), *The positive sum strategy: Harnessing technology for economic growth* (pp. 275-304). Washington DC: National Academy Press.

Koberg, C. S., Uhlenbruck, N., & Sarason, Y. (1996). Facilitators of organizational innovation: The role of life-cycle stage. *Journal of Business Venturing, 11*(2), 133-149.

Kogut, B. (1991). Joint ventures and the option to expand and acquire. *Management Science, 37*(1), 19-33.

Koka, B. R., & Prescott, J. E. (2002). Strategic alliances as social capital: A multidimensional view. *Strategic Management Journal, 23*(9), 795-816.

Krackhardt D. (1992). The strength of strong ties: The importance of philos in organizations. In N Nohria & R. G. Eccles (Eds.), *Networks and organizations: Structure, form, and action* (pp. 216-239). Boston, MA: Harvard Business School Press.

Lane, P. J., & Lubatkin, M. (1998). Relative absorptive capacity and interorganizational learning. *Strategic Management Journal, 19*(5), 461-477.

Laursen, K., & Salter, A. (2006). Open for innovation: the role of openness in explaining innovation performance among U.K. manufacturing firms. *Strategic Management Journal, 27*(2), 131-150.

Lavie, D. (2006). The competitive advantage of interconnected firms: An extension of the resource-based view. *Academy of Management Review, 31*(3), 638-658.

Lavie, D. (2007). Alliance portfolios and firm performance: A study of value creation and appropriation in the US software industry. *Strategic Management Journal, 28*(12), 1187-1212.

Lavie, D., & Miller, S. R. (2008). Alliance portfolio internationalization and firm performance. *Organization Science, 19*(4), 623-646.

Mansfield, E., & Rapoports, J. (1975). The costs of industrial product innovations. *Management Science, 21*(12), 1380-1386.

Marin, P. L., & Siotis, G. (2007). Innovation and market structure: An empirical evaluation of the "bounds approach: in the chemical industry. *Journal of Industrial Economics*, *55*(1), 93-111.

McFadyen, M. A., & Cannella, A. A., Jr, (2004). Social capital and knowledge creation: Diminishing returns of the number and strength of exchange relationships. *Academy of Management Journal*, *47*(5), 735-746.

McGill, J. P., & Santoro, M. D. (2009). Alliance portfolios and patent output: The case of biotechnology alliances. *IEEE Transactions on Engineering Management*, *56*(3), 388-401.

McGrath, R. G. (1997). A real options logic for initiating technology positioning investments. *Academy of Management Review*, *22*(4), 974-996.

Mohr, L. B. (1969). Determinants of innovation in organizations. *The American Political Science Review*, *63*(1), 111-126.

Mone, M. A., Mckinley, W., & Barker III, V. L. (1998). Organizational decline and innovation: A contingency framework. *Academy of Management Review*, *23*(1), 115-132.

Nahapiet, J., & Ghoshal, S. (1998). Social capital, intellectual capital and the organizational advantage. *Academy of Management Review*, *23*(2), 242-266.

Nelson, R. R., & Winter, S. G. (1982). *An evolutionary theory of economic change*. Cambridge, MA: Belknap Press/Harvard University Press.

Nohria, N., & Gulati, R. (1996). Is slack good or bad for innovation? *Academy of Management Journal*, *39*(5), 1245-1264.

Obstfeld, D. (2005). Social networks, the tertius iungens and orientation involvement in innovation. *Administrative Science Quarterly*, *50*(1), 100-130.

Ozcan, P., & Eisenhardt, K. M. (2009). Origin of alliance portfolios: Entrepreneurs, network strategies, and firm performance. *Academy of Management Journal*, *52*(2), 246-279.

Pennings, J. M., & Harianto, F. (1992). Technological networking and innovation implementation. *Organization Science*, *3*(3), 356-382.

Phelps, C. C. (2010). A longitudinal study of the influence of alliance network structure and composition on firm exploratory innovation. *Academy of Management Journal*, *53*(4), 890-913.

Piatier, A. (1984). *Barriers to innovation*. London, England: Frances Pinter.

Powell, W. W., Koput, K. W., & Smith-Doerr, L. (1996). Interorganizational collaboration and the locus of innovation: Networks of learning in biotechnology. *Administrative Science Quarterly*, *41*(1), 116-145.

Provan, K. G., Fish, A., & Sydow, J. (2007). Interorganizational networks at the network level: A review of the empirical literature on whole networks. *Journal of Management*, *33*(3), 479-516.

Rosner, M. M. (1968). Economic determinants of organizational innovation. *Administrative Science Quarterly*, *12*(4), 614-625.

Roth, K., Schweiger, D. M., & Morrison, A. J. (1991). Global strategy implementation at the business unit level: Operational capabilities and administrative mechanisms. *Journal of International Business Studies*, *22*(3), 369-402.

Rothaermel, F. T., & Deeds, D. L. (2006). Alliance type, alliance experience and alliance management capability in high-technology ventures. *Journal of Business Venturing*, *21*(4), 429-460.

Rothaermel, F. T., Hitt, M. A., & Jobe, L. A. (2006). Balancing vertical integration and strategic outsourcing: Effects on product portfolio, product success, and firm performance. *Strategic Management Journal*, *27*(11), 1033-1056.

Rowley, T., Behrens, D., & Krackhardt, D. (2000). Redundant governance structures: An analysis of structural and relational embeddedness in the steel and semiconductor industries. *Strategic Management Journal*, *21*(3), 369-386.

Ruef, M. (2002). Strong ties, weak ties and islands: Structural and cultural predictors of organizational innovation. *Industrial and Corporate Change*, *11*(3), 427-449.

Sampson, R. C. (2007). R&D alliances and firm performance: The impact of technological diversity and alliance organization on innovation. *Academy of Management Journal 50*(2), 364-386.

Sarkar, M. B., Aulakh, P. S., & Madhok, A. (2009). Process capabilities and value generation in alliance portfolios. *Organization Science*, *20*(3), 583-600.

Shan, W., Walker, G., &, & Kogut, B. (1994). Interfirm cooperation and startup innovation in the biotechnology industry. *Strategic Management Journal*, *15*(5), 387-394.

Shipilov, A. V. (2009). Firm scope experience, historic multimarket contact with partners, centrality, and the relationship between structural holes and performance. *Organization Science*, *20*(1), 85-106.

Srivastava, M. K., & Gnyawali, D. R. (2011). When do relational resources matter? Leveraging portfolio technological resources for breakthrough innovation. *Academy of Management Journal*, *54*(4), 797-810.

Stuart, T. E. (2000). Interorganizational alliances and the performance of firms: A study of growth and innovation rates in a high-technology industry. *Strategic Management Journal*, *21*(8), 791-811.

Teece, D. J. (1986). Profiting from technological innovation: Implications for integration, collaboration, licensing and public policy. *Research Policy*, *15*(6), 285-305.

Teece, D. J. (1996). Firm organization, industrial structure, and technological innovation. *Journal of Economic Behavior & Organization*, *31*(2), 193-224.

Thomke, S. H. (2003). *Experimentation matters: Unlocking the potential of new technologies for innovation*. Boston, MA: Harvard Business School Press.

Tiwana, A., & Keil, M. (2007). Does peripheral knowledge complement control? An empirical test in technology outsourcing alliances. *Strategic Management Journal*, *28*(6), 623-634.

Tsai, W., & Ghoshal, S. (1998). Social capital and value creation: The role of intrafirm networks. *Academy of Management Journal*, *41*(4), 464-476.

Uzzi, B. (1996). The sources and consequences of embeddedness for the economic performance of organizations: The network effect. *American Sociological Review*, *61*(4), 674-698.

Vanhaverbeke, W., Gilsing, V., Beerkens, B., & Duysters, G. (2009). The role of alliance network redundancy in the creation of core and noncore technologies. *Journal of Management Studies*, *46*(2), 215-244.

Vassolo, R. S., Anand, J., & Folta, T. B. (2004). Nonadditivity in portfolios of exploration activities: A real options-based analysis of equity alliances in biotechnology. *Strategic Management Journal*, *25*(11), 1045-1061.

Vasudeva, G., & Anand, J. (2011). Unpacking absorptive capacity: A study of knowledge utilization from alliance portfolios. *Academy of Management Journal, 54*(3), 611-623.

Wassmer, U. (2010). Alliance portfolios: A review and research agenda. *Journal of Management, 36*(1), 141-171.

Wellman, B. (1988). *Structural analysis: From method and metaphor to theory and subtance*. Cambridge, MA: Cambridge University Press.

Williamson, O. (1985). *The economic institutions of capitalism*. New York, NY: Free Press.

Yli-Renko, H., Autio, E., & Sapienza, H. J. (2001). Social capital, knowledge acquisition, and knowledge exploitation in young technology-based firms. *Strategic Management Journal, 22*(6-7), 587-613.

Zaheer, A., & Bell, G. G. (2005). Benefiting from network position: Firm capabilities, structural holes, and performance. *Strategic Management Journal, 26*(9), 809-825.

CHAPTER 6

TECHNOLOGY VERSUS WORK VERSUS LIFE

Lucy R. Ford and Gayle Porter

ABSTRACT

Technology devices, such as smartphones, are becoming ubiquitous. In this chapter we explore whether new technologies of this type are helping or hindering peoples' relationship with their work, and whether the disappearing of boundaries between work and nonwork should be of concern. In addition, we address the broader societal impact of the use of technology devices for both work and nonwork purposes, in the context of a society in which people are working ever harder. The advent of these devices has resulted in an ability to get work done at any time, in any place. Coupled with increasingly long work hours and higher levels of work intensity than in the past, such concerns as stress, dangerous use of devices while driving, and attention losses from attempts to multitask, have become serious concerns for society in general. These issues cannot be solved by any one stakeholder group alone. We issue a call to action, and provide suggestions for individuals, employers, technology manufacturers, and society in general.

Global Perspectives on Technological Innovation, pp. 157–182
Copyright © 2013 by Information Age Publishing
All rights of reproduction in any form reserved.

INTRODUCTION

Weaver's hand, sprout-picker's thumb, stitcher's wrist, cotton-twister's hand, cubist's thumb or Rubik's wrist, and BlackBerry thumb. What meaning do we attach to these strangely labeled body references? Some may sound familiar, others completely foreign. Each is a name for an ailment derived primarily from repeated movements that are both small and fast, creating an intensity of hand use that exceeds the capacity of our skeletal and muscular structures. These ailments all became common enough to merit a special description, but came about in different ways. The first four—weaver's hand, sprout-picker's thumb, stitcher's wrist, and cotton-twister's hand—were terms in usage during the 19th century (Tenner, 1997). They were disorders connected to work, and much of this type of work has since been automated to a large extent. Therefore, these terms are not familiar to most people today.

In contrast, cubist's thumb or Rubik's wrist both refer to medical conditions that are specifically derived from the use of a toy that was introduced in the 1960s, and continues to be used today. Rubik's Cube is considered the "best selling toy ever," not only due to the total sales of "more than 350 million" since its introduction, but also due to the fact that it is still popular enough to have generated "9.2 million of those [sales]" as a yearly total as recently as 2009 (Kadaba, 2010). Worldwide competitions continue for overall speed in solving the puzzle, including by age bracket (e.g., the 4-year old who, in 2007, solved it in less than a minute and a half), as well as for solving one handed, blind-folded, or using feet rather than hands (Kadaba, 2010). For most enthusiasts, though, a Rubik's Cube means devotion of a great deal of time turning and twisting the cube to finally achieve the result of a solid color on each side or, having succeeded, to work at increasing speed or demonstrate repeatedly one's proficiency with its complexity.

The commonality across all these hand/wrist ailments is that they are caused by rapid and small motions, either due to work-related or leisure endeavors. Where, then, does BlackBerry Thumb fit into the classification? The term BlackBerry Thumb was adopted by the American Physical Therapy Association in 2006 to refer to the pain and numbness caused by overuse of handheld devices (American, 2006). Research in Motion, the company offering the actual BlackBerry product, began with a business strategy that emphasized business application, which would suggest that BlackBerry Thumb might be similarly focused on excess work-related use. However, other brands of hand held devices have proliferated in recent years, without that business focus. Under the general terminology of "smartphones," they collectively have become fairly ubiquitous in personal life, as well as business application.

In other words, we cannot attribute the hand ailments caused by use of these devices exclusively to work or to leisure activity. The technology has crossed that work/nonwork boundary to a level never seen before, and our society has embraced this crossing, by accepting that having the technology to blur the boundaries between our work and nonwork lives means that it is a good or an acceptable choice to do so.

We will discuss a range of technology, but with particular emphasis on smartphones, defined as handheld devices that typically offer telephonic functions, access to the Internet, appointment calendars, recordkeeping, a camera, and an increasingly large number of games and other "apps" that might facilitate both work and leisure activities. The list of possibilities continues to grow on a daily basis. In April, 2012, the Apple application store contained more than half a million separate work applications available for Apple smartphones (Apple, n.d.), with the number rising daily.

As implied by the title, this chapter will consider (1) whether technology is helping or hindering people's relationship to their work, (2) whether the shifting (or disappearing) of boundaries between work and other aspects of life should be more of a concern, and (3) the broader implications of technology in modern life, particularly if work and nonwork are entangling irreversibly. We include a discussion of who might take responsibility for making improvements where technology has created problems.

TODAY'S WORKPLACE

While not all modern work involves the use of computers, a government report of more than 20 years ago (Bureau of the Census, 1991) was already reporting that more than 1 in 3 adults used a computer at work, a proportion that has most certainly increased significantly since then. Further, the computer is now just one of several technological devices used in the workplace, particularly in white-collar professions. A report by Korn/Ferry International (2006) reported that 81% of the surveyed 2,300 executives around the globe were connected to work all the time through use of cell phones and other mobile devices. With the advent of tablet devices, defined as touch screen mobile computers ("Definition of Tablet Computer," n.d.), we will almost certainly see such devices becoming more common in the workplace. In a November 2010 survey of IT purchasers, it was found that 7% of employers were providing tablets to their employees, while an additional 14% were planning to do so in the first quarter of 2011 (Carton, 2010).

At a conference session, one of the presenters put up a list of the electronic devices he routinely uses on a daily basis. About a dozen different

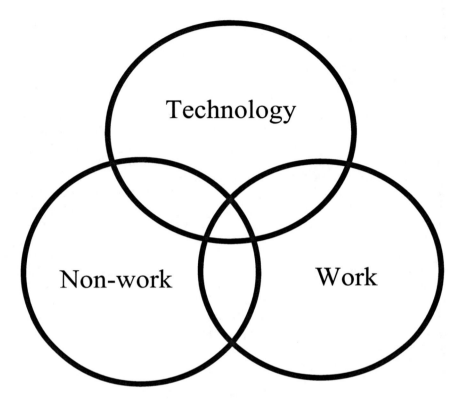

Figure 6.1.   Three topics of discussion with 2-way and 3-way relationships.

devices were listed, and he expressed his confidence that he was an average user, at least within the legal profession. The trend toward having many devices may be reversing, however, with the introduction of tablets, and other devices that combine the functions of multiple earlier devices. For example, the smartphone has already replaced the need to have a telephone *and* a personal digital assistant device, as both functions are available in the smartphone.

It seems as though there is no turning back the tide of technology adoption in the workplace, but there are many who question whether the proliferation is living up to its promise of improving either productivity or the quality of life for workers. For example, technology allows us to work faster on many things, but the length of the workweek in the U.S. has increased rather than decreased. Authors generally point to the period around the 1970s as the time when longer workweeks began increasing above 40 hours (Golden, 2006; Nye, 2006; Schor, 1993), after having steadily declined for decades. In research on work-family conflict, Williams and Boushey (2010) reported that middle-income employees worked an average of 11 hours more per week in 2006 than in 1979. Although this lengthening of the workweek may have contributed to improved productivity, the trend continues.

In 1995, Rifkin wrote about the success of shorter workweeks in countries such as France, and predicted that Americans would see shortened workweeks in the coming decades, while the unemployed would become a permanent underclass. But, in what she called the "betrayal of the great promise of technology," (p. 207), Bunting, (2004) reported not only long work hours in the U.S. being accompanied by employees failing to use all available vacation days but, further, that in general it is now the higher salaried employees who are working the longest hours. But at the time of her writing, even Bunting felt that the situation had reached a tipping point and that we would see a shift toward shorter working hours. The economic downturns since then have, instead, resulted in reduced employment, so that those with jobs face even greater demands, as well as insecurity about the continuation of their employment. So the predicted reduction in work hours has failed to materialize.

Does the increasing use of technology have anything do with creating longer workweeks? Is it a need arising out of those longer workweeks? Or is it simply a disappointing coincidence? Those who think that technology is causal often point to the proliferation of information to which we are exposed, and which we must manage. There is likely some truth to this, but it is partially because we have made the choice to have access to such information, and must therefore devote the time to manage it. Historian David Nye (2006) proposes that technology is not something external to society that has an impact on our lives but is instead "an expression of our social world" and "shaped by social context" (p. 47). This would suggest that while we have oft expressed hope that technology will lead to more leisure time, we have in fact neglected our own social pressures in the opposite direction, in particular the extent to which we prioritize work success. In fact, in our society, for many, work identity is the primary identity, and without work, life may feel meaningless (Helliker, 2009). As advances in technology allow us to do more than we could in the past, we are using the technology to work more than we did in the past, thereby increasing the chances of work success (or at least, so we believe).

Once new technologies begin to take hold, people may be swept into usage that ultimately is found to have unintended (and unwanted) consequences (Tenner, 1997). Postman (1993) suggests that technology is not in and of itself neutral, to the extent that the user does not have complete control over whether that technology is harmful or not. The technology is designed for a particular application and its use, therefore, impacts how we live. This is probably why workers sometimes report feeling that technology controls them rather than the other way around. For example, the availability of e-mail allows quick communication, but responding to dozens or even hundreds of e-mails per day shapes how time is spent at work and is considered burdensome to many (especially weeding through all those "cc" messages that do not add value but are incredibly easy to generate "just in case") (Beaton, 2007). In fact, this problem has become so intractable that there is a move afoot in the online community to take back control of a technological innovation that consumes perhaps more time than it saves (E-mail charter, n.d.).

THE CHANGE TO WORK AT ANY TIME, ANY PLACE

As mentioned above, technology that is physically in the workplace is no longer the complete picture. Small easily transportable devices have increased workers' ability to stay connected to work at any time and any place with almost, if not completely, the same capabilities formerly identified with a physical space and prescribed work times. A recent article in *Financial Times* (Taylor, 2010) reported that although "feature phones" (the older generation that included a camera and some multimedia features) then accounted for 70% of US phone sales, that proportion was rapidly shifting. Their prediction was that within 18 months 50% of U.S. phone sales would be smartphones, moving toward the day when all phones will be smartphones. Their prediction was right on target, as the Wall Street Journal reported that smartphones accounted for 49.7 of all mobile telephone sales in the United States in February, 2012 (Poletti, 2012).

In a recent study that examined work-related use of smartphones, almost half (43%) of the 627 respondents were current smartphone users, but more than a third (38%) of the nonusers indicated that they were thinking about becoming a user within the next 6-12 months (Porter, 2009). While the majority of the current users had devices supplied by their employer, which was no doubt a factor in their adoption, not all were employer-supplied. Employee usage of the devices spanned both work and nonwork activities, regardless of who originally purchased the devices. The blurring of the demarcation between work and nonwork activities due to the use of smartphones for both parallels the increased blurring of time boundaries between work and nonwork.

Since the introduction of these devices, without which we all functioned until recently, our expectations have been raised on all fronts. At a championship baseball game in Philadelphia, fans were angered by their inability to call, e-mail, text, or access the Internet during the sold-out game, due to overload of the wireless network in that area—too many users concentrated in one limited space. Complaints prompted a network upgrade, to better handle the 5,000 to 10,000 users estimated to be in the full stadium.

Today, smartphone users expect continuous and reliable service, and this often extends to an expectation that those to whom they send messages will reply more or less instantaneously. While this might create friction between friends or family members, the potential is significantly more serious in the workplace, when it involves messages between a worker and the boss, or with important customers. If a manager sends out e-mails long after work hours, employees seeing the e-mail at work the next day might become concerned that their responses were considered too slow. If job anxiety is high enough, they may begin to alter sleeping habits in order to check for overnight messages in the future. Some bosses might have a real expectation of immediate response that supports this fear, while others might be unaware of the implications of their actions. Either can induce worker anxiety and additional attention to work in what was previously considered private time.

Another topic of recent study is work intensification—the mental and physical effort devoted to getting more work done in a prescribed block of time (Green, 2004, 2008). A study on flexible working conditions (Kelliher & Anderson, 2010), found three types of intensification. The first was imposed intensification—that which is directly required as job performance. The second was enabled intensification—an experience of heightened focus, usually mentioned by workers in remote locations and therefore not subject to the usual workplace distractions. The third was reciprocal intensification, the one of most interest in this discussion. Reciprocal intensification is extra effort applied to work, and which is offered to the employer in exchange for flexible working conditions.

This willingness to work *more intensely* in exchange for flexibility is akin to the finding that people will also willingly work *longer* in exchange for flexibility (Porter, 2009). For example, a parent who wants to eat dinner with his family, and spend time with them before they go to bed, might be willing to return to work activity in the later evening hours. This option, although not the same as working less, might be a better solution for that parent than staying late at the office and not seeing the children. Likewise, the ability to leave work early to attend to nonwork matters (such as a child's recital) might be willingly traded for longer work hours on the other days of the week. Technology has increased the possibilities for adjustment of work time in this manner, as the worker can accomplish the work from any location, and can be accessed if necessary. Information technology, as one might imagine, has been argued to be the single biggest factor in creating work intensification (Bunting, 2004).

It is clear that work and nonwork activities are becoming woven together in new patterns, very different from the clearly containerized work day and leisure time separation of the past, and furthermore that technology is at the heart of many of the threads of change. New patterns which blur the lines between work and nonwork are not necessarily bad, if there is no loser—no one is exploited by the change. There is evidence to suggest, though, that the employee tends to lose out, as evidenced by the steady increase in average work hours. Yet the employer may not be benefitting to the degree that one might expect. In addition, as workers' time is more and more consumed by their jobs, there is an overall societal impact to consider. Our use of technology may well serve as a reflection of what we are as a society, but as undesired consequences are realized, we need not blindly continue in a particular direction. We may in fact choose to alter our interactions with technology.

SOCIETAL IMPACT OF ADVANCING TECHNOLOGY

Fifteen years ago, Tenner (1997) wrote about technology using the word "REVENGE." He was not drawing attention to the side-effects of technological advances, but instead to the consequences of the use of technology for its intended purpose. For example, technology in the workplace held the promise to eliminate certain dangers and diseases and, thereby, be a positive addition for workers. While this is true in many cases—for example, factory floor advances in robotics—technology is directly related to various health issues, in the form of eyestrain, back problems, tendonitis, and exhaustion even from sedentary work, among others. These attacks on muscles, vertebrae and tendons are now common place among white-collar workers. So, technology did not eliminate physical problems in the workplace, it simply traded one type for another. Eventually the "price of health may require the reduction—if not the avoidance—of the intensity that newer technology makes possible" (p. 234).

Stress

Increasing work hours and work intensification leads to an increase in stress. Historically considered to be a side effect of physical trauma, mental stress is now recognized as a health issue in its own right, and represents a substantial cost for employers in terms of productivity and health care costs. In spite of the growing attention to sustainability in the workplace, we seem more attuned to applying these concepts to our physical environment than to human sustainability. "Human beings have finite resources, physical and emotional, and the overwork culture eats into them" (Bunting, 2004, p. 177).

Loyalty between employers and employees has diminished in the past 10-20 years, making long-term employment in one company increasingly rare. Furthermore, some companies seem to follow a strategy of pushing employees to their very limits, with the hope of getting a few good years from them before they reach total burnout (Bunting 2004). While the public might be appalled to see physical exploitation of workers, such as unsafe working conditions, there seems to be less awareness of the severity of exploitation that occurs when employees are expected to work longer and harder.

Failure to protect individual workers from this type of stress erodes the well-being of our society at both a macro- and a microlevel. Chronic stress is related to a number of issues such as domestic violence and suicide, in addition to the frequent individual outcomes of depression, weight gain and drug abuse. There has been some recognition in the United Kingdom that an employer has a "duty of care" to employees that includes avoidance of stress (Bunting, 2004). In the United States, concern about work stress has historically revolved around whether work-related stress must be addressed only within the confines of workers' compensation or might be considered more broadly. Currently there is increasing focus on work-related stress as a disability under the Americans With Disabilities Act (1990). There is little doubt these debates will continue in the United States legal arena, as stress and other mental health issues continue to increase, much of it related to the demands of the workplace, and likely exacerbated by technology.

Another outcome of stress may be disruption to sleep patterns. Additionally, in recent years, many workers—particularly parents—are self-imposing sleep deprivation as a means to create more waking hours in the day for dealing with the combined demands of home and work. The morning hours starting at 4:00 A.M. provide a time for household tasks before others arise to start the day, and this is followed by a 9-10 hour work day. While this seems effective in the short run, those individuals will be more prone to ill health. Also, that time at work is less productive than it would be with a full night's sleep. Studies have long shown that loss of sleep impairs performance on many tasks to the same level of detriment as alcohol consumption (e.g., Wilkinson, 1961).

Road Safety

Technology also causes societal problems when drivers make calls, text, surf the web, or read/write e-mails while driving their cars. The National

Safety Council (2009) offers the following points in its appeal to drivers to eliminate this behavior (and to businesses to enact policies to prohibit it among their employees):

- Use of cell phones contributes to 636,000 crashes each year.
- Hands-free devices do not make usage safe.
- While there are other activities that may distract a driver, the use of a telephone while driving is so pervasive that it contributes to a significantly higher number of accidents than other dangerous behaviors.
- The temptation to multitask is particularly strong when driving time can be used to conduct business, but employers need to realize the potential liability they are assuming should they allow their employees to use their phones while driving.
- Only a small number of companies report having policies prohibiting on-road use of cell phones but, of those who do, 85% say the policies do *not* lead to less productivity.

Assigning liability to the employers is not restricted to accidents that happen while the employee is on a business call. In cases where the company supplied the phone to their employee, the company may be found liable, regardless of whether the call at the time of the accident was related to business (Browning, 2006). The executive order signed by President Obama, banning federal employees from texting while driving, clarified that it applied to federal employees both when they are using government-provided cars or cellphones for personal purposes, and when they are using their personal phones and cars to conduct government business (Richtel, 2009a). It seemingly covers all combinations of car and cellphone ownership. Some individual states have passed their own laws on cell phone use while driving, most commonly going only so far as to require hands-free operation. Pennsylvania has recently gone a step further, by banning texting while driving (Pennsylvania Antitexting Law, 2011). In some cities there have also been attempts to specifically curtail cab drivers' calling and texting while behind the wheel, but it has been difficult to enforce (Grynbaum, 2009). In spite of getting some laws on the books, regulation is spotty across the U.S. and enforcement is very difficult, as a police officer must observe the behavior, which in turn requires them to take their eyes off the road.

It is often the employees themselves who want exemption from any legislation banning texting while driving. For example, truck drivers claim the cost is too high, as do tradesmen and delivery drivers—stopping for needed communication adds clear expense to their operation (Richtel,

2009b). Resistance also comes from professional groups in technology and telecommunications industries, as well as legislators, who share concern about stakeholder groups they may alienate if they do not take this stand (Richtel, 2009c). Although some of these authors spoke specifically about basic cellphone use and/or the use of computers in vehicles, their views are pertinent to a discussion of smartphones, which offer the same functionality and the same risks.

The National Safety Council (2009) specifically addressed the temptation to multitask among drivers who are trying to stay in touch with work in their report. Interestingly, the lure of multitasking is based on erroneous assumptions about the capabilities of the human brain. There is strong evidence that in a multitasking situation, such as driving and texting, people are not performing in the way they think they are. It has been consistently demonstrated (e.g., Gorlick, 2009; Loukopoulos, Dismukes, & Barshi, 2009) that people overestimate their ability to divide their attention among tasks, failing to recognize that it is simply not possible to perform two cognitively demanding tasks simultaneously; it is, however, possible to combine tasks that require low cognitive processing. Driving a car and texting would be two cognitively demanding tasks; watching television while eating lunch would be two low cognitive processing tasks.

What people are doing when they multitask is rapidly switching their attention from one task to the other—each shift in focus taking attention away from the other task. While originally researchers thought people who heavily relied on multitasking were those particularly adept at making these quick attention changes, research has shown that that is not the case. Heavy multitaskers are actually *more* susceptible to distracting information, indicating that their focus on the intended work is not as intense as those who less frequently try to multitask (Gorlick, 2009; Loukopoulos et al., 2009). Additionally, the high multitaskers may spend 50% more total time on completion of all tasks than if they had simply completed one before starting on the next (Nye, 2006).

Time

A common theme that emerges as a problem related to the use of new technologies is time pressure. The assumption that technology should save us time is overridden by the issues created as people try to squeeze technology use into inappropriate time (driving), or try to perform multiple tasks at the same time, facilitated by the technology (the myth of multitasking). In creating pressure to work either longer hours or more intensely, technology creates stress and related health problems (including physical symptoms connected directly to the technology itself), and pressures people into life habits such as forgoing sleep (leading to more stress and impaired productivity). The overall picture is one that cannot be addressed with singular actions. Nor can one look at any of the issues in isolation.

In this section of the chapter we have summarized a nonexhaustive selection of issues arising from the interaction of technology, work activities, and nonwork activities. In the next section we will discuss possible actions that may be taken across four domains of responsibility.

DOMAINS OF RESPONSIBILITY/CALLS TO ACTION

It is clear that there currently exists a dysfunctional interaction among technology, work activities and nonwork activities, and without a change of course it is only likely to worsen. We contend that there are four domains of responsibility for changing this course, and that these four domains are to a degree interdependent (Figure 6.2). First are the individuals who, while possibly feeling pressure from their employers, real or imagined, should not forget that they do have the option of exercising their personal choice. Second are the companies whose work is being accomplished using these devices. Employers have significant influence over the norms that drive the level of separation between work and nonwork, or lack thereof. Third are the technology companies who supply the tools that become means for either improvement, or placement of further demands on the individuals within their employers' operations. Finally, society in general has a stake in resolving these issues, so it is also critical to realize the responsibilities in that domain—particularly consideration of how broader attitudes and behaviors can effect change. We consider that governmental action would be part of this domain where it is appropriate as one path toward remedy.

Individuals

While personal choice has not entirely disappeared from our lives, many may feel that their options have been reduced even further than in the past. We have allowed so much of our personal sense of worth to become intrinsically tied not just to the nature of the work we do, but also to specific job titles, pay levels and professional recognition. Furthermore, we tend to be overly critical when we fail to realize our ambitions within a certain timeframe. "If you believe the American Horatio Alger credo of pulling oneself up the ladder and then you fall off, it must be because you

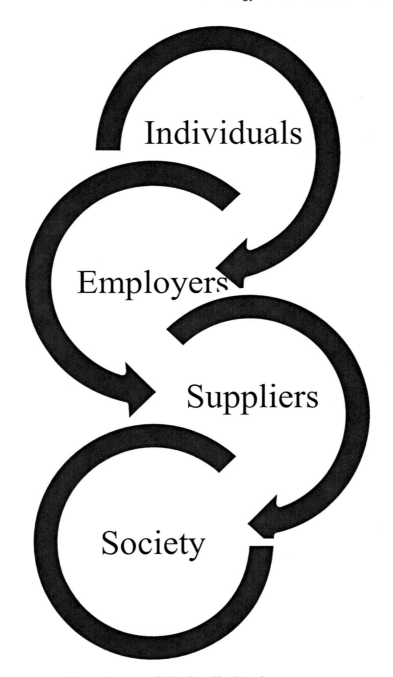

Figure 6.2.   Parties with responsibility for effecting change.

mis-stepped" (Rayman, 2001, xvi). In other words, as a society we tend to believe achieving personal success is simply a matter of hard work, and as a result, if we fail to achieve that success, especially after working extremely hard, then we can only ascribe that failure to personal deficiency. Intellectually, while we understand that jobs have disappeared, the economy is struggling, and a business decision doesn't equate to a personal judgment, we do not readily accept those rationales when applied to ourselves. Instead we are likely to believe that we are deficient, or did not work hard enough.

In the early 1990s, Juliet Schor (1993) wrote about Americans' shift to longer hours, suggesting that the shift was a result of a pursuit of more and more material goods. In 2000, Robert Reich suggested that new anxieties had arisen around income security. He suggested that the shift to a knowledge-based economy was resulting in an increased lack of confidence in individual future earning capability, and that that lack of confidence was creating a felt need to get things *now*, just in case. In addition, he suggested that workers were increasingly recognizing the growing disparity between haves and have-nots. As the gap widens, it is likely that people will work even harder to make sure they stay on the 'have' side of the divide. When difficult choices arise "you don't have to scale the wall, but the consequence of not doing so is harder, and the reward for doing so is sweeter, than you have ever encountered before" (Reich, 2000, p. 224). In the intervening decade, we have experienced a significant economic downturn, which has resulted in even less job security. However, workers still strive to acquire material goods, and particularly to have more than their parents did, so that they can give their children a strong start in life. This incremental improvement by generation is an important element of the American Dream, and one which people will work very hard to maintain.

The personal drive to work beyond external demands has its roots in a desire to establish self-worth, and builds on the fear that self-worth will crumble if the individual is no longer receiving workplace validation of their worth. The extent to which an individual might be driven to overwork, however, can reach an excess that resembles addiction (Porter, 1996; Robinson, 1989). Hard work is pursued to a degree that is not necessary for financial reward, and is distinctly different from high work engagement (e.g., Schaufeli, Taris, & van Rhenen, 2008). Using the term "workaholism" to distinguish this extreme version of working long hours, it is also an identification of compulsive behavior that includes obsessive behaviors like thinking about work when away from it and attempts to control the work of others (Mudrack & Naughton, 2001; Porter, 1996; Scott, Moore, & Miceli, 1997). As with any addiction (or addiction like behavior), we can point to others as supporting or enabling this behavior, but it is the individual who must realize that when work has become such a singular interest in life, they are opting to sacrifice all other involvements.

In one study that focused on a very high pressure organization (Porter, 2006), the 14 managers studied differed in their demonstration of behaviors consistent with workaholism. They were categorized into four groups: workaholics, at-risk (showing stronger tendencies than average but not yet as extreme), moderates, and nonworkaholics (those most unlike workaholics). The managers were assessed on measures of various health issues that had occurred in the immediately preceding 6 months (e.g., headaches, indigestion, chest pain, ulcers), and it was found that while not everyone who had frequent health issues was a workaholic, the workaholics almost all had frequent health issues. This is entirely consistent with our prior suggestion that working longer hours leads to stress, and a wide variety of related health issues.

It is clear that working excessively hard is related to health issues, and that the individual must take responsibility for that. It is entirely possible that extreme levels of work are self-imposed, as opposed to being expected by the employer. In the Porter (2006) study, three of the managers were categorized as workaholics, and were not reported as being any more successful than those who did not engage in such extreme workaholic behaviors, yet worked in the same high pressure environment.

People who have previously engaged in workaholic behaviors, and subsequently change their behavior, typically have some manner of realization about their own personal responsibility in creating the need for workaholism. One executive in a fast-paced marketing firm reported making changes after reading Covey's book on 7 *Habits of Highly Effective People* (1989). He explained that he had previously worked extreme hours, always running to put out one fire after another, until he changed his behavior and realized he had been the one setting the fires. This relates to the workaholic tendency to seek or create crisis situations in order to maintain an insurmountable amount of work and get the temporary ego boost of resolving these extreme work tasks (Porter, 1996).

Another example is that of a divorced executive who decided to remarry and start a second family. His new wife insisted that, barring an extreme emergency, he would always be home by 7 P.M. or she would not agree to have children. The agreement was made, and years later he commented that he was amazed how easy it had been to meet the terms of the agreement, once he set his mind to it. Additionally, he then began to realize how much he had missed out on with the children from his earlier marriage, when he was the more typical absent, busy executive. Advances in technology did help him keep to his promise, which demonstrates that we do have the power to choose to use the technology to help rather than to hurt us. Compare this, however, to the yoga professional who was mystified by neck and back problems, having always given high priority to his health and physical awareness. Someone else had to point out to him that his physical complaints started when he purchased his first smartphone, and spent significant time in an unnatural sitting position with shoulders and head bent over viewing the screen.

So, technology can facilitate the alleviation of work demands, or it can introduce new habits that lead to health problems. As pointed out by Porter and Kakabadse (2006), people with a tendency toward overwork are enabled by the increasing convenience of small, easily carried (and easily hidden) connectivity devices. Additionally, people with a tendency toward addictive behavior with technology can fall back on excuses about the demands of work to keep their devices always with them. This mutually supportive relationship may be contributing to even higher numbers of people showing excess behavior at that intersection of work and technology. While friends and family can highlight the excess, it is up to the individual to decide to listen, to assign some credibility to these complaints, and to affirmatively decide on a positive change in priorities. There are even suggested therapeutic solutions (e.g., Chen, 2006), and 12-step groups, but the individual must want help.

While not everyone that works hard suffers from full-blown workaholism, we have used this extreme behavior to demonstrate that change must begin with the individual. To the extent that an individual is less guilty of using technology to let work interfere with either health or nonwork relationships, the consequences might be correspondingly less, but nonetheless, it is a matter of personal choice.

Employers

Employers seem to be aware that advances in technology merit explicit policies around that technology. Yet, there are some difficulties even with this awareness. First, the problems are identified through experience – which is not surprising as they are new situations created by new technological capabilities. However, this places the employer in a position of being reactive rather than proactive, and attempting to "fix" a problem rather than to prevent it. For example, at a recent leadership workshop conducted by one of the authors, the senior executive team of the client firm discussed their own excessive work behaviors (such as sending e-mails late at night, or from their smartphones while out to dinner with their families, or calling in every day while on vacation) as they are recognizing that such behaviors have sent an unintended message to others in the organization, and they wish to turn that around, as wellness is a concern for them. Further, perhaps partly connected to the "playing catch-up" position just noted, the first changes considered are all too often focused on reducing cost to the company, rather than improving employee wellbeing.

William Herbert (2008) pointed out the negatives of e-mail use in the workplace, including "miscommunication and employee alienation, as well as workplace disruptions," including the possibility that e-mail usage might undermine the workplace culture. He also noted that "few employers proactively address the issue of e-mail overuse or conduct trainings on e-mail etiquette" (p. 73). It is even less likely that an employer would consider policies governing the use of electronic communications during nonwork hours, and in nonwork settings. Such policies need not be harsh and rigid. A simple reminder that, while e-mail is an effective asynchronous communication tool, the company does not expect employees to monitor e-mail 24 hours per day, and might even articulate a clear cut-off time. Another possibility is to ask that even if e-mails are written during nonwork hours, they be sent only during work hours, in order not to create an expectation of immediate response.

There has been increasing concern about "time theft" in the workplace, when employees are spending time at work on nonwork activities (e.g., Henle, Reeve & Pitts, 2010), which might be construed to include their time with personal e-mails, doing web searches, shopping or other activities that are not connected to their work, and that have become increasingly attractive as technology has progressed. As companies search for ways to ensure that their employees are engaged only in work activities at work, it would be nice to see equal attention given to how they might also alleviate unnecessary overflow of work into time that should reasonably be kept as personal.

For telecommuting employees who are working from home locations, there are logical gains for both employee and employer. For people with substantial commuting distance, working at home automatically puts time back into the "available" category that otherwise would be spent on the road. Telecommuters frequently talk about increases in productivity, due to control over their time and lack of interruptions. At the same time, when the telecommuter is using this freedom to work hours that are not parallel to those of the rest of the organization, it becomes difficult to coordinate activities with the in-office personnel (Meinert, 2011). In this case it is a simple matter for the company to provide guidelines around core working hours and expected response times during the standard business day.

Regardless of whether the devices are used exclusively at work, or are carried by the employee back and forth from home, employers understandably have concerns about the security of the physical property *and* the information available on the device, or using the device. Policy recommendations include ensuring employees understand the importance of looking after the company property; clarifying confidentiality expectations and company ownership of related files, servers, and so on; and delineating "rules" limiting employees' use of their computers and other devices (Kamm, 2010). These are all important aspects of having employees carry electronic connections to the office, but the proliferation of smartphones has complicated things further. On the one hand, a personal smartphone provides options to connect to the workplace and work tasks, but does not belong to the company. On the other hand, a company supplied smartphone is likely to become an indispensable personal tool for that employee. While some people do maintain two phones—one for work and one for nonwork, many others blur that line of use and ownership in the same way work and nonwork time has blurred.

One example of a dilemma caused by this blurring of use and ownership occurred as companies explored ways to cut back labor expense without laying people off. One suggestion was to implement furloughs, a time period during which the furloughed employee is not working, and is not paid, but expects to return to work at the end of the furlough. On the surface, it seems like a good idea—everyone gets a little less, so nobody loses their job. Concerns arose, however, about how to ensure that furloughed employees were not actually working during that time, particularly those who had company supplied smartphones for the very purpose of being able to stay connected. Possible solutions were to physically take the phones as the furloughed employees left for their time off, or to arrange discontinuance of service during that time. Employees' negative reactions, however, demonstrate the extent to which the device was incorporated into their personal lives. A smartphone allows an employee to keep both their business and personal calendars in one place, and to store all their contacts, both business and personal, also in one place. While on furlough, they still wanted access to nonwork information stored on the device. While the incorporation of all this personal information onto a work provided device might be good news to the extent that it might increase motivation to not lose the device, it also created an unanticipated dilemma. No one had thought to issue a policy to protect the employees when losing access to their smartphone on short notice. The company certainly had the right to take the smartphones from furloughed employees, but all constituents were caught off-guard by the degree to which personal and work activity had been combined in the evolving use of this technology.

Human resource (HR) management professionals typically advise that company policies related to the use of technology be developed with the usual team of lawyers, IT personnel and HR, as well as some employee representation. It has been suggested that in particular, the millennial generation should be included, as they are the group most likely to demand the use of available technologies, but that inclusion on this basis did not seem to be happening yet (Roberts, 2008). That same logic, however, might justify incorporating a broad range of employee perspectives into the preliminary policy review. For example, do the policies adequately take into account the needs of all employees using the technology —younger and older, men and women, people of different races, backgrounds and pay levels? Do the policies give adequate consideration to parents of young children and those facing eldercare responsibilities?

Based on the preceding comments about individual responsibility, a good perspective to maintain both in creating policies and in the day-to-day management of technology use would be to assess whether the company is creating a situation that will encourage and support workaholism, or whether it is setting norms to prevent such excess. Having clarified that the individual bears final responsibility, it is also worth saying that the company can help or hinder those who would like to avoid excess work by not creating a culture that considers that the norm (regardless of what the formal policies say). One author estimates that one in eight people show signs of addiction to the internet (Fox, 2007), which suggests that employers have an opportunity to provide discipline or treatment for employees whose behaviors indicate a problem. While this might be considered a reasonable suggestion regarding addictive behavior with computer usage, it does not translate well to the tendency toward working too much. One study found that employers almost never refer employees to their employee assistance program for workaholic behavior, unless it is couched in terms of individual symptoms, such as problems with interpersonal relations (Porter & Herring, 2006).

Suppliers of the Technology

It is not adequate for the companies that create and sell the technology to say they are simply responding to the demands of the market. After all, many of the devices and features currently available are things they taught us to need. The younger generations, who do not remember a time without many options for connectivity, will be more demanding. When mobile telephones were first conceived, there was significant resistance, but through movies and other popular media we learned that a portable phone could be "cool" (even though the first generation portable phones were the size of a small briefcase). In a leap from sci-fi to reality that seemed unrealistic not too long ago, we can now embed tracking devices into people, communication devices can be made as small as a shirt button, and it is likely that within a matter of years, communications tools that today seem to be pure fantasy will in fact be reality.

Earlier discussion about the use of smartphones while driving empha-sized the public safety aspect of this dangerous behavior. Could some-thing be built into the devices to alleviate this tendency? One suggestion might be a feature that disables keyboard use when the device senses vehicular motion. Of course, this would also have to have a release to allow passengers to text when sitting on a train, or when some other motion is interpreted incorrectly. Employers might even support this, to avoid the liability when employees have accidents because of interacting with their electronic devices, instead of watching the road. Some custom-ers would consider it a negative feature in their smartphones, but the act of having to override the safety feature would at least provide a quick reminder that one might be about to engage in ill-advised behavior. Those determined to do so would certainly override and continue with their texting, but in doing so they would accept responsibility for that decision.

Due to the enactment of state laws, people have moved to more use of hands free phone calls. A similar shift is occurring from the use of a key-board to voice recognition. The technology has existed for years that would enable a driver to hear e-mail messages and respond by voice, but the accuracy of voice recognition has been questionable in the past. In recent months, Apple has released a new version of the iPhone software that includes "Siri," a character with whom the user can interact (and select their preferred gender and accent) (Siri, n.d.). The accuracy of Siri's voice recognition has improved over previous generations, and is backed up by a vast and growing database of knowledge. Why did it take so many years for a previously existing technology to finally receive the attention it deserved? Interestingly, Apple appears to be promoting Siri as a source of information (as you can orally query the database) as opposed to a tool for voice recognition that might result in safer driving behaviors. This is not an attempt to blame technology companies for bad choices that individuals make. But the creative teams at the leading technology companies are aware of what capabilities are on the horizon long before we, as consumers, make our buying decisions. It would be nice to see some of the marketing dollars include information to help us become responsible users, at the same time they are highlighting the "sexy" new features of their product.

Only the technology companies are in a position to elaborate on what they might do in the future to assist in altering the current course of tech-nology use. They are the ones who can identify enhancements such as reminders, alerts, instructions, or constraints that would eliminate some of the issues created by use of these devices. Beyond those concerns related to individual use of the devices, they might collaborate more with industry to devise ways in which technology used in the workplace could create a more positive interface between work and nonwork. We are not suggesting that the technology companies are at fault; only that there is an opportunity for them to be part of the solution.

Society at Large

As a society we have had a hand in creating the environment in which individuals, employers and technology companies operate. Any change is likely to require that we collectively become more explicit about what we do not want to accept. Bunting (2004) titled her book *Willing Slaves* to communicate that people have chosen to work to excess. She also makes the point that people have a finite amount of energy, so the more energy we expend on things that we say we do not want, the less time we have to devote to things that we say we do want. Apparently, as a society we agree with her assessment that a primary issue today is overexpenditure of energy, as now there is a thriving market for several hours of energy in a small bottle. It is inexpensive, not too unpleasant tasting and, as the television commercials explain, a good solution for people who do not want to waste time making and drinking a cup of coffee in the morning. Many people have bought this product (authors included). Why, when we note exhaustion of our energy supply, do we not look to the root cause, and make more substantive changes to the behavior that put us into that situation, rather than routinely consuming a chemical to eke out a little more from our depleted reserves?

Many of us complain about social norms regarding cell phone use. How unpleasant and distracting it is to hear one side of a stranger's conversation, with those conversations often containing personal information that might be whispered in a face-to-face meeting but must be nearly shouted through a cell phone. It seems that people now even spend time texting or checking e-mail on their phones, rather than facing the discomfort of personal interaction with strangers. Are these new social norms that we really want to accept? Movie theaters now include, along with messages that we can no long smoke in the theater (which has been true for decades), reminders that all electronic devices must be turned off. Most of us have, however, been disturbed by brightly lit smartphone screens, and ringtones during movies. One author recently experienced a woman standing up, turning around to those behind her in the theater audience, and snapping a picture!

These examples are, at best, peripherally related to the workplace. They focus more on the interaction between technology and life in general. An important point, however, is that social norms have lagged behind the capabilities of the technology. Until we are willing, collectively, to establish new societal norms around how technology is generally used in shared times and places, we cannot be overly critical of employers who have not implemented policies that consider employee wellbeing, or be too impatient with the technology companies for not doing a better job of protecting us from ourselves.

As a result of our society's tendency to overly identify with work in creation of our self-image, many people use the word workaholic like a badge of honor. This of course hinders the kind of recognition of workaholism as a problem that would assist those individuals who want to change their behavior. Similarly, we aspire to skill in multitasking as if we cannot have a successful future without it, all the while failing to recognize that it is impossible to actually do two cognitively challenging tasks at the same time. Until we recognize these as issues, and withdraw our social support, workaholism and multitasking will continue to be considered desirable rather than destructive and impossible. So, as a society, we need to be more purposeful in thinking about technology related to work, life, and the intersection between the two.

CONCLUSION

A number of authors have offered observations that resonate. Bunting (2004) pointed out that "the point of primary emotional focus has shifted from home to work" (p. 241). Although many people seem to yearn for the type of refuge from the world that home used to provide, we now have turned it into a "canvas on which to paint the escape fantasies which console us" (p. 242). The proliferation of print and televised media devoted to home improvements/replacements are held up as examples of how this plays out; we often hire the energy of others to create this depiction of our fantasy, because we cannot muster enough of our own time and energy to do so. The more we work, the more we want a refuge, but the less time we have to create it. Add to that the technology-enabled intrusion of work into our home space, and the resulting boundary erosion makes it even more difficult to use home as a place for true replenishment; instead it becomes a quick "pit stop" (p. 245) rather than a shared space for interweaving lives and activities not related to work.

Postman (1993) warned that "When a method of doing things becomes so deeply associated with an institution that we no longer know which came first—the method or the institution—then it is difficult to change the institution or even to imagine alternative methods for achieving its purposes" (p. 143). As new generations enter the workforce, will they wonder whether it was the work that required the blurring of the boundaries between work and nonwork, or whether it was that prior generations chose an emphasis on work that necessitated enabling technology? Can we even be sure now?

The overall question might be to ask what outcome it is that we are hoping for, and whether our current activities have any hope of getting us there. Bunting offers the metaphor of standing under a downpour of gravel to explain how people often feel about their work. No matter how desperately one digs toward the top, the downpour does not stop. This paints a rather bleak picture of a situation that is out of our control. Charles Handy (1999), in comparison compares the feeling to riding a bicycle with knowledge that you are only OK as long as you keep peddling; if you stop peddling, you fall (p. 17).

Perhaps both serve to remind us that we might look to technology, not for a more complex dump truck or a faster bicycle but, rather, for remote access to the off switch of the dumping mechanism or for the motor on the bicycle. Technology offers enormous potential, if we only think through how we use it, and take responsibility for path corrections as needed.

REFERENCES

American Physical Therapy Association. (2006). BlackBerry Thumb. Retrieved from http://www.apta.org/

Americans with Disabilities Act of 1990. (1991). Pub. L. No. 101-336, § 2, 104 Stat. 328.

Apple iTunes Store. (n.d.) Retrieved from http://www.apple.com/iphone/from-the-app-store/

Beaton, E. (2007, July/August). Work is driving me crazy. *Atlantic Business, 18*(4), 36-45.

Browning, J. G. (2006). Put liability on hold with a cellphone use policy. *In-House Defense Quarterly, 1*(1), 17-18.

Bunting, M. (2004). *Willing slaves: How the overwork culture is ruling our lives*. London, England: HarperCollins.

Bureau of the Census. U.S. Department of Commerce, Economics and Statistics Administration. (1991). *The growing use of computers* (SB/91-11). Retrieved from http://www.census.gov/population/socdemo/computer/sb91-11.pdf

Carton, P. (2010). An explosion in corporate tablet demand. Retrieved from http://www.investorplace.com/2010/12/explosion-in-corporate-tablet-demand/

Chen, C. P. (2006). Improving work-life balance: REBT for workaholic treatment. In R. J. Burke (Ed.), *Research companion to working time and work addiction* (pp. 310-329). Northampton, MA: Edward Elgar.

Covey, S. R. (1989). *The 7 habits of highly effective people*. New York, NY: Free Press.

Definition of Tablet Computer. (n.d.) In *PCMag.com's Encyclopedia*. Retrieved from http://www.pcmag.com/encyclopedia_term/0,2542,t=tablet+computer&i=52520,00.asp

Email charter. (n.d.). 10 Rules to reverse the email spiral. Retrieved from www.emailcharter.org

Fox, A. (2007, December 1). Caught in the web. *HR Magazine*. Retrieved from http://www.shrm.org/Publications/hrmagazine/EditorialContent/Pages/1207Fox2_cover.aspx

Golden, L. (2006). How long? The historical, economic and cultural factors behind working hours and overwork. In R. J. Burke (Ed.), *Research companion to working time and work addiction* (pp. 36-60). Cheltenham, England: Edward Elgar.

Gorlick, A. (2009, August 24). Media multitaskers pay mental price, Stanford study shows. *Stanford Report*. Retrieved from http://news.stanford.edu/news/2009/august24/multitask-research-study-082409.html

Green, F. (2004). Why has work effort become more intense? *Industrial Relations*, *43*(4), 709-741. doi:10.1111/j.0019-8676.2004.00359.x

Green, F. (2008). Work effort and worker well-being in the age of affluence. In R. J. Burke & C. L. Cooper (Eds.), *The long work hours culture: Causes, consequences and choices* (pp. 115-136). Bingley, England: Emerald Group.

Grynbaum, M. (2009, August 3). Cabbies stay on their phones despite ban. *The New York Times*. Retrieved from http://www.nytimes.com/2009/08/04/nyregion/04taxi.html

Handy, C. (1999). *The hungry spirit*. London, England: Hutchinson.

Helliker, K. (2009). You might as well face it: You're addicted to success. *The Wall Street Journal*. Retrieved from http://online.wsj.com/article/SB123423234983566171.html

Henle, C. A., Reeve, C. L., & Pitts, V. E. (2010). Stealing time at work: Attitudes, social pressure, and perceived control as predictors of time theft. *Journal Of Business Ethics*, *94*(1), 53-67. doi:10.1007/s10551-009-0249-z

Herbert, W. (2008). The electronic workplace: To live outside the law you must be honest. Retrieved from http://www.americanbar.org/content/dam/aba/administrative/labor_law/meetings/2011/tech/d_04.authcheckdam.pdf

Kadaba, L. S. (2010, June 23). Happy Birthday to Cube. *The Philadelphia Inquirer*, p. D1-2.

Kamm, N. (2010, January 1). Bodyguard for electronic information. *HR Magazine*, Retrieved from http://www.shrm.org/Publications/hrmagazine/EditorialContent/2010/0110/Pages/0110legal.aspx

Kelliher, C. & Anderson, D. (2010). Doing more with less? Flexible working practices and the intensification of work. *Human Relations*, *63*(8), 83-106. doi:10.1177/0018726709349199.

Korn/Ferry International (2006). Press Releases. Retrieved January 6, 2008 from http://www.kornferry.com/Library/Process.asp?P=PR_Detail&CID=1743&LID.

Loukopoulos, L. D., Dismukes, R. K., & Barshi, I. (2009). *The multitasking myth*. London, England: Ashgate.

Meinert, D. (2011, June 1). Make telecommuting pay off. *HR Magazine*, Retrieved from http://www.shrm.org/Publications/hrmagazine/EditorialContent/2011/0611/Pages/0611meinert.aspx

Mudrack, P. E., & Naughton, T. J. (2001). The assessment of workaholism as behavioral tendencies: Scale development and preliminary empirical testing. *International Journal Of Stress Management*, *8*(2), 93-111. doi:10.1023/A:1009525213213

National Safety Council. (2009, January). National safety council calls for nationwide ban on cell phone use while driving. Retrieved from http://www.nsc.org/Pages/NationalSafetyCouncilCallsforNationwideBanonCellPhoneUseWhileDriving.aspx

Nye, D. E. (2006). *Technology matters: Questions to live with*. Cambridge, MA: MIT Press.

Pennsylvania Anti-Texting Law, Pennsylvania Motor Vehicle Code Ch. 75 § 3316. (2011).

Poletti, T. (2012, March 29). Smartphone sales hit 49.7% of U.S. mobile market in Feb. Retrieved from http://blogs.marketwatch.com/thetell/2012/03/29/smartphone-sales-hit-49-7-of-u-s-mobile-market-in-feb/

Porter, G. (1996). Organizational impact of workaholism: Suggestions for research the negative outcomes of excessive work. *Journal of Occupational Health Psychology*, *1*(1), 70-84. doi:10.1037/1076-8998.1.1.70

Porter, G. (2006). Profiles of workaholism among high-tech managers. *Career Development International*, *11*(5), 440-462. doi:10.1108/13620430610683061

Porter, G. (2009). Implications of employer-supplied connectivity devices on job performance, work-life and business culture. *World at Work Journal*, *19*(2), 6-21.

Porter, G., & Herring, R. (2006). The unlikely referral of workaholics to an employee assistance program. In R. J. Burke (Ed.), *Research companion to working time and work addiction* (pp. 242-269). Northampton, MA: Edward Elgar.

Porter, G., & Kakabadse, N. K. (2006). HRM perspectives on addiction to technology and work. *Journal Of Management Development*, *25*(6), 535-560. doi:10.1108/02621710610670119

Postman, N. (1993). *Technopoly: the surrender of culture to technology*. New York, NY: Vintage Books

Rayman, P. M. (2001). *Beyond the bottom line: The search for dignity at work*. New York, NY: St. Martin's Press.

Reich, R. B. (2000). *The future of success*. New York, NY: Knopf.

Richtel, M. (2009a, October 1). Texting while driving banned for federal staff. *The New York Times*. Retrieved from http://www.nytimes.com/2009/10/02/technology/02distracted.html

Richtel, M. (2009b, September 30). At 60 m.p.h., office work is high risk. *The New York Times*. Retrieved from http://www.nytimes.com/2009/10/01/technology/01distracted.html

Richtel, M. (2009c, July 18). Drivers and legislators dismiss cellphone risks. *The New York Times*. Retrieved from http://www.nytimes.com/2009/07/19/technology/19distracted.html

Rifkin, J. (1995) *The end of work: The decline of the global labor force and the dawn of the post-market era*, New York, NY: Tarcher.

Roberts, B. (2008, October 1). Stay ahead of the technology use curve. *HR Magazine*. Retrieved from http://www.shrm.org/Publications/hrmagazine/EditorialContent/Pages/1008roberts.aspx

Robinson, B. E. (1989). *Work addiction*. Deerfield Beach, FL: Health Communication.

Schaufeli, W. B., Taris, T. W., & van Rhenen, W. (2008). Workaholism, burnout, and work engagement: Three of a kind or three different kinds of employee well-being? *Applied Psychology: An International Review, 57*(2), 173-203. doi:10.1111/j.1464-0 597.2007.00285.x

Schor, J. (1993). *The overworked American: The unexpected decline of leisure*. New York, NY: Basic Books.

Scott, K. S., Moore, K. S., & Miceli, M. P. (1997). An exploration of the meaning and consequences of workaholism. *Human Relations, 50*(3), 287-314. doi:10.1023/A:1016986307298

Siri. (n.d.). Retrieved from http://en.wikipedia.org/wiki/Siri_%28software%29

Taylor, P. (2010, March 30). Smartphone sales boom is poised to set the tone in us. *Financial Times*. Retrieved from http://www.ft.com/cms/s/0/1d7e83b8-3b93-11df-a4c0-00144feabdc0.html

Tenner, E. (1997). *Why things bite back: Technology and the revenge of unintended consequences*. New York, NY: Vintage Books.

Wilkinson, R. T. (1961). Interaction of lack of sleep with knowledge of results, repeated testing, and individual differences. *Journal Of Experimental Psychology, 62*(3), 263-271. doi:10.1037/h0048787

Williams, J. C., & Boushey, H. (2010, January). *The three faces of work-family conflict: The poor, the professionals, and the missing middle*. Retrieved from http://www.worklifelaw.org/pubs/ThreeFacesofWork-FamilyConflict.pdf

CHAPTER 7

TOWARD A NEW CONCEPTUALIZATION OF TECHNOLOGY TRANSFER MANAGEMENT

Kheng Boon Quek and Yue Wang

ABSTRACT

To compete in a globalized competitive business environment, companies are increasingly investing in new technologies. The successful transfer, adoption, and integration of new technologies has emerged as a primary source of competitive advantage. Although the subject of technology transfer has been widely studied, there is a lack of conceptual integration. In this article, we deepen the study of technology transfer by operationalizing Agmon and von Glinow's (1991) typology in order to investigate how to effectively manage the transfer process of three types of technologies, namely product-, process-, and person-embodied technologies. We propose a conceptual model to establish linkages among the transferring processes of the three types of technologies. Based on the model, a set of hypotheses is developed to explore a variety of factors that might impact the effectiveness of the technology transfer.

Global Perspectives on Technological Innovation, pp. 183–205
Copyright © 2013 by Information Age Publishing
All rights of reproduction in any form reserved.

INTRODUCTION

Facing the competitive pressures of a globalized market environment, companies are increasingly investing in new technologies to reduce operational costs and shorten production lead times in order to enable a fast response to market or customer needs. In particular, the time-to-market dimension of product introduction has become a crucial determinant of competitive advantage in a fast-moving environment. Firms operating in a knowledge-intensive environment require the successful transfer of technologies in order to improve their competitive advantage. Therefore, the successful transfer and adoption of new technologies has emerged as a primary source of competitive advantage for firms.

The subject of technology transfer has been extensively studied in many academic fields, including engineering and management. In the past, researchers focused on investigating the factors that affect technology transfer at both the macro- and microlevels. At the macrolevel, the emphasis has been placed on economic factors (Contractor & Sagafi-Nejad, 1981; Jensen & Scheraga, 1998; Marton, 1986; Pugel, 1978), while at the micro level, the impact of a wider range of factors, such as culture, social norms, management policies, and organizational relationships, has been studied (Al-Ghailani & Moor, 1995; Godkin, 1988; Jensen & Scheraga, 1998; Kedia & Bhagat, 1988; Simon, 1991); in particular, when a transfer can occur within the realms of science and technology, within a societal level from one geographical location to another, and from a societal level to an international level (Osman-Gani, 1991, 1996). Nevertheless, the subject of technology transfer itself will have to be established through study at the micro level. Only in this way can we develop a closer understanding of how to manage the transfer process of technology effectively.

At the microlevel, technology transfer is often viewed as a problem to be solved by different organizational or contractual arrangements (Amesse & Cohendet, 2001). The contexts have been differentiated as being internal (within an organization) or external (between organizations), and as pertaining to the innovation process (creating technology) or to the diffusion process (reproducing the technology) (see Figure 7.1). Amesse and Cohendet (2001) contend that the main problem of technology transfer for situation I is how to move technology efficiently from the lab to the market, while the main problem for situation II is how to efficiently manage the contribution of specialized suppliers.

In situation III, the main issues in technology transfer are the nature of the emitting capacity of the technology source and the receiving capacity of the subsidiaries and divisions. Finally, in situation IV, the technology transfer problems are shaped by the transfer of technology between firms. The incidence of all of these transfer problems can be predicted to some

	Within Organization	Between Organizations
Creating technology	I Managing Innovation	II Contracting out R&D and Outsourcing
Reproducing and diffusing technology	III Transferring to Divisions or Subsidiaries	IV Buying or Selling Proven Technologies

Source: Amesse & Cohendet (2001).

Figure 7.1.   Four types of technology transfer contexts.

extent by analyzing the properties of the transfer process. Therefore, the main contribution of this chapter is to develop a conceptual model for analyzing the properties of the transfer process in order to manage the transfer of technology effectively.

To investigate the effectiveness of the technology transfer from a management perspective, Agmon and Glinow (1991) provided a useful classification of technology transfer: product-embodied, process-embodied, and person-embodied. To operationalize the typology in order to investigate how to manage the technology transfer process effectively, this chapter develops a conceptual model to explore the following research questions:

(a)   What are the technology characteristics of these three types of technologies?
(b)   What elements of the transfer environment should be considered when dealing with the transfer of the three types of technologies?

Our chapter unfolds as follows: First, we review the extant literature on the basic concepts of technology transfer, and distinguishes the three types of technologies. Next, a conceptual model to improve the overall management of technology transfer is proposed. Based on the conceptual model, hypotheses are developed to distinguish the key dimensions of the three types of technology transfer and explore a variety of factors that might impact the effectiveness of the technology transfer. Finally, we conclude with a summary of the model and an outline for future research.

LITERATURE REVIEW

To understand the overall process of effective technology transfer, this section reviews the extant literature on the concept of technology and decomposes technology transfer into its components (product-, process-, and person-embodied technologies).

Definition of Technology

The meaning of the term *technology* has long been the subject of debate in the field of technology management (Gomory, 1983; Layton, 1974). A traditional conceptualization of technology views it as the tangible result of science and engineering—technology is the system by which a society applies science and engineering to provide its members with those things that are needed or desired. Science can be thought of as a large pool of knowledge that is accumulated from basic research (Gomory, 1983), and it is the cumulative effect of science and social needs that create technologies. From this point of view, science and engineering are embedded in products and processes via technology (Roussel, Saad, & Erickson, 1991). These conceptualizations of technology are in line with the definition provided by the World Intellectual Property Organization (1977):

> Technology means systematic knowledge for the manufacturing of a product, the application of a process or the rendering of a service, whether that knowledge be reflected in an invention, an industrial design, a utility model, or a new plant variety, or in technical information or skills, or in the services and assistance provided by experts for the design, installation, operation or maintenance of an industrial plant or for the management of an industrial or commercial enterprise of its activities. (World Intellectual Property Organization, 1977)

More recent views define technology as a process rather than an outcome. Davidow (1986), for example, views technology as an incomplete product (a product not yet ready for sale). This view resonates with the idea that research and development provides raw knowledge and prototypes that cannot be readily used by end users. Similarly, Lundquist and Thompson (1999) define technology as the ability to produce a functional design, based on science and engineering, that meets specific performance criteria. A functional design is the commonly understood result, such as a prototype, of a step in product development. This view explains that technologies are not only prototypes, but also the knowledge and the skills that are needed to produce a design that works. Without the right skills, experience, and tools to make another prototype that works, no technology exists. Chen (1996, p. 2) states that:

> Technology does not have a fixed shape, consisting mainly of design, documents and prescriptions. It can be diffused through oral dictation and

illustration. It does not need reproduction to be used and transferred multiple times. Therefore, its marginal cost is almost zero.

In this chapter, we combine the elements of the two dominant views, and define technology as a tangible object transformed from the accumulated basic scientific research, knowledge, and operations/routines required to fulfill a social need.

Definitions of Technology Transfer

After defining the term *technology* for this chapter, we can move on to define *technology transfer*. Several researchers have offered definitions of the term. Souder, Nashar, and Padmanabhan (1990), for example, define technology transfer as the managed process of conveying a technology from the sender of the technology to its adoption by the receiver of the technology. Lundquist and Thompson (1999) define technology transfer as the movement of the ability to realize a technology from one person or group to another, as confirmed by the demonstration of performance according to agreed-upon requirements.

Nevertheless, the term *technology transfer* is often used interchangeably with *knowledge transfer*, another term found in the literature. While knowledge transfer and technology transfer are interdependent activities, they serve different purposes. For instance, Levinson and Minoru (1995) argue that the creation of new knowledge involves the understanding and absorption of certain new technologies. Tornatzky and Fleischer (1990) explain that, compared to the broad concept of knowledge, technology refers more specifically to new tools, methodologies, processes, and products, and, as such, is primarily an instrument used for changing the environment. Similarly, Grant (1996) believes that knowledge embodies broader learning, as evidenced by changes in the strategic thinking, culture, and problem-solving techniques used by a firm. In an attempt to explore the differences between technology transfer and knowledge transfer, Gopalakrishnan and Santoro (2004) argue that knowledge and technology are distinct constructs that embody different activities.

In this chapter, we argue that technology transfer and knowledge transfer are intrinsically related constructs, but not identical concepts. For example, technology transfer is the process by which science and technology are diffused throughout human activity. This can be either a transfer from more basic scientific knowledge into technology, or the adaptation of an existing technology into a new use (Brooks, 1966). On the other hand, knowledge transfer occurs at an individual level, in terms of "how knowledge acquired in one situation applies (or fails to apply) to another"

(Singley & Anderson, 1989). It is often referred to as the "transferring of best practice[s]" within a firm (Szulanski, 1996). As such, knowledge transfer is seen as dyadic exchanges of organizational knowledge between a source and a recipient—the replication of a superior internal practice within the organization (Winter & Szulanski, 2002).

The confusion between the two theoretical constructs arises from the fact that, when defining technology transfer, many authors do not specify the types of technology being transferred. Following Kedia and Bhagat (1988), we define technology transfer as the movement of three types of technology from a sender to a receiver, and we define the three types as product-embodied, process-embodied, and person-embodied technologies. We argue that the transfers of the three types of technology do not have to take place at the same time; however, to state anything practically meaningful about the overall effectiveness of technology transfer, we must first distinguish among the three types of technology.

Product-Embodied Technology

A product is something that is created in a factory in large quantities, usually in order to be sold. In marketing terms, a product is anything that can be offered to a market that might satisfy a want or need. Furthermore, a service is considered to be a product because a service is a nonmaterial equivalent of a product, a process of either a change in customers; a change in physical possessions; a change in intangibles; or the selling of some level of skill, ingenuity, experience, and ideas to other firms that need it. In this chapter, a product is defined as something that is created in the form of physical objects or services that can be offered to a market and/or customers.

Product-embodied technologies are physical objects or services with appropriate technologies that can be offered to a market and/or customers. They are a set of ideas embodied in the products themselves. As such, product-embodied technology transfer involves the transfer of the physical product itself.

Corporate prosperity depends on new product introduction: successful new products account for significant profits and growth for many companies (Cooper, 1993). New product failures can result in major losses of time, money, reputation, and market position. Thus, better management of product-embodied technology transfer gives firms access to a greater variety of new technology options and improves their abilities to offer significantly differentiated products, as well as to enhance their competencies.

Process-Embodied Technology

A process is a means of transferring the requisite inputs into the product. It is a sequence of operations and events, taking up time, space, expertise, or other resources to create the product. Process-embodied technologies include the machines, equipment, and devices that help firms transform materials, and information in order to add value and fulfill the firms' strategic objectives (Slack, Chambers, & Johnston, 2001). Thus, process-embodied technology transfer involves transferring scientific processes and engineering details from a sender to a receiver.

Process-embodied technology is vital for firms' competitiveness. It allows firms to manage capacity, in terms of both scale and scope, which creates opportunities to satisfy often-changing market needs. It also facilitates incremental firm-specific learning in routine and tacit knowledge, thus making it hard for other firms to copy or imitate the firms' technological success (Teece, Pisano, & Shuen, 1997). Process- and product-embodied technologies are often equal partners in innovation. Process-embodied technology has to be in place to support new product innovations; without this capability, new product developments will fail.

Person-Embodied Technology

Person technology has not been well defined in the literature. Gotz (2001, p. 80) refers to Boethius's (A.D. 475-525) definition of a person as "an individual substance of rational nature," and argues that *person technology* emerged from the development of our species at an early age when tools were being manufactured. He suggests that:

> As tools became more diversified and complex, brain size doubled and the canine teeth became smaller, for their use was being supplanted by tools. This would seem to indicate that the kind of knowing that was emerging was at least partially instrumental—as it was defined as technological—because the basic problems of tool making were intellectual rather than motor. They involved knowledge of what the tool was good for based on experience. (Gotz, 2001, p. 75)

In this chapter, we define *person technology* as human beings who possess *know-how* skills, and have the capability to analyze, make judgments, and act, based on their wisdom, experience, and perspective.

Person-embodied technology is "knowledge embodied in a human being" that must be utilized in such a way that it establishes the preconditions needed to create something of value to a society. The person requires a certain degree of capability or expertise to process the information and knowledge. This ability to process information is the essence of technological know-how, as humans are still the essential element in any dealings with science and technology. This is because productive activities require human cognition in order to be carried out.

Person-embodied technology is one of the most important organizational assets. Many organizations have difficulty managing person-
embodied technology due to cultural factors (Buch & Rivers, 2001), organizational inertia (Welsch, Liao, & Stoica, 2001), or lack of absorptive
capacity (Bosch, Volberda, & Boer, 1999; Cohen & Levinthal, 1990; Minbaeva, Pedersen, Bjorkman, Fey, & Park, 2003). The term *absorptive capacity* is defined as the firm's ability to identify, assimilate, and exploit
external knowledge (Cohen & Levinthal, 1989, 1990). Thus, better management of *person-embodied technology* is essential for operating successfully
in a knowledge-intensive environment. The effective management of
knowledge or know-how can also facilitate quick access to the current and
accurate knowledge that is required to perform various tasks, improve
decision making, and enable the sharing of knowledge throughout the
organization.

THE CONCEPTUAL MODEL

Having provided definitions for the basic concepts, this section develops a
conceptual model for managing technology transfer and addressing the
two research questions posed in this chapter. First, we will deconstruct the
concepts of technology and technology transfer into their components

Table 7.1. Summary of Key Definitions

Term	Definition
Technology	A tangible object embodied with science that is accumulated from basic research and operates to fulfill a social need
Technology transfer	The movement of the three types of technology from one party to another party
Product	Something that is created in the form of physical objects and services that can be offered to market and/or customer needs
Process	A means of transferring the requisite inputs into a product
Person	An individual of a rational nature
Product technology	Physical objects or services with appropriate technologies that can be offered to a market and/or customer needs
Process technology	Machines, equipment, and devices that help firms transform materials, information, and customers to add value and fulfill the firms' strategic objectives
Person technology	Human beingswho possess know-how skills, and have the capability to analyze, make judgments, and act, based on their wisdom, experience, and perspective

(product-, process-, and person-embodied technologies) in order to better understand the overall process of technology transfer. Figure 7.2 shows how successful technology transfer depends on interdependence among the three types of technology. For example, a customer purchases a set of unassembled metal bookshelves (product-embodied technology). When the customer opens the packaging, he/she finds a set of instructions for assembling the bookshelves, the shelves, and a bag of accessories, such as screws, bolts, and nuts. In this example, the product-embodied technology is transferred from the firm to the end user. Despite the successful transfer of the product to the customer, the bookshelves cannot be used unless they are assembled. Consequently, in order for the customer to enjoy the "embodied ideas" of the product, he/she needs to possess some basic knowledge (person-embodied technology) about using a screwdriver and following a procedure (process-embodied technology) in order to assemble the bookshelves. This simple example demonstrates the interrelationships among the product-, process-, and person-embodied technologies in the context of technology transfer.

Second, we expand Figure 7.2 to a full model in Figure 7.3, by taking into account a range of factors that interact with the three types of technology to hinder technology transfer. For instance, recall the example of the customer who bought a set of unassembled bookshelves. If the customer does not have basic tools, such as a screwdriver (process-embodied technology: physical infrastructure in Figure 7.3), basic knowledge of how to use the screwdriver (person-embodied technology: absorptive capability), and an understanding of the procedure (process-embodied technology: human infrastructure; person-embodied technology: absorptive capability) that guides the customer to build the bookshelves, he/she will not be able to enjoy the embodied idea of the product itself. In this case, before the customer makes the decision about whether or not to buy the bookshelves, he/she needs to know whether he/she (1) can read and understand the assembly procedures, (2) possesses the necessary tools to build the bookshelves, and (3) knows how to use the basic tools.

Let us consider another example. A sales manager wants to export automobiles in order to increase his/her sales target. Before the sales manager makes any decisions, he/she needs to understand the market characteristics and the state of social development of the country to which he/she wants to export. The sales manager will not want to sell automobiles to a country that has no roads and limited access to fuel (product-embodied technology: social state of development), a small population (product-embodied technology: market characteristics), or a population that lacks a basic understanding of automobiles (person-embodied technology: absorptive capability).

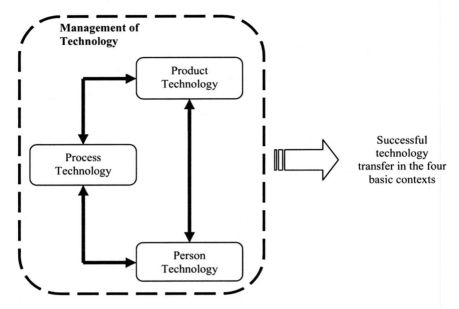

Figure 7.2.   Interrelationships among product-, process-, and person-embodied technology for successful technology transfer.

HYPOTHESES DEVELOPMENT

We used two figures and two examples to illustrate the conceptual model and demonstrate the relevance of the model to the understanding and improvement of the management of technology transfer. Based on the model, we will examine the determinants of technology transfer effectiveness and cluster them into four main attributes: technology characteristics, transfer environment, diffusion factors, and observability.

Baranson (1970) argued that technology transfer depends on (1) the complexity of the product and production techniques, (2) the transfer environment of the donor and recipient, (3) the absorptive capabilities of the recipient, and (4) the transfer capability of the donor. Mansfield (1961, 1963) investigated factors that govern the rate of imitation and diffusion of an innovation. The author presented strong empirical evidence that the number of users of a new technique grows slowly at the start, then accelerates, and finally decreases when full equilibrium of the demand is reached. The author's investigation also showed that the diffusion of technology depends on the profitability of the investment in the innovation, the age of the technology at that time, and the size of the firm.

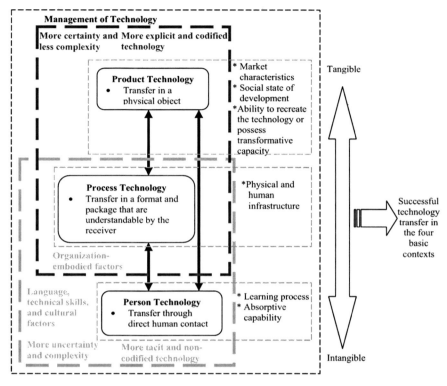

Figure 7.3.   A proposed conceptual model of technology transfer management.

Teece (1998) explained that technologies that can be replicated or imitated are easier to transfer, while Gopalakrishnan and Santoro (2004) stated that technology transfer effectiveness depends on the key dimensions of technology and knowledge transfer, such as the breadth of the construct, observability, overarching characteristics, the management phase(s) of most consequence, organizational learning, and the nature of the interactions. Several other authors have also studied the characteristics of technology transfer (Kogut & Zander, 1993; Nonaka & Takeuchi, 1995), as well as how these factors impact the effectiveness of technology transfer. Despite such rich research in technology transfer effectiveness, the current literature has not teased out the key dimensions of the three types of technology as described above, and, therefore, has difficulty in determining the key factors that influence transfer effectiveness.

Technology Characteristics

The technology's characteristics have a significant effect on technology adoption. Although some technologies are easily transferred, the transfer of most technologies is difficult because it includes a large amount of tacit knowledge: that is, the new knowledge is not easily visible, not easily expressible, highly personal, hard to formalize, and difficult to communicate (Nonaka & Takeuchi, 1995). Some researchers have proposed several dimensions to characterize the nature of technology. Table 7.2 summarizes the key dimensions of technology in the extant literature on technology transfer.

While this research discusses the dimensions of technology, the authors did not make a distinction among the characteristics of product-, process, and person-embodied technologies; therefore, their work makes a limited contribution to our understanding of how these generic technology characteristics impact technology transfer and adoption. In this section, the technology characteristics are discussed in relation to these three types of technology. We will then develop hypotheses about how the relationships among the technology characteristics and the types of technology impact the effectiveness of technology transfer.

Product-embodied technology is generally more explicit and codified. The transfer of this type of technology is more certain and less complex. Process-embodied technology falls between explicit and codified, and tacit and noncodified technology. There are two broad possibilities for the transfer of this type of technology. First, if the process is standardized to the extent that it can be stored easily in blueprints, technical papers, or other formal documents, such as operational manuals, it is considered

Table 7.2.   Important Research on the Key Dimensions of Technology

Authors	Complexity	Maturity	Codification	Teachability	Observability
		Dimension of Technology			
Teece (1977)		√			
Wu (1993)	√	√	√		
Kogut & Zander (1993)	√		√	√	
Nonaka & Takeuchi (1995)			√		
Teece (1998)			√		√
Gopalakrishnan & Santoro (2004)			√		√

explicit and codified. Consequently, the transfer of this type of explicit process-embodied technology is more likely to be certain and less complex. On the other hand, if the process-embodied technology is not currently in use or readily quantifiable, it is considered tacit and noncodified technology. The transfer of this type of tacit process-embodied technology is uncertain and more complex, as the nature of the technology is not easily understood by the sender and/or the receiver.

Person-embodied technology can be considered largely tacit technology. It lacks physical embodiment and is not easily codified; it is often stored inside a person's mind. Because "one can know more than one can tell," person-embodied technology is, therefore, harder to identify, locate and quantify, map, or value (Polanyi, 1966, p. 8). The transfer of this type of technologies is uncertain and complex. As Teece (1998) argued, uncodified or tacit knowledge is slow and costly to transmit in comparison to the transfer of product- and process-embodied technology. Because know-how cannot be replicated the way product-embodied technology can, successful transfers involve learning, demonstration, observation, and possible hands-on practices in order to be understood (Burghart, 1992; Teece, 1998). This leads to the following hypotheses:

> **Hypothesis 1.** The transfer of tacit technology is slower than the transfer of explicit technology.

> **Hypothesis 1a.** The transfer of person-embodied technology is slower than the transfer of product-embodied technology.

> **Hypothesis 1b.** The transfer of noncodified process-embodied technology is slower than the transfer of codified process-embodied technology.

Transfer Environment

The transfer environment is another important attribute to be considered for effective technology transfer. For instance, product-embodied technology transfer will be unsuccessful if a technology supplier fails to consider market characteristics, such as market size (Davidson & McFetridge, 1985) and market/end user needs. As soon as a new product is brought to the consumer market, consumers' decisions about whether to purchase and adopt the new technology depend to a large extent on whether it fulfils their needs, as well as the nature of the benefits and costs. In addition, the successful transfer of product-embodied technology depends on the social state of development. For example, the relative advantage of an iPad depends on the speed of a computer as compared to the iPad and the availability of a Wi-Fi infrastructure within which a user can use the iPad. Without the wider availability of complementary input, the transfer of product-embodied technology will be slow or unsuccessful.

In contrast to product-embodied technology, process- and person-embodied technology transfers will never occur without some overarching organizational framework (Agmon & Glinow, 1991). Significant changes in structure and administrative practices are required for diffusion and successful adoption (Nasbeth & Ray, 1974). For the transfer of process-embodied technology, the value accrued through the successful adaptation of the process innovation is realized through the simultaneous use of external and internal integration mechanisms, including external integration with customers, integration of design and manufacturing with suppliers, and integration of the firm's organizational structures, to foster its successful adoption (Ettlie & Reza, 1992). A high degree of communication, coordination, and cooperation among organizations must also exist for the successful transfer of process-embodied technology. In short, a new hierarchical structure and the three related factors (communication, coordination, and cooperation) are required for the successful transfer of process-embodied technology.

Successful person-embodied technology transfer can also be constrained by organizational learning capability. Organizational learning is a mediating process between collaborative interaction and the acquisition of technology competences (Steensma, 1996). The development of technology competence depends heavily on an organization's ability to learn (Hamel, 1991; Prahalad & Hamel, 1990) and the organization's culture. To improve organizational learning capability, two criteria must be met in order for the recipient to understand and value the new external knowledge (Cohen & Levinthal, 1990):

1. The receiver must possess some amount of prior knowledge basic to the new knowledge.
2. Some fraction of the sender's knowledge must be fairly diverse in order to permit effective, creative utilization of the new knowledge by the recipient.

In other words, for the successful transfer of person-embodied technology, it is important to acquire the required level of competence and/or to improve the firm's absorptive capacity. Consequently, the firm will need to invest in training. However, organizational learning capability can be affected by organizational culture in terms of attitudes, values, and experiences within an organization. This is because much of organizational learning is tacit, occasioned through experiences of the artifacts of the organization's culture that are part of the daily organizational routine (Cook & Yanow, 1993). Therefore, we suggest the following hypothesis:

Hypothesis 2. The transfer of product-embodied technology is related to market characteristics or the social state of development, whereas the transfer of process- and person-embodied technology is related to organizational factors.

Diffusion Factors

Some researchers suggest that product-embodied technology is not a form of technology transfer. Because the important ingredient is not know-how, but show-how, the core technologies are, in fact, embodied within the physical items. The most important factor leading to the acceptance of products in any society is the ability for the society to assimilate both the products and the technologies associated with them (Burghart, 1992). A basic understanding of the use of the object and its capabilities must either be present or be created. People who have adopted technology previously or who are already familiar with the technological aspect of the product will probably adapt to the new product more readily than those who are not familiar with it. Consequently, the overall state of society's development plays a larger role in how a firm exploits the opportunities a new product can offer. Moreover, transfer effectiveness also depends on the society's ability to recreate the technology or build upon it. If the society lacks transformative capacity (Garud & Nayyar, 1994) or is unable to reproduce the product (i.e., it does not have the necessary technological skills), it will be dependent on outside sources to provide the product.

Process-embodied technology transfer must come in a format that is readily understood by those receiving it (Burghart, 1992). These transfers involve the movement of designs, blueprints, and the know-how to manufacture the designed products or equipment (Agmon & Glinow, 1991). The purpose is to provide the basic information, data, and guidelines needed to create the desired capability. Thus, the effectiveness of the transfer relies on the complexity of the process involved (Burghart, 1992). Accurate descriptions may not be of any use if the receiving body is incapable of executing the process described. Differences in language, technical skills, and culture may hinder the implementation of the instructions. Moreover, infrastructure, comprised of both the facilities needed to exploit a given technology and the people who are trained and qualified to use those facilities, must be present before a given technology can be put into practical use (Rosenberg, 1972).

Person-embodied technology transfers know-how, or intangible knowledge and/or information. In some circumstances, information that is transferred is not actually possessed; that is, the provision of the know-how and the software is not simply to manufacture existing products but, more importantly, to innovate and adapt existing technologies and products, and ultimately, to design new products (Agmon & Glinow, 1991). These transfers depend on the phase of learning—specifically, how to learn and use what others have learned (Mansfield, 1975). Since a successful transfer depends on learning type (Meyers, 1990) and the absorptive capacity within an organization, person-embodied technology, among the three types of technologies, is the most difficult to transfer and the most costly to achieve. As Burghart (1992) explained, activities that can be quantified and described in the technical literature are easier to demonstrate and learn by actual application. However, transfer effectiveness can still be affected during direct human contact due to differences in language, technical skill, and culture between sender and receiver. Therefore, the following hypotheses are introduced:

Hypothesis 3a. The transfer of product-embodied technology is faster with a higher level of societal development.

Hypothesis 3b. The transfer of process-embodied technology is faster with a well-developed physical and human infrastructure, such as facilities, common language, technical skills, and culture.

Hypothesis 3c. The transfer of person-embodied technology is faster when the receiver has a good learning process and both sender and receiver have a common language, technical skills, and culture.

Observability

Product-embodied technologies are transferred in terms of physical objects, such as finished products, tools, equipment, or machinery (Mansfield et al., 1982). As such, they are observable, even after the products are sold. A scanner, printer, or computer is available for conceptual imitation and reverse engineering once it has been introduced into the market. Because of this observability, receivers are able to visualize and adopt the technology more easily.

Process-embodied technology transfer falls somewhere between the tangible and the intangible. It can be transferred in a standard form of knowledge through technical papers or journals, patent information, manufacturing procedures, and other forms of documentation that allow the receiver to duplicate the process. On the other hand, the complexity of the technology can restrict the sender from having the technical information detailed in written or other forms of media, making it difficult for the receiver to visualize and duplicate the process.

Person-embodied technology transfer can be classified as intangible. This technology is about know-how that includes elements of human judgment, the ability to possess information, and the handling of exceptions. It also includes accumulated practical skill or expertise that allows one to do something smoothly and efficiently. All of this know-how or knowledge is embodied in individual humans and difficult to replicate (Teece, 1998). The relevant routines that support a particular competence may not be transparent (Nelson & Winter, 1982). Therefore:

> **Hypothesis 4.** The transfer of product-embodied technology is faster than that of person-embodied technology, because product-embodied technology is easier to observe and easier to replicate or imitate than person-embodied technology, which is a nonobservable object.

In sum, we have explained the key factors that hinder the transfer effectiveness of the three types of technologies, and we have clustered them into four main attributes, as shown in Table 7.3. Of the three, product-embodied technology is likely to be the most explicit and codified. Since the transfer of tacit technology is slower than that of explicit technology, product-embodied technology is more certain and less complex than process- or person-embodied technology. Moreover, product-embodied technology is transferred in a physical form; therefore, it is easier to replicate or imitate than process- or person-embodied technology. Finally, the transfer effectiveness of product-embodied technology depends on market characteristics and societal development rather than on organizational factors and physical and human infrastructure; therefore, product-embodied technology is easier to transfer than process- or person-embodied technology. Although organizational and human factors play an important role in the transfer effectiveness of process- and person-embodied technology, person-embodied technology is more difficult to transfer than process-embodied technology, because person-embodied technology is transferred in the form of know-how or intangible information/knowledge, which is more tacit and noncodified. These transfers depend on the learning type and absorptive capacity within an organization. Table 7.3 summarizes the key factors that influence product-, process-, and person-embodied technology transfer effectiveness.

DISCUSSIONS AND CONCLUSION

This chapter conceptualizes technology transfer as the dynamic process of managing the transfer of three distinctive, yet interrelated, types of technologies: product-, process-, and person-embodied technologies.

A model is proposed to guide managers in analyzing and investigating the issues that may arise during the technology transfer process in the four basic contexts. By identifying the factors that influence the effectiveness of

Table 7.3.   Key Factors of Product-, Process- and Person-Embodied Technology Transfer

	Product Technology	*Process Technology*	*Person Technology*
Technology characteristics	More explicit and codified	Can be explicit and codified or tacit and non-codified, depending on the complexity of the process technology	More tacit and non-codified
	More certainty and less complexity	Ranges from the certain and less complex to the uncertain and complex	More uncertain and complex
Transfer environment	Depends on market characteristics, such as market size and market/enduser needs, as well asthe social state of development	Depends on organization-embodied factors	
Diffusion factors	Transfer of physical objects, such as finished products, tools, equipment, or machinery	Transfer in a form that is understood by the receiver	Transfer in the form of know-how or intangible information and knowledge. Sometimes, information can be transferred without first acquiring it.
	Depends on society's overall state of development and the ability to recreate the technology, build on it, or possess transformative capacity	Depends on the development of physical and human infrastructure, such as language, technical skill, and culture	Depends on the type of learning process, absorptive capability, and human factors, such as language, technical skill, and culture
Observability	Tangible and easy to replicate or imitate	May be tangible and/or intangible, depending on the complexity of the process technology	Intangible and unable to be replicated

the transfer of the three types of technologies, the model enables users to analyze and understand the complex issues that they face in technology transfer, and therefore, to improve the overall management of technology transfer in the four basic contexts. First, we argued that product-embodied technology is easily replicated and imitated, by comparing it to the other two types of transfer. Consequently, many firms are more hesitant to transfer their process- and person-embodied technology overseas than their product-embodied technology, because the diffusion of process- and person-embodied technology is harder to control (Chatterji, 1990). This argument is consistent with the literature that confirms that a product-embodied technology is the easiest form to transfer (Kedia & Bhagat, 1988; Mansfield, 1975). Second, we proposed that product-embodied technology transfer depends on market characteristics, such as market size or market need, rather than on organizational factors. As long as the product satisfies the end user's needs, and the market size is attractive to the technology supplier, there are fewer barriers to transferring and adopting the technology. Finally, person-embodied technology is likely to be tacit knowledge and, therefore, as Teece (1998) points out, is difficult, slower, and costly to transfer.

Implications for Public Policy

In the past, researchers focused on investigating the factors that affect technology transfer at both the macro- and microlevel. The study of public policies for domestic technology transfer focus on technology transfer from government to private sector or transfer within the private sector (from one company to the next). This model, which identifies the potential issue of technology transfer, provides a policymaker with an idea of how to start to formulate or evaluate a policy in addressing the most important unmet problem: barriers in transferring and adopting the technology in the market. The model rests on the analysis of the transfer of product-, process-, and person-embodied technologies, and aims to identify areas where the market cannot be expected to work well. Acquiring such information will allow a policymaker to design a policy that deals with the structure of market incentives and capabilities in assisting a successful technology transfer in the four contexts.

Directions for Future Research

The model and hypotheses presented above outline a set of relationships among the four main attributes (technology characteristics, transfer environment, diffusion factors, and observability) and the three types of technology being transferred (product-, process-, and person-embodied). The level of conceptual detail should aid in the development of sound, theoretically grounded measures of these constructs. This, in turn, should enhance the reliability and validity of future empirical tests. Tests of this model, using a variety of methodologies ranging from qualitative case studies of a few firms to quantitative studies, such as large sample survey studies, are encouraged.

Limitations of This Study

This model has some limitations. Currently, it does not consider the mode of the technology transfer. Davidson & McFetridge (1985) suggest that there are some relationships between the mode of transfer (licensing, direct investment, etc.) and the participants involved in the transfer. Further empirical study should examine the relationships between the mode of the technology transfer and the three types of technologies. Second, the age of the given technology, which might constitute one of the transfer barriers (Teece, 1977), is not taken into account in this model. The age of the technology is defined as the number of years since the beginning of the first commercial application of the technology anywhere in the world and the end of the technology transfer program. As the age of the technology increases, more individuals have the opportunity to acquire this noncodified knowledge. However, when the length of stay of corporate personnel begins to be outstripped by the age of the technology, the noncodified dimensions of the design knowledge may be lost to the firm. Future research should investigate the relationship between the age of the technology and the three types of technologies discussed in this chapter.

REFERENCES

Agmon, T., & von Glinow, M. A. (1991). *Technology transfer in international business*. New York, NY: Oxford University Press.

Al-Ghailani, H. H., & Moor, W. C. (1995). Technology transfers to developing countries. *International Journal of Technology Management, 10*(7/8), 687-703.

Amesse, F., & Cohendet, P. (2001). Technology transfer revisited from the perspective of the knowledge-based economy. *Research Policy, 30*, 1459-1478.

Baranson, J. (1970). Technology transfer through the international firm. *The American Economic Review, Papers and Proceedings of the Eighty-second Annual Meeting of the American Economic Association, 60*(2), 435-440.

Bosch, F. A. J. V., Volberda, H. W., & Boer, M. D. (1999). Coevolution of firm absorptive capacity and knowledge environment: Organization forms and combinative capabilities. *Organization Science, 10*(5), 551-568.

Brooks, H. (1966). *National science policy and technology transfer*. Proceedings of a conference on technology transfer and innovation. Washington DC: National Science Foundation Publication No. NSF 67-5.

Buch, K., & Rivers, D. (2001). TQM: The role of leadership and culture. *Leadership & Organization Development Journal, 22*(7/8), 365-371.

Burghart, D. L. (1992). *Red microchip: Technology transfer, export control, and economic restructuring in the Soviet Union*. Brookfield, VT: Dartmouth.

Chatterji, M. (1990). Innovation, management and diffusion of technology: A survey of literature. In M. Chatterji (Ed.), *Technology transfer in the developing countries* (pp. 3-18). London, England: Macmillan Press.

Chen, M. (1996). *Managing international technology transfer*. London, England: International Thomson Business Press.

Cohen, W. M., & Levinthal, D. A. (1989). Innovation and learning: The two faces of R&D. *The Economic Journal, 99*(397), 569-596.

Cohen, W. M., & Levinthal, D. A. (1990). Absorptive capacity: A new perspective on learning and innovation [Special issue: Technology, organizations, and innovation]. *Administrative Science Quarterly, 35*(1), 128-152.

Contractor, F. J., & Sagafi-Nejad, T. (1981). International technology transfer: Major issues and policy responses. *Journal of International Business Studies, 12*(2), 113-135.

Cook, S. D. N., & Yanow, D. (1993). Culture and organizational learning. *Journal of Management Inquiry, 2*(4), 373-390.

Cooper, R. G. (1993). *Winning at new products* (2nd ed.). Reading, MA: Addison-Wesley.

Davidow, W. H. (1986). *Marketing high technology: An insider's view*. New York, NY: The Free Press.

Davidson, W. H., & McFetridge, D. G. (1985). Key characteristics in the choice of international technology transfer mode. *Journal of International Business Studies, 16*(2), 5-21.

Ettlie, J. E., & Reza, E. M. (1992). Organizational integration and process innovation. *The Academy of Management Journal, 35*(4), 795-827.

Garud, R., & Nayyar, P. R. (1994). Transformative capacity: Continual structuring by intertemporal technology transfer. *Strategic Management Journal, 15*(5), 365-385.

Godkin, L. (1988). Problems and practicalities of technology transfer: A survey of the literature. *International Journal of Technology Management, 3*(5), 587-603.

Gomory, R. E. (1983). Technology development. *Science, New Series, 220*(4597), 576-580.

Gopalakrishnan, S., & Santoro, M. D. (2004). Distinguishing between knowledge transfer and technology transfer activities: The role of key organizational factors. *IEEE Transactions on Engineering Management, 51*(1), 57-69.

Gotz, I. L. (2001). On person, technology and education. *Educational Theory, 51*(1), 75-89.

Grant, R. M. (1996). Prospering in dynamically-competitive environments: Organizational capability as knowledge integration. *Organization Science, 7*(4), 375-387.

Hamel, G. (1991). Competition for competence and interpartner learning within international strategic alliances [Special issue]. *Strategic Management Journal, 12*, 83-104.

Jensen, O. W., & Scheraga, C. A. (1998). Transferring technology: Costs and benefit. *Technology in Society, 20*, 99-112.

Kedia, B. L., & Bhagat, R. S. (1988). Cultural constraints on transfer of technology across nations: Implications for research in international and comparative management. *Academy of Management Review, 13*(4), 559-571.

Kogut, B., & Zander, U. (1993). Knowledge of the firm and the evolutionary theory of the multinational corporation. *Journal of International Business Studies, 24*(4), 625-645.

Layton, E. T., Jr. (1974). Technology as knowledge. *Technology and Culture, 15*(1), 31-41.

Levinson, N. S., & Minoru, A. (1995). Cross-national alliances and interorganizational learning. *Organizational Dynamics, 24*(2), 50-63.

Lundquist, G., & Thompson, J. (1999, July). *Technology quality management, Part 1*. Technology Transfer Society Proceedings.

Mansfield, E. (1961). Technical change and the rate of imitation. *Econometrica, 29*(4), 741-766.

Mansfield, E. (1963). Intrafirm rates of diffusion of an innovation. *The Review of Economics and Statistics, 45*(4), 348-359.

Mansfield, E. (1975). International technology transfer: Forms, resource requirements and policies. *American Economic Review, 65*(2), 372-376.

Mansfield, E., Romeo, A., Schwartz, M., Teece, D., Wagner, S., & Brach, P. (1982). *Technology transfer, productivity, and economic policy*. New York, NY: W. W. Norton & Company.

Marton, K. (1986). *Multinationals, technology and industrialization*. Lexington, MA: Lexington Books.

Meyers, P. W. (1990). Nonlinear learning in large technological firms: Period four implies chaos. *Research Policy, 19*, 97-115.

Minbaeva, D., Pedersen, T., Bjorkman, I., Fey, C. F., & Park, H. J. (2003). MNC knowledge transfer, subsidiary absorptive capacity and HRM. *Journal of International Business Studies, 34*, 586-599.

Nasbeth, L., & Ray, G. F. (1974). *The diffusion of new industrial processes: An international study*. London, England: Cambridge University Press.

Nelson, R. R., & Winter, S. G. (1982). *An evolutionary theory of economic change*. Cambridge, MA: Harvard University Press.

Nonaka, I., & Takeuchi, H. (1995). *The knowledge-creating company: How Japanese companies create dynamics of innovation*. New York, NY: Oxford University Press.

Osman-Gani, A. A. M. (1991). *International transfer of management technology within a MNE: A cross-national study of managers' perceptions*. (Unpublished doctoral dissertation). The Ohio State University, Columbus, OH.

Osman-Gani, A. A. M. (1996). International technology transfer for competitive advantage: A conceptual analysis of the role of HRD. *Competitiveness Review, 9*(1), 9-18.

Polanyi, M. (1966). *The tacit dimension*. New York, NY: Anchor Day Books.

Prahalad, C. K., & Hamel, G. (1990). The core competence of the corporation. *Harvard Business Review, 63*(3), 79-91.

Pugel, T. (1978). *International technology transfer and neo-classical trade theory: A survey* [Working paper]. New York, NY: New York University.

Rosenberg, N. (1972). Factors affecting the diffusion of technology. *Explorations in Economic History, 10*(1), 3-33.

Roussel, P. A., Saad, K. N., & Erickson, T. J. (1991). *Third generation R & D: Managing the link to corporate strategy*. Boston, MA: Harvard Business School Press.

Simon, D. (1991). International business and the trans-border movement of technology: A dialectic perspective. In T. Agmon & M. A. Von Glinow (Eds.), *Technology transfer in international business* (pp. 5-28). New York, NY: Oxford University Press.

Singley, M. K., & Anderson, J. R. (1989). *The transfer of cognitive skill*. Cambridge, MA: Harvard University Press.

Slack, N., Chambers, S., & Johnston, R. (2001). *Operations management* (3rd ed.). Harlow, England: Pitman.

Souder, W. E., Nashar, A. S., & Padmanabhan, V. (1990). A guide to the best technology-transfer practices. *Journal of Technology Transfer, 15*(1,2), 5-13.

Steensma, H. K. (1996). Acquiring technological competencies through interorganizational collaboration: An organizational learning perspective. *Journal of Engineering Technology Management, 12*, 267-286.

Szulanski, G. (1996). Exploring internal stickiness: Impediments to the transfer of best practice within the firm. *Strategic Management Journal, 17*, 27-43.

Teece, D. J. (1977). Technology transfer by multinational firms: The resource cost of transferring technological know-how. *The Economic Journal, 87*(346), 242-261.

Teece, D. J. (1998). Capturing value from knowledge assets: The new economy, markets for know-how, and intangible assets. *California Management Review, 40*(3), 55-79.

Teece, D. J., Pisano, G., & Shuen, A. (1997). Dynamic capabilities and strategic management. *Strategy Management Journal, 18*(7), 509-533.

Tornatzky, L. G., & Fleischer, M. (1990). *The processes of technological innovation*. Lexington, MA: Lexington Books.

Welsch, H., Liao, J., & Stoica, M. (2001). *Absorptive capacity and firm responsiveness: An empirical investigation of growth-oriented firms*. In the Proceedings of the 2nd USASBE/SBIDA Conference, An Entrepreneurial Odyssey, Orlando, FL. Retrieved from http,//www.usasbe.org/

Winter, S. G ., & Szulanski, G. (2002). Replication of organizational routines: conceptualizing the exploitation of knowledge assets. In N. Bontis & C. W. Choo (Eds.), *The strategic management of intellectual capital and organizational knowledge: A collection of readings* (pp. 207-222). New York, NY: Oxford University Press.

World Intellectual Property Organization. (1977). *Licensing guide for developing countries: A guide on the legal aspects of the negotiation and preparation of industrial property licenses and technology transfer agreements appropriate to the needs of developing countries*. Geneva, Switzerland: Author.

Wu, F. S. (1993). *University-industry technology transfer: An empirical study of the industrial firms' organizational practices*. (Unpublished doctoral dissertation). Rensselaer Polytechnic Institute, Troy, New York, NY.

CHAPTER 8

UNCOVERING THE HIGH-END DISRUPTION MECHANISM

When the Traditional Start-Up Wins

Juan Pablo Vazquez Sampere

ABSTRACT

Empirical evidence indicates both superior and inferior technologies can be successfully used to launch a new firm that seriously threatens the incumbent's sustainability. Using the traditional criteria of cost and performance to measure the superiority or inferiority of a new technology this research isolates when and why a superior technology can predictably displace the incumbent. Primary data comes from semistructured interviews that were obtained from a very successful start-up that operates in the Spanish real estate market. I use a newly designed mixed methods methodological approach both to separate the explanatory from the predictability variables and to measure their distances and relationships. A start-up can be successful using a superior technology if: (1) it uses a fully interdependent business model; (2) uses a revenue model different from that of the incumbents and; (3) exploits a distribution channel where the incumbents are either not present or minimally present. This strategy will work if the industry has these

Global Perspectives on Technological Innovation, pp. 207–259

characteristics; (1) the superior technology must enable the possibility of making the start-up business model more efficient than that of the incumbents; (2) customers are currently experiencing variability when using the incumbents service; (3) incumbents disaggregation prevents them from reacting and; (4) incumbents performance has remained flat or nearly flat if observed from the point of view of the customer. This research also suggests that the limited supply of high-end customers is a limiting factor for the introduction of superior technologies. Explaining why superior technologies were more likely to succeed in the past than in the future.

INTRODUCTION

Predicting when and why a new technology will displace an established firm is at the heart of firm sustainability. Still, despite both the extant literature and the remarkable research efforts, this much sought after ability to predict—with a reasonable degree of certainty—when and why a new and superior technology will displace the established one is still remarkably limited. For the last several decades the preferred method for determining the potential of a new technology has relied on assessing whether if the new technology is technically either superior or inferior compared to the one currently used. This way of categorizing the potential of new technologies has become widespread. It is used today in all kinds of industries, from very technology intensive industries such as semiconductors, smartphones, and so on, to industries where the technology that is being used appears disguised in a variety of forms. An example of the latter case is the transatlantic cruise lines that during the 19th and 20th centuries dominated the market of transporting passengers from Europe to the United States. In this industry, companies such as the Hamburg America Line or the White Star Line had to observe powerlessness how nonstop transatlantic flights essentially took over their business in what's a clear case of how a superior technology takes over a market. The very same phenomenon that has been both observed and researched in a variety of industries. In this particular case the main performance metric for a technology to cross the Atlantic was *average speed*. At the time speed was so important that the passenger liner with the highest record average speed was distinguished with an unofficial accolade named the *Blue Riband*. For instance, in the 1870s the White Star Line received the *Blue Riband* by displacing Cunard. Cunard's response consisted on obtaining substantial loans and subsidies from the British Government to develop a new steam-based technology that would be embedded in a new ship design named the *superliner*. Two well-known superliners are the Titanic and the Queen Mary. However after some time the technology that supports manned flight matured just enough as to enable these companies to transport passengers across the Atlantic. Jet-based propulsion is so fundamentally superior to steam-based propulsion that even the main performance metric had to change its units of measurement from months to hours, and therefore a rather fast technological substitution process started. This is a quite clear case of a superior technology taking over an industry and taking out of business the entire cohort of previously established firms. However there are many situations where technological superiority is not at all that clear. For instance, this case doesn't explain the Concord anomaly. The Concord was a plane capable of reducing by half the time it takes to cross the Atlantic, however its service was discontinued in 2003.

Research that tries to isolate the pattern that predicts when a superior technology will displace the incumbents still faces a variety of anomalies. In the case of the inferior technology there seems to be an established pattern that has been encapsulated into what has been called the disruptive innovation theory. For instance, continuing with the Transatlantic Cruise lines example; starting in the 1930s some of these lines used to sail their boats to the Caribbean when rough made the Atlantic impassable. In 1964, when a new port was opened in Miami, Florida, these lines stumbled into a new emerging industry: the pleasure cruises. Surprisingly, while they were still exploring this opportunity, they had to watch again how dozens of startups, such as Royal Caribbean and Carnival, retrofitted existing ships to offer pleasure cruises, building an entirely new travel and leisure category that continues to grow today (Sull, 2011).

The performance metric of the pleasure cruises industry obviously isn't speed, it is instead related to the ability of the cruise to offer a variety of amenities for passengers during the time they are on board. At its inception, this business was very unattractive for the transatlantic cruise lines. Their resource allocation was focused on investing in improving speed and they were used to passengers willing to pay more for that. The profitability of the leisure traveler was much less than what they were used to earn with their core business and on top of that they still had to incur in major investments to modify the ships extensively so they could meet these very different needs. From their point of view modifying a ship in ways that does not favor speed was viewed as making an inferior ship, something companies can rarely do because their resource allocation usually prevents them from doing so. New startups such as Royal Caribbean or Carnival did not have to face this problem. The profitability was not an issue because they did not even have profits to start with. In addition they did not have to reallocate resources from the speed performance metric to modify the ships. In other words, their ships, while more adapted to the comfort of the passenger, and so on. were viewed by the transatlantic cruise liners as inferior ships. These situations, when the issue of technological competences masks a fundamental problem of investment is precisely what the disruptive innovation theory describes as the mechanism through which an inferior technology takes over the incumbents.

Scholars have been studying the failure of incumbents since at least when Schumpeter (1942) identified the failure of most of the leading firms in an industry because new entrants with new methods of production either reshaped or rejuvenated it while relentlessly putting the prior wave of companies out of business. Examples of this phenomenon are the introduction of the mechanized factory, the electrified factory, the chemical synthesis industries or in modern times the iPhone. And yet after all these years the result of these research efforts is a variety of constructs, frameworks and models that compete against each other. Each explaining a portion of the phenomena but suffering anomalies they cannot explain on their own. Although the predictive ability of the literature is still noticeably limited there are three categorization schemes that have gained prominence. There seems to be a general agreement on the fact that these categorization schemes must be accounted for when trying to predict technologically-based industry change.

The first categorization scheme is the distinction between one firm vs. an entire generation of firms. As the example above illustrates, it's not that Hamburg, White Line, or Cunard failed independently and that the rest of competitors stayed in business. What really happened is that this entire generation of businesses disappeared. Research indicates the number and size distribution of firms in an industry affects significantly the rate of sustaining and disruptive innovations (Clark, 1985)

The second categorization scheme is the distinction between an established firm and a new entrant. In the previous example the established firms couldn't find a new sustainable business in the pleasure cruises business. The reason is that established firms and newly formed firms fundamentally vary in the number and types of internal and external forces they need to adapt to (Leonard-Barton, 1995; March & Simon, 1958)

The third categorization scheme is the previously mentioned superiority or inferiority of a technology compared to the main performance metric of the technology that is at the moment used by incumbents. However, in this categorization, the majority of research efforts have been addressed at understanding the superior technology phenomena and, in order to do that the most common procedure has been describing the variety of attributes of each technology and justifying the outcomes as if these attributes were the causal mechanism that caused the incumbents to fail (Murmann & Frenken, 2006; Schumpeter & Opie, 1934).

I argue in this chapter that the research method used to develop the disruptive innovation theory, a theory that describes some instances of when an inferior technology can displace the incumbents, can also be used to find the causal mechanism that predicts when and why an established firm will fail in front of a superior technology. While doing so I plan to introduce a new way to do research on technological change that separates between the descriptive and prescriptive portions of a theory and offers much more specific recommendations and constructs to look for to predict industry change.

THE CONTRIBUTION OF DISRUPTIVE INNOVATION TO THE DEVELOPMENT OF PREDICTIVE THEORIES OF TECHNOLOGICAL CHANGE

The question of when will a superior technology take over is still one of the fundamental questions in the technological change research field. This question has been researched using a variety of angles and using several research methods either alone or combined. Among the most frequently used research methods are both inductive and deductive reasoning, empirical and theoretical research, quantitative and qualitative studies and a variety of industry-related research studies. All these studies shared the same purpose: to find an explanatory and predictive theory exhaustive enough to answer the question.

Contrary to intuition, theory development in any field shows all these iterations are not only far from being failures but also instrumental for developing a strong corpse of theory. These iterations are not only very frequent but also quite indispensable in the never ending process of fully explaining and fully predicting a given phenomenon. In this portion of the chapter I use a methodological view (see Figure 8.1) to help visualize the fundamental architecture of a theory and to briefly explain how—using this methodology—theories are developed. I believe that understanding theory development is fundamental for isolating the theoretical contribution of disruptive innovation. There are a variety of ways to organize a body of literature. The reason for choosing the one introduced by Christensen and Carlile (2006) is that it explicitly separates between the portions of research that are explanatory (descriptive) from the causal (normative). It also separates between constructs, frameworks, and models is in each of these portions. This emphasis on making these distinctions are very helpful for understanding which research efforts builds upon which and how new anomalies emerge.

The natural evolution of a theory usually starts from the ground up. The first studies of a particular phenomenon are usually addressed at describing *constructs* (Bagozzi, Yi, & Phillips, 1991; Campbell, 1957; Campbell & Fiske, 1959; Campbell & Stanley, 1963; Gibbert, Ruigrok, & Wicki, 2008). Constructs are abstractions—that must be observable by

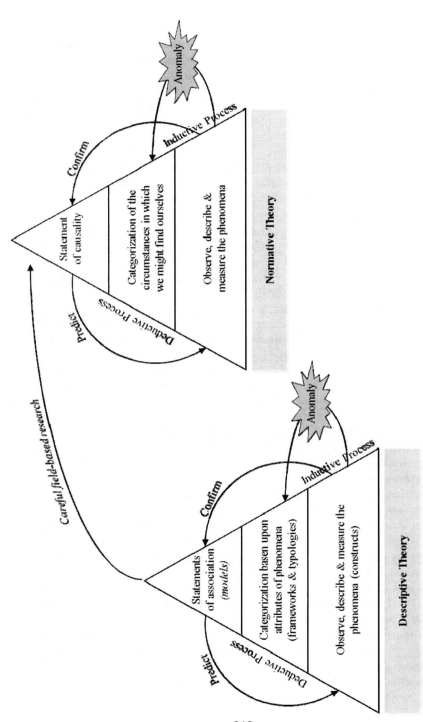

Source: Christensen & Carlile (2009).

Figure 8.1. The process of theory building.

everyone—that help us rise above the messy detail to understand the essence of what the phenomenon is and how it operates (Christensen & Carlile, 2006). Once the first constructs are identified scholars start focusing both in measuring them and in developing more. During this period hundreds of constructs are usually introduced. For example, functionality, reliability, incumbent, start-up, radical technology, incremental technology, market niche, and so on, are all constructs that have been identified in the extant literature. At this stage these constructs represented a fundamental improvement for both scholars and practitioners. Once they have been identified scholars can focus their attention toward them as opposed to as how it was before, when they had nothing specific or agreeable to focus on. Surprisingly enough, even at this very early stage of theory development the first "prescriptions" start to emerge. For instance, sentences such as "if you build a radical product you will succeed in this market" or "if you enter this market developing a platform-mediated network you will for sure kill the incumbent". Unfortunately, empirical evidence shows that having that particular attribute is no prescription for anything. And still, despite the overwhelming evidence, this happens much more often than expected.

Luckily enough scholars' research impetus does not stop here. As research efforts start showing constructs that either overlap or that refer to completely different things and never appear together, scholars start classifying constructs in a mutually exclusive and collectively exhaustive way (Agresti, 1996, 2002). This is the origin of the next step in theory building process: the first *frameworks* (Edmondson & McManus, 2007; Walsh, Tushman, Kimberly, Starbuck, & Ashford, 2007). For example, the Architectural framework is a way to classify the four previously identified constructs *Incremental, Modular, Radical* and *Architectural* (Henderson & Clark, 1990). Another framework is the "superior technologies vs. inferior technologies," which determines if a technology is superior compared to another by comparing their respective attributes (Markides, 2006). This stage of the theory building process also generates a variety of frameworks, and again each of them "prescribes" that if a particular phenomenon falls inside one of its categories a particular result will happen, but then again, anomalies are still mostly the norm.

Still not happy with this, the tireless scholar's research impetus continues in such a way as to look for better and more comprehensive ways to explain the phenomena. They use statistical methods such as regression or correlation analysis to identify several frameworks that—when combined—can explain a larger portion of the phenomena. We call the result of these research efforts *models* (Hoetker, 2007). Two particularly well known models are the industry life cycle (Klepper, 1997; Polli & Cook, 1969) and the technology S-curve (Foster, 1986). At this stage the limitations of the models researched becomes widespread, for instance, there are technologies that do not seem to follow the S-curve development pattern (Comin, Hobijn, & Rovito, 2006; Tellis, Hauser, & Griffin, 2006). And again at this stage "prescriptive" recommendations appear. For instance, sentences such as "don't enter a market that is in its mature stage." These "prescriptive" indications have become so frequent today that it's not unusual to find technological change papers that use a descriptive analysis technique (such as a correlation or regression) to predict future outcomes using the word "if." Most of these papers assume that a high statistical significance also describes a causal relationship.

As described in the left hand side portion of Figure 8.1, once the three building blocks (constructs, frameworks, and models) have been established, scholars start looking both inductively and deductively for research data to test them. Specifically they look for three situations. First, cases where previous research explains well enough the phenomena (usually called *literal replications*); Second, cases where the research results are not what was expected but the models still can explain why (*theoretical replications*) and; Third, cases where research results are not explained at all in the extant literature (*anomalies*) (Yin, 2003). The natural evolution of a theory—and an indispensable and fundamental step—improves throughout this process by having tireless scholars circling around up and down the left-hand side pyramid of Figure 8.1 while trying to falsify previous research efforts. And in doing so finding new variables and helping us understand the myriad relationships between them and between the constructs, frameworks and business models.

Unfortunately after some time a variety of symptoms of fatigue start to emerge. First, it becomes unclear where does a new piece of research fit into the existing body of literature. Scholars start having difficulties understanding which body of work builds upon which prior's scholar's effort. Second, there are countless constructs, frameworks and models that not only overlap but also rival in trying to explain the same portion of the phenomena while each of them suffer anomalies on their own and; Third, the research field's *scientific rigidity* becomes quite noticeable (Bourdieu & Wacquant, 1992).

When *scientific rigidity* is high scholars are able to recite long lists of articles from the literature but struggle to define new research questions or deploy research designs more likely to yield new research insights. As a result it is not unusual to see how the number of empirical papers rises much more than that of theoretical papers (Hillman, 2011). However, most importantly it is also a sign that the theory building process is about to make a fundamental transition.

This fundamental transition usually emerges from case-based research combined with ethnographic studies (Edmondson & McManus, 2007).

Using case study research to make a transition and switching the research stream from description to prediction is not new to scholars. Doctoral programs introduce students to the works of Kuhn (1962), Glaser and Strauss (1967) or Yin (2002, 2003) that document the process of having several competing research lines (Lakatos & Musgrave, 1974) and how the natural evolution of these lines, usually through case based research, causes research to eventually transition into a set of causal norms (Chalmers, 1976).

What exactly this transition consists of is leaving the descriptive attribute-based realm that permeates constructs, frameworks and models to enter a normative stage where the correct identification of the circumstances drives causality. An accurate and systematic assessment of the circumstances obtained in a case study creates a new classification scheme where the causality between the circumstances and expected phenomena are linked unequivocally. This change usually happens accidentally, when scholars find a change in a variable that can't be accommodated in the Descriptive pyramid of theory building. If it cannot be accommodated it is usually because this variable is not an attribute, and when this new variable is present a portion of the attributes previously researched plays a particular role, and when it is absent those attributes lose relevance in front of others or just express themselves in a different way. When this happens both scholars and managers at last start to understand in what circumstances the deliberate actions they are engaging in will deliver the expected results (Levitt, 1974). For example, investing in complementary assets (a descriptive model) to increase the firm's sustainability by profiting from technological innovation (Teece, 1986, 2010) was suggested to be always a safe alternative for incumbents that want to be sheltered against new entrants. However, subsequent circumstance-based research prescribed circumstances where complementary assets are a liability both in economic and organizational terms, that is, obsessively serving the most profitable customers or raising the level of commitment of the firm to its environment (Christensen, 1997a; Sull, Tedlow, & Rosenbloom, 1997). While walking upwards the descriptive side of the pyramid Tripsas (1996) indicates that complementary assets are still safer because of their *buffer effect*. It was not until scholars identified in what circumstances the interactions of firms drive complementarities that a normative theory was made explicit (Porter & Siggelkow, 2008).

In the case of Disruptive Innovation Christensen (2006) writes (p. 43): It became clear that the causal mechanism of the outcomes we observed—the incumbent leaders excelled at sustaining innovation but rarely succeeded at disruption—was resource dependence as manifested in the resource-allocation process. In other words, the theory of disruption, at this initial stage boils down to using this circumstance-based categorization scheme to identify—on a case per case basis—which of the previously researched constructs, frameworks or models from the previous extant literature on the technological change literature are valid in a particular situation (see Figure 8.2).

Once the first building block of the normative theory building process is in place scholars have the opportunity to complete the rest of the right hand side pyramid in just the same way they completed the descriptive side. However, they must be aware of the limitations of the previously used research methodologies such as correlation analysis to do research at the circumstance-based level. In this realm primary data sources are almost always necessary to obtain normative research results and the distinction between *contingency* and *causality* must be carefully observed.

Although the normative portion of the theory building process is also improved in the same way its components are fundamentally different. *Constructs, frameworks* and *models* become now *normative-constructs, circumstances* and *paradigms*.

There are three types of normative-constructs. First there are constructs that at the end of the study remain identical as the descriptive constructs identified ex-ante. This usually means that the circumstance the research controls for doesn't affect this construct in particular. Second, constructs that have been affected by the circumstance researched in the study, in other words, they have suffered an alteration ex-post. It can be in how they appear or in how are they being measured. Third, new constructs that only appear ex-post.

Although the separation between the descriptive and the normative portion of the theory building process is relatively new, scholars' concern about developing methodologies to control for the circumstances is not new at all. Starting in the 1960s a variety of methodologies emerged to help us classify the phenomena according to its circumstances. For example, Lawrence and Lorsch (1967) (p. 157) write: These findings suggest a contingency theory of organization which recognizes their systemic nature and organizational variables are in a complex interrelationship with one another and with conditions in the environment. Another example is Glaser and Strauss (1967) treatise. Where they indicate a theory has two stages the *Substantive* (descriptive) stage and the *Formal* (normative) stage.

Thomas Kuhn (1962) describes in his book how the proliferation of nonattribute based phenomena helps researchers transition from descriptive to normative. He describes how the preliminary period of confusion and debate plants the seeds for the emergence of a paradigm. A paradigm shapes the way subsequent scholars conduct research and defines the major ways of thinking about a particular research problem, something that usually generates resistance from scholars that are fully identi-

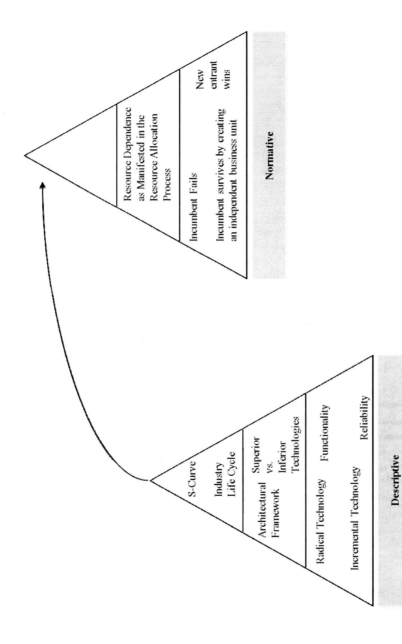

Figure 8.2. The circumstance-based categorization scheme of disruptive innovation.

fied with the previous paradigm. This usually slows the adoption of the new paradigm significantly.

As described above, the contribution of the disruptive framework consists of incorporating a circumstance-based categorization scheme that introduces *prediction* in the literature of technological change. I think it is important to highlight I am not claiming the disruptive innovation model is correct, or that the theory of disruption is precise. In fact some research seems to contradict some of its findings. For instance, Danneels (2004, 2006) argues that what Christensen really does is naming disruptive any case where the new entrant caused the incumbents to fail and he goes on to research instances when not listening to their main customers has been detrimental for established firms. Di Benedetto (2006) indicates no company can launch a disruptive new business without unlearning about their current business model and that that is nearly impossible to do so while exploiting it. Henderson (2006) indicates neoclassical theory has studied this problem before and that research results show that, in the absence of cannibalization, the incumbent always responds to the threat posed by the new entrant. Henderson explains that in those instances where the incumbent doesn't respond this is normally because of some kind of organizational rigidity. Govindarajan and Kopalle (2006) argue that a disruptive innovation can only be identified ex-post and that in any case this type of innovation has the positive effect of lowering the technological costs for all firms. Utterback and Acee (2005) explain this model's categorization scheme is not correct and that business models should have been considered in more depth. Markides (2006) also describes how inferior technologies do not really displace established firms while Slater and Mohr (2006) explain that new technologies are successful if the initial customer is selected correctly. Adner (2002) and Adner and Zemsky 2006) explain customers are more heterogeneous than what the theory describes. Additionally McKelvey (2004) argues this model has no external validity because it was obtained from technology-intensive industries while Tellis (2006) explains that he tried to replicate Christensen's findings with data from the disk drive industry but was not able to. He also acknowledges that all technologies, irrespective of who brings them to the market, are inferior when they are initially developed but that they seem to have an advantage because of this inferiority (Sood & Tellis, 2010).

I believe the case of the introduction of the disruptive innovation research has been unfortunate. Christensen (2006) not only addresses most of the concerns described above but also mentions he should have used the term "business model" instead of "technology" because the latter created confusion. I believe the biggest misunderstanding comes from introducing disruption as a way to explain when a superior technology can displace the incumbents when in reality this theory tries to explain the opposite, which is when do inferior technologies displace the incumbents. This difference is abysmal, irrespective of the evidence that shows that in both cases the incumbent fails or ends up tremendously compromised.

In my view, the criticisms to the theory reviewed above coupled with this misunderstanding represent fantastic opportunities for new causal-based research. When does a superior technology (a high-end technology) beats the incumbent is still an open question. When does an inferior technology (a low-end technology) beats the incumbent has one answer and has left us with one circumstance-based categorization scheme. This chapter uses this circumstance-based categorization scheme and a mixed method research design to uncover this much sought after high-end disruption mechanism.

EARLIER VIEWS OF FACTORS INFLUENCING THE SUCCESS OF SUPERIOR TECHNOLOGIES IN THE MARKETPLACE

For the last 80 years the advent of policies focused on reducing significantly the presence of monopolies have altered the industries appropriability regimes increasing the incentives of start-up companies to invest in radical innovation (Arrow, 1962; Gilbert & Newbery, 1982). This policy change has had a significant multiplier effect when a variety of technologies started to cross over industry boundaries (Tripsas, 2008). Because of the disparity in the industry's cycle times (Fine, 1998) the best way to appreciate this changes in detail is by examining the products that are being commercialized today. Products such as cell phones, DVDs, eBay, digital imaging scanners, personal computers, and so on, all live in industries that share a fundamental difference. In some of them incumbents managed to maintain their market position. In other instances the introduction of some of these products represented the incumbent's ultimate demise.

The technological change literature is not short on research efforts that try to determine if the new technology provided an unusual advantage that led to the failure of the incumbent. For instance, at the construct level Dosi (1982) identified the *technological discontinuities*, Utterback and Acee (2005) were able to measure the increase in market size as a lagging effect of *radical innovation*, Teece (1986) notes the variety of behaviors and the associate profitability of the *appropriability regime* and Tripsas's *buffer effect* (1997) indicates that in front of a technological threat incumbents have a temporary advantage available that they might want to use in their favor.

However, the abundance of empirical papers coupled with the absence of theoretical papers (Hillman, 2011) and, specifically papers that helped develop a strong theoretical classification in the literature of technological change provoked a change in focus in the literature toward other explanations for the incumbents failure, such as the entrant's business model or the firm's internal or external market environment. This line of research tries to develop a categorization scheme that sheds some light on the mechanism that predicts when a new technology coupled with a business model can displace the incumbents. For instance, incremental versus radical innovations (Abernathy & Clark, 1985), organizational competences (Henderson, 2006; Tushman & Anderson, 1986) or the ability to exploit the incumbent's rigidities (Leonard-Barton, 1995) are examples of these efforts.

Figure 8.3 describes the theoretical framework Christensen (2006) used to develop the disruptive innovation mechanism. Christensen explains he used Henderson and Clark's (1990) architectural innovation as a descriptive framework and resource dependence (Pfeffer & Salancik, 1978) as a circumstance-based categorization scheme. This approach led him to observe three normative constructs named *incumbent fails*, *new entrant wins* and most importantly *incumbent survives creating an independent business unit*. Each of these constructs has been operationalized using a variety of measurements. Also, as explained in the previous section, while some of them can only be observed ex-post there are others that had been identified before.

Table 8.1 lists the eight possible cases derived from this descriptive and normative combination. Table 8.1's columns list the portion of the descriptive and normative frameworks analyzed in each case, the type of innovation identified (using the disruption lingo), the prescriptive result expected and a brief explanation of this outcome.

Case 1.1. This case analyzes what will happen to a start-up that enters the market with a technology that is fundamentally based on the same technological paradigm (Dosi, 1982) than the one the incumbent is using. In most of the cases this technology comes from the incumbent's R&D efforts (Cans & Stern, 2000; Rivette & Kline, 2000). In addition it does so using a business model that makes the new entrant want to try to enter into the market by designing better products that can be sold for better margins to the incumbent's best customers. In the disruptive innovation model this type of entry strategy is described as competing against the sustaining trajectory of improvement of the incumbent. The incumbent is motivated to use all of its resources (Nelson & Winter, 1982) to introduce the improvements itself. The result of this strategy is the failure of the new entrant (Christensen, 1997a; Christensen, Anthony, & Roth, 2004).

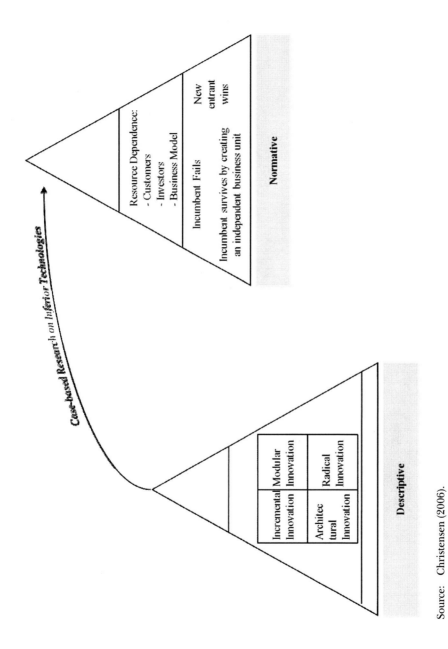

Source: Christensen (2006).

Figure 8.3. Theoretical mechanism.

221

Table 8.1. Framing the Technological Change Literature

Case	Descriptive	Normative	Innovation	Result	Reason
1.1	Incremental	Financially Attractive	Sustaining	Incumbent Wins	Incumbent has all the incentives to implement the innovation
1.2	Incremental	Financially Unattractive	Not Implemented	Nobody Wins	This R&D normally stays in the company's shelves...
1.3	Modular	Financially Attractive	Displacement	Incumbent Wins	Incumbent improves a specific product feature or reduces costs
1.4	Modular	Financially Unattractive	Low-End Disruption	New Entrant Wins	Resource Dependence prevents the incumbent from investing leaving room for the new entrant to gain foothold
1.5	Architectural	Financially Attractive	Sustaining or Breakthrough	Incumbent Wins	Neoclassical Theory: The incumbent has all the incentives to implement this platform-based innovation
1.6	Architectural	Financially Unattractive	New Market Disruption	New Entrant Wins	Resource Dependence shows the new business platform is unattractive for the incumbent because it captures nonconsumers
1.7	Radical	Financially Attractive	Breakthrough	Incumbent Wins	Introduced as a way to reduce costs or as a fundamentally superior technology (analog vs digital telephone line)
1.8	Radical	Financially Unattractive	High-End	New Entrant Wins	Incumbent's growth rate stagnates. The new entrant takes over the incumbent's most valued customers

222

Case 1.2. In this case, the technology is again based on the same technological paradigm than that of the incumbent. However the business models this technology enables are not attractive from the incumbent's point of view when measured in terms of margins or preferred customer demands. Again, this type of technology is normally developed at the incumbent's lab. The incumbent's Resource Dependence process makes sure this technology never gains *impetus* (Bower, 1986). The most usual result of this situation is to have the technology stored in the "company's shelves" until somebody takes it away when it leaves the company to become an entrepreneur (Bhidé, 2000).

Case 1.3. Displacement occurs when the technological paradigm of the start-up is the same as the one of the incumbent but there is a new component that makes the product empirically more attractive for the incumbent's preferred customers. This component' addition or substitution increases the customers' willingness to pay. Although in some instances the start-up gains some traction in the market the company fails to gain momentum when the incumbent introduces this modular component. The end result of this process is the failure of the new entrant (Christensen et al., 2004).

Case 1.4. In this case the technological paradigm of the start-up is still fundamentally equal than that of the incumbent. However the start-up has deliberately modified it. In this case the start-up has deliberately reduced the incumbent's most valued functionalities; the ones that the incumbent's preferred customers usually value the most. The reason is that the start-up is trying to introduce a product whose main functionalities are unequivocally worse than those of the incumbent. This product "simplification" generates huge savings that the new entrant reinvests in both lowering the price and adding modules that significantly improve the product's convenience or usability. This technological change enables a business model that makes the start-up profitable despite having margins several times smaller than those of the incumbent. In this case resource dependence works perfectly well. It makes this initiative unattractive for the incumbent and therefore it won't invest. If the incumbent's has not been alerted from this particular type of competitor's threat the new entrant will not only gain foothold in the market but also experience significant growth becoming after some time a profitable threat (Christensen, 1997a). Although this case is consistent with the technological change and the innovation literatures, recent research—still not empirically tested—indicates that if instead of a new entrant there are several of them the incumbent might decide otherwise and end up investing (Amaldoss & Shin, 2011).

Case 1.5. In this case the new entrant reconfigures an established system, often introducing a new component that enables improvements that weren't possible before. Although the scientific and engineering knowledge remain the same (Henderson & Clark, 1990, p. 12) this new architecture poses a serious threat to the incumbent because most of what the company knows is useful but the part that is not is built on solid processes that are extremely hard to change. Resource allocation is an iterative process that for example favors initiatives that propose cost reductions before the ones that propose new products (Bower & Gilbert, 2005). This causes the incumbent to respond ineffectively (Henderson, 1993) at first. However, the incumbent's incentives to serve its best customers will finally cause the new entrant to fail or to stagnate (Nelson & Winter, 1982).

Case 1.6. When the new entrant develops an architectural innovation that is financially unattractive for the incumbent. This usually translates into having a new platform that has been significantly improved in one of the following features: price, skills, time or access (Christensen & Raynor, 2003). As opposed to the previous case this improvement doesn't increase the willingness to pay of the incumbent's most valuable customers. A particularly distinctive feature of the business model enabled using this technology is that it normally gains foothold outside the boundaries of the industry. It normally develops within groups of consumers that have only purchased occasionally or in nonconsumers. This new business model, tightly coupled to this new technological design, keeps improving until it eventually transitions from the fringes of the industry into an industry's first set of customers, there's where it gains foothold (Tripsas, 2008). This process has been labeled new-market disruption and, although the incumbent usually ignores the appearance of such a competitor, when the new entrant has improved enough as to enter into the mainstream industry, there is no way for the incumbent to stop it (Christensen et al., 2004).

Case 1.7. A technology is radical when it satisfies the same need with a different dominant design (Schoenmakers & Duysters, 2010). Radical innovation has been studied for a very long time (Schumpeter, 1942; Schumpeter & Opie, 1934). As Henderson (2006) points out Neoclassical Theory (Nelson & Winter, 1982) indicates that if the radical technology is attractive to the incumbent's best customers (hence increasing their willingness to pay) or it significantly reduces costs incumbents have all the incentives to adopt it. Regardless of how much adopting it might cost incumbents will use all their assets and capabilities to succeed at that. Incumbents will go as far as to lead themselves into one of these rare circumstances where they allow themselves to lose money for some time. It is very difficult for a new entrant to match the level of commitment and resources needed to commercialize a radical innovation under these circumstances. That is the reason why in this case a new entrant will not be successful (Teece, 1986, 2006; Tushman & Anderson, 1986).

Case 1.8. This case describes the traditional research question in the field of technological change: When does a superior technology displace the established one causing the leading firms to fail? In this case the incumbent's best customers indicate their increase in willingness to pay for the new technology but still the incumbent's resource dependence theory frames the technology as unattractive. For example, in real estate advertising, the supe-riority of the Internet over newspapers is unequivocal. Not only that, news-papers had all the assets and capabilities required to succeed in the classifieds business. Additionally the classifieds' business unit accounts for over 40% of revenues on average for a newspaper in Spain. How is it possi-ble they lost already more than half of the market and are on their way of losing the rest? Previous research indicates there are several potential causes of incumbent failure, the most frequent ones are: reluctance to cannibalize existing products (Chandy & Tellis, 1998), the failure to identify this envi-ronmental change as a threat (Gilbert, 2006), not listening appropriately to the incumbent's best customers (Danneels, 2006), organizational rigidities (Henderson, 2006; March & Simon, 1958), the group of high-end consum-ers where the new entrant gains foothold (Slater & Mohr, 2006), the previ-ous commitments the incumbent had incurred into throughout the company's history (Sull et al., 1997) and the learning provided by the exploitation of complementary assets (Tripsas, 1997).

The case of radical technologies that replace the very foundations of a business model and in the process challenge the sustainability of estab-lished firms has been studied extensively. In the example at the beginning of the chapter; the case of the Transatlantic Cruise lines, we see how these technologies can come from direct competitors (in that case the fastest radical technology had the *Blue Riband* accolade) or from new entrants, in that case represented by the aviation companies. These very same phe-nomena has also been observed in literally thousands of industries. For example cars versus carriages, the steam engine, electricity versus oil can-dles, jet engines versus helix engines, xerography versus carbon copies, and so on (Freeman & Soete, 1997; Marquis, 1969; Myers & Marquis, 1969; Simon, 2001). Even Christensen acknowledges this "High-End" anomaly in the disruptive innovation model (George, Works, & Watson-Hemphill, 2005) while Anthony (2006) tries to untangle this phenomena calling it "Sustain and Win."

This variety of cases coupled with a very long research history has gen-erated a very noticeable scientific rigidity and the corresponding scholar's loss of interest. The prescriptive ability of what has been previously researched is extremely limited when it comes to predict if a new technol-ogy that is being introduced today will displace the established one. And it is not because of the scarcity of constructs, frameworks or models, quite the opposite, scholars and practitioners have a variety to choose from. Since technological change is one of the main driving forces that explain industry and organizational change we need not only a descriptive but also a prescriptive theory that helps us control and predict with much more accuracy this evolutionary process.

RESEARCH METHODS

Using a multicase design I follow a "replication logic" where a set of cases is treated as a series of experiments. Each case serving to confirm or disconfirm inferences from another (Yin, 2003). The multicase research design is based on "qualitizing data" (Fielding & Lee, 1998; Lee & Forthofer, 2005). I use qualitative data transformed into numerical codes that can be analyzed statistically (Miles & Huberman, 1994). My purpose with data qualitization is threefold. First, capture as much descriptive and context information as possible (Glaser, 1978), and in this sense qualitative research is particularly useful for exploratory analysis (Strauss, 1987), especially for the context-related data obtained (Audretsch, 1995; Child, 2009). Second, maximize the use of a multimethod design (Campbell & Fiske, 1959). Specifically, I use the foundational basis of grounded theory (Glaser & Strauss, 1967) together with cluster analysis (Bailey, 1983) to increase the internal validity of the model (Campbell, 1957). Third I use the tactic (Fine & Elsbach, 2000) *repertory grid technique* (RGT) that is specifically designed to produce a map of an individual's knowledge construction system (Loef, 1990). To design the interviews, develop constructs from qualitative data, calculate the distance between constructs and cluster them using additive tree structures (Sattath & Tversky, 1977).

In the research process I use sensitizing strategy as a mixed method design (Tashakkori & Teddlie, 2003). Figure 8.4 describes the methodological separation between the qualitative and the quantitative parts of the study. The architecture of the study is modular in nature with the objective of using a mixed method in a way that increases its complementary strengths and nonoverlapping weaknesses (Brewer & Hunter, 1989). Although this methodological approach takes a grounded theory orientation (Lee, 1999) it should not be considered a grounded theory research. The reason is that I have intentionally replaced grounded theory methodological techniques in favor of quantitative techniques in areas where the use of qualitative methods have been either more controversial (Suddaby, 2006) or more subject to researcher bias (Strauss, 1987). Scholars should consider this research design a multimethod research that is modular in nature and where quantitative techniques have replaced qualitative techniques when possible. This substitution strategy has increased both the robustness and the internal validity of the research.

A detailed explanation of Figure 8.4 reveals the details of the study; in the first step I create the hermeneutic unit and assign the documents listed in Table 8.2 to it. In the second step I use open coding to obtain the codes and quotations. Although this process is potentially very sensible to

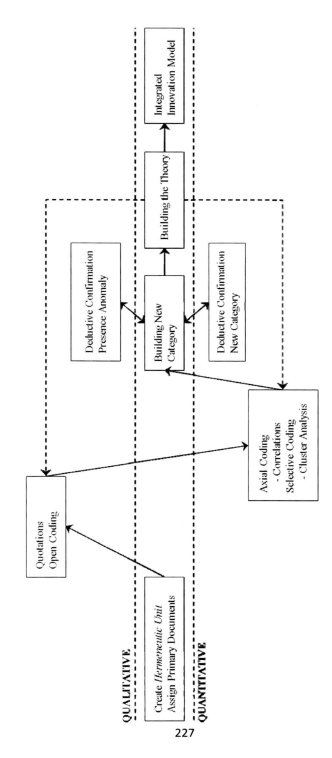

Figure 8.4. Mixed-method research design.

227

researcher bias (Glaser, 1978) I found a way to isolate my theoretical sensitivity throughout this particular rationale: There are two types of codes. The first are the "unequivocal" codes, which are usually labeled *in vivo* codes in grounded theory. They empirically express what is going on in the passage, that is, if subject says "our cash burn rate was very high" it is observable "burn-rate" is a unequivocal code. The second type is *open coding*, this is where the researchers' theoretical sensitivity is at play. Codes must have a "trigger factor" that causes the researcher to interpret them in a particular way. Because of the trigger effect all codes are—up to a debatable extent—partially correct. Finding a code that is partially correct usually means at a deeper level that we are facing a situation in which that particular code is neither mutually exclusive nor collective exhaustive. This is exactly the situation of continuous variables. This is the reason why I use Euclidean distance to measure distances between variables. Using this research methodology these variables are continuous in nature, this ensures the percentage of attribution of the researcher into the code is taken into account. In the third step of the methodology I replace qualitative axial coding techniques with quantitative methods. I use correlation analysis for axial coding in order to separate codes from constructs. In addition I have also replaced the qualitative technique for obtaining the central category. Instead of using selective coding I use cluster analysis. Since descriptive and normative theory building requires a central category I use the context provided in the quotations and the results from the Euclidean distances to develop the categorization schemes. Fourth, I finish the inductive part of the research process by building the new category. On a parallel track I also build on the previous research of the literature of Disruptive Innovation to deductively fail to disconfirm the presence of the anomaly. I then use correlation of the deductive variables to test the anomaly empirically and to confirm if it is mutually exclusive and collectively exhaustive compared to the resource dependence categorization scheme. In the fifth step of the process I introduce the new categorization scheme into the descriptive and normative disruptive innovation theory. The sixth and final step integrates disruptive innovation with the previous literature on innovation. The final visual of the research results is very useful for determining new areas of future research.

DATA SOURCES

The primary unit of analysis is a company I will name "Stratemic" founded in the year 2000 that sells only online real estate advertising and they only do that through the internet. This company is fundamentally different from the other companies in this industry because it is

Table 8.2. Sources of Data

Primary Documents	Quotations	Quotations %	Interviews Quota %	Inductive(I)/ Deductive(D)	Data: Primary (P)/ Secondary
P 1: 1_Interview August 9th 2007	33	4.1	4.1	I	P
P 2: 2_Dossier_Stratemic_ES_2007	33	4.1		I	P
P 3: 3_Dossier_ Stratemic _ES_2008	42	5.2		I	P
P 4: 4_Interview August 13th 2007	98	12.2	12.2	I	P
P 5: 5_Interview August 17th 2007	101	12.5	12.5	I	P
P 6: 6_Values_Stratemic	13	1.6		I	P
P 7: 7_Presentation_Services_Stratemic	49	6.1		I	P
P 8: 8_Business Plan Stratemic	38	4.7		I	P
P 9: 9_Business Plan Stratemic Exec Summary	34	4.2		I	P
P10: 10_Comunication Labels Launch Stratemic	6	0.7		I	P
P11: 11_Big_Idea	30	3.7		I	P
P12: 12_Contract A	9	1.1		I	P
P13: 13_Contract B	14	1.7		I	P
P14: 14_Reasons Fragmentation	10	1.2	1.2	I	P
P15: 15_case	3	0.4		I	P
P16: 16_How do Business on the Internet	22	2.7	2.7	I	P
P17: 18_Internal_Usability Stratemic	8	1.0		I	P
P18: 19_Interview EL MUNDO	17	2.1	2.1	I	S
P19: 20_internal_paper_Jose	11	1.4		D	S
P20: 21_Fragmented_Dissagregated_email	4	0.5	0.5	I	P
P21: 22_The Innovators Solution Book	200	24.8		D	S
P22: 23_The Innovators Dilemma Book	4	0.5		D	S
P23: 24_The External Control of Organizations	7	0.9		D	S
P24: 25_When Mkt Fragmented Jump Platform	19	2.4		I	S
TOTAL	805	100	35.4		

"extremely" interdependent; company founders developed the entire company in-house. Dozens of direct competitors were incorporated at the time in Spain, all of them focused on the very same market and all of them were trying to satisfy the very same customer need. However, having analyzed most of them (the most relevant 20 companies that account for over 96% of the entire market), I could not find another who was fully interdependent in nature. There are mainly three types of competitors in this market: The first type is the incumbent's subsidiaries. These are corporate ventures that were created as independent business units to exploit the new internet channel (Gilbert, 2006). This companies use the incumbent's assets and most of them are even located at the incumbent's offices. The second group is startup companies that have developed a partnership with an incumbent. They have a modular organizational structure (Baldwin & Clark, 2000) and are specialized in exploiting that particular asset from the incumbent; they outsource almost all their other activities. Usually the asset they have licensed from the incumbent is their database. The third group is formed of companies that provide the service for free and that base their projected revenue on advertising (Anderson, 2009). These companies are trying to leverage the power of user generated content to increase demand. In 2007 all these companies but two were either languishing or had already disappeared. One of them is Stratemic the other is a subsidiary of a large company that operates in the classifieds market and that it is not a newspaper. Figure 8.5 shows Stratemic's revenues. In the real estate online advertising market, Stratemic is by far the first company in revenues. In its industry, it is also the first company in number of visitors in Spain. The most demanding consumers per segment (brokerage agencies, personal seller or buyers, etc.) rate Stratemic as the best provider of the service in the industry and the company is still experiencing almost exponential sales growth (in 2010 Stratemic's revenues passed the €20 million mark). On the other hand due to the company's interdependent organizational structure it was by far the most expensive company to create, their set-up costs were about 15 times higher than those of the industry's average. Why did they choose to be interdependent? What were they trying to accomplish that needed a start-from-the-scratch to deliver that kind of service? Why target the incumbent's most valuable customers? In an industry where the newspaper companies are the incumbents and whose specialized assets are still useful and with plenty of resources, strong political connections, and large amounts of cash, why was not Stratemic neutralized by them?

I examined this company because I identified it as a high-end disruption. I was given full access to the data and the top management was willing to give me a substantial portion of their valuable time. I worked at the circumstance-based categorization level to understand the mechanism

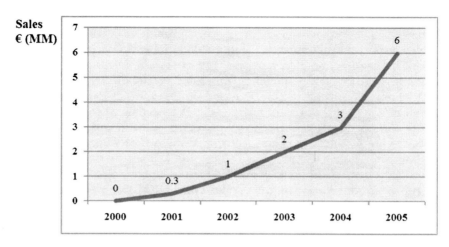

Figure 8.5.   Stratemic sales.

that causes an incumbent to be incapable to react in front of a disruptive threat. I developed the research sequentially and both the CEO and the management team were kind enough to help me understand the way they designed their market entry. They were also kind enough as to provide me with all the information needed to introduce into the research an exhaustive list of both descriptive and normative factors in chronological order (Yin, 2003). *The repertory grid technique* (RGT) kept me very close to the data (Eisenhardt, 1989) and was very helpful in clinically refining the constructs and their expressions (Gibbert et al., 2008). This is an ongoing process that I kept pushing until both the company's deliberate strategy and the elements of the high-end anomaly were explicit and understood (Eisenhardt & Graebner, 2007).

The RGT technique used in the interviews works eliciting an individual's *triages* of constructs by presenting a series of events. It then invites the individual to indicate the similarities and differences among the elements. One of the differences between grounded theory and the mixed method used is that although in grounded theory (Strauss & Corbin, 1990) it is recommended to capture direct observations I included all the information in the transcripts, without being selective at all. I used only my theoretical sensitivity for the axial coding (Glaser, 1978). The data collected from structured interviews and archival documents was organized in chronological order. No additional step was started before having fully analyzed the previous one. Results were compared to the expected solutions indicated in the disruptive innovation model and divergences were used to compare construct design and to develop the new set of constructs that were to be elicited. This methodology helps new theories emerge while conducting the research (Glaser, 1992). Table 8.2 displays the number of quotations obtained per item, the quotation percentage, the total amount of information that comes from interviewing directly the management team (35.4%), if the item was used for inductive or deductive theory development and if the source of the data was primary or secondary. All the documentation I requested was provided on time and therefore the interviewing sequence used to confirm and disconfirm facts and hypotheses was kept intact (Strauss & Corbin, 1990). The interviewing period lasted 3 months.

Two main sources of data were collected: (1) RGT semistructured interviews, (2) Archival documents. In studies such as this one *triangulation* is used to address the potential problems of construct validity because the multiple sources of evidence essentially provide multiple measures of the same phenomenon (Jick, 1979).

Interviews

In total, 24 hours of interview time were transcribed distributed in seven in-depth interviews that were conducted with members of the management team and shareholders. Three of them were conducted with the CEO. All were in-depth interviews and none lasted less than 3 hours. One interview lasted almost 6 hours nonstop. By the sixth interview more than 70% of the entries had already appeared in previous interviews. The seventh interview was the last one because at that point it was clear the interview process had reached its *theoretical saturation* point. One of the advantages of narrowing the research question in this study is that there is no need to conduct a large number of interviews to reach the saturation point. The *theoretical sampling* strategy had the following rationale: Together with the RGT I used a semistructured interview questionnaire that listed all the elements of a low-end and a new-market disruption. I asked each member of the management team why they violated specific areas of these theories and why. Every question contained context specific aspects that were necessary to understand what market conditions they elicited. Several questions addressed how these context specific aspects evolved over time. Consistently with the resource dependence theory the management team very often emphasized the difficulties of raising funds and the role of investors in managing the company. This symptom was particularly acute in this case because of the very interdependent nature of Stratemic, which made it a start-up with a very high burn rate. Another set of questions addressed competitors and their expected reaction. In the competitors section I included nonconsumption as a competitor (Christensen & Raynor, 2003), this is important because in Spain there is no multiple listing service and about 50% of the market neither uses advertising nor hires real estate agents. 100% of the interviews were transcribed and strict case-study protocol was followed. I used triangulation obtained from multiple informants and cross-checking information against archival and public documents to avoid retrospective bias in the interviews.

Archival Documents

This documentation was used to cross-check information provided in the interviews. The documents used for the inductive part of theory building are business plans, internal memos, external information, client's contracts, conferences offered by members of the management team, and interviews. There were also e-mails sent to clarify some specific points of view of the industry, specifically the concept of fragmentation. For the deductive part of theory building and for some specific parts of theory testing, the documentation used is mainly books and a business plan from a well-established competitor that launched a subsidiary to compete against Stratemic. This subsidiary is no longer operating. Table 8.2 lists some of the titles of these documents. Some of them were confidential and I have to thank Stratemic's management for both granting me access and letting me include them in this research (Yin, 2003).

A NOTE ON THE SUPERIORITY OF THE TECHNOLOGY

Mainstream customers evaluate and at the end choose a product on the basis of a selected group of attributes (Govindarajan, Kopalle, & Danneels, 2011; Thompson, Hamilton, & Rust, 2005), real estate Internet advertising is a superior technology compared to newspaper-based real estate advertising. In terms of the four main groups of attribute-based performance metrics Internet-based real estate advertising is unequivocally superior in all four of them (Christensen, 1997b).

Functionality

Internet ads include many more product description categories (fields of information) than newspaper ads. They also include pictures, videos and several additional functionalities that just cannot be supported with newspaper ads. In Spain, if on average a typical Real Estate Newspaper ad has 10 fields of information an Internet-based ad usually has well over 40.

Reliability

Internet-based ads are much more reliable. They not only provide more information to mainstream customers but also are updated much more frequently than newspaper ads. The moment a property is sold its ad is subsequently removed from the website so many potential customers who are still looking will not even get to see the ad and therefore will never make the initial phone call. This prevents them from being disappointed because the property is already been sold while it also makes them feel confident that if they call the property will still be on sale.

Convenience

Internet-based ads are not only adaptable to multiple display devices but also permit the properties to be searched more effectively. For instance, a newspaper ad usually permits making a search based on location or property size. With an Internet-based ad you can perform searches using any of its more than 40 fields of information. This not only ends up providing much more precise results but only saves a substantial amount of time.

Price

Internet-based ads are much cheaper than newspaper ads. Not only because of the inherent costs of these two platforms but also in terms of audience reached.

ANALYSIS OF THE DATA

Emergence of Codes

Following one of the two main research lines on building grounded theory (Strauss & Corbin, 1990) I reviewed the extant literature on Innovation and prepared a list of the different codes, constructs, categorization schemes and models that had been already identified. Since this is an inductive research there are no hypotheses to test, there are just constructs to elicit and classify. However—in order to build a mutually exclusive and collectively exhaustive categorization scheme—it is critical to clearly identify ex-ante the elements that have been already researched (Dent-Brown & Wang, 2006). I use this information as the metadata to insert in the semistructured interviews. Table 8.3 lists the codes that were obtained and their meaning. Table 8.4 lists the groundedness per code (the number of times the code is linked to the quotation in the text and therefore to a particular circumstance), the percentage of groundedness compared to the total, the groundedness cumulative percentage and the quartile where each code fits in this normal distribution (Kolmogorov-Smirnov $Z = 0.94$ [0.32]).

Preliminary results depicted in Table 8.4 confirm both that this is an anomaly according to the disruptive innovation literature and that this is

Table 8.3. List and Definition of Inductive and Deductive Codes

Code	Definition
Users underserved	Instances when the founders or the customers expressed they would value improvements in the traditional performance characteristics of the service.
Interdependent	Characteristic of a business model where the company owns the entire value chain (also named fully integrated company). Instrumental for improving the functionality or reliability of an industry that is largely underserved because *"you have to own everything to do anything"*.
Buyer match wants vs can-afford (job)	A customer variability measure. Indicates quotations where the real estate company offered to the customer a product outside it's willingness-to-pay.
Buyer concern exhaustivity	A measure of underserved customers. Indicates customers are not able to be exhaustive on their searches. Therefore when they finally buy a house they still have the doubt of whether there is another somewhere they would like better or they would get better value for their investment.
Buyer's variability	A measure of underserved customers, indicates every time the consumer undertakes an action that doesn't deliver the expected result. For example, calling a real estate company to ask for a product only to find they no longer have it for sale but they use the phone call to try to sell to them something else, or going to visit a place only to find the number of rooms is not the one desired.
Modular Deductive	This code comes from empirically validating the anomaly. Indicates a business that is not interdependent at the time of entering an industry.
Property information key	A very specific industry variable. In the real estate market in Spain most of the products are not sold using exclusivity contracts, therefore real estate companies are very reluctant to disclose the address of the product because that would cause another agency to contact the buyer so they can add it to their portfolio. This code captures the problems, efforts and initiatives Stratemic had to undertake to overcome that constraint.
Buyer more convenient (access and product info)	Indicates quotations related with convenience, for example that the database doesn't have duplicities, the number of functionalities per advertisement, the usability, etc.
internet	This code is used as both a dummy code for indicating if the business model was enabled with the internet and as a way of indicating the use of a channel where the incumbents are either not present or the channel doesn't represent substantial earnings for them.
Seller lower WTP	In the spanish market a significant number of transactions are made without a real estate brokerage because they reduce the willingness-to-pay of the buyer and of the seller. This code captures the quotations where the seller expresses this concern.

Continued on next page

235

Table 8.3. (Cont.)

Code	Definition
Burn rate	A frequently used term in the venture capital industry, this code indicates the money a company needs per unit of time (usually months) to keep its operations running.
Buyer time needed (less)	This code captures the instances of all the activities the buyer's undertake and that represent a waste of time, i.e. searching in media, learning how a real estate web page works, visiting properties, etc.
Defragmented	This codes indicates quotations that indicate the industry is fragmented. The name of the code indicates the opposite because of the structure of the questionaire.
Dissaggregated	This codes refines the previous one in the sense that includes weak economic substitutes and the effects of localization in the anatomy of the industry.
Efficient (biz model)	This code indicates quotations that refer to the traditional meaning of efficiency; the ability to deliver a service at an inferior unit of cost than that of a competitor.
Efficient (services you pay in other biz models or don't have)	This code indicates efficiency in the sense of having the possibility of delivering more services for the same unit of cost, it's not the trational sense of the term that indicates delivering the service for an inferior unit of cost.
Buyer skills needed (less)	This code captures quotations that refer to problems buyers have when searching for a property and that come from lack of knowledge of the internet, the real estate industry, search strategies, etc.
Not intuitive agencies pov RPV	This code captures the real estate agencies points of view in front of an infrastructural innovation such as the internet. It also indicates how the agencies Resources, Processes and Priorities (Values) have shaped the way they see the world.
Communication push	All the quotations that refer to initiatives for launching marketing campaigns in any type of media are included in this code.
Incumbent wrong RPV	This code captures the Resouces, Processes and Priorities (Values) of the incumbents in the industry. Specifically it not only captures the transition from threat to opportunity but also why their initiatives have been usuccessful.
Free service	This code is a dummy variable for buyers, sellers and agencies. It captures those instances when any of these entities expected to receive the service for free.
Communication push generates demand pull	This code captures an unexpected phenomena. It includes those quotations that indicate an unexpected demand pull originated from the operating actions used to lunch Stratemic into the market.
Investors	This code captures the investors' mind set. Quotations referred to the breakeven time, payback periods, type of business model adopted or strategies to retaliate in front of a competitor are captured here.

Continued on next page

Table 8.3. (Cont.)

Code	Definition
Interdependent Deductive	This code, created to test empirically the model, captures the quotations that indicate when an interdependent business model is going to capture the lion share of income of a particular industry.
Independent commercial system	This code complements the "internet" code. It captures those quotations that are pointing out to "soft" characteristics of an independent commercial system that comprises a channel where the incumbent is minimally present.
Incumbent service no improvement 20 years	This code captures the mismatch between the trajectory of improvement of the incumbent and the consumers' absorptive capacity.
Interindustry boundaries	This code captures the quotations -- made either by the incumbents or by the Strategic management team -- that indicate a specific action or goal exceeds the industry boundaries.
Users underserved Deductive	This code was developed to test empirically the model. It refers to those instances that deal with underserved consumers in the Disruptive Innovation literature.
Users overserved Deductive	This code was developed to test empirically the model. It refers to those instances that deal with overserved consumers in the Disruptive Innovation literature.
Product not proprietary	This code captures the industry's way of competing from the point of view of the agencies. Specifically it deals with their concen of not having the exclusivity for selling a property and the measures they have to take to prevent competitors from selling "their products".
Modular	This code captures instances that indicate a business model is modular in nature.
Short-term orientation (investors)	This code refines the "investors" code. Specifically it introduces the investor's concern of recovering the investment in the minimum possible time.
Upsurge demand	This code captures an environmental change. Specifically it controls for upsurges in demand, a circumstance the Spanish real estate market has experienced extensively for the last 10 years.
Industry outsiders	This code captures the Stratemic's management team specific attributes they "brought in" the Real Estate industry. Specially because none of them had any previous experience in this industry.
No cash	This code captures the quotations where the Stratemic management team indicates there is a cash shortage.
No regulator	This code captures the quotations that refer to the absence of a regulator and the advantages and disadvantages of that situation.
Layoffs	This code captures the situation where the Stratemic team had to layoff employees to continue running the company's operations.

also a given situation in the traditional superior technologies challenge described in the extant innovation literature. According to disruption, the first five codes are consistent with the incumbent's sustaining innovation strategy, not with the new entrant's. The usual codes for a new entrant are *users-overserved* (a code that has not even been mentioned once in all the research process!), organizational modularity and some measurement of convenience for the customer. Regarding the traditional research question: When do superior technologies coupled with a business model can displace the incumbents? Table 8.4 provides some hints about the business model: It is interdependent in nature. Specifically, according to the quotations and consistent with prior observations, Stratemic's business model is interdependent up to the very extreme of that continuum. They have built all the pieces of the value chain in-house and from scratch. Paradoxically, they explained that at the beginning they didn't want to but at the end they had no option but to do so. Throughout the interview process managers described how they initially tried to outsource as much as possible. However at the end they had no option but to develop everything in-house because the outsourced services they were offered were not nearly good enough for the quality of service they wanted to deliver. This observation is consistent with the prior literature on innovation in the sense that interdependent business models have a higher performance than the modular ones. Interdependent business models would only hire suppliers or partners when they are forced to for noneconomic reasons (i.e., bandwidth providers). Still, in order to build prescriptive theory, we need to know when a new interdependent entrant will be successful in front of the incumbent. Table 8.4 provides more hints in that direction in the sense that is quite remarkable that an industry that is at least 200 years old is still so underserved and has consumers that experience such a high-variability and low-reliability in service. In fact, more than 20% of the quotations refer to different underserved customer characteristics. These are the most valuable customers for the incumbent and are exactly the customer groups Stratemic has targeted very successfully. The business model architecture chosen to do that is shown in the form of lagging variables in the first quartile of the distribution of codes. This quartile contains 49% of the groundedness of the study. This makes very clear the first nine codes (the code *modular-deductive* belongs to the deductive part of theory building) were prioritized very aggressively from the very beginning of the venture.

Axial Coding: From Codes to Concepts and From Concepts to Constructs

Consistent with the mixed methods approach used in this research I have used correlation analysis to obtain the concepts and the constructs. The

Table 8.4.   Code's Groundedness

CODE	Groundedness	%	Cumulative %	Quartile
1. users underserved	220	8.4	8.4	1
2. interdependent	186	7.1	15.6	1
3. buyer match wants vs can-afford (job)	141	5.4	21.0	1
4. buyer concern exhaustivity	133	5.1	26.1	1
5. buyer's variability	128	4.9	31.0	1
6. modular deductive	102	3.9	34.9	1
7. property information key	99	3.8	38.7	1
8. buyer more convenient (access and product info)	95	3.6	42.3	1
9. Internet	88	3.4	45.7	1
10. seller lower WTP	87	3.3	49.0	1
11. burn rate	79	3.0	52.1	2
12. buyer time needed (less)	79	3.0	55.1	2
13. defragmented	78	3.0	58.1	2
14. dissaggregated	78	3.0	61.1	2
15. efficient (biz model)	78	3.0	64.0	2
16. efficient (services you pay in other biz models or don't have)	70	2.7	66.7	2
17. buyer skills needed (less)	66	2.5	69.3	2
18. not intuitive agencies pov RPV	66	2.5	71.8	2
19. communication push	61	2.3	74.1	3
20. incumbent wrong RPV	61	2.3	76.5	3
21. free service	60	2.3	78.8	3
22. communication push generates pull	56	2.1	80.9	3
23. investors	53	2.0	82.9	3
24. interdependent Deductive	52	2.0	84.9	3
25. independent commercial system	51	2.0	86.9	3
26. incumbent service no improvement 20 years	41	1.6	88.5	3
27. interindustry boundaries	41	1.6	90.0	3
28. users underserved Deductive	37	1.4	91.5	3
29. users overserved Deductive	36	1.4	92.8	4
30. product not proprietary	34	1.3	94.1	4
31. modular	30	1.1	95.3	4
32. short-term orientation (investors)	28	1.1	96.4	4
33. upsurge demand	28	1.1	97.4	4
34. industry outsiders	24	0.9	98.4	4
35. no-cash	22	0.8	99.2	4
36. no regulator	11	0.4	99.6	4
37. layoffs	10	0.4	100.0	4

reason is that this quantitative technique increases the internal validity. Therefore, instead of relying on the researcher's theoretical sensitivity (Glaser, 1978) this step in the process is completely replicable. The measurement used to separate codes from concepts is the statistical correlation. The rationale to create the concepts is built on the grounded theory's *labeled phenomenon* approach (Strauss & Corbin, 1990). When there is a significant correlation between codes each code transcends its meaning in the sense that it is also part of the explanation of a construct. Hence, the union of two or more concepts represents a construct. Constructs are the building blocks for building theory inductively. Table 8.5 depicts the constructs relevant for theory building. To increase internal validity only constructs with a correlation coefficient of 80% or higher and statistically significant at least at 95% ($p < 0.05$) have been selected. Since these constructs are solidly grounded in the contexts I can go back to the quotations and get a context-specific meaning for each of them. Table 8.6 depicts the constructs, the concepts they contain, the name I have assigned to the construct and the context-specific meaning of the construct for this research.

We are now in the descriptive constructs portion of theory building. The portion Glaser and Strauss (1967) labeled a substantive theory or, in other words, the construct area of the descriptive process of theory building (Christensen & Carlile, 2009). However only developing a formal (or circumstance-based categorization scheme) the theory will have predictive power. These constructs must be separated in two central categories, one descriptive and one normative. That is what selective coding is for. According to Glaser (1998) the central category has the highest variance, and that makes the research valid but the concepts it generates imprecise. To develop the selective coding I have replaced qualitative central category determination with cluster analysis. I use the Euclidean distance between concepts to measure the strength of the relationships between constructs (Kuckartz & Kuckartz, 2006). These Euclidean distances have a heuristic value that permits to separate the variables in the appropriate number of clusters. Although there are methodologies to uncover the appropriate number of clusters I have used the hierarchical cluster methodology to increase the internal validity by showing each concept behavior depending on the different number of clusters.

The concepts *users underserved, independent channel* (Internet) and *interdependent* are not only the ones most solidly grounded in the research but also the most distant ones from the rest of the concepts. There are two ways to separate the results of the cluster analysis into descriptive and normative. The first one is analyzing the quotations of the groups of variables per cluster; this is the qualitative way of doing it. The second way is using the agglomeration schedule of the cluster analysis. I have triangulated this step

Table 8.5.   From Codes to Constructs

Concept	burn_rate	buyer's variability	buyer concern exhaustivity	buyer match wants vs can-afford (job)	buyer more convenient (access and product info)	buyer time needed (less)	communication push generates pull	disaggregated	efficient biz (model)	efficient (services you pay in other biz models or don't have)	incumbent_wrong_RPV	interdependent	investors	not_intuitive_agencies_pov_RPV	product_not_proprietary
1 buyer's variability	0.859** (0.00)														
2 buyer concern exhaustivity		0.871** (0.00)													
3 buyer match wants vs can-afford (job)		0.895** (0.00)	0.926** (0.00)												
4 buyer more convenient (access and product info)		0.889** (0.00)	0.870** (0.00)	0.883** (0.00)											
5 buyer time needed (less)				0.898** (0.00)											
6 communication push generates pull		0.818** (0.00)													
7 disaggregated							0.960** (0.00)								
8 efficient (services you pay in other biz models or don't have)									0.838** (0.00)						
9 incumbent_wrong_RPV							0.821** (0.00)								
10 interdependent		0.806** (0.00)					0.863** (0.00)								
11 not_intuitive_agencies_pov_RPV							0.859** (0.00)					0.858** (0.00)			
12 property_information_key							0.817** (0.00)				0.804** (0.00)	0.820** (0.00)			
13 seller lower WTP				0.821** (0.00)										0.835** (0.00)	
14 short-term orientation (investors)													0.809* (0.00)		
15 users_underserved				0.805** (0.00)						0.808** (0.00)				0.817** (0.00)	0.881** (0.00)

** p<0.01 (2-tailed)
* p<0.05 (2-tailed)

Table 8.6. From Constructs to Concepts (1/2)

Num.	Concepts Included	Number Quot	Construct Name	Explanation Considering the Context Related Quotations
1	buyer's variability burn_rate	1	1_Variab_burn	Developing and improving the service to reduce consumer error has a severe and direct effect on the cost structure and requires interdependency
2	buyer_ concern_exhaustivity buyer's variability	67	2_exhaustive_variab	The consumer considers the randomness in the service and the concern for being as exhaustive as possible as two tightly coupled variables
3	buyer match wants vs can afford (job) Buyer_ concern_exhaustivity buyer's variability	48	3_match_exhaustive_variab	Randomness and exhaustivity are not enough, the offers received must be compatible with the consumer's willingness-to-pay. The consumer must find what he wants in less than 5 phone calls
4	Buyer more convenient (access and product info) buyer match wants vs can afford (job) Buyer_ concern_exhaustivity buyer's variability	32	4_access_match_exhaust_variab	Randomness, exhaustivity and tailor fitted willigness-to-pay offers are not enough, the consumer wants all that diplayed in an understandable way and available through different channels (computer, cell phone, etc.)
5	Buyer time needed (less) Buyer skills needed (less)	59	5_time_skills	Buyers and consumers with no expertise in searching must be able to find what they are looking for as quickly as possible
6	Communication push generates pull Buyer's variability	11	6_pull_variab	Unexpected pull demand originated from setting up the company's operations provides very helpful feedback for reducing buyer's variability
7	Dissaggregated Degragmented	70	7_dissaggreg_defrag	Incumbent's response is severely weakened when the market is not only fragmented but also full of weak economic substitutes and geographically dispersed
8	efficient (services you pay in other biz models or don't have) Efficiente(biz model)	43	8_efficient_services	Company efficiency (compared to the incumbent's) is instrumental for providing services the incumbent just can't provide without either raising costs or investing substantially in modifying or building an asset
9	Communication push generates pull Incumbent_wrong_RPV	3	9_pull_IwrongRPV	The incumbent's performance trajectory (especially the way it makes money) is incompatible with those very clear demands underserved consumers have expressed in the past

Table 8.6. (Cont.)

Num.	Concepts Included	Number Quot	Construct Name	Explanation Considering the Context Related Quotations
10	Interdependent Buyer's variability Communication push generates pull	9	10_interd_variab_pull	Pull demand and their explicit needs are intimately related to reducing buyers' slack and need an interdependent business model to be appropriately met
11	Not intuitive agencies Pov RPV Communication push generates pull interdependent	2	11_agenRPV_pull_interd	Real estate agencies priorities also generate substantial consumer's waste and became Stratemic's clients because of its interdependent business model (that reduced substantially consumer's waste)
12	Property information key Incumbent wrong RPV Interdependent Not intuitive agencies Pov RPV Product not proprietary	1	12_key_IwrongRPV_interd_age nRPV_propiet	These codes are tightly linked to each other and describe a 2-sided platform with a high level of encroachment. Property information key and the incumbent's interest in improving in other variables is connected interdependently with the way agencies compete because of the non-proprietary nature of the product
13	Seller lower WTP Buyer match wants vs can afford (job) Communication push generates pull Not intuitive agencies Pov RPV	0	13_WTP_match_pull_agenRPV	Sellers' willingness-to-pay for advertising or selling their properties is very low (this is the main cause of nonconsumption in this industry), agencies try to compensate this attracting the consumer and have developed selling capabilities that do not fit neither consumers' clearly expressed underserved needs nor the offer of properties adjusted to their purchasing power
14	Investors Short_term_orientation (investors)	14	14_ivest_shortterm	Investors apply the usual financial metrics and are particularly concerned about the payback period, they also have a strong view against emergent strategies and favor deliberate strategies above all the others
15	Users_underserved Buyer match wants vs can afford (job) Efficient (services you pay in other biz models or don't have)	15	15_unders_match_efficient	The financial view of underserved users favors limiting the offers to those they can afford and using free high-value added services the incumbent can't introduce because they are incompatible with their profit architecture

243

Table 8.7.   Typology of Clusters

Cluster	Variables	Classification-Scheme
1	Users underserved	Formal (Normative)
2	property information_key	Formal (Normative)
3	Internet	Formal (Normative)
4	interdependent	Formal (Normative)
5	Efficient (biz model) Efficient (services you pay in other biz models or don't have)	Substantive (Descriptive)
6	Buyer's variability Buyer concern exhaustivity Buyer march wants vs can-afford (job)	Substantive (Descriptive)
7	Burn rate Buyer more convenient (access and product info) Buyer skills needed (less) Buyer time needed (less) Communication push Communication pull Defragmented Dissaggregated Free service Incumbent service no improvement 20 years Incumbent wrong RPV Independent commercial system Industry outsiders Inter-industry boundaries Investors Layoffs Modular No cash No regulator Not intuitive agencies Product not proprietary Seller lower WTP Short-term orientation (investors) Upsurge demand	Substantive (Descriptive)

and have obtained the same results (Jick, 1979). Other cluster techniques also deliver the same results not only for finding the optimal number of clusters but also for determining if they are descriptive or normative in nature (see Table 8.7).

Controlling for the Presence of the Anomaly

As previously mentioned Table 8.4 confirms we are in the presence of an anomaly according to the disruptive innovation literature. To confirm

**Table 8.8.   Empirical Demonstration of
the High-End Disruption Anomaly**

	Interdependent_ Deductive	Modular_ Deductive	Users_Overserved_ Deductive
modular_deductive	.988**		
	0.00		
users_overserved_ deductive	.979**	.992**	
	0.00	0.00	
users_underserved_ deductive	.988**	1.000**	.992**
	0.00	0.00	0.00

** $p < 0.01$ (2-tailed)

* $p < 0.05$ (2-tailed)

the presence of this anomaly I have codified the documents 19, 22, 23 and 24 from Table 8.2. These documents are the books *The Innovator's Dilemma* (1997a), *The Innovator's Solution* (2003), *The External Control of Organizations* (1978) and the business plan of a competitor that wanted to launch a subsidiary to capture a portion of the real estate advertising market. The objective is to determine if the anomaly is present in this literature. Table 8.8 depicts the constructs that result from conducting this deductive part of the research.

All constructs depicted in Table 8.8 are consistent with the disruptive innovation theory but one, the construct that indicates instances where an interdependent business model gains traction with overserved users (marked in italics). This indicates a breakthrough innovation that causes an industry turmoil (Abernathy & Clark, 1985; Utterback, 1994). This is exactly the original research question: a superior technology coupled with a business model that displaces the incumbent.

RESULTS

This research shows that the case of a superior technology displacing the incumbents, contrary to what (at the descriptive level) had been researched before is not a technological problem per se. At a deeper level it seems to be an industry architecture problem. Research findings indicate there is a particular industry architecture that disables the incumbent's ability to respond rendering it powerless in front of a new entrant.

However separating from descriptive to normative research leaves us with more insights. The descriptive industry architecture identified is not enough for the new entrant to succeed. The new firm must deliberately define a particular strategy for the industrial architecture to be engaged. The normative portion of the research shows it must target underserved consumers throughout an interdependent business model and using a commercialization channel where incumbents are either minimally or not present at all.

Figure 8.6 describes both the descriptive and normative research results. I have labeled the new category "incumbent's reach" because the incumbent's forceful reaction to maintain its market position is largely insufficient. The reason is that this reaction requires being able to have influence in environments where the incumbent's complementary assets are inexistent. There are two attributes and four constructs that enable the high-end disruption. The first attribute *efficient* indicates that the new entrant's business model is more efficient in both the traditional sense of the construct and in the sense that it delivers several free products and services the incumbent cannot afford because of its capabilities or priori-

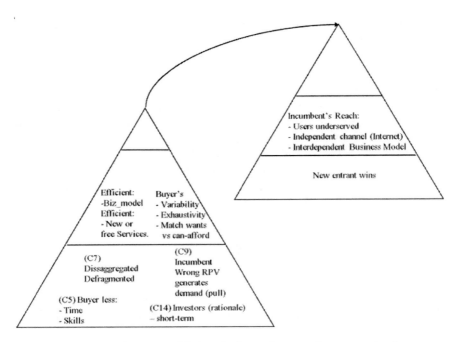

Figure 8.6.   "Incumbent's reach" descriptive and normative categorization scheme.

ties, for example, Stratemic only charges for publishing ads. Users on the other hand browse the ads for free. The second attribute is related to the incumbent's technological path dependence (Schilling, 1998). It describes dominant designs that—although represented significant improvements when they were introduced—their performance's variability in the products and services they are encapsulated in is unacceptable for today's standards. These two descriptive categories are already present in the innovation literature. These research findings help us understand previously unexplained phenomena. It seems that if new entrants used the *efficient* and *superior technology* attributes but were unsuccessful in challenging the incumbents is because they didn't adopt the normative business model design introduced above. As explained previously it is not *efficiency* or *technological superiority* per se what will cause the new entrant's success, it's building a causal (normative) mechanism on top of these two enablers.

Research results also indicate the four constructs that describe the characteristics of an industry where a high-end disruption strategy is enabled and therefore can be engaged had also been identified in the innovation literature. These are:

1. *Buyers:* there must be consumers with difficulties for using or hiring the incumbent's services. These difficulties can either come from their unwillingness to invest too much time learning how to use the incumbent's service or from their unwillingness to develop the skills needed to obtain an acceptable result from the incumbent's service.

2. *Fragmented/Disaggregated:* Although Anthony (2006) mentions fragmentation might prevent effective incumbent response this research indicates that there is more going on than the standard fragmentation described in Porter (1980). Specifically this construct indicates that, when an industry is very large and plagued with weak economic substitutes, even if a company or group of companies have a large part of the market share the market effect of their actions is limited. Refining this construct is not one of the objectives of this research. But this might be a good opportunity for further research. The separation of fragmentation from disaggregation might also be useful for explaining previously described phenomena. For instance, in Tushman and Anderson (1986) the CT scanners case describes an industry that at the time was also both fragmented and disaggregated.

3. *Incumbent wrong RPV generates pull:* consistent with the anxiety derived from the variability in the consumer experience. This construct indicates that although the incumbent invests significantly

in improving its platform consumers just do not perceive these improvements. The reason is that the industry is locked into an inferior technology that is improving on features consumers no longer value. This anxiety and frustration provokes consumers to abandon the incumbent rather quickly when a more fitted alternative is introduced into the market. This phenomenon has also been observed in sectors with competing technologies such as nuclear energy, cars, metallurgy and multimedia (Malerba, 2002).

4. *Investors' rationale—short term:* Viewed from the point of view of the incumbents. In mature industries investors and shareholders are very reluctant when it comes to developing a new platform because they view the current platform as still good enough and (most importantly) fully paid.

Previous literature on innovation introduces both radical and incremental innovations (Abernathy & Utterback, 1978), architectural innovation (Henderson & Clark, 1990) and modularity and interdependence (Baldwin & Clark, 2000; Christensen, Chesbrough, & Westerman, 2002) as two sides of the same continuum. The combination of these innovation alternatives, a selection of business models, and both market and nonmarket forces must drive us to a contingent theory that predicts when a new entrant can cause an incumbent to fail. The additional circumstance-based categorization scheme introduced in this chapter completes an exhaustive list of the three circumstances identified. These circumstances should alert the incumbent in such a way as to carefully evaluate the potential threat of that specific new entrant. Figure 8.7 depicts these circumstances. The first one *financially attractive within reach* represents all the initiatives incumbents pursue while continuing along their own trajectory of improvement. Resource dependence indicates which initiatives gain impetus and their enforcement can be measured through the resource allocation process. Needless to say competition ensues established firms already live a busy life even if they are not experiencing a disruptive threat. Companies need to execute in this circumstance just to keep up with what's going on in their industry. The second one, *not financially attractive* represents initiatives that are not undertaken because they either cannibalize existing products (Henderson, 2006; Nelson & Winter, 1982) or because their business model architecture is not designed in such a way as to make money with it (Christensen, 1997a). Last, the third one *financially attractive without reach* represents circumstances where the incumbent's dominant design is solidly grounded in a technology and a channel and does not permit the incumbent to switch paths (Malerba, 2002). A new entrant in the first circumstance has almost no chances to survive. In the second circum-

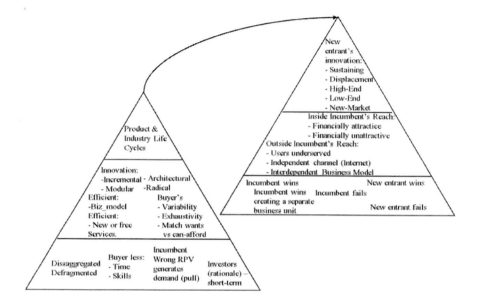

Figure 8.7.   Integrated innovation model for firm sustainability.

stance it will represent a threat to the incumbent—especially in the long-term—if it either pursues a low-end or a new-market disruption. If a new entrant perceives that the high-end disruption is enabled in an industry, gets funding to develop an interdependent business model solidly grounded in today's customer needs and brings it to market through a channel where incumbents don't have a solidly established dominance it will gain market foothold almost immediately and will start capturing a large portion of the mass market. Incumbents will see how their most valuable customers flee with no intention to return.

As Figure 8.7 intuitively describes doing research while controlling for descriptive and normative variables is very useful for pointing out where there is an anomaly current research can't account for. For instance, the limitations of this case study research show that this research attribute-based categorization scheme is only preliminary. I am sure the case study described in this research has only found the tip of the iceberg in the descriptive portion that tries to itemize the industry architecture that enables the high-end disruption mechanism. As mentioned, some constructs and frameworks have been already identified in the previous literature on innovation. Two particularly intriguing ones are the *buffer effect* and the *appropriability regimes*.

Although the nature of this case study research helps increase both the robustness and the internal validity of the study this usually happens at the expense of the external validity. Therefore, I can only guess this additional circumstance-based categorization scheme is also available in all industries. And that only future research that specifically separates between descriptive and normative categorization will allow us to visualize in its entirety the mechanism that enables the possibility of entering through a high-end disruption.

CONCLUSIONS

This study began with the aim of solving an anomaly in the disruptive innovation literature (Christensen, 2006). This anomaly is also coincidentally one of the most fundamental questions in the technological change literature: when and why a superior technology displaces the established firms. Disruptive innovation describes two additional causes of the established firms' ultimate demise, but both of them consider exclusively inferior technologies. Therefore disruptive innovation is not answering the original question. Using the disruptive innovation methodology for conducting this research (Christensen & Carlile, 2009) I was able to inductively uncover an additional circumstance-based categorization scheme named "Incumbent's Reach". This new circumstance-based categorization scheme is not rooted in the resource dependence theory—as disruptive innovation is – but in the industrial organization theory. This transforms the problem from a dilemma of resource allocation to an enabling characteristic that remains inherent in an industry architecture this research identifies.

Figure 8.7 introduces the resulting integrated model for a firm's sustainability. As previously described in the case of inferior technologies resource dependence acts as a resource prioritization system that is tied up to the incumbent's most profitable customers. These are not necessarily the most demanding customers but the ones closer to be monetized if the incumbent is willing to commit a sufficient amount of resources (Ethiraj, Ramasubbu, & Krishnan, 2012). Since no firm can target all customers the groups of unattended underserved customers can become either *lead users* and create their own products (Von Hippel, 1988) or become fertile ground for new companies that will target them with a superior technology. And this is where superior technologies usually gain market foothold.

However the results of this research show introducing a high-end disruption is not an easy task. The causal mechanism that enables the high-end disruption is less and less frequent because the natural evolution of industries makes them improve on a yearly basis leaving less and less underserved customers unattended (Fine, 1998). And superior technologies view these highly demanding groups of high-end customers as fertile ground to gain foothold in a new market. Additionally, creating an inter-dependent company from the scratch is not only a managerial challenge but also a financial one, especially if the new company must master a new fully-fledged independent commercial system. It's important to keep in mind that this research also shows these deliberate strategic decisions will only work if the industry architecture meets the following criteria: (1) it encroaches the new technology with a business model that provides a set of highly valued services for free, (2) the superior technology helps the customer experience significantly less variability when using the service (as well as more convenience and easiness of use), (3) one of the dominant technologies is not fragmented, (4) incumbent's retaliation capacity is marginal and 5) the performance trajectory of the incumbent is flat or nearly flat from the customer's point of view.

Finally, Figure 8.7 also helps visualize the limitations of this study as well as the potential areas for future research. As mentioned previously in the theory building process, constructs that overlap when describing two different phenomena need subsequent research so they can be refined according to the circumstance where they appear. For instance, the disag-gregation vs. fragmentation construct represents a good opportunity for research. As it has the potential to help us visualize more accurately when does the incumbent's reach becomes more actionable. Also, because of the number of interviews in this research this theory building process is unfin-ished. This research describes the causal model through which a superior technology will displace the incumbents. Disruptive innovation describes two causal instances where an inferior technology will overtake the incum-bents. However there are at least four new anomalies none of which nei-ther this nor to my knowledge previous research can account for. The first one is the effect of M&As and build-ups in new market entry; The second one is what are the changes resource dependence suffers when the com-pany is owned or run by its employees; The third one is which new market entry alternatives are enabled if the incumbent does not use margins but market share to maintain its competitive position and; The fourth one is what are the new market entry alternatives when the market is very small (like that of a very small country) and competition is forced to compete using tit-for-tat (Davis, Schoorman, & Donaldson, 1997) as an strategic response in front of any competitive threat.

I believe that using this research public policy officials, managers and scholars will be able to predict ex-ante when and why a new superior tech-nology will gain market foothold. They can do so by looking at the three deliberate decisions and the several technological and industrial charac-teristics described. Public policy officials must be able to regulate accord-ingly to keep these industry characteristics available in every industry.

The reason is that managers will now be capable of introducing new superior technologies with a much more acceptable success rate. Especially in the case of new companies that are intensively based on engineering or that use the Internet very intensively and whose business model rationale is grounded in the superiority of these technologies compared to the one currently used.

This research poses a profound dilemma for public policy decisions. Public policy officials must reconcile the objective of cherishing the R&D of new superior technologies with the objective of satisfying the incumbent's lobbies that focus on preventing these superior technologies from being introduced into the market by a new firm. For instance, blocking the commercialization channel—according to this research a fundamental causal requirement for a new superior technology to enter into the market successfully—is systematically blocked by the incumbent's lobbies. They have successfully passed laws and acts that prevent either the technologies or the service they provide to be offered outside a specific channel the incumbent usually controls. A very notorious example is how the music industry started to lobby more aggressively to protect themselves against internet-based business models. There are examples like that one in almost every industry. This is one of the reasons that explain why health care costs are so high in the United States (Christensen, Grossman, & Hwang, 2008). I believe these research findings and the integrated model depicted in Figure 8.7 are particularly useful for public policy officials who want to incentivize entrepreneurship or internationalization while at the same time maximizing their scarce resources. Between 1960 and 2000 established firms' volatility of revenues, employment and profitability have more than doubled (Sull, 2009). This increase in market turbulence creates opportunities public policy officials can capitalize on to deliberately revitalize their industries and make them evolve.

ACKNOWLEDGMENTS

This chapter has benefited extensively from the comments of the assistants to the Darden Entrepreneurship and Innovation Conference held in April 2010 in Charlottesville, Virginia. The author would like to especially thank Professor Mary Tripsas for her helpful comments and Professor Mauro Guillén for his support. All errors and omissions remain mine.

REFERENCES

Abernathy, W. J., & Clark, K. B. (1985). Innovation: Mapping the winds of creative destruction. *Research Policy, 14*(1), 3-22.

Abernathy, W. J., & Utterback, J. M. (1978). Patterns of industrial innovation. *Technology Review*, *80*(7), 40.

Adner, R. (2002). When are technologies disruptive? A demand-based view of the emergence of competition. *Strategic Management Journal*, *23*(8), 667-688. doi:10.1002/smj.246

Adner, R., & Zemsky, P. (2006). A demand-based perspective on sustainable competitive advantage. *Strategic Management Journal*, *27*(3), 215-239. doi:10.1002/smj.513

Agresti, A. (1996). *An introduction to categorical data analysis* (1st ed.). Gainesville, FL: Wiley-Interscience.

Agresti, A. (2002). *Categorical data analysis*. Gainesville, FL: Wiley-Interscience.

Amaldoss, W., & Shin, W. (2011). Competing for low-end markets. *Marketing Science*, *30*(5), 776-788. doi:10.1287/mksc.1110.0664

Anderson, C. (2009). *Free: The future of a radical price* (1st ed.). New York, NY: Hyperion.

Anthony, S. D. (2006). When Can You Sustain and Win? *Strategy & Innovation*, *4*(January-February), 6-9.

Arrow, K. J. (1962). Economic welfare and the allocation of resources for inventions. In R. Nelson (Ed.), *The rate and direction of inventive activity: Economic and social factors* (pp. 609-662). Princeton, NJ: Princeton University Press.

Audretsch, D. B. (1995). *Innovation and industry evolution*. Cambridge, MA: MIT Press.

Bagozzi, R. P., Yi, Y., & Phillips, L. W. (1991). Assessing construct validity in organizational research. *Administrative Science Quarterly*, *36*(3), 421-458.

Bailey, K. D. (1983). Sociological classification and cluster analysis. *Quality & Quantity*, *17*(4), 251-268. doi:10.1007/BF00167543

Baldwin, C. Y., & Clark, K. B. (2000). *Design rules*. Cambridge, MA: MIT Press.

Bhidé, A. (2000). *The origin and evolution of new businesses*. New York, NY: Oxford University Press.

Bourdieu, P., & Wacquant, L. J. D. (1992). *An invitation to reflexive sociology* (1st ed.). Chicago, IL: University of Chicago Press.

Bower, J. L. (1986). *Managing the resource allocation process: A study of corporate planning and investment*. Boston, MA: Harvard Business School Press.

Bower, J. L., & Gilbert, C. G. (2005). *From resource allocation to strategy*. Oxford, England: Oxford University Press.

Brewer, J., & Hunter, A. (1989). *Multimethod Research: A Synthesis of Styles*. Newbury Park, CA: SAGE.

Campbell, D. T. (1957). Factors relevant to the validity of experiments in social settings. *Psychological Bulletin*, *54*(4), 297-312.

Campbell, D. T., & Fiske, D. W. (1959). Convergent and discriminant validation by the multitrait-multimethod matrix. *Psychological Bulletin*, *56*(2), 81-105.

Campbell, D. T., & Stanley, J. (1963). *Experimental and quasi-experimental designs for research*. Chicago, IL: Wadsworth.

Cans, J. S., & Stern, S. (2000). Incumbency and R&D incentives: Licensing the gale of creative destruction. *Journal of Economics & Management Strategy*, *9*(4), 485-511.

Chalmers, A. F. (1976). *What is this thing called science?: An assessment of the nature and status of science and its methods*. St. Lucia, Q: University of Queensland Press.

Chandy, R. K., & Tellis, G. J. (1998). Organizing for radical product innovation: The overlooked role of willingness to cannibalize. *Journal of Marketing Research, 35*(4), 474-487.

Child, J. (2009). Context, comparison, and methodology in chinese management research. *Management and Organization Review, 5*(1), 57-73. doi:10.1111/j.1740-8784.2008.00136.x

Christensen, C. M. (1997a). *The innovator's dilemma: When new technologies cause great firms to fail*. Boston, MA: Harvard Business School Press.

Christensen, C. M. (1997b). Patterns in the evolution of product competition. *European Management Journal, 15*(2), 117-127. doi:10.1016/S0263-2373(96)00081-3

Christensen, C. M. (2006). The ongoing process of building a theory of disruption. *Journal of Product Innovation Management, 23*(1), 39-55. Blackwell. doi:10.1111/j.1540-5885.2005.00180.x

Christensen, C. M., & Carlile, P. R. (2006). Practice and malpractice in management research (Unpublished working paper). Harvard Business School.

Christensen, C. M., & Carlile, P. R. (2009). Course research: Using the case method to build and teach management theory. *Academy of Management Learning & Education, 8*(2), 240-251.

Christensen, C. M., & Raynor, M. E. (2003). *The innovator's solution: Creating and sustaining successful growth*. Boston, MA: Harvard Business School Press.

Christensen, C. M., Anthony, S. D., & Roth, E. A. (2004). *Seeing what's next: Using the theories of innovation to predict industry change*. Boston, MA: Harvard Business School Press.

Christensen, C. M., Chesbrough, H. W., & Westerman, G. (2002). Disruption, disintegration and the dissipation of differentiability. *Industrial and Corporate Change, 11*(5), 955-993.

Christensen, C. M., Grossman, J. H., & Hwang, J. (2008). *The Innovator's prescription: A disruptive solution for health care*. New York, NY: McGraw-Hill.

Clark, K. B. (1985). The interaction of design hierarchies and market concepts in technological evolution. *Research Policy, 14*(5), 235-251.

Comin, D., Hobijn, B., & Rovito, E. (2006). Five facts you need to know about technology diffusion. *National Bureau of Economic Research Working Paper Series, No. 11928*.

Danneels, E. (2004). Disruptive technology reconsidered: A critique and research agenda. *Journal of Product Innovation Management, 21*(4), 246-258. Blackwell. doi:10.1111/j.0737-6782.2004.00076.x

Danneels, E. (2006). Dialogue on the effects of disruptive technology on firms and industries. *Journal of Product Innovation Management, 23*(1), 2-4. doi:10.1111/j.1540-5885.2005.00174.x

Davis, J. H., Schoorman, F. D., & Donaldson, L. (1997). Toward a stewardship theory of management. *Academy of Management Review, 22*(1), 20-47.

Dent-Brown, K., & Wang, M. (2006). The mechanism of storymaking: A grounded theory study of the 6-part story method. *The Arts in Psychotherapy, 33*(4), 316-330. doi:10.1016/j.aip.2006.04.002

Di Benedetto, C. A. (2006). Welcome to a new volume of JPIM! *Journal of Product Innovation Management.* doi:10.1111/j.1540-5885.2005.00173.x

Dosi, G. (1982). Technological paradigms and technological trajectories: A suggested interpretation of the determinants and directions of technical change. *Research Policy, 11*(3), 147.

Edmondson, A. C., & McManus, S. E. (2007). Methodological fit in management field research. *Academy of Management Review, 32*(4), 1155-1179.

Eisenhardt, K. M. (1989). Making fast strategic decisions in high-velocity environments. *The Academy of Management Journal, 32*(3), 543-576.

Eisenhardt, K. M., & Graebner, M. E. (2007). Theory building from cases: Opportunities and challenges. *Academy of Management Journal, 50*(1), 25-32. Academy of Management.

Ethiraj, S. K., Ramasubbu, N., & Krishnan, M. S. (2012). Does complexity deter customer-focus? *Strategic Management Journal, 33*(2), 137-161. doi:10.1002/smj.947

Fielding, N., & Lee, R. M. (1998). *Computer analysis and qualitative research.* London: Sage.

Fine, C. H. (1998). *Clockspeed?: Winning industry control in the age of temporary advantage.* Reading, MA: Perseus Books.

Fine, G. A., & Elsbach, K. D. (2000). Ethnography and experiment in social psychological theory building: Tactics for integrating qualitative field data with quantitative lab data. *Journal of Experimental Social Psychology, 36*(1), 51-76.

Foster, R. N. (1986). *Innovation: The attacker's advantage.* New York, NY: Summit Books.

Freeman, C., & Soete, L. (1997). *The economics of industrial innovation* (3rd ed.). Cambridge, MA: The MIT Press.

George, M. L., Works, J., & Watson-Hemphill, K. (2005). *Fast innovation: Achieving superior differentiation, speed to market, and increased profitability.* New York, NY: McGraw-Hill.

Gibbert, M., Ruigrok, W., & Wicki, B. (2008). What passes as a rigorous case study? *Strategic Management Journal, 29*(13), 1465-1474. doi:10.1002/smj.722

Gilbert, C. G. (2006). Change in the presence of residual fit: Can competing frames coexist? *Organization Science, 17*(1), 150-167. doi:10.1287/orsc.1050.0160

Gilbert, R. J., & Newbery, D. M. G. (1982). Preemptive patenting and the persistence of monopoly. *American Economic Review, 72*(3), 514-526.

Glaser, B. G. (1978). *Theoretical sensitivity: Advances in the methodology of grounded theory.* Mill Valley, CA: Sociology Press.

Glaser, B. G. (1992). *Basics of grounded theory analysis. Emergence vs forcing.* Mill Valley, CA: Sociology Press.

Glaser, B. G. (1998). *Doing grounded theory. Issues and discussions.* Mill Valley, CA: Sociology Press.

Glaser, B. G., & Strauss, A. L. (1967). *The Discovery of Grounded Theory; Strategies for Qualitative Research.* Chicago, IL: Aldine.

Govindarajan, V., & Kopalle, P. K. (2006). Disruptiveness of innovations: Measurement and an assessment of reliability and validity. *Strategic Management Journal*, 27(2), 189-199. doi:10.1002/smj.511

Govindarajan, V., Kopalle, P. K., & Danneels, E. (2011). The effects of mainstream and emerging customer orientations on radical and disruptive innovations. *Journal of Product Innovation Management*, 28(s1), 121-132. doi:10.1111/j.1540-5885.2011.00865.x

Henderson, R. M. (1993). Underinvestment and incompetence as responses to radical innovation: Evidence from the photolithographic alignment equipment industry. *The Rand Journal of Economics*, 24(2), 248.

Henderson, R. M. (2006). The innovator's dilemma as a problem of organizational competence. *The Journal of Product Innovation Management*, 23(1), 5.

Henderson, R. M., & Clark, K. B. (1990). Architectural innovation: The reconfiguration of existing product technologies and the failure of established firms. *Administrative Science Quarterly*, 35, 9-30.

Hillman, A. (2011). Editor's comments: What is the future of theory? *The Academy of Management Review*, 36(4), 606-608.

Hoetker, G. (2007). The use of logit and probit models in strategic management research: Critical issues. *Strategic Management Journal*, 28(4), 331-343. doi:10.1002/smj.582

Jick, T. D. (1979). Mixing qualitative and quantitative methods: Triangulation in action. *Administrative Science Quarterly*, 24(4), 602-611.

Klepper, S. (1997). Industry life cycles. *Industrial & Corporate Change*, 6(1), 119-143.

Kuckartz, A. M., & Kuckartz, U. (2006). Qualitative Text Analysis Using MAXQDA. In J. Andreu Abela (Ed.), *Journal of Political and Social Applied Research* (pp. 24-46). Andalusian Bar Association of Doctors and Graduates in Political Science and Sociology.

Kuhn, T. S. (1962). *The structure of scientific revolutions*. Chicago, IL: University of Chicago Press.

Lakatos, I., & Musgrave, A. (1974). *Criticism and the growth of knowledge*. Cambridge, England: Cambridge University Press.

Lawrence, P. R., & Lorsch, J. W. (1967). *Organization and environment: Managing differentiation and integration*. Boston, MA: Division of Research, Graduate School of Business Administration, Harvard University.

Lee, E. S., & Forthofer, R. N. (2005). *Analyzing complex survey data: Quantitative applications in the social sciences*. Thousand Oaks, CA: SAGE.

Lee, T. W. (1999). *Using qualitative methods in organizational research. Organizational research methods*. Thousand Oaks, CA: SAGE.

Leonard-Barton, D. (1995). *Wellsprings of knowledge: Building and sustaining the sources of innovation*. Boston, MA: Harvard Business School Press.

Levitt, T. (1974). The managerial merry-go-round. *Harvard Business Review*, 52(4), 120-129.

Loef, M. M. (1990). *Understanding teachers' knowledge about building instruction on children's mathematical thinking: Applications of a personal construct approach* (Unpublished doctoral dissertation). University of Wisconsin-Madison.

Malerba, F. (2002). Sectoral systems of innovation and production. *Research Policy, 31*(2), 247-264. doi:10.1016/S0048-7333(01)00139-1

March, J. G., & Simon, H. A. (1958). *Organizations*. New York, NY: Wiley.

Markides, C. C. (2006). Disruptive innovation: In need of better theory. *Journal of Product Innovation Management, 23*(1), 19-25. doi:10.1111/j.1540-5885.2005.00177.x

Marquis, D. G. (1969). The anatomy of successful innovations. In E. B. S. O. Innovation (Ed.), *Managing Advancing Technology. Volume I* (pp. 35-48). New York, NY: American Management Association.

McKelvey, B. (2004). Toward a complexity science of entrepreneurship. *Journal of Business Venturing, 19*(3), 313-341. doi:10.1016/S0883-9026(03)00034-X

Miles, M. B., & Huberman, A. M. (1994). *Qualitative Data Analysis: An expanded sourcebook* (2nd ed.). Thousand Oaks, CA: SAGE.

Murmann, J. P., & Frenken, K. (2006). Toward a systematic framework for research on dominant designs, technological innovations, and industrial change. *Research Policy, 35*(7), 925-952. doi:10.1016/j.respol.2006.04.011

Myers, S., & Marquis, D. G. (1969). *Successful industrial innovations; A study of factors underlying innovation in selected firms*. Washington, DC: National Science Foundation.

Nelson, R. R., & Winter, S. G. (1982). *An evolutionary theory of economic change*. Cambridge, MA: Belknap Press of Harvard University Press.

Pfeffer, J., & Salancik, G. R. (1978). *The external control of organizations: A resource dependence perspective*. New York, NY: Harper & Row.

Polli, R., & Cook, V. (1969). Validity of the product life cycle. *Journal of Business, 42*(4), 385-400.

Porter, M. E. (1980). *Competitive strategy: Techniques for analyzing industries and competitors*. New York, NY: Free Press.

Porter, M. E., & Siggelkow, N. (2008). Contextuality within activity systems and sustainability of competitive advantage. *Academy of Management Perspectives, 22*(2), 34-56.

Rivette, K. G., & Kline, D. (2000). *Rembrandts in the attic: Unlocking the hidden value of patents*. Boston, MA: Harvard Business School Press.

Sattath, S., & Tversky, A. (1977). Additive similarity trees. *Psychometrika, 42*(3), 319-345. Springer. doi:10.1007/BF02293654

Schilling, M. A. (1998). Technological lockout: An integrative model of the economic and strategic factors driving technology success and failure. *Academy of Management Review, 23*(2), 267-284.

Schoenmakers, W., & Duysters, G. (2010). The technological origins of radical inventions. *Research Policy, 39*(8), 1051-1059. doi:10.1016/j.respol.2010.05.013

Schumpeter, J. A. (1942). *Capitalism, socialism, and democracy*. New York, NY: Harper & Brothers.

Schumpeter, J. A., & Opie, R. (1934). *The theory of economic development: An inquiry into profits, capital, credit, interest, and the business cycle*. Cambridge, MA: Harvard University Press.

Simon, H. A. (2001). What makes technology revolutionary. *Educause*, 28-39.

Slater, S. F., & Mohr, J. J. (2006). Successful development and commercialization of technological innovation: Insights based on strategy type. *Journal of Product Innovation Management, 23*(1), 26-33. doi:10.1111/j.1540-5885.2005.00178.x

Sood, A., & Tellis, G. J. (2010). Demystifying disruption: A new model for understanding and predicting disruptive technologies. *Marketing Science, 30*(2), 339-354. doi:10.1287/mksc.1100.0617

Strauss, A. L. (1987). *Qualitative analysis for social scientists.* New York, NY: Cambridge University Press.

Strauss, A. L., & Corbin, J. M. (1990). *Basics of qualitative research: Grounded theory procedures and techniques.* Newbury Park, CA: SAGE.

Suddaby, R. R. (2006). From the editors: What grounded theory is not. *Academy of Management Journal,* 633-642.

Sull, D. N. (2009). *The upside of turbulence: Seizing opportunity in an uncertain world* (p. 288 pages). New York, NY: Harper Business.

Sull, D. N. (2011, Autumn). 10 clues to opportunity. *Strategy+Business, Booz, Allen & Hamilton, 64,* 5.

Sull, D. N., Tedlow, R. S., & Rosenbloom, R. S. (1997). Managerial commitments and technological change in the us tire industry. *Industrial and Corporate Change, 6*(2), 461-501.

Tashakkori, A., & Teddlie, C. (2003). *Handbook of mixed methods in social & behavioral research.* Thousand Oaks, CA: SAGE.

Teece, D. J. (1986). Profiting From technological innovation: Implications for integration, collaboration, licensing and public policy. *Research Policy, 15*(6), 285-305. doi:10.1016/0048-7333(86)90027-2

Teece, D. J. (2006). Reflections on "Profiting from Innovation." *Research Policy, 35*(8), 1131-1146. doi:10.1016/j.respol.2006.09.009

Teece, D. J. (2010). Business models, business strategy and innovation. *Long Range Planning, 43*(2-3), 172-194. doi:10.1016/j.lrp.2009.07.003

Tellis, G. J. (2006). Disruptive technology or visionary leadership? *Journal of Product Innovation Management, 23*(1), 34-38. doi:10.1111/j.1540-5885.2005.00179.x

Tellis, G. J., Hauser, J., & Griffin, A. (2006). Research on innovation: A review and agenda for marketing science. *Marketing Science, 25*(6), 687-717. doi:10.1287/mksc.1050.0144

Thompson, D. V., Hamilton, R. W., & Rust, R. T. (2005). Feature fatigue: When product capabilities become too much of a good thing. *Journal of Marketing Research, 42*(4), 431-442.

Tripsas, M. (1996). *Surviving radical technological change: An empirical study of the typesetter industry* (Unpublished dissertation). Massachussets Institute of Technology.

Tripsas, M. (1997). Unraveling the process of creative destruction: Complementary assets and incumbent survival in the typesetter industry. *Strategic Management Journal, 18*(Special Issue), 119-142.

Tripsas, M. (2008). Customer preference discontinuities: A trigger for radical technological change. *Managerial and Decision Economics, 29*(2-3), 79-97. doi:10.1002/mde.1389

Tushman, M. L., & Anderson, P. (1986). Technological discontinuities and organizational environments. *Administrative Science Quarterly, 31*(3), 439-465.

Utterback, J. M. (1994). *Mastering the dynamics of innovation: How companies can seize opportunities in the face of technological change.* Boston, MA: Harvard Business School Press.

Utterback, J. M., & Acee, H. J. (2005). Disruptive technologies: An expanded view. *International Journal of Innovation Management, 9*(1), 1-17.

Von Hippel, E. (1988). *The sources of innovation.* New York, NY: Oxford University Press.

Walsh, J. P., Tushman, M. L., Kimberly, J. R., Starbuck, B., & Ashford, S. (2007). On the relationship between research and practice: Debate and reflections. *Journal of Management Inquiry, 16*(2), 128-154. doi:10.1177/1056492607302654

Yin, R. K. (2002). *Applications of case study research* (2nd ed.) Thousands, Oak, CA: SAGE.

Yin, R. K. (2003). *Case study research: Design and methods* (3rd ed.). Thousand Oaks, CA: SAGE.

CHAPTER 9

CHEAP SOLUTIONS

Managing a Coproducing Crowd of Strangers to Solve Your Problems

Brendan M. Richard

ABSTRACT

The growing phenomenon of Crowdsourcing has introduced new opportunities and challenges for managers. The opportunities include inviting a worldwide group of talented and educated people to contribute to coproducing solutions for organizational problems. The challenges include redesigning the organization structure, incentive system, and information platform to allow a crowd of stranger's access to the organization and its intellectual property. This chapter focuses on the facilitating factors that enable crowdsourcing, the contingency factors that shape how crowdsourcing is implemented and the outcomes that ensue. The key factors that can enable managers to effectively assess how they can use a crowd of strangers to coproduce solutions to their problems are presented and discussed.

Global Perspectives on Technological Innovation, pp. 261–287
Copyright © 2013 by Information Age Publishing
All rights of reproduction in any form reserved.

CROWDSOURCING: A NEW ORGANIZATIONAL STRATEGY

In his work on the wealth of networks, Benkler (2006) described in detail the two emerging trends which allow for the rise of the networked information economy: the proliferation of the Internet and personal computers, and the rise of an economy based upon information production. The increasingly networked information economy has become a potential platform for mass collaboration and, when harnessed and focused by a firm, for crowdsourcing projects that problem solve. Separately O'Reilly (2005) called attention to the post dotcom boom centered on the emerging trend of what he termed Web 2.0. Web 2.0 marked a shift in the way that the Internet was being utilized, from people passively consuming to actively participating. YouTube, Wikipedia, Facebook, Twitter and countless other online participation platforms are examples of Web 2.0. This cultural shift in the usage of the Internet has opened the door for mass collaboration for problem solving and the use of the growing phenomena of Crowdsourcing.

Crowdsourcing itself is when a networked group is invited to participate in helping to find solutions to a firm's problems. These problems can be general or specific. A general problem would be contributing to a Wiki for example where the crowd adds knowledge to a data base or information source. A specific solution is where the crowd is invited to help solve a problem that a specific organization has such as new source code development for a software application or the design of clothing. The applications of crowdsourcing are amazingly broad with reported uses by the entertainment, graphic design, medical and financing industries as well as within the academic, scientific and artistic communities. The challenge for organizations seeking to use crowdsourcing as a cheap alternative to employing a panel of experts or consultants to help solve its problems is in how to successfully manage this new organizational structure where strangers are coproducing solutions with the organization.

Managers must learn how to successfully manage nonemployees who are invited into the organization to help it solve problems. This chapter describes the preconditions for organizations to successfully utilize crowdsourcing, the organizational factors that must be managed to use a crowd of strangers, the factors associated with the problems that lend themselves to crowdsourcing, and some suggestions for further research into this largely unexplored topic.

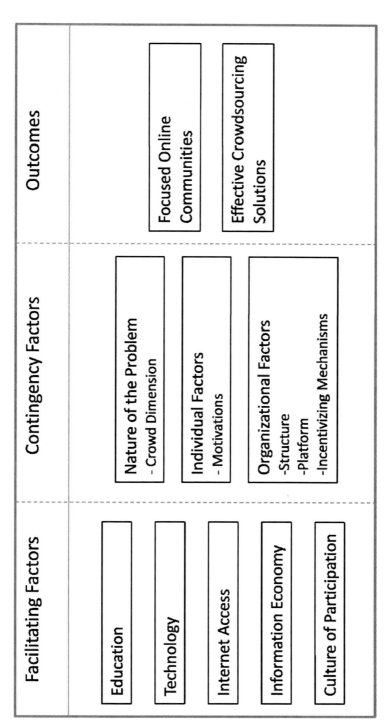

Figure 9.1. Crowdsourcing model.

CROWDSOURCING: FACILITATING FACTORS

Several trends have enhanced the ability of the networked information economy to become an environment ripe for mass collaboration. First there has evolved a surplus of underemployed and educated talent that is looking for opportunities to use their talent and skills in their discretionary time. Second there has grown a commitment to online communities (Howe, 2008) by the group of people that have talent and time. This has led to a search by this educated group for opportunities to use their underutilized skills on their easily accessed networks. This has created a critical mass of participants (Sharma, 2010) willing to contribute a minor investment of their discretionary time (Heylighen, 2007). Finally the old Web 1.0 model, which "primarily supported webpage publishing and e-commerce" has been replaced with the "Web 2.0 model [which] is focused on collaborative design environments, social media, and social networks creating feasibility spaces for new cultures that allow people to participate rather than being confined to passive consumer roles" (Fischer, 2010, p. 4). The recent trend of educated talent with discretionary time in conjunction with access to Web 2.0 has created the rise of online communities. These communities offer an outlet for participatory interaction of these talented people for social purposes and have set the stage for also extending their participation into problem-solving purposes (Howe, 2008; Kozinets, Hemetsberger, & Schau, 2008).

Beyond the mere existence of the Internet, its ubiquitous nature, and the recently developed culture of participation by talented, educated people with discretionary time, there are several features of the Internet itself that can change the way an organization is structured different from traditionally conceived markets and hierarchies. Howe (2008) notes that the Internet minimizes transaction costs which are normally the key consideration in organization design strategy. In addition, contributors operate in a near perfect meritocracy, as they are judged on the merits of their contributions, not on their demographic characteristics (age, race, gender, income, location, education, etc.). The networked information economy also has the ability to foster the creation of nonrivalry of information. Traditional economic models assign value assuming the finite nature of goods or services, but this is not true for information. The Internet and its participatory platforms allow for essentially zero publishing costs, free replication, and partial excludability (difficulty in preventing transfer of information) (Heylighen, 2007).

Benkler asserts that we are in the midst of a radical transformation in how we create our information environment. "The networked information environment has dramatically transformed the marketplace, creating new modes and opportunities for how we produce and consume information.

Crowdsourcing is used to create value in information technology, the arts, basic research, and retail business" (Kazman & Chen, 2009, p. 76). Benkler (2006) notes that within this new environment, most startling is "the rise of effective, large-scale cooperative efforts—peer production of information, knowledge, and culture.... We are beginning to see the expansion of the model not only to our core software platforms, but beyond them into every domain of information and cultural production" (p. 4). It is within this networked information economy ripe for mass collaboration, achieved through technological, educational, network access and cultural advancements that firms can undertake crowdsourcing projects to find solutions to their problems. Understanding the nature of the problem, and how best to manipulate organizational (structure, platforms and mechanisms) and individual (motivation) factors will lead to the creation of focused online communities and effective crowdsourcing solutions.

WHY WOULD AN ORGANIZATION WANT A CROWD TO SOLVE ITS PROBLEMS?

Crowdsourcing is a relatively low-cost, flexible, and rapid method for obtaining a better idea or a more valuable service. By utilizing mass collaboration a vast repository of knowledge can be created, organized and integrated into a solution that is beneficial to the firm. Kazman and Chen (2009, p. 1) note that "the importance of this form of production is undeniable; as of May 2009 five of the 10 most popular Web sites—Myspace.com, YouTube.com, Facebook.com, Wikipdiea.com and Blogger.com—were produced this way, according to Alexia.com; with the exception of Wikipedia, all are for-profit enterprises." Crowdsourcing is also scalable on demand, from no expenditure to full spending as required, and is a lower cost option for firms because it avoids using internal staff or professional services for lower level tasks. Effective crowdsourcing allows firms to reduce the time it takes to bring new products and services to the market. All of this is possible because unlike traditional hierarchical firm structures, by crowdsourcing a firm is managing the crowd itself, not individuals, and because under certain circumstances a crowd is more effective and efficient than professional service providers (Dawson & Bynghall, 2011).

Within a traditional firm, human resources is concerned with the hiring of specific individuals who hold certain skill sets and experiences. The search for new hires to fill open positions is limited by funding, time, and demographic characteristics of potential candidates such as geographical location, age, education, and citizenship. These limitations do not exist when a firm employs a crowdsourcing solution. Crowdsourcing effectively mitigates the downsides of traditional hiring practices. By outsourcing a firm's project to a crowd, it is relying on the diversity of the masses. The more contributors to a project, the greater the diversity of contributors, the more likely those contributors with skills required by the project will be involved.

It is important to understand the concept of collective creativity and how it can be beneficial to crowdsourcing. Kozinets and colleagues (2008, p. 341), note that

> most studies of consumer creativity thus far take as their focus the individual consumer, perhaps the lone inventor working alone in her garage, or the individual consumer creating a world of imagination from mass culture.... Yet actual studies of lived creative behavior reveal that it is highly collaborative and often more innovatively applied to real-world problems than many theorists previously suspected. (p. 341)

Individually, the two main ingredients for creativity are curiosity and drive, where curiosity can be viewed as openness and a willingness to explore and drive as working hard and having perseverance (Csikszentmihalyi, 1996). Collective creativity differs from individual creativity though, as it requires social interactions to occur, which take the form of four sets of interrelated activities: help seeking, help giving, reflective reframing, and reinforcing behavior (Hargadon & Bechky, 2006). The more individuals a firm has within a crowd, each with their own unique background and experiences, undertaking these interrelated activities, the greater the variation in ideas generated will be. These multitudes of diverse individuals will also bring their experience to bear in developing the criteria of idea selection, as well as in developing the chosen ideas, propagating and promoting them (Kozinets et al., 2008).

Howe (2008) notes the existence of a phenomenon in which diversity trumps ability. This phenomenon is supported by Page's (2007) work on collective intelligence in which he seeks to explain why a random collection of problem solvers can outperform a collection of individuals with the most ability. It is based on the notion that those at the top echelons of ability are actually a relatively homogenous group, and it is this lack of diversity that hinders them from obtaining the most valuable solutions to problems. Furthermore, firms benefit from the hybrid nature of idea generation that is employed in crowdsourcing. Girotra, Terwiesch, and Ulrich (2010) propose that a hybrid idea generation method, in which an individual is allowed to brainstorm independently before meeting in a team, is more beneficial than a purely independent or teamwork based method. Crowdsourcing allows for this hybrid method as individuals are able to contribute both independently and/or rely on the contributions of others to improve their own work.

Surowiecki (2004) breaks down the advantages of crowd wisdom into three categories: cognition, coordination and cooperation. He posits that processing power will be faster and more reliable, that the coordination of information and tasks will be streamlined and more efficient, and that within free market conditions individuals can form networks of trust without a centralized information processing system dictating their actions. Taken together, a firm can obtain increased processing power, access to vast amounts of knowledge, a greater variety in idea generation, increased levels of creativity, and faster implementation, all at lower cost. Firms that implement crowdsourcing to develop solutions to their problems can do so at both a lower cost and with increased benefits over the more traditional methods for idea generation and task completion.

The Value of Effectively Crowdsourcing Solutions

If a firm has not contemplated how it might be able to effectively implement crowdsourcing, it is likely that its competitors have. Fisher (2009) surveyed 100 top marketing executives in regard to crowdsourcing, to determine their familiarity with it and its perceived benefits. Over 70% of respondents acknowledged familiarity with the term and possessing knowledge of its perceived benefits. Summarizing the results of his study Fisher writes:

> The 2008 survey uncovered two startling results: 1) senior executives rated crowdsourcing and consumer collaboration groups as effective as internal R&D staff for developing ideas for new product/services; 2) one half of the executives believed crowdsourcing would produce cost efficiencies ranging from 10% to 30% over either traditional in-house approaches or external professional services. Fully 90% of the executives indicated that crowdsourcing is attractive based on these findings. (p. 2)

These expressions of faith in crowdsourcing are not merely limited to the results of Fisher's survey though; there are several tangible examples of firms undertaking successful crowdsourcing projects. In *Wikinomics* Tapscott and Williams (2006) retell the story of Goldcorp, a struggling gold-mining firm. Rob McEwen, CEO, inspired by Linus Torvalds and the development of the Linux operating system, decided to crowdsource the process of locating gold deposits. McEwen was willing to go against the prevailing culture of secrecy within the industry by releasing all of the firm's intellectual property, geological data collected since 1948, to the public. Offering a total of $575,000 in prize money, the results of the challenge led to the discovery of approximately 8 million ounces of gold, estimated to be worth over $3 billion. This example is important because it dispels the myth that crowdsourcing is only valuable to Web 2.0 firms such as YouTube and Wikipedia.

Fast forward to 2012 and several large companies, organizations and government agencies have observed and recognized the benefits of crowdsourcing solutions, and are at present implementing their own. Wal-Mart Labs, Wal-Mart's innovation division has initiated a campaign entitled "Get on the Shelf," in which companies can compete for placement on Wal-Mart's website. Interested parties post videos of their products onto Wal-Mart's online system, at which point they are voted on publically over the Internet (Kelly, 2012). The U.S. Department of Defense has also come around to the benefits of utilizing crowdsourcing, and is working on "fun to play" games that contain software that could potentially have bugs or vulnerabilities. At a time when defense spending in the United States has flat lined, and the United States military is finding it difficult to allocate funding toward testing weapon systems software, the "Crowdsourced Formal Verification" program will leverage a huge user base of casual game players, acting as code reviewers, that would otherwise be impossible through traditional hiring or outsourcing methods (McGlaun, 2012). Finally Mountain Dew, Coca-Cola and Sam Adams have all allowed crowds the ability to craft new products by having a say in determining the product features. Budweiser even asked its fans to be the ones who decided which commercials it would run during the super bowl. (Wasserman, 2012).

Crowdsourcing is not limited geographically either; crowdsourced tasks are being completed by citizens in underdeveloped nations, both to benefit firms in developed nations and the communities that they themselves live in. In countries such as India, citizens are taking part in Amazon's Mechanical Turk program, a crowdsourced Internet marketplace, by completing Human Intelligence Tasks that computers are as of now still unable to perform. The compensation is small relative to that in developed nations, but to those individuals in developing nations it can be quite beneficial. Ipeirotis (2010) conducted a survey revealing that 34% of Mechanical Turk workers come from India. From those workers surveyed who were in India, approximately 26% noted that they were utilizing Mechanical Turk as their primary source of income, with approximately 36% listing it a as secondary source of income.

Glickhouse (2012), who wrote an article titled a "Crowdsourcing guide to Latin America," details how crowdsourcing has become a popular method for involvement by citizens in law enforcement, public health, consumer rights and social issues. She describes how in Argentina the Antidrug Association created a narcotics trafficking map utilizing Google maps, so that citizens could post tips on suspected locations of drug sales and smuggling routes. Glickhouse goes on to note the existence of similar crime prevention and reporting collaboration tools across the region including in Brazil, Chile, Costa Rica, Mexico, Panama, Peru, and Venezuela. By being a member of the crowd and contributing, citizens within these countries are helping to rid crime from their own communities.

WHAT ARE THE FACTORS THAT INFLUENCE THE ABILITY OF AN ORGANIZATION TO EFFECTIVELY USE CROWDS?

The Nature of the Problem

Crowdsourcing utilizes the networked information economy to outsource to and influence a crowd to meet its goals. For a firm to use crowdsourcing, it has to create a relationship with a crowd. That means it must identify and connect with the right crowd with the right knowledge for the problem it wishes to engage their participation. Moreover, it must have a platform in place that permits access to organizational data relevant to the problem the crowd is asked to help solve. Finally the firm must have organizational enabling mechanisms in place such as managers receptive to external input from strangers and a process for recognizing and rewarding those members of the crowd who add value to the organization. Thus, the relationship between a firm and the crowd must be built on identifying the goals of the crowd, and the inducements the crowd expects from the firm to influence, motivate, regulate and support it. It is necessary to understand the nature of the crowd and the desired communities within it because they are the foundation upon which crowdsourcing resides.

Understanding the Crowd

It is advantageous for a firm to tap into and effectively crowdsource a community that is already in existence. Firms should actively scan the online environment to determine if an existing community shares the same basic purpose and/or goals as the firm. If a community does not exist, and a firm decides to establish one to suit its needs, it should proceed delicately as any action that is perceived by potential participants as being exploitative would be detrimental to the firm's ability to crowdsource to solve its problems.

Online communities can take on several unique configurations, and firms should be aware of which it is dealing with. Kozinets and colleagues (2008) classified online creative consumer communities into a framework consisting of four groups in order to explain collective consumer creativity and innovation: crowds, hives, mobs and swarms. The four groups are organized within a framework by two dimensions, the extent to which a community is goal oriented and its level of concentration. The first dimension, designated collective innovation orientation, depicts whether a community has a goal related orientation, or is community oriented, in which innovations are a random by-product of day-to-day interactions. The second dimension is collective innovation concentration, which depicts the percentage of the community that contributes, where a high concentration has relatively few contributors and vice-versa. The nature of a firm's problem will influence the type of community it focuses its efforts on.

Crowds

Crowds are large organized groups that are formed in order to complete specific, well defined projects. Crowds have a lower concentration of collective innovation because the innovation is spread across a larger number of individuals. They are focused on the completion of a single project and so they tend to be well organized and focused in their efforts. As the name implies crowds are the most frequently used type of online community by firms seeking to crowdsource projects. If a firm's goal involves the collection of information, or the generation of specific ideas or tasks that can be completed by a broad subset of the general public, the

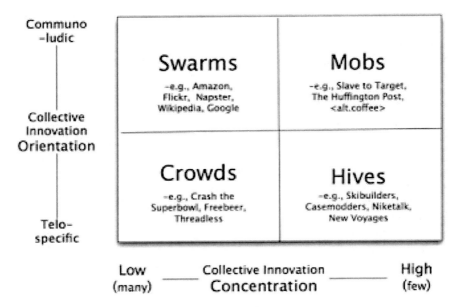

Figure 9.2.   Typology of online creative consumer communities by Kozinets and colleagues (2008).

most beneficial group orientation is crowds, which has a low collective innovation concentration, resulting in mass collaboration from the most possible contributors. The T-shirt design outsourcing website Threadless is a classic example of a crowd focused around a specific goal, that of designing innovative, popular T-shirts. Neither submitting designs, nor voting on the submitted designs requires rare skills or talents and so a large percentage of the online community can participate should they so choose (Kozinets et al., 2008).

Hives

Hives, like crowds, are focused on the completion of a specific goal, but if a firm is seeking the generation of complex ideas or more advanced tasks which can only be completed by a highly talented subset of the population, then the usage of a hive community would be more appropriate. Hives are centers of skills and excellence. They typically consist of well educated skilled individuals who finding themselves unchallenged at work seek out opportunities to intellectually occupy themselves. "On sites, such as Niketalk or SourceForge, where collectives of consumers/users self-select, get organized around a common interest, develop rules, hierarchies, and workflow applications to invent new shoe designs and software from scratch, we can also see the networking, systematization, high individual contributions, and project-focus of Hive" (Kozinets et al., 2008, p. 348). The motivation behind individual's participation within a hive community, as opposed to crowds, is more intrinsic. Firms should tread carefully in attempting to utilize a hive community, as this type of online community is resistant to, and might be disinterested in extrinsic benefits such as minute direct payments.

Mobs

Mobs, like hives, consist of a narrow subset of individuals, who are skilled and talented, although unlike hives, their efforts aren't directed toward the completion of a specific goal. Their contributions are directed toward the community in general or prolific individuals who act as sources of inspirational leadership. While the community tends to form around these influential sources, the goal still remains fluidic, and can change at any point in time with relative ease. Since this form of community has no specific goal that defines its existence, if a firm were to seek out an influential source, it would have the potential to direct the contributions of the community toward its ends.

Swarms

Swarms are low in both collective innovation concentration and innovation; they consist of masses of individuals, a community who contribute in minute ways, and have no overarching goal. These are individuals who embrace Web 2.0, rating products, tagging pictures and commenting on whatever might interest them. While individually their contributions might be miniscule, aggregated to the whole swarm community, the contributions reflect a higher quality, a harnessed collective intelligence.

> Yet this is a particular kind of collective intelligence: the collective intelligence of relatively larger groups, doing relatively invisible informational labor, unaware for the most part that their online activities are, en masse, contributing value to the capital ventures of corporations. (Kozinets et al., 2008, p. 350)

In addition to seeking to understand a given crowd's orientation, a firm should actively seek out existing crowds that are wise. Surowiecki (2004) adds to the concept of crowds based on goals and participant concentrations, identifying criteria with which crowds can become wise, and as a result more useful to firms. Surowiecki lists four criteria that influence a crowd's level of wisdom as: diversity of opinion, independence, decentralization and aggregation. Optimally a wise crowd would consist of a system in which each person has private information, has their own opinions separate from those of the group, has the opportunity to specialize, and whose contributions are aggregated into the collective.

The challenge of the firm is to align the goal of the crowd with its own, forming a focused online community dedicated to solving the firm's problem. It is important for firms to remember though that communities are not appreciative of being controlled. Communities appreciate the feeling of ownership in their contributions, not exploitation solely for a firm's profitability. To effectively crowdsource firms should form focused online communities, but in a manner in which it does not appear that the firm is taking advantage of the community.

Individual Factors: Motivations

Once a firm has identified an online community that has the potential to solve its problem, it becomes necessary to identify and understand the motivations that drive individuals within that community to become participants. Traditionally monetary compensation has been the primary incentive given to agents to perform tasks. Motivations to participate in a crowd that will use a social network to coproduce solutions for an unaffiliated company or organization are more complex and numerous though than mere monetary compensation. Studies have shown the following factors motivate individuals to contribute to peer production in crowds: self-advancement (Heylighen, 2007), recognition and esteem from within the community (Heylighen, 2007; Lerner, 2002), altruism (Heylighen, 2007), improved status/reputation, desires to benefit society and pass on knowledge, curiosity and joy of practicing a craft (Csikszentmihalyi, 1975, 1990, 1996), feelings of connectedness and social integration, and deriving pleasure from cultivating talent (Lakhani & Wolf, 2005).

Kaufmann, Schulze, and Veit (2011) sought to understand worker motivation in crowdsourcing by developing a model from an amalgamation of motivation constructs. Crowdsourcing motivations are categorized based on whether they are intrinsic or extrinsic, where

> Intrinsic motivation exists if an individual is activated because of its seeking for the fulfillment generated by the activity (e.g., acting just for fun). In the case of extrinsic motivation the activity is just an instrument for achieving a certain desired outcome (e.g. acting for money or to avoid sanctions). (Kaufmann et al., 2011, p. 3)

Specific to crowdsourcing, Kaufman and colleagues classify intrinsic motivations as those that are either enjoyment based or community based, whereas extrinsic motivations involve immediate payments, delayed payments or social motivations. A proper understanding of individual's motivations to contribute, both intrinsic and extrinsic, will influence how a firm creates mechanisms to guide the crowd in solving its problems.

Altruism

Contributing to the community doesn't need to be on a grand scale within the world of peer production. As Heylighen (2007) notes, while traditional economic models assume that resources are scarce and consumable, information is nonmaterial in nature, it can be replicated in vast numbers at almost no cost, and can be easily shared and distributed via the Internet, again at almost no cost. As a result information is deemed to be representative of a nonrival economic model and operates differently from traditional transaction costs. For those among the community that wish to act altruistically in regard to information sharing, the barriers to doing so are almost nonexistent. If an individual has already taken the time and resources to create information for self-benefit, the additional effort required to share it with the community is minimal. This does not imply that everyone within a community will act altruistically and contribute, rather only that those individuals that wish to share have the ability to share. Kazman and Chen (2009) developed the metropolis model to illustrate the interactions between the various players in the crowdsourcing process. In concentric rings: the kernel is the inner circle which consists of the firm's structure and the platform it creates, the periphery are those users that choose to actively participate in the peer-production process is some way (motivated by various reasons, influenced by the firm's mechanisms), and finally the outer ring consists of the masses, those who primarily consume. The beauty of crowdsourcing is that the masses don't by themselves damage the peer-production process. The masses consumption of peer-produced information does not result in the producers of the information benefiting less than if the masses did not exist. Quite the contrary, the masses are an audience to the contributors, which spurs motivation and provides benefits that make it advantageous to be in the periphery (Heylighen, 2007).

Enjoyment

Csikszentmihalyi (1975 1990, 1996) has shown that when users are engaged in creative tasks they tend to lose sense of time, allocating more time to the task then they had initially intended. Lakhani and Wolf (2005) conducted several web-based survey studies looking into the motivations of contributors within the Free/Open Source software (F/OSS) Source-Forge.net community. Results showed that 73% of the survey respondents lost track of time when programming. In addition 61% of survey respondents indicated that working on a F/OSS project was a time in their lives when they felt "the most productive, creative or inspired" (Lakhani & Wolf, 2005, p. 10).

Lakhani and Wolf found three major categories of motivations based upon the survey of F/OSS participants, the most prominent of which was determined to be "enjoyment-based intrinsic motivations" (2005, p. 11). The response with the greatest frequency (44.9%) to the question of why participants choose to contribute to projects was that it was intellectually stimulating. The F/OSS community survey also indicated that a significant percent of participants (33%) were motivated by an obligation to the community through their belief that "source code should be open" (Lakhani & Wolf, 2005, p. 12). In addition F/OSS participants (42% strongly agree, 41% somewhat agree) responded with the belief of a strong sense of group identification. To summarize participation within a community was found to be positively correlated with; feelings of productivity, creativity, inspiration, enjoyment, intellectual stimulation, and group identification.

Kaufman and colleagues (2011) in their model for Worker's motivation in crowdsourcing defined enjoyment based motivation with five factors: skill variety, task identity, task autonomy, direct feedback from the job, and a pastime. These factors respectively reflect the extent to which an individual: utilizes diverse skill sets, perceives the tangibility of the work he undertakes, has freedom with which to pursue the task, has a perceived sense of achievement and undertakes a task to avoid boredom. In testing their motivation model and its constructs by surveying contributors to Amazon's Mechanical Turk, Kaufmann et al. found that behind direct payment (an extrinsic motivation), the next highest motivation constructs were task autonomy, skill variety, and task identity, all intrinsic motivations.

Self-Advancement

Firms can benefit from the relaxation of their intellectual property and its release to the crowd to stimulate rapid low-cost development (Tapscott & Williams, 2006) in order to obtain a competitive advantage against their competitors. This release of intellectual property is a facet of crowdsourcing traditionally viewed as a macroperspective, but this process is also played on a microlevel between individuals. When individuals choose to contribute to an online community or a crowdsourcing project they are in essence giving away rights they have to their own intellectual contributions. One reason individuals might choose to freely share information is that in return the community might provide the contributor with feedback. This feedback might be valuable, enhancing the contributor's knowledge of the subject or acting as a springboard for the development of their own work (Heylighen, 2007). What appears to be a purely altruistic action can in fact be motivated by the desire to advance one's knowledge through feedback from an online community.

Recognition and Esteem

Maslow (1970) proposed a hierarchy of needs to explain to complexity of human behavior, which is often represented in a pyramid consisting of two levels. The lower half contains physiological needs; physiological, safety, belongingness and esteem, all of which it is proposed must be satisfied before an individual can progress to the second level, self-actualization. While the layering of the pyramid and the ordering of the needs is contentious, the needs themselves are valid determinants of human behavior. Esteem includes behaviors motivated by confidence and respect. Heylighen (2007) notes that contributing to the collective makes individuals visible within the community, which in turn allows for recognition. Recognition for contributions can lead to a positive reputation, which in turn can lead to a higher level of status within the community. Transparency and the free movement of and access to information within the community ensure that outsiders are able to view the contributions of individuals, which might not be the case in closed commercially developed projects. In an online community contributors typically retain all of the praise from their efforts. In an open-source project the contributor is his or her own boss, has complete control over the nature of the contribution, and is entirely responsible for its success or failure. This is in contrast to a contribution within a commercial project, where coworkers, peers, and/or supervisors might edit, modify and share responsibility for contributions (Lerner, 2002).

Financial Incentives.

Financial incentives can take two forms; direct, whereby participants are rewarded monetarily based on their contributions to a project, and indirect, whereby participants expect to receive rewards such as consultancy fees or honorariums from recognition obtained from their contributions. In regard to direct payments Howe (2008) notes that typically participants in crowdsourced projects contribute with the expectation that they will be receiving an insignificant or nonexistent financial reward. On the other hand though, if for example the contributed software is complex and distributed to a mass of users, it is entirely possible that the contributor's knowledge and skills will be required to provide guidance on usage of the software, in the form of a consultancy fee (Heylighen, 2007). This phenomenon is described in Simon's work on personal attention. Simon contends that in an information society, in which the nonrivalry of information makes it replicable and abundant, it is personal attention that becomes scarce (1971). This scarcity fits within Kelly's proposition that to counter information nonrivarly, valuable intangibles must be produced, one of which is interpretation, which consists of support and guidance (2008). The magnitude of the consultancy fee a contributor obtains will be partially correlated to the amount of recognition a contributor has received from within the community.

Organizational Factors: Structure, Platform & Incentivizing Mechanisms

Once a firm understands the nature of the problem, and the motivations that drive individuals to contribute to solve a problem, it has three responsibilities: first to create an environment within the firm in which crowdsourcing can exist and be accepted, second to create a platform that can be utilized by the crowd to solve the firm's problem, and third to put in place mechanisms on top of the platform to incentivize effective crowdsourcing. Features of the platform that are important in maximizing participation are: a metadesign focus, an open system, allowing continuous evolution, backwards compatibility, ubiquitous operations, accounting for unstable resources and bifurcated requirements, distributing delivery, maintenance and testing between the platform and the contributors, designing for modular and granular work, and establishing a low-cost method of integration (Benkler, 2006; Fischer, 2010; Kazman & Chen, 2009; Lieberman, Paterno, & Wulf, 2006). Once the platform has been developed based on the above recommendations, it now has the potential to draw in the contributions of the crowd, but in order to be truly successful the firm must manage the project through the usage of incentivizing mechanisms. These incentivizing mechanisms fall into several distinct categories based upon their intended goal: recommendation and reputation, recognition, task-sorting, trust and safety, collaboration, integration, and oversight (Benkler, 2006; Heylighen, 2007; Kazman & Chen, 2009; Kriplean, Beschastnikh, & McDonald, 2008; Shneiderman, 2007; Wattenberg, Viegas, & Hollenbach, 2007). Each mechanism plays a unique role in ensuring the success of the crowdsourcing project.

Respecting the Crowd: Firm Structure

The process of accepting and appreciating crowdsourcing can be difficult for a firm. In the United States, a shift occurred in the economy from one that was goods dominated, to its present state, service dominated. Under the goods dominated system firms "treated customers as isolated entities—recipients of value—neglecting the customer's own resources and networks for dynamic collaboration value cocreation" (Kazman & Chen, 2009, p. 77). Firms that are still stuck in their ways have not yet been enlightened as to the potential value of integrating customers, among others, into the design process as cocreators. Firms must now think of their customers as members of a crowd, a crowd that they can utilize to overcome the downsides of firm-centric value creation.

Before a firm can begin the process of creating a crowdsourced project it must align its operations, procedures, and culture to provide a fertile environment for crowdsourcing to prosper. Tapscott and Williams (2006) seek to explain the combination of mass-collaboration and open-source technology, referring to it as "wikinomics" he postulates that to be competitive firms need to focus on the principles of openness, sharing, peering and acting globally. In order to be successful within the principles of wikinomics (the same that determine the success of crowdsourcing), Tapscott and Williams develop structural steps to be taken by firms to foster and effectively manage mass collaboration through open-source technology. He advocates the removal of: hierarchical structures, reliance on internal employees, protection of all intellectual property, and the focus on shareholders. In addition he advocates the strengthening of the firm's culture of collaboration and a focus on empowering the net generation, as they will be the core proponents of crowdsourcing efforts. Within a firm it is important to develop a culture that is both willing to initiate a crowdsourcing project, but also eager to accept the results of the project and integrate the new knowledge or ideas back into the firm to strengthen its competitive position.

Gathering the Crowd: Platforms

The creation and deployment of a platform to the crowd is necessary for a firm to successfully crowdsource. The platform is responsible for accepting, coordinating and integrating the contributions of the crowd. Furthermore, the platform will allow for incentivizing mechanisms designed to influence the behavior of the crowd. Several authors have stressed the importance of the platform to crowdsourcing; its optimal structure, necessary features, and functions. Benkler (2006) provides the following recommendation for the structure of what he defines as commons-based peer production; that it allow for the creation of modular and granular work, where modular refers to the ability of work done to be divisible, and granular suggests it should be fine-grained and small in size. This is in line with Heylighen's conjecture (2007) that when a minimal amount of time is required, projects that are divisible and fine-grained can be worked on by a greater percentage of the populace, increasing the diversity of agents, in turn increasing the likelihood that those agents best suited to work on a particular project, will be working on it.

Fischer (2010) discusses a variety of platform features to encourage and optimize end-user development of a project, which themselves are a result of the emerging participatory web (Web 2.0) and the culture of participation. To be successful a system must be metadesigned with a focus on open systems. These systems take into account the uncertainty of future needs and requirements by allowing for significant modifications by the end-user. These systems optimally remain in a state of "beta" or continuous improvement, in contrast to traditional commercially released products. Within metadesign, Lieberman and colleagues (2006) recommend a design based on computational artifacts, specifically those that allow for customization, personalization, and end-user modifiability. Kazman and Chen (2009) reinforce the "never finished" continuous evolution requirement of the platform, in addition noting that the platform should optimally contain: bifurcated requirements, a fragmented implementation, distributed testing, distributed maintenance and ubiquitous operations. Together these requirements implore a firm to ensure that the platform is small, heavily tested, stable, backwards compatible, easy to learn and simple to use. In contrast, the periphery (consisting of users who contribute) should deliver the vast majority of end-user value, should not have its activities planned or coordinated, should be loosely tested, and should strive for 100% operational uptime to ensure the maximum amount of contributions.

Motivating the Crowd: Mechanisms

Once a firm has successfully built a platform through which individuals can contribute to the crowdsourced project, it must look toward the successful completion of the project, and ways in which it can ensure maximum output, in both quality and quantity, from the crowd. How can the firms keep contributors active, engaged and productive? Kazman and Chen (2009) posit that

> when building a city, infrastructure and rules must be in place to create the social and technical mechanisms needed to engage long-term participation, encouraging community custodianship, recognizing merits of individuals, promoting them through a hierarchy of "ranks" or allowing them to move to a different realm, and finally protecting the community by barring malicious or dangerous participants. (p. 80)

Broken down into tasks and aggregated into categories, firms must take manage the following sets of mechanisms in order to ensure the success of their crowdsourced project: system development tasks, reputation, task-sorting, trust & safety, participant growth, integration and administrative action.

System Development Tasks

In their metropolis model, Kazman and Chen (2009) seek to explain the relationships between the various players involved in crowdsourcing; the kernel (platform), periphery (contributors), and the masses (participants). As part of this effort Kazman outlines several system development tasks that ensure the success of coproduction activities. These tasks are overarching goals built into the platform to oversee, protect, recognize and reward the contributors for their efforts. The development tasks into the following categories: performance-management modeling, crowd engagement, community protection, task alignment with volunteer's values, and the provision of requirements to the crowd. The features of the platform in conjunction with the above system development tasks have led to the development of several mechanisms, discussed in this section, the goal of which are to optimize the adoption and usage of the platform by guiding the actions of the contributors.

Recommendation and Reputation

A mechanism that establishes the reputation of contributors and allows them to receive recommendations is essential to the success of a crowdsourcing project. With the firm's expectation that contributors will seek to establish a positive reputation, the first goal must be dealing with newcomers to the system and teaching them the basics. Furthermore, the development of transparent requirements will foster an open culture in which the barriers to learning, especially for new members, are low. Placing the requirements and training materials on a publically available wiki or share-site is a frequently used method in open-source and crowdsource projects. Once beginners have been trained, encouraging desirable activity becomes essential, and so mechanisms that bolster a contributor's reputation are recommended. In addition, it is desirable for the firm to develop a mechanism that allows for the ability to identify trustworthy partners to work well within the community (Kriplean et al., 2008). Kriplean and colleagues (2008) describe the importance of allowing for acknowledgement, both by the platform and fellow contributors within the community. To ensure that this recognition is fair and effective, it is recommended that firms provide for: dedicated space for open communication between contributors, a means to make every agent's work visible, and the encouragement of a gift-giving culture.

Task-Sorting

Several authors warn against succumbing to the temptation to control periphery members. Any attempt to directly control the activities of the periphery members will weaken the online community, and only serve to demotivate the contributors. Kazman and Chen (2009) instead recommend attempting to inspire, persuade and motivate contributors. Intelligent task routing systems are an attempt to gently persuade instead of control the contributors (Kriplean et al., 2008). Their primary purpose is to make the most important tasks stand out, displaying collective demand where it is needed most (Heylighen, 2007). One example of a recently designed task routing system in practice is embedded within Locationary, a location mapping wiki. Locationary utilizes missions and need to do notifications to offer contributors the opportunity to earn extra recognition (through shares and tickets) if they complete the firm's recommended tasks (Ingram, 2010).

Trust and Safety

Trust within the community is built when accurate records are kept, those records are public, the actions of other agents can be seen by all, and the platform facilitates open discourse (Benkler, 2006; Shneiderman, 2007). Safety within the community can be encouraged by ensuring safe exchanges and by protecting agents against dangerous participants. When participant activities and exchanges are made public and easily accessible, administrators are able to view dishonest or disreputable activity, and take the appropriate actions against the offending contributor.

Participant Growth

Shneiderman (2007) contends that creativity support tools should be designed to have low thresholds, high ceilings, and wide walls. Novice or new users to a creativity tool require low thresholds that make it easy for these users to utilize the platform without extensive training or support from more experienced users. Low ceilings are designed to maximize the adoption rate and usage of the platform. The firm optimally wants the kernel to be usable by the lowest common denominator of users, although it is by no means desirable to exclude the more advanced users as a result. Shneiderman notes that one possible solution to this problem is the implementation of a multilayer interface design, which allows for the progression of users to more advanced features, or the clear separation of basic and advanced tools. This is apparent in most online search tools that usually are set by default to a novice level for ease of use, but allow for the usage of an advanced tools setting. Kazman and Chen (2009) recommend promoting agents through a hierarchy of ranks, or allowing them to progress to different realms, potentially containing more challenging assignments, or unique activities. This reward system appears to be akin to those found within popular video games, where you level-up, or progress to a new area based upon the successful completion of tasks.

Integration

In order to successfully peer produce a project a firm must develop an efficient mechanism for the integration of individual contributor's inputs into the overall system. Benkler (2006) notes that this mechanism should be low-cost and contain quality controls. If the integration mechanism is expensive, the more users that contribute to the project, the more expensive it will become, negating the benefits of mass collaboration. Quality controls are needed to ensure that inputs into the project are not malicious in nature, or actively detract from the progress of the project. Optimally the integration mechanism will be automated, as that will be the least costly and most efficient method.

Administrator Action

Administrators serve a vital role within online communities and crowdsourced projects, as they alone are able to handle problems too complex or delicate for automated mechanisms. Wattenberg and colleagues (2007) distinguishes between two roles that administrators undertake within the community; systemic and reactive. Systemic tasks are generic actions that are required to ensure the proper functioning of the project and can take the form of other mechanisms such as recognition, recommendation and task sorting. Ideally these tasks would be automated, although that is not always possible due to development time and cost considerations. Reactive tasks can take the form of ensuring trust and safety within the community by actively watching for those users that attempt to undermine the project. It can also consist of positive activities such as welcoming new members into the community, a task that is more valuable when it is completed by an administrator instead of an automated mechanism.

ENCOUNTERING, OVERCOMING AND AVOIDING
FAILURE AT CROWDSOURCING

Encountering Difficulties

Not all crowds will be successfully formed, and even when they are all crowds will not produce satisfactory work. As this paper has described, in order for a firm to successfully crowdsource a project it must understand: the motivation that drives individuals, the various configurations that online communities can take, the need to internally accept a crowdsourcing culture, the proper methods to building a platform, and finally the proper utilization of platform mechanisms to motivate the crowd. Surowiecki (2004) posits that crowds break down and are only as successful as its best individuals when the decision-making environment is not set up to encourage the crowd to contribute effectively.

Surowiecki (2004) details five factors that can result in the failure of a crowdsourced project: homogeneity, centralization, division, imitation, and emotionality. Homogeneity, a state in which the composition of the crowd lacks diversity, results in a lack of unique private information, a similar thought process, and ultimately a lack of variance in task solutions. Centralization is a result of a platform in which a hierarchical bureaucracy forms that limits the attention paid to the contributions of lesser participants, resulting in less diversity and a nonoptimization of informational synergies. Issues with control and division occur when individuals are not allowed to choose which tasks they will work on, or when the platform is fractured and the right hand does not know what the left is doing. When individuals are not allowed to choose the tasks they work on, task completion is not optimized by the skill of the participants, and instead it is regulated by a central authority. When a platform is fractured, and individuals cannot easily access other participant's contributions, work is repeated or completed less efficiently. Imitation is the result of a process in which participants only view the latest iterations of a task, and are therefore unable to pass judgment or contribute to earlier assumptions. This is the platform equivalent of a house of cards, in which a task is completed on a weak base on contributions. Finally emotional factors can lead to peer pressure within the community, which if unchecked can lead to situations in which individuals do not make rational decisions based on their unique perspective and instead succumb to groupthink.

To succeed in crowdsourcing firms should choose the right crowd based on the requirements of the project, ensure that it is utilizing the proper motivations to engage the crowd, encourage participation by keeping individual tasks as small and simple as possible, from time to time provide gentle guidance and direction to the crowd, and seek to optimize the manner in which the contributed tasks are aggregated.

Potential Solution: Outsourcing Crowdsourcing

While every attempt has been made in this chapter to assist a firm in understanding the challenges involved and opportunities available in crowdsourcing, some firms understandably might not be able to take the plunge. It might be that it would be too difficult to modify the firm's culture to be accepting of crowdsourced solutions, or that the firm doesn't have the time or resources available to invest in properly selecting, forming, motivating, and managing a crowd to complete its goals, or that the firm does not have the technical ability to create an effective platform.

Thankfully a solution exists for those firms that do not feel prepared, or don't believe it is worthwhile, to pursue a crowdsourced project internally. Firms can outsource crowdsourcing to emerging groups of service providers who can handle any or all aspects of the crowdsourcing process. Firms desiring to initiate crowdsourcing can find services that will provide: platforms, crowd processes, crowd services and marketplaces. Platform firms such as IdeaScale, Klusterm Consensus Point and Napkin Labs provide services such as complete crowd platforms and idea management. Crowd process firms such as Data discoverers, Crowd flower, Scalable Workforce and Smart sheet provide services that offer value-added processes or integration capabilities to existing crowds. Crowd services, such as access to labor pools or crowd management, are provided by firms such as Think speed, V&S, Clickadvisor, and Genius Rocket among others. Finally online marketplaces exist, such as Amazon's Mechanical Turk, Freelancer, and Kickstarter, that will match buyers and sellers of services. Should a firm choose to do so, the entire crowdsourcing process could be outsourced (Dawson & Bynghall, 2011).

WHAT DO WE NEED TO DO NEXT TO BETTER UNDERSTAND HOW FIRMS CAN EFFECTIVELY CROWDSOURCE?

The field of crowdsourcing would benefit from empirical results to support the underlying model and its propositions. Literature on crowdsourcing is heavily weighted to the listing of successful examples (Wikipedia, YouTube, Linux, etc.). Two drawbacks exist with a majority of these examples; first a significant portion of the projects discussed have the sole purpose of enriching the community, mostly through the formation of nonprofit organizations, which limits generalizability, and second frequently these firms are viewed from an outside perspective based on the success of the project. In-depth case studies in which researchers embed themselves in the crowdsourcing process itself would yield more substantial results than merely reporting the financial success of the venture.

What can be done to address specific gaps within the framework provided above? Since most crowdsourcing projects are studied once they are already in existence, an important research topic is how and why do crowdsourcing projects fail before firms are able to release them to the public. Specifically, how does a firm know if it has created the proper environment internally necessary to support a crowdsourcing project? Some aspects of this process are more tangible and therefore measurable than others, for instance the willingness to open up a firm's intellectual property to outside analysis and reducing reliance on internal employees. Other factors such as empowering the net generation and deepening a culture of participation are more difficult to measure. A study that looks into the moderating factors of the formation of crowdsourcing projects within a firm would be beneficial to firms considering whether or not to pursue a project.

In regard to the challenges of successfully crowdsourcing there is a need to assess the influence of individual mechanisms and their effect on the overall success of the project. Each mechanism is designed specifically to help guide or motivate the community to effectively meet the firm's goals, as such the extent to which they're each applied is a variable controlled by the firm. Too little usage of a mechanism and the community could become chaotic, losing focus, and ultimately potentially disbanding. On the other hand heavy handedness by the firm in the usage of mechanisms could result in a lessoning of the firm's legitimacy to oversee the project in the eyes of the crowd. An inverted U-shape is predicted on the extent to which mechanisms are deployed and the resulting success of the project.

Several mechanisms and their influences could be explored. Task routing, which is meant to provide subtle direction to the crowd, could be seen as an attempt by the firm to exploit the community. Ensuring the safety of the crowd, which in itself appears on the surface to be well-intentioned, could result in the firm being labeled as a big brother instead of the more desirable and innocuous perception as a neighborhood watch. Finally the ability to offer a monetary reward for contributions could backfire if it actively disenfranchises the substantial portion of the crowd that is contributing based on nonmonetary motivations.

Finally, a study that conducted a cost/benefit analysis on the cost of pursuing a crowdsourcing project versus the measurable returns (cost savings and increased revenues) across a wide range of industries to ensure generalizability would be beneficial to firms. While Fisher's (2009) survey showed that approximately 50% of marketing executives expected a cost savings of 10%-30%, this is perceived, not actual savings. In addition the costs associated with effectively implementing a crowdsourcing project, such as structural changes to the firm, the development and deployment of a platform, and the development and oversight of incentivizing mechanisms is relatively unknown.

ACKNOWLEDGMENT

I would like to acknowledge Dr. Robert C. Ford, who encouraged me to write this chapter, and provided me with much needed guidance and support.

REFERENCES

Benkler, Y. (2006). *The wealth of networks: How social production transforms markets and freedom*. New Haven, CT: Yale University Press.

Csikszentmihalyi, M. (1975). *Beyond boredom and anxiety: The experience of play in work and games*. San Francisco, CA: Jossey-Bass.

Csikszentmihalyi, M. (1990). *Flow: The psychology of optimal experience*. New York, NY: Harper & Row.

Csikszentmihalyi, M. (1996). *Creativity: Flow and the psychology of discovery and invention*. New York, NY: Harper Collins.

Dawson, R., & Bynghall, S. (2011). *Getting results from crowds: The definitive guide to using crowdsourcing to grow your business*. San Francisco, CA: Advanced Human Technologies.

Fischer, G. (2010). End-user development and meta-design: Foundations for Cultures of participation. *Journal of Organizational and End User Computing, 22*(1), 52-82. Retrieved from http://l3d.cs.colorado.edu/~gerhard/papers/2010-JOEUC.pdf

Fisher, S. (2009). *Crowdsourcing: Innovate or die*. Retrieved from http://www.mengonline.com/docs/DOC-1896

Girotra, K., Terwiesch, C., & Ulrich, K. T. (2010). Idea generation and the quality of the best idea. *Management Science, 56*(4), 591-605.

Glickhouse, R. (2012). Technology update: A crowdsourcing guide to Latin America. Retrieved from http://www.ascoa.org/articles/3887/A_Crowdsourcing_Guide_to_Latin_America/

Hargadon, A. B., & Bechky, B. A. (2006). When collections of creatives become creative collectives: A field study of problem solving at work. *Organization Science, 17*(4), 484-500.

Heylighen, F. (2007). Why is open access development so successful? Stigmergic organization and the economies of information. In B. Lutterbeck, M. Bärwolff, & R. A. Gehring (Eds.), *Open source jahrbuch* (pp. 165-180). Cologne, North Rhine-Westphalia, Germany: Lehmanns Media.

Howe, J. (2008). *Crowdsourcing: Why the power of the crowd is driving the future of business*. New York, NY: Crown Business.

Ingram, M. (2010). *Locationary wants to be the Wikipedia of Location*. Retrieved from http://gigaom.com/2010/09/20/locationary-wants-to-be-the-wikipedia-of-location/

Ipeirotis, P. (2010). Demographics of Mechanical Turk. Retrieved from http://archive.nyu.edu/bitstream/2451/29585/2/CeDER-10-01.pdf

Kaufmann, N., Schulze, T., & Veit, D. (2011) More than fun and money. Worker motivation in crowdsourcing—A study on mechanical turk. *Proceedings of the Seventeenth Americas Conference on Information Systems*, Detroit, Michigan.

Kazman, R., & Chen, H. (2009). The metropolis model: A new logic for development of crowdsourced systems. *Communications of the ACM, 52*(7), 76-84.

Kelly, K. (2008). Better than free. Retrieved from http://www.edge.org/3rd_culture/kelly08/kelly08_index.html

Kelly, M. (2012). Wal-Mart lets gadget companies compete for a spot on its shelves. Retrieved from http://venturebeat.com/2012/01/18/walmart-get-on-the-shelf/

Kozinets, R., Hemetsberger, A., & Schau, H. J. (2008). The wisdom of consumer crowds: Collective innovation in the age of networked marketing, *Journal of Macromarketing, 28*(4), 339-354.

Kriplean, T., Beschastnikh, I., & McDonald, D. W. (2008). Articulations of wiki-work: Uncovering valued work in Wikipedia through barnstars, *CSCW'08*, San Diego, CA.

Lakhani, K., & Wolf, R. (2005). Why hackers do what they do: Understanding motivation and effort in free/open source software projects. In J. Feller, B. Fitzgerald, S. Hissam, & K. Lakhani (Eds.), *Perspectives on free and open source software* (pp. 3-22). Cambridge, MA: MIT Press

Lerner, R. M. (2002). *Developmental assets and asset-building communities: Implications for research, policy, and practice*. New York, NY: Plenum.

Lieberman, H., Paterno, F., & Wulf, V. (Eds.) (2006): *End user development*. Dordrecht, The Netherlands: Springer.

Maslow, A. (1970). *Motivation and personality* (2nd ed.). New York, NY: Harper & Row.

McGlaun, S. (2012). DoD eyes crowdsourced bug hunting for weapon systems. Retrieved from http://www.tgdaily.com/security-features/60927-dod-eyes-crowdsourced-bug-hunting-for-weapon-systems

Page, S. (2007). *The difference: How the power of diversity creates better groups, firms, schools, and societies*. Princeton, NJ: Princeton University Press.

O'Reilly, T. (2005). Design patterns and business models for the next generation of software. Retrieved from http://oreilly.com/web2/archive/what-is-web-20.html

Sharma, A. (2010). Crowdsourcing critical success factor model: Strategies to harness the collective intelligence of the crowd. Retrieved from http://irevolution.files.wordpress.com/2010/05/working-paper1.pdf

Shneiderman, B. (2007). Creativity support tools: Accelerating discovery and innovation, *Communications of the ACM, 50*(12), 20-27.

Simon, H. A. (1971). Designing organizations for an information-rich world. In M. Greenberger (Ed.), *Computers, communication, and the public interest* (pp. 37-72). Baltimore, MD: The Johns Hopkins Press

Surowiecki, J. (2004). *The wisdom of crowds: why the many are smarter than the few and how collective wisdom shapes business, economies, societies and nations*. New York, NY: Random House.

Tapscott, D., & Williams, A. (2006). *Wikinomics: How mass collaboration changes everything*. New York, NY: Penguin Group.

Wasserman, T. (2012) Facebook app lets Sam Adams fans crowdsource a tap. Retrieved from http://mashable.com/2012/01/19/sam-adams-crowdsources-beer-facebook/

Wattenberg, M., Viegas, F., & Hollenbach, K. (2007). Visualizing activity in wikipedia with chromograms. *INTERACT'07 Proceedings of the 11th IFIP TC 13 international conference on human-computer interaction—Volume Part II* (pp. 272-287). Heidelberg, Germany: Springer-Verlag Berlin.

CHAPTER 10

LIMINALITY AND THE ETHICAL CHALLENGES PRESENTED BY INNOVATIVE MEDICAL PROCEDURES

Nanette Clinch and Asbjorn Osland

ABSTRACT

International commercial gestational surrogacy in India, gender selection, and female cosmetic genital surgery are sometimes offered commercially as services where legally permitted. The technology for each has been developed enough to offer the services but given the embryonic stage of development of these services, numerous ethical issues are apparent. New technologies sometimes elude regulation in the early stages, taking a marginal place in the legal environment. Yet ethical responses to new technologies can be very strong, since such technologies represent man-made alternatives to human life as it has been known for generations. Such distinctive technologies thus may offer unusual insights into the purpose and nature of ethical analysis as well as the value of the enterprises that occupy what may be viewed as liminal spaces. In striking new ground, such enterprises are relatively free to stage new modes of experience, develop new rituals, and, in the midst of delivering what might seem fantastic, potentially deliver as well unexpected and unwanted transformations of humanity. The ultimate aim of this paper is to further discussion of the ethics of these controversial technologies with a primary focus on liminality. People engaged in any of these innovative medical practices enter a liminal space where they are between what they were and what they might become.

INTRODUCTION

We begin with a brief description of the three technologies, followed by a brief discussion of their legitimacy. Since the technologies appear to offer what some consumers want, one might think them admirably progressive, yet ethically, they all may represent, for humanity, a step into precarious space. Examining these technologies requires an effort to step back and be objective regardless of predictable ethical concerns. The ethical discussion covers the following topics: sustainability, discordant philosophical perspectives, liminality as a heuristic device illuminating ethical issues, and the liminal experience presented by the three.

INTERNATIONAL COMMERCIAL GESTATIONAL SURROGACY

International commercial gestational surrogacy (ICGS), a form of medical tourism, is at first glance a radical new medical service. Outsourced surrogacy is more complicated than a call center for credit cards. Though shocking initially, medical services that were once seen as radical, such as "test-tube babies" of the 1970s, are now accepted since so many Americans require the use of fertility clinics and in vitro fertilization (IVF). The attitudinal differences toward ICGS between cultures and jurisdictions are reflected in legislation. In some areas, commercial gestational surrogacy is forbidden whereas in others, such as India and California, it is available to all comers.

ICGS seems to promote a win-win service for all concerned providing the legal requirements are respected: parents get the child they long for and the surrogate is paid what she perceives as enough. Whether commercializing the womb leads to greater liberation of women or furthers exploitation of reproduction and of women in particular remains ethically problematic. Furthermore, there are implementation problems: citizenship can be problematic in some cases; for example, gays and lesbians as prospective parents are treated differently in other parts of the world than in California; humble Indian women are not in a strong negotiating position since other poor women would likely take their place if they asked for more money; governments dramatically limit the options of infertile couples in some jurisdictions. Commercializing the womb is not a simple issue but perhaps stands to gain increasing acceptance, as has been true of IVF services in general. ICGS would simply become one of the services such clinics provide.

GENDER SELECTION

According to the literature, prospective parents of Indian, Chinese, and South Korean ethnicity residing in the United States sometimes expressed a cultural preference for sons. If they had already had daughters the likelihood of desiring a son was still greater. Parents desiring a specific gender sometimes resorted to abortions as a form of gender selection. Gender selection through abortion was rampant in China, India and South Korea (Puria, Adams, Ivey, & Nachtigall, 2011; Roan, 2011; Roberts, 2009).

Fertility clinics in California were largely free to offer whatever services were technically possible and marketable, even when professional bodies raised questions about services such as sex selection. The issue had become complicated in other jurisdictions with antiabortion groups using sex selection as a reason to support legislation prohibiting abortion for that purpose (e.g., Arizona—Schwinn & Robson, 2011).

Gender selection is morally reprehensible in many societies where it is forbidden yet freely practiced in parts of Asia, and fertility clinics in California openly offer the service.

Discussion of the ethics of gender selection, based on reasoned debate, should occur at the level of professional societies prior to politicians imposing regulations based on political pressures, especially when associated with hot issues such as abortion. Innovation is promoted in environments where openness prevails as in California. To prohibit gender selection through PGD could limit the growth of the technology and unforeseen new knowledge. It could also lead to additional limitations on fertility clinics (e.g., banning commercial surrogacy). The Catholic Church is the most prominent foe of IVF because of the destruction of embryos but non-Catholics may not hear its message. It appears that where legal, gender selection is freely offered to all comers generally without discussion of the ethical consequences of the practice due to commercialization of the practice.

FEMALE COSMETIC GENITAL SURGERY (FCGS)

The Second Global Symposium on Cosmetic Vaginal Surgery was held on September 23-25, 2010 in Las Vegas. Plastic surgeons have established FCGS as a service promoted on the Internet, including vaginal rejuvenation and tightening, labia reduction and beautification, and reconstruction of the hymen ("virginity" can be culturally important in cases such as rape or incest), with before and after photos of external changes to the clitoris or labia.

Several professional societies voiced their opposition. The Royal Australian and New Zealand College of Obstetricians publicly opposed FCGS (Braun, 2010). The American College of Obstetricians and Gynecologists (ACOG, 2007) voiced reservations.

FCGS could face legal challenges for malpractice if women perceive that they are harmed. Reproductive health is a valid area for engagement. FCGS is also located, ethically and legally, in cosmetic surgery, where the appeal to the "liminal person" merits significant consideration (see Schouten, 1991).

FCGS is currently offered by plastic surgeons free of regulation and the surgeons providing the service are not intimidated by the reservations expressed by professional societies. The FDA tightly regulates pharmaceutical products and devices but FCGS seems to operate in a regulatory and ethical vacuum; women request and pay for services that they believe will make them more desirable. Surgeons capitalize on this desire to offer what appears to be a commercially viable business until the malpractice claims become onerous. The government and professional societies seem to have stepped aside with the courts perhaps destined to be the discussion forum of last resort after women have been damaged. Legitimacy will perhaps have to await their future decisions.

GENERAL DISCUSSION

In order of legitimacy, we would assert that FCGS is less ethically challenging than the other two. Cosmetic surgery directly bears on concepts of personhood. The United States Supreme Court has recognized the significance of personhood and "choices central to personal dignity and autonomy" (discussion of childbearing rights in *Planned Parenthood of Southeastern Pennsylvania v. Casey*, 1992, 505 U.S. 833 at 851). Gender selection can be used to avoid gender-based genetic defects but all too often is used to have sons, reflecting a sexist traditional view. ICGS, though providing adults with genetically related children, potentially commodifies the surrogate, breaking with biological and cultural conceptions of motherhood and childhood associated with the birth process. The potential stigmatization of women as primarily reproductive utilities could nourish the kind of male preference that informs gender selection on a large and perhaps hazardous scale.

Although all three technologies described above clearly have some legitimacy, whether such legitimacy can be broadened and sustained is questionable given their distance from normal procedures. FCGS could conceivably be required in cases of genitalia so malformed that normal activities would be highly uncomfortable or the individual could be stigmatized for a perceived abnormality. However, not all women need to wear thong bikinis to feel complete and beautiful. Such preoccupation with sexuality as a mechanism detracts from true beauty. Traditional forms of birth might be somewhat unusual in cases of artificial insemination, but actually having a child carried by another woman is far from the norm (see Shreffler, Johnson, & Scheuble, 2010). Many women have wished for the birth of a son throughout human history, yet having access to technological assurance could undermine consideration of the real reasons for that preference, which could be simple social and economic discrimination. Whether any of the services are sought depends, in part, on the strength and coherence of the ethical outlook of the potential consumers. These technologies arguably undermine sustainability, and ethical justification depends on one's philosophical outlook.

SUSTAINABILITY

A sustainable world welcomes men and women as equals in dignity and thus equally entitled to opportunities to flourish. Yet these technologies, over time, could reduce the dignity of women, eroding the Self in the pursuit of some notion of personal satisfaction. FCGS, for example, could be decried as symptomatic of the "medicalization" of women (New View Campaign, 2010; New View Campaign, Manifesto, 2010).

Human dignity, a mark of a sustainable world, is undermined by the legitimizing of certain types of bargains. All forms of slavery are condemned, and any notion a person could voluntarily agree to slavery, even for a week, in exchange for compensation, would be abhorrent even if legal. Gestational surrogacy is easily associated with the commodification of the person. Compensating carriers could lead to exploitation, as can the sale of organs. Thus legislative remedies can prohibit compensation to avoid the specter of using economically disadvantaged women to supply the needs of those who are financially stable (Ford, 2005). Pfeffer (2011) thus compares organ selling to egg selling by women in the fertility industry as illustrative of injustice. Serving as a 9-month carrier of another's child reflects those occupations that keep women "stuck at a low level of the occupational hierarchy" and sustains their sense of their own "lack of entitlement to resources" (Pfeffer, 2011, p. 640).

Gender selection practices offer the most disturbing, and possibly irreversible, picture of the future. Two troubling aspects of gender selection are the evident preference for males over females and the potential consequences of a world populated by too many men, made aggressive given the absence of women; "technology, declining fertility and ancient prejudice are combining to unbalance societies" ("The Worldwide War On Baby Girls" 2010, p. 77). Bumgarner, in 2007, expressed concerns that given the preference for men over women in China and India, "rape, kidnapping, prostitution and trafficking of women" (p. 1301) will only rise, all to the detriment of women.

In India and China, preferences for male children surface as animosity toward females and the implications are global, often escaping "the usual tools of demographic analyses" (George, 2006, p. 608). The problem is receiving considerable attention (see Roan, 2011; Roberts, 2009).

Abrevaya (2008), while acknowledging the possible "high incidence of hepatitis B in many Asian Countries" as a reason for unusually high rates of boy births in Asia, describes a study "From Gleicher and Barad (2007), who examined the experience of couples that underwent gender-selective IVF cycles" with "Asian and Indian couples overwhelmingly selecting for male embryos" (p. 27). Even though data on abortions based on fetal sexing in the U.S. is hard to obtain, census data suggest that while families in the U.S. seek a mix of genders, certain couples whose racial background is Chinese, Indian or Korean display a preference for sons (Abrevaya, 2008).

Should the scientists and businesses be responsible for this? How to identify particular social responsibilities is a pressing issue in theory and practice (see Dahlsrund, 2006).The concept of corporate sustainability (CS) is gaining attention. Hediger (2010) argues businesses should be concerned not just with ethical practices within the market but other costs that can lead to "an inefficient allocation of scarce resources and social welfare losses" (Hediger, 2010, p. 2).

DISCORDANT PHILOSOPHICAL PERSPECTIVES

The absence of full ethical legitimacy is particularly exposed when one sets aside utilitarianism or consumer demand as some sort of justification. The temptation to justify these technologies by invoking utilitarianism is particularly superficial. Utilitarianism fails to provide any measurement of what are good and just objectives for happiness; any kind of concern for moral justification focuses on assessments of ascertainable pain or harm, customarily manifested in some physical (not metaphysical) form. Utilitarianism becomes a convenient theory for consumer satisfaction theories, which work well in economic contexts with questionable assumptions, such as the idea that individuals make rational choices and thus should be left alone (see Nixon, 2007). Indeed, utilitarianism suggests it is wrong to judiciously weigh forms of happiness; utility—the prevalence of the desire—is what matters. If questioning certain desires is wrong then proclaiming certain desires as immoral certainly is not essential to the utilitarian scheme.

Setting utilitarianism aside permits a more judicious view of virtues and vices, justice and inequalities, the self as an integral whole and the self as a fragmented being, possibly wavering between impetuous ego and collective demands.

FCGS

To the extent FCGS is a means of enhancing one's sexual ego, the service hardly instills or furthers virtues, nor is obsession with sexuality temperate in an Aristotelian sense. Patients using FCGS sometimes use a pornographic standard. In pornography, humans are instruments of pleasure and nothing more. Kant opposed instrumentalism. For Nussbaum (1999), sex is not the enemy to free agency and individual dignity agency, but pornography is the enemy. The distortion of the other is required in order to erase concerns about the other that would interfere with present pleasure. The other is to be used; its feelings are "other" and can be ignored. The pornographic associations therefore may trouble those adhering to a deontological approach.

Gestational Surrogacy

Aristotle believed people should aim toward a telos that gave life meaning in a world where one could contribute or undermine community (MacIntyre, 1988). For the Greeks, family and kinship were central to life; religious outlooks required high regard for familial and community bonds.

Gestational birth contracts interrupt natural ties by suppressing, through the power of contractual law or statutes, the birth mother's natural interest in a relationship to the child. Interestingly, Jadva, Murray, Lycett, MacCallum, and Golombok (2003, p. 2202) point out that 77% (i.e., 26) of the 34 surrogate mothers participating in a 2003 study believed the child should be informed about the surrogate birth.

The idea that natural bonds of love can be eliminated through legal coercion is certainly not presented as the truth in Sophocles' play *Antigone*. The tragedy presents the legitimacy of virtue, illustrated in familial bonds of love and honor, exposing the limitations of the seeming legitimacy of human law. Creon, in trying to prevent Antigone from giving an honorable burial to her traitorous brother, uses the force of legal authority to disrupt natural ties. Creon subsequently suffers irreversible shame and horror, including the loss of his own son, as a consequence of Antigone's courageous protection of her brother's spiritual rights. Gestational surrogacy attempts an arguably similar fiction, using using not governmental coercion but contracts to exclude the birth mother as legitimate mother.

Kant asserted that no person should be treated as a means to an end, yet it is hard to see how that is avoided in the situation of commercial gestational surrogacy. A contractual promise to give up a bond of love does not clearly fit within Kant's philosophical outlook of a world where doing what is right depends on universalizing the rules: how would one feel as the other?

Gender Selection

Aristotle believed deeply in the virtue of justice. Justice calls for balance; exclusion of individuals on the basis of sex preference does not serve justice.

Certainly, Kant's rule of universalization, demanding mutual respect, does not easily accommodate preferences on the basis of sex, or individual actions that would sustain or further discrimination against women. Yet if gender selection did not result in discrimination on the basis of sex, the rational choices of the parties might justify gender selection, as it empowers parents to choose the ideal sex and could result in improved parental duties through a "a more positive rearing experience" (Daar, 2005, p. 271).

Some might argue that these technologies must be made available to women on the ethical grounds that women have the right to determine what to do with their bodies. The rights theory fails to address those who raise the rights of all forms of human life, namely the embryos inevitably discarded in IVF procedures designed to produce a person for a woman who desires a particular kind of person: genetically related or one of a particular sex.

LIMINALITY AS A HEURISTIC DEVICE ILLUMINATING ETHICAL ISSUES

Although there are many benefits to exploring technologies through different philosophical lenses, engaging in comprehensive philosophical dialogue calls for deep consideration of the phenomena. The ethical implications of these technologies might easily escape notice, owing to the novelty of the phenomena and the application of traditional assumptions. One way to gain appreciation of the ethical implications and what is morally at stake is through examination of the actual experience of its participants, including children born of the technologies. Does moral reasoning matter to them or are they only interested in the utilitarian objective? How well do the agents of these technologies serve these individuals in an ethical sense? Does the experience of these technologies reassure those who doubt their ethical legitimacy or does it raise new concerns?

By stepping back to see reality from the vantage point of accepting life's tenuousness, one may gain new appreciation of human experience and its contingent reliance on various constructions of meaning. Human anxiety over the transitory nature of life, described so well by Martin Heidegger, is expressed in the many liminal stages of human life.

In *Being and Time*, Heidegger (1962/2008) explored the contingent nature of Being in human life. Humans must find their way around this place of ongoing assumptions of roles and predictably utilitarian use of materials without losing sight of their potential authenticity. The German word for being, *Dasein* (being-there) (Heidegger, 1962/2008, note by translators Macquarrie & Robinson, p. 27) is a way of contemplating both the significance of existence and the philosophical question evident in Plato and Socrates: how to be. One sense of *Dasein*, of being "thrown" or hurled into life at birth (Heidegger, 1962/2008), invigorates the inquiry: everyone is projected into a world made by others, for others. How does one make that world one's own place, how does one project oneself intentionally, toward what end? All these questions become critical to avoiding consumption of the authentic self by culture and demands of others.

Liminality is not a new approach in the social sciences, but its most productive use, when examining experiences, might well depend on appreciation of its original conception in anthropological contexts. The anthropological concept of liminality focuses on transformative stages of life that are common to most humans and are meaningfully bound up with cultures through rites of passage. Most of these transitional states are associated with physical states such as formal social acknowledgements of transitions from adolescence to adulthood, retirement and aging; adulthood and marriage; birth, illness and death (van Gennep, 1908/1960; Turner, 1982, 1987).

Turner (1982, 1987), building on van Gennep's work, extended the study of liminality beyond rites of passage. Turner (1982) explained the importance of distinguishing liminality in reference to rites of passage and metaphorical applications of the concept, which pertained to large-scale complex societies, where rites of passage are vanishing because they become individualized. Thus, a person undergoing cosmetic surgery is undertaking the rite of passage personally (Schouten, 1991). The woman seeking FCGS is engaging in a process that she hopes will transform her physically and psychologically, making her feel more sexualized.

Exploring these technologies through a lens of liminality reveals the exploratory and tenuous satisfaction of the seemingly consumer-oriented and scientifically grounded transformational process for those who seek its remedies. Each woman has an objective; each wants her life transformed; yet what each will also encounter, whether recognized or not, is the liminal experience that accompanies the technological process. The nature of this liminal experience can be explored, drawing on van Gennep (1908/1960), in terms of three stages of passage. The three stages prove useful: awakening to the potential transformation, the ensuing liminal state, and reincorporation into ordinary life, though in some instances, the liminal state initiated by the desire coupled to technology might not be resolved.

THE TRANSFORMATION PROCESS: AWAKENING, LIMINAL STAGE, RETURN TO ORDINARY LIFE

The idea that a transformation is pending is the awakening stage. In illness, this awakening arrives upon a prognosis or receipt of medical information that is ambiguous but may portend future ill health (Forss, Tishelman, Widmark, & Sachs, 2004; Little, Jordens, Paul, Montgomery, & Philipson, 1998). Little and colleagues (1998) find the threshold awakening or awareness of disease as a stage manifested by acceptance or even outright denial, revealed in rejection of treatment. Women informed of ambiguous results of a pap smear are similarly awakened to potential illness and thus fall into liminal states (Forss et al., 2004). The objective is clearly to restore health.

Awakenings can also be moments of awareness that one might be freed from a liminal state: infertility or rejection of one's physical limitations. A sought for transformation is within reach. A woman without children can suddenly envision fitting into society with a family. Individuals unhappy with their appearance might awaken to cosmetic surgery as a means of transformation and proceed to move through the liminal state of transition (Schouten, 1991). Fantasies turn into potentially achievable objectives.

During the liminal phase that follows awakening, individuals must make sense of the liminal space and its mixing of old and new, sacred and profane.

In the liminal stage, one does not feel firmly connected to society; rather, one is moving through an otherworld where all that seemed securely understood is now fragmented. This alienation from society and the awareness of one's singular state is a feature of a rite of passage (van Gennep, 1908/1960) and it marks the experience of those undergoing cosmetic surgery (Schouten, 1991) as well as the agony of those coping with serious or anticipated medical illness (Kelly, 2008; Little et al., 1998).

Alienation might be exacerbated by the secrecy associated with users of these technologies, further obscuring appreciation of the effect of these technologies on the users. The use of reproductive technologies is often shrouded in secrecy; this is also true of cosmetic surgery. Women who seek FCGS sometimes do not reveal their interest in aesthetic improvement even to the physician, fearing the physician will only consider medical reasons such as discomfort (Triffin, 2010). Couples interested in fertility treatments strive to project optimism to the potential provider, to show they are good candidates (Cussins, 1998).

The liminal phase might terminate upon achievement of the objective, but these new technologies, setting new standards for birth and sexual attractiveness, might actually create permanent liminal states for some who use them. Failure to achieve the desired objective might also prolong a liminal state. For example, not being provided a mode of moving out of the liminal state of cancer, the patients are confined to liminality (Little et al., 1998).

Table 10.1 shows the individuals who are in liminal states and the characteristics of those states.

The Liminal Experience of Gestational Surrogacy

The Surrogate

A woman may have an awakening that opens an unexpected window of opportunity: enough money to move up the social ladder of success. This awakening may come from learning of the commercial advantages from the media or clinic marketing. In India, the monetary compensation would be otherwise unattainable.

In the United States, research suggests most surrogates are economically near dire straits, lacking employment, often dependent on governmental assistance (Drabiak, Wegner, Fredland, & Helft, 2007). The agencies promoting surrogacy project the message that serving as a surrogate can enhance self worth through providing a critical service (Drabiak et al., 2007). In the United States, the compensation could be between $13,000 and $24,000, which could serve as an incentive but also open them to exploitation (Drabiak et al., 2007, p. 303); more is even possible.

The law, through a contract, can diminish recognition of the surrogate's uncertainty experience by relying on rationality and free choice. In the United States, "ninety-five percent of surrogacy contracts involve IVF, so most surrogates are not the genetic mothers of the children they bear" (Scott, 2009, p. 139). Establishing that the birth mother lacks parental rights rests on the intending parents' genetic contribution, with

Table 10.1.   Liminality and International
Commercial Gestational Surrogacy

Individual	Awakening and Objective	Transformation Stage (Liminal)	Transformed Identity and Return to Ordinary Life or Prolonged Liminal Stage
Commercial surrogate	For the commercial surrogate, awareness of the opportunities may come through clinic marketing efforts or other media. The objective is to increase income in order to improve economic and social circumstances that would otherwise be out of reach.	The liminal space might end with compensation upon delivery of the child to the intending parents.	Surrogate returns to community with enough money to improve her economic or social circumstances (sending children to college, building a house). Surrogates could also suffer from profound postpartum depression and long term regret or lowering of self-esteem, and continued rejection by the community.
Intending parents	Awareness of opportunities may come from Internet searches or, in states or countries where gestational surrogacy is legal, from medical professionals or fertility clinics. The objective is to have a genetically-related child.	The intending mother is never pregnant, so the normal liminality of pregnancy must be fulfilled in other ways since her expected delivery of a child is never publicly produced for social inspection. The liminal space might end with delivery of a healthy child. The new child presumably has the appropriate documentation to become a citizen of the parents' home country.	Parents return to community with a healthy child who is genetically related to them. The liminal space might continue if the child is unhealthy, if the surrogate asserts parental rights, or if the community becomes aware of the procedure and views the parents as unethical. The liminal space may be revived when the child is told of the gestational surrogacy and the existence of a birth mother.
Child born of gestational surrogacy.	When the child learns of the existence of the surrogate, the child will realize he or she differs from other children, whose biological mother is also the birth mother. The objective of the child will be to reconcile this difference, perhaps by seeking out the birth mother.	The liminal space for a child aware of a birth mother could result in questions about identity, familial duties and kinship.	The child is content with identity and the process that brought him or her into being and either dismisses the role of the surrogate as incidental or embraces her role and incorporates the surrogate into identity.

Table 10.2. Liminality and Gender Selection

Individual	Awakening and Objective	Transformation Stage (Liminal)	Transformed Identity and Return to Ordinary life or Prolonged Liminal Stage
Woman desiring a child of one sex	The internet, media, or fertility clinics might provide advice on gender preference for economic or social reasons or forfamily balancing. In states or countries where gender selection is legal, awakening could occur through conversations with medical professionals or fertility clinic providers	The parents direct destruction of embryos not matching desired gender preference. This state might end when the child of the correct sex is born. However, if the child is the correct sex but does not meet the family's gender expectations, the liminal stage might continue as the child is a disappointment.	The parents present the child of the chosen sex to society, taking pleasure in their balanced family or in many cases the advantages of having a boy who might promote their economic and social status.
Child born through use of gender selection	When the child learns of the process, the child might have the objective to fulfill the family's gender expectations even if those expectations conflict with the child's preferences	The liminal stage might end if the child goes through life meeting gender expectations.	For the boy born as a result of the gender selection the liminal space could last a life time if he is born into a society with an imbalance of men and women.
Men and women	As the technology becomes socially familiar, society will become awakened to gender selection. Society might feel social objectives are met. Society might begin to accept cultural preferences for men over women as representative of freedom of choice.	The liminal space will be one of discovering the consequences of the technology and whether the objectives are met. Should gender selection result in more men than women, humans might find themselves in a liminal space where marriage is unavailable to many men, who may become more aggressive. Women, turned into a rarity, might be made vulnerable to aggressive efforts to be claimed as wives.	If women and men suffer from the effects of a preference for males, society might prohibit gender selection technologies. Otherwise, the same technology might be forcibly used by political regimes to restore the natural balance by insisting on a preference for girls.

301

Table 10.3.   Liminality and FCGS

Individual	Awakening and Objective Individual	Transformation Stage (Liminal)	Transformed Identity and Return to Ordinary life or Prolonged Liminal Stage
The patient	In FCGS the patient seeks an improved sexuality through cosmetic surgery. Awareness may come from consultations with cosmetic surgeons, the internet, or a partner.	The patient has to measure herself against standards of female anatomy that might not be natural and assume the risks that come with surgery. The liminal stage ends with successful surgery and few, if any, side effects.	The liminal stage might never end if the surgery is unsuccessful or if the sexual expectations related to partners' or spousal approval and sexual interest fail.
Partners	The partner might discover the availability of the surgery through the media and promote it. The partner has the objective of improving the woman's sexuality by reconfiguring her genitalia.	If a partner is involved, he or she would presumably be involved with the patient as she goes through the surgical process.	The partner may be disappointed or leave the woman for various reasons, and remain in a liminal stage of protracted sexual desire for the perfect genitalia.

the resulting sense that it is appropriate to emphasize the contractual nature of the relationship (Ford, 2008).

The rational choice argument relies on informed consent of the surrogate, yet whether the surrogate appreciates what she will be giving up in exchange is not clear, given the emotional consequences (Walker Wilson, 2005). Even the law foresees such emotional consequences in some jurisdictions. In New Hampshire, the surrogate has the ability to claim parental rights within 3 days of the child's birth (Ford, 2008, p. 90.)

On the contractual surface, the surrogate removes herself from motherhood even as she bears the child, requiring her to be reconceived as a substitute for normal pregnancy where the gestational carrier is presumed, through this labor, to be delivered into a new phase of motherhood entailing even deeper attachment. Yet it is not just the body that is partitioned out to intending parents: there are equally compelling claims on the surrogate's mind. She's not a machine.

Further distancing the surrogate from the creative process of giving birth are features of the process that alter the relationship between the surrogate and the medical caregivers. The surrogate is not even clearly the patient in the medical context. As Drabiak-Syed (2011) points out, the intending parents might influence whether the fetus is tested, and whether, if a fetus appears disabled, the surrogate must undergo an abortion.

Sense-making for surrogates means not entirely breaking the mold of motherhood roles but emphasizing anchors in the traditional concept. A study of 34 surrogates in the United Kingdom suggested that nongestational and gestational surrogates were perfectly capable of distancing themselves from the pregnancy. Jadva and colleagues (2003) concluded the idea of bonding is misplaced, yet the study did show:

> Eleven women (32%) experienced some difficulties in the weeks following the handover, and one surrogate mother experienced moderate difficulties. The remainder reported no difficulties. Five women (15%) reported some difficulties a few months after the handover, and the remaining 29 (85%) reported no difficulties. The number reporting some difficulties had decreased to only two (6%) at 1 year on, with 32 (94%) reporting no difficulties. (p. 2200)

The depth of the difficulties remains obscure for this study: "Since the child was born, three women (9%) had visited a general practitioner for psychological problems and one woman … made regular visits to a clinic regarding such problems" (Jadva et al., 2003, p. 2201).

Whether counseling is offered will depend on the provider and the contract (See Lee, 2009). Counseling might really amount to a managerial oversight of surrogates that speaks of suspicion and distrust (Pande, 2011) even as it would complement informed consent of surrogates (Blyth, Thorn, & Wischmann, 2011).

Some problems in readjusting may relate to the cultural context as well as individual outlooks on life. In the United States, where there are diverse types of families, where donating sperm and eggs is not uncommon, having no interest in parenting a child, however biologically related, might be disapproved but it certainly is part of the social fabric. Perhaps it is thus not surprising that in the United States, few surrogates express regret and tend instead to "view themselves as performing a service of great social value" (Scott, 2009, pp. 138-139).

As Palattiyil, Blyth, Sidhva, and Balakrishnan (2010) observe, the Indian surrogates seek justification for surrogacy as an unselfish act associated with "good karma" (p. 691). They may overlook more immediate consequences to their health and social standing. Indian surrogates might express their role as spiritual agency (Pande, 2011). Similarly, the payment could be seen as less commercial and more as a gift to a "needy" Indian (Pande, 2011, p. 621). Pande (2011) describes the anomalous situation of Indian surrogates, who, culturally discouraged to be seen as wage earners, construe their role as both providers of a gift of a child and beneficiaries of the intending mothers. Such constructions may well be defenses against the surrogates' sense of their own "disposability within the process of gestational surrogacy (Pande, 2009a)" (Pande, 2011, p. 622).

Gestational surrogates who are satisfied with the contract nevertheless may be in liminal places once they return to their homes where they may often conceal what they have done given cultural norms and religious perspectives.

The clinics presumably want to ensure the health of surrogates, but lawsuits can arise for failure to provide each surrogate with screening for psychological issues or infectious diseases (James, Chilvers, Havemann, & Phelps, 2010).

Few couples would boast about generating embryos in a petri dish; that machinery hardly fits into the normal imagery of the birth process. Ragoné (1998) maintains that in gestational surrogacy arrangements, all parties try to downplay the mechanical or technical aspects of surrogacy that represent a departure from tradition. Thus, a Mexican American surrogate who gave birth to a child for a Japanese couple felt "'In a way, she will always be my Japanese girl; but she is theirs'" (Ragoné, 1998, p. 125).

Many Indian women might not want any further contact with the parents or the child, given their interest in pursuing their own lives and also in light of community disapproval of the procedure (Parks, 2010).

The Intending Parents

Since gestational surrogacy services are becoming more publicized, would-be parents might be exposed to the idea through the media or physicians. The norms of medical practice themselves have to adjust to the liminality of the new process, in part by devising a new medical norm by "creating" as Elliot (2003) argues, a disease, namely infertility (p. 42). It is normal to seek treatment for a disease; it is normal to follow a physician's recommendations.

The ability to point to the legality of a procedure as evidence of its morality is limited for gestational surrogacy. The lack of clarity in the law furthers the liminal dimensions of the practice, which may have unpredictable results with gestational surrogates claiming a child or genetic parents rejecting one (James et al., 2010).

The awakening offers an opportunity that cannot be deeply interrogated if having the child is an unquenchable desire. Nevertheless, in some instances that desire might be constrained if the parents choose to examine the reality: what to do in the absence of giving birth, and what to do, if gestational surrogacy is chosen, with the real birth mother.

Pregnancy is a social symbol of fertility and generational power that the intending parents will never enjoy. The public would not know whether one had undertaken IVF cycles, but the infant appearing without being heralded by pregnancy would have to be explained to close family members, friends and even associates in the workplace.

Gestational surrogacy seems to eliminate the problem of biological motherhood and nurturing motherhood that arises for traditional surrogates using artificial insemination of sperm (Ragoné, 1998, p.123). However, the intending mother is always deprived of experiencing the emotional and physical sensations hailing a pending birth.

The biological contribution of the surrogate has to be diminished to retain the purity of the objective, which is going to justify, after all, severance from the birth mother. There is, for example, current research on the placental amnion, part of the fetal tissue, and its role in pregnancy and parturition (Han et al., 2008). Research on the amino placenta suggests it is possible the placenta contributes genetically to the parturition of the child (Han et al., 2008). If this is the case, then the emphasis on genetic connections as physical connections might suddenly provide the surrogate mother with a significant role over the lifetime of the child, a biological presence unanticipated by the intending parents.

An intending parent in liminal space might creatively substitute ways to prepare for the birth that will engage skills and efforts to make up for the absence of pregnancy. Haworth (2007) interviewed Jessica Ordenes, one intending parent in a gestational surrogacy arrangement. Ordenes is described as a 40-year old woman with one child from a prior marriage determined to have a child despite the lack of a uterus by using a surrogate. However, in New Jersey, surrogates cannot be compensated, and the woman, who called the waiting "the most demoralizing experience of my life" (Haworth, 2007, p. 7) traveled to the clinic of Dr. Patel in India. Although successful implantation becomes risky given Ordenes' age, Ordenes, after becoming acquainted with her surrogate, left India:

> Jessica Ordenes is not sure she can stick around for the embryo transfer—Patel has scheduled it for the following week. "I really want to stay to be with Najima," she says, "but I need to get home because I've arranged to have my basement renovated." She quickly realizes how that sounds and adds a qualifier. "Well, you know, good workmen are very hard to find. And the renovations are for the baby." (p. 7)

Intending parents understandably might focus not on the birth, where the fractured birth process is most evident, but on the nurturing of the child and his or her swift removal out of the liminal state of Indian mother and Indian birth site. It would certainly be beneficial to have the support of others.

Intending parents must try to find services. Although gestational surrogacy "accounts for approximately 95% of all surrogate pregnancies in the United States" (Smerdon, 2008/2009, p. 17), in the United States, surrogacy laws differ widely from state to state (James et al., 2010). One attraction India offers for gestational surrogacy is clarity on parenthood: under pending legislation, the surrogate would "relinquish all parental rights" (Palattiyil et al., 2010, p. 692). In contrast, in the United States, some state laws, sensitive to the natural relationship between mother and child, give surrogates an option, immediately after birth, to raise parental claims (see, e.g., Ford, 2008).

Not everyone will be able to afford this procedure, often not covered by insurance in the United States (Inhorn, 2011, p. 586.). Therefore, traveling to India, where the commercial costs are far less than in the United States, and the process may be undertaken without months of delay, may be appealing (Parks, 2010; Palattiyil et al., 2010).

If one has the determination, then the liminal stage begins, a journey where the intending parents must struggle to make sense of the process that is filled with the unexpected and not easily framed by normal conceptions of pregnancy, birth, and the concept of family.

Whether one is seeking gestational surrogacy or gender selection abroad, it is the woman's responsibility to access and filter reliable information. The Internet offers privacy, a way to avoid public disapproval, and information as well as "virtual communities" (Inhorn & Gürtin, 2011, p. 669). Interviews of North American women who had sought fertility treatments in the Czech Republic revealed the solitary effort: "'Doing the research' was an apt phrase used by many women" (Speier, 2011, p. 594), yet also patients spoke of randomly finding information, as if this success was not related to methodical effort but rather "aligned reproductive travel with fate" (Speier, 2011, p. 595).

Women seeking gestational surrogacy may have to confront the criteria that are surfacing on a global scale. According to the International Federation of Fertility Societies Surveillance 2010 (2010), accepted reasons for "IVF surrogacy" include a physical inability to conceive and carry a fetus to term or serious risk. Convenience is not a valid reason.

Even in the United States, where the practice is legal, physicians might discourage women from considering its use. Within fertility clinics there can be stressful ethical dissensions over practices where consultations go to those who can afford to pay, even if they have children, yet might be withheld from those without any children if they are deemed to lack the financial wherewithal to manage expenses (Cussins, 1998).

Clinics also strive to generate standards of civility in order to reduce anticipated stress or disappointment, perhaps through counseling, for what medical professionals may regard as a "major life crisis" (Cussins, 1998, p. 74).

Reproductive tourism results when women travel to other countries for services, often because those services are not available where they reside. The plight of Italian women who seek to be single parents, for example, means choosing a nation, perhaps based on advice from friends since many physicians might support the law prohibiting such use of IVF and the Catholic perspective of family that informs it (Zanini, 2011).

Many Muslims might find themselves in a similar quandary, since "the dominant Sunni branch of Islam—constituting nearly 90% of the world's Muslims—disallows any form of third-party reproductive assistance" though such services are permitted for Shia Muslims, so "donor technology and surrogacy are now widely practiced in Iran and also in Lebanon" (Inhorn, 2011, p. 588).

The ability to trust the medical professionals would also enter into passing the threshold awakening stage. Many Arab Americans feel more comfortable using IVF services in the Middle East, where the language and culture would be familiar and any sense of discrimination against Muslims would be alleviated (Inhorn, 2011). Being forced to travel, however, because of unfavorable laws thrusts intending parents deeply into liminal space: another country, another language, and physicians they might not trust (see, e.g., Zanini, 2011).

Travel could offer secrecy or promise some tourist distractions from a potentially stressful IVF or surrogacy process (see, e.g., Inhorn, 2011).

The personal rite and comfort might be constructed through the small community of fellow seekers that meet at a clinic and then decide to maintain contact (Inhorn & Gürtin, 2011; Speier, 2011).

Upon delivery of the child, the parents' liminal state may end. Yet if the intending parents, perhaps upon discovering the child was fathered by another male, reject the child, the child might remain with the surrogate. This could put the child, the surrogate, and the intending parents in a liminal state. Ragoné (1998) observes there are indications that parents, though rationally accepting a nonbiologically related child, nevertheless seek similarities in the children. A surrogate required to raise the child, if the intending parents refuse, would also find this easier if there were racial resemblance.

The Child Born of Gestational Surrogacy

The transfer of the child becomes liminal too, largely because the parenthood of the child, being legally constructed in contracts, is subject to ambiguous results and is not entirely logical in the firm assignment of legal parenthood.

The health of the fetus could be impacted by a surrogate who tries to remove herself from any emotional connection to the child: "her stress or ambivalence could negatively impact the fetus' psychological and emotional development" (Drybiak-Syed, 2011, p. 561).

A Canadian couple, after seeking screening of the fetus, which was discovered to have Down's syndrome, directed the surrogate to abort the fetus or they would withdraw their interest in claiming the child (Drabiak-

Syed, 2011). The question of prescreening for the health of the child also implicates the health of the surrogate, since certain prescreening tests could increase chances of miscarriage or have other effects, including discomfort (Drabiak-Syed, 2011).

In another case, when a baby was born through a surrogacy arrangement in India, the Japanese intending parents divorced and the biological mother and surrogate mother refused to claim the child. In India, a female child cannot leave the country without consent of the mother. Eventually, a court issued a "certificate of identity, which is given to individuals who are stateless or cannot get a passport" and allowed the paternal grandmother to take the baby to Japan (Parks, 2010, p. 333).

A child awakened to his or her unusual birth circumstances might also fall into a liminal state of doubt about identity. Some of that doubt might stem from a sense the child was viewed as a commodity. This is reinforced by the way that the law actually handles gestational surrogacy. Is one dealing with a child or fetal tissue? One U.S. law seeking to address the problem of predictable commercialization of these nonchildren could be interpreted as restraining clinics in the U.S. from focusing on remuneration for gestational surrogacy contracts (i.e., Section 289g-2 of the U.S.C.A. titled "Prohibitions regarding human fetal tissue") (see James et al., 2010, p. 865).

The shaky legality of gestational surrogacy contributes to the liminality of the state of those who are generated in this manner. Berys (2006) explores several contract models, focusing on goods and services, and concludes the surrogacy contract is more like a personal service contract than a sale of goods contract, arguing in part that personal services cannot be delegated. However, surrogacy can be delegated at any time prior to successful implantation, just as delegation could occur in the sale of "future goods" to be delivered by breeding horses or cows. One might object to a new tutor for one's children or a new portrait painter because one is sensitive about who is present with one's children and how one's self is fixed in an artistic medium. Yet what would-be parents would object if one gestational carrier, a healthier one, were substituted for another prior to implantation?

The child might be marginalized into liminal space by conflicting laws. Michigan and the District of Columbia, for example, provide criminal penalties as part of the legal schemes outlawing gestational surrogacy arrangements (James et al., 2010). If the parties decide that such conduct or concealment by a birth mother constitutes a material breach, then the parents could walk away from the genetic child. One restraint might be a law, a statute that declared the parents have to accept the child, probably allowing them legal recourse against the surrogate, which might be limited to return of the fee if the surrogate has no other assets.

The society that receives these new children is unprepared. The law addresses common problems, not highly unusual problems. Gestational surrogacy on a commercial level is hardly something the law is prepared to address. Patricia Mendell and Stuart Bell (2011), Cochairs of the American Fertility Association, released a statement that concluded in part,

> There is something very wrong when gourmet food trucks operate under more regulations than surrogacy and donor agencies. With the advent of the internet, anyone can operate an agency and appear to be legitimate. We need standardized and uniform rules that all agencies operate under. There ought to be licensing and background checks. There should be mandatory medical and psychological screening. There should be requirements that all parties be represented by independent legal counsel, that contracts be in place prior to the commencement of any medical procedures and safeguards in place to make sure all participants have informed consent. There needs to be oversight of trust accounts and clear and transparent cost sheets so that Surrogates, Egg Donors and Intended Parents can make informed decisions and be secure in the handling of their life savings. We need to ensure that adequate insurance is available to cover the Surrogates, Egg Donors and the resulting children. These issues can no longer be ignored and left to the judgment of individual agencies.

Citizenship is another concern. The child born of gestational surrogacy also poses potential problems of his or her identification as a citizen. When Aki Mukai, a famous entertainment figure in Japan, sought gestational surrogacy in Nevada, the eventual birth of twins was greeted with joy, marred only by authorities in Japan because the birth mother was not Japanese. Addressing this case, de Alcantara (2010) writes,

> The two most common forms of acquisition of citizenship by birth are *ius soli* and *ius sanguini*. The former confers citizenship unconditionally to all persons born in the state's territory. The latter confers citizenship to persons with a citizen parent or parents. (p. 420)

In the United States, those born within the United States are citizens; in Japan, a country of *ius sanguini*, the child's parent must be a Japanese citizen (de Alcantara). While Mukai was finally able to adopt, without providing the name of the surrogate on the documents, the Japanese position on surrogacy, as communicated through the Science Council of Japan in 2008, recommended prohibition of surrogacy, insisting surrogates would be the legal mother of the child, "the right to know one's origins should be guaranteed considering the child's welfare" and that there be recognition of the need for further "policy planning" (p. 426).

Germany poses similar problems, recently determining that a child born out of a surrogacy arrangement in India (using the German parents' gametes) could not obtain German citizenship (Blyth et al., 2011).

The U.S. State Department has interpreted citizenship requirements to extend citizenship to any child born of a noncitizen abroad so long as there is a genetic relationship to one or both U.S. citizen parents (de Alcantara, 2010, p. 423). This would assist U.S. citizens undertaking gestational surrogacy abroad.

Current reproductive practices challenge the significance of identity by working contractually to conceal the full identity of the beings involved. However, the International Federation of Social Workers has produced a policy seeking "noncommercialization of surrogacy and gamete and embryo procurement" (Blyth et al, 2011, p. 647). The same policy opposes practices of keeping donors' identities anonymous (Blyth et al., 2011).

A child who is informed of surrogacy origins is placed in a different liminal state, one where the identity of the birth mother will probably be underplayed and treated as incidental and not related to the child's identity. Yet identity is self-forming and the process of differentiating oneself from other carries over a lifetime, so the liminal state might endure.

Gender Selection

The Woman Seeking Gender Selection

A woman desiring a child of a certain sex might believe her life incomplete or inadequate without this. The idea of a high success rate will encourage use of the technology.

As noted above, women seeking fertility treatments may find it essential to gain expertise in researching online. Gender selection is legal in the US but illegal in many others. In cultures where males are preferred, information about sex determination may be highly accessible.

All the cultural reasons for preferring sons, and in many instances, a need (or a policy) limiting the number of children, contribute to sex discrimination practices, as is apparent in China, India, and other nations, including to some degree the United States (see Bumgarner, 2007; Abrevaya, 2008). The reality of a world where women continue to suffer, and the public as well, has been compellingly set out in 2010 in the *Economist* ("Sobs," "The War on Baby Girls," "The Worldwide War").

The mother may have been pressured into accepting cultural preferences for sons, thus diminishing her own value as a woman. To find some sense of self-worth, sex selection may offer "relational autonomy"

(Zilberberg, 2007, p. 518). If women feel socially obligated to make this choice, the autonomy of the decision is suspect (see, e.g., Bumgarner, 2007).

Women seeking gender selection might find themselves being morally judged. The morality of choosing a child based on sex is debatable. Scully, Banks, and Shakespeare (2006) conducted a study on attitudes toward sex selection in the United Kingdom that involved 48 individuals in 10 groups who ranged in age from 14 to over 80 from various backgrounds, with none convened on the basis of a religion. Results showed that 83% disagreed "with the use of prenatal social sex selection" and "a small minority thought prenatal sex selection was morally unacceptable in all circumstances (including selection to avoid an impairment)" (Scully et al., 2006, p. 23). The authors were also "surprised at the high degree of ambivalence that participants showed toward the idea of choice" (p. 24), suggesting that choice offers inadequate evidence the decision maker has engaged in moral contemplation and that, therefore, his or her decision should be respected as ethical.

A survey in Brazil of 723 physicians, at a conference for obstetricians and gynecologists, revealed that "opinions about sex selection were influenced by gender, as men were two times more likely to be in favor of sex selection" (Caldas, Caldas, Araújo, Bonetti, Leal, & Costa, 2010, pp. 159-160). Those disputing sex selection indicated "all children are welcome (70.6%), it was unnatural (17.4%), it was as playing god (8.9%) and worry with sex-ratio unbalance (3.1%)," though "in the context of a sex-linked disease, however, a large majority of the respondents (94%) reported that they would use sex selection to obtain healthy embryos" (p. 160),

Puria and Nachtigall (2010), interviewing 40 primary care physicians (PCPs) and 15 sex selection technology providers, found PCPs more likely to question desires for sex selection, whereas the sex selection technology providers, "understood their role as translating scientific advances into expanded reproductive options for their patients and did not express strong emotional sentiments about sex selection" (p. 2112).

As noted above in the section on sustainability, the practice of preferring one sex can result in damaging discrimination. The cultural reality obscures this because girls can be an economic burden. In many cultures, a dowry must accompany their marriage, and girls would not be contributing, through employment, to the economic welfare of the household. Many cultures are patriarchal where men have the last word or dominate legal and economic institutions, occupying the main sites of hegemonic power. To have a son is to have potential access, for a mother, to such power, albeit indirectly. Even in the Unites States, where women share equal political rights with men, cultural traditions shape the lives of citizens, many of whom use technologies, including abortion, to avoid bearing girls.

The Child Born of Gender Selection

The child born of gender selection, awakened to this choice, might feel compelled to match the gender expectations of the parents. The child would also be aware that other embryos, possibly healthy, were generated with the recognition they would be destroyed in the search for the right sex. This knowledge could raise questions about the personhood of such cellular life and the humanity of such generation and destruction in the name of personal preferences.

In a world where gender selection becomes common, men might dominate the planet. Both sexes could find themselves in liminal states, with men becoming more aggressive toward others, including the women they must obtain, and women living in greater fear and suppression. Reproductive freedom could lead to reproductive chaos. This liminal condition in the future might only end through termination of gender selection or some political and dictatorial mandate that it be used coercively to ensure the birth of more women. Termination of the liminal condition probably requires more than a ban on the technology: what is needed above all is improved social conditions for women (Zilberberg, 2007).

FCGS

Women seeking FCGS may be prompted to do so through advertising promising sexual happiness, yet without a healthy sense of self, many women may find even greater dissatisfaction with their lives. The promises of improved sexual pleasure draw on cultural genitalia emphasis, including pornography with its lens directed at genitalia. These cultural projections of beauty turn the potentially healthy quest for self-embodiment into a distorted desire for sexual approval (Braun, 2006; Braun, 2010). Cultural obsession with appearance can make cosmetic surgery "medical treatment for the inferiority complex" (Elliot, 2003, para. 17).

Yet for FCGS in particular, how the body measures up socially depends not on what people see on the street but what people imagine to be present beneath the apparel. Disappointment could lead, in some cases, to serious depression, as has been shown in recent research on suicides following breast implants (Lipworth et al., 2007).

A woman seeking FCGS wants to be happy and for her, satisfaction with her sexual being as reconceived by FCGS may well achieve this. Women's perceptions of genital attractiveness relate to many aspects of happiness (see Schick, Calabrese, Rima, & Zucker, 2010). How to determine whether one's body is satisfactory is complex in a world infiltrated by the subjective. "Sexual self-schemas" register how much one believes one meets the standard through consideration of those "personal characteristics that are associated with participation in intimate sexual relationships and behavioral openness to sexual experiences and encounters" (Donaghue, 2009, p. 37). Research has demonstrated "women's feelings about themselves and their happiness and satisfaction with life are highly influenced by embodied aspects of self (Fredrickson, Roberts, Noll, Quinn, & Twenge, 1998); in this case, satisfaction with their bodies and their sexual confidence" (Donaghue, 2009, p. 40).

Increased physical comfort or adjustment of obvious abnormalities that could be eliminated through surgery is certainly possible through FCGS (Braun, 2010), but body image also relates to health as a balance of body and mind (Braun, 2010). Self-consciousness and worries of inadequacies may depend upon how one measures up to standards of appearance (Schick et al., 2010, p. 2). How much body image contributes to sexual satisfaction is in dispute, but this may be owing to measurements of satisfaction with the body as a whole as opposed to particular parts (Schick et al., 2010). The consideration that women may view themselves as an assortment of parts, explains how "some body parts are more vulnerable to negative self-evaluation than others" (p. 3).

Women awakened to the advantages of FCGS might hesitate to speak of sexual satisfaction to surgeons, preferring to keep the real reason for transformation secret. As Braun (2010), writes, "reasons given for surgery may be the ones women think surgeons want to hear; functional accounts may be emphasized" (p. 1399).

The psychological results of women studying their own sexual organs are still being researched. Women's self consciousness during sex has led researchers to consider self-objectification. This can result in negative outcomes for women's functioning (Calogero & Thompson, 2009, p. 145).

Exploration of women's sexuality has become socialized where women compare themselves to desired images (Braun, 2006; Braun, 2010; Calogero & Thompson, 2009, p. 148). This unrealistic picture of the normal fits a liminal state. The kinds of vulva sought through FCGS reflect what is found in much "heterosexual male-oriented pornography" (Braun, 2005, p. 413). Schick and colleagues (2010) assert that pornographic displays of "unrealistic vulvas and the rising popularity of FGCS may enhance feelings of distress about genital appearance (Braun & Tiefer, 2010; Davis, 2002; Green, 2005)" particularly for young women (p. 9). Ethical physicians should be concerned about the desires of their patients (see Goodman et al., 2007). Technological promises of sexual beauty could undermine the ability of a woman to appreciate the limitations of how much FCGS can resolve her personal dissatisfaction with her sexuality (Liao & Creighton, 2007).

One might go so far as to suggest that unreality is a persistent problem of liminal conditions, for in being exposed to the old and new, the challenge of selecting the appropriate new arrangement is quite formidable, particularly since liminality does not necessarily introduce clarification. To experience liminality is not the same as struggling to witness, phenomenologically, the liminality of lived-out lives. Those who undertake these technologies are primarily interested in gaining the desired outcomes; the process is something to be endured, not an opportunity for enlightenment.

Schouten (1991) asserts that the person who chooses to be transformed through cosmetic surgery is the actor driving the rite to self with a newly perceived status.

Yet the pursuit of cosmetic surgery might create an endless liminal state of constant body scrutiny and criticism. Surgery alone does not connect women with their ability to solve problems, with the result that some women just become preoccupied with the next defect to be fixed (Liao & Creighton, 2007, p. 1091).

DISCUSSION AND CONCLUDING COMMENTS

Implications for Public Policy

From a commercial view the above technologies are legitimate where practiced in that they fulfill perceived needs. Barren women can have biological offspring, families that want a boy can have one, and women that feel the need for a transformed genitalia can do so. From a utilitarian perspective one could say that ICGS meets the needs of participants while minimizing potential risk and harm as does FCGS. Gender selection where practiced to avoid gender related disorders would clearly be utilitarian in the avoidance of harm to the desired child. Other forms of gender selection would be acceptable if demanded as a form of happiness, one benefit being reduction of abortions, which in the United States, though framed by certain procedural restrictions, or potentially limited by some states, could largely be done for any reason, including sexism. Should gender selection be used to promote sexism that would emerge as identifiably harmful to society, as in a significant number of abandoned or abused girls, the utilitarianism of the technology would be diminished.

However, at a more profound value level, ICGS uses surrogates as a means to an end and risks dehumanizing them. Gender selection is inherently wrong when used to promote advantages for men at the expense of women's integrity. FCGS objectifies women's sexuality and in so doing dehumanizes the participants.

Engagement in dialogue is the most promising way to ensure that approaches to these technologies accord with significant interests of humanity in the well-lived life. Although one should be cautious at out-right prohibitions, professional oversight from associations could encourage practitioners to consider the ethical consequences of their services. Public awareness and dialogue would contribute valuable perspectives beyond potential patients that could, in part, provide potential patients with a richer context for making decisions about using these technologies. Such discussion ultimately benefits legislators and the courts when legal authority is sought for differences and disputes that cannot be resolved in the private sector.

Directions for Future Research

Should these technologies be regulated to avoid the above mentioned shortcomings? ICGS could be limited to the hopelessly childless and not offered to help the wealthy avoid the inconvenience of pregnancy. Furthermore surrogates could be offered counseling support to ensure that they have considered the risks of undertaking surrogacy. Governments could also protect them from exploitive clinics. Gender selection could be limited to the avoidance of gender specific genetic problems. FCGS could be reviewed professionally to evaluate outcomes of patients already treated and clinicians should be forced to demonstrate the efficacy of assorted techniques through peer reviewed research. Future research could assess the outcomes of services performed to determine the consequences to patients.

Limitation of the Study

The study is based on observations of some enterprises and participants. Thus, there is limited understanding of the consequences of the services. Any observations would have to be limited to the specific services performed that are not performed in large numbers.

Professional societies and regulatory bodies should review the liminal experiences of participants in the above mentioned technologies to determine how they were served and what problems were encountered. In some cases such analyses need to be done longitudinally since the impact of procedures may not be apparent immediately.

But society must not leap too quickly to judgment. Preimplantation genetic diagnosis was very controversial initially and still is for Catholics and others. However, fertility clinics have proven popular given the fertility problems so many couples experience. Adoption was always the alternative to infertility but it can take years and cost a great deal now that people tend to adopt internationally given the lack of available babies in the developed world. Thus ICGS may grow dramatically in the future. Again, gender selection is unsupported from an ethical perspective and medical professional societies and governments should work to limit it. FCGS can be unnecessary but pre- and postphotos on plastic surgeons website show the transformation of some patients. One can readily question the practice given its cosmetic approach but assessing the liminal responses of patients over time would be the prudent course of action. How women feel about their bodies is obviously important. Courts and legislatures may also evaluate the outcomes of these services in some jurisdictions and determine what is legal in the future.

Liminality focuses on the transformational experience. One can judge too quickly without understanding the long-term consequences of such new technologies.

REFERENCES

Abrevaya, J. (2008). Are there missing girls in the United States?: Evidence from birth data. Retrieved from http://papers.ssrn.com/sol3/papers.cfm?abstract_id=824266#

ACOG. (2007). ACOG advises against cosmetic vaginal procedures due to lack of safety and efficacy data. Retrieved from http://www.acog.org/from_home/publications/press_releases/nr09-01-07-1.cfm

Berys, F. (2006). Interpreting a rent-a-womb contract: How California courts should proceed when gestational surrogacy arrangements go sour. *California Western Law Review, 42,* 321-353.

Blyth, E., Thorn, P., & Wischmann, T. (2011). CBRC and psychosocial counseling: Assessing needs and developing and ethical framework for practice. *Reproductive Biomedicine Online, 23,* 642-651.

Braun, V. (2005). In search of (better) sexual pleasure: Female genital "cosmetic" surgery. *Sexualities, 8,* 407-424. doi:10.1177/1363460705056625

Braun, V. (2006). Making sense of female genital alteration practices. Women's Health Action Trust. Retrieved from http://www.womens-health.org.nz/index.php?page=making-sense-of-female-genital-alteration-practices.

Braun, V. (2010). Female genital cosmetic surgery: A critical review of current knowledge and contemporary debates. *Journal of Women's Health, 19*(7), 1393-1404. doi:10.1089/jwh.2009.1728

Bumgarner, A. (2007). A right to choose?: Sex selection in the international context. *Duke Journal of Gender Law & Policy, 14,* 1289-1309.

Caldas, G. H., Caldas, E., Araújo, E. D., Bonetti, T. C. S., Leal, C. B., & Costa, A. M. (2010). Opinions concerning pre-implantation genetic diagnosis and sex selection among gynecologist-obstetricians in Brazil. *European Journal of Obstetrics & Gynecology and Reproductive Biology, 148,* 158-162.

Calogero, R. M., & Thompson, J. K. (2009). Potential implications of the objectification of women's bodies for women's sexual satisfaction. *Body Image, 6,* 145-148.

Cussins, C. (1998). Producing reproduction: Techniques of normalization and naturalization in infertility clinics. In S. Franklin & H. Ragoné (Eds.), *Reproducing reproduction: Kinship, power, and technological innovation* (pp. 66-101). Philadelphia, PA: University of Pennsylvania Press.

Daar, J. F. (2005). ART and the search for perfectionism: On selecting gender, genes, and gametes. *The Journal of Gender, Race & Justice, 9,* 241-272.

Dahlsrund, A. (2006). How corporate social responsibility is defined: An analysis of 37 definitions. *Corporate Social Responsibility and Environmental Management, 15,* 1-13. doi:10.1002/cst.132.

de Alcantara, M. (2010). Surrogacy in Japan: Legal implications for parentage and citizenship. *Family Court Review, 48*(3), 417-430.

Donaghue, N. (2009). Body satisfaction, sexual self-schemas and subjective well-being in women. *Body Image, 6,* 37-42.

Drabiak, K. C., Wegner, C., Fredland, V., & Helft, P. R. (2007, Summer). Ethics, law and commercial surrogacy: A call for uniformity. *Journal of Law, Medicine & Ethics, 35*(2), 300-309.

Drabiak-Syed, K. (2011). Waiving informed consent to prenatal screening and diagnosis. Problems with paradoxical negotiation in surrogacy contracts. *Journal of Law, Medicine & Ethics, 39*(3), 559-564.

Elliot, C. (2003). American bioscience meets the American dream. *The American Prospect, 14*(6) 38-42. Retrieved from ABI/Inform database.

Ford, M. (2008). Gestational surrogacy is not adultery: Fight against religious opposition to procreate. *Barry Law Review, 10,* 81-109

Forss, A., Tishelman, C., Widmark, C., & Sachs, L. (2004). Women's experiences of cervical cellular changes: An unintentional transition from health to liminality? *Sociology of Health & Illness, 26*(3), 306-325.

George, S. M. (2006). Millions of missing girls: From fetal sexing to high technology sex selection in India. *Prenatal Diagnosis, 26,* 604-609. doi:10.1002/pd.1475

Goodman, M. P., Bachmann, G. Johnson, C. Fourcroy, J. L., Goldstein, A., Goldstein, G., & Sklar, S. (2007). Is elective vulvar plastic surgery ever warranted, and what screening should be conducted preoperatively? *Journal of Sex Medicine, 4,* 269-276. doi:10.1111/j.1743-6109.2007.00431.x

Han, Y. M., Romero, R., Kim, J., Tarca, A. L., Kim, S. K., & Draghici, S. (2008). Region-Specific gene expression profiling: Novel evidence for biological heterogenity of the human amnion. *Biology of Reproduction, 79,* 954-961.

Haworth, A. (2007, July 29). Surrogate mothers: Womb for rent. *Marie Claire.* pp. 1-7. Retrieved from http://www.marieclaire.com/world-reports/news/surrogate-mothers-india

Hediger, W. (2010). Welfare and capital-theoretic foundations of corporate social responsibility and corporate sustainability. *Journal of Social Economics, 39*(4), 518-526. Retrieved from Science Direct. doi:10.1016/j.socec.2010.02.001

Heidegger, M. (2008). *Being and time.* (J. Macquarrie & E. Robinson, Trans.). New York, NY: Harper Perennial (Original translation published 1962).

Inhorn, M. C. (2011) Diasporic dreaming: Return reproductive tourism to the Middle East. *Reproductive Biomedicine Online, 23,* 582-591.

Inhorn, M. C., & Gürtin, Z .B. (2011). Cross-border reproductive care: A future research agenda. *Reproductive Biomedicine Online, 23,* 665-676. doi:10.1016/h/rbmo.2011.08.002.

International Federation of Fertility Societies Surveillance. (2010). In H. W. Jones, I. Cooke, R. Kempers, P. Brinsden, & D. Saunders (Eds.). *Fertility and sterility* (accepted August 9, 2010). doi:10.1016/j.fertnstert.2010.08.011.

Jadva, V., Murray, C., Lycett, E., MacCallum, F., & Golombok, S. (2003). Surrogacy: The experiences of surrogate mothers. *Human Reproduction, 18*(10), 2196-2204. doi:10.1093/humrep/deg397.

James, S. Chilvers, R., Havemann, D., & Phelps, J. Y. (2010). Avoiding legal pitfalls in surrogacy arrangements. *Reproductive Biomedicine Online, 21,* 862-867.

Kelly, A. (2008). Living loss: An exploration of the internal space of liminality. *Mortality, 13*(4), 335-350.

Lee, R. L. (2009). New trends in global outsourcing of commercial surrogacy: A call for regulation. *Hastings Women's Law Journal, 20,* 275-300.

Liao, M. L., & Creighton, S. M. (2007). Requests for cosmetic genitoplasty: How should healthcare providers respond? *BMJ, 334,* 1090-1092.

Little, M., Jordens, C. F. C. , Paul, K., Montgomery, K., & Philipson, B. (1998). *Social Science Medicine, 47*(10), 1485-1494.

Lipworth, L., Nyren, O. Ye, W., Fryzek, J., Tarone, R. E., & McLaughlin, J. K. (2007). [Abstract]. Excess mortality from suicide and other external causes of death among women with cosmetic breast implants. *Annals of Plastic Surgery, 59*(2), 119-123. Retrieved from https://mail.google.com/a/sjsu.edu/?ui=2&view=bsp&ver=ohhl14rwmbn4

MacIntyre, A. (1988). *Whose justice? Which rationality?.* Notre Dame, IN: University of Notre Dame Press.

Mendell, P., & Bell, S. (2011). The AFA and the need for regulation. The Spin Doctor. Retrieved from http://www.eggdonor.com/blog/

New View Campaign. (2010) Retroeved from http://www.fsd-alert.org

New View Campaign. (2010) Retrieved from http://www.fsd-alert.org/manifesto3.asp

Nixon, M. G. (2007). Satisfaction for whom? Freedom for what?: Theology and the economic theory of the consumer. *Journal of Business Ethics, 70,* 39-60.

Nussbaum, M. C. (1999). *Sex and social justice.* New York, NY: Oxford.

Palattiyil, G., Blyth, E., Sidhva, D., & Balakrishnan, G. (2010). Globalization and cross-border reproductive services: Ethical implications of surrogacy in India for social work. *International Social Work 53*(5), 686-700. doi:10.1177/0020872810372157 2010 53.

Pande, A. (2011). Transnational commercial surrogacy in India: Gifts for global sisters?. *Reproductive Biomedicine Online, 23,* 618-625. doi.10.1016/j.rbmo.2011.07.007.

Parks, J. A. (2010). Care ethics and the global practice of commercial surrogacy. *Bioethics, 24*(7), 333-340.

Pfeffer, N. (2011). Eggs-ploiting women: A critical feminist analysis of the different principles in transplant and fertility tourism. *Reproductive Biomedicine Online, 23,* 634-641.

Planned Parenthood of Se. Pennsylvania versus Casey, 505 U.S. 833, 874 (1992).

President's Council on Bioethics. (2003). *Beyond therapy: Biotechnology and the pursuit of perfection, Chapter Two, Better children, selecting embryos for desired traits.* Retrieved from http://www.bioethics.gov/reports/beyondtherapy/chapter2.html

Puria, S., & Nachtigall, R. D. (2010). The ethics of sex selection: a comparison of the attitudes and experiences of primary care physicians and physician providers of clinical sex selection services. *Fertility and Sterility, 93*(7). doi:2107-2114. doi:10.1016/j.fertnstert.2009.02.053

Puria, S., Adams, V., Ivey, S., & Nachtigall, R. D. (2011). "There is such a thing as too many daughters, but not too many sons:" A qualitative study of son preference and fetal sex selection among Indian immigrants in the United States. *Social Science & Medicine, 72*(7), 1169-1176. doi:10.1016/j.socscimed.2011.01.027

Ragoné, H. (1998). Incontestable motivations. In S. Franklin & H. Ragoné (Eds.), *Reproducing reproduction: Kinship, power, and technological* innovation (pp. 118-131). Philadelphia, PA: University of Pennsylvania Press.

Roan, S. (2011, March 14). In China, India, sex selection means there are too many males. *Los Angeles Times.* Retrieved from http://articles.latimes.com/2011/mar/14/news/la-heb-sex-selection-20110314

Roberts, S. (2009, June 14). U.S. births hint at bias for boys in some Asians. *New York Times.* Retrieved from http://www.nytimes.com/2009/06/15/nyregion/15babies.html?_r=1&pagewanted=all

Scott, E. S. (2009). Show me the money: Making markets in forbidden exchange: Surrogacy and the politics of commodification. *Law & Contemporary Problems, 72,* 109-146.

Schick, V. R., Calabrese, S. K., Rima B. N., & Zucker, A. N. (2010). Genital appearance dissatisfaction: Implications of women's genital image self-consciousness, sexual esteem, sexual satisfaction, and sexual risk. National Institute of Health. *Psychology Women Quarterly, 34*(3), 394-404.

Schwinn, S. D., & Robson, R. (2011, March 30). Arizona abortion law: Requiring an affidavit excluding race or sex as reasons. Constitutional Law Prof Blog. Retrieved from http://lawprofessors.typepad.com/conlaw/2011/03/arizona-abortion-law-requiring-an-affidavit-excluding-race-or-sex-as-reasons.html)

Schouten, J. W. (1991). Selves in transition: Symbolic consumption in personal rites of passage and identity reconstruction. *Journal of Consumer Research, 17,* 412-425.

Scully, J. L., Banks, S., & Shakespeare, T. W. (2006). Chance, choice and control: Lay debate on prenatal social sex selection. *Social Science & Medicine, 63*(21), 31. doi:10.1016/j.socscimed.2005.12.013.

Shreffler, K. M., Johnson, D. R., & Scheuble, L. K. (2010). Ethical problems with infertility treatments: Attitudes and explanations. *The Social Science Journal, 47,* 731-746. doi:10.1016/j.soscij.2010.07.012.

Smerdon, U. R. (2008/2009). Crossing bodies, crossing borders: International surrogacy between the United States and India. *Cumberland Law Review, 39*(1), 15-85.

"Sobs on the night breeze." (2010, March 6-12). *The Economist, 394*(8672), 104.

Sophocles. *Antigone*. (1967). In M. Hadas (Ed.) & Jebb, R. C. (Trans.), *The Complete Plays of Sophocles* (pp. 121-155). New York, NY: Bantam Books, .

Speier, A. R. (2011). Brokers, consumers and the internet: How North American consumers navigate their infertility journeys. *Reproductive Medicine Online, 23*, 592-599. doi:10.1016/j.rbmo.2011.07.005.

Triffin, M. (2010, July). Warning: These doctors may be dangerous to your vagina. *Cosmopolitan*, 159-161. http://cosmo.itgo.in/cosmopolitan/story.jsp?sid=7945&page=1

Turner, V. (1982). *From ritual to theatre: The human seriousness of play*. New York, NY: PAJ.

Turner, V. (1987). *The anthropology of performance*. New York, NY: PAG.

Van Gennep, A. (1960). *The rites of passage* (M. B. Vizedom & B. L. Caffee, Trans.). Chicago, IL: University of Chicago Press. (Original work published 1908)

Walker Wilson, M. J. (2005). Precommitment in free-market procreation: Surrogacy, commissioned adoption, and limits on human decision making capacity. *Journal of Legislation, 31*, 329-350.

"The war on baby girls: Gendercide." (2010, March 6-12) *The Economist, 394*(8672), 13.

"The worldwide war on baby girls." (2010, March 6-12). *The Economist, 394*(8672), 77-80.

Zanini, G. (2011). Abandoned by the state, betrayed by the church: Italian experiences of cross-border reproductive care. *Reproductive Biomedicine Online, 23*(5), 565-572.

Zilberberg, J. (2007). Sex-selective abortion for social reasons: Is it ever morally justifiable?: Sex selection and restricting abortion and sex determination. *Bioethics, 2*(9), 517-519.

CHAPTER 11

PATENT WARS

Staying Ahead of the Curve

Avimanyu Datta and Len Jessup

ABSTRACT

With this work we extend the research on radical innovation to established firms' commitment toward future markets. We used patent filings from 1996 through 2009 from the information technology (IT) industry within the S&P-500 database. We selected the top ten patents in each of the categories of radicalness: *novelty to past innovations, uniqueness to present innovations,* and *impact on future innovations.* Twenty four unique patents were collected of which only 14 met the criteria of radicalness specified by Dahlin and Behrens (2005): a patent is radical if it is either (a) both unique and novel, or (b) has an impact on future technologies, or (c) both. These 14 patents came from eight firms (AMD, Agilent, EMC, IBM, Intel, Microsoft, SanDisk, and Xerox). Discussing each of these firms, we linked the technical content of the patents with future markets that were 5 to 15 years from each patents' date of filing. While one cannot truly say whether accidental technological breakthroughs open market opportunities or whether vision of markets leads to deliberate breakthroughs, we conclude

Global Perspectives on Technological Innovation, pp. 321–371

that continuous commitment toward research on technology increases the chance of both accidental and deliberate discovery of future markets.

INTRODUCTION

The failure to predict future markets is a root cause of organizational collapse (Christensen & Bower, 1996; Cordell, 1973). Future markets generally can be captured with successful introduction of radical innovations (Dahlin & Behrens, 2005; Di Benedetto, DeSardo & Song, 2008; Golder, Shacham & Mitra, 2008; Malhotra, Majchrzak, Carman, & Lott, 2001; Rice, Kelley, Peters & O'Connor, 2001; Soosay & Hyland, 2008). Radical innovations differ inherently from existing products or technologies (Aboulnasr, Narasimhan , Blair & Chandy, 2008; Andriopoulos & Lewis, 2010; Chandy, Hopstaken, Narasimhan & Prabhu, 2006; Di Benedetto et al., 2008; Schilling & Phelps, 2007), and within an industry, dominant firms tend to value radical innovations more than do nondominant firms (Sorescu, Chandy & Prabhu, 2003). Further, a firm's inability to bring radical innovations to market likely compromises its survival chances (O'Reilly & Tushman, 2004; Tushman & O'Reilly, 1996a, 2002; Veliyath, 1992).

Successful radical innovations tend to provide firms with an opportunity to gain sustainable competitive advantages, such that they can earn economic rents by capturing future markets (Achilladelis, Schwarzkopf, & Cines, 1990; Harhoff, Narin, Scherer, & Vopel, 1999). Research specifically links radical innovations to commercial value using measures of patent citations (Hall, Jaffe, & Trajtenberg, 2005), firm longevity (Burgelman & Grove, 1996; O'Reilly & Tushman, 2004; Tushman & O'Reilly, 1996a, 2002), and sustainable competitive advantages that generate economic rents (Achilladelis et al., 1990; Ray, 1980; Harhoff et al., 1999). Radical innovations are particularly critical in dynamic industries with short product lifespans (Bourgeois & Eisenhardt, 1988; Dess & Beard, 1984; Jansen, Vanden Bosch & Volberda, 2006; Miller & Friesen, 1983; Sidhu, Volberda & Commandeur, 2004), such as the information technology (IT) industry, for which windows of opportunity open and shut quickly (Ladd, Datta, & Sarker, 2010). Despite extensive innovation research (Bharadwaj, 2000; Bharadwaj, Bharadwaj, & Konsynski, 1999; Bhatt & Grover, 2005; Brynjolfsson, 1993; Brynjolfsson & Hitt, 1996; Brynjolfsson & Mendelson, 1993; Ferneley & Bell, 2006; Hitt & Brynjolfsson, 1996; Joshi, Chi, Datta, & Han, 2010; Lyytinen & Rose, 2003; Sambamurthy, Bharadwaj, & Grover, 2003; Santhanam & Hartono, 2003; Swanson & Ramiller, 2004; Tippins & Sohi, 2003), the IT literature continues to ignore radical innovations in terms of their novelty, uniqueness, and impact on future innovations or ability to address the needs of future markets.

The radicalness of an innovation is a function of its newness and difference. That is, it must be novel compared with past innovations, unique compared with present innovations, and likely to influence future innovations (Dahlin & Behrens, 2005). To determine whether radicalness exists with just one of these characteristics or requires all of them, Dahlin and Behrens (2005) investigate tennis racket patents and find three categories of radical patents: (1) both unique and novel, (2) an impact on future technologies, or (3) both 1 and 2. We adopt this three-criterion system to investigate the top patents in each category (uniqueness to past, novelty to present, impact on future) in the IT industry.

In addition, whereas Dahlin and Behrens (2005) consider granted patents, we investigate the firms that file patents to determine if the content of radical patents contributes to a firm's knowledge of future market opportunities. To do so, we attempt to link the technological content of an innovation (approximated by patents) with future markets, considering the necessary lag time between a patent announcement, the relevant product introduction, and potential market success (Nerkar & Shane, 2007; Soh, 2003). The filing of a radical patent ultimately may lead to the fulfillment of market needs in the future (Nerkar & Shane, 2007; Soh, 2003), such that a patent filing implies a firm's commitment to future markets. Accordingly, this study adopts a dual purpose. First, it identifies the most radical patents in the IT industry in the past 15 years. Second, by reviewing individual firms, we attempt to show how firms, through their radical patents, contribute to addressing the needs of a future market. In turn, we gain a greater understanding of how firms might make innovation choices that tap emerging opportunities and position themselves competitively for the future.

RADICAL INNOVATIONS: DEFINITIONS, INDICATORS, AND RESEARCH QUESTIONS

Radical or breakthrough innovations are defined as "those foundational innovations that serve as the basis for many subsequent technical developments" (Ahuja & Lampert, 2001). Radical innovations serve as a source for many subsequent innovations, because their technical content can be used by many successive innovations (Trajtenberg, 1987, 1990; Trajtenberg, Henderson & Jaffe, 1997). This notion is consistent with Dahlin and Behrens's (2005) requirement that radical inventions have an impact on future innovations, along with being novel and unique compared with past or present innovations. In a similar vein, we consider all innovations that serve as important antecedents for later innovations as radical. Our definition thus concurs with Dahlin and Behrens's (2005) work: An innovation is radical to the extent it is novel and unique or has an impact on future technology, where

1. *Novel to past* indicates that the innovation is dissimilar from prior innovations.
2. *Unique to present* means the invention is dissimilar from current innovations.
3. *Impact on future* implies the innovation influences the content of future innovations.

To measure radicalness on all three dimensions, Dahlin and Behrens use patents and citations. If an innovation fulfilled the novel and unique criteria, they could ex ante claim that it was radical; if it met the impact criterion, they could assert ex post that as a successful change agent, it caused a radical technological change in the industry (Dahlin & Behrens, 2005). Thus, though novelty and uniqueness indicate radicalness, in some cases, an innovation can exert a high impact on future technologies, even if it was not novel or unique at the time of its filing.

Dominant firms in an industry tend to value radical innovations more than nondominant ones (Sorescu et al., 2003), and the ability to develop radical new products without destroying existing markets increases firms' longevity (O'Reilly & Tushman, 2004; Tushman & O'Reilly, 1996b, 2002). Although not all firms effectively develop radical innovations, because they cannot transcend their core rigidities (Galunic & Eisenhardt, 1996; Leonard-Barton, 1992), it remains unclear if a firm really must be radical in all three dimensions for it to bring radical innovations to the market. On one hand, an innovation might be novel but have no impact on future technologies, such that the firm created a radical innovation, but the market did not perceive it as such. On the other hand, an innovation may not be novel from the firm's perspective, but it could have an impact on future technologies. That is, a firm may have the capability to be innovative on all three radicalness levels, but each innovation does not necessarily score high in all categories. It is worth discerning whether an individual patent indicates a radical innovation, even if it does not meet all three criteria.

Furthermore, the need for radical innovation is particularly intense in certain industries, especially dynamic ones with short product lifespans (Bourgeois & Eisenhardt, 1988; Dess & Beard, 1984; Jansen et al., 2006; Miller & Friesen, 1983; Sidhu et al., 2004). IT is one such "high velocity" industry (Bourgeois & Eisenhardt, 1988), notable for its scientific and commercial advances, high patenting rates, reliance on interfirm collaborations, and diversity of participating organizations (e.g., universities, public research institutions, venture capital firms, financial institutions, small enterprises). Sources of scientific leadership thus are widely dispersed and rapidly developing, and the skills and resources needed to produce new products are broadly distributed. No single organization, thus, can master and control all the competencies required to develop new products, and the fast pace of technical advances makes it increasingly difficult for any organization to stay abreast of all developments. Accordingly, the need to be radical in this industry is matter of survival, rather than leadership.

Most prior studies of the radicalness of innovations rely on patent citations, because patents that are more widely cited by future innovations achieve higher commercial value (Tobin's Q) than those that are less frequently cited (Hall et al., 2005). Such calculations of commercial value require the consideration of firm-level variables as well. Therefore, though we look to citations to determine radicalness, we also investigate how the radical patents of specific firms help them tap emerging opportunities for the future.

We also note the time lag between a patent announcement and its conversion into a product (Nerkar & Shane, 2007; Soh, 2003). A radical patent filing includes content that likely addresses the needs of a market sometime in the future—perhaps even 5-15 years into the future. If a firm can see the future market potential of a technology, it can create a blueprint through a patent, such that the patent should provide a reasonable idea of future market potential. If we consider a 10-year old patent, we can also determine the firm's current technological expertise and thus recognize whether its commitment to the market, as manifested by the 10-year old patent, had a positive influence. Yet prior literature largely has ignored the technical content of patents as indicators of a firm's vision and commitment to future markets.

These discussions together reveal the theoretical and practical interest of determining the leading radical innovations in the IT industry, identifying the firms involved in those innovations, and recognizing how the innovations could be linked to future markets, distant at the time of the patent announcement. We therefore consider two key research questions:

RQ1. *What are the top radical patents in each of the three categories of radicalness?* We looked specifically at the top-ranked radical patents for each of Dahlin and Behren's (2005) categories: both unique to past, and novel to present, with an impact on future technologies, or both. Then we identified the firms that filed these patents and how the firms were positioned across the three criteria. We also addressed the cumulative patenting behavior of these firms, in terms of total patents filed and granted and the number of patents that were novel to present, unique to past, and impactful for future innovation s. Thus, this research question centers on the patents and the firms as originators of those patents.

RQ2. *What are the future markets, and how did the radical innovations help firms address the needs of those markets?* For this question, we shifted analysis from patents to firms, which enabled us to link the technical content of the radical innovation described by the patent with accumulated R&D and future markets. In turn, we could determine how each firm addressed the needs of emerging opportunities with radical innovations and stayed of competition. We graphically represent the core premises of these research questions in Figure 11.1.

METHODS

Data Collection: Patents as Innovation

In line with prior research, we used patents as a proxy for innovation (Basberg, 1987; Cohen, Goto, Nagata, Nelson, & Walsh, 2002; Dahlin & Behrens, 2005; Grindley & Teece, 1997; Katila, 2002; Katila & Ahuja, 2005) and their citations as a measure of radicalness (Fleming, 2001; Fleming & Sorenson, 2001; Katila, 2002; Katila & Ahuja, 2005; Rosenkopf & Almeida, 2003; Rosenkopf & Nerkar, 2001; Sorenson, Rivkin, & Fleming, 2006; Stuart & Podolny, 1996). Searching for sources of innovation is a problem-solving activity (Nelson & Winter, 1982); that is, firms solve problems by combining knowledge elements and thus create new products (Katila, 2002). Because a patent describes a technical problem

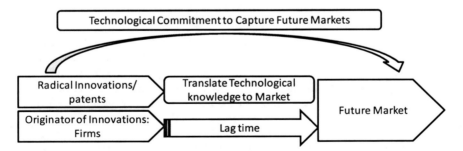

RQ1: Centers on patents and discusses firms as originator of patents.
RQ2: Centers on individual firms where patents are R&D initiative taken to address needs of future market opportunities.

Figure 11.1.   Radical innovations and technological commitments towards future markets.

and its solution, patent data offers a detailed, consistent chronology of how firms solve problems and the manner in which they search for those solutions.

For a patent to be granted, the information underlying it must be novel, nontrivial, and useful. A granted patent creates a legal title that indicates the name of the inventor or inventing firm, the relevant technology types (Rosenkopf & Almeida, 2003), and the technological antecedents of the focal knowledge.

Patents with more forward citations likely have more economic value for firms that possess them (Harhoff et al., 1999). Furthermore, forward citations are good indications of the technological importance of an invention (Dahlin & Behrens, 2005). Finally, patent citation counts approximate the technological importance of innovations (Albert, Avery, Narin & McAllister, 1991; Narin, Noma, & Perry, 1987); highly cited patents are more likely to feature radical innovations (Trajtenberg, 1990). A patent has an impact on future technology if it is cited by future patents and has a high forward-to-backward citation ratio. When a citation to prior technology appears in a new patent, the inventor has successfully received and built on the knowledge underlying the earlier patent (Sorenson et al., 2006).

Data Collection Strategy and Sampling

We selected U.S. firms from Standard & Poor's (S&P) 500 list, which covers approximately 75% of the U.S. equity market by capitalization. We identified 81 firms from the IT industry and confirmed their industry setting by checking standard industrial classification codes: 7379 (computer systems and design services), 7376 (computer facilities management), 3571 (electronic computer manufacturing), 7371 (custom computer programming services), and 8748 (other scientific and technical consulting services). Of the 81 firms, only 69 had filed patents. We therefore collected the patents for all 69 firms from the U.S. Patent and Trademark Office (USPTO) database (January 1, 1996-June 30, 2009). Across all 69 firms, we collected 192,070 patents and more than 2 million citations for the analysis.

Radicalness

We select the top 10 radical innovations in each category of radicalness.

Novel From Past

To be novel, by definition, an innovation must be dissimilar from prior innovations (Dahlin & Behrens, 2005). Thus novelty is a measure of the distinction of the focal technology in a patent application compared with the firm's own core competences with existing technology. From a patent-level perspective, we first noted the technology class match, a percentage calculation of how similar a technology is to a firm's previous cited works, which we subtracted from 1 to compute technology distinction. Technology distinction thus is the degree to which a patent's technology differs from the technology of the patents it cites, so backward citations offer a measure of novelty (Carpenter, Narin, & Woolf, 1981; Dahlin & Behrens, 2005). Radical inventions should be more likely to cite patents from patent classes other than that to which the radical invention belongs (Dahlin & Behrens, 2005; Rosenkopf & Nerkar, 2001).

Our measure reflects and extends Dahlin and Behrens's (2005) efforts to attain a backward match of a new, exclusive classification with the technology class of the patent and its cited patents. We devise a more fine-grained method to determine technology similarity. A patent examiner and applicant determine the primary classification for any patent, so Patent X may have a primary classification of "514/252.01," because it falls into the 514 class (drug, bioaffecting, and body-treating compositions) and the 252.01 subclass. These additional classifications describe the patent's technological breadth. For Patent X, the 514 primary classification appears eight times in its backward citations, each time defining a unique subclass.[1] In addition, the 544 class appears three times, the 546 class twice, the 548 class once, and the 549 class is mentioned twice. Therefore, the class match score describes an overlap of any two patents, X and Y, according to the USPTO's classification system, defined as follows:

$$ClassMatch(X, Y) = Prob(C_{x_i}) \cap Prob(C_{y_i}).$$

The technology distinction (D) score is $1 - Prob(C_{x_i}) \cap Prob(C_{y_i})$, where C is class match attained through citations.

Unique to Present

For an innovation to be unique, by definition it must be dissimilar from current inventions (Dahlin & Behrens, 2005). A ratio of forward-looking to backward-facing citations can represent this uniqueness (Dahlin & Behrens, 2005): For a unique innovation, the number of forward citations will exceed the number of backward citations. The most basic formula to represent uniqueness is $F/(1 + B)$ (Dahlin & Behrens, 2005), where F represents the number of forward citations, and B is the number of backward citations.

An alternative would be use a weighted ratio. If a backward citation is unique, it should reduce the uniqueness of the current patent (X); if not, it should not affect the focal patent. Conversely, if a forward citation is unique, it should enhance the uniqueness of the current patent (X); if it is not, X is not distinct from current innovations. In this case, we would calculate the uniqueness of each patent by each firm as $\dfrac{(1 + (f)F)}{(1 + (b)B)}$, where F is forward citations, f refers to the forward class match, B indicates a backward citation, and b is the backward class match.

Impact for Future

An innovation has an impact on future technologies when it influences the content of future innovations (Dahlin & Behrens, 2005), which implies the innovation has been adopted. In line with Ahuja and Lampert (2001), we use forward patent citation counts to identify this form of radicalness; they are good estimators of the technological importance of inventions (Albert et al., 1991; Narin et al., 1987). Highly cited patents also offer an important indicator of radical innovations' significant impact on future technologies (Trajtenberg, 1990).

FINDINGS

When we take the top ten patents in each category of radicalness, we find the 24 patents in Table 11.1, which contains descriptions of their patent numbers, filing dates, grant dates, owner firms, radicalness scores, categories of radicalness, future markets, and key products (name or category) that received the application of the patented knowledge.

RQ1: Patents, Categories, and Firms

The 24 unique patents came from 11 firms: AMD, Agilent, Cisco, EMC, HP, IBM, Intel, Micron, Microsoft, SanDisk, and Xerox. Most of the patents entailed processes to create a product or system configurations, such as flash memories, server virtualization, storage, hosted collaborations, memory construction (e.g., EPROMS), enterprise applications, content management, network interfaces, dynamic RAM, search engine optimization, Internet security, cloud computing, and document management.

However, only five patents represented more than one category of radicalness: 5675537 (AMD), 7026834 (Agilent), 6157955, 6362082 (both Intel), and 5815665 (Microsoft). Only Microsoft's patent 5815665 featured all three categories. In Figure 11.2, we depict the relative position of the 11

Table 11.1. Twenty four Radical Patents, Descriptions, Radicalness, Future markets and Products

Firm	Patent No	Granted	Filed	Description	Novelty	Unique ness	Impact	Future Market	Product
						Radicalness		Market and Product	
				Patent and Firm					
AMD	5675537	7-Oct-97	22-Aug-96	An improved erasing structure for performing a programming back operation and a concurrent verify operation subsequent to application of an erasing pulse in an array of multiple bits-per-cell flash EEPROM memory cells on a more effective and efficient basis.	Y	Y		Efficient memory usage to switch between programs for Computers, game consoles, embedded system applications	Athlon 64; AMD Quad FX platform Bioanalytical measurement instruments and equipment for measurement and evaluation:
Agilent	7026834	11-Apr-06	8-Sep-05	A method for probing a plurality of sets of receptacles and/or probes of a device under test (DUT).	Y	Y		Electronic and bioanalytical measurement instruments and equipment for measurement and evaluation. Also Microelectromechanical systems and nanotechnology.	oscilloscopes, logic analyzers, spectrum analyzers, vector network analyzers, Atomic Force Microscope (AFM), automated optical inspection, automated x-ray inspection (5DX),

(Table continues on next page)

Table 11.1. (Cont.)

Firm	Patent No	Granted	Filed	Description	Novelty Unique Impact	Future Market	Product
							in-circuit test, and electronic design automation (EDA) software (EEsof); Life Science and Chemical Analysis: DNA microarrays, HPLCs, capillary electrophoresis systems, mass spectrometers, gas chromatographs, and data analysis software (GeneSpring)

Header groupings: *Patent and Firm* spans Firm, Patent No, Granted, Filed, Description. *Radical ness* spans Novelty, Unique, Impact. *Market and Product* spans Future Market, Product.

(Table continues on next page)

Table 11.1. (Cont.)

| Firm | Patent and Firm | | | | Radical ness | | | Market and Product | |
	Patent No	Granted	Filed	Description	Novelty	Unique	Impact	Future Market	Product
Cisco	5852607	22-Dec-98	26-Feb-97	Fundamentally it is about interconnecting two or more networks at a media-access level of a data-link layer and techniques or apparatus which process the address information field for switching the packet of information.	Y			Data Center, Vitual LANS & Hosted Collaboration Solutions and Switching Technologies	Storage: Symmetrix, CLARiiON, Celerra, Iomega; Virtualization: VMware, VPLEX; Backup recovery and archiving: DataDomain, Avamar, Mozy, RecoverPoint, SRDF, NetWorker, Centera, SourceOne;

(Table continues on next page)

Table 11.1. (Cont.)

Firm	Patent No	Granted	Filed	Description	Novelty	Unique	Impact	Future Market	Product
									Cloud Computing:Atmo s, vBLOCK, Mozy; IT Management: Ionix, SMARTS; Data-Warehousing/ Business Intelligence: Greenplum

Patent and Firm | Radical ness | Market and Product

(Table continues on next page)

333

Table 11.1. (Cont.)

Firm	Patent No	Granted	Filed	Description	Novelty	Unique	Impact	Future Market	Product
						Radical ness		Market and Product	
EMC	5742792	21-Apr-98	28-May-96	A system for automatically providing remote copy data storage.			Y	Storage, Backup, recovery, Archiving, Virtualization, Cloud Computing, IT Management, Enterprise Content Management & Information Governance;	Storage: Symmetrix, CLARiiON, Celerra, Iomega; Virtualization: VMware, VPLEX; Backup recovery and archiving: DataDomain, Avamar, Mozy, RecoverPoint, SRDF, NetWorker, Centera, SourceOne;

(Table continues on next page)

Table 11.1. (Cont.)

| | Patent and Firm | | | | Radicalness | | | Market and Product | |
Firm	Patent No	Granted	Filed	Description	Novelty	Unique	Impact	Future Market	Product
								Data-Warehousing/ Business Intelligence,	Cloud Computing: Atmos, vBLOCK, Mozy; IT Management: Ionix, SMARTS; Data-Warehousing/ Business Intelligence: Greenplum
HP	5844553	12/1/ 1998	3/29/ 1996	Application sharing technology that enables sharing of many single-user nonmodified applications between two or more workstations. It provides concurrent sharing of existing multiple applications with no change in a distributed environment.	Y			Enterprise Application Software (EAS); Servers	HP Openview; HP Enterprise Services

(Table continues on next page)

Table 11.1. (Cont.)

Firm	Patent No	Granted	Filed	Description	Novelty	Unique	Impact	Future Market	Product
						Radicalness		**Market and Product**	
				Patent and Firm					
IBM	5640343	17-Jun-97	18-Mar-96	A nonvolatile magnetic random access memory (MRAM) is an array of individual magnetic memory cells. Each memory cell is a magnetic tunnel junction (MTJ) element and a diode electrically connected in series. The storage element is a thin film cell which has a thickness of approximately 1 to 12,000 angstroms.			Y	High Speed Random Access Memory; Semiconductor design and manufacturing form Mobile application and Game consoles.	PowerPC tri-core processor; Cell BE microprocessor; Gekko, Broadway
IBM	5650958	22-Jul-97	18-Mar-96	A magnetic tunnel junction (MTJ) device is usable as a magnetic field sensor or as a memory cell in a magnetic random access (MRAM) array. The storage element is a thin film cell which has a thickness of approximately 1 to 12,000 angstroms.			Y	High Speed Random Access Memory; Semiconductor design and manufacturing form Mobile application and Game consoles.	PowerPC tri-core processor; Cell BE microprocessor; Gekko, Broadway

(Table continues on next page)

Table 11.1. (Cont.)

Firm	Patent No	Granted	Filed	Description	Radical ness Novelty	Radical ness Unique Impact	Future Market	Product
IBM	5727129	10-Mar-98	4-Jun-96	A communication system for facilitating communication between a user and a network of information resources at respective remote network nodes, the system comprising local node having a user interface program, for allowing a user to interface with the network and request a download of information items from the information resources; a network interface coupled between the local node and the network; a user interface including (i) means for receiving user commends representative of user actions and (ii) means for displaying received network responses of network information for viewing by a user; means for recording a sequence of successive user actions and network responses; means for developing a profile of user activities based on the user actions and network responses monitored in the step of monitoring; and means for actively facilitating user activities based on the developed profile.		Y	Enterprise Application Software (EAS); Software-as Services; Servers	Lotus Notes; Red Hat Enterprise Linux; Sametime; Websphere; Tovoli; DB2

(Table continues on next page)

Table 11.1. (Cont.)

Firm	Patent No	Granted	Filed	Description	Novelty	Unique Impact	Radical ness	Future Market	Product
								Market and Product	
				Patent and Firm					
IBM	5804803	8-Sep-98	2-Apr-96	Mechanism for retrieving information using data encoded on an object. A method in a client computer system for retrieving a document, comprising the machine executed steps of scanning data encoded on an object; creating a uniform resource locator (URL) from said scanned encoded data, wherein said URL identifies a first server connected to said client computer system via a network and a location of said document on said first server, and wherein said URL is created from information retrieved from a second server using said scanned encoded data as a key into said information and wherein said creating step further comprises creating said URL by substituting values into said scanned encoded data from a customer data record wherein said customer data record is retrieved to said client computer system from said second server; transmitting said URL to said first server; and receiving said document from said first server wherein said document is different from said object.			Y	Electronic shopping cart; content management	IBM Lotus Web Content Management; Webspehere; Tovoli; DB2

(Table continues on next page)

338

Table 11.1. (Cont.)

					Radical ness			Market and Product	
Firm	Patent No	Granted	Filed	Description	Novelty	Unique	Impact	Future Market	Product
IBM	6012088	4-Jan-00	10-Dec-96	An Internet access device uses an automatic configuration process to handle the task of configuring the Internet access device at a customer site for communication with the Internet. Method where large blocks of data (e.g., streamed data) are transferred between a remote file server and a requesting computer.			Y	Enterprise Application Software (EAS); Servers	Lotus Notes; Red Hat Enterprise Linux; Sametime
IBM	6226618	1-May-01	13-Aug-98	A method of securely providing data to a user's system, said method comprising the steps of: (a) encrypting the data using a first encrypting key; encrypting a first decrypting key using a second encrypting key;(b) transferring the encrypted data, which has been encrypted with the first encrypting key, to the user's system; (c) transferring the encrypted first decrypting key, which has been encrypted with the second encrypting key, to the user's system; (d) transferring the encrypted first decrypting key, which has been encrypted with the second encrypting key, to a clearing house that possesses a second decrypting key; (e) decrypting the first decrypting key using the second decrypting key; and (f)transferring the decrypted first decrypting key to the user's system.			Y	on-demand content management and blade server computing resources	IBM Lotus Web Content Management; Websphere; Tovoli; DB2

(Table continues on next page)

Table 11.1. (Cont.)

Firm	Patent No	Granted	Filed	Description	Novelty	Unique	Impact	Future Market	Product
						Radicalness		Market and Product	
Intel	5784581	21-Jul-98	3-May-96	An apparatus capable of operating as either a master device or a slave device on a communication link such as a Universal Serial Bus (USB). Comprises of :(a)first communication port utilized when said apparatus is operating as a slave device; (b) second communication port utilized when said apparatus is operating as a master device; and (c) a device controller coupled to said first communication port and said second communication port, said device controller enabling said first communication port or said second communication port in response to detection of the presence or absence of an active host controller coupled to said first communication port.	Y			Memory, Processors, Network Interface cards	Motherboard chipsets, network interface controllers and integrated circuits, flash memory, graphic chips, embedded processors, Bluetooth wireless interconnect
Intel	6157955	5-Dec-00	15-Jun-98	A system comprising: (a)an application processor having a host interface; (b) a bus bridge coupled to said host interface; and (c) a policy engine coupled to said bus bridge to classify packets according to at least one of a plurality of application-specific classification policies and to enable at least one of a plurality of actions to be performed on said classified packets responsive to said packet classifications.	Y	Y		Memory, Processors, Network Interface cards	network interface controllers and integrated circuits, Bluetooth wireless interconnect

(Table continues on next page)

340

Table 11.1. (Cont.)

Firm	Patent No	Granted	Filed	Description	Novelty	Unique	Impact	Future Market	Product
						Radicalness		Market and Product	
Intel	6362082	26-Mar-02	28-Jun-99	A method of improving short channel effects in a transistor. It comprises of: (a) implanting a substance in a substrate; (b) annealing said substrate such that said implanted substance forms a void in said substrate; and, (c) forming a transistor on said substrate, in which a channel region of said transistor includes said void to inhibit lines of force from a drain of said transistor from terminating at a source of said transistor.	Y	Y	Y	Memory, Processors, Network Interface cards	Motherboard chipsets, network interface controllers and integrated circuits, flash memory, graphic chips, embedded processors, Bluetooth wireless interconnect
Intel	6586761	1-Jul-03	7-Sep-01	Reducing heat loss in memory chips. Comprises of (a) a support structure; (b) an insulator over said support structure, said insulator having an opening defined in said insulator; and (c) a cup-shaped phase change material in said opening, said phase change material including an upper surface and said insulator including an upper surface, said upper surfaces of said insulator and said phase change material being substantially coplanar.		Y		Memory, Processors, Network Interface cards	Motherboard chipsets, network interface controllers and integrated circuits, flash memory, graphic chips, embedded processors

(Table continues on next page)

Table 11.1. (Cont.)

Firm	Patent No	Granted	Filed	Description	Novelty	Unique	Impact	Future Market	Product
							Radicalness	**Market and Product**	
Micron	5997384	7-Dec-99	22-Dec-97	An apparatus for controlling planarizing characteristics of a microelectronic substrate, comprising: (a) a carrier positionable with respect to a polishing medium to move with a microelectronic substrate during planarization on a planarizing surface of the polishing medium, (b) the carrier comprising a microelectronic substrate holder having a chuck and a rim; and (c) a modulator having a contact element, the modulator being attached to the substrate holder to position the contact element radially outwardly from a perimeter edge of the substrate so that at least a portion of the contact element is in front of the leading edge of the substrate during planarization and superadjacent to an exposed portion of a standing wave on the planarizing surface, the modulator being configured to cause the contact element to selectively engage the exposed portion of the standing wave to modulate a contour of a residual portion of the standing wave on the planarizing surface under a perimeter region of the substrate, and wherein the modulator comprises a passive modulator and the contact element has a desired contour to attenuate an amplitude of the residual portion of the standing wave under the perimeter region of the substrate.			Y	DRAM Memory components	NAND Flash memory; High Speed NAND, eMMC, eUSB, Serial NAND, and SSDs.

(Table continues on next page)

Table 11.1. (Cont.)

					Radicalness			Market and Product	
	Patent and Firm				Novelty	Unique	Impact		
Firm	Patent No	Granted	Filed	Description				Future Market	Product
Micron	6326698	4-Dec-01	8-Jun-00	A method of packaging at least one semiconductor device substrate, comprising: (a)providing at least one semiconductor device substrate with at least one contact pad exposed to an active surface thereof; (b) submerging said at least one substrate in a photopolymeric liquid material to a depth forming a thin layer thereof on at least a portion of said active surface; and(c) selectively subjecting said thin layer of photopolymeric liquid material to polymerizing radiation to form a layer comprising at least semisolid polymer material on said active surface.		Y		DRAM Memory components	NAND Flash memory, High Speed NAND, eMMC, eUSB, Serial NAND, and SSDs.
Microsoft	5815665	29-Sep-98	3-Apr-96	An online brokering service provides user authentication and billing services to allow users to anonymously and securely purchase online services from service providers (SP) sites (e.g., World Wide Web sites) over a distributed public network, which may be an untrusted public network.	Y	Y	Y	Web Security, Digital Rights Management, Web Content Management, Cloud Computing	Internet Explorer; Zune, Windows Operating Systems

(Table continues on next page)

Table 11.1. (Cont.)

Firm	Patent No	Granted	Filed	Description	Radical ness Novelty Unique Impact	Future Market	Market and Product Product
Microsoft	5883810	16-Mar-99	24-Sep-97	An online commerce system facilitates online commerce over a public network using an online commerce card. The "card" does not exist in physical form, but instead exists in digital form. The online commerce card is issued electronically to a customer by an issuing institution. Automatic transaction system with a dynamic display and methods of its operation. Steps comprises of: (A) Issuing an electronic commerce card to a customer during a registration phase, the commerce card having a permanent number associated therewith to identify the customer; and (B) during an online commerce transaction phase, issuing a proxy number that is associated with the permanent number for use in an online commerce transaction in place of the permanent number on the commerce card.	Y	Web Security, Digital Rights Management, Web Content Management, Cloud Computing	Internet Explorer

(Table continues on next page)

Table 11.1. (Cont.)

		Patent and Firm			Radicalness			Market and Product	
Firm	Patent No	Granted	Filed	Description	Novelty	Unique	Impact	Future Market	Product
Microsoft	6006218	21-Dec-99	28-Feb-97	A method of retrieving information for a user; the method, comprising the steps of: (a) generating a set of search results including a plurality of entries, at least some of said entries not being known to the user; and (b) arranging the set of search results for presentation to the user from top to bottom, using estimates of the probability that the entries are known to the user; the step of arranging being performed so that entries having a higher probability of being known to the user are less likely to be placed at the top of the arranged set of search results then entries which have a lower probability of being known to the user.	Y			Search Engines	Microsoft Search Engine, Bing
Microsoft	6029126	22-Feb-00	30-Jun-98	A coder stored on computer readable memory of a computer system for coding an input signal, the coder comprising a multiresolution transform processor for receiving the input signal and producing a nonuniform modulated lapped biorthogonal transform having transform coefficients and a weighting processor with a masking threshold spectrum processor for masking quantization noise by spectrally weighting and partially whitening the transform coefficients. Essentially, either an expansion or reduction of the bandwidth required for transmission of a sound signal.	Y			Multimedia, Games	Media Player, Xbox, Zune

(Table continues on next page)

Table 11.1. (Cont.)

Firm	Patent No	Granted	Filed	Description	Novelty	Unique ness	Impact	Future Market	Product
						Radicalness		*Market and Product*	
				Patent and Firm					
SanDisk Corporation	6222762	24-Apr-01	7-Aug-97	Maximized multistate compaction and more tolerance in memory state behavior is achieved through a flexible, self-consistent and self-adapting mode of detection, covering a wide dynamic range.			Y	Flash memory, memory cards, USB removable drives	Memory Stick, Memory Stick PRO (2003), Memory Stick Duo, Memory Stick Pro Duo, Memory Stick PRO-HG Duo, Memory Stick Micro (M2). SD cards (2001), miniSD Cards (2003), and microSD Cards (2005)

(Table continues on next page)

Table 11.1. (Cont.)

	Patent and Firm				Radicalness			Market and Product	
Firm	Patent No	Granted	Filed	Description	Novelty	Unique	Impact	Future Market	Product
SanDisk Corporation	6522580	18-Feb-03	27-Jun-01	A method of operating a nonvolatile memory system wherein values stored in some of storage elements of an array of memory elements affect values read from others of the storage elements because of at least electric field coupling between storage elements, comprising: comprising; because of at least field coupling between them, thereby to facilitate accurate reading of the first set of data from the first group of storage elements.			Y	Flash memory, memory cards, USB removable drives	Memory Stick, Memory Stick PRO (2003), Memory Stick Duo, Memory Stick Pro Duo, Memory Stick PRO-HG Duo, Memory Stick Micro (M2). SD cards (2001), miniSD Cards (2003), and microSD Cards (2005)
Xerox	5692073	25-Nov-97	30-Jul-96	A processor is provided with first and second document images. The first image represents an instance of a reference document to which instance a mark has been added. The second image is selected from among a collection of document images and represents the reference document.			Y	Document management System, Desktop publishing, network publishing	Document management System, Desktop publishing, network publishing

(Table continues on next page)

347

firms in terms of their capabilities with regard to the three dimensions of radicalness, as exhibited by their 24 radical patents. It also shows how each firm fared in terms of total patents, categories, and intersections among categories. Among the 24 patents, overlaps only occurred between novel and unique and among novel, unique, and impact. No overlaps arose between novel and impact or between unique and impact. By definition, for a patent to be impactful when it is novel, it must also be unique, and vice versa.

Following Dahlin and Behrens (2005), we required a radical patent to (1) be unique and novel (N∩U), (2) have an impact on future technologies (I), or (3) all three (N∩U∩I). Therefore we look at patents that fulfill (N∩U) ∪ (I) ∪ (N∩U∩I). The first criterion reveals four patents: 5675537 (AMD), 7026834 (Agilent Technologies), 6157955, and 6362082 (both Intel). The second indicates only one patent: 5815665 (Microsoft). Finally, with the third criterion, we identify nine patents: 5640343, 5727129, 5804803, 6012088, 6226618 (all IBM), 5742792 (EMC), 6222762, 6522580 (both SanDisk), and 5692073 (Xerox). Thus, eight IT companies produced fourteen truly radical patents (Dahlin & Behrens, 2005) between January 1, 1996, and June 30, 2011.

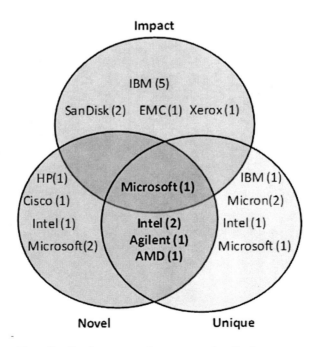

Figure 11.2.   Firm distribution across three areas of radicalness as per top 10 patents in each category. Number of patents is in parenthesis.

In Figures 11.3–11.7, we graph the cumulative patenting curves of these eight firms for patents filed during the study period, which we then compare with the S&P 500 average for the IT industry. To obtain these curves, we relied on the number of patents filed (Figure 11.3), patents granted (Figure 11.4), measures of novelty (Figure 11.5), measures of uniqueness (Figure 11.6), and measures of impact (Figure 11.7) for the eight firms, by year of patents filed. Then we added each year, compared with previous years, to discern cumulative growth from 1996 to 2009.

RQ2: Radical Patents, Firms, and Future Markets

This research question centers on individual firms, with patents representing the R&D initiatives taken to address the needs of emerging opportunities. We look into each of the eight firms to determine how the technological content of their radical innovations is associated with finding emerging opportunities. That is, do the patents indicate commitment to future markets?

A radical patent may be ahead of its time, in the sense that it adjusts technological expertise and diffuses a product even before an established market has become saturated (Christensen, 1992a; Christensen, 1992b; Christensen, 1997; Christensen & Bower, 1996; Christensen & Raynor, 2003). Figure 11.8 indicates how radical innovations help decrease the time and effort needed to capture a future market. A firm can pursue insights into a future market while still retaining a strong foothold on established markets. The time difference (t2 – t1) indicates how far ahead the underlying technology was in its ability to address a future market, where t2 is the time an average player enters the market to capture some rents. We conceive of t3 as the time when the market is no longer emerging and the majority of laggards have entered; it is already populated with t1 and t2 entrants. An early technological commitment makes it easier for a focal firm to understand the needs of the emerging market, so it focuses its R&D on creating fundamental innovations that become core products in an emerging market—leading to a patent for a radical innovation. An early commitment also flattens the learning curve and technological performance trajectories associated with innovation. When the opportunity translates into a real market, the firm has the necessary knowledge already; even if this firm decides not to turn the innovation into a product, it can license its technology to other firms and earn substantial rents (Hill, 1992; Lyles & Salk, 2006; Madhok & Tallman, 1998; Song, Droge, Hanvanich, & Calantone, 2005).

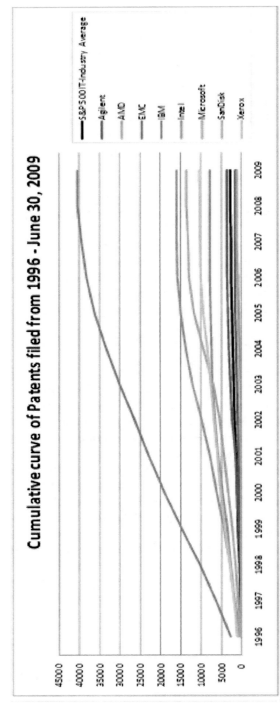

Figure 11.3. Comparative cumulative curve of patents filed by nine firms and industry average

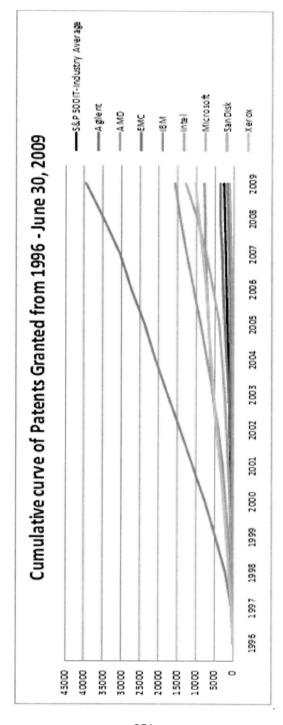

Figure 11.4. Comparative cumulative curve of patents granted by nine firms and industry average.

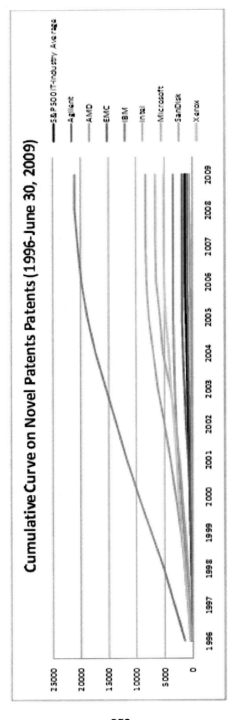

Figure 11.5.   Comparative cumulative curve of novel patents by nine firms and industry average.

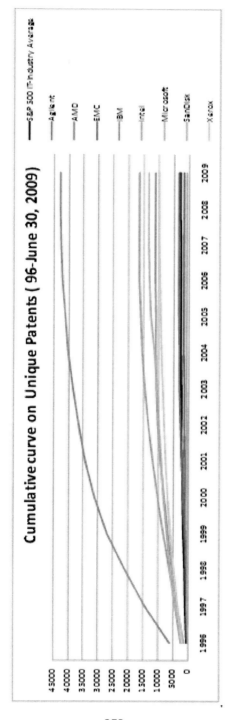

Figure 11.6. Comparative cumulative curve of unique patents by nine firms and industry average.

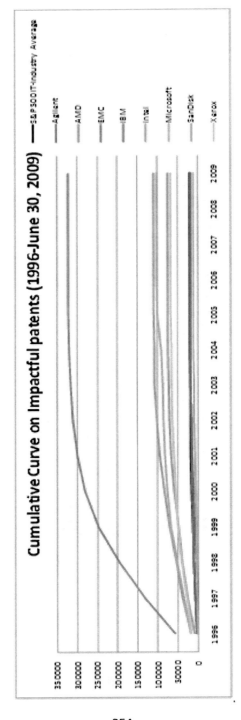

Figure 11.7. Comparative cumulative curve of Impactful patents by nine firms and industry average.

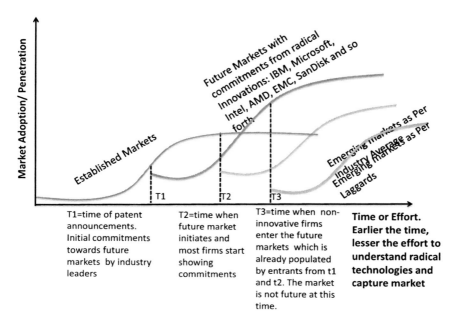

Figure 11.8.   Commitment through patent announcements to capture future markets. Concept adopted from Christensen (1992a and 1992b).

We now conduct minicase studies of each firm to outline how their radical innovations helped pave the way and position them for the future. For some firms, the innovations led to massive transformations in products or services (e.g., IBM); for others, they created diversification (e.g., Intel); and for still other firms, the innovations enabled them to take advantage of a changing environment (e.g., Microsoft).

IBM. IBM holds more patents than any other U.S.-based technology company, coming from its nine research laboratories worldwide (IBM, 2010c). Its employees have earned five Nobel Prizes, four Turing Awards, nine National Medals of Technology, and five National Medals of Science (IBM, 2010a). The company has undergone several organizational changes since its inception, such as when it acquired SPSS (2009) and PwC Consulting (2002) or spun off SAP (1972) and Lexmark (1991). Of the 14 radical patents we identified, 5 came from IBM. As Figures 11.3 and 11.4 show, from 1996 to mid-2009, IBM filed and received approximately 40,000 patents—equal to about 8 patents per day.

All five of IBM's radical innovation patents were filed between 1996 and 1998 and exerted strong impacts on future technologies. The date of filing is more interesting than the grant date, because filing signals the firm's commitment to radical innovation and the emergent opportunity of technological innovations. The patent grant just indicates the USPTO's acceptance. During 1996-1998, IBM was a major player in the desktop and laptop industry (Kanter, 2009; Marquis & Kanter, 2010; O'Reilly, Herreld, & Tushman, 2009), but competition was shrinking its margins (Kanter, 2009; Marquis & Kanter, 2010; O'Reilly et al., 2009). Although it was the first mover in many technologies, IBM could not control the market. For instance, it developed the first router, but Cisco went on to dominate the market (Kanter, 2009; Marquis & Kanter, 2010; O'Reilly et al., 2009). IBM developed the first technologies to accelerate Internet performance, but Akamai had better product vision and captured the market (O'Reilly et al., 2009). IBM also developed the first speech recognition software, only to be eclipsed by Nuance (O'Reilly et al., 2009). Thus, IBM's works have impacts on future technologies that other firms commercialize. IBM has ignored opportunities in enterprise information systems, leading SAP to develop as a separate subsidiary (March, 1996).

At the turn of the 21st century, IBM underwent a colossal transformation, including selling its computer division to Lenevo in 2003 (Marquis & Kanter, 2010; O'Reilly et al., 2009) and acquiring PricewaterhouseCoopers (PwC) in 2002 (Marquis & Kanter, 2010; O'Reilly et al., 2009). A leading IT consultant, PwC focuses on technological advisory and SAP implementation (March, 1996), so its acquisition signaled IBM's commitment to entering the enterprise application software (EAS) and software-as-service businesses. By selling its laptop and desktop businesses, IBM also showed its commitment to exiting these lines, with their shrinking margins. The five radical patents by IBM further indicated its realization of the potential in emerging IT markets. Four patents, 5727129, 5804803, 6012088, and 6226618, relate to applications in the enterprise computing, IT service management, enterprise content management, on-demand content management, and blade server fields, as depicted by both the content of the patents and their forward citations. The associated technologies and processes included Lotus Notes, Sametime (a chat tool embedded in Lotus Notes), Web Content Management, Tivoli, DB2, and Websphere, which currently represent established markets for IBM but were future markets in the late 1990s, when the patents were filed (Marquis & Kanter, 2010; O'Reilly et al., 2009). Thus, though IBM's acquisition and divestment moves in the early 2000s increased its consulting foothold, it has committed to entering the future markets of enterprise computing, IT service management, enterprise content management, on-demand content management, and blade server in its patents in the late 1990s. Thus in Figure 8, the time difference $(t2 - t1)$ indicates that IBM was 5 years ahead in addressing the needs of a future market.

Also in the late 1990s, research focused heavily on high speed random access memory (RAM) and semiconductor designs but did not consider applications in the domain of game consoles or mobile technologies (Marquis & Kanter, 2010; O'Reilly et al., 2009). However, IBM's patent 5640343 (see Table 1), filed on March 1996, formed the cornerstone for designing magnetic RAM for captive devices and game consoles. The core technology, as the forward citations of this patent show, provided a foundation for products such as the PowerPC tri-core processor, Gekko processor, and Cell BE microprocessor; all latest generation console gaming systems thus use microprocessors developed by IBM. For example, the Xbox 360 contains a PowerPC tri-core processor, designed and produced by IBM in less than 24 months (IBM, 2010b), whereas Sony's PlayStation 3 features the Cell BE microprocessor, designed jointly by IBM, Toshiba, and Sony (IBM, 2010b). Nintendo's seventh-generation Wii console features an IBM chip with the codename Broadway (IBM, 2010b), and its GameCube used the Gekko processor (IBM, 2010b). From Figure 11.8, the time difference (t2 − t1) shows that IBM was approximately 10 years ahead of the curve with this patent. Thus, IBM's five radical patents and their significant impacts on future technologies demonstrate the company's strong commitment to future markets, captured around a decade after the patent filings.

Microsoft. Microsoft is a key player in PC operating system market, at both client and server levels, particularly with its Windows operating systems (Rangan & Bell, 2009). The Wintel (Windows and Intel) architecture owns more than 80% of the market, is the de facto standard in PCs, and has contributed to the deverticalization of the computer industry (Burgelman & Grove, 1996; Casadesus-Masanell, Yoffie, & Mattu, 2010; Grove, 1996). Microsoft has a sizeable stock of patents. From Figures 3 and 4, we find that Microsoft filed and was granted around 13,000 patents during our study period, or approximately 3 patents per day. However, only one of these patents meets Dahlin and Behrens's (2005) criteria, though patent 5815665 is the only one to intersect all three categories of radicalness (novelty, uniqueness, and impact). This patent was filed in 1996 and granted in 1998.

During the 1990s and early 2000s, Microsoft introduced some famous products, such as Windows operating systems (Versions 95, 98, NT, Millennium, 2000, and XP) and the Office Suite (95, 97, 2000, XP, 2003, 2007) (Lerner & Leamon, 2010; Rangan & Bell, 2009). The release of Windows 95 on August 24, 1995, featured preemptive multitasking, a completely new user interface with a novel "Start" button, and 32-bit compatibility. It provided Win32 API (Cope, 1996; Lerner & Leamon, 2010; Pietrek, 1996; Rangan & Bell, 2009) but also came bundled with MSN online services and Internet Explorer, a web browser (Lerner & Leamon,

2010; Rangan & Bell, 2009; Thurrott, 2005). During the early and mid-1990s, the convergence of telecommunications, cable, Internet, and IT had appeared inconceivable (Burgelman, Christensen, & Wheelright, 2006; Lerner & Leamon, 2010; Rangan & Bell, 2009). Products were offered separately, with no value-added services. Firms in each area developed products in their respective vertical chains, driven by myopic visions. Microsoft first envisioned the potential of value-added services, and in 1996, it branched out into new markets by partnering with NBC Universal to create a new 24/7 cable news station, MSNBC (Burgelman et al., 2006; Lerner & Leamon, 2010; Rangan & Bell, 2009). The Windows CE 1.0 operating system also was designed for personal devices, with low memory demands or other constraints (Lerner & Leamon, 2010; Rangan & Bell, 2009; Tilly, 2008).

In the mid-1990s, electronic commerce was also a future market; Amazon.com launched in 1995. Consumers' initial response to Amazon was modest, out of fears of user authentication and identity theft issues (Applegate, 2010; Cott & Palepu, 2001; Huckman, Pisano, & Kind, 2008; Palepu, 2001). Microsoft's patent 5815665 involved technology that supported user authentication by allowing users to purchase, anonymously and securely, from online service providers' sites over a distributed public network. This knowledge formed the cornerstone for 128- and 256-bit encryption technologies. Microsoft added this technology to Internet Explorer (Netscape and Firefox eventually adopted it as well), which increased consumers' trust of online purchases. During the early 2000s, Microsoft expanded its product offerings to include networking and web-based services. The forward citations of patent 5815665 until 2007 also indicate that it provided a foundation for authentication in cloud computing applications, including the design of the core technologies of the Azure Service Platform (Lerner & Leamon, 2010; Rangan & Bell, 2009). Cloud computing still remains a somewhat future market, so its radical patent in 1996 clearly showed Microsoft's commitment to future markets, at least 15 years into the future. In Figure 11.8, the time difference (t2 − t1) shows that Microsoft was 15 years ahead of the needs of this future market.

Intel. Intel constitutes the other half of the de facto Wintel industry standard, where Win refers to the Windows architecture by Microsoft. Intel's core competencies with microelectronics enabled it to transform itself from a pioneering, struggling RAM manufacturing firm to the most successful microprocessor firm by the early 1990s (Casadesus-Masanell et al., 2010). Like IBM and Microsoft, Intel has a sizeable stock of patents; between 1996 and 2009, Intel filed and received about 16,000 patents, or approximately 3 patents per day (Figures 11.3 and 11.4). During the mid-1990s to early 2000s, the PC market was plagued by competition, which strained the margins of the major players that were Intel's main customers, such as Dell, Hewlett-Packard, Compaq, and IBM (Lenovo). This competition, coupled with an overreliance on Microsoft, led Intel to look for alternative opportunities and find promise in mobile computing, connectivity between cell phones and computers, and wireless connectivity (Burgelman, 2007; Shih & Thurston, 2009, 2010). Intel's two radical patents, 6157955 and 6362082, were filed in 1998 and 1999, respectively. Both patents describe systems to enhance connectivity and share data between devices, leading to interoperability and connectivity across hardware interfaces. Intel's Architecture Lab (IAL) in turn created many hardware innovations related to personal computers, such as the PCI Bus, PCI Express (PCIe) bus, Universal Serial Bus (USB), Bluetooth wireless interconnect, and the now-dominant architecture for multiprocessor servers. In its attempt to reduce its reliance on Microsoft, Intel allied with Apple, ensuring that Apple computers run on Intel's Xeon processors (Yoffie & Slind, 2007). Apple provides superior plug-and-play features compared with Windows (Yoffie & Slind, 2007), and Intel's experience with patents 6157955 and 6362082 helped it improve these capabilities, as evidenced in the technical content and future citations. The knowledge associated with the patents also influenced the content of Intel's Core Duo processor and Classmate PC, a leading low-cost computer (Burgelman, 2007; Shih & Thurston, 2009, 2010). From Figure 11.8, the time difference shows about that Intel was around 7 years ahead in addressing the needs of a future market.

AMD. After Intel, AMD is the second-largest global supplier of microprocessors, which are based on the x86 architecture, as well as one of the largest suppliers of graphics processing units (Ofek & Barley, 2007; Shih & Ofek, 2009). Its main products include microprocessors, motherboard chipsets, embedded processors and graphics processors for servers, workstations and personal computers, and processor technologies for handheld devices, digital television, automobiles, game consoles, and other embedded systems applications (Ofek & Barley, 2007; Shih & Ofek, 2009). As Figures 11.3 and 11.4 show, during the study period, AMD filed and received around 8,000 patents, or approximately half as many as its closest rival, Intel. Similar to Intel, in late 1990s AMD felt the need to expand its offerings beyond the PC industry (Ofek & Barley, 2007; Shih & Ofek, 2009), though it attempted to diversify into graphics and audio devices, using research into EPROM memory. Advanced graphics and sound, especially for game consoles and embedded systems, were future markets in the early to late 1990s. Patent 5675537 (filed in 1996, granted in 1997) confirmed AMD's commitment to EPROM, a fundamental building block for game console applications. Forward citations appear in the patents for processors such as the Althon 64 and AMD's Quad FX platform, which still are used in computers and game consoles. From Figure 11.8, t2 – t1 shows about that AMD was 8 to 10 years ahead of the needs of this future market.

EMC. As the IT industry evolved from mainframes to TCP/IP architectures, the capacities of hard drives increased, while their size decreased (Christensen, 1992a; Christensen, 1992b; Christensen & Bower, 1996). The use of networked computing also produced networked storage platforms. As the largest provider of data storage platforms worldwide, EMC competes with IBM, Hewlett-Packard, and Hitachi Data Systems, with a product line ranging from enterprise storage arrays to content management systems to storage area networks, backup, recovery, and archiving solutions, and information security. In comparison with some top IT players, EMC's patent stock is relatively modest, at approximately 1,600 patents from 1996-2009, lower than the industry average.

The company's most radical patent is 5742792, which describes a process and apparatus for automatically providing remote copy data storage. Two data storage systems can be interconnected by a data link for remote data mirroring, such that each volume of data gets configured as local, primary in a remotely mirrored volume pair, or secondary in a remotely mirrored volume pair. The patent was filed in 1996 and granted in 1998. Although this patent refers to fundamental technologies for storage, backup, recovery, and archiving, it also provides a cornerstone for the then-future markets of cloud computing, IT management, enterprise content management & information governance, data warehousing, and business intelligence. Most of these markets matured around 2003-2007 but were emerging when the patent was filed. Forward citations appear in all these aforementioned future markets, as well as in patents for products such as Atmos, vBLOCK, and Mozy (cloud computing); Ionix and SMARTS (IT management); and Greenplum (business intelligence, data warehousing). In Figure 11.8, the time difference shows about that EMC was seven to 11 years ahead.

SanDisk. This multinational corporation designs and manufactures flash memory card products. SanDisk produces many different types of flash memory, including various memory cards and a series of USB removable drives. SanDisk markets to both high-end and low-end sectors to meet their demand for premium quality flash memory; it markets to other equipment makers as well as end consumers. Its global leadership in flash memory cards spans research, manufacturing, and product design, as well as consumer branding and retail distribution. SanDisk's product portfolio includes flash memory cards for mobile phones, digital cameras, and camcorders, as well as digital audio/video players, USB flash drives for consumers and enterprises, embedded memory for mobile devices, and solid-state drives for computers.

Unlike the top IT players, SanDisk's patent stock is relatively modest, at around 1,100 patents in the 13 years of our study, which is lower than the industry average. Two of these patents meet the radical criteria (Dahlin & Behrens, 2005): 6222762 (filed in 1997, granted in 2001) and 6522580 (filed in 2001, granted in 2003). Both patents entail technologies related to portable storage devices for USB drives, flash drives, and portable storage. In the late 1990s, SanDisk recognized that digital cameras would need digital storage, and computers could become more mobile and light, in which case they would require similar storage technology.

Although the market did not mature until 2004, these two radical patents show SanDisk's commitment to creating competencies through technological breakthrough and pursuing opportunities in a future market. Forward citations show that some of the products that use these patents' technologies include the Memory Stick, Memory Stick PRO (2003), Memory Stick Duo, Memory Stick Pro Duo, Memory Stick PRO-HG Duo, Memory Stick Micro (M2), SD cards (2001), miniSD Cards (2003), and microSD Cards (2005). From Figure 11.8, the time difference shows about that SanDisk was 3 to 5 years ahead in addressing future market needs.

Xerox. Founded in 1906, Xerox Corporation is a global document management company that manufactures and sells a range of color and black-and-white printers, multifunction systems, photo copiers, digital production printing presses, and related consulting services and supplies (Chang, 2010; Lerner, 1998; Rangan, 2002). From 1996 to 2009, according to Figures 11.3 and 11.4, Xerox filed and was granted approximately 10,000 patents, though only one (5692073, filed in 1996, granted in 1997) made it onto our radical innovation list. It addresses the technological needs for high-end multifunction printers and document management systems—markets that were emerging at the time of the filing and matured only around 2006–2007. The forward citations of this patent show that its technological content is a cornerstone for some Xerox's most successful products, such as the iGen4 Press, Phaser printers, and document management software such as DocuShare, MarketPort, and FlowPort. According to Figure 11.8, t2 – t1 shows that Xerox was approximately 10 years ahead in addressing the needs of the future market.

Agilent Technologies. Agilent Technologies designs and manufactures electronic and bioanalytical measurement instruments and equipment (Burg, Ghosh, & Arenas, 2004). Although it was established only in 1999, by 2009, it had filed approximately 3600 patents (see Figures 11.3 and 11.4) and been granted about half. The company arose as a subsidiary of Hewlett-Packard, designated to pursue future markets, conduct research, and manufacture scientific instruments, semiconductors, optical networking devices, and electronic test equipment for telecom and wireless fields.

One patent by Agilent (7026834, filed in 2005, granted in 2006) made the radical innovation list; it provides a technology for measuring and testing electrical properties (Table 11.1) and thus informs research and production of measurement instruments and equipment. Such products include oscilloscopes, logic analyzers, spectrum analyzers, vector network analyzers, atomic force microscopes, automated optical inspection, automated x-ray inspection, in-circuit test, and electronic design automation software (Burg et al., 2004). The time difference in Figure 8 shows that Agilent was approximately 2 to 3 years ahead in addressing the needs of a future market.

DISCUSSION

Summary

For this study, we adopt Dahlin and Bheren's (2005) definition of radical innovations to achieve two research goals: to identify the top patents in each category (uniqueness, novelty, impact) in the IT industry and to determine how radical innovations indicate show commitment to emerging opportunities. Accordingly, we collected data from 192,070 patents filed by IT firms on the S&P 500 list from 1996 through 2009. We then calculated and ranked the patents according to their novelty, uniqueness, and impact. The identification of the top ten patents in each category led to 24 unique patents from 11 firms, though only 14 patents met Dahil and Behrens's (2005) criteria. These 14 patents represent 8 firms (AMD, Agilent, EMC, IBM, Intel, Microsoft, SanDisk, and Xerox). We thus outlined how each firm's patents reveal technological content that could address the needs of a market that was 5 to 15 years in the future.

In particular, IBM's patents filed between 1996 and 1998 showed its commitment to enterprise computing, captive devices, and game consoles—markets that came into being around 2000 but have yet to mature. Similarly, Microsoft's radical patent, filed in 1996, provided a cornerstone for user authentications for e-commerce applications, as well as for cloud computing, still a future market in 2011. However, the behaviors of the eight firms and their innovations cannot truly reveal whether technological breakthroughs are premeditated, based on a market vision, or if the technological breakthroughs opened market opportunities accidently. In either case, continuous commitments to R&D, in the form of attention to radical innovations, maximizes the probability of positive outcomes, whether deliberate or serendipitous.

Implications for Theory, Practice, and Research

Despite some studies of innovation lag times (Baker, Miner, & Eesley, 2002; Boynton & Victor, 1991; Goldfarb & Henrekson, 2003; Nerkar & Shane, 2007; Soh, 2003), little research has linked patents to future markets, especially in the IT domain. In contrast, IT literature, despite its important contributions, has largely ignored the novelty, uniqueness, and impact of radical innovations or their ability to address the needs of future markets.

This study weaves together literature on (1) radical innovations (Achilladelis et al., 1990; Dahlin & Behrens, 2005; Di Benedetto et al., 2008; Golder et al., 2008; Kumar, Scheer, & Kotler, 2000; Lane, Koka, & Pathak, 2006; Majchrzak, Cooper, & Neece, 2004; Malhotra et al., 2001; Rice et al., 2001; Soosay & Hyland, 2008; Sorescu et al., 2003), (2) information technology, (3) future markets (Christensen & Bower, 1996; McCann, 1991; Mitchell, 1989; O'Reilly et al., 2009; Sidhu et al., 2004; Tsai, Lin, & Kurekova, 2009), and (4) patents (Chandy & Tellis, 1998; Golder & Tellis, 1997, 2004; Henderson, Jaffe, & Trajtenberg, 1998; Levin, Klevorick, Nelson, Winter, Gilbert & Griliches, 1987; Trajtenberg et al., 1997). Some prior studies use patent citations to establish innovations' radicalness (Chandy & Tellis, 1998; Dahlin & Behrens, 2005; Golder & Tellis, 1997, 2004) or understand the value of radical patents (Hall et al., 2005; Trajtenberg, 1987), but the coevolution of these disciplines has been overlooked, such that each research area has grown in separate vacuums. Merging these disciplines can produce theory that helps clarify what makes a firm a true visionary and the indicators of such a vision. For example, a firm's inability to produce radical innovations compromises its longevity (O'Reilly & Tushman, 2004; Tushman & O'Reilly, 1996b, 2002). The contents of radical patents highlight the notable foresight of firms, which enables them to address future needs with a new product or process. Therefore, additional research should continue to use patent radicalness as a measure of success. The content of the patents also can be linked to the firm's vision of the future, with the patent signaling a commitment to that market.

From a practical standpoint, this research suggests greater collaborations between management and research scientists. Path-breaking research can suggest new markets, but managers must be committed to the innovation for the market to open. The technical content of a patent cannot reveal for certain that a firm or its scientists had *a priori* knowledge of the future market or if the technological breakthrough created those future markets. However, collaborations between management and scientists increase the chances that technological breakthroughs become market opportunities, as is evident from IBM, Microsoft, Intel, and AMD cases. Firms should create incentives for scientists to translate their technological breakthroughs into market opportunities and for managers to see market opportunities in breakthroughs.

Limitations and Directions for Future Research

Every study has limitations, and this work is no exception. First, the relevance of these findings may be limited to the IT industry or industries that are typically fast paced. Future research should try to replicate this work with different industries, such as biotechnology, pharmaceuticals, automobiles, aerospace, and defense. Second, the relevance may be restricted to industries where the patents are meaningful indicators of innovations. Third, while the patents correlate to new products, they are not commercialized products per se. Thus, the radicalness of patents only partially captures the radicalness of innovation. Future research should consider the novelty of commercialized products and the technology architecture to judge distinctness from the firm's current portfolio.

CONCLUSIONS

Although we do not know for certain if accidental technological breakthroughs open market opportunities or if predictions about markets lead to deliberate breakthroughs, we show that highly radical patents have great potential to address market needs, 5 to 15 years down the road. It is often difficult to discern a vision of future markets by long-lived firms, but their patents stocks, contents, and citation indexes can indicate a firm's commitment to markets of the future. Such continuous commitments increase the chances of both accidental discovery and deliberate efforts to meet the needs of future markets.

NOTE

1.   Classes, as the primary component of the USPTO classification system, are more stable over time than class-subclass combinations.

REFERENCES

Aboulnasr, K., Narasimhan, O., Blair, E., & Chandy, R. (2008). Competitive response to radical product innovations. *Journal of Marketing, 72*(3), 94-110.
Achilladelis, B., Schwarzkopf, A., & Cines, M. (1990). The dynamics of technological innovation: The case of the chemical industry. *Research Policy, 19*(1), 1-34.

Ahuja, G., & Lampert, C. M. (2001). Entrepreneurship in the large corporation: A longitudinal study of how established firms create breakthrough inventions. *Strategic Management Journal, 22*(6/7), 521-543.

Albert, M. B., Avery, D., Narin, F., & McAllister, P. (1991). Direct validation of citation counts as indicators of industrially important patents. *Research Policy, 20(3)*, 251-259.

Andriopoulos, C., & Lewis, M. W. (2010). Managing innovation paradoxes: Ambidexterity lessons from leading product design companies. *Long Range Planning, 43*(1), 104-122.

Applegate, L. M. (2010). Amazon.com: The brink of bankruptcy. *Harvard Business School Case*, 9-809-014.

Baker, T., Miner, A. S., & Eesley, D. T. (2002). Improvising firms: bricolage, account giving and improvisational competencies in the founding process. *Research Policy, 32*(2), 255-276

Basberg, B. L. (1987). Patents and the measurement of technological change: A survey of the literature. *Research Policy, 16*(2-4), 131-141.

Bharadwaj, A. S. (2000). A resource-based perspective on information technology capability and firm performance: an empirical investigation. *MIS Quarterly, 24*(1), 169-196.

Bharadwaj, A., S., Bharadwaj, S., G., & Konsynski, B., R. (1999). Information technology effects on firm performance as measured by Tobin's Q. *Management Science, 45*(7), 1008-1024.

Bhatt, G. D., & Grover, V. (2005). Types of information technology capabilities and their role in competitive advantage: An empirical study. *Journal of MIS, 22*(2), 253-277.

Bourgeois, L. J., III, & Eisenhardt, K. M. (1988). Strategic decision processes in high velocity environments: Four cases in the microcomputer industry. *Management Science, 34*(7), 816-835.

Boynton, A. C., & Victor, B. (1991). Beyond flexibility: Building and managing the dynamically stable organization. *California management Review, 34*(1), 53-66.

Brynjolfsson, E. B. (1993). The productivity paradox of information technology. *Commun. ACM, 36*(12), 66-77.

Brynjolfsson, E., & Hitt, L. (1996). Paradox lost? Firm-level evidence on the returns to information systems spending. *Management Science, 42*(4), 541-558.

Brynjolfsson, E., & Mendelson, H. (1993). Information systems and the organization of modern enterprise. *Journal of Organizational Computing, 3*, 245-255.

Burg, C., Ghosh, A., & Arenas, M. D. C. (2004). Agilent technologies. *Richard Ivey School of Business, Case no. 904A04.*

Burgelman, R., A. (2007). Intel in wireless in 2006: Tackling the cellular industry. *Stanford Graduate School of Business Case, SM-165.*

Burgelman, R. A., Christensen, C. M., & Wheelright., S. C. (2006). *Strategic management of technology and innovation*. New York, NY: McGraw-Hill.

Burgelman, R. A., & Grove, A. S. (1996). Strategic dissonance. *California Management Review, 38*(2), 8-28.

Carpenter, M. P., Narin, F., & Woolf, P. (1981). Citation rates to technologically important patents. *World Patent Information, 3*(4), 160-163.

Casadesus-Masanell, R., Yoffie, D., & Mattu, S. (2010). Intel Corporation 1968-2003. *Harvard Business School Case, 9-703-427*.

Chandy, R., Hopstaken, B., Narasimhan, O., & Prabhu, J. (2006). From invention to innovation: Conversion ability in product development. *Journal of Marketing research, 43*(3), 1547-7193

Chandy, R. K., & Tellis, G. J. (1998). Organizing for radical product innovation: The overlooked role of willingness to cannibalize. *Journal of Marketing Research, 35*(4), 474-487.

Chang, V. (2010). Xerox and affiliated computer services (ACS). *Stanford Graduate School of Business Case, SM-187*.

Christensen, C. M. (1992a). Exploring the limits of the technology s-curve. Part I: Component technologies. *Production and Operations Management, 1*(4), 334-357.

Christensen, C. M. (1992b). Exploring the limits of the technology s-curve. Part II: Architectural technologies. *Production and Operations Management, 1*(4), 358-366.

Christensen, C. M. (1997). *The innovator's dilema: When new technologies cause great firms to fail*. Cambridge, MA: Harvard Business School Press.

Christensen, C. M., & Bower, J. L. (1996). Customer power, strategic investment, and the failure of leading firms. *Strategic Management Journal, 17*(3), 197-218.

Christensen, C. M., & Raynor, M. E. (2003). *The innovator's solution: Creating and sustaining successful growth*. Cambridge, MA: Harvard Business School Press.

Cohen, W. M., Goto, A., Nagata, A., Nelson, R. R., & Walsh, J. P. (2002). R&D spillovers, patents and the incentives to innovate in Japan and the United States. *Research Policy, 31*, 1349-1367.

Cope, J. (1996). New and Improved. *Smart Computing, 4(3)*.

Cordell, A. J. (1973). Innovation, the multinational corporation: Some implications for national science policy. *Long Range Planning, 6(3)*, 22-29.

Cott, J., & Palepu, K. (2001). Amazon.com in the year 2001: The question of Going Concern. *Harvard Business School Case, 9-101-112*.

Dahlin, K. B., & Behrens, D. M. (2005). When is an invention really radical?: Defining and measuring technological radicalness. *Research Policy, 34*(5), 717-737.

Dess, G. G., & Beard, D. W. (1984). Dimensions of organizational task environments. *Administrative Science Quarterly, 29*(1), 52-73.

Di Benedetto, C. A., DeSardo, W. S., & Song, M. (2008). Strategic Capabilities and Radical Innovation: An Empirical Study in Three Countries. *IEEE Transactions on Engineering Management, 55*, 420-433.

Ferneley, E., & Bell, F. (2006). Using bricolage to integrate business and information technology innovation in SMEs. *Technovation, 26*(2), 232-241.

Fleming, L. (2001). Recombinant Uncertainty in Technological Search. *Management Science, 47*(1), 117-132.

Fleming, L., & Sorenson, O. (2001). Technology as a complex adaptive system: Evidence from patent data. *Research Policy, 30*(7), 1019-1039.

G. F. Ray. (1980). Innovation as the source of long term economic growth. *Long Range Planning, 13*(2), 9-19.

Galunic, D. C., & Eisenhardt, K. M. (1996). The evolution of intracorporate domains: Divisional charter losses in high-technology, multidivisional corporations. *ORGANIZATION SCIENCE, 7*(3), 255-282.

Golder, P. N., Shacham, R., & Mitra, D. (2008). Findings--Innovations' Origins: When, By Whom, and How Are Radical Innovations Developed? *Marketing Science*, mksc.1080.0384.

Golder, P. N., & Tellis, G. J. (1997). Will it ever fly? Modeling the *Takeoff of Really New Consumer Durab*les. *Marketing Science, 16*(3), 256-270.

Golder, P. N., & Tellis, G. J. (2004). Growing, growing, gone: Cascades, diffusion, and turning points in the product life cycle. *Marketing Science, 23*(2), 207-218.

Goldfarb, B., & Henrekson, M. (2003). Bottom-up versus top-down policies towards the commercialization of university intellectual property. *Research Policy, 32*(4), 639-658.

Grindley, P. C., & Teece, D. J. (1997). Managing Intellectual Capital: Licensing and Cross-Licensing in Semiconductors and Electronics. *California management Review, 39*(2), 8-41.

Grove, A. S. (1996). *Only the paranoid survives: Exploit the crisis point that challenge every company and career*. New York, NY: Doubleday.

Hall, B. H., Jaffe, A., & Trajtenberg, M. (2005). Market value and patent citations. *The RAND Journal of Economics, 36*(1), 16-38.

Harhoff, D., Narin, F., Scherer, F. M., & Vopel, K. (1999). Citation Frequency and the Value of Patented Inventions. *The Review of Economics and Statistics, 81*(3), 511-515.

Henderson, R., Jaffe, A. B., & Trajtenberg, M. (1998). Universities as a source of commercial technology: A detailed analysis of university patenting, 1965-1988. *Review of Economics and Statistics, 80*(1), 119-127.

Hill, C. W. L. (1992). Strategies for exploiting technological innovations: When and when not to license. *ORGANIZATION SCIENCE, 3*(3), 428-441.

Hitt, L. M., & Brynjolfsson, E. (1996). Productivity, business profitability, and consumer surplus: Three different measures of information technology value. *MIS Quarterly, 20*(2), 121-142.

Huckman, R. S., Pisano, G. P., & Kind, L. (2008). Amazon web services. *Harvard Business School Case, 9-609-048*.

IBM. (2010a). Awards & Achievements. Retrieved from http://www.research.ibm.com/resources/awards.shtml

IBM. (2010b). IBM delivers Power-based chip for Microsoft Xbox 360 worldwide launch. *IBM news Release*. Retrieved from http://www-03.ibm.com/technology/index.html

IBM. (2010c). IBM maintains patent lead, moves to increase patent quality. *IBM News Room*. Retrieved from http://www-03.ibm.com/press/us/en/index.wss

Jansen, J., Vanden Bosch, F. A. J., & Volberda, H. W. (2006). Exploratory innovation, exploitive innovation and performance: Effects of organizational antecedents and environmental moderators. *Management Science, 52*(11), 1661-1674.

Joshi, K. D., Chi, L., Datta, A., & Han, S. (2010). Changing the competitive landscape: Continuous innovation through IT-enabled knowledge capabilities. *Information Systems Research, 21*(3), 472-495.

Kanter, R. M. (2009). IBM in the 21st Century: The coming of the Globally Integrated Enterprise. *Harvard Business School Case, 9-308-105.*

Katila, R. (2002). New product search over time: Past ideas in their prime? *Academy of Management Journal, 45*(5), 995-1010.

Katila, R., & Ahuja, G. (2005). Something old, something new: A longitudinal study of search behavior and new product introduction. *Academy of Management Journal, 45,* 1183-1194

Kumar, N., Scheer, L., & Kotler, P. (2000). From market driven to market driving. *European Management Journal, 18*(2), 129-142.

Ladd, D. A., Datta, A., & Sarker, S. (2010, August). Trying to outrun a speeding environment: Developing "high-velocity" strategic DSS Evaluation criteria. 16th Americas Conference on Information Systems. Lima, Peru.

Lane, P. J., Koka, B. R., & Pathak, S. (2006). The reification of absorptive capacity: A critical review and rejuvenation of the construct. *Academy of Management Review, 31*(4), 833-863

Leonard-Barton, D. (1992). Core capabilities and core rigidities: A paradox in managing new product development. *Strategic Management Journal, 13,* 111-125.

Lerner, J. (1998). Xerox technology ventures: January 1997. *Harvard Business School Case, 9-298-109.*

Lerner, J., & Leamon, A. (2010). Microsoft's IP ventures. *Harvard Business School Case, 9-810-096.*

Levin, R. C., Klevorick, A. K., Nelson, R. R., Winter, S. G., Gilbert, R., & Griliches, Z. (1987). Appropriating the returns from industrial research and development. *Brookings Papers on Economic Activity, 1987*(3), 783-831.

Lyles, M. A., & Salk, J. E. (2006). Knowledge acquisition from foreign parents in international joint ventures: an empirical examination in the Hungarian context. *Academy of International Business, 38*(1), 3-18.

Lyytinen, K., & Rose, G. M. (2003). The disruptive nature of information technology innovations: The case of Internet computing in systems development organizations. *MIS Quarterly, 27,* 557-595.

Madhok, A., & Tallman, S. B. (1998). Resources, transactions and rents: Managing value through interfirm collaborative relationships. *ORGANIZATION SCIENCE, 9*(3), 326-339.

Majchrzak, A., Cooper, L. P., & Neece, O. E. (2004). Knowledge reuse for innovation. *Management Science, 50*(2), 174-188.

Malhotra, A., Majchrzak, A., Carman, R., & Lott, V. (2001). Radical Innovation without Collocation: A Case Study at Boeing-Rocketdyne. *MIS Quarterly, 25*(2), 229-249.

March, A. (1996). SAP America. *Harvard Business School Case, 9-397-057.*

Marquis, C., & Kanter, R. M. (2010). IBM: The corporate service corporation. *Harvard Business School Case, 9-409-106.*

McCann, J. E. (1991). Design principles for an innovating company. *The Executive, 5*(2), 76-93.

Miller, D., & Friesen, P. H. (1983). Strategy-making and environment: The third link. *Strategic Management Journal, 4*(3), 221-235.

Mitchell, W. (1989). Whether and when? Probability and timing of incumbents' entry into emerging industrial subfields. *Administrative Science Quarterly, 34*(2), 208-230.

Narin, F., Noma, E., & Perry, R. (1987). Patents as indicators of corporate technological strength. *Research Policy, 16*(2-4), 143-155.

Nelson, R. R., & Winter, S., G. (1982). *An evolutionary theory of economic change.* Cambridge, MA: Harvard University Press.

Nerkar, A., & Shane, S. (2007). Determinants of invention commercialization: An empirical examination of academically sourced inventions. *Strategic Management Journal, 28*(11), 1155-1166.

O'Reilly, C. A., Herreld, J. B., & Tushman, M. L. (2009). Organizational Ambidexterity: IBM and emerging Business Opportunities. *California management Review, 51*(4), 74-99.

O'Reilly, C. A., & Tushman, M. L. (2004). Ambidextrous organization. *Harvard Business Review 82*(4), 71-81.

Ofek, E., & Barley, L. (2007). AMD: A Customer-Centric Approach to Innovation. *Harvard Business School Case, 9-507-037.*

Palepu, K. (2001). Amazon.com in the year 2000. *Harvard Business School Case, 9-101-045.*

Pietrek, M. (1996). *Windows 95 System Programming Secrets.* Foster City, CA: IDG Books.

Rangan, V. K. (2002). Xerox: Book-In-Time: The new way to market, order, print, and fulfil books one at a time, just in time, worldwide. *Harvard Business School Case, 9-599-119.*

Rangan, V. K., & Bell, M. (2009). Microsoft's Unlimited Potential *Harvard Business School Case, 9-508-072.*

Rice, M., Kelley, D., Peters, L., & O'Connor, G. C. (2001). Radical innovation: triggering initiation of opportunity recognition and evaluation. *R&D Management, 31*(4), 409-420.

Rosenkopf, L., & Almeida, P. (2003). Overcoming local search through alliances and mobility. *Management Science, 49*(6), 751-766.

Rosenkopf, L., & Nerkar, A. (2001). Beyond Local Search: Boundary-Spanning, Exploration, and Impact in the Optical Disk Industry. *Strategic Management Journal, 22*(4), 287-306.

Sambamurthy, V., Bharadwaj, A., & Grover, V. (2003). Shaping agility through digital options: Reconceptualizing the role of information technology in contemporary firms. *MIS Quarterly, 27*(2), 237-263.

Santhanam, R., & Hartono, E. (2003). Issues in linking information technology capability to firm performance. *MIS Quarterly, 27*(1), 125-153.

Schilling, M. A., & Phelps, C. C. (2007). Interfirm Collaboration Networks: The Impact of Large-Scale Network Structure on Firm Innovation. *Management Science, 53*(7), 1113-1126.

Shih, W., & Ofek, E. (2009). Intel 2006: Rising to the graphics challenge. *Harvard Business School Case, 9-607-136.*

Shih, W., & Thurston, T. (2009). Intel NBI: HandHeld Graphics Organization. *Harvard Business School Case, 9-608-098.*

Shih, W., & Thurston, T. (2010). Intel NBI: Intel Corporation's new business initiatives. *Harvard Business School Case, 9-609-043*.

Sidhu, J., S, Volberda, H. W., & Commandeur, H., R. (2004). Exploring exploration orientation and its determinants: Some empirical evidence. *Journal of Management Studies, 41*(6), 913-932.

Soh, P.-H. (2003). The role of networking alliances in information acquisition and its implications for new product performance. *Journal of Business Venturing, 18*(6), 727-744.

Song, M., Droge, C., Hanvanich, S., & Calantone, R. (2005). Marketing and technology resource complementarity: an analysis of their interaction effect in two environmental contexts. *Strategic Management Journal, 26*(3), 259-276.

Soosay, C., & Hyland, P. (2008). Exploration and exploitation: the interplay between knowledge and continuous innovation. *International Journal of Technology Management*, 20-35.

Sorenson, O., Rivkin, J. W., & Fleming, L. (2006). Complexity, networks and knowledge flow. *Research Policy, 35*(7), 994-1017.

Sorescu, A. B., Chandy, R. K., & Prabhu, J. C. (2003). Sources and financial consequences of radical innovation: Insights from pharmaceuticals. *The Journal of Marketing, 67*(4), 82-102.

Stuart, T. E., & Podolny, J. M. (1996). Local search and the evolution of technological capabilities. *Strategic Management Journal, 17*(S1), 21-38.

Swanson, E. B., & Ramiller, N. C. (2004). Innovating mindfully with information technology. *MIS Quarterly, 28*(4), 553-583.

Thurrott, P. (2005). MSN: The inside story. *winsupersite.com (Penton Media)*. Retrieved from http://www.winsupersite.com/showcase/msn_inside_01.asp

Tilly, C. (2008). The history of Windows CE *HPC:Factor*. Retrieved from http://www.hpcfactor.com/support/windowsce/

Tippins, M. J., & Sohi, R. S. (2003). It competency and firm performance: Is organizational learning a missing link? *Strategic Management Journal, 24*(8), 745-761.

Trajtenberg, M. (1987). Patents, citations and innovations: Tracing the links. NBER Working Paper Series Vol. w2457.

Trajtenberg, M. (1990). A penny for your quotes: Patent citations and the value of innovations. *The RAND Journal of Economics, 21*(1), 172-187.

Trajtenberg, M., Henderson, R., & Jaffe, A. (1997). University versus corporate patents: A window on the basicness of invention. *Economics of Innovation and New Technology, 5*(1), 19 - 50.

Tsai, Y., Lin, J. Y., & Kurekova, L. (2009). Innovative R&D and optimal investment under uncertainty in high-tech industries: An implication for emerging economies. *Research Policy*, 1388-1395.

Tushman, M. L., & O'Reilly, C. A. (1996a). Ambidextrous organizations: Managing evolutionary and revolutionary change. *California Management Review, 38*(4), 8-30.

Tushman, M. L., & O'Reilly, C. A. (1996b). Ambidextrous organizations: Managing evolutionary and revolutionary change. *California management Review, 38*(4), 8-30.

Tushman, M. L., & O'Reilly, C. A. (2002). *Winning through innovation: A practical guide to leading organizational change and renewal.* Boston, MA: Harvard Business School Press.

Veliyath, R. (1992). Strategic planning: Balancing short-run performance and longer term prospects. *Long Range Planning, 25*(3), 86-97.

Yoffie, D., & Slind, D. (2007). Apple Computer, 2006. *Harvard Business School Case, 9-706-496.*

CHAPTER 12

WHAT REALLY IMPACTS LOCAL BUSINESS CLIMATE

Evidence of the Need for Entrepreneurship-Friendly Policy and Entrepreneurial Role Models

Eric W. Liguori, Joshua Maurer,
Josh Bendickson, and K. Mark Weaver

ABSTRACT

This chapter explores the perceptual side of business climate, arguing that individual perceptions of local business climate are directly impacted by views of external factors. To illustrate this, a conceptual scheme is proposed which highlights the cumulative nature of these factors and the impact they have on one's perception of the local business climate. The conceptual scheme focuses on six primary determinants that past research has linked to the emergence of entrepreneurs: government, role models, media coverage, colleges and universities, bankers and investors, and community groups and organizations. Tested over a 3 year period from 2008-2010, using data from 2,000 U.S. small and medium sized enterprises, results indicate that favorable government policy and the existence of entrepreneurial role models have the strongest and most consistent impact on perceptions of the local business climate. Implications for climate perceptions and their determinants are discussed.

INTRODUCTION

Development of an attitudinal climate that views entrepreneurship as good and enables entrepreneurial behavior is essential to long-term economic success. Krueger and Brazeal (1994) point out that "providing a reasonable supply of entrepreneurs first requires providing an environment congenial to creating potential entrepreneurs" (p. 99). Given 70% of new products and 80% of the new jobs created each year result from the entrepreneurial sector (Hisrich & Grachev, 1993), encouraging entrepreneurship is imperative to stimulate growth in a growth conscious world (Baumol, 1968), especially when considering the current economic situation faced by not only the United States, but many other developed nations as well.

> There is no doubt that the U.S. government has shown greater interest in and support for entrepreneurship in recent years. Discussions of job growth now frequently address the importance of new business creation, and elected officials today regularly emphasize the need for innovation and entrepreneurship to revive our failing economy. (Strom, 2012, p. 1)

The phrase "local business climate" is commonly used in both the mass media and the academic literature, yet it remains elusive. Though no commonly agreed upon definition exists, "the local economic conditions that foster or retard the birth or growth of firms" (Bittlingmayer, Eathington, Hall, & Orazem, 2005, p. 1) accurately captures the core essence of the phrase, both from an economic and perceptual perspective. Yet, it remains important to distinguish between economic and perceptual approaches to assessing climate. While many economic measures quantifying a "business climate" within a geographic area exist, they fail to capture the more human element of climate given they are based solely on hard economic indicators. This economic base negates the role of individual perceptions.

Simon (1957) proposed that people are boundedly rational; that individuals make decisions based upon the limited cognitive ability they possess. Inherent to this notion is that individual perceptions impact subsequent behavior (e.g., Ajzen, 1988, 1991; Ajzen & Fishbein, 2005; Fishbein & Ajzen, 1975; Krueger, Reilly, & Carsrud, 2000). Likewise, limited cognitive ability forces individual's to make decisions based upon perceptions of reality that may not always (or ever) be based upon economic indicators. Thus, this chapter explores the perceptual side of business climate, largely because it is individual perceptions and not economic reality that directly impact entrepreneurial behavior. For example, the vast majority of business owners considering relocation attribute their consideration to the perceived attractiveness of alternate communities (Dennis, 2006; Weaver, Liguori, & Vozikis, 2011). Additionally, past research has shown that nascent entrepreneur's (i.e., individuals engaging in activities meant to result in a feasible business start-up; Aldrich & Martinez, 2001) perceptions of local business climate favorableness impacts whether or not a new firm is ever even created (Bird, 1988, 1989; Krueger, 2009; Krueger & Carsrud, 1993; Mueller & Goic, 2003). Ultimately, what an entrepreneur perceives is more important than any objective reality; in essence "perceptions are critical" (Krueger & Brazeal, 1994, p. 99).

Climates perceived as favorable are associated with reduced poverty levels (Walters, 1990), higher rates of innovation and economic prosperity (Drucker, 1999), and increased economic growth (European Commission, 2003). In essence, favorable climates are vital to economic health (Henderson & Robertson, 2000), and policymakers who seek to stimulate new business or retain existing business need to consider the numerous factors affecting individual climate perceptions. By identifying and understanding what factors contribute to local business climate perceptions, scholars and practitioners alike can be provided with a more solid base of information to draw from when making informed decisions.

This chapter proceeds as follows. First, a conceptual scheme of factors impacting business climate perceptions is offered, and each factor is explained in detail. Then, the conceptual scheme is tested and results from a 3 year cross-sectional study are presented and discussed. Last, limitations are discussed and directions for future research are offered.

PERCEIVED BUSINESS CLIMATE: A CONCEPTUAL SCHEME

Figure 12.1 is a conceptual scheme illustrating the contributory factors we posit impact local business climate perceptions. This conceptual scheme was developed by reviewing past research into local business climate perceptions (viz., a review of the 2006 NFIB National Small Business Poll Results; Dennis, 2006). The figure is not intended to be tested as a fully specified model; rather it is intended to merely illustrate the cumulative nature of the contributory factors. Given individuals make decisions based on a plethora of personal construals (e.g., Hambrick, 2007; Hambrick &

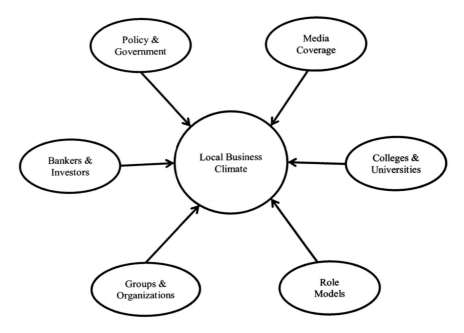

Figure 12.1.   Business climate perceptions conceptual scheme.

Mason, 1984), and that these construals undoubtedly vary by individual, it is not reasonable to derive a fully specified model of climate perceptions. Accordingly, the term "conceptual scheme" is used in lieu of the term "model."

Role Models

The existence and availability of role models in a given environment play an interesting and critical role in determining how favorable the environment is perceived to be. In studying entrepreneurial intentions, Scott and Twomey (1988) empirically found that exposure to role models is important. Individuals who venture out and form their own organization tend to be celebrated and admired for their drive, determination, hard work, and business acumen (Goetz, 2008). In the United States, business world entrepreneurs represent the majority of successful role models; and society celebrates both these individuals and their successes (Aronsson, 2004). This celebration of role models transcends a superficial "kudos" type pat on the back; individual's behaviors are often learned from observing others (Bandura, 1977a, 1977b), and thus role model behaviors are often mimicked.

Past research has demonstrated a significant and consistent link between the presence of entrepreneurial role models and the emergence of entrepreneurs (Cooper, Woo, & Dunkelberg, 1988; Kolvereid, 1997; Matthews & Moser, 1995; Shapero & Sokol, 1982; Timmons, 1986). By watching another individual succeed, one's own efficacy judgment about their ability to succeed is elevated (Scherer, Adams, Carley, & Wiebe, 1989). When one witnesses someone they consider to be a peer (or someone of comparable knowledge, skills, and ability) successfully start a new business, they are able to envision themselves behaving in a similar way, while at the same time benefiting from information cues toward venturing (e.g., Katz, 1992).

Role models also bring a level of respect and credibility to the table. Respect given to local business owners from the community is often taken into high consideration when pursuing an occupation (Dennis, 2006). People value respect and find it to be a social reward. In fields where respect is pervasive, role models and mentors are often readily available (Dennis, 2006). In a linked fashion, credibility often ties together with respect from an entrepreneurial standpoint. The availability of credible role models in one's life can readily affect ones desire to become an entrepreneur. For example, at Babson College greater than half of undergraduate students who study entrepreneurship have families who own businesses (Bygrave & Cowling, 2007), illustrating the impact of entrepreneurial role models on entrepreneurial behavior.

Family members and friends need not be the primary location for one to find entrepreneurial role models. In fact, Liñán and Santos (2007) found that the strongest influence came from nonfamily (or community-based) role models. Exemplar communities have an abundance of role models everywhere: rotary meetings, coffee shops, town halls, government, and even in education. Likewise, they exist at all levels, ranging from the independent consultant or small coffee shop owner, all the way up to Bill Gates in Silicon Valley. McCollister (2011) goes so far as to say that any prominent figure who illustrates to youth what is possible when you have a dream and commit to it can be considered an entrepreneurial role model. He includes not only Facebook Founder Mark Zuckerberg as an entrepreneurial role model, but also other media and sports figures such as Justin Bieber, LeBron James, and Trevor Bayne; a sentiment shared by Suster (2011).

Yet, let us distinguish for all intents and purposes that we consider figures such as Bayne and Bieber to be inspirational to youth, encouraging them to believe in their dreams and to persevere, but not to necessarily behave entrepreneurially or seek self-employment. Behavior is likely learned at a more local or regional level, given norms and policies vary at these levels. Thus, roles models take many forms. Some illustrate the power of perseverance (e.g., Bieber, James, & Bayne), where others help raise efficacy perceptions (e.g., Young's 2011 interview with Red Jacket Fire Arms owner Will Hayden; Maraist's 2011 profile of Buckfins and Feathers founder Kelly Neuville) and impart behavioral cues (Katz, 1992).

Overall, the existence (or lack thereof) of entrepreneurial role models does impact one's perceptions of the favorableness of the local business climate. After all, if the climate was favorable, should not examples of successful individuals be prevalent? And, if prevalent role models exist, then not only must the climate be favorable (holding all else constant), but individuals will also feel more self-confident in their ability to venture. Ultimately, the presence of role models has the ability to facilitate a positive climate which creates better conditions for future business ventures at various levels in the economy.

Media Coverage

The media plays an important and critical role in disseminating information about local business climate. Aside from just conveying news, media coverage also generates publicity, increases community involvement and awareness, highlights success stories, and generally engages individuals at a personal level. Local media coverage can use various avenues including magazines, newspapers, newsletters and local TV in order to publicize entrepreneurs' endeavors and bring those efforts to the attention of the general populous. For example, Descant's (2011) *The Advocate* (a Baton Rouge, LA based newspaper) article describes a local start-up weekend brainstorming and business development workshop, highlighting activities and portraying entrepreneurship in a positive light. By describing entrepreneurial events in the media, subjective norms that entrepreneurial behavior is acceptable become more ingrained in the culture, offering local entrepreneurs more support and legitimacy. Similarly, local news stations covered the start-up weekend and are known for occasionally writing biographies about local entrepreneurs. It is not uncommon for local media coverage to do a story on a new or expanding entrepreneurial venture, explaining what the venture does and interviewing the entrepreneur (Scram, 2011). In addition, local business news magazines typically provide biographies of local entrepreneurs and can help promote entrepreneurship by giving out awards including business person of the year, entrepreneur of the year, and young business person of the year, similar to that of The Greater Baton Rouge Business Report. Not only are these award winners recognized within these magazines, but are also recognized through other mediums. It would not be uncommon for entrepreneurs receiving awards from one medium or agency to transcend through multiple media platforms. As described above, a positive entrepreneurial climate would see multiple media platforms and competing media firms covering similar stories related to entrepreneurship.

Publicizing entrepreneurial successes tend to increase perceptions that starting a business is feasible (Krueger & Brazeal, 1994). Media portrayals of entrepreneurial role models and positive activities can increase one's desire for self-employment through entrepreneurial venturing. The reverse effect may also occur; media may also paint a negative picture of entrepreneurship, causing a decline in a potential entrepreneur's desire to start a new venture. Thus, exposure to media coverage on the local business environment can influence one's perceptions of the favorableness of the environment in both positive and negative ways. Indeed, one of Birch, Haggerty, and Parsons's (1999) 10 criteria used to assess the entrepreneurial-ness of a community was whether local newspapers wrote about and celebrated entrepreneurs. It is clear that there is a role for media in entrepreneurship and a greater understanding of this role creates opportunity for media to facilitate new business ventures within a community.

Getting the community involved is essential for a healthy entrepreneurial climate. One way to do this is by sharing what local entrepreneurs are accomplishing. Stories involving economic and social contributions made by entrepreneurs in the community will increase the public's awareness of the essential improvements made by these individuals and their businesses (Rightmyre, Johnson, & Chatman, 2004). This serves as an inspiration to potential entrepreneurs and helps to legitimize individual entrepreneurs to financial institutions, investors and other resource allocators. In a similar fashion, the romanticism associated with entrepreneurs, as they tell their stories, comparing their accomplishments to war, parenting, freedom, and the journey of a lifetime can help plant the seed of entrepreneurship within a community (Hustedde, 2007). In accordance, the publication and coverage of award ceremonies and other entrepreneurial recognitions can help stimulate an entrepreneurial climate.

Publicity not only generates immediate sales, but also provides a longer-term understanding for those seeking knowledge regarding the problems and opportunities involved in business ownership (Dennis, 2006). From this regard, media coverage provides insight as to how a business owner might find success or avoid failures. The media can be viewed as a great community asset in facilitating climate and shedding light on business creation. In sum, the media has the potential to share entrepreneurial stories, publicize new business ventures, and spread credible knowledge and insight to prospective future entrepreneurs. Through diligent and appropriate media coverage, these capabilities can provide a great deal of awareness to the community.

Colleges and Universities

Colleges and universities present many opportunities to advance business and provide desirable climates. A few prominent components to consider when addressing the roles of colleges and universities are governmental policies, education and learning, and community advancement. First, as many universities are public, there is a fair amount of overlap between government and university procedures involving entrepreneurial activity. Governments believe that the promotion of entrepreneurial based education programs can increase the amount of new entrepreneurial business formation and colleges and universities are a primary contributor to these educational efforts. State and local governments that invest in colleges and universities also help support effective intellectual property transfer programs which can intern, help to stimulate economic growth (Markley & Macke, 2002). Educators and researchers are concerned with the demands raised by politicians, practitioners, and the general public for the promotion of entrepreneurial activity. In a reciprocal role, academics studying entrepreneurship can provide information and insight that may influence or support political action. Their involvement provides understanding and insight into the importance of small business creation, allowing for policymakers to take heed of potential effects on entrepreneurial activity (Strom, 2012). In addition, they may also have a direct impact on policy formation if they move from academia to governmental positions. This may be similar to two senior economic advisors who provide greater attention to the demands and needs of small businesses, further encouraging venture and birthrate growth (Strom, 2012). Higher total education expenditures are also very attractive to various industries (Plaut & Pluta, 1983). The links among government, policy, and education are unavoidable. For better or worse, these links present a variety of opportunities to impact business climate.

Beyond the educational structure as designed by both public and private institutions, the heart of what colleges and universities are creating is learning environments and opportunities. An implied objective of all entrepreneurship education is the creation of more (and more skillful) entrepreneurs (Ronstadt, 1985); thus increasing the self-efficacy of the population of entrepreneurs and stimulating firm birthrates (Sternberg, 2009). Entrepreneurial activity has been increasingly linked to educational experience, especially in regards to business development and intellectual capital curriculums, which helps to create a healthy foundation to build an entrepreneurial economy. Education systems must teach the future entrepreneurs how to adapt, innovate, and react to changes, uncertainties and complexities, or in other words, how to be entrepreneurial (Fayolle, 2007). Rightmyre et al. (2004) use findings from the global entrepreneurship monitor (GEM) to demonstrate the strong relationship between education and entrepreneurial activity, thus indicating the need for strong educational programs that provide education and resources for potential entrepreneurs and their future employees. Raposo and do Paco (2010) counter that while the entrepreneurial education—entrepreneurial linkage is not definitive, there is a significant amount of research suggesting a positive relationship exists.

Education can lead to major impacts in the entrepreneurial climate, community, and knowledge spillover. More than just transferring knowledge, universities play a strong institutional role in developing innovation systems and this support has great impact on community actors and partners (Wolfe, 2007). Universities provide communities with skilled labor and the ability to sustain an education labor force (Erickson, 1987); and the educational attainment of the venture team is often used as a criterion to determine venture financing decisions (Liguori & Muldoon, 2012). Among many other things, universities are educated labor forces and more likely to produce knowledge spillover. Research has shown that knowledge created in universities tends to spillover to practitioners for commercial use which helps to generate innovative activity (Feldman & Audretsch, 1996; Mansfield, 1995). Knowledge spillovers trigger entrepreneurial communities and result in higher rates of city and regional growth (Audretsch, Keilbach, & Lehmann, 2006). The value of knowledge spillover may depend on the amount, type, and transferability but generally speaking, spillover is beneficial to the community and proximate to universities.

Similar to educating potential entrepreneurs, universities can offer and support entrepreneurs in the local community by building relationships. Entrepreneurs who are able to cultivate relationships and partner with academics are able to harness new knowledge capabilities and possibly integrate external knowledge. Individuals who are effective at cultivating relationships and engage in more communication with others including academics and the services they provide are more successful and less likely to fail (Duchesneau & Gartner, 1990). Indeed, business owners who create a valuable social network, interact effectively, and form a favorable reputation are more likely to be financially rewarded (Baron & Markman, 2003).

This knowledge and technical assistance can greatly help one grow and cultivate a business based on relationships or training and counseling provided by these educational services (Velazquez et al., 2009). Universities also work through small business and development centers (SBDC) throughout the nation which give them access to a broader base of knowledge to bring back to their community partners. To stimulate entrepreneurial growth, local governments consciously implement formal programs like SBDCs with a vast majority of them being housed in universities (Liguori, Koutroumanis, & Solomon, 2012). Programs such as SBDCs have a profound effect on both the number of new ventures created and their future success (Liguori et al., 2012). Entrepreneurs who receive counseling and similar support services provided by universities, have a greater survival rate and have an increased ability to innovate and grow (Chrisman & McMullan, 2000). Without guidance from these types of programs, entrepreneurs are more susceptible to their inabilities to overcome complications and are prone to limitations in their long-term success (Dodge & Robbins, 1992; Rice & Matthews, 1995).

Ultimately, colleges and universities can have many impacts. In addition to the numerous impactful services provided above, they create a climate that initiates communities which work more closely together, build cooperative relations between schools and the business community, and create the means to help organizations and new businesses become more successful (Dennis, 2006). On average, small business owners are well educated and tend to be more inclined to work in communities with supportive colleges and university assistance (Dennis, 2006). Last, and

> perhaps most importantly, professors who conduct research on entrepreneurship bring it into their classrooms, ultimately educating the next generation of voters and entrepreneurs about the importance of new business creation and fostering the ingenuity and industriousness that they will need for success. (Strom, 2012, p. 1)

Bankers and Investors

The availability of resources improves perceptions of business creation feasibility to potential entrepreneurs. Initial and continual financing for the start-up of a new business is likely to promote or deter the creation and development of new enterprises. Some form of financing is usually essential for start-up or expansion of business. Without this financing to develop marketing, production, and other business essentials, an innovative idea or product may never come to fruition. Increased access to funding of loans is one of the most commonly identified ways to improve a business's potential success (Juneau Economic Development Council., 2011). Understanding how, why, when, and the challenges entrepreneurs face in regards to financing is important in order for local communities to develop successful business climates.

Capital obtained for business creation can come from many sources. Although firms may typically rely on entrepreneurs, family, or friends to finance their formation, the cost and availability of capital through traditional means becomes critical once a business is operational (Dunkelberg, Scott, & Dennis, 2003). Surprisingly, only about 14% of initial financing comes from banks, venture capital institutions or angel investors (Markley, 2007). Since the amount of venture capital investment available in an economy is related to entrepreneurial activity and opportunity recognition (Bygrave, 2002), it seems measures should be taken to instigate these types of funds. Crane and Meyer (2006) suggest that governments should encourage the availability of venture capital through both private equity and angel funds.

Entrepreneurs may need funding for multiple reasons and at various times. Markley (2007) identifies four stages in which a business venture may need capitalization. During the first stage an individual tests and generates ideas. This could include surveys or developing a prototype product. The second stage involves the initial start-up which requires additional capital for equipment, inventories, property, and other business necessities. It has been estimated that these initial two stages have typically averaged around $25,000, but the demand for capital may fluctuate as entrepreneurs continue to operate (Markely, 2007). It can become difficult for entrepreneurs to cover current operating costs with the proceeds from current income (Markely, 2007). The final stage at which an entrepreneur may require funding is when it is necessary to grow the firm. Therefore, even after the initial investment in a firm, the ease at which business owners get continued financial support becomes crucial.

As alluded to, obtaining financing is not an easy process for entrepreneurs. Studies have found that a lack of financial resources is one of the most important obstacles faced by entrepreneurs (Bitzenis & Nito, 2005; Chatman, Altman, & Johnson, 2008). Crane and Meyer (2006) suggest that lack of seed money, lack of venture capital, and lack of angel investors can be a major obstacle to entrepreneurial development. Obtaining capital is not the only challenge. Entrepreneurs must also be cognizant as to the types and rates they are receiving. Lower loan rates and fees are critical in allowing small businesses to make payments and avoid going deeper in debt in early start-up stages. Lower rates can help them to make payments, access credit, and increase their chances of survival. Unfortunately, understanding how to obtain capital, and the nuances is one of the most challenging aspects for small business owners (Velazquez et al., 2009). This becomes even more complicated and exaggerated by financial crisis, leaving many small business owners with few options to obtain capital. Though other challenges exist, these are arguably most pressing at present time.

Due to financing complexities, placing a national priority on informational seminars to help business owners (and potential business owners) gain understanding regarding available capital would be a noteworthy effort (Velazquez et al., 2009). This could also be an initiative which could be tied together locally through colleges and universities. Sutaria and Hicks (2004) linked regional development (of new firms) to the availability of local financial capital. Presently, creating a flow of capital is more challenging. However, local communities who find ways to do so will greatly enhance their business climate and likely see a rise in business ventures.

Community Groups and Organizations

Community groups and organizations play a valuable role for entrepreneurs by facilitating knowledge sharing, providing support, creating and developing business relationships, expediting networking, and increasing the entrepreneurial community's political voice. Within these groups, entrepreneurs are able to voice concerns, benefit from the experience of others and meet potential suppliers or clients. A favorable entrepreneurial climate that includes positive perceptions of a community's groups and organizations may indicate that there is a strong support network that may aid entrepreneurs during the evolution of their ventures from inception to growth.

Community groups may take the form of local chamber, rotary, local economic development authority and even social activist groups (Dennis, 2006). Various groups and organizations can provide help and opportunities to business owners (and prospective business owners) in a community. These opportunities are important for a number of reasons. For one, social support and community assistance have been linked to perceptions of feasibility. Social support in a community can be crucial to encouraging entrepreneurship by affecting an individual's desire to start a business. In addition, community groups can collaborate to stretch limited resources. These groups work together to achieve mutual objectives maximizing (their already) strained financial resources. This community support may influence a potential entrepreneur's beliefs that starting a business is both desirable and attainable (Krueger & Brazeal, 1994). These perceptions are critical in developing a community of entrepreneurs. Community groups can provide three fundamental benefits: collaboration, information sharing, and networking opportunities.

Collaborating with other local business owners can have many benefits. Although many of the local businesses may be competitors to some extent, improvement based cooperation has the potential to help the group as a whole. This is something that is not always recognized by business owners who are in competition. Improving climate, even if it is for your competitors, can provide a great deal of spill-overs for your business (Dennis, 2006). Through regular meetings, collaboration can present an abundance of opportunity in discussing improvements and issues that are affecting small businesses in the community (Velazquez et al., 2009).

Large quantities of information can be shared through community groups. When individuals share information and tell stories about their struggles and achievements as an entrepreneur, it provides valuable insight into complexities of different organizational functions associated with marketing, financing, developing, and managing (Hustedde, 2007). By associating with other entrepreneurs, an individual is able to tap into a collective wisdom held and shared between the group members (Chojnowski, 2010). It is not uncommon for entrepreneurs to argue that a vast majority of what they learn is from other entrepreneurs (Bandura, 1977a, 1977b; Chojnowski, 2010). Additionally, entrepreneurial failures do not have to be looked at with a negative stigma, but instead can often contribute to this collective wisdom which can be a valuable learning agent for new business formation (Chojnowski, 2010). Duboc (2002) similarly suggests that failure is recognized as having the potential to teach important business lessons; and entrepreneurs who fail are not necessarily cut off from the rest of the entrepreneurial community. In fact, they may even be held in higher esteem than those who have not gone through similar learning experiences. Successful businesses, lessons learned, and overall wisdom all represent valuable information sharing potential which occurs in various community groups.

Collaboration and information sharing often occur due to networking. Through networking, information uncertainties, knowledge of risk, and mobilization of social resources can all increase (Chatterjee & Lakshmanan, 2009). Network opportunities are essential for small business owners. It is important to hold these regular meetings not only to share information as addressed above, but also to identify barriers that can be resolved through practice or by local policymakers. This increases opportunities to exchange information, meet other entrepreneurs, obtain potential funding sources, and identify ways to support small business development (Rightmyre et al., 2004).

There are other facets of networking which can lead to additionally important connections. Entrepreneurship is a continuous process and while a business owner may have had some great ideas in the past, continuously meeting and discussing with other entrepreneurs may help inspire new opportunities. Entrepreneurs may try to identify these new opportunities by networking beyond their professional or social network by identifying "connectors." Connectors are individuals who have meaningful relationships with you and with others, providing a means for introductions and the building of additional relationships (Stephenson, 2008).

As seen, community groups can have many roles for collaboration, information sharing and networking which can intern lead to a whole host of possibilities. Chatterjee and Lakshmanan (2009) point out a number of these possibilities.

> These organizations have several functions: policy activism identifying unmet goals and demanding new policies, supplementing and facilitating markets for targeted services, promotion of increased transparency in governance, and engagement in socioeconomic coordination jointly with the public and the private sector agents. (Chatterjee & Lakshmanan, 2009, p. 109)

Finally, Cowen and Cowen (2010) strongly believe in the potential of community groups and that the relationships built locally (or also on larger scales) are critical to gaining a strategic position to obtain resources. Community groups clearly present a great deal of opportunity. They help position a local economy for greater entrepreneurial activity by creating productive and connected groups of business leaders and entrepreneurs.

Local Government and Policy

Local business owners greatly value community support and an interconnected community of people working together, both items that were addressed in prior sections. On the other end of the spectrum, business owners often least value government interference, taxes, and general costs of doing business (Dennis, 2006). Despite a general disliking toward governmental regulation, there are many things a local government can do to support, promote, and attract business ventures. The following section introduces a variety of important local governmental issues associated with local business climate. This includes an overview of general policy issues as well as a more in depth look at, taxation, laws, and economic growth.

To begin, it is appropriate to ask what local government can do to create a good business climate. According to Plaut and Pluta (1983), there are a number of components including low state and local taxes, little union activity, and a cooperative government structure. Other somewhat location based factors can provide benefits. They also identify cost and availability of labor, raw materials and transportation facilities (Plaut & Pluta, 1983). Additionally, maximum freedom to develop new ideas and businesses without hindrance from taxation, regulation, and other barriers is conducive to produce a favorable entrepreneurial climate (VanMetre & Hall, 2007). Furthermore, one of Birch et al.'s (1999) 10 principals used in identifying whether or not a community was entrepreneurial was whether government officials consistently met with entrepreneurs to for their advice. Business climate is often heavily linked to taxes and state employment growth; and high taxes convincingly deter business growth (Pluat & Pluta, 1983). Much of the literature on governmental implications draw attention to lawmaking and taxation and accordingly, the following section will address some of these concerns.

Policymakers can develop laws and programs influencing the jurisdictional business climate. The ultimate goal for these policymakers is to insure that the government provides enough protection for firms but not to the extreme that costs dwarf their benefits (Campbell, Heriot, Jauregui, & Mitchell, 2012). These policies including tax laws, education, and regulations can create both incentives and constraints for potential entrepreneurs. Both taxes and the public services brought by these taxes influence a business climate (Steinnes, 1984). It is suggested that in regards to economic growth, the most important elements of business climate are tax and regulatory burdens imposed on firms (Bittlingmayer et al., 2005). Similarly, Bast (2010) argues that minor changes in taxes and policies can lead to businesses losing employees, customers, and even business failure or relocation. His primary principal is keeping the total tax burden low arguing that what, who, or how something is taxed is less important than the overall tax burden, which when high results in reduced growth. Secondarily, he calls for a simplification and reduction in taxes, specifically targeting small businesses. Bast (2010) argues that by simplifying and lowering theses taxes (i.e., capital gains taxes and personal income taxes), it will help to encourage a favorable entrepreneurship climate. In addition, policymakers should implement policies that allow for affordable housing and that attract creative individuals. Affordable housing increases the labor supply while policies directed at attracting creative individuals increase a community's supply of potential entrepreneurs. Entrepreneurs are especially vulnerable to high income taxes, lawsuit abuse and inflexible labor policies (Bast, 2010).

An excessive amount of governmental burdens placed on entrepreneurs is negatively effecting job creation and economic growth at an increasing rate (Keating, 2011). The conflicting goals that policymakers face may limit their ability to maximize venture creation and limit entrepreneurial failure (Campbell et al., 2012). Consequently, this makes these government officials the dominant decision makers with power to influence many factors contributing to a positive entrepreneurial climate. These officials design the support facilities and develop the policies in order to create and develop new business ventures (Fayolle, 2007).

The primary concern for many policymakers is to reduce unemployment and grow their economies. Since policymakers require a continued supply of jobs to maintain their positions, entrepreneurial business creation remains as one of their primary focal points. Public policy helps to shape the business environment in which an organization operates. The buy or not buy decision by potential entrepreneurs can depend strongly on the business climate an individual finds themselves in. A key issue facing the policymakers is developing mechanisms that promote employment creation and economic growth. Varying mechanisms have been attempted on national, regional, and local levels. Aldrich (1999) and Aldrich and Kim (2005) posit that the greater the political and social legitimacy of business creation in a state, region, or nation, the more likely individuals are to engage in entrepreneurial activity. It is predicted that entrepreneurial development activities, including tax incentives, enterprise zones, new venture development and training programs, may create a favorable entrepreneurial climate for small firms (Isserman, 2007). Support from the local community in the form of social, political, and business leaders are all essential to encouraging new ventures (Krueger & Brazeal, 1994). Adopting policies that produce an atmosphere supportive to a high level of new business formations spanning numerous industries is a key factor to creating a healthy entrepreneurial climate and growth development. These polices should support an assorted base of small and new firms in various sectors making communities resilient and adaptive to technological and economic changes. The policies that promote a more stable community also provide a community that is better prepared to capitalize on new opportunities and sustain economic growth throughout the future.

There are a few final policy implications to keep in mind. Many policies are designed to help the local business climates. Unfortunately though, there are a number of negative components that have become bothersome to the entrepreneurial spirit. Fifty percent of entrepreneurs do not believe that local governments go out of their way to improve the local business climate (Dennis, 2006). Some entrepreneurs also argue that the government is treating them unfairly. This view of fairness affects the overall climate and is at least partially the responsibility of the local government. "Tax abatements, tax increment financing, and other location incentives are often seen as unfair by local businesses. Zoning, taxes, and provision of public services can also signal a community's fairness to small businesses" (Chatman et al., 2008, p. 74). Therefore, it is prudent to look beyond just tax cuts or a comparison of different state taxes in assessing a business climate. Some policies may also provide a favorable environment to larger organizations while ignoring the needs of entrepreneurs. Local entrepreneurs are keen to these items and may seek business climates which are more favorable.

As Shapero (1981) illustrates, policies that emphasize the relocation of firms instead of new firm formation may be more costly, more risky, and more likely to fail. Often a community will go out of its way to attract new organizations by offering tax breaks, inexpensive land, interest incentives, buildings, and improved infrastructure. However, this often leads to a few firms holding the rest of the community hostage to their demands; and a community should be concerned with establishing conditions favorable to firm formation as opposed to servicing specific industries and plants (Shapero, 1981). This approach will strengthen the community as a whole, making it more resilient to economic shifts and plant closures. Thus, as VanMetre and Hall (2011) suggest, it is important to understand what the policymakers should focus on when trying to create incentives that support entrepreneurial activity and focus specifically on small businesses and enterprise development.

In some jurisdictions, policies have been developed to promote financing and limit barriers to entrepreneurial business creation. Examples include the Bayh-Dole Act allowing universities to more easily transfer technology and a Michigan law allowing state pension funds to invest venture capital in potential businesses. Examples of barriers include outdated laws and regulations that demand unnecessary and/or large investments. State and local governments increasingly have the power to influence education, taxation, zoning, planning, and the environment in which an entrepreneur operates and indeed, these powers influence economic development activity (Goetz & Freshwater, 2001).

Policies can also be established by promoting local patronage such as town festivals, increased parking, and downtown revitalization programs in order to support local entrepreneurs (Chatman et al., 2008). As shown, beyond just tax implications, different policies can have a vast array of impacts on the local community and the local business climate.

Ultimately, the nature of law-making is complex and interrelated. Encouraging economic growth is a fundamental goal. However, the goals may not be quite as clear as it seems. For example, to create a community with great education and good infrastructure, while at the same time keeping taxes low, can become very difficult to achieve (Kolko, Neumark, & Mejia, 2011). Local policy and lawmakers must abide within the federal and state restrictions while also doing as much as they can to attract, maintain, and develop favorable business climate. As mentioned, taxation, lawmaking and policymaking can all have a great impact on the local business climate and furthermore, the complexities have a great deal of interplay. In the long term, there are numerous challenges but also excellent opportunities for local governments to impact the local business climate.

METHOD AND MEASURES

This study is based on a 3 year (2007, 2008, and 2009) data collection conducted in the fall of 2007, 2008, and 2009. Data were collected from a cross-sectional sample of small firm owners and managers in Louisiana. We began with a respondent pool of Louisiana-based firms listed in the InfoUSA database, and then stratified the pool to only include firms with between 1 and 250 employees.

All surveys were conducted by a professional public polling research firm experienced in large-scale data collection best practices. A mixed mode approach was employed (phone, internet, and mail) to ensure maximum participation. To ensure candor, respondents were assured that individual responses would be kept confidential and that only aggregate data would be reported. The cooperation rate (reported in lieu of a response rate because initial respondent eligibility was unknown) was 41.5% and was calculated using the American Association for Public Opinion Research's (2008) Cooperation Rate 4 measure. Reasons for nonresponses were primarily refusals (98%), though some responses had to be discarded due to noncompletion of the full survey instrument (< 1%).

Table 12.1, categorized by year, provides a detailed overview of the sample descriptive statistics. Overall, respondent gender and education were equally balanced, and respondents' averaged 48 years of age. As expected from a small firm sample (e.g., Miller, LeBreton-Miller, & Scholnick, 2008), the majority of respondents were the firms' owner/manager, though some nonowner managers and nonmanager owners were also included in the sample.

Table 12.1. Descriptive Statistics

Category	Description	2007	2008	2009
N	Sample Size	571	562	621
Age	Average	49.75	47.25	47.95
Gender	% Female	38%	52%	47%
Education	% College Educated	48%	46%	56%
Respondent Ownership Status	% Owner (only)	11%	9%	3%
	% Owner/Manager	67%	54%	60%
	% Manager (only)	22%	37%	37%
Industry	% Services	47%	54%	63%
	% Retail	24%	28%	26%
	% Manufacturing	5%	4%	7%
	% Other	24%	14%	4%

Arguably, the large sample size(s) allow for ample representation of a variety of industries and locations through the state. The industries represented in our sample included manufacturing, retail, services (e.g., professional, personal, financial, educational, technical, scientific and administrative), and a variety of others (e.g., construction, wholesale trade, warehousing, and entertainment & recreation).

The survey instrument was adopted with permission from the National Federation of Independent Business's National Small Business Poll (NSBP), a commonly accepted measure in the business climate and entrepreneurship literature (e.g., Dennis, 2006; Dennis, 2011a, 2011b; Weaver et al., 2011). The NSBP consists of affirmative statements regarding business owner or manager perceptions of the determinants of local business climate (explanatory variables), and their perception of their community's business climate favorableness (dependent variable). The survey solicited 5-point Likert-type responses anchored "strongly disagree" to "strongly agree." A representative explanatory variable item is "Local community groups and organizations go out of their way to support local businesses, including people trying to start them."

The survey statement used to calculate the dependent variable (business climate favorableness) read as follows: "Overall, is your community's business climate very favorable, favorable, neither favorable nor unfavorable, unfavorable, or very unfavorable?" Higher scores reflect more positive (favorable) perceptions of the business climate. Control variables (industry, gender, age, education, and ownership status) were also included.

RESULTS AND DISCUSSION

To test the extent to which each of the six aforementioned factors (role models, media coverage, area colleges and universities, bankers and investors, community groups and organizations, and policy & government) impact local business climate perceptions we used hierarchal linear regression. Controlling for industry, as well as respondent age, gender and level of education, we ran each year of data independently. Results for each year are reported in Tables 12.2, 12.3, and 12.4, respectively. Then, all 3 years of data were combined, an additional control variable titled year was added, and the model was rerun. Results of this analysis are presented in Table 12.5. Table 12.6 summarizes the significance of each factor across all analyses. Overall, the percentage of explained variance in all four analyses is low, but that is as to be expected. Remember, the conceptual scheme presented in Figure 12.1 was never intended to be a fully specified model; certainly other factors also impact climate perceptions.

Table 12.2.   Hierarchical Regression Analysis Results (2007 Data)

Variable	R^2	ΔR^2	β
Step 1 *(control variables)*	−0.004	0.003	
Industry			0.001
Age			0.008
Gender			0.057
Education			0.010
Step 2 *(focal variables)*	0.060***	0.057***	
Industry			0.001
Age			0.020
Gender			0.063
Education			0.027
Bankers & Investors			0.018
Role Models			0.111*
Media Coverage			0.100*
Policy & Government			0.137**
Community Groups & Orgs.			0.042
Area Colleges & Universities			0.002

Note: $N = 571$. Standardized beta coefficients are shown.
† $p < .10$; * $p < .05$; ** $p < .01$; *** $p < .001$

Role models and policy and government were the only two factors that were universally statistically significant across four analyses. Given these two factors also consistently had the largest impact, policymakers seeking to improve climate perceptions in an effort to foster entrepreneurial behavior could consider these areas a starting point. In a U.S. study of regulations at the national level, Hahn (2005) found that many regulations impose costs much greater than the benefits they create. A focus group of California-based entrepreneurs conducted by Liguori (2011) yielded similar results, with several respondents expressing their frustration with the cost of compliance to local and state legislation (viz., emissions, workers compensation, and mandated safety and healthcare programs at the state level). To quantify the impact of compliance costs, consider that economists estimate that every $15 million in regulatory compliance costs stimulates one fatality due to lost income (Lutter, Morrall, & Viscusi, 1999).

The 2008 results reported in Table 12.3 were interesting in that it was the only analysis where five of the six factors were significant. This may be in part due to the increased awareness of one's environment leading up to a U.S. presidential election (Bowler & Donovan, 1998). It seems reason-

Table 12.3. Hierarchical Regression Analysis Results (2008 Data)

Variable	R^2	ΔR^2	β
Step 1 (control variables)	0.00	0.01	
Industry			0.08†
Age			0.02
Gender			0.04
Education			0.01
Step 2 (focal variables)	0.23***	0.23***	
Industry			0.04
Age			0.01
Gender			0.03
Education			0.00
Bankers & Investors			0.10*
Role Models			0.21***
Media Coverage			0.10*
Policy & Government			0.11*
Community Groups & Orgs.			0.14**
Area Colleges & Universities			0.06

Note: $N = 562$. Standardized beta coefficients are shown.
† $p < .10$; * $p < .05$; ** $p < .01$; *** $p < .001$

able to suspect, for example, that media coverage of entrepreneurial-related topics was heightened during the fall of 2008 as the nation prepared for November's presidential election, especially given the state of the U.S. economy at the time (i.e., the need for jobs). Essentially, we posit that as Election Day approached, both news coverage and efforts to mold public opinion intensified; a hypothesis consistent with findings in the political awareness literature (e.g., Nicholson, 2003).

Several reasons may exist for why area colleges and universities universally failed to significantly impact overall climate perceptions. First, the nature of the sample was limited in that very few high-technology firms were interviewed. It is these types of firms that would be most impacted by area colleges and universities (cf. Cha & Bae, 2010; Chell & Allman, 2003; George, Jain, & Maltarich, 2005). Second, it is possible the public does not associate entities like the Small Business Develop Center network under the "area college and university" umbrella. Though SBDCs are primarily housed in university settings, perhaps respondents viewed them as independent community groups or organizations, thus diluting the impact of area colleges and universities as conceptualized in this

Table 12.4.   Hierarchical Regression Analysis Results (2009 Data)

Variable	R^2	ΔR^2	β
Step 1 *(control variables)*	0.01*	0.02*	
Industry			0.08[†]
Age			0.01
Gender			0.07
Education			0.06
Step 2 *(focal variables)*	0.20***	0.20***	
Industry			0.04
Age			0.05
Gender			0.05
Education			0.06
Bankers & Investors			0.13**
Role Models			0.22***
Media Coverage			0.02
Policy & Government			0.20***
Community Groups & Orgs.			0.07[†]
Area Colleges & Universities			0.05

Note: $N = 621$. Standardized beta coefficients are shown.
† $p < .10$; * $p < .05$; ** $p < .01$; *** $p < .001$

study. Third, with the exception of the state's flagship LSU campus in Baton Rouge, Louisiana universities do little to support or foster entrepreneurial behavior as compared against other state university systems (e.g., FL). Last, as many entrepreneurship educators have recently speculated, perhaps universities are not the entrepreneurial factories they proclaim to be (e.g., Pilegaard, Moroz, & Neergaard, 2010).

Ultimately, a confluence or syntheses of factors are needed to foster a positive business climate. While we painstakingly sought to independently measure the effects of each of the factors included in our conceptual scheme, it is likely that they work in unison. Media coverage can influence perceptions of climate favorableness just by what topics are or are not covered. For example, media outlets can highlight local entrepreneurs giving rise to the perception of role models, thus increasing the perception that business venturing is feasible (Krueger & Brazeal, 1994). Policies can be put in place to establish mentoring programs. Public-private partnership efforts can spin out organizations to further support venturing. Ultimately, this study sought to separate the effects of each factor in an effort to find which factors have the greatest

Table 12.5. Hierarchical Regression Analysis Results (2007-2009)

Variable	R^2	ΔR^2	β
Step 1 (control variables)	0.06***	0.07***	
Industry			0.08***
Age			0.01
Gender			0.03
Education			0.02
Year			0.41***
Step 2 (focal variables)	0.19***	0.13***	
Industry			0.07**
Age			0.01
Gender			0.04†
Education			0.03
Year			0.44***
Bankers & Investors			0.01
Role Models			0.11***
Media Coverage			0.01
Policy & Government			0.13***
Community Groups & Orgs.			0.07*
Area Colleges & Universities			0.04†

Note: $N = 1754$. Standardized beta coefficients are shown.
† $p < .10$; * $p < .05$; ** $p < .01$; *** $p < .001$

impact; it would be naïve to believe a synthesis is not required to create favorable business climates.

LIMITATIONS AND FUTURE RESEARCH DIRECTIONS

Several limitations and areas of future research exist and should be noted. First, the study sample was constrained to only Louisiana-based firms under 250 employees. Thus, while it is reasonable to generalize the results to Louisiana-based small businesses, generalizing results to outside of the state or presuming they apply to larger firms should be done with caution. Second, this study sought to explore the sources of business climate perceptions because these sources impact perceived climate favorableness and entrepreneurial behavior. Future research should seek to explore what differences, if any, exist in responses from firm non-man-

Table 12.6.   Summary of Findings (2007-2009)

Variable	2007	2008	2009	All 3
Industry	n.s.	n.s.	n.s.	*
Age	n.s.	n.s.	n.s.	n.s.
Gender	n.s.	n.s.	n.s.	n.s.
Education	n.s.	n.s.	n.s.	n.s.
Year	–	–	–	*
Bankers & Investors	n.s.	*	*	n.s.
Role Models	*	*	*	*
Media Coverage	*	*	n.s.	n.s.
Policy & Government	*	*	*	*
Community Groups & Orgs.	n.s.	*	*	*
Area Colleges & Universities	n.s.	n.s.	n.s.	n.s.

Note. * = significant findings in that year; n.s. = not significant.

ager-owners verses owner-managers verses manager-non-owners. Third, this study was limited to only perceptual data. Going forward, researched may consider blending perceptual and objective data together to more completely look at business climate favorableness.

Fourth, future research may consider distinguishing between community colleges and colleges and universities, in large part because regarding community impact, their goals are quite different. Last, this study did not seek to make any comparisons of local parish or county differences, though the popular press often uses surveys like the one employed here to "rank" business climates at state and national levels. In the future, researchers may want to explore local parish or country differences within a given state, but it should be done so with more rigor than is commonly employed by the popular press. Insights from such an endeavor may help enlighten policymakers who are seeking to stimulate economic development at the local level.

ACKNOWLEDGMENT

The support of the National Federation of Independent Businesses and NFIB Senior Research Fellow William (Denny) Dennis is gratefully acknowledged. Funding for the data collection was provided by the Shell Oil Economic Development and Counseling Stewardship Project.

REFERENCES

American Association for Public Opinion Research. (2008). *Standard definitions: Final dispositions of case codes and outcome rates for surveys* (5 ed.). Lenexa, Kansas: Author.

Aronsson, M. (2004). Education matters—but does entrepreneurship education? An interview with David Birch. *Academy of Management Learning & Education, 3*(3), 289-292.

Ajzen, I. (1988). *Attitudes, personality, and behavior*. Chicago, IL: The Dorsey Press.

Ajzen, I., & Fishbein, M. (2005). The influence of attitudes on behavior. In D. Albarracín, B. T. Johnson, & M. P. Zanna (Eds.), *The handbook of attitudes*. Mahwah, NJ: Erlbaum.

Aldrich, H. E. (1999). *Organizations evolving*. Thousand Oaks, CA: SAGE.

Aldrich, H. E., & Kim, P. H. (2005, November). *Against all odds: The impact of financial, human, and cultural capital on becoming a nascent entrepreneur*. Paper presented at the conference Nascent Entrepreneurship: The Hidden Potential, Durham, NC.

Aldrich, H. E., & Martinez, M. A. (2001). Many are called, but few are chosen: An evolutionary perspective for the study of entrepreneurship. *Entrepreneurship Theory & Practice, 25*(4), 41-56.

Audretsch, D. B., Keilbach, M. C., & Lehmann, E. E. (2006). *Entrepreneurship and economic growth*. New York, NY: Oxford University Press.

Bandura, A. (1977a). Self-efficacy: Toward a unifying theory of behavioral change. *Psychological Review, 84*, 191-215.

Bandura, A. (1977b). *Social learning theory*. Englewood-Cliffs, NJ: Prentice-Hall.

Baron, R. A., & Markman, G. D. (2003) Beyond social capital: The role of entrepreneurs' social competence in their financial success. *Journal of Business Venturing, 18*, 41-60.

Bast, J. (2010). *Ten principles for improved business climate*. (Legislative Principles Series, Vol. 8). Chicago, IL: The Heartland Institute.

Baumol, W. J. (1968). Entrepreneurship in economic theory. *The American Economic Review, 58*(2), 64-71.

Birch, R., Haggerty, A., & Parsons, W. (1999). *Entrepreneurial hot spots: The best places in America to start and grow a company*. Cambridge, MA: Cognetics.

Bird, B. (1988). Implementing entrepreneurial ideas: The case for intention. *Academy of Management Review, 13*(3), 442-453.

Bird, B. (1989). *Entrepreneurial behavior*. Glenview, IL: Scott Foresman.

Bittlingmayer, G., Eathington, L., Hall, A. P., & Orazem, P. F. (2005). *Business climate indexes: Which work, which don't, and what can they say about the Kansas economy?* Topeka, KS: Kansas, Inc.

Bitzenis, A., & Nito, E. (2005). Obstacles to entrepreneurship in a transition business environment: The case of Albania. *Journal of Small Business & Enterprise Development, 12*(4), 564-578.

Bowler, S., & Donovan, T. (1998). *Demanding choices: Opinion, voting, and direct democracy*. Ann Arbor, MI: University of Michigan Press.

Bygrave, W. (2002, November). *Risk capital in Canada: Breaking down barriers, increasing access.* Panel discussion at the Canadian Foundation for Investor Education Symposium Series, Montreal, Quebec.

Bygrave, W., & Cowling, M. (2007). Entrepreneurship, welfare provision and unemployment: Relationships between unemployment, welfare provision, and entrepreneurship in thirty-seven nations participating in the Global Entrepreneurship Monitor (GEM) 2002. *Comparative Labor Law & Policy Journal, 28*(4).

Campbell, N. D., Heriot, K.C., Jauregui, A., & Mitchell, D.T. (2012). Which state policies lead to U.S. firm exits? Analysis with the economic freedom index. *Journal of Small Business Management, 50*(1), 87-104.

Cha, M.-S., & Bae, Z.-T. (2010). The entrepreneurial journey: From entrepreneurial intent to opportunity recognition. *Journal of High Technology Management Research, 21*, 31-42.

Chatman, D., Altman, I., & Johnson, T. (2008). Community entrepreneurial climate: An analysis of small business owners' perspectives in 12 small towns in Missouri, USA. *Journal of Rural and Community Development, 3*, 60-77.

Chatterjee, L., & Lakshmanan, T. R. (2009). The fashioning of dynamic competitive advantage of entrepreneurial cities: Role of social and political entrepreneurship. In C. Karlsson, A. E. Andersson, P. C. Cheshier & R. R. Stough (Eds.), *New Directions in Regional Economic Development* (pp. 107-120). New York, NY: Springer.

Chell, E., & Allman, K. (2003). Mapping the motivations and intentions of technology oriented entrepreneurs. *R & D Management, 33*(2), 117-134.

Chojnowski, B. (2010). Turning Failfield, Iowa into a rural renaissance city. *Economic Development Journal, 9*(4), 30-34.

Chrisman, J. J., & McMullan, W. E. (2000). A preliminary assessment of outsider assistance as a knowledge resource: The longer-term impact of new venture counseling. *Entrepreneurship Theory & Practice, 24*(3), 37-54.

Cooper, A., Woo, C., & Dunkelberg, W. (1988). Entrepreneurs' perceived chances for success. *Journal of Business Venturing, 3*, 97-108.

Cowen, A. P., & Cowen, S. S. (2010). Rediscovering communities: Lessons from the Hurricane Katrina crisis. *Journal of Management Inquiry, 19*(2), 117-125.

Crane, F. G., & Meyer, M. (2006). The entrepreneurial climate in Canada: The entrepreneur's viewpoint. *Journal of Small Business and Entrepreneurship, 19*(3), 223-232.

Dennis, W. J. (2006). Local Business Climate. *NFIB Small Business Poll, 6*(2), 1-32.

Dennis, W. J. (2011a). Entrepreneurship, small business, and public policy levels: Part 1. *Journal of Small Business Management, 49*(1), 92-106.

Dennis, W. J. (2011b). Entrepreneurship, small business, and public policy levels: Part 2. *Journal of Small Business Management, 49*(2), 149-162.

Descant, S. (2011, November 16). Startup Weekend: Business cram session. *The Advocate.* Retrieved from http://theadvocate.com/home/1328164-125/startup-weekend-business-plan-cram.html

Dodge, H. R., & Robbins, J. E. (1992). An empirical investigation of the organizational life cycle model for small business development and survival. *Journal of Small Business Management, 30*(1), 27- 37.

Drucker, P. (1999). *Innovation and entrepreneurship* (2 ed.). Oxford, England: Butterworth-Heinemann.

Duboc, S. (2002, November). *Risk capital in Canada: Breaking down barriers, increasing access.* Panel discussion at the Canadian Foundation for Investor Education Symposium Series, Montreal, Quebec.

Duchesneau, D. A., & Gartner, W. B. (1990). A profile of new venture success and failure in an emerging industry. *Journal of Business Venturing, 5,* 297–312.

Dunkelberg, W. C., Scott, J. A., & Dennis, W. J. (2003). *Small business indicators of macroeconomic activity.* Washington DC: National Federation of Independent Businesses.

Erickson, R. A. (1987). Business climate studies: A critical evaluation. *Economic Development Quarterly, 1*(1), 62-71.

European Commission. (2003). *The commission's green paper: Entrepreneurship in Europe.* Brussels, Belgium: DG Enterprise.

Fayolle, A. (2007). *Entrepreneurship and new value creation.* Cambridge, England: Cambridge University Press.

Feldman, M. P., & Audretsch, D. B. (1996). R&D spillovers and the geography of innovation and production. *American Economic Review, 86,* 630-640.

Fishbein, M., & Ajzen, I. (1975). *Belief, attitude, intention, and behavior: An introduction to theory and research.* Reading, MA: Addison-Wesley.

George, G., Jain, S., & Maltarich, M. (2005, March). *Academics or entrepreneurs? Entrepreneurial identity and invention behavior of university scientists.* Paper presented at the Technology Transfer Society Conference, Kansas City, MO.

Goetz, S. J. (2008). *State entrepreneurial climate estimates: An update based on the Kauffman Index.* University Park, PA: The Northeast Regional Center for Rural Development at The Pennsylvania State University.

Goetz, S. J., & Freshwater, D. (2001). State-level measures of entrepreneurship and a preliminary measure of entrepreneurial climate. *Economic Development Quarterly, 15*(1), 58-70.

Hahn, R. W. (2005). *In defense of the economic analysis of regulation.* Washington DC: AEI-Brookings Joint Center for Regulatory Studies.

Hambrick, D. C. (2007). Upper echelons theory: An update. *Academy of Management Review, 32*(2), 334-343.

Hambrick, D.C., & Mason, P. (1984). Upper echelons: The organization as a reflection of its top managers. *Academy of Management Review, 9*(2), 193-206.

Henderson, R., & Robertson, M. (2000). Who wants to be an entrepreneur? Young adult attitudes to entrepreneurship as a career. *Career Development International, 5*(6), 279-287.

Hisrich, R. D., & Grachev, M. V. (1993). The Russian entrepreneur. *Journal of Business Venturing, 8*(6), 487-497.

Hustedde, R. (2007). What's culture got to do with it? Strategies for strengthening an entrepreneurial culture. In N. Walzer (Ed.), *Entrepreneurship and local economic development* (pp. 39-58). Lanham, MD: Lexington Books.

Isserman, A. (2007). State economic development policy and practice in the United States. In Plane, Mann, Button & Nijkamp (Eds.), *Regional planning: Classics in planning* (Vol. 4). Cheltenham, England: Edward Elgar.

Juneau Economic Development Council. (2011). *Southeast Alaska business climate survey.* Juneau, AK: Author.

Katz, J. (1992). A psychosocial cognitive model of employment status choice. *Entrepreneurship Theory & Practice, 17*(1), 29-37.

Keating, R. J. (2011, December 14). Baby steps to a biz-friendly New York, *New York Post.* Retrieved from http://www.nypost.com/f/print/news/opinion/opedcolumnists/baby_steps_to_biz_friendly_new_york_BeN0z1pTAWCDa1nTdSeNgI

Kolko, J., Neumark, D., & Mejia, M. C. (2011). *Business climate rankings and the California economy.* San Francisco, CA: Public Policy Institute of California.

Kolvereid, L. (1997). Prediction of employment status choice intentions. *Entrepreneurship Theory & Practice, 21,* 47-57.

Krueger, N. (2009). Entrepreneurial intentions are dead: Long live entrepreneurial intentions. In A. L. Carsrud & M. Brannback (Eds.), *Understanding the entrepreneurial mind.* New York, NY: Springer.

Krueger, N., & Brazeal, D. V. (1994). Entrepreneurial potential and potential entrepreneurs. *Entrepreneurship Theory & Practice, 18*(3), 91-104.

Krueger, N., & Carsrud, A. (1993). Entrepreneurial intentions: Applying the theory of planned behavior. *Entrepreneurship & Regional Development, 5,* 315-330.

Krueger, N. F., Reilly, M. D., & Carsrud, A. L. (2000). Competing models of entrepreneurial intentions. *Journal of Business Venturing, 15*(5-6), 411-432.

Liguori, E. W. (2011, November). *Determinants of local business climate perceptions.* Roundtable discussion hosted by the Craig School of Business, Fresno, CA.

Liguori, E. W., & Muldoon, J. (2012). Credentials. In M. Marvel (Ed.), *Encyclopedia of New Venture Management* (pp. 342-343). Thousand Oak, CA: SAGE.

Liguori, E. W., Koutroumanis, D., & Solomon, G. T. (2012). Public policy: Government stimulation of start-ups. In M. Marvel (Ed.), *Encyclopedia of New Venture Management* (pp. 152-154). Thousand Oak, CA: SAGE.

Liñán, F., & Santos, F. J. (2007). Does social capital affect entrepreneurial intentions? *International Advances in Economic Research, 13,* 443-453.

Lutter, R., Morrall, J. F., & Viscusi, W. K. (1999). The cost-per-life-saved cutoff for safety-enhancing regulations. *Economic Inquiry, 37*(4), 599-608.

Mansfield, E. (1995). Academic research underlying industrial innovations: Sources, characteristics, and financing. *The Review of Economics and Statistics, 77*(1), 55-65.

Maraist, C. M. (2011). Entrepreneur: Kelly Neuville. *Greater Lafayette Business Journal, 4*(5), 28.

Markley, D. M. (2007). Building communities through entrepreneurship development: Financing entrepreneurs and entrepreneurial support systems. In N. Walzer (Ed.), *Entrepreneurship and local economic development* (pp. 125-144). Lanham, MD: Lexington Books.

Markley, D., & Macke, D. (2002). Entrepreneurs & entrepreneurship [Monograph] Center for Rural Entrepreneurship. Retrieved from http://www.ruraleship.org/index_html ?page=content/monographs.htm

Matthews, C. H., & Moser, S. B. (1995). Family background and gender: Implications for interest in small firm ownership. *Entrepreneurship & Regional Development, 7,* 365-377.

McCollister, R. (2011, March 8). Young people, entrepreneurs are key. *Baton Rouge Business Report*. Retrieved from http://www.businessreport.com/artile/ 20110308/BUSINESS REPORT0201/303089971/0/businessreport0402

Miller, D., LeBreton-Miller, I., & Scholnick, B. (2008). Stewardship vs. stagnation: An empirical comparison of small family and non-family businesses. *Journal of Management Studies, 45*(1), 51-78.

Mueller, S. L., & Goic, S. (2003). East-West differences in entrepreneurial self-efficacy: Implications for entrepreneurship education in transition economies. *International Journal of Entrepreneurship Education, 1*(4), 613-632.

Nicholson, S. P. (2003). The political environment and ballot proposition awareness. *American Journal of Political Science, 47*(3), 403-410.

Pilegaard, M., Moroz, P. W., & Neergaard, H. (2010). An auto-ethnographic perspective on academic entrepreneurship: Implications for research in the social sciences and humanities. *Academy of Management Perspectives, 24*(1), 46-61.

Plaut, T. R., & Pluta, J. E. (1983). Business climate, taxes and expenditures, and state industrial growth in the United States. *Southern Economic Journal, 50*(1), 99-119.

Raposo, M., & do Paco, A. (2010). Entrepreneurship and education-links between education and entrepreneurial activity. *International Entrepreneurship and Management Journal, 3*(6), 1-2

Rice, M. P., & Matthews, J. B. (1995). *Growing new ventures, creating new jobs: Principles and practices of successful business incubation*. Westport, CT: Quorum Books.

Rightmyre, V. M., Johnson, T. G., & Chatman, D. (2004). *Growing entrepreneurs from the ground up*. Columbia, MO: Community Policy Analysis Center, University of Missouri—Columbia.

Ronstadt, R. (1985). The educated entrepreneur: A new era of entrepreneurial education is beginning. *American Journal of Small Business, 10*, 7-23.

Scherer, R., Adams, J., Carley, S., & Wiebe, F. (1989). Role model performance effects on development of entrepreneurial career performance. *Entrepreneurship Theory & Practice, 13*(3), 53-81.

Scott, M., & Twomey, D. (1988). The long-term supply of entrepreneurs: Students' career aspirations in relation to entrepreneurship. *Journal of Small Business Management, 26*(1), 5-13.

Scram, K. (2011, February 11). *Young entrepreneur expands family business*, [Television broadcast]. Baton Rouge, LA: Knight Broadcasting.

Shapero, A. (1981). Entrepreneurship key to self-renewing economies. *Economic Development Commentary, 5*, 19-22.

Shapero, A., & Sokol, L. (1982). The social dimensions of entrepreneurship. In C. A. Kent, D. L. Sexton, & K. H. Vesper (Eds.), *Encyclopedia of Entrepreneurship* (pp. 72-90). Englewood Cliffs, NJ: Prentice-Hall.

Simon, H. A. (1957). *A behavioral model of rational choice models of man, social and rational: Mathematical essays on rational human behavior in a social setting*. New York, NY: Wiley.

Steinnes, D. N. (1984). Business climate, tax incentives, and regional economic development. *Growth & Change, 15*(2), 38-47.

Stephenson, K. (2008). The community network solution. *Strategy and Business, 49,* 1-6.

Sternberg, R. (2009). Regional dimensions of entrepreneurship. *Foundations and Trends in Entrepreneurship, 5*(4), 211-340.

Strom, R. (2012, January 9). Academia's emerging role in entrepreneurship policymaking. *The Huffington Post.* Retrieved from http://www.huffingtonpost.com/robert-strom/academias-entrepreneurship-policymaking_b_1194477.html

Suster, M. (2011, March 1). What every entrepreneur could learn from Justin Bieber. *TechCrunch.* Retrieved from http://techcrunch.com/2011/03/01/what-every-entrepreneur-could-learn-from-justin-bieber/

Sutaria, V., & Hicks, D. (2004). New firm formation: Dynamics and determinants. *Annuals of Regional Science, 38,* 241-262.

Timmons, J. A. (1986). Growing up big: Entrepreneurship and creation of high-potential ventures. In D. Sexton & R. Smilor (Eds.), *The art and science of entrepreneurship* (pp. 223-239). Cambridge, MA: Ballinger.

VanMetre, B. J., & Hall, J. C. (2007). How friendly to entrepreneurs are "business friendly" policies? Some preliminary results. *Journal of Business and Economics Perspectives, 28*(1), 105-116.

Velazquez, N. M., Moore, D., Shuler, H., Dahlkemper, K., Schrader, K., Kirkpatrick, A., et al. (2009, February 11). *Full committee hearing on the state of the SBA's entrepreneurial development programs and their role in promoting an economic recovery.* Washington DC: U.S. Government Printing Office.

Walters, S. J. K. (1990). Business climate and measured poverty: The evidence across states. *Atlantic Economic Journal, 18*(1), 20-26.

Weaver, K. M., Liguori, E. W., & Vozikis, G. S. (2011). Entrepreneur business climate perceptions: Developing a measure and testing a model. *Journal of Applied Business and Economics, 12*(1), 95-104.

Wolfe, D. A. (2007). The role of higher education and new forms of governance in economic development: The Ontario case. In S. Yusuf & K. Nabeshima (Eds.), *How universities promote economic growth* (pp. 119-138). Washington, DC: The World Bank.

Young, R. (2011). Thriving in economic recession: *Red Jacket Firearms* [Radio]. United States: WKRF (NPR).

CHAPTER 13

TECHNOLOGY AND ITS IMPACT ON HIGHER EDUCATION

Christina Partin and Kathleen P. King

ABSTRACT

This chapter reveals the major issues surrounding the adoption of innovative instructional technology in higher education and presents an interdisciplinary model for framing changes in perspectives, action and policy. The review of existing literature illuminates the great need for colleges and universities to be more relevant and address student expectations and needs for technology integration while coping with faculty concerns about the same. The proposed model shifts away from a system that devalues innovative teaching to one that cultivates effective and innovative technology use in education even in research-focused institutions.

The foundational research and literature of this chapter includes research and theory across higher education, sociology, ethics, adult learning, faculty development and educational psychology. The chapter presents a four-stage interdisciplinary **integrative innovation model for higher education,** which builds upon several environmental variables that extend across policy and management issues, cultural issues, and faculty development issues. We will discuss aspects of these environmental variables such as (1) ethics and respect for colleagues, management, and support persons; (2) motivation and willingness to change; and (3) academic freedom including consideration of faculty voice. We recognize these variables as essential for encourag-

Global Perspectives on Technological Innovation, pp. 403–433
Copyright © 2013 by Information Age Publishing
All rights of reproduction in any form reserved.

ing faculty creativity and willingness to innovate with technology. The chapter's discussion extends from technology implementation and student success to new aspects of cultural issues and organizational thinking. A valuable feature of this chapter is the use of scenarios and case studies to provide a new perspective for effecting and sustaining change in institutions which are often bureaucratic and static.

INTRODUCTION

Institutions of higher education are burdened with a conflict: they recognize a need for innovative instructional methods but their faculty often lack the training or readiness to deliver instruction in these ways. This conflict emerges not only from the rapid innovation of technology, but also its widespread social adoption for most daily and workplace needs. As higher education remains slow to integrate technology in instruction, a critical disconnect in validity and relevance grows (Bok, 2003; Burns & Lohenry, 2010; Kosak et al, 2005; Tapscott, 2008). This chapter explores the literature related to major issues surrounding the adoption of innovative instructional technology in higher education and presents an interdisciplinary model, the **integrative innovation model for higher education (IIMHE)**, to provide new strategies for framing and implementing recommended perspectives, action and policy. Instead of continuing to stigmatize innovative teaching, a critical characteristic and outcome of this model is that it recognizes the importance of innovation in education, even in research-focused institutions. The four-stage, interdisciplinary model is built on a theoretical foundation that draws from three major areas, each pertaining to different facets of faculty career development: policy and management issues, cultural issues, and faculty development issues. First, the policy and management issues reveal the complexity of competing demands and conflicting values within higher education, which interfere with both instructional innovation and technology adoption. For instance, in many research universities, publication and research hold the highest value in the evaluation of a faculty member's tenure application (Alstete, 2000). In such a context, pursuing anything else, such as pursuing faculty development in distance learning or developing online courses, has been viewed "as a waste of time" for tenure earning faculty.

Next, our review of literature will reveal how cultural issues influence instructional technology adoption, showing the lack of faculty voice in decision making regarding all institutional aspects of the issue. While colleges and universities derive their strategic plans from their mission, the organizational culture is less firmly rooted in mandates and specifics. Instead, organizational culture survives on a fluid foundation of conflicting characteristics. For example, while organizational culture may be collectively developed, it is also often guided by a leader, and while dependent on group buy-in, it can be influenced by individuals or organizational norms. Moreover, an emphasis on teaching often results in a lack of monetary, economic capital (Fairweather, 2005), and those who endeavor to enhance their classes through innovative teaching methods are denied other forms of capital as well. For instance, according to Bourdieu (1992), symbolic capital may be denied to those who place an emphasis on innovative teaching as it is less desirable in the academic system. This discussion extends from technology implementation and student success to new aspects of cultural issues and organizational thinking.

Finally, a comprehensive but focused review of related faculty development issues demonstrates research which can guide future efforts. Existing literature demonstrates that faculty are hesitant to incorporate innovative teaching techniques in their classes because they have anxieties about using these methods (King, 2003). The anxieties stem from a lack of training and a great concern that they may be devalued by their institution or colleagues because of their desire to teach effectively. At least one model (Boyle & Boice, 1998) found success in mentoring faculty and saw positive impacts of systematic professional development on improved success in teaching and job satisfaction, so whether teachers can effectively incorporate innovations into their classes seems to be a null question. The real question, based on these issues and others, is how the perception of innovative teaching can move from a stigmatized activity to a valuable aspiration.

The four-stage interdisciplinary model that we propose is based on (1) ethics and respect for colleagues, management, and support persons; (2) adult learning and the ability to build on prior experience, as well as faculty ownership; and (3) motivation and willingness to change. The authors build upon research and theory across higher education, sociology, ethics, adult learning, faculty development and educational psychology in order to provide a new perspective of how to effect and sustain change in traditionally bureaucratic and static institutions. The chapter presents the model in detail, while also illustrating more features of it through cases and scenarios. These vehicles cultivate a deep understanding of the needs, issues, and decisions related to implementing the model in varied contexts.

UNDERSTANDING THE CONTEXT

Historical Roots of Higher Education: The Road From Exclusiveness to Accessibility

The roots of United States higher education are not what many people believe them to be. With the founding of the Ivy League, the U.S.'s first colleges in the 1600s, only the upper class had access to institutions of "higher learning" (Rudolph & Thelin, 1990). These colleges were in fact seminaries as the most learned people of the community were clergy. Gradually, the focus of studies in higher education widened to include medical studies, law, and business. Women did not have access to higher education until the mid-1800s when women's colleges emerged in the Midwest and later in the Northeast (Thelin, 2004). Teacher colleges were another trend as these "normal schools" primarily prepared women in a few months to two years. However, it was not until the mid-1880s through 1940s that that legislation began to set aside many of their exclusions of class, status, religion, gender, race, or other various social or demographic characteristics that previously restricted access.

Two major types of legislation did more to advance the education of the "masses" (nonelite) than anything else. The first are the land grant legislations passed in 1796-1864 to allocate public property for the establishment of "land grant universities" (thus providing the large campuses of our state universities), the most famous of which is the Morrill Act legislation of 1864 (Thelin, 2004). One can recognize the commitment to higher education upon noting that these land grants included appropriations from 46,000 to 100,000 acres (p. 75). The other major class of legislations are military veteran educational benefits. The most prominent of these is the post-World War II era GI Bill, which provided scholarships for returning veterans. However, the U.S. government continues to allocate these benefits in new forms and dimensions as seen in the post-9/11 GI Bill (the Yellow Ribbon Program) which provides full tuition for public colleges and universities or up to $17,500 for tuition and fees at participating private institutions (U.S. Department of Veterans Affairs, 2011).

The increased democratization of higher education surged in the 1960s as college student protests leveraged and merged with the efforts of the Civil Rights Movement (Rudolph & Thelin, 1990). The results include the development of student services and the introduction of student-centered learning in higher education Schrecker (2010).

A third major legislation shifted higher education from not only elite to mass education, but to universal education as the expectation (Thelin, 2004). These legislations established the federal financial aid system and included the 1964 Higher Education Act and 1976 Basic Educational Opportunity Grant (BEOG), now known as the Pell Grants. At this point, enrollment in higher education became an entitlement of every qualified U.S. high school graduate and thus, 40-50% of all high school graduates enrolled as college students. Social and legal trends led to a dramatic change in the students enrolled in U.S. institutions of higher learning, but even more dramatic changes were yet to come.

Higher education in the United States had slowly transitioned across 200 years from the elite class to everyone attending colleges and universities; however, the early 1990s brought the means of still greater transformation. The first online classes launched as the general public gained access to desktop computing and Internet. By 2000, most accredited higher education institutions delivered classes and complete programs/degrees online (Allen & Seaman, 2008). Flexibility drove the popularity of this delivery format. People seeking to complete a degree no longer had to attend on campus classes. Instead, logging in from their homes increased student access as it reduced many barriers such as travel time, transportation, scheduling conflicts, childcare, and so on (Allen & Seaman, 2008; Bates & Sangra, 2011). However, faculty lagged in the adoption of technology, and specifically distance learning, compared to industry, the general public and student needs (Bok, 2003; Fischman, 2010; Schmidt, Shelley, Van Wart, Clayton, & Schreck, 2000).

A new wave of pressure for change in U.S. higher education dawned with distance learning, in part due to the inability of traditional colleges and universities to move quickly in adopting it. The age of for-profit institutions burst upon the landscape of higher education and became an academic phenomenon, which institutions had to notice by 2000. However, the American 2008 Financial Crisis pushed this need much further. The high tuition costs of several for-profit institutions lured students to enroll with false job expectations and promises of financial aid despite exorbitant tuition rates. Unfortunately, a combination of a poor job market with high unemployment rates, coupled with a lack of valid lack of preparation left many of these graduates unable to secure employment, and ultimately, as many Americans endured the mortgage crisis, many students battled the student loan crisis bubble that followed. (Cohn, 2010; PremierStudentLoans.com, 2008; Sanchez, 2008). As a result, currently U.S. legislators are exploring mandates for higher education institutions to demonstrate the employability/earning potential of all degree and certificate programs (Donoghue, 2011). Never called upon before to correlate the pursuit of higher education with employability, U.S. higher education faces a new crossroads to challenge the demands placed before it or to reinvent itself.

The Current State of Technology in Higher Education

Despite these significant changes, the institution of higher education is steeped in tradition, which helps to explain many activities or behaviors that might seem strange outside of their context. While society has changed drastically, much has remained the same within the ivy walls of higher education. For instance, we can easily illicit the image of the way that Plato, Aristotle, or other "enlightened individuals" taught. The community considered them the authority on a subject, and revered them seeking their insights. Listening to either lectures or questions, the students, looking to become enlightened, sat mostly as passive recipients. Paolo Freire (1970) referred to this process as the "banking method of education," which describes the top-down approach that centers on the teacher as the authority in the classroom. Despite all the societal transformation outside of the classroom, inside of the classroom this tradition has persisted. In the spirit of academic freedom, professors have discretion to run their classrooms and research agendas in whatever way they see appropriate (Bok, 2003). As such, they often model after those who taught them (Blackburn, Chapman, & Cameron, 1981; Donald, 2003), even when those methods are ineffective or outdated.

In recent years, the influx of technology threatens some of the tradition in higher education. Professors, once the sole authority and dispensers of information, now compete with Google, Wikipedia, or Ask.com—websites that offer answers to questions at the click of a mouse. In the midst of this "information age," the structure of higher education is beginning to shift. The focus in higher education, at least as it is articulated in mission statements and strategic plans, is evolve away from simply providing knowledge to providing sets of skills to students. Technology is helping to shape this change, but not all individuals inside the institution have responded with the same fervor. Faculty members often feel pressure from administration and students to use technology in their classes, yet many find inadequate training and support from their institutions (Olcott & Wright, 1995; Wilson & Stacey, 2004).

People today are constantly using twenty-first century technologies in their daily lives for work, family, entertainment, and socialization (i.e., ATMs and cell phones to deposit checks, e-mail, IM and webcams to communicate with work and family worldwide, etc.). As this technology continues to decrease in both cost and physical size, access to technology continues to grow. As a result, people of all ages now possess inexpensive devices which fit into their pockets, but have the computing power of a desktop PC. In our constantly evolving and increasingly computerized world, mobile Internet browsing and social networking capabilities have changed the way that people connect and learn about each other and their worlds. However, in higher education classrooms, many of these technologies are untapped: at best, these technologies are considered bothersome—at worst, disrespectful and distracting (Burns & Lohenry, 2010).

It is important to realize that in the last decade, the traditional students who entered college classrooms were exposed to computers, cell phones, and other advanced technologies since birth (Tapscott, 2008).

These individuals, commonly referred to as "digital natives" (a term in part coined and popularized by Marc Prensky in 2001), tend to be more comfortable and accepting of new technologies in their day-to-day activities. In fact, current research suggests that digital natives' attachment to their technologies is so great that they view their devices as an extension of their own physical bodies (Oksman & Rautianen, 2003). On the other hand, the literature often refers to nontraditional students, along with many professors or instructors, as "digital immigrants." Digital immigrants are people who adopt technology later in life, and while they accept the change, they less fully embrace or understand the technology as quickly as their native counterparts.

As "baby boomers" near retirement in this current area, a large portion of the workforce currently falls into the digital immigrant category, although the first wave of digital natives and other early adopters of technology are making their way into classrooms as young professors. In other words, while digital natives continue to enter the universities in droves, university leadership and faculty remain dominated by digital immigrants who may not fully understand the population they serve.

Fortunately, some researchers and educators persist in devising and researching methods to introduce these technologies into classroom lectures, discussion and activities with significant outcomes—including greater student engagement and success. Prior research indicates that the introduction of multimedia encourages a student culture of active learning in both higher and secondary classroom environments (Mayer, 2008). Other indications reveal that introducing technology into college instruction can be a useful pedagogical practice for engaging students in the learning process (Mollborn & Hoekstra, 2010). Thereby, effective use of technology in higher education advances the essential elements of student success, which include learner engagement, active learning, class attendance, and retention (Kuh, Kinzie, Schuh, & Whitt, 2010).

Challenges and Issues: Obstacles to Implementation

With research indicating that using technology produces positive student outcomes, it begs the question why all educators are not using technology in their classes. According to Tennant, McMullen, and Kaczynski (2010), many educators are resistant to technology for a variety of reasons. For instance, lack of technology resources, instructional technology training, administrative watchdogs, and time to learn how to use the technology effectively for their teaching and research needs (Bok, 2003; Tennant, McMullen, & Kaczynski, 2010). In addition to these reasons, another persistent explanation for faculty resisting technology is fear.

These obstacles block progress toward instructional technology implementation, and are a part of the larger issues addressed in this chapter—issues related to management and policy, culture, and professional development.

While many faculty will not outright state they are fearful of using technology in their teaching, research by King (2003) confirms this is a major barrier. Many readers might ask why would they be fearful? However, consider the role and identity of faculty as depicted earlier and persisting through the history of higher education. Professors are expert academicians expected to understand and communicate all knowledge to their students without hesitation. From the perspective of the professor, how does the prospect of fumbling with an LCD projector or Smartboard augment or detract from this role? If faculty cannot immediately access the wiki, blog or website they want to use to make a point, how will that situation make them look to their students? And worse case situation, if one has to call for technical support or ask the class for assistance, what thread of authority be retained?

Based on extensive discussion with faculty, we can confirm that these are the very real and frequent fears which haunt faculty and keep them from taking risks with technology. In addition, another major fear is that perhaps they will not know well enough how to teach with technology. After all, they were never taught like with technology; they have no model to follow. Instead, current faculty have learned quite well how to imitate the pedagogical style of their senior faculty. Why take a risk in our teaching and the student evaluations, when we KNOW how to teach another way? (Donald, 2003) The stakes are large indeed. Student evaluations will impact faculty tenure and merit pay (annual raises); if faculty have too many technical problems or they are ineffective with it, the students will surely lambast their performance. These are examples of some of the predominate fears which faculty have about using technology in their teaching.

It is therefore dismaying when we realize that most administrators, faculty developers, information technology (IT), and instructional design staff do not hear and see these fears and concerns. Instead, they watch and listen to what amounts to resistance. Faculty who do not want to use technology, will often just state their decision without extended discussion. However, consider the alternative. Who wants to tell another adult that you are afraid of failure or risk when you are supposed to be "The Expert?" The cognitive and emotional dissonance is enough to confuse most people and certainly create behavior of avoidance.

Obviously, these examples include issues spanning organizational and individual dimensions and scope. Any strategies which will be successful on a broad basis in engaging faculty in using technology in teaching will have to include addressing management and policy, culture, and professional development. The choices being made, whether to adopt technology or not, are embedded in culture, policy and preparation. The good news is that all of these elements may be altered to address the concerns. The reality of the situation is, however, these changes happen slowly and need to planned and implemented in manners consistent with the sociocultural context of the individual institution and respecting authority and ownership of faculty (Caffarella, 2001; Lawler & King, 2000). The next section discusses more of these issues in depth.

INTERDISCIPLINARY PERSPECTIVES FOR AN INTEGRATIVE, RESPONSIVE APPROACH

Later in this chapter, we will introduce a two-part model. This model signifies a reciprocal relationship between various entities of the academy, and ways that these entities interact and influence one another. The first part of this model pertains to the environment necessary for implementation of the model. We discuss these environmental variables in depth below and assert them as a prerequisite for encouraging faculty creativity and for the integrative model's successful implementation.

Ethics and Respect

In an environment with such a diversity of knowledge and skills, ethics and collegiality become increasingly important topics for discussion. Because of the rigid hierarchy in university, the increased emphasis on research over teaching, and the varying motivation or technological skill level of individuals within the university, the ethical principle of recognizing and respecting the intrinsic value of others becomes necessary. Only upon recognizing and embracing this ethical principle can the skills of each individual be thought of as equal contributions, so it becomes possible to see the institution of higher education as a place for technological innovation as well as traditional teaching—as a place that values the instructor as well as the researcher—and as a collection of people who embrace the opportunity to learn new skills at any rank, length of service, or level in the institution.

Craft (2010) notes that ethics is more than taking correct actions in given situations—being ethical also requires the skill and ability to critically question and create logical arguments. These skills can be taught and honed at any level. Having an established ethical background provides faculty with the tools needed to foster an environment of respect and collegiality, major themes in many codes of ethics. Emphasizing the importance of maintaining a culture whereby people can acknowledge the contributions of others, and can praise their value, creates a more productive, collegial, and ethical work environment.

The major source for discussion in faculty ethics emerges from the professional associations. It is herein that many faculty, such as in the medical sciences, social sciences, counseling, social work, and so on, find their code of ethics developed, discussed, and upheld. It is curious that the discussion of ethics is held outside of the university and that rarely does one see evidence of a code of ethics or discussion about ethics among colleges and departments.

While the academic profession is supposed to be a collegial community by its shared purpose of discovering, discussing and sharing knowledge, faculty experience is often dominated by strife among colleagues. As any book about tenure will testify, academia has a culture guided by a rigid hierarchy related to rank. Entry to the ranks is a closely guarded process with many obstacles of production, achievement and group approvals. Pretenured faculty are encouraged to take great caution in their relationships with other professors, to avoid controversy or disagreement and to be supportive of senior faculties' agendas and needs. The reason for this strategy is that, unlike most other professions, in higher education professions the continuation of one's contract is based on peers' choice, rather than the discretion of a supervisor.

It would therefore make sense that once faculty achieve tenure, they completely understand and appreciate the needs of pretenure faculty who follow them in the timeline. Unfortunately, it seems that this environment breeds a more frequent response of competition. Instead of understanding the needs of "the other," once tenured, faculty quickly begin to assume a role of defending the quality and purity of their ranks.

Even aside from these dynamics of oppression and competition, the traditional standards for tenure do not value teaching as highly as the premiere criteria: research and publication (Tennant, McMullen, & Kaczynski, 2010). Therefore, junior and senior faculty alike find the statutes and procedures reward a lack of attention to teaching in order to advance one's research and publication agenda. When tenure and promotion committees reject faculty with excellent teaching reputations and classroom evaluations because of less than stellar achievements in publishing, faculty hear a critical message about priorities. However, the committees magnify the message when they award tenure to faculty who receive dismal student evaluations and student complaints about their teaching, but have excellent publishing records. In these ways, the culture of not valuing good teaching persists and grows on our campuses.

These examples and explanations should demonstrate the importance of creating a culture whereby people can acknowledge the contributions that each person makes, even when those contributions are different between the individuals. When one faculty member is stronger in teaching and another in research, a powerful perspective would be to consider the unit as a team whereby each individual has a different role complementing the talents and skills of the others. A new opportunity emerges of replacing a competitive culture, which devalues teaching in the tenure process at the expense of research and publication, with a collegial and collaborative culture of multitalented and diverse experts. When higher education faculty are free to use the lessons learned from industry and management regarding team building, team work, and collaboration we will have a new order of the academy reaching towards a new light.

Motivation

One difficulty in implementing any change is mustering the motivation of those "in the trenches" who are affected most directly by the change. Previous research suggests that motivation can be increased or decreased when participants aren't given a voice in the process (Wlodkowski & Ginsberg, 2010), and when participants do not understand the importance of the task (Alexander & Jetton, 1996; Bandura, 1993; Caffarella, 2001).

When beckoned to incorporate technology into their classrooms, young professors have reason to answer the call. First, they may be more comfortable using the technology themselves depending on their age and prior access. More importantly, however, they are at the beginning of a career ladder and especially during this time, it behooves them to comply with the requests of administration. Exiting faculty, however, may not sense the same urgency. Having established teaching methods that they feel are effective, they are less likely to seek ways to make changes in the curriculum. Additionally, for those who have already earned tenure, less is at stake for noncompliance.

Furthermore, faculty who would prefer to spend their time conducting research might be less inclined to incorporate new pedagogies or techniques into their teaching because restructuring their classes takes time away from their research agendas. The current trend in higher education includes added value placed on research, with value lost on teaching. This trend is evidenced not only in research intensive universities, but often in liberal arts and community colleges as well. Fairweather (2005) evaluated faculty salaries and showed through statistical models that greater emphasis on research is a predictor for higher salary, whereas emphasis on teaching is a negative predictor and is associated with lower salary. This salary disparity is the case even after national initiatives for enhancing the value of teaching were put into place. In a society where monetary rewards are often considered a marker for success, it is clear that teaching is not being treated as an equal activity to the research counterpart.

Unfortunately, due to the rigid hierarchical structure of what constitutes success in higher education, motivation toward innovative teaching decreases. According to Ames (1992), the motivation for participation can be directly linked to understanding and valuing the importance of the task. Placing a greater value on teaching, and ensuring that faculty understand the importance of innovative teaching methods, would motivate faculty participation for technology incorporation and adoption in the classroom. Faculty development efforts, especially when coupled with data and research on student success, can show faculty members how teaching with technology can be effective, and can relieve anxiety about technological savvy and competence. However, without an institutional emphasis on the importance of teaching, motivation is not likely to rise.

Motivation among faculty can also be cultivated in other ways. Building greater faculty understanding about the availability of support, faculty development, instructional design, efficiencies and other benefits of integrating technology can be stronger motivators/incentives for technology adoption. In each of these items, information and perception are key elements.

As we all have likely experienced, anticipation can be worse than reality. Similarly, perceptions can be the cause of anxiety and threat, rather than reality. Simple activities such as exposure to information or circumstances, visualization and education in supportive settings can reduce such emotions greatly (King, 2003). Providing this support with respect, encouraging faculty input and suggestions, and accommodating their need for confidentiality like all adult learners are examples of ways to encourage participation. At the very least, reducing or neutralizing the barriers increases motivation. In the best situations, the hesitant or fearful faculty may become an advocate.

Academic Freedom and Faculty Voice

In the private sector, most organizations maintain policies to guide ethical behavior. Individuals within those organizations are accountable to an authority with higher rank in the organizational hierarchy. While ethical dilemmas may be complex, the outcomes are simple—guidelines are followed based on preconceived standards, and organizational policies are upheld. In the institution of higher education, things are not so straightforward. In her book *The Lost Soul of Higher Education*, Ellen Schrecker (2010) details some of the historical underpinnings that have led to a rather unique work environment that consists of varying and often ambiguous ethical guidelines with a strong emphasis on self-regulation rather than organizational enforcement.

During the era of expansion of the academic profession in the United States, faculty embraced the German notion of academic freedom. Americans, however, expanded this notion beyond professional independence. They asserted that they

> had a higher calling than other workers; their activities benefited the common good of the entire society ... and as a result they had to be free from meddling from outsiders who did not share their special knowledge and commitment. (Schrecker, 2010, p. 12)

Professors reconceived the notion of academic freedom to include all aspects of their work, especially as they sought tenure. While professors were technically employees of their universities, they argued that the universities lacked the specialized competence to judge their efforts, and thus, they created an incestuous system of regulation wherein the creation, maintenance, and oversight of professional standards is the responsibility of those who are held accountable to those standards.

Academic freedom was intended to give professors the ability to teach and research their subject areas without external interference as the "subject matter experts" who had the expertise to make such judgments and decisions. In the midst of a hostile work environment where employees feel threatened by colleagues, peers, and administrators, freedom is being used as a defense mechanism rather that a protection. For instance, when called upon to make changes to the structure of their classrooms by incorporating instructional technology, resistant professors cite "academic freedom" as their rationale for rejecting the directive.

In addition to academic freedom, several policies and practices in higher education illustrate the role of faculty voice and the autonomous nature of faculty. The system of faculty governance ensures direct faculty participation in the protection of their rights, needs, and concerns. Moreover, unlike most other professions, job retention (tenure) and promotions are dominated by faculty peers rather than supervisors or managers. Faculty committees also conduct employment searches and interviews. A final example is that faculty control course, program and curriculum design entirely from design to review, and throughout any revisions. These examples of the institutionalization of faculty voice illustrate that faculty expect to be decision makers based on embedded practices and concurrent expectations. Skirting their voice/ownership or delivering top-down edicts will not be favorably received in higher education institutions.

Differences Addressed

Indeed, in recent years we have also witnessed the fact that not all people adopt technology at the same rate or in the same way. While some people will follow the "bleeding edge" of technology innovation into the nether regions of obscurity and fads despite the cost or risk, other people are more prone to watch, observe the results and make a calculated evaluation of the risks and benefits before adopting new instructional technology or strategies. Of course, there is also a group of people, including faculty, who are reluctant to change at any cost. Even when confronted with copious evidence, demands and requests, they hold fast to the traditional strategies.

One of the errors that many instructional technology and professional development programs have made over the years is to think that all three of these groups will learn and use technology in identical ways. Evidence reveals this is simply a false expectation and very costly in jeopardizing the reputation and success of well-purposed faculty development initiatives. Instead of this one-size-fits-all approach, the design of faculty development needs to fit the needs, comfort levels and expectations of the faculty members being served at that specific time (Schmidt, Shelley, Van Wart, Clayton, & Schreck, 2000). More customized instructional technology training initiatives prove successful, including drop in centers and on-demand support (Kosak et al., 2005).

This situation is further compounded by the fact that professionals who enter careers in information technology or instructional technology faculty support tend to be people who are more adept at technology and are often early adopters themselves. In addition, this is a more recent career path and therefore many are younger than the faculty they support. All totaled we have many people who are digital natives seeking to guide less technology adept faculty. Based on their personal experience, such developers cannot understand the needs of less technophilic individuals. Therefore, it becomes urgent for the developers to have sufficient training in how and why to make faculty feel comfortable, safe, and supported in the learning process. Building skills among developers in not only technical and instructional technology areas but also strong human relations skills, facilitation and interview skills, as well as instructional design will help greatly in developing greater faculty cooperation, ownership and adoption of technology.

Figure 13.1 displays the environmental variables discussed above and illustrates the interactive relationship among them. When higher education institutions cultivate all of these essential variables in interdependent ways, our understanding is that faculty experience greater encouragement and support for innovation and creativity. Later, this figure will become the center of our integrative model.

Figure 13.1.   Environmental variables needed to encourage faculty creativity.

Consider working in a college or university where you as faculty experience disrespect, or no opportunities for voice and participation. What is the benefit of being creative if you will be penalized? What is the motivation for expending time and energy on innovative planning or development if your ideas are always rejected? By creating such organizational climates, the institution eliminates participation, motivation, and ownership. Moreover, many highly authoritarian or bureaucratic systems often exclude these same positive characteristics. This chapter describes a very different paradigm; instead of squelching creativity, it encourages participation and innovation. Building a positive environment in which faculty experience positive feedback for their discoveries and original suggestions, continues this cycle of motivation, respect and ethics. This interactive system is the critical core, the hub, of the more detailed model proposed in the next sections.

THE IMPACT OF FACULTY CAREER DEVELOPMENT: THE BIGGER PICTURE

The theoretical foundation for this chapter draws from three major areas which explain different facets of faculty career development: policy and management issues, cultural issues, and faculty development issues. We form the model which follows by examining, combining, and using these separate facets.

Management and Policy Issues

To exemplify the unequal distribution of value of research in higher education, it is only necessary to examine the tenure process.

In faculty lives, the implementation of tenure and promotion statutes includes management of policies and processes in a complex cultural organization. Faculty, as well as supporting administrators and colleagues, must make decisions daily about career choices based on the specific institutions' tenure and promotion statutes in which they are employed (Alstete, 2000). Consider that in many research universities, publication and research hold the highest value in the evaluation of a faculty member's tenure application. In such a context, pursuing faculty development in distance learning, developing online courses, or making other innovative changes in the use of technology in the classroom has been viewed "as a waste of time" for tenure earning faculty. New faculty members are advised by senior faculty to spend their precious time more wisely on research and publication which they will need to secure tenure.

The current trend in higher education includes added value placed on research, with value lost on teaching. This trend is evidenced not only in research intensive universities, but often in liberal arts and community colleges as well. Fairweather (2005) evaluated faculty salaries and showed through statistical models that greater emphasis on research is a predictor for higher salary, whereas emphasis on teaching is a negative predictor and is associated with lower salary. This salary disparity is the case even after national initiatives for enhancing the value of teaching were put into place.

Several studies confirm that when faculty are unproductive with their research agenda, it is not uncommon for their teaching loads to be raised (Burgan, 2006; Colbeck, 2002). While administrators of legislative mandates might consider that such actions will increase the productivity of faculty, the measures may be counterproductive in several ways. Additional time assigned to teaching requires more class preparation, in class hours, office hours and grading. Therefore, any faculty members who had hopes of reviving their research record become buried in greater responsibilities which tax their time and energy. In addition, students pay a steep price for this policy. When faculty engage in less research, they will be in less contact with current publications and findings. Therefore, the classes and students such faculty teach run the risk of receiving outdated information.

Cultural Issues

Issues related to faculty learning and using technology remain deeply embedded within the organizational culture and the unique roles of different faculty groups. While colleges and universities derive their strategic plans from their mission, the organizational culture is less firmly rooted in mandates and specifics. Instead, organizational culture survives on a fluid foundation of conflicting characteristics. For example, while organizational culture may be collectively developed, it is also potentially leader guided, and while dependent on group buy-in, it can be influenced by individuals or organizational norms.

Due to the rigid hierarchical structure of the academy, faculty members may comply with the departmental or organizational culture, but they may not identify with these behaviors or internalize the norms (Kelman, 1958). Further, they may feel insecure in speaking up or voicing dissenting ideas that differ with the ideas of higher ranking "colleagues." While faculty members may not openly disagree with colleagues or influential individuals, if they have not internalized the organizational goals or norms, they are less likely to genuinely "buy-in" or exert effort to align their beliefs with those organizational expectations. Thus, while organizational norms are thought of as collectively created and maintained, the reality is that the "collective" may not be a true representation of all voices.

For example, faculty members often have competing sets of expectations in their roles. Many faculty members are expected to teach, and may be accountable to dozens of students, while they are also pressured to produce high quality research. Their successes earn them capital, which may come in different forms. Previously, we discussed the lack of monetary, economic capital that comes from an emphasis on teaching (Fairweather, 2005). Additionally, it is relevant to note that those who endeavor to enhance their classes through innovative teaching methods may be denied other forms of capital as well. For instance, according to Bourdieu (1992), symbolic capital may be denied to those who place an emphasis on innovative teaching as it is less desirable in the academic system. Symbolic capital includes capital that is earned through social efforts to achieve status, merit, honor, or distinction. Bourdieu explains that the accumulation of symbolic capital represents an accrual of actual power. Without this power, it is difficult to advance successfully through the social and bureaucratic hierarchy. Those who do earn symbolic capital may then use symbolic violence to repress those who are less powerful as a result of their lower symbolic social standing. In a culture that rewards research and disregards an emphasis on teaching, a culture of fear develops under this model. For instance, if a faculty member (even one who has already earned tenure) decides to focus on teaching, that person may be stigmatized by colleagues for wasting time or efforts, or simply for breaching the norm expected by the culture. As a result, this faculty member may be excluded from conversations about departmental decisions or his or her opinions may be less valued by colleagues, demonstrating the way that a loss of symbolic capital can become a loss of actual power. If faculty are aware that this can happen, a culture of fear can develop which would hinder even the idea of any such innovations.

Aside from facing a culture that discourages innovation, faculty are often confronted with contradictory expectations. This is especially true for faculty members who desire to innovate in their teaching endeavors but are told to focus largely on their research agendas. This dissonance causes faculty to experience a strain from the stress associated with trying to meet these conflicting expectations, and sometimes find that they are unable to achieve the institutionally prescribed goals (Merton, 1938; Piscopo, 1994). Some faculty members may find innovative ways to accomplish both the institutionally established goals as well as their own. Without institutional support, however, faculty members may respond by performing their work as ritualists who determine what is minimally required and subsequently avoid change in their routines. Others still might retreat entirely—especially after earning job security through tenure. A faculty member in this circumstance might stop showing up to faculty meetings and avoid engaging with colleagues, and all research productivity as well as innovation with technology, would likely halt.

Faculty Development Issues

While research has been done on ethics in mentoring as it is related to human resource development (Hezlett & Gibson, 2005; McDonald & Hite, 2005), there is a gap in the literature about the effects of ethical mentoring on graduate student outcomes or successful performance in the role of teaching assistant, where future faculty are often first establishing their identity as colleagues in higher education institutions. According to Brandstetter and Handelsman (2000), best practices for professionalization can be established by implementing an ethical training program with graduate teaching assistants. This model, however, does not take into account structural challenges to implementing such a program, such as departmental participation, or motivation for the students to participate.

Preservice educators (PSEs) and graduate teaching assistants (GTAs) often experience anxiety when approaching, developing, and delivering their own courses or course materials (Cho, Kim, Svinicki, & Deckey, 2011). Because of this anxiety, these beginning educators are likely to stay within their comfort zones by replicating what they have seen from their teaching mentors. PSEs and GTAs, then, are not likely to seek or embrace technological innovations in their instructional methods. However, when their mentors demonstrate a willingness to implement innovative technologies,

PSEs and GTAs may begin to critically reflect on their instructional abilities and contemplate ways in which they might use technology as they deliver their own course materials. Based on connections between extant literature (Mezirow, 1995; King, 2003, 2005), it becomes clear that mentors can create transformative learning experiences which instill the confidence and competence necessary for career success in a classroom filled with technologically savvy students (Partin & Lauderdale, 2011). Considering the influx of digital natives, as well as the pressure from institutions to incorporate technology into teaching, we have to ask whether it is ethical to send faculty members into their roles without the proper training. Unfortunately, the value of ethical behavior is a component of faculty development and mentoring programs that is often omitted or overlooked (Moberg & Velasquez, 2004).

Boyle and Boice (1998) examined existing models of professional development to determine which had the best outcomes for mentors and their mentees. The researchers conducted studies of two professional development programs—one for new faculty at a comprehensive university, and one for graduate teaching assistants at a Research One university. The participants in these programs were volunteers, although the researchers admit than many were not initially enthusiastic about participating and may have been persuaded by visits of the researchers. They were interested in determining how well mentees would perform upon receiving mentoring, and as a result of this interest and research, Boyle and Boice developed a model for mentoring that is replicable in diverse settings (new faculty and graduate teaching assistants) as well as a guideline for skills of effective mentors.

Through a content analysis of meetings and statistical analysis of the results of mentoring surveys, the researchers determined that structured, systematic mentoring is an effective way to increase job satisfaction and performance. They found that the outcomes are more effective when the mentor has at least 3-5 years of experience already completed, and that it does not matter whether the pairs are homogenous in social categories such as race. Interestingly, they found that pairing new faculty with someone from another department was helpful because the new faculty members felt safer in exposing concerns or weaknesses. For graduate students, they found that pairing within the department was more successful because GTAs were not as concerned about external judgments and were able to learn more about department dynamics and politics. They determined that the components required for successful mentoring are "planning, structure, and assessment" (Boyle & Boice, 1998, p. 173). In both studies, one major significant finding was that group meetings seemed to facilitate the best professional development, as they allowed for the generation of new ideas through collaboration.

Boyle and Boice's (1998) study suggests that innovation for teaching can be encouraged through the use of faculty development and mentoring relationships. Unfortunately, due to the rigid hierarchical structure of what constitutes success in higher education, motivation toward innovative teaching decreases. According to Ames (1992), the motivation for participation can be directly linked to understanding and valuing the importance of the task. Placing a greater value on teaching, and ensuring that faculty understand the importance of innovative teaching methods would motivate faculty participation for technology incorporation and adoption in the classroom. Faculty development efforts, especially when coupled with data and research on student success, can show faculty members how teaching with technology can be effective, and can relieve anxiety about technological savvy and competence. However, without an institutional emphasis on the importance of teaching, motivation is not likely to rise.

The existing literature confirms that faculty are hesitant to incorporate innovative teaching techniques in their classes because they have anxieties about using these methods. The anxieties stem from a lack of training and a greater concern that they may be devalued by their institution or colleagues for their desire to teach effectively. At least one model (Boyle & Boice, 1998) found success in mentoring faculty and the positive impacts of systematic professional development on improved success in teaching and job satisfaction, so whether teachers can effectively incorporate innovations into their classes seems to be a null question. The real question, based on these issues, is regarding how the perception of innovative teaching can move from a stigmatized activity to a valuable aspiration.

THE MODEL:
INTEGRATIVE INNOVATION MODEL FOR HIGHER EDUCATION

Based on the above extensive literature review of interdisciplinary research and theory, Figure 13.2 reveals the proposed IIMHE.

The IIMHE places the essential environmental variables identified earlier in the chapter (1. ethics and respect for colleagues, management, and support persons; 2. academic freedom, as well as adult learning and the importance of faculty voice; and 3. motivation and willingness to change) at the core of the model. Furthermore, the model provides a fully integrative and responsive approach to incorporate needs and changes within the organization and constituency (faculty). This paradigm is in stark contrast to designing faculty development initiatives isolated from organizational policies and process (Caffarella, 2001).

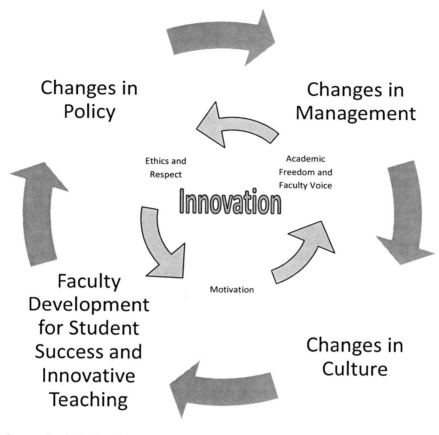

Source: Partin & King (2011).

Figure 13.2.   Integrative innovation model for higher education (IIMHE).

The outer ring of the model reveals the essential actions which need to interact and inform one another, in order to encourage faculty creativity and innovation with technology. The result is a four-stage model of institutional action which moves dynamically back and forth among (1) changes in policy, (2) changes of management, (3) change in culture, and (4) faculty development for student success and innovative teaching.

As we have demonstrated through our review of literature, the environmental aspects of this model must be in place to support the best outcomes from implementation of this model. These environmental variables (including ethics and respect, academic freedom and faculty voice, and motivation) are central to the model as depicted in the center of Figure 13.2. Once the environment is ripe, the changes in action (depicted in the outer ring of the model) can be implemented successfully.

The IIMHE encourages a paradigm shift involving recognizing the critical importance of organizational climate and culture, while addressing the breadth or issues involved in cultivating higher education innovation. The model uniquely weaves the usually disjointed sectors of higher education institutions to create a powerful synergy. This approach includes each of the following actions: creative interpretation of current policy and revisions in future iterations to reflect teaching values, a change in management and implementation of the policies and evaluations, and subsequently, and change in the culture surrounding the credence and merit given to faculty for their varied contributions to their institutions.

Using the IIMHE as a model for institutional change and support provides integrated systems approach to faculty development and institutional innovation. Instead of replicating our usual isolated efforts, the focus is on sustaining a healthy organizational climate which scaffolds resources, abilities and opportunities.

The next section of this chapter provides scenarios and cases, which further explain applications of the IIMHE to different higher educational contexts and situations specifically as related to policy, processes, culture, and action.

APPLICATION AND DISCUSSION

The IIMHE has the potential to cultivate change in higher education management, policy, culture and actions if applied thoughtfully to the specific context and needs at hand. The following scenarios illustrate a few examples of the how the model may emerge in college or university. The cases, which follow, provide opportunities for readers to pose their unique decision-making skills in applying the IIMHE in situations, which will be instructive in developing deeper understanding of the model's characteristics, capabilities and nuances.

Scenarios: Seeing the Model in Action

This section of the chapter illustrates how to implement the model and its application in a few scenarios. Based on these examples, readers may consider new strategies and specifics of implementation in their own contexts.

Scenario 1: The Consequences of Success

Escoheag Community College (ECC) launched their online accounting associate's degree in 2002 in response to students' requests for greater flexibility in course scheduling. Since then, the program had become quite successful in earning national awards for student achievement, retention and faculty support of learning. However, with recognition also comes greater press and this dynamic resulted in larger enrollments not from the surrounding county but across the nation. The difficulty faculty encountered now is that they no longer "know" the students they teach. The ECC faculty "knew" how to teach and support well the rural students in neighboring towns. These were Midwest communities, many with connections to farming and extended families who lived in the area for four or more generations. Today their online classes had a diversity of students across geography, race, employment, occupation, immigration status, etc. The students did not understand their typical agrarian examples, nor relate to the references to budgets for extended families and local economic issues.

ECC met the challenge by forming a distance learning faculty and student taskforce, with students and faculty drawn from those involved in the online classes. Their charge was to determine how to reframe the courses to address diverse populations. The Provost's office had designated money for faculty stipends and technical support for the redesign of the classes. The established timeline would span two years and include data gathering, design, pilot, development, evaluation, revision, and rollout.

Reflection Questions

- What were the major issues which had to be addressed in this scenario?
- What did ECC do, which helped their effort be successful?
- What else could they have done?
- What other issues might arise which cause online courses to need redesign?
- How can colleges monitor for such needs?

Scenario 2: There is Trouble in River City

The faculty at River City's Cavalier College prided themselves in being an elite, high standards institution. They only hired the very best faculty and they only admitted the very best students. These faculty were indeed the "best of the best," the very definition of experts. Therefore, the regional accreditation report documenting their failure to deliver quality online courses sent tidal waves of anger and indignation across the campus and cyberspace.

Dr. Willows convened campus wide meeting for faculty, administration and staff. All work stopped, phones and e-mail placed on auto response as the crowd assembled to hear the president declare they would leave the accrediting group. However, Dr. Willows had a better understanding of the situation and wisely guided the assemblage to understand that without regional accreditation, they would need to close their physical and virtual doors within a few short years. Instead, she had a plan.

Based on a detailed review of the report, Dr. Willows recognized the major issue was that Cavalier College did not have an infrastructure to evaluate the design and delivery of courses. The problem was not so much with the courses, but with the data to support their value and merit. She requested a cross section of volunteers across faculty, administration and staff, and the major departments to become a distance learning committee. Such an approach would ensure understanding the needs and resources of all critical functions and sectors of the college. While the committee developed a plan to remediate the issue over the next two years, his office would work with the chair of the committee to draft a response letter to the regional accreditation body.

Reflection Questions

- What were the major issues which had to be addressed in this scenario?
- What did the president do, which helped her effort?
- Why did she make each of her decisions? (For instance, why did she not just send a campus-wide memo?)
- What else could she have done?
- What issues must the committee address during the evaluation planning and implementation?

  o What strategies can the committee use to ensure cooperation across campus?
  o How can the committee monitor their progress, meet their deadlines, and make sure their decisions are relevant to all campus constituencies?
  o What other difficulties might the committee encounter? How can they address them?

- How can higher education institutions be sure they plan distance learning to meet all the requirements of their many stakeholders?

Cases: Taking Your Turn at Bat

The specific cases presented here provide opportunities for reader reflection and application of the chapter's concepts. Consider the parameters and dynamics of the situations presented as you reflect on the accompanying questions. This activity builds greater capacity applying the chapter to your unique needs and setting.

Case 1: Technology Crisis at Woodland College

Woodland College, a small liberal arts school has been undergoing its regional reaccreditation process. As part of this process, the accreditation committee has dedicated its institution to providing students with technological competence. In order to fulfill that mission, the institution has determined that all faculty will begin using the institution's learning management system to post syllabi, all course documents (like assignment prompts or instructions), and at least one assessment which must be completed online. During the annual faculty meeting, two weeks before the beginning of the semester, Provost Redwood proudly shares the new requirements and announces that "we will now be certain that our students are leaving our college with 21st century skills for success." After a brief moment of awkward silence, the room erupts with questions, concerns, anxiety, and frustration. Dr. Maple, a professor of chemistry, breaks through the murmur, "This all sounds nice, but I've never used that technology—I can't even create a PowerPoint." She goes on, "How can I be ready for this in only two weeks?" An English composition professor, Mr. Cherrywood follows up by stating, "I don't mind posting my notes—that's easy. But I don't want to read a bunch of papers online. I have to write extensive comments on these papers. I guess I won't be able to do that now." Finally, Mrs. Willow, a statistics instructor asks, "After the meeting, can someone show me how to put a syllabus online?" She asks the Provost, "Is there any training available for us?"

This situation seems to be spiraling downward quickly.
Think about the change in policy:

- Why did the faculty react in this matter?
- Are their concerns warranted?
- How could this topic have been broached differently to prevent faculty panic?
- What should happen now to help the faculty get onboard?
- How could future policies be implemented differently for a more positive outcome?

Reflecting on the concerns of the faculty:

- What needs to happen to prepare the faculty for the next semester?
- In the event of a major policy change such as this, what kind of provisions (made in advance) could help the faculty cope with the change?

Case 2: Shifting the Burden of Teaching at Presidential State University

Presidential State University, a large research intensive university, has not been offering enough sections of the required courses, and as a result the undergraduates are having a difficult time finishing their degree programs in a timely manner. The solution, as the administration sees it, is to require faculty with low research productivity to teach more of these classes. In the U.S. History Department, Dr. Hoover, the department chairperson, announces the new policy at a faculty meeting. Dr. Garfield, a top researcher in the department weighs in, "This is a great policy. Maybe people will start carrying their weight around here." Dr. McKinley agrees, and adds, "I think we should just hire a bunch of adjuncts to teach those courses. After all, anyone can teach those classes, but no one else can do the research I'm doing." A puzzled Dr. Carter asks for clarification, "I don't understand how productivity is measured. Is it by quantity or quality? How will I know if I am doing enough?" Before the chairperson has the opportunity to respond, Dr. Cleveland asks, "Can my teaching load please be reduced so that I can have the time needed to restart my research agenda?" Dr. Hoover replies by saying, "I'll work with each of you individually to make sure that your hard work and efforts are aptly rewarded. Keep up the good work with your scholarship." He then dismisses the meeting. Many faculty members leave the meeting with a renewed interest in their research agendas, although the adjuncts and full-time instructors sit silently wondering if the changes will have an impact on their workloads.

Reflect on the culture of this department:

- Are some skills or attributes valued more than others?
- Are these dynamics conducive to teamwork or collegiality?
- How do faculty members view their peers?
- Is this the kind of climate you want to work in?
- If you were the chairperson, would you take steps to change the culture of your department?

- In this case, is the chairperson contributing to the culture in the department?
  - How?
  - What could be done differently?

What are your reactions to this situation if you are:

- A student in the department?
- An adjunct or full-time instructor in the department?
- A professor with low research productivity?
- A professor with high research productivity?
- A professor who loves dividing time between research and teaching?
- The department chairperson?
- An administrator in the dean's office?

Future Research

Based on the provided literature review, proposed model, and extensive consideration of policy, management and culture issues discussed in the cases and scenarios of this chapter, it is clear that there is abundant opportunity for future research in this area. We would first recommend that future studies examine the connection between the theory and dynamic praxis of Figure 13.1. These environmental variables have been suggested as best practices to encourage innovation in higher education, but we realize that proposing such a model is different than implementation. As such, it is imperative to address the obstacles encountered in establishing an atmosphere that supports ethics and respect, motivation, and academic freedom and faculty voice, and to find ways to challenge any obstacles in order to promote innovation.

Further, once an atmosphere of integrative innovative instruction has been successfully established in an institution, it would be ideal to examine faculty and administrator perceptions of the broader IIMHE. Through the use of quantitative and qualitative analyses, potential findings could lead to "best practices" for a 21st century higher education environment. If the goal is to encourage innovation in higher education, future researchers will need to carefully consider implications of context and constituents, including management, policy and those individuals affecting or affected by both.

CONCLUSION

This chapter introduced the IIMHE model to facilitate and encourage a paradigm shift within institutions of higher education. Specifically, we examined the literature for theory and research to develop a more complete understanding of the dynamics and needs for higher education faculty's adoption of technology. Critical interdisciplinary insight emerged from the literature related to social, and economic capital, organizational culture, faculty development, and adult learning.

The model encourages faculty and administrators to build creative interpretations of current policy and revisions in future, ever-improving, iterations. The goal of these cycles of improvement are to reflect teaching values better and build a supportive structure of policies and evaluations. Such strategies hold the potential of changing the culture, credence, and merit awarded faculty for their varied contributions to their institutions, thus better serving the need to incorporate technology changes into instruction.

REFERENCES

Alexander, P. A., & Jetton, T. L. (1996). The role of importance and interest in the processing of text. *Educational Psychology Review, 8*, 89-121.

Allen, I. E., & Seaman, J. (2008). *Online nation: Five years of growth in online learning*. Sloan Foundation Report. Retrieved from, http://www.sloan-c.org/publications/survey/pdf /online_nation.pdf

Alstete, J. (2000). Posttenure faculty development: building a system for faculty improvement and appreciation. *ASHE–ERIC Higher Education Report 27*(4). San Francisco, CA: Jossey-Bass.

Ames, C. (1992). Classrooms: Goals, structures, and student motivation. *Journal of Educational Psychology, 84*, 261-271.

Bandura, A. (1993). Perceived self-efficacy in cognitive development and functioning. *Educational Psychologist, 28*, 117-148.

Bates, A., & Sangra (2011). *Managing technology in higher education*. San Francisco, CA: Jossey-Bass.

Blackburn, R., Chapman, D., & Cameron, S. (1981). "Cloning" in academe: Mentorship and academic careers. *Research in Higher Education 15*(4), 315-327.

Bok, D. (2003). *Universities in the marketplace: The commercialization of higher education*. Princeton, NJ: Princeton University Press.

Bourdieu, P. (1992). *Language & symbolic power*. Cambridge, MA: Harvard University Press.

Boyle, P. & Boice, B. (1998). Systematic mentoring for new faculty teachers and graduate teaching assistants. *Innovative Higher Education, 22*(3), 157-179.

Brandstetter, S., & Handelsman, M. (2000). Graduate teaching assistants: Ethical training, beliefs, and practices. *Ethics & Behavior, 10*(1), 27-50.

Burgan, M. (2006). *What ever happened to the faculty?: Drift and decision in higher education*. Baltimore, MD: The Johns Hopkins University Press.

Burns, S., & Lohenry, K. (2010). Cellular phone use in the classroom implications for teaching and learning: A pilot study. *College Student Journal, 44*(3), 805-810.

Caffarella, R. (2001). *Planning programs for adult learners* (2nd ed.). San Francisco, CA: Jossey-Bass.

Cho, Y., Kim, M., Svinicki, M. D., & Deckey, M. L. (2011). Exploring teaching concerns and characteristics of graduate teaching assistants. *Teaching in Higher Education, 16*(3), 267-279.

Cohn, S. (2010, Dec 21). Student loans leave crushing debt burden. *MSNBC.com* Retrieved from, http://www.msnbc.msn.com/id/40772705/ns/business-cnbc_tv/t/student-loans-leave-crushing-debt-burden/

Colbeck, C. L. (2002, Jan 21). State policies to improve undergraduate teaching: Administrator and faculty responses. *The Journal of Higher Education, 73*(1), 3-25.

Craft, J. (2010). Making the case for ongoing and interactive organizational ethics training. *Human Resource Development International 13*(5), 599-606.

Donald, J. (2003). *Learning to think: Disciplinary perspectives*. San Francisco, CA: Jossey-Bass.

Donoghue, F. (2011, June 20). The gainful-employment rule: New developments and implications. *The Chronicle of Higher Education*. Retrieved from, http://chronicle.com/blogs/innovations/the-gainful-employment-rule-new-developments-and-implications/29690

Fairweather, J. (2005). Beyond the rhetoric: Trends in the relative value of teaching and research in faculty salaries. *The Journal of Higher Education, 76*(4), 401-22.

Fischman, J. (2010, Jan.) Colleges lag in technology and teaching quality a top education official says. *The Chronicle of Higher Education* Retrieved from http://chronicle.com/blogs/wiredcampus/colleges-lag-in-technologyteaching-quality-a-top-education-official-says/20419

Freire, P. (1970). *Pedagogy of the oppressed*. New York, NY: Continuum.

Hezlett, S., & Gibson, S. (2005). Mentoring and human resource development: Where we are and where we need to go. *Advances in Developing Human Resources, 7*(4), 446-469.

Kelman, H. (1958). Compliance, identification, and internalization: Three processes of attitude change. *The Journal of Conflict Resolution, 2*(1), 51-60.

King, K. P. (2003). *Keeping pace with technology: Educational technology that transforms. Vol. 2: The challenge and promise for higher education faculty*. Cresskill, NJ: Hampton Press.

King, K. P. (2005). *Bringing transformative learning to life*. Malabar, FL: Krieger.

Kosak, L., Manning, D., Dobson, E., Rogerson, L., Cotnam, S., Colaric, S., & McFadden, C. (2005). Prepared to teach online? Perspective of faculty in the University of North Carolina system. *ISTE NECC Annual Conference*. Retrieved from http://center.uoregon.edu/conferences/ISTE/uploads/NECC2005/KEY_7248775/Dobson_necc_paper_RP.pdf

Kuh, G. D., Kinzie, J., Schuh, J. H., & Whitt, E. J. (2010). *Student success in college: Creating* conditions that matter. San Francisco, CA: Jossey-Bass.

Lawler, P., & King, K. P. (2000). *Effective faculty development: Using adult learning principles.* Malabar, FL: Krieger.

Mayer, R. E. (2008). Applying the science of learning: Evidence-based principles for the design of multimedia instruction. *American Psychologist, 63*, 760-769.

Mezirow, J. (1995). Transformation theory of adult learning. In M. R. Welton (Ed.), *In defense of the lifeworld* (pp. 39–70). New York, NY: SUNY Press.

McDonald, K., & Hite, L. (2005). Ethical issues in mentoring: The role of HRD. *Advances in Developing Human Resources, 7*(4), 569-582.

McKenzie, B., Mims, N., Bennett, E., & Waugh, M. (2000, Winter). Needs, concerns and practices of online instructors. *Online Journal of Distance Learning Administration, III*. Retrieved from, http://www.westga.edu/~distance/ojdla/fall33/mckenzie33.html

Merton, R. (1938). Structural strain and anomie. *American Sociological Review 3*(5), 672-682.

Moberg, D., & Velasquez, M. (2004). The ethics of mentoring. *Business Ethics Quarterly, 14*(1), 95-122.

Mollborn, S., & Hoekstra, A. (2010, March). A meeting of minds: Using clickers for critical thinking and discussion in large Sociology courses. *Teaching Sociology, 38*(1), 18-27.

Oksman, V., & Rautiainen, P. (2003). Perhaps it is a body part: How the mobile phone became an organic part of the everyday lives of Finnish children and teenagers. In J. Katz (Ed.), *Machines that become us: The social context of personal communication technology* (pp. 293-320). New Brunswick, NJ: Transaction.

Olcott, D., & Wright, S. (1995). An institutional support framework for increasing faculty participation in postsecondary distance education. *American Journal of Distance Education 9*(3), 5-17.

Partin, C., & Lauderdale, S. (2011, October). *Facilitating transformative learning experiences for pre-service educators and graduate teaching assistants: Ways that mentors can promote career readiness through the use of technology in teacher education and graduate teaching assisted courses.* Paper presented at the Florida Association of Teacher Educators Conference, St. Petersburg, FL.

Piscopo, B. (1994). Organizational climate, communication, and role strain in clinical nursing faculty. *Journal of Professional Nursing 10*(2), 113-119.

Prensky, M. (2001). Digital natives, digital immigrants. *On The Horizon, 9*(5), 1-6. Retrieved from http://www.marcprensky.com/writing/Prensky%20-%20Digital%20Natives,%20Digital%20Immigrants%20-%20Part1.pdf

PremierStudentLoans.com (2008). Subprime mortgage problem hindering student loans. Retrieved from http://www.premierstudentloans.com/news-opinions/subprime-mortgage-hindering-student-loans/

Rudolph, F., & Thelin, J. R. (1990). *The American college and university: A history.* Athens, GA: University of Georgia Press.

Sanchez, C. (2008). Student loan crunch may have lasting impact. *National Public Radio (NPR)* Retrieved from http://www.npr.org/templates/story/story.php?storyId=90111746

Schmidt, S., Shelley, M., Van Wart, M., Clayton, J., & Schreck, E. (2000). The challenges to distance education in an academic social science discipline. *Education Policy Analysis Archives*. Retrieved from http://168.144.129.112/articles/
the%20challenges%20to%20distance%20education%20in%20an%20academic%20social%20science%20discipline--
the%20case%20of%20political%20science.rtf

Schoepp, K. (2005). Barriers to technology in a technology rich environment. Learning and teaching in higher education: *A Gulf Perspective, 2,* 1-24. Retrieved from http://citeseerx.ist.psu.edu/viewdoc/
download?doi=10.1.1.87.5771&rep=rep1&type=pdf

Schrecker, E. (2010). *The lost soul of higher education: Corporatization, the assault on academic freedom and the end of the American University.* New York, NY: The Free Press.

Tapscott, D. (2008). *Grown up digital: How the net generation is changing your world.* New York, NY: McGraw-Hill.

Tennant, M., McMullen, C., & Kaczynski, D. (2010). *Teaching, learning and research in higher education.* New York, NY: Routledge.

Thelin, J. R. (2004). *A history of American higher education.* Baltimore, MD: The John Hopkins University Press.

U. S. Department of Veterans Affairs. (2011). Benefits of the Yellow Ribbon Program. Retrieved from http://gibill.va.gov/benefits/post_911_gibill/yellow_ribbon_program.html

Wilson, G., & Stacey, E. (2004). Online interaction impacts on learning: Teaching the teachers to teach online. *Australasian Journal of Educational Technology 20*(1), 33-48.

Wlodkowski, R., & Ginsberg, M. (2010). *Diversity and motivation: Culturally responsive teaching* (2nd ed.). San Francisco, CA: Jossey Bass.

CHAPTER 14

BUSINESS MODELS AND INNOVATION ACTIVITIES WITHIN NEW INDUSTRIES

The Case of Medical Biotechnology

Terje Grønning

The concept of business models has in recent years become popular in connection with researching company level organizational change. Using the example of medical biotechnology this chapter introduces, after a brief review of the business models literature, a perspective which theorizes business models as belonging to various business model classes. These business model classes are organized according to two dimensions, where the first is running between a focus predominantly on exploration of knowledge and a focus predominantly on exploitation of knowledge. The second dimension is running between end market proximity versus end market distance. The market distant business models exclusively serve other firms, whereas end market proximate business models serve the end market with finished products or services. This analytical way of envisioning the medical biotechnology sector differs from perspectives which may overgeneralize similarities, and it also differs from descriptive perspectives operating with a great amount of detail when distinguishing between business models. The matrix with nine classes of business models may be especially useful in policy contexts, since firms and

Global Perspectives on Technological Innovation, pp. 435–459
Copyright © 2013 by Information Age Publishing
All rights of reproduction in any form reserved.

their business models may be grouped according to the analytical dimensions, and subsequent policy measures can become more adapted to subaggregate levels.

INTRODUCTION

The themes of how organizational resources and strategies relate to the way environmental factors place constraints upon the organization have been at the essence of organization theory for decades (Child, 1972; Nadler & Tushman, 1999). The relatively new concept of business models seems to have renewed this debate, and has in recent years become increasingly popular among academia, business, and policymaking (Magretta, 2002; Zott, Amit, & Massa, 2011). The concept is, however, often used in a wide and abstract manner within the literature, and has also been used in a number of different meanings. Recent studies on business models have therefore urged for placing a renewed attention on the business model concept with the aim of furthering its theoretical and methodological usefulness (Teece, 2010; Zott et al., 2011). The purpose of this chapter is to contribute to this field by way of suggesting one way of operationalization of the concept at the sectoral level. In spite of the multiple meanings and applications of the business model concept, can the concept nevertheless be used as a stepping stone towards increased understanding of similarities and differences between intrasector firms?

This research objective will be achieved by way of, first, giving a brief overview of the emergent literature on business models, both when it comes to the way the concept has hitherto been used in general, as well as the way it has been applied to the medical biotechnology sector, that is, development of biopharmaceuticals and the supporting tools, techniques and services. Second, I will attempt to make the business model concept operational on an analytical rather than on a purely descriptive basis. The existing propositions regarding business models contain a number of important insights, however, they seem to miss a simple, albeit effective, way of grouping business models according to their analytical properties regarding knowledge intensity and their relation to the end market. It is, however, possible to conceptualize and distinguish between different business models based on applying these two analytical dimensions: The distinction between exploration and exploitation of knowledge, and the distinction between proximity versus distance from the end market. The proposed approach builds in parts on existing perspectives on exploration and exploitation issues and on existing perspectives on business models within medical biotechnology.

In addition to explaining the logic behind selecting and using these two dimensions as criteria, the paper provides some empirical examples based on selected firms in the Kansai region of Japan. One of these firms has been visited, however, the information within this chapter is extracted from publicly available sources both in the case of this firm as well as the other firms in order to keep consistency and address up to date information.

I will in the next section first provide a background on the increased interest in the business model concept, and then in the subsequent section provide a brief review of selected parts of the existing literature on the business model concept. The final sections present and discuss the main dimensions of the proposed framework for classifying business models within medical biotechnology. The paper concludes by stating that the business model concept may be a promising avenue towards accounting for intrasector differences. It is within both research and policy not optimal to operate with either too few and overgeneralized, nor with too many and technical, distinctions. The suggestion which is being proposed within this chapter is that the analytical basis or starting point for a middle way solution is to develop analytical categories of business model classes which range from knowledge explorative to knowledge hybrid or knowledge exploitative, as well categories of business model classes which range from being end market distant to being end market proximate.

THE BUSINESS MODEL CONCEPT

It is important to remark that the business model concept has been used in a number of different ways in recent years (Onetti, Zucchella, Jones, & McDougall-Covin, 2010; Zott et al., 2011). This brief and delimited review first introduces a background to the emergence of the concept, and subsequently a description of selected different usages.

Background

There have in recent years been significant theoretical advances regarding the importance of a firm's resources and capabilities when it comes to the positioning of the firm within the marketplace. Large parts of this discussion have focused on the opportunities these resources and capabilities place upon the optimal management of the firm's innovation activities (Barney, 2001; Child, 1972; Teece, Pisano, & Shuen, 1997). One basic tenet behind this recent wave of theorizing is that all firms are unique in one way or the other, since they may possess resources in the form of knowledge which may be difficult to imitate or replicate. While this observation is valid in a narrow sense, there is at the same time an acknowledged methodological need for well-founded generalizations regarding identifiable patterns across firms and industries when it comes to the key characteristics of innovation activities. Without such generalizations it will be difficult to advance research, as well as suggest policy improvements. A solution towards the other extreme consists in generalizing that a majority of firms within a particular sector share significant similarities due to, for example, their allegedly shared knowledge base (Asheim & Coenen, 2005) or the way they source innovations (Tidd & Trewhella, 1997). While also these observations may be true in a broad sense, the assumption that the entire sector shares the same or similar characteristics may conceal important intrasector structures and mechanisms.

The introduction of the business model concept has been one effort in the direction of cautious categorizations and generalizations which aim at striking a balance between intrasector homogeneity and heterogeneity. This effort has been in the form of trying to achieve an overall theoretical integration between a focus on strategic, agency-related aspects on the one hand, and structural, resource-related aspects on the other hand (Teece, 2010; Zott et al., 2011). Second, there have been various and tentative applications of the business model or similar concepts at a sectoral level, such as within biotechnology (Casper, 2000; Fisken & Rutherford, 2002; Luukkonen, 2005; Mangematin, 2000; Pisano, 2006; Rasmussen, 2010; Rothman & Kraft, 2006) as well as a voluminous literature on "e-business" (Dubosson-Torbay, Osterwalder, & Pigneur, 2002). In either case, in the event there is a successful theoretical merger between a focus on the structural composition of a firm's resources and a focus on its strategic orientation, the result might be an increased level of understanding into inter-firm differences as well as similarities.

The business model concept has, however, been used in a considerable number of ways. According to Zott et al. (2011) it has been used in the meaning of "a *statement* …, a *description* …, a *representation* …, an *architecture* …, a *conceptual tool or model* …, a *structural template* …, a *method* …, a *framework* …, a *pattern* …, and as a *set*" (pp. 1022, italics in original). There have. however, emerged some common themes, as shown in the results of the extensive literature review conducted by Zott et al.: First, the business model literature in the strategy field has focused primarily on: "(1) The networked nature of value creation; (2) The relationship between business models and firm performance, and (3) The distinction between the business model and other strategy concepts" (p. 1031). Scholars within this field have also concentrated their research efforts on how to define the borders of the business model concept, and arrived at conclusions such as: A business model does not involve a linear mechanism for value creation;

it is not the same as product-market strategy; and it cannot be reduced to issues that concern the internal organization of firms (pp. 1031-1032).

It is, however, possible to subdivide the literature further into three subgroups according to the predominant assumptions and perspectives: A *normatively* oriented body of literature, a *descriptively* oriented perspective, and an *analytically* oriented view. This is not to say that the first two perspectives lack analytical components, but rather indicates where the theorist's main emphasis lies when it comes to normative, descriptive and analytical concerns. Although this chapter is most at home within the third and analytical perspective, a brief review of all three is in its place.

Normative and Descriptive Perspectives

Osterwalder and his colleagues have in recent years strived to advise practitioners about how the firm's business model should be reformulated on a continuous basis (Osterwalder & Pigneur, 2010; Osterwalder, Pigneur, & Tucci, 2005). According to Osterwalder, a business model is:

> a conceptual tool that contains a set of elements and their relationships and allows expressing a company's logic of earning money. It is a description of the value a company offers to one or several segments of customers and the architecture of the firm and its network of partners for creating, marketing and delivering this value and relationship capital, in order to generate profitable and sustainable revenue streams. (Osterwalder, 2004, p. 15)

Oesterwalder and his colleagues recommend with their proposed "Business Model Canvas" (Osterwalder & Pigneur, 2010) a mapping of the various elements of the business model, divided between internal and externally directed aspects. As a column directed both towards internal and external aspects stands the element "value propositions," whereas internally directed elements include "key activities," "key resources," "key partners" and "cost structure." Externally directed elements include "customer relationships," "communication, distribution, and sales channels," "customer segments," and "revenue streams" (Osterwalder & Pigneur, 2010).

Compared to the heavy strategy orientation of Osterwalder and colleagues, Teece's contributions to the field (Teece, 2007, 2010) are placed more in a long-range stream of empirical and theoretical works originating in the resource-based theory of the firm:

> A business model articulates the logic and provides data and other evidence that demonstrates how a business creates and delivers value to customers. It

also outlines the architecture of revenues, costs, and profits associated with the business enterprise delivering that value. (Teece, 2010, p. 173)

Teece (2010) is thus also concerned with the constraints that may be placed upon successful business model design. Nevertheless, his contribution is of a normative kind, since the basic assumption is that the conception serves to show that there in many sectors is a necessity for firms to develop and maintain a sounder business model concept than what is prevalent today. Indeed, Teece's starting point is actually descriptive, in that he maintains that all firms have a business model: "Whenever a business enterprise is established, it either explicitly or implicitly employs a particular business model that describes the design or architecture of the value creation, delivery, and capture mechanisms it employs" (p. 172). The firm must, however: "select or create a particular business model that defines its commercialization strategy and investment priorities" (Teece, 2007, p. 1327).

In contrast to this normatively oriented view urging firms to adopt particular types or levels of business models, there exists a *descriptive view*, where the strategic element mainly comes into play whenever a firm aspires to change from one business model to another. A concrete approach attempting a descriptive conceptualization has been proposed by Hedman and Kalling (2003). They propose a "generic business model" conceptualization, which includes seven different components: customers, competitors, offering, activities and organization, resources, supply of factor and production inputs, and lastly a longitudinal process component. The latter is included in order to "cover the dynamics of the business model over time and the cognitive and cultural constraints that managers have to cope with" (p. 53). Subsequently their conceptualization "integrates firm-internal aspects that transform factors to resources, through activities, in a structure, to products and offerings, to market" (p. 53).

Cavalcante, Kesting, and Ulhøi (2011) are proponents of a similar, descriptive view: "We conceptualize a business model as a systematic analytical device, partly for evaluation and action ... with respect to organizational change in general, and partly for addressing innovation ... activities in particular" (p. 1328). They use the business model concept as a synonym to a firm's "core repeated standard processes," and the business model is subsequently in their view "an abstraction of the principles supporting the development of the core repeated standard processes necessary for a company to perform its business" (pp. 1328-1329). Processes are within their analyses ranked according to whether they are considered as core processes or more peripheral processes. The core processes are of key importance to the business and performed on a continuous basis, and should constitute its boundaries. Consequently, any "changes in core repeated standard processes ... imply a change in the business model" (pp. 1329-1330). In overall, they specify "four different types of business model change: business model creation, extension, revision, and termination" (p. 1327). Another approach constitutes a rather literal application of the descriptive method, since it consists in mapping the entire scope of conceivable resource categories with relevance to the business model concept (Seppänen, 2009). The approach identifies six groups of resources ranging from human resources to legal and relational resources, with a total of 36 categories (Seppänen, 2009, p. 107).

One variant of the descriptive approach, albeit not using the business model concept as such, can be found in the classification of sub-sectors according to an interpretation of the main activities of firms within the industry. When it comes to the biotechnology industry, for example, the firms can be divided into sub-sectors such as "genetically modified organisms", "pharmaceuticals," "industrial biotechnology and bioremediation," and so on (European Union, 2005). In some cases it can be useful to classify according to the "scientific and technological drivers for innovation", ranging from e.g. molecular design to bio-informatics (Gassmann, Reepmeyer, & Von Zedtwitz, 2008). Within industry itself, one example of the descriptive approach is when the bioindustry development association in the Kansai region in Japan (cf. also case examples in next section) decided to present their 96 medical biotechnology ventures as of 2010 as divided into firms within "drug discovery and regenerative medicine" (16 firms), "drug discovery related" (28 firms), "drug design, testing, diagnosis and imaging" (25 firms), and "the advanced analytical equipment field" (27 firms) (NPO Kinki Bio-industry Development Association, 2010).

The normative and descriptive approaches seem to work well when it comes to their respective objectives, that is, pointing towards the needs and benefits for formulating normative business model conceptions in relation to organizational change at a company level, and pointing towards the elements to be included within descriptive contexts respectively. One theoretical problem when it comes to the former perspective is that one effect resulting from applying the approach appears to be a great difficulty in distinguishing between a multitude of different existing and potential business models. In theory the approach encourages the proliferation of virtually limitless business models according to some selected value-oriented criteria, whereas there is little material available within the approach which can help distinguish or theorize between the resulting types of business models. In contrast, the descriptive approach is quite detailed in explaining the constituting elements of business models. The main problem with this approach is that the number of components is relatively high, which in turn can result in difficulties when it comes to theorizing their interrelationships as well as in connection with the practical side of effectively researching or implementing the components.

Analytical Perspectives.

As proponents emphasizing the need for an *analytical* view emphasizing both an organization's objectives as well as actual activities, Amit and Zott define a business model as depicting "the content, structure, and governance of transactions designed so as to create value through the exploitation of business opportunities" (Amit & Zott, 2001, p. 511). They elaborate by way of proposing an "activity system" perspective:

> We conceptualize a firm's business model as a system of interdependent activities that transcends the focal firm and spans its boundaries. The activity system enables the firm, in concert with its partners, to create value and also to appropriate a share of that value. (Zott & Amit, 2010, p. 216)

Elsewhere the same authors have elaborated this definition by stating that the business model "elucidates how an organization is linked to external stakeholders, and how it engages in economic exchanges with them to create value for all exchange partners" (Zott & Amit, 2007, p. 181). Behind the emergence of a particular firm's business model lie a series of managerial choices. Depending on the choices the firm may end up with different business models. In other words, the end result may be "a different set of activities, as well as the resources and capabilities to perform them—either within the firm, or beyond it through cooperation with partners, suppliers or customers" (Zott & Amit, 2010, p. 217). Schweizer (2005) has within a similar resource based view of the firm developed a typology based on the tree dimensions (1) value chain constellation, (2) market power of innovators and complimentary assets owners respectively, and (3) total revenue potential, resulting in business models titled "integrated," "layer maker," "market maker," and "orchestrator."

Analytical approaches have in some form or the other also been applied within studies of medical biotechnology or other parts of biotechnology (Fisken & Rutherford, 2002; Mangematin, 2000; McKelvey, 2008; Onetti et al., 2010; Rasmussen, 2010; Rothman & Kraft, 2006). Mangematin (2000) understands business models as "organisational models covering the targeted market (final or intermediate market), networks of partners, and shareholders" (p. 182). A business model thus "corresponds" to: "a set of key resources for the firm's development *and* to a mode of securing these resources within the organization" (p. 182, my italics). He subsequently operates in his analyses with a distinction between four dominant business models: Firms with good development potential; firms which develop in niches; firms attached to a group; and new biotech firms.

Similarly, Fisken and Rutherford (2002), as well as Rothman and Kraft (2006), divide between four business models within biotechnology, namely: "the fully integrated pharmaceutical company" (FIPCO) business model, the product business model, the platform or tool business model, and the hybrid business model, with the latter also being referred to as "a new 'dual' business model that combines established platform capabilities with drug development" (Rothman & Kraft, 2006, p. 86). Onetti and his colleagues (2010) do on the other hand criticize their predecessors for lacking a geographical dimension within the conception of business models. They define the business model concept as "the way a company structures its own activities in determining the focus, locus and modus of its business" (p. 24). Focus refers to the "selection of activities on which the company's efforts are concentrated"; modus refers to "the relationships with other players and about organizational boundaries" (such as "insourcing and outsourcing of activities along social and inter-organizational ties, inward-outward relationships with other players, [and] strategic alliances"); and locus refers to the geographical location of activities, i.e. "local vs. foreign based activities, inward-outward relationships with space, entry modes, [and] local embeddedness" (p. 4).

According to Rasmussen (2010), the business model's function is "to select and filter a range of possible technologies for development into products, which are then offered to the market" (p. 15). The business model is thereby vital in connection with the commercialization of technology: "It acts as the value creation construct that mediates between the technical and economic domains, selecting and filtering technologies and packaging them into particular configurations to be offered to the market" (p. 5). Rasmussen goes on to operate according to a division between three dominant business models. They are denominated as "drug discovery," "platform technology," and "large biotech" respectively, and have distinctive "technological regimes" (p. 6).

Another attempt at theorizing business models within medical biotechnology has been provided by McKelvey (2008), who first identifies as two "dominant models" the "classical biotech model" and the "vertically integrated model" (p. 47). The former relies on long-term, basic research, and is thus a specialized supplier, however, relying on collaboration with institutes or with incumbent firms in related industries. The vertically integrated model is akin to an integrated pharmaceutical firm's business model, which in addition to focusing on the discovery process also has the manufacturing and sales capabilities. She subsequently identifies 10 emerging as well as "speculative" (which do not seem to yet exist) business models. Her framework is built upon two dimensions, where the first is whether there is emphasis on in-house competencies or on coordination across actors, and the second is whether the business model is geared towards competition based on technology or on the end market. Business models with emphasis on in-house competencies and competing on technology are the platform model, contract research and the hybrid technology model. The latter consists of selling combinations of technological platforms, services and goods, for example, diagnostics. In contrast, business models which likewise place emphasis on in-house competencies, albeit compete on the market, are the service provider and "market maker" models. The latter entails innovation through introducing new "business logics," such as the creation of a localized market for personalized medicines. Business models with emphasis on coordination across actors and competing on technology are the information business model, "pure tool and component," the "systems integrator" and the "open source" business models. Last, a market competing and cross-actor coordinating business model is denominated as "the orchestrator model" (Schweizer, 2005), meaning a business model geared towards "helping other firms develop the desired collaboration and co-ordination effects within specific production and knowledge networks" (McKelvey, 2008, p. 50).

Some possible critical remarks towards the existing analytical approaches include observing a possible inherent vagueness within the general approaches proposed by, for example, Amit and Zott (2001; Zott & Amit, 2008). While their focus on "activity systems" is appealing, a further narrowing down or operationalization of the general approach is necessary, in order to avoid the risk (shared with the descriptive approach reviewed above) of possibly facing a situation where there is a large number of "activities" which are difficult to discriminate between when it comes to their actual relation to or function within the business model concept. As for the approaches proposed by Mangematin (2000) and Rasmussen (2010), the analytical rigor is indeed present, however, the fact that their ideal types contain only a few select business model categories makes it difficult to assess the applicability of their approaches to a more detailed analysis including, for example, "hybrid" cases. As for the McKelvey (2008) and Onetti et al. (2010) approaches the interesting elements within their approaches are somewhat overshadowed by their inclusion within their business model conceptions of aspects which may be viewed as purely strategic concerns. The essence within the Zott et al. (2011) call for a business model conception which clearly distinguishes between the strategy and business model domains respectively, is in a way diluted by the McKelvey typology distinguishing between business models based on the mode of in-house development versus cooperation as one main dimension. This is because forms of collaboration are strategic decisions, and not necessarily part of a business model archetype. It is, however, possible to theorize that some forms of collaboration are more likely within particular business models compared to other models. Similarly, the Onetti et al. (2010) inclusion of particular location preferences in a geographic sense is also more a matter of strategy, rather than part of a business model archetype.

This review has served as a selective overview into the debate on varying applications of the business model concept. There are many valuable lessons to be learnt from both the normative, descriptive, and, especially, analytical approaches, but there are nevertheless areas open for further theorizing. In the next section I will make an attempt at contributing in such a respect by way of suggesting a typology based on a knowledge intensity dimension, in addition to the dimension included by some of the earlier theorists (e.g., Mangematin 2000; McKelvey, 2008) regarding position in relation to the end market.

Operationalization of the Business Model Concept in the Case of Medical Biotechnology

With the reservations listed above regarding the multiple usages of the business model concept, the purpose of this section is to make the concept operational in connection with empirical observation and analysis at a sector level. The version of the business model conception which lies as a foundation for the section is the Amit and Zott (2001) definition stating that a business model depicts "the content, structure, and governance of transactions designed so as to create value through the exploitation of business opportunities" (p. 511). However, this definition, as well as their later elaborations of it, still remains at a relatively abstract level, hence as mentioned the need for efforts at further theorizing and operationalization.

Bidimensional Classification of Business Model Classes Within Medical Biotechnology

In the case of medical biotechnology it should be possible to envision variations and similarities according to the character and type of a business model in terms of two dimensions. The two dimensions are, first, the character of activities and visions when it comes to knowledge-intensity. A business model can in overall be geared towards "exploration" or "exploitation" of knowledge. The second dimension is constituted by a firm's proximity versus distance to the end market. A business model can on these terms be classified according to whether it is geared towards intermediate business-to-business (B2B) markets, to the end consumer market, or towards a duality in this respect.

A business model, and hence the corporate activities, can in overall be geared towards either "exploration" or "exploitation" of knowledge. The notion of exploration versus exploitation obviously builds upon the seminal work by March (1991), and his distinction between these two opposites on a continuum has led to a steady stream of research discussing the necessity for many firms to achieve an "ambidextrous" balance between the two (He & Wong, 2004). The conceptual set has also been applied to the study of innovation activities at the level of the firm (Gupta, Smith, & Shalley, 2006; Ichijo, 2002), alliances between firms (Lavie & Rosenkopf, 2006; Rothaermel & Deeds, 2004), the innovation system (Gilsing & Noteboom, 2005) as the well as the region (Cooke, 2005), with the conceptual set being expanded with "examination" as a separate category rather than as a sub-category of exploitation within the latter perspective (Cooke, 2005).

Here we borrow the original conception as proposed by March (1991), but use it in the context of identifying whether a business model is geared towards predominantly exploration of (unknown) knowledge on the one hand versus exploitation of (known) knowledge on the other hand. Indeed, a business model of the exploitative kind would still need to maintain explorative activities (and vice versa). But the main aspect we are interested in capturing in this context is in what way the business model may be characterized as knowledge intensive by way of using the two concepts exploitation and exploitation as indicative guidelines (Table 14.1). A firm operating within a competitive system will rarely be explorative in the same sense as, for example, basic research projects within the higher education or institute sector (Levin, Klevorick, Nelson, & Winter, 1988). With this reservation in mind, it will nevertheless be possible to distinguish between firms which operate with relatively long term perspectives and large innovation projects aiming at developing incremental or even radical innovations, that is, the exploration of "new" knowledge, whereas there may on the other hand be firms where the operations are geared towards marketing less ambitious products and services based on more short term perspectives and smaller innovation projects, that is, predominantly the exploitation of existing knowledge.

We are, however, not interested in doing the classification too simple, since the framework may then be too far from the realities of medical biotechnology as a sector (cf. also critique in previous section of approaches which contain only a select, few categories). Thus, a segment in-between the opposites of exploration and exploitation titled hybridity is included, in order to accommodate any business models catering explicitly to both the exploration and exploitation of knowledge.

Table 14.1.   Nine Classes of Business Models According to the Exploration—Exploitation and Market

	Exploration	*Hybridity*	*Exploitation*
cursive: End market proximity	Explorative end-market serving	Hybrid end-market serving	Exploitative end-market serving
cursive: Market duality	Explorative market duality	Hybrid market duality	Exploitative market duality
cursive: End market distance	Explorative end market distant	Hybrid end market distant	Exploitative end-market distant

The second dimension is constituted by a firm's proximity versus distance to the end market. In this context distance obviously refers to market relationship in terms of whether the sales, or projected sales, are in terms of finished goods or services directly to end customers, and not distance in geographic terms. In the case of medical biotechnology it is useful to conceive of the end market in terms of patients, doctors, and hospitals. Obviously, in the case of preventive measures healthy citizens may be part of the end market as well. After all the actual consumption of the products and services is what ultimately creates value. However, the industry proliferates with B2B relationships, and sometimes these kinds of B2B transactions may be both the first and the ultimate activity of a firm. Examples of such transactions include providing services in the form of testing or supplies in the form of laboratory equipment.

Based on these two dimensions related to knowledge and the end market it becomes possible to distinguish between large categories or types of business models. Similar to the "hybridity" category along the knowledge intensity axis, a category titled market duality is included on the market related axis, meaning simply that in contrast to a business model geared towards the end market (market proximity) or only towards development of ideas or products meant for B2B transactions (market distant), the additional category accommodates for any business models which are catering explicitly to both the end and B2B markets. Taking the point of departure in the knowledge intensity axis, however, the three major classes of business models may be termed as the explorative, the exploitative and hybrid business model classes, and we will in turn describe their characteristics by way of providing some examples.

Explorative, Exploitative, and Hybrid Business Model Classes

Exploration is per definition likely to take time, and the time and resources spent until reaching eventual rewards is justified by way of getting, if successful, high levels of revenues. Explorative business models are thus associated with high risk and high revenue, as well as with large and lengthy innovation projects.

AnGes MG was founded in December, 1999, and listed on the Tokyo Stock Exchange (on the so called "Mothers" list for "high-growth and emerging stocks") in September 2002. As of 2011, AnGes employs about 70 people and is capitalized at 9,460,618,000 yen. The scientific foundation is genetics, in the sense that the firm wants to explore the potential of human genes within drug discovery and development. The firm conceives of itself as having two axes, whereas one is horizontal and constituted by genetic medicine, and one is vertical constituted by lifestyle-related diseases and chronic conditions. The firm's strategy is subsequently to divide activities into two stages, where the first is to study lifestyle-related diseases and chronic conditions, "for which no satisfactory effects can be obtained with conventional drugs" (AnGes MG, 2011). Second, the firm investigates the possibility of genetic medication and thereby become specialized in genetic and nucleic acid medicine (AnGes MG, 2011).

As of 2011 the company has got nine projects in its R&D pipeline which are distributed as follows: Four are at the preclinical stage, one is clinical trial phase I; one is phase II; one is phase III; one is at the investigational new drug (IND) application preparation stage; one is at the IND application preparation stage in Japan at the same time as it is in phase I in the United States; and one is at an application research stage. In connection with the development of these projects the firm has as of 2011 established joint research related to one of the mentioned projects with two different small companies, and joint development with another small company in connection with another project. In addition, there is one project where the firm has established agreement regarding codevelopment and marketing rights with a pharmaceutical company, and two projects with marketing rights agreements with another pharmaceutical company (AnGes MG, 2011). As for the origin of AnGes MG's projects these are not necessarily developed in-house, but rather the purchase of patenting rights from an university or research institute in exchange for a cash fee or royalties (Ohtaki, 2005, p. 17).

Thus AnGes MG relates to partners both downstream in connection with idea and patent scouting, to horizontal partners in connection with collaboration, and upstream in connection with licencing out. Based on these criteria one might conceive of the company as belonging to the end-market distant explorative business model class. The firm has, however, licensed-in a product from a firm in the United States and is the marketer in Japan for this product. It hence possesses some marketing skills and may be classified as belonging to the dual-market business model class, even though the vast majority of activities pertain to the end market distant type.

Disregarding the fact that AnGes MG may actually be conceived of as dual-market and explorative, we focus in the following on the explorative and market-distant business model class, that is, one which deals exclusively on the intermediate market. This in turn implies that the activities to be most prevalent within this business model class are likely to include commercialization relations with other firms rather than with the end consumers. Obviously the explorative scientific activities in connection with drug discovery are in focus, and may be conducted (like even in the AnGes MG dual case) either in-house or in collaboration with other firms. In addition, crucial activities may include (like in AnGes MG's case) the development and maintenance of competency when it comes to the acquisition of patenting rights or other types of external sourcing.

If a firm is within the explorative end-market distant business model class it implies that it can choose to aspire towards vertical integration, stay where it is and abstain from further development of the product and rather license it out, or let the company itself be acquired by another firm before the product or technology is developed in full. It remains to be seen how AnGes MG develops in terms of a continued limited dual position, or a strive towards vertical business model class transformation in the sense of a fuller market duality and start to market also its own products when the time comes.

The hybrid business model class is clearly represented by Carna Biosciences, which appears to have transitioned into this class from the exploitative class. Carna Biosciences was founded in April, 2003, and publicly listed in March, 2008, on the NEO market. As of 2010, Carna Biosciences

Table 14.2. The Location of Selected Japanese Firms Within Business Model Classifications

	Classification in This	KBDO Classification	Likely Classification Within Existing Approach
AnGes	Explorative dual-market	Drug discovery and regenerative medicine	
CosMED	Hybrid end-market proximate		Product
Carna Biosciences	Hybrid end-market distant	Drug discovery related	Hybrid/dual
Transgenic	Exploitative end-market distant		Platform

Notes: "KBDO-classification" according to KBDO (2010). "Existing approach" derived from Rothman & Kraft (2006).

employs about 50 people, and is capitalized at 2,125,632,000 yen. The scientific foundation is to focus on a catalyzing enzyme called kinase, and aims to be "a leading provider of integrated platforms of proprietary kinase drug discovery technologies designed to aid in the identification and optimization of kinase inhibitors" (Carna Biosciences, 2011).

Core activities are within, first, ("exploitative") drug discovery support, and second, ("explorative") drug discovery and development. Concerning the former and major activity area, the firm provides drug discovery supporting products and services within four distinct fields: Kinase proteins, profiling services; assay development, and crystallography. All their kinase proteins are active human recombinant proteins. The firm is also able to provide custom protein production as well as special order mutated forms of specific protein kinases. Concerning the second drug discovery and development activity area, the aim is to identify and develop new medicines primarily for the treatment of cancer and anti-inflammatory diseases. Here the firm plans to use its own kinase drug discovery platform.

Carna Biosciences collaborates with the Japanese pharmaceutical company Astellas through a collaboration and service agreement with the Astellas subsidiary OSI Pharmaceuticals, Inc. (agreement signed in October 2007, that is, before OSI was acquired by Astellas in 2010). As indicated in Table 14.2 the firm belongs to the end market distant class of the hybrid column, although the majority of activities are still of the exploitative kind.

Another hybrid case is CosMED Pharmaceutical Co. Ltd., which defines its core business area as "transdermal drug delivery" (CosMED, 2011), in other words drug delivery through the human skin. It was established in 2001 and employs as of 2011 about 20 people. It is capitalized at 50,000,000 yen, which is by far the most modest sum among the companies presented here. In a narrow sense, drug delivery could be conceived of as belonging to the exploitative class. However, it is more appropriate to classify the firm as belonging to a hybrid class since CosMED is conducting explorative research and development related to transdermal drug delivery systems within areas ranging from pain issues to various therapeutic areas. It holds three original technologies as of 2011. It should be noted that the company is within the end-market serving segment, since it offers completed products to the end market rather than to other firms. This entails that a considerable amount of activities must be concentrated to marketing and sales, in addition to research and development. As for the exploitative business models class, the company TransGenic, Inc. appears to be a representative case. While being another highly knowledge-intensive firm, this exploitative, end-market distant firm was established in April, 1998, and has as of 2010 got ca. 40 employees (TransGenic Inc.,

2011). It is capitalized at 855,000,000 yen. Exploitation of knowledge entails another type of risk, compared to exploration, since the activities will be highly specialized and allow for little diversification (Pisano, 2006, p. 169). The origin of the company in question was based on the initial attempts at commercialization of new processes developed by a university in Southern Japan. In 2005 another contract regarding technology transfer from another university was signed (Bio Centre, 2005, pp. 468-469). The main activities as of 2011 are organized as three different research themes: Development of antibody products is in order to gain short-term revenue; the development of "diagnostic reagents using biomarkers" a midterm strategy; and potential identification of innovative "druggable" targets is a mid- to long-term strategy (TransGenic Inc., 2011).

There are two fundamental technologies in use, namely technology for producing "knockout mice" (i.e., genetically engineered mice where an existing gene has been inactivated or "knocked out") and antibody-producing technology. The company has as a result of these activities arrived at six product groups, which are: Knockout mice and a phenotype database; custom production of knockout mice; other mouse-related products for research purposes; custom production of antibodies and proteins; and antibody-related products (approximately 600 of them). The company can in addition conduct drug-discovery support services.

One problem in connection with the initial years of development was that exclusive contracts signed with three different pharmaceutical firms in 2001 and 2004 turned out to be unfavorable to TransGenic. Although overall turnover was considerable, profitability was suffering. The development costs of the particular products specified within the exclusive contrasts turned out to vastly outnumber the terms outlined in the contracts (Bio Centre, 2005). This is perhaps a good example of the challenge such an exploitation oriented firm meets when it comes to managing one of its core activities, namely the terms when it comes to develop and deliver to its clients and collaborators.

DISCUSSION AND CONCLUSIONS

The business model concept has come into wide usage in recent years, something which even the delimited review provided within this chapter has shown. Usage has been within a variety of fields, and different meanings have been ascribed to the concept. In the chapter we have delimited to the literature and approaches conceptualizing business models as representing the relationship between the structural, resource-related attributes of an organization on the one hand and its agentic objectives on the other hand, and observed that one may distinguish between the subgroups normative, descriptive and analytical approaches within this kind of literature. When applied to the case of medical biotechnology, the existing business model conceptualizations have been valuable contributions to the field, however, they may be improved by way of attempting further efforts of an analytical kind. This is because the existing approaches either offer relatively few analytical or too many technical categories for distinguishing between distinct business models. As a supplement to the existing approaches this study has contributed a new way of classifying classes of business models, based on the dimensions exploration versus exploitation and end market distance versus end market proximity (cf. Table 14.1).

Implications for Public Policy.

In connection with the formulation and implementation of public policy this new way of distinguishing between classes of business models offers the advantages of retaining a relatively simple classification scheme, at the same time as the peculiarities of the business models represented within the sector may be addressed in a feasible way (cf. examples in Table 14.2). There might in a particular nation or region be plans for developing a biotechnology related labor market, infrastructure or innovation policies. Regarding the latter one concern might be the fostering of particular skills deemed especially necessary for certain segments of the cluster, for example, marketing, collaboration, negotiation, or general management skills. In connection with subsequent plans for targeted interventions, policymakers invariably confront a cluster of medical biotechnology firms, which might be difficult to have a complete, or even partial, overview of. One easy way out would be to perceive of the entire cluster as consisting of more or less homogenous firms, and implement uniform policy measures for the entire cluster. An alternative could be to draw support from existing descriptive accounts based on particular technical areas, however, this might turn out to be a challenging task in itself as well as result in unintended consequences of the implemented policies. The proposed approach may, depending on further refinement, provide aid in such situations, since single subclasses or entire business model classes may be targeted in connection with the interventions.

It should be possible to perform policy related analyses of an entire cluster according to the business models classes perspective, and subsequently arrive at conclusions as to whether the firms which are being studied belong to the targeted categories. In other words, the results of an analysis can for example tell if a policy appropriate for a type of activities dominant within explorative business model classes is in the process of being implemented towards exploitative business model classes, or vice versa.

Directions for Future Research

While the advantage of the proposed approach is the ability to operate at a level between the sector and microdescriptive levels, it is simultaneously a disadvantage of the proposed approach that some of the resulting categories are rather broad. The two business model classes termed as exploitative and hybrid are within existent approaches each inhabited by a number of different business models. This is in one sense not inconsistent with the proposed approach when it comes to distribution along the vertical axis (end market distance or proximity), but may be the source of problems in connection with, for example, policy formulation. For instance, in the case of the exploitative business model class, there may be as different end market distant business models such as various types of consultancy firms (the "Orchestrator model" in McKelvey (2008) or Schweitzer (2005) terms), bioinformatics firms and other information related firms such as biobanks (McKelvey's "information model"), contract research firms (McKelvey's "contract research model"), and firms specializing within a specific field, such as TransGenic Inc. (McKelvey's "pure tool and component model"). A similar situation may arise within the hybrid business model classes, as these may be perceived of as accommodating rather disparate concrete cases such as "theranostics" (Gilham, 2002), that is, an integration between the therapeutic and diagnostic fields, as well as combinations between delivery techniques and therapeutics like in the CosMED case. Carna Biosciences was in this paper assessed as a predominantly exploitative firm due to the focus on drug discovery support, but its business model is nevertheless appropriately located within the hybrid class due to the simultaneous drug discovery support, drug discovery, and drug development activities. Given the importance and increase of such hybrid business models within the sector (Rothman & Kraft, 2006) focus on the nature of hybridity could be a separate and prioritized area for further research.

In order to overcome this potential disadvantage the overall framework proposed here could be combined with developing the hybrid and exploitative "columns" at more detailed levels whenever necessary, at the same time as the broad trends and patterns regarding exploration versus exploitation and end market proximity versus distance is kept at the centre of the analysis.

The current study is based mostly on a qualitative and interpretative assessment of the way the firms present their own activities, supplemented with available quantitative information regarding products, technologies, number and types of alliances, and the like for each firm. Methodologically, it will in connection with more full-fledged surveys be necessary with more explicit and concrete criteria for classifying activities according to the exploration—exploitation dimension as well as according to the market distance—proximity dimension. Such objective criteria will necessarily have to be developed and tested in the context of concrete research or policy implementation projects. However, limited to the knowledge exploration versus exploitation dimension, some indicators could include the following:

- Amount and type of capitalization
- Ratio of scientists in relation to overall workforce
- Ratio of R&D expenditures in relation to turnover
- Patents or patent applications
- Number and type of products or services in terms of complexity
- Assumed and actual time for developing a product or service
- Number and types of horizontal and upstream networking and collaboration activities
- Expenditures on training and education

For the vertical market distance—proximity dimension a tentative and first list could be as follows:

- Turnover
- Number of products on the market
- Number of products or services in the pipeline
- Number and types of commercial networking and collaboration activities, including types of clients or customers

Limitation of the Study

This study was focusing on some of the methodological issues regarding classification, while focusing on innovation activities and relations with clients, customers and collaborators. Hence, the study did not focus explicitly in an extensive degree on another "core" element of the business models discourse, that is, value creation mechanisms and relations with venture capitalists or shareholders. The lack of a holistic approach including reflections on actual or potential value creation mechanisms resulting from being placed within particular business model classes is due first and foremost to a need for delimitating the study. Nevertheless, the presentations and discussions are obviously implicitly relevant to the issue of value creation, such as in the construction of the overall framework where placement towards the exploitative end of the continuum assumes short term investments and short term revenues, compared with vice versa towards the explorative end of the continuum. Incidentally, the increase of hybrid forms have been interpreted as precisely the attempt at creating a balance between these two strategies (Rothman & Kraft, 2006).

Furthermore, the study is predominantly methodological and tentative in nature. The empirical examples are limited, and, as mentioned in the previous subsection, a more large scale application of the perspective according to rigorous criteria for assessment is warranted for in order to demonstrate the usefulness of the perspective for research and, not least, policy formulation.

CONCLUSIONS

The study contains implications for theory and policy concerns as follows. For theory development, the call for theoretical advancement of the business concept, as formulated by, for example, Teece (2010) and Zott et al. (2011), has within this chapter been addressed by way of retaining simplicity and consistency, at the same time as an advancement from the abstract and general level into a more operational level is suggested. Regarding policy-related concerns, it might in some cases be a tendency towards using rather broad conceptualizations regarding sectors, firms and (more recently) business models in connection with formulating and implementing innovation policies and other policies. If the medical biotechnology sector is regarded as consisting of only a few and dominant business models, such a perspective might result in a challenging policy process at best, or the risk for serious errors underway at worst. Alternatively, if the sector is considered as consisting of a multitude of business models, which is in essence true, it becomes equally difficult to handle both research and policy tasks. At the same time policymakers are aware of the need for new approaches and alternative conceptualizations (McKelvey, 2008), and analytically based approaches such as the one proposed here might be useful in such a context. It is unfeasible to operate with too many and detailed technical distinctions within the policy context, but it will perhaps be both possible and useful to be able to observe and distinguish analytically between business models at the intermediate level. The suggestion being proposed here is that the analytical basis or starting point for such an endeavor is to develop analytical categories such as knowledge explorative, hybrid or exploitative, as well as end market distant, dual or proximate.

In sum, both within the theory and policy domains the business model concept may be a promising avenue towards increased and simultaneous attention being placed on both agency and structure aspects of organizations, and thereby enable meaningful analytical distinction between firms within one and the same sector. There is, however, considerable work remaining when it comes to relating the abstract and general treatment of the concept on the one hand, and theoretically based nevertheless more operational and empirically informed conceptualizations on the other hand. Hopefully this chapter has been able to contribute in such a respect.

ACKNOWLEDGMENTS

The author would sincerely like to thank for the hospitality in connection with a visit to AnGes MG in 2008, and also like to thank discussant Laura James and other participants at the workshop *Perspectives on knowledge dynamics and innovation* in Oslo, 6 December 2011, for helpful comments when presenting a draft version of the chapter.

REFERENCES

Amit, R., & Zott, C. (2001). Value creation in e-business. *Strategic Management Journal, 22*(6-7), 493-520. doi:10.1002/smj.187

AnGes MG. (2011). AnGes MG, Inc. Retrieved from http://www.anges-mg.com

Asheim, B. T., & Coenen, L. (2005). Knowledge bases and regional innovation systems: Comparing Nordic clusters. *Research Policy, 34*(8), 1173-1190. doi:10.1016/j.respol.2005.03.013

Barney, J. B. (2001). Is the resource-based "view" a useful perspective for strategic management research? Yes. *Academy of Management Review*, 41-56.

Bio Centre (Ed.). (2005). *Bio Venture Dai-Zen*. Tokyo: Nikkei Biotech/Nikkei Bio Business.

Carna Biosciences. (2011). Carna Biosciences. Retrieved from http://www.carnabio.com

Casper, S. (2000). Institutional adaptiveness, technology policy, and the diffusion of new business models: The case of German biotechnology. *Organization Studies, 21*(5), 887-914. doi:10.1177/0170840600215003

Cavalcante, M. S. A., Kesting, P., & Ulhøi, J. P. (2011). Business model dynamics and innovation: (Re) establishing the missing linkages. *Management Decision, 49*(8), 1327-1342. doi:10.1108/00251741111163142

Child, J. (1972). Organizational structure, environment and performance: The role of strategic choice. *Sociology, 6*(1), 1-22. doi:10.1177/003803857200600101

Cooke, P. (2005). Rational drug design, the knowledge value chain and bioscience megacentres. *Cambridge Journal of Economics, 29*(3), 325-341. doi:10.1093/cje/bei045

CosMED. (2011). CosMED Pharmaceutical Co. Ltd. Retrieved from http://cosmed-pharm.co.jp

Dubosson-Torbay, M., Osterwalder, A., & Pigneur, Y. (2002). E-business model design, classification, and measurements. *Thunderbird International Business Review, 44*(1), 5-23. doi:10.1002/tie.1036

European Union. (2005). *European Union fact sheet: The Biotechnology Industry 4.* Luxembourg: Publications Office of the European Union

Fisken, J., & Rutherford, J. (2002). Business models and investment trends in the biotechnology industry in Europe. *Journal of Commercial Biotechnology, 8*(3), 191-199.

Gassmann, O., Reepmeyer, G., & Von Zedtwitz, M. (2008). *Leading pharmaceutical innovation: Trends and drivers for growth in the pharmaceutical industry.* Berlin, Germany: Springer Verlag.

Gilham, I. (2002, Fall). Theranostics: An emerging tool in drug discovery and commercialization. *Drug Discovery World,* 17-23.

Gilsing, V., & Noteboom, B. (2005). Exploration and exploitation in innovation systems: The case of pharmaceutical biotechnology. *Research Policy, 35,* 1-23. doi:10.1016/j.respol.2005.06.007

Gupta, A. K., Smith, K. G., & Shalley, C. E. (2006). The interplay between exploration and exploitation. *The Academy of Management Journal, 49*(4), 693-706.

He, Z. L., & Wong, P. K. (2004). Exploration vs. exploitation: An empirical test of the ambidexterity hypothesis. *Organization Science, 15*(4), 481-494. doi: 10.1287/orsc.1040.0078

Hedman, J., & Kalling, T. (2003). The business model concept: Theoretical underpinnings and empirical illustrations. *European Journal of Information Systems, 12*(1), 49-59. doi:10.1057/palgrave.ejis.3000446

Ichijo, K. (2002). Knowledge exploitation and knowledge exploration. In C. W. Choo & N. Bontis (Eds.), *The Strategic Management of Intellectual Capital and Organizational Knowledge* (pp. 477-483). Oxford: Oxford University Press.

NPO Kinki Bio-industry Development Association. (2010). Kansai Bio-venture View 2010. Osaka, Japan: Author.

Lavie, D., & Rosenkopf, L. (2006). Balancing exploration and exploitation in alliance formation. *Academy of Management Journal, 49*(4), 797-818.

Levin, R. C., Klevorick, A. K., Nelson, R. R., & Winter, S. G. (1988). Appropriating the returns from industrial research and development. *Cowles Foundation Discussion Paper* (Vol. 1987). New Haven, CT: Yale University.

Luukkonen, T. (2005). Variability in organisational forms of biotechnology firms. *Research Policy, 34*(4), 555-570. doi:10.1016/j.respol.2005.03.004

Magretta, J. (2002). Why business models matter. *Harvard Business Review, 80*(5), 86-93.

Mangematin, V. (2000). Competing business models in the French biotech industry. In J. De la Mothe & J. Niosi (Ed.), *The economic and social dynamics of biotechnology* (pp. 181-204). Dordrecht: Kluwer Academic.

March, J. G. (1991). Exploration and exploitation in organizational learning. *Organization science*, 71-87. doi:10.1287/orsc.2.1.71

McKelvey, M. (2008). Health biotechnology: Emerging business models and institutional drivers *OECD International Futures Programme, 33*, 1-60.

Nadler, D. A., & Tushman, M. L. (1999). The organization of the future: Strategic imperatives and core competencies for the 21st century. *Organizational Dynamics, 28*(1), 45-60. doi:10.1016/S0090-2616(00)80006-6

Ohtaki, Y. (2005). Business model to business plan. In BioCentre (Ed.), *Bio Venture Dai Zen* (pp. 14-23). Tokyo: Nikkei Biotech/Nikkei Bio Business.

Onetti, A., Zucchella, A., Jones, M. V., & McDougall-Covin, P. P. (2010). Internationalization, innovation and entrepreneurship: Business models for new technology-based firms. *Journal of Management and Governance* (Online First), 1-32. doi:10.1007/s10997-010-9154-1

Osterwalder, A. (2004). The business model ontology: A proposition in a design science approach. *Academic Dissertation, Universite de Lausanne, Ecole des Hautes Etudes Commerciales, 2*.

Osterwalder, A., & Pigneur, Y. (2010). *Business model generation: A handbook for visionaries, game changers, and challengers*. Hoboken, NJ: Wiley.

Osterwalder, A., Pigneur, Y., & Tucci, C. L. (2005). Clarifying business models: Origins, present, and future of the concept. *Communications of the association for Information Systems, 16*(1), 1-25.

Pisano, G. P. (2006). *Science business: The promise, the reality, and the future of biotech*. Boston, MA: Harvard Business School Press.

Rasmussen, B. (2010). *Innovation and commercialisation in the biopharmaceutical industry: Creating and capturing value*. Cheltenham, England: Edward Elgar.

Rothaermel, F. T., & Deeds, D. L. (2004). Exploration and exploitation alliances in biotechnology: A system of new product development. *Strategic Management Journal, 25*(3), 201-221. doi:10.1002/smj.376

Rothman, H., & Kraft, A. (2006). Downstream and into deep biology: Evolving business models in top tier genomics companies. *Journal of Commercial Biotechnology, 12*(2), 86-98.

Schweizer, L. (2005). Concept and evolution of business models. *Journal of General Management, 31*(2), 37-56.

Seppänen, M. (2009). Empirical classification of resources in a business model concept. *Intangible Capital, 5*(2), 102-124. doi:10.3926/ic.2009.v5n2.p102-124.

Teece, D. J. (2007). Explicating dynamic capabilities: the nature and microfoundations of (sustainable) enterprise performance. *Strategic Management Journal, 28*(13), 1319-1350. doi:10.1002/smj.640

Teece, D. J. (2010). Business models, business strategy and innovation. *Long Range Planning, 43*(2-3), 172-194. doi:10.1016/j.lrp.2009.07.003

Teece, D. J., Pisano, G., & Shuen, A. (1997). Dynamic capabilities and strategic management. *Strategic Management Journal, 18*(7), 509-533. doi:10.1002/(SICI)1097-0266(199708)18:7

Tidd, J., & Trewhella, M. J. (1997). Organizational and technological antecedents for knowledge acquisition and learning. *R&D Management, 27*(4), 359-375. doi:10.1111/1467-9310.00071

TransGenic   Inc.   (2011).   TransGenic   Inc.   Retrieved   from   http://
www.transgenic.co.jp
Zott, C., & Amit, R. (2007). Business model design and the performance of entrepreneurial firms. *Organization science, 18*(2), 181-199. doi:10.1287/
orsc.1060.0232
Zott, C., & Amit, R. (2008). The fit between product market strategy and business
model: Implications for firm performance. *Strategic Management Journal,
29*(1), 1-26. doi:10.1002/smj.642
Zott, C., & Amit, R. (2010). Business Model Design: An activity system perspective. *Long range planning, 43*(2-3), 216-226. doi:10.1016/j.lrp.2009.07.004
Zott, C., Amit, R., & Massa, L. (2011). The business model: Recent developments
and future research. *Journal of Management, 37*(4), 1019-1042. doi:10.1177/
0149206311406265

CHAPTER 15

MANAGING INNOVATION IN SOFTWARE ENGINEERING IN JAPAN

Yasuo Kadono

ABSTRACT

The objective in this chapter is to better understand the mechanisms of how software engineering capabilities relate to IT firms' business performance and business environment in a challenging era for the Japanese software industry. To this end, we designed a research survey to look into software engineering capabilities, and administered it, together with Japan's Ministry of Economy, Trade and Industry. Focusing on management of software engineering innovation, the common order effects originating with human resource development along the paths of service innovation, product innovation, and process innovation were empirically verified based on the data-centric approach. Based on the panel analysis, several series correlations among the software engineering capabilities were proved. The longitudinal analysis suggested positive relationships among software engineering capabilities and profitability in the long-term. However, the relationships among the software engineering capabilities and business performance vary significantly depending on the origin of a vendor: maker-turned, user-turned or independent. Therefore, in formulating public policy

Global Perspectives on Technological Innovation, pp. 461–496

proposals to promote software engineering innovation, we should consider both the individual characteristics and the organizational inertia, broken down by type of vendor.

INTRODUCTION

Many companies in Japan that use enterprise software have not been fully satisfied with the quality, cost, and productivity of software that IT vendors deliver, or the speed of delivery. At the same time, IT vendors in Japan are facing drastic changes in their business environment, such as technological innovations and new entrants from emerging countries, for example, China and India. Also, there are particular issues that are present in the IT industry in Japan, such as vendors relying on multilayer subcontractors and on business models that depend on supplying custom-made applications for the domestic market (Cusumano, 2004; Kadono, 2007). In fact, in 2009, the information service industry was a 10.5 trillion yen market in Japan, of which 7.6 trillion yen was for software development and programming; orders for software totaled 6.4 trillion yen, accounting for 60.3% of the entire information service industry, while the software products market was 1.2 trillion yen (Ministry of Economy, Trade and Industry [METI], 2010).

The structure of the software industry in Japan is shown in Figure 15.1, analyzed using the five forces model (Porter 1980). The buyers in the right-side box include IT user companies, while the suppliers in the left-side box include hardware vendors and temporary staffing as a variable cost. The central box shows three types of origin of software vendors in Japan, namely, maker-turned, user-turned, and independent vendors. Maker-turned vendors are hardware suppliers or subsidiary companies of them, that is, computer makers. User-turned vendors are subsidiary companies of buyers, that is, IT user-companies such as financial firms, and iron and steel companies. The independent vendors are neither maker-turned vendors nor user-turned vendors. The upper box shows new competitors: offshore IT vendors from China and India are emerging in the Japanese market. The lower box shows the recent trend in which Japanese purchasers expect to obtain packaged software and cloud computing, instead of custom-made software. Policymakers, such as the Japanese government, especially the METI, who used to be very active in the high-speed growth era of the Japanese economy, are considered to be a sixth force.

Informed by the five forces model, we interviewed experts in the IT industry and searched the literature, and so came up with the following as environmental threats to the industry: new entrants, for example, China and India; U.S./EU vendors; difficulty in recruiting bright people; low-profitability; low-growth; mature oligopoly; packaged software, for example, enterprise resource planning (ERP); decline in IT demand; quick delivery requests by clients; price-cutting requests by clients; quality requirements by clients; region of interest (ROI) requirements by clients; low IT literacy of clients; self-development by clients; shortage of subcontractors; new technology adoption; product differentiations; switching vendors by clients; software engineering capability erosion; decreasing numbers of bright IT students; turnover problem; M&A; retirement of senior software engineers; stagnation in IT innovation (Kadono, Tsubaki, & Tsuruho, 2009).

In order for the IT industry in Japan to meet these challenges, an important step is to understand how software engineering capability as a core competence for the industry is significant for achieving medium- and long-term success. Therefore, we designed a research survey on software engineering capabilities and administered it in 2005, 2006, and 2007, in collaboration with METI and Information-Technology Promotion Agency (IPA).

The objectives of the research were to:

1. assess the achievements of the software engineering discipline, as represented by IT vendors in Japan, and

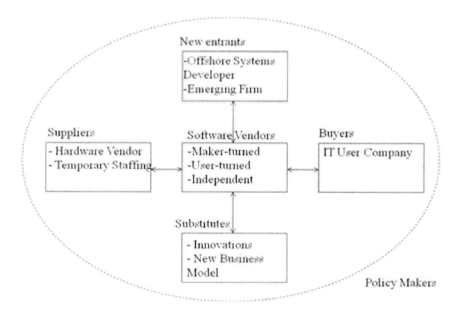

Figure 15.1.   The five forces model of software industry in Japan.

2. better understand the mechanisms of how software engineering capabilities relate to IT vendors' business performance and business environment.

To achieve these objectives, we developed a measurement tool called software engineering excellence (SEE), which can be used to evaluate the overall software engineering capabilities of IT vendors based on these seven factors: deliverables, project management, quality assurance, process improvement, research and development, human resource development, and customer contact. We introduced two other indicators as well: business performance and business environment. Business performance indicates the overall business performance of individual IT vendors, such as profitability, growth, productivity, and efficiency of the management. Business environment expresses the company profile and structure of an IT vendor, including, for example, origin of vendor, number of software engineers, average age of employees, business model, customer base, corporate culture. The business environment complements the relationship between the SEE and the business performance of software vendors (see Figure 15.2).

In the 2005 SEE survey, we preliminarily analyzed the relationships among SEE, business performance and business environment based on data collected from 55 major IT vendors in Japan. We conducted path analysis, by which we found that SEE factors exert a direct positive impact on business performance, and that the competitive environment directly and indirectly (i.e., via SEE) affects business performance (Kadono, Tsubaki, & Tsuruho, 2006). In the 2006 SEE survey, we increased the

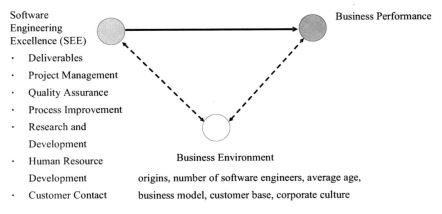

Figure 15.2.   Structural model of software engineering excellence (SEE) survey.

number of surveyed Japanese IT vendors from 55 to 78, in order to more deeply investigate the impact of software engineering on business performance and the business environment. In the 2007 SEE survey, we collected data from the top 100 major IT vendors in Japan. Since the sample size of each type of vendor, that is, maker-turned, user-turned and independent, is thought to be large enough to perform stratified analysis, we statistically investigated the differences in characteristics attributable to vendors broken down by origin.

This chapter is organized as follows. In the next section, our research model, that is, measurement models, is discussed in connection with related literature. Then, the SEE survey is introduced. In the subsequent sections, the structural models, the analysis results, and the implications for the management of software engineering innovation are presented, based on the following research questions. Finally, the contributions of the present chapter and directions for future work are discussed.

Research Question 1 (RQ1): What are the common causal relationships among the seven SEE factors and business performance, discoverable from SEE2006 and SEE2007?

Research Question 2 (RQ2): What are the differences in the causal relationships among the seven SEE factors and business performance, looking separately at each type of vendor, maker-turned, user-turned and independent?

Research Question 3 (RQ3): How does each SEE factor influence the other SEE factors within a given year; the same SEE factor in the future; and the other SEE factors in the future?

Research Question 4 (RQ4): Do IT firms with high software engineering capabilities tend to keep and improve a high level of profitability in the long-term?

RESEARCH MODEL

The model we used to measure SEE (Kadono, Tsubaki, & Tsuruho, 2006) was originally developed based on interviews conducted with over 50 industry experts in Japan and the United States, and on literature searches done during the surveys period (Barney, 2007; Carnegie Mellon University, n.d.; Dierickx & Cool, 1989; Fujimoto, 2003; IEEE, Computer Society, 2004; Ministry of Economy, Trade and Industry; Portor, 1980). The measurement model for 2007 was modified slightly based on: the response rate for each question item; the statistical significance of each observed response obtained in the 2005 and 2006 SEE surveys; and recent changes in technology and market trends.

An aim of this research is to encourage innovation, so, in developing our measurement model, we also surveyed state-of-the-art cases, paying attention to the management of innovation, especially service, process, and product. Therefore, the scope of the survey included the resource-based view of vendors, informed by which we also paid attention to factors such as degree of rarity and inimitability of the management resources (Barney, 2007). Moreover, informed by the viewpoint of service science, we see that project management and customer contact are on the border-line between user and vendor of software, so we expanded the questionnaire to include user-side items.

The SEE measurement model is also understood to be complementary to existing models, such as Fujimoto's manufacturing capability model, software engineering body of knowledge (SWEBOK), and Carnegie Mellon University's capability maturity model integration (CMM/CMMI).

First, based on the manufacturing capability model (Fujimoto, 2003) in the automobile industry, we went into greater depth, with question items exploring IT vendors' routines and deep competitiveness, that is, human resource development, project management, quality assurance, process improvement, research and development, and customer contact; and superficial competitiveness, that is, deliverables.

Second, existing Process Improvement models in the field of software were explicitly included inside the SEE model in the following way. Regarding SWEBOK (IEEE, Computer Society, 2004), we reviewed the SWEBOK knowledge areas and adopted the following areas into the SEE model to address IT vendors' innovative capabilities in process and product: software requirements, software design, software construction, software testing, software maintenance, software configuration management, software engineering management, software engineering process, software engineering tools and methods, and software quality. Regarding CMM/CMMI (Carnegie Mellon University), we adopted into the SEE model the certification levels from one to five, so as to access the process improvement factor, since we considered these levels to be a symbolic assessment measure of Process Improvement capability in software engineering.

Third, as already mentioned, since project management and customer contact are on the borderline between vendor and user of software, we enhanced the question items on these factors, for example, top management involvement, and quality of user requirement specification, consistent with insights obtained from service science (Stauss, Engelmann, Kremer, & Luhn, 2008).

Based on these considerations, we came up with the SEE measurement model. The SEE measurement model has a hierarchical structure with three layers: observed responses to question items, seven detailed factors, and SEE as a primary indicator. SEE as we have defined it consists of the following seven factors:

- Deliverables: achievement ratios on quality, cost, speed, and productivity; understanding of project information;
- Project Management: project monitoring, assistance to project managers, project planning capability, PMP (project management professional) ratio;
- Quality Assurance: organization, methods, review, testing, guidelines, management of outsourcers;
- Process Improvement: data collection, improvement of estimation, assessment methods, CMM/CMMI (Carnegie Mellon University's capability maturity model integration);
- Research and development: strategy, organization, sharing of technological skills, learning organization, development methodology, intellectual assets, commoditized software, readiness for state-of-the-art technology;
- Human resource development: training hours, skill development systems, incentive schemes, measurement of human resource development, moral support;
- Customer contact: ratio of prime contracts, scope of services offered, direct communication with customers' top management, deficit prevention, and clarification of user specifications.

Business environment includes the following items:

- origin of vendor: maker-turned, user-turned, or independent,
- number of software engineers, including programmers,
- average age of employees,
- business model: ratio of customized development, ratio of prime contractors,
- customer base: manufacturing, service, utility, etc.
- corporate culture: aspirations of senior managers, spirit of challenge, information sharing, agility.

Business performance includes items such as:

- profitability: operating profit ratio,

- growth: sales growth ratio,
- productivity: sales per person,
- efficiency: capital ratio.

SURVEY ON SOFTWARE ENGINEERING EXCELLENCE

Based on the measurement model, we conducted surveys on Software engineering excellence in 2005, 2006, and 2007, together with Japan's METI, and IPA. We designed a questionnaire on the practice of software engineering and the nature of the responding company. This questionnaire was sent to the CEOs of major Japanese IT vendors with over 300 employees, as well as the member firms of the Japan Information Technology Services Industry Association (JISA), and was then distributed to the departments in charge of software engineering.

In the 2005 survey, there were 55 valid responses, a response rate of 24%; and in the 2006 survey, there were 78 valid responses, a response rate of 15% (Table 15.1). In the 2007 SEE survey, responses were received from 117 companies, with a total of 100 valid responses, a response rate of 10%. In the 2007 SEE survey, the sample size of each type of vendor, that is, maker-turned, user-turned, and independent, was large enough to perform stratified analysis. For the panel analysis in the subsequent sections, we have integrated the 233 valid responses received over the three years into a new database including 151 unique companies, consisting of 42 maker-turned vendors, 33 user-turned vendors, and 76 independent vendors.

After collecting data from vendors in 2005, 2006, and 2007, we calculated the standardized factor loadings of the seven factors—deliverables, project management, quality assurance, process improvement, research and development, human resource development, and customer contact—through confirmatory factor analysis, based on the responses received to

Table 15.1.   Software Engineering Excellence Surveys

Year	2005	2006	2007	Total*
Questionnaires sent	230	537	1,000	NA
Valid responses	55	78	100	151
Maker-turned	17	27	27	42
User-turned	15	15	20	33
Independent	23	36	53	76
Response rate (%)	24	15	10	NA

*Total number of unique respondents over the three surveys.

the questions relevant to the measurement model described in the previous subsection.

For example, the deliverables score of SEE is estimated using responses to the relevant question items, such as achievement ratios of quality, cost, and delivery, productivity, and understanding of project information. The median quality, cost, and delivery achievement ratios are over 70% for all three types of vendor (Figure 15.3). Quality, cost, and delivery achievement levels for user-turned vendors tend to be higher than those for maker-turned vendors and independent vendors.

One of the SEE questions used to measure human resource development asks about the number of training hours for new recruits. For new recruits, the median is over 400 training hours per year (Figure 15.4), whereas for other experienced software engineers, another Human Resource Development measurement item queried in the survey, the median is almost 40 hours per year (Figure 15.5). This tendency observed in the 2007 survey results was also observed in the 2005 and 2006 results. Maker-turned vendors tend to invest relatively more time training engineers than do other types of vendors.

The measurement model is fitted to the data by confirmatory factor analyses to estimate the scores for the seven SEE factors. Then we estimate the overall SEE score each year by principal component analysis,

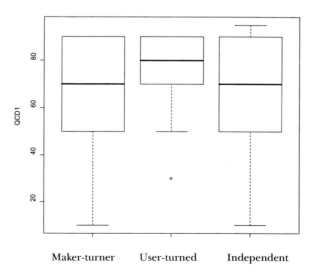

Figure 15.3.   Quality, cost and delivery achievement ratios (%) for SEE survey respondents in 2007.

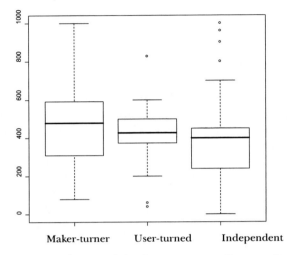

Figure 15.4.   Software engineer training hours per year for experienced workers.

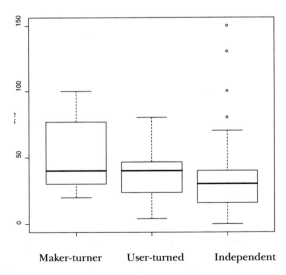

Figure 15.5.   Software engineer training hours per year for new recruits.

that is, SEE2005, SEE2006 and SEE2007. For example, a histogram of deviations of the SEE2006 score is shown in Figure 15.6, and a scatter plot diagram matrix of the seven factors and SEE2006 is shown in Figure 15.7.

Figure 15.8 contains box-and-whisker plots showing that the median SEE of the maker-turned vendors is higher than that of the user-turned vendors, which, in turn, is higher than that of the independent vendors. However, the maximum SEE of the independent vendors is higher than that of the user-turned vendors. This tendency in SEE2007 is the same as in SEE2005 and SEE2006.

In the subsequent sections, to further investigate the relationships among the SEE factors, business performance, and business environment, we perform statistical analyses such as path analysis, cross-section analysis, and panel analysis, based on the SEE surveys for 2005 through 2007 and financial data in the long-term.

BASE MODEL AND CROSS-SECTION ANALYSIS RESULTS

The purpose of this section is to clarify, through cross-section analysis based on the 2007 survey, the common mechanism of how the management of software engineering innovation relates to the business performance of IT vendors. By analyzing data collected from 100 major IT vendors, we reproducibly observe that a higher effort level on human resource development, quality assurance, and project management is

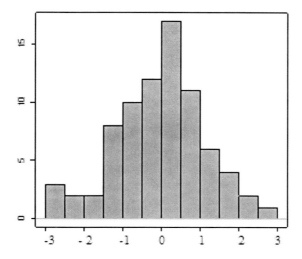

Figure 15.6.   Histogram of deviations of SEE2006.

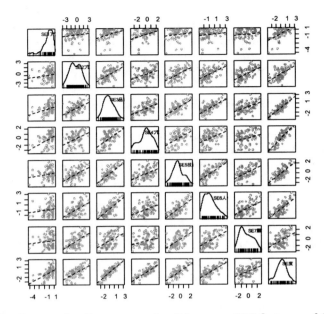

Figure 15.7.   Scatter plot diagram matrix of the seven SEE factors and SEE2006.

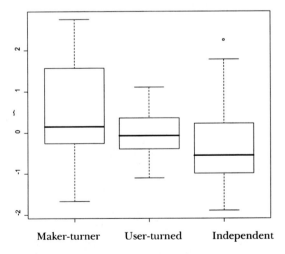

Figure 15.8.   Deviations of SEE by origin of vendors.

associated with better performance in customer contact, research and development, process improvement, and deliverables, consistent with the 2006 survey results.

However, the relationships among the above capabilities and business performance differ significantly by origin of vendor, that is, maker-turned, user-turned or independent. In maker-turned vendors, indicators of innovation, including service innovation, for example, project management, and customer contact; process innovation, for example, quality assurance, and process improvement; and product innovation, for example, research and development; are all mutually interrelated, effectively originating with human resource development. By contrast, in user-turned vendors, indicators of software engineering innovation are probably attributable to a management policy of paying extra attention to business performance. Among independent vendors, human resource development is the only factor that positively and significantly influences the other software engineering capabilities and business performance.

Structural Model and Hypothesis

In this section, we will think about the following research questions.

Research Question 1 (RQ1): What are the common causal relationships among the seven SEE factors and business performance, discoverable from SEE2006 and SEE2007?

Research Question 2 (RQ2): What are the differences in the causal relationships among the seven SEE factors and business performance, looking separately at each type of vendor, maker-turned, user-turned, and independent?

In order to answer the research questions, we construct the structural model, based on the empirical results of the 2006 SEE survey, interviews with IT industry experts, and literature searches.

First, we consider the hypothesis underlying the structural model for SEE2007, based on the empirical results from SEE 2006. On the basis of the data collected from 78 firms in SEE2006, we succeeded, by a trial and error method, in constructing a well-fitted path model (CFI = 1.0), where all the existing path coefficients are significant at the 5% level (Kadono, Tsubaki, & Tsuruho, 2008). As shown in Figure 15.9, superior deliverables and business performance correlate significantly with effort expended, particularly on human resource development, quality assurance, research and development, and process improvement. In more detail, we found the following from SEE2006, through the use of a structural equation model (Bollen, 1989).

Among the SEE factors, human resource development is positioned in the uppermost stream. Human resource development has a positive impact on quality assurance, project management and customer contact. Quality assurance and customer contact have direct negative impacts on the operating profit ratio. These paths suggest that the costs of quality assurance and customer contact do not pay off. However, indirectly, quality assurance and customer contact have positive impacts on the operating profit ratio via a positive influence on process improvement, deliverables, and research and development. Research and development has a direct positive impact on the operating profit ratio. Also, Process Improvement has a positive impact on the operating profit ratio via Deliverables. These tendencies are similar to the results from the previous study, SEE2005 (Kadono, Tsubaki, & Tsuruho, 2006).

Second, based on the interviews with IT vendors and experts in Japan and the United States, we identified three key factors for successful innovations: sales force management, operational improvement, and R&D. Some vendors who manage their sales force effectively succeed in efficiently assigning their software engineers to upcoming customer projects. As a result, one such vendor operates at an average of 90% capacity. Other

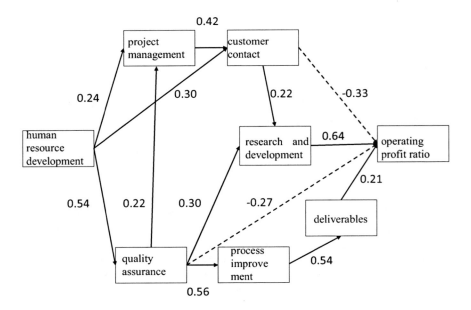

Figure 15.9.   Path analysis results from the 2006 SEE survey.

profitable vendors have accumulated data on quality, cost, delivery, and productivity for more than 30 years in order to improve their operations (Kaizen). Most large-scale system integrators in Japan work very hard on R&D activities, in addition to doing effective sales force management and efficiently improving their operations. These three key factors are considered to be innovations in service, process, and product, respectively (Dodgson, Gann, & Salter, 2008).

Third, we conducted literature searches relating to innovation. The manufacturing capability model (Fujimoto, 2003) for the automobile industry suggests that organizational routines finally influence business performance through both deep competitiveness, for example, quality, productivity, product, and development lead-time; and superficial competitiveness, for example, cost, delivery time, and product appeal power. Therefore, we considered the order effect on the three innovation paths in the structural model: IT vendor's routines and deep competitiveness, for example, from project management to customer contact, and from quality assurance to process improvement; superficial competitiveness, that is, deliverables; and business performance, that is, operating profit ratio.

As shown in Figure 15.10, we assume the structural model hypothesis, proceeding from development of human resources development through refinement of deliverables toward improvement in business performance by leverage from the following three types of innovation in the management of software engineering:

- Service innovation: proceeding from human resource development to project management and customer contact, shown in the upper level;
- Product innovation: proceeding from human resource development to research and development, shown in the middle level; and
- Process innovation: proceeding from human resource development to quality assurance and process improvement, shown in the lower level.

Results

Addressing RQ1, that is, comparison of causal relationships between 2006 and 2007, based on the structural model in Figure 15.10 and the data collected from 100 major IT vendors in the 2007 SEE survey, we constructed a well-fitted path model by a trial and error method as shown in Figure 15.11. Compared with the results from the 2006 SEE survey (Figure 15.9), we reproducibly observed that a higher level of

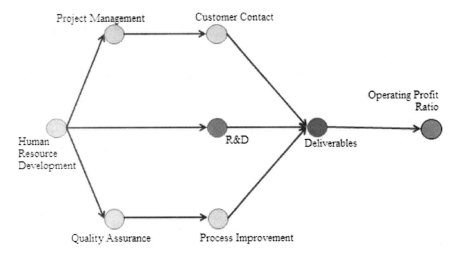

Figure 15.10.   Structural model hypothesis.

effort expended on human resource development, quality assurance, and project management significantly improved the performance of IT vendors in Japan in customer contact, research and development, process improvement, and deliverables, the same tendency that we found in 2006 (Kadono, in press). On the other hand, the paths from customer contact, research and development, quality assurance, and deliverables to operating profit ratio are not significant.

Addressing the management of innovation (Dodgson, Gann, & Salter, 2008) and the manufacturing model (Fujimoto, 2003), the process innovation paths from human resource development through quality assurance and process improvement, that is, routines and deep competitiveness, do not reach operating profit ratio, that is, business performance, but do significantly reach deliverables, that is, superficial competitiveness. However, the deep competitiveness paths of service and product innovations relating to project management, customer contact, and research and development, reach neither superficial competitiveness nor business performance. Also, no relationship was observed between superficial competitiveness and business performance.

Addressing RQ2, that is, the differences among types of vendors, the causal relationships differ significantly depending on vendor origin, i.e. whether the business is a maker-turned vendor, a user-turned vendor or an independent vendor.

First, we constructed a well-fitted path model for the maker-turned vendors (CFI = 1.0, p = 0.84), where all the path coefficients are signifi-

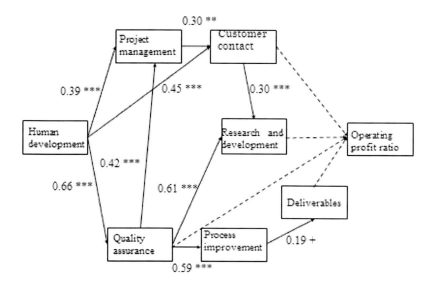

*** p < 0.001, ** p < 0.01, * p < 0.05, + p<0.10

Figure 15.11.   Path analysis results of the 2007 SEE survey

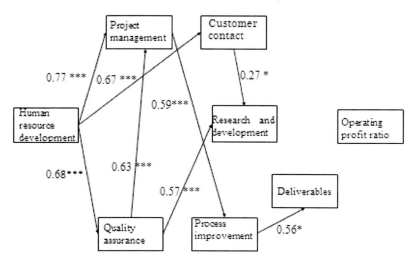

*** p < 0.001, ** p < 0.01, * p < 0.05

Figure 15.12.   Path analysis results for maker-turned vendors, from SEE2007.

cantly positive at the 5% level. The causal relationships of the maker-turned vendors shown in Figure 15.12 are similar to the overall structure found in the 2007 SEE survey (Figure 15.11) except for the following points. The path from project management to process improvement is significantly positive. Moreover, the path coefficient 0.56 from process improvement to deliverables is much higher than that in the overall model (0.19). In addition, the paths from human resource development to research and development through quality assurance and customer contact are significantly positive. However, the path from quality assurance to process improvement and the path from project management to Customer Contact are not significant.

Second, we constructed a well-fitted path model for the user-turned vendors (CFI = 1.0, p = 0.89), where all the path coefficients are significantly positive at the 5% level. As shown in Figure 15.13, it is a salient feature of the user-turned vendors that all of the seven SEE factors are connected to operating profit ratio either positively or negatively. The direct paths from project management, research and development, and process improvement to operating profit ratio are significantly positive. On the other hand, the direct paths from human resource development, quality assurance, customer contact, and deliverables to operating profit ratio are significantly negative.

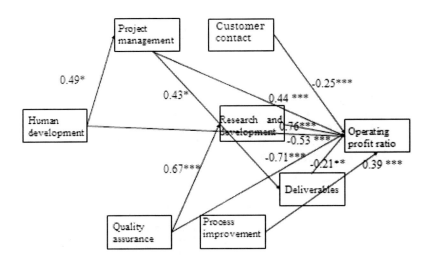

*** p < 0.001, ** p < 0.01, * p < 0.05

Figure 15.13.   Path analysis results for user-turned vendors, from SEE2007.

Third, we constructed a well-fitted path model for the independent vendors (CFI = 1.0, p = 0.79), where all the path coefficients are significantly positive at the 5% level. It is remarkable in Figure 15.14 that human resource development significantly and positively influences all the other factors of deep competitiveness, superficial competitiveness, and business performance, that is, project management, quality assurance, process improvement, customer contact, research and development, operating profit ratio and deliverables (at the 10% significance level), whereas the positive direct paths from human resource development to quality assurance, project management, and customer contact are similar to those shown in the overall structure in Figure 15.9. In addition, there are significant relationships from quality assurance to project management, from project management to process improvement, and from process improvement to customer contact.

Implications and Discussion

The purpose of the SEE surveys, carried out in collaboration with METI and IPA, was to clarify the mechanism of how software engineering capabilities are reflected in the business performance of IT vendors. In this chapter, we have described the structural model arrived at through

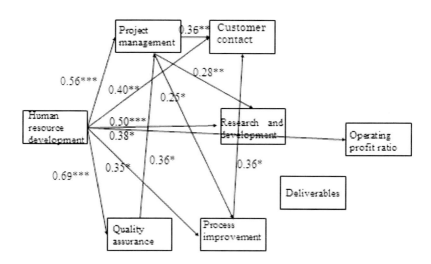

*** p < 0.001,   ** p < 0.01,   * p < 0.05

Figure 15.14.   Path analysis results for independent vendors from the 2007 SEE.

interviews with IT industry experts, literature searches and the results obtained empirically from the SEE surveys administered in 2005 and 2006. We have then investigated and compared the causal relationships among the seven SEE factors and business performance, paying attention to any differences between the 2006 SEE survey results and the 2007. Also, based on the 2007 survey, we have analyzed the differences in the causal relationships, broken down by origin of IT vendor, that is, maker-turned, user-turned, and independent.

We have analyzed the data collected from 100 major IT vendors in Japan in the 2007 SEE survey, and reproducibly observed that the more effort they put into human resource development, quality assurance and project management, the better their performance in customer contact, research and development, process improvement, and deliverables. This is consistent with a similar tendency that emerged from the 2006 SEE survey. In the context of Fujimoto's manufacturing model, we have found, through a cross-section analysis of the 2007 SEE survey results, that IT vendors' routines and deep competitiveness bring about improved superficial competitiveness, but they do not significantly improve business performance. However, we have also found that the relationships between the SEE factors and business performance factors vary significantly depending on vendor origin.

In the case of the maker-turned vendors, the causal relationships are similar to the overall causal relationships found in the 2007 SEE survey (Figure 15.11) except that the path from project management to process improvement is significantly positive and that the path coefficient from process improvement to deliverables is much higher than that in the overall model. In the causal relationships for maker-turned vendors it is salient that the paths from human resource development through quality assurance, project management and process improvement toward deliverables are connected positively and highly significantly. Also, human resource development has an overall positive impact on the other factors at the 15% significance (Kadono et al., 2009)

Focusing on the management of software engineering innovation, these results suggest that service innovation, process innovation and product innovation are mutually interrelated, effectively originating with human resource development in the maker-turned vendors. However, these innovations do not lead to improvement in business performance, that is, operating profit ratio, but reach superficial competitiveness, that is, deliverables, partially through process improvement.

In the case of the user-turned vendors, a salient characteristic among the causal relationships is that all of the seven SEE factors exert an effect on the operating profit ratio, either positively, as with project management, research and development, and process improvement, or negatively, as with human resource development, quality assurance, customer contact, and deliverables. It is notable that only project management as deep competitiveness positively and significantly influences both superficial competitiveness, that is, deliverables, and business performance, that is, operating profit ratio, as evaluated by standardized overall effects, including both direct and indirect effects.

Although the paths from human resource development to operating profit ratio by way of project management are significantly positive, the direct path from human resource development to operating profit ratio negates these positive effects overall. Similarly, although the paths from quality assurance to operating profit ratio by way of research and development are significantly positive, the direct path from quality assurance to operating profit ratio negates these positive effects overall. These results suggest that negative sources, such as human resource development, quality assurance, customer contact, and deliverables, do not pay off in the short-term, similar to the way in which the paths from quality assurance and customer contact to operating profit ratio are significantly negative in the 2006 SEE survey results. Even so, these efforts might possibly be expected to exert longer-term effects on other SEE factors.

Focusing on the management of software engineering innovation, each software engineering capability should probably be considered separately, without considering order effect of the innovations. In other words, if we focus on the operating profit ratio affected by each SEE factor, as shown in Figure 15.13, it appears that the parent companies of user-turned vendors might not care about the negative relationships, but do pay attention to their business performance attributable to management policy. Probably this indicates that management focuses strongly on business performance and makes it a priority.

In the case of the independent vendors, human resource development significantly and positively influences all the other factors including deep competitiveness, superficial competitiveness, and business performance. Also, human resource development is the only one of the seven SEE factors that has overall significantly positive impact on deliverables, that is, superficial competitiveness, and on operating profit ratio, that is, business performance. These characteristics are unique to the independent vendors, distinguishing them from maker-turned vendors and user-turned vendors (Kadono et al., 2009).

Overall, research and development is positively and significantly influenced by human resource development, project management, quality assurance, and process improvement; however, research and development does not exert significant influence on either deliverables, that is, superficial competitiveness, or operating profit ratio, that is, business performance. It appears to be difficult for independent vendors to get a payoff in the short-term from Research and Development.

These results imply that Human Resource Development in particular is a key success factor for independent vendors. There are also significant relationships from quality assurance to project management, from project management to process improvement, and from process improvement to customer contact. These paths suggest that there are mutual connections between service innovation and process innovation, which has implications for the management of software engineering innovation.

To better understand the relationships between the SEE factors and the business performance of Japanese IT vendors, panel analysis in the long-term should be an effective method. Beyond the cross-section analysis results presented in this section, we go on in the next section to perform a panel analysis on the software engineering capabilities of the uniquely identified firms that responded to the SEE surveys in 2005 through 2007. Then, in the subsequent section, we conduct a panel analysis including both the software engineering capabilities and the long-term financial data of the firms.

RELATIONSHIPS AMONG SOFTWARE ENGINEERING CAPABILITIES

We integrated 233 valid responses to the SEE surveys received over three years into a new database and identified 151 unique IT firms (Table 15.1). Then we conducted panel analyses of the seven SEE factors, using the three years of data, to clarify what influence SEE factors have within a year, year-to-year, and midterm.

Based on the results of the panel analysis, our first observation is that most SEE factors in one year have significant positive influences on the same factor the next year. Second, within a year, there are three paths to improving the level of deliverables, that is, through project management, quality assurance and research and development. Third, some SEE factors have significant positive influence diagonally on different SEE factors in the following year. Fourth, there are some negative paths, implying that efforts put toward a particular factor do not pay off within the duration of our research. Even so, these efforts might be expected to exert longer-term positive effects on other SEE factors.

Structural Model and Hypothesis

In this section, we think about the following research question.

Research Question 3 (RQ3): How does each SEE factor influence the other SEE factors within a given year; the same SEE factor in the future; and the other SEE factors in the future?

In other words, the research question here is how a SEE factor influences the other SEE factors horizontally, vertically or diagonally, as illustrated in Figure 15.15.

As discussed in the previous section, based on the interviews with successful IT vendors in Japan, we identified three key factors for successful vendors: sales force management, operational improvement, and R&D. Some vendors who manage their sales force effectively succeed in efficiently assigning their software engineers to upcoming customer projects. For example, a user-turned vendor with successful sales force management operates at an average of 90% capacity; and other profitable vendors have accumulated data on quality, cost, delivery, and productivity for more than 30 years, in order to improve their operations. Most large-scale system integrators in Japan emphasize the importance of R&D activities, in addition to doing effective sales force management and efficiently improving their operations.

The hypothetical structure within each year (horizontally) is approximately consistent with the empirical results obtained from the SEE 2006 and the SEE 2007 surveys, as shown in the previous section. Therefore, within each year (horizontally), we assume three paths to improvement of deliverables, for example, quality, cost, and delivery, which relate to the management of technological innovation (Dodgson, Gann, & Salter, 2008) as follows: in the upper level of Figure 15.15, service innovation, from human resource development to project management and customer contact; in the middle level, product innovation, from human resource development to research and development; and, in the lower level, process innovation, from human resource development to quality assurance and process improvement.

Also, vertically, year-to-year, we assume that each SEE factor at a firm has series correlation. For example, if a vendor has a high human resource development factor score in 2005, it also has a high human resource development factor score in 2006: the tendency should continue in 2007. In addition, diagonally, we assume mid-term effects among SEE factors. For example, if a vendor invests in human resource development in 2005, we look to see good R&D results in 2006.

Concepts of service science provide useful insights when considering users and vendors of IT. Out of the seven SEE factors, project management and customer contact are on the borderline between users and vendors of the software; and deliverables are the common goal of both users and vendors. Vendors alone should be responsible for the other SEE factors,

namely, human resource development, quality assurance, process improvement, and R&D. In this section, we also investigate the relationships among
the seven factors from the viewpoint of service science (Stauss, Engelmann,
Kremer, & Luhn, 2008).

Results

Based on the structural model hypotheses, we conducted a panel analysis of the data from the 233 valid responses we had received from 151
unique firms in the 2005, 2006, and 2007 surveys. The results of the
panel analysis are shown in Figure 15.16. We found the following to be
characteristics of the relationships among the seven SEE factors over the
3 years.

Vertically, year by year, most SEE factors each have significant influence
on the same factor in the following year. For example, human resource
development in 2005 influenced human resource development in 2006,
which, in turn, influenced in 2007. The same holds true for quality assurance and deliverables. There are two exceptions. Project management in

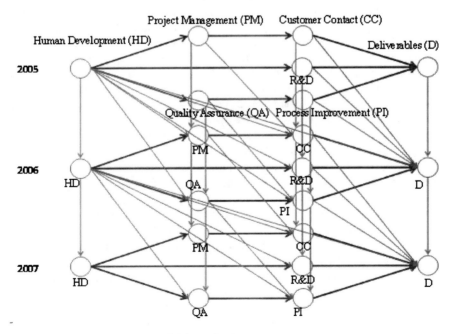

Figure 15.15.   Structural model hypothesis.

2005 did not seem to affect PM in 2006, nor did process improvement in 2005 seem to influence PI in 2006. Horizontally (within each year), most causal relationships are similar, and they are generally consistent with the results of the 2006 SEE survey.

Diagonally, some SEE factors have significant influence on different factors in the following year. Examples are human resource development in 2005 and 2006, which influenced R&D in 2006 and 2007, respectively; and process improvement in 2005 which impacted deliverables in 2006. There are some negative paths, such as R&D in 2005 and 2006 which negatively influenced deliverables in 2006; process improvement in 2006 which had a negative impact on deliverables in 2007; and project management in 2006 which negatively influenced customer contact in 2007 (Kadono, 2011).

Implications and Discussion

In this section, we integrated 233 valid responses to three surveys on software engineering excellence into a new database and identified 151

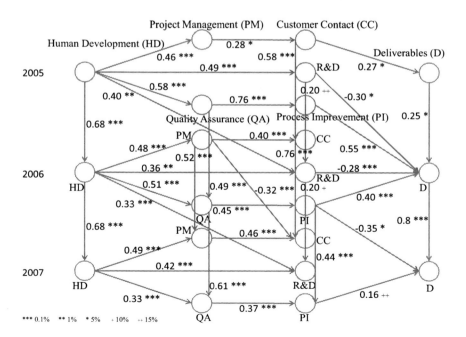

Figure 15.16.   Panel analysis results ($N = 151$).

unique IT vendors in Japan, of whom 42 were maker-turned vendors, 33 were user-turned vendors and 76 were independent vendors. We investigated the relationships among the SEE factors over 3 years to clarify how they influence future SEE factors horizontally, vertically and diagonally. Within a year (horizontally), we assumed three paths toward improved deliverables (quality, cost, and delivery): through service innovation, which includes project management and customer contact; through product innovation, including R&D; and through process innovations, including quality assurance and process improvement. Also, year-to-year (vertically), we assumed that each factor would be consistent due to series correlation. In addition, diagonally, we assumed midterm effects, such as that vendors who invest in human resource development in 2005 may be expected to see the results of that investment in their R&D in 2006.

On the basis of the structural model hypotheses, we conducted panel analysis using the integrated data from the 2005, 2006 and 2007 SEE surveys. As a result of panel analysis, we found characteristic relationships among the seven SEE factors for the three surveyed years. Vertically, most SEE factors each have significant influence on the same SEE factor in the following year. Thus human resource development in 2005 influences human resource development in 2006, which in turn affects human resource development in 2007. These results indicate that IT vendors build on the SEE factor levels that they have achieved thus far. Horizontally, most causal relationships each year are similar and are generally consistent with the results of the SEE 2006 survey results. The structural consistency between different years implies that there are three paths to improving the level of deliverables through service innovation (project management and customer contact), related to service science; through product innovation (R&D); and through process innovation (quality assurance and process improvement). Diagonally, some SEE factors have significant influence on different SEE factors in the following year, such as the case of human resource development in 2005 and 2006, which influenced R&D in 2006 and 2007, respectively. These influences suggest medium-term positive effects. However, there are some negative paths, such as from R&D in 2005 and 2006 to deliverables in 2006; from process improvement in 2006 to deliverables in 2007; and from project management in 2006 to customer contact in 2007. The negative paths imply that effort expended on some factors does not pay off. Even so, these efforts might be expected to have positive long-term effects.

Comparing with existing models, we empirically confirmed part of Fujimoto's manufacturing capability model for automobile companies (Fujimoto, 2003). This model hypothesized that the organizational routines and deep competitiveness, for example, quality, productivity, and product development lead-time, influence the superficial competitiveness, for example, cost and delivery time, as well as business performance. In the context of the software industry, we have empirically proved in this section that superior deliverables, for example, quality, cost, and delivery, an aspect of superficial competitiveness, has significant correlations with effort expended on routines and deep competitiveness, that is, human resource development, project management, quality assurance, process improvement, R&D, and customer contacts, as shown horizontally within a year in Figure 15.16.

Statistically, we confirmed the series correlation. Once a factor loading of a certain SEE factor becomes high, it tracks itself in the next year and continues to be high. For example, we empirically proved high path coefficients among human resource development factors in 2005 through 2007. Similar tracking phenomena were observed generally, except for the paths of project management between 2005 and 2006, and process improvement between 2005 and 2006.

From the viewpoint of service science, project management and customer contact are on the borderline between users and vendors of the software. In each year (horizontally), project management significantly influences customer contact. And, vertically, year by year, customer contact in 2005 and 2006 exerts significant influence on the same factor in the following years. Also, project management in 2006 significantly influenced project management in 2007.

In the panel analysis in this section we have focused on software engineering capabilities in 2005, 2006, and 2007; however, the full range of relationships among capabilities, business environment, and business performance, which are discussed qualitatively in Fujimoto's manufacturing capability model, are also fundamental issues in this chapter (Figure 15.1).

Regarding the business environment, we analyzed the relationships of threats, strengths/weaknesses and the number of software engineers, broken down by vendor type, that is, maker-turned, user-turned and independent vendors (Kadono, Tsubaki, & Tsuruho, 2009). The results of analysis suggested that the maker-turned vendors significantly tend to expand business by, for example, new acquisition of patents, well-resourced R&D, offshore system development, and offshore client development. In contrast, the user-turned vendors seem to depend heavily on demand from their parent companies; thereby, some of them are thought to gain inimitable capabilities, including knowhow on a specific function and inimitable products/services. In contrast again, many of the independent vendors, lacking specific strengths, merely supply temporary staff to principal contractors. However, some independent vendors that do have inimitable assets and are not threatened by industry stagnation seem to be role models for software vendors in Japan.

To expand the results of the present section, it is important to better understand the long-term relationships between the SEE factors and business performance of Japanese IT vendors. Simultaneously, we need to further investigate the series correlation we have discussed in this section. Therefore, in the next section, we perform a panel analysis on the relationships between software engineering capabilities and business performance, that is, long-term financial data of the 151 identified firms, based on longitudinal modeling.

LONG-TERM RELATIONSHIPS BETWEEN SOFTWARE ENGINEERING CAPABILITIES AND PROFITABILITY

This section aims at better understanding the relationships among software engineering capabilities and profitability, as a component of, and representing, business performance, of software vendors in the drastically changing IT industry in Japan. To do so, by characterizing both intra-class and serial correlation among the repeated measurements of each firm, we apply a latent growth curve model including latent factors corresponding to the level and the growth of the long-term business performance in 1999 through 2008. Based on longitudinal modeling of the 3-year SEE data and ten-year operating profit ratio of the 151 respondents to the SEE surveys, we empirically verify that IT firms who have excellent software engineering capabilities tend to maintain and improve their business performance in the medium and long term.

Structural Model

In this section, we think about the following research question.

Research Question 4 (RQ4): Do IT firms with high software engineering capabilities tend to keep and improve a high level of profitability in the long-term?

Recalling the empirical results obtained from the 2006 SEE survey, and in particular the finding that superior deliverables and business performance correlated with the effort expended particularly on human resource development, quality assurance, research and development, and process improvement at 5% significance, and recalling also our interviews with successful IT vendors in Japan, we hypothesize that the firms that have excellent software engineering capabilities do tend to maintain and improve their business performance in the medium and long term.

Therefore, we assume a path model as shown in Figure 15.17. Here, SEE consists of SEE2005, SEE2006 and SEE2007. Taking the operating profit ratio as a component of, and representing, business performance, we identified 151 unique IT firms that responded to the three SEE surveys, and we calculated their operating profit ratios from 1999 through 2008, relying on accounting data supplied by a Japanese credit research firm. To better and more effectively characterize both intraclass and serial correlation among the repeated measurements of each firm, we adopted a latent growth curve model (Meredith & Tisak, 1990), including two latent factors corresponding to the level (intercept) and the growth (slope) of the operating profit ratio for 10 years.

Results

Based on the hypothetical structural model shown in Figure 15.17, we conducted path analysis of the data from the 233 valid responses we had

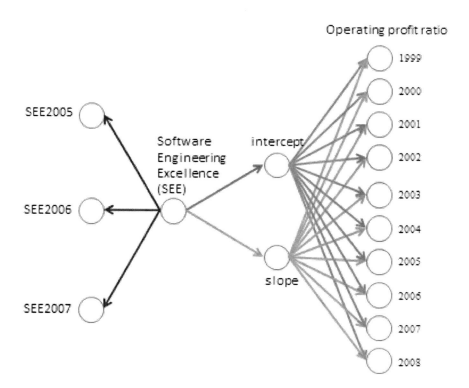

Figure 15.17.   Structural model hypothesis.

received to the 2005, 2006, and 2007 surveys from 151 unique firms (Bollen, 1989). The result of the path analysis is shown in Figure 15.18. We found the following to be characteristics of the significant relationships among 3-year SEE scores and 10-year operating profit ratios (CFI = 0.415). Regarding SEE, overall SEE is related to SEE2005, SEE2006 and SEE2007 at 0.1% significance. Overall SEE has a positive impact on the intercept of operating profit ratio for 10 years at 10% significance. Also, overall SEE has a positive impact on the slope of operating profit ratio for 10 years at 5% significance (Kadono, Tsubaki, & Tsuruho, 2011).

Implications and Discussion

In this section we significantly verified that firms that have excellent software engineering capabilities tend to maintain and improve their business performance, that is, operating profit ratio, in the medium and long term. We arrived at this conclusion by longitudinal modeling, drawing on the data obtained from the three annual SEE surveys and 10 years of financial data obtained from IT vendors who responded to the SEE surveys. We focused

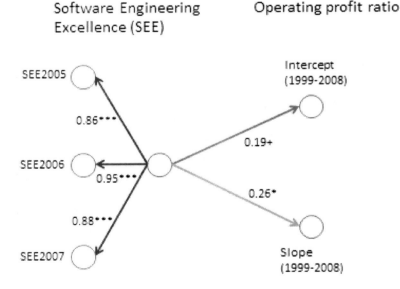

***: p<0.001   * : p<0.05   + : p<0.1

Figure 15.18. Path analysis results.

on the relationship between an overall SEE score, derived from the three surveys, and the 10-year operating profit ratio, as a component of, and representing, business performance (Figures 15.17 and 15.18). In other words, the contribution of the research is to empirically verify the relationship between the software engineering innovation level just before the cloud computing era began, and long-term financial data for the period just before Lehman's fall. However, it is a limitation of this research that SEE scores are available extending over only 3 years.

For a future study, we intend to expand this initial longitudinal model so that we can analyze the relationships among the seven SEE factors, that is, deliverables, project management, quality assurance, process improvement, research and development, human resource development, and customer contact, as against financial indicators such as productivity, and stability of management, in addition to profitability.

CONCLUSIONS

The objective in this chapter was to better understand the mechanisms of how software engineering capabilities relate to IT vendors' business performance and business environment in a challenging era for the Japanese software industry. To this end, we designed a research survey to look into software engineering capabilities, and administered it in 2005, 2006 and 2007, together with Japan's METI and IPA. We received responses to the 2007 SEE survey from 117 companies, of which a total of 100 were valid, a response rate of 10%. There were 55 valid responses to the 2005 survey (a response rate of 24%), and 78 for 2006 (a response rate of 15%), including the largest class system integrators in Japan.

For further analysis, we integrated the 233 valid responses received over the three years into a database including 151 unique companies consisting of 42 maker-turned vendors, 33 user-turned vendors, and 76 independent vendors. Then we performed several statistical analyses upon the standardized software engineering capability scores for the 3 years and the financial data for 10 years, for examples, path analysis, cross-section analysis, panel analysis, longitudinal analysis, stratified analysis, and the latent growth model.

Through the cross-section analysis on the 2007 survey, we reproducibly observe that a higher effort level on human resource development, quality assurance, and project management brings about better performance in customer contact, research and development, process improvement, and deliverables; this was consistent with the 2006 survey results. Focusing on management of software engineering innovation, the common order effects originating with human resource development along the paths of service innovation, product innovation, and process innovation were empirically verified based on the data-centric approach.

Based on the panel analysis of the seven SEE factors, several series correlations among the software engineering capabilities were proved. Our first observation is that most SEE factors in 1 year had significant positive influences on the same factor the next year. Second, within a year, there were three paths to improving the level of deliverables, that is, through project management, quality assurance, and research and development. Third, some SEE factors exerted significant positive influence on different SEE factors in the following year diagonally. Fourth, there were some negative paths, implying that effort put toward a particular factor did not pay off. These results suggest that each IT vendor needs to know its own nature based on the path dependency and make the most of what it has.

The longitudinal analysis based on the latent growth model suggested relationships among software engineering capabilities and profitability, as a component of, and representing, business performance, in software vendors in the drastically changing IT industry in Japan. Based on the panel analysis of the 3-year SEE data and 10-year operating profit ratio of the 151 respondents to the SEE surveys, we significantly verified that IT firms that have excellent software engineering capabilities tend to maintain and improve their business performance in the medium and long term. Equally, the series correlations of a firm's financial performance were observed to correspond to those of its software engineering capabilities.

However, the relationships among the seven SEE factors and business performance vary significantly depending on the origin of a vendor: maker-turned, user-turned or independent. If we focus on the management of innovation, then, in maker-turned vendors, service innovation, process innovation, and product innovation are effectively connected. However, in user-turned vendors, any indicated software engineering innovation is probably attributable to a management policy of paying extra attention to business performance. In independent vendors, human resource development is the only factor that positively and significantly influences the other capabilities and business performance.

Implications for Public Policy

These results imply the following contemporary perspectives on technological innovation, management and policy. Based on the longitudinal analysis, we verified that there are significant positive relationships between the sophistication of software engineering capabilities and the superior performance of IT vendors in the long-term. At the same time, through the panel analysis of the seven SEE factors, several series correlations among the software engineering capabilities were proved. For example, most SEE factors in 1 year had significant positive influences on the same factor the next year. It follows that the structure of the software engineering capabilities and the financial results of IT vendors should be considered to be entrenched in the long-term.

On the other hand, the relationships among the seven SEE factors and business performance vary significantly depending on the type of vendor. For example, through the stratified analysis, we found that the innovation path, that is, including service innovation, product innovation, and process innovation, varies significantly depending on the origin of a vendor, that is, maker-turned, user-turned or independent. Also, having regard to the size of vendors, we found that vendors who have a larger number of software engineers tend to get a higher SEE score (METI, IPA, 2007).

Therefore, in formulating public policy proposals to promote software engineering innovation, we should consider both the individual characteristics and the organizational inertia, broken down by type of vendor. For example, the government should encourage maker-turned vendors, especially large-scale system integrators, to accelerate state-of-the-art product innovations; to this end, the government should commission huge nationwide IT projects. On the other hand, the government should financially support small or medium-size independent vendors to help them develop human resources in software engineering. To help shape sound public policy, we think it crucial that (1) a stable measurement tool be established, such as the SEE survey, by which to measure the management of innovation in the software industry in Japan, and (2) financial reporting standards be adopted in common by corporate managers.

Limitations of the Study

Since the SEE surveys were a large-scale and costly research method, it was not practical to continue administering the surveys routinely, year after year. Therefore, we integrated the 233 valid responses received over the 3 years, 2005 through 2007, into a database including 151 unique companies, the better to perform several statistical analyses, such as a longitudinal analysis of the relationships between the SEE scores and the financial data from 1999 through 2008. We proved several findings that are statistically significant; however, the amount of the SEE data is not necessarily sufficient to perform some other statistical analyses that would be desirable, for example, stratified analysis of the SEE scores by type of vendor for any given year.

Directions for Future Research

In this chapter, we have focused on the three types of vendor, but components of the business environment, such as the number of software engineers and the business model, should also be brought into the account so as to clarify the mechanism by which they leverage software engineering innovations. For example, as noted earlier, vendors who have a larger number of software engineers tend to get a higher SEE score. This tendency is evident in the results of the three SEE surveys, 2005 through 2007. Equally, regardless of vendor type, vendors who have a larger number of software engineers tend to be less profitable. This tendency also is evident in the results of the three SEE surveys, 2005 through 2007. We need to investigate any trade-off between the advantages of scale, notably, higher SEE scores, versus the disadvantages, notably, lower profitability. In other words, the causal relationships among the SEE factors, and business performance and business environment, including, for example, the number of software engineers, business model, and average age of employees, remain to be analyzed and understood in the future (Figure 15.1).

In the global cloud computing era, to further study issues associated with the management of software engineering innovation in the Japanese IT industry, we suggest doing global comparisons of IT industry architecture; in particular, we suggest comparing the multilayered subcontractor industry in Japan with the industries in the United States, and other Asian countries, such as China, India, and others. Also, we think it important to simulate the future possible industry architecture in more detail, based on a data-centric approach and continuing fact-finding investigations, such as the SEE surveys, so as to formulate an effective national strategy for the software industry in Japan.

ACKNOWLEDGMENTS

The author gratefully acknowledges the valuable suggestions and support received from Professor Hiroe Tsubaki at the Institute of Statistical Mathematics; the Japanese Ministry of Economy, Trade and Industry (METI); the Software Engineering Center, Information-Technology Promotion Agency, Japan (SEC, IPA); Dr. Seishiro Tsuruho; the Japan Information Technology Services Industry Association (JISA); and the Management Science Institute Inc. (MSI). This research was partially supported by the grants-in-aid for scientific research from the Japan Society for the Promotion of Science (B: 20310090; C:24530497).

REFERENCES

Barney, J. B. (2007). *Gaining and sustaining competitive advantage.* Saddle River, NJ: Pearson Prentice Hall.

Bollen, K. (1989). *Structural equation with latent variables.* Hoboken, NJ: Wiley-Interscience.

Carnegie Mellon University, Software Engineering Institute. (n.d.). Retrieved from http://www.sei.cmu.edu/cmmi/

Cusumano, M. (2004). *The business of software.* New York, NJ: Free Press.

Dierickx, I., & Cool, K. (1989, Winter). Asset stock accumulation and sustainability of competitive advantage. *Management Science*, 1504-1511.

Dodgson, M., Gann, D., & Salter, A. (2008). *The management of technological innovation.* Oxford, Englang: Oxford University Press.

Fujimoto, T. (2003). *Capability-building competition.* Japan: Chuokoron-Shinsha.

IEEE, Computer Society. (2004). Guide to the software engineering body of knowledge (SWEBOK). Retrieved from http://www.computer.org/portal/web/swebok

Kadono, Y. (2007). The issues on IT industry in Japan. *Nikkei Net.* Retrieved from http://it.nikkei.co.jp/business/news/index.aspx?n=MMITac000017122007

Kadono, Y. (2011, July-September). A study on management of software engineering capability in japan using panel analysis. *International Journal of Service Science, Management, Engineering, Technology*, 20-32.

Kadono, Y. (in press). The differences in structural relationships among software engineering capabilities and business performance depending on origin of IT firm in Japan. *International Journal of Innovation and Learning.*

Kadono, Y., Tsubaki, H., & Tsuruho, S. (2006). A study on the reality and economy of software development in Japan. *Proceedings of the sixth Asia Pacific Industrial Engineering Management Systems Conference*, Bangkok, Thailand.

Kadono, Y., Tsubaki H., & Tsuruho, S. (2008). A survey on management of software engineering In Sio-long Ao (Ed.), *Current themes in engineering technologies* (pp. 267-277). College Park, MD: The American Institute of Physics.

Kadono, Y., Tsubaki, H., & Tsuruho, S. (2009). A study on characteristics of software vendors in Japan from environmental threats and resource-based view. *Proceedings of Pacific Asia Conference on Information Systems*, Indian School of Business, Hyderabad, India.

Kadono, Y., Tsubaki, H., & Tsuruho, S. (2011). Longitudinal modeling of the software engineering capabilities and profitability of software companies in Japan. *Proceedings of Technology Innovation and Industrial Management.*

Meredith, W., & Tisak, J. (1990). Latent curve analysis. *Psychometrika*, *55*, 107-122.

Ministry of Economy, Trade and Industry, and Information-Technology Promotion Agency, Japan. (2007). *Fact-finding investigation on software engineering capabilities of enterprise systems in Japan.* Retrieved from sec.ipa.go.jp/reports/20071204/SE_level_research_2006_2.pdf

Ministry of Economy, Trade and Industry, Japan. (2010). *Fact-finding investigation on the software industry in Japan.* Japan: Author.

Porter, M. (1980). *Competitive Strategy.* New York, NY: Free Press.

Stauss, B., Engelmann, K., Kremer, A., & Luhn, A., (2008). *Services science: Fundamentals, challenges and future developments.* Berlin, Heidelberg: Springer-Verlag.

ABOUT THE CONTRIBUTORS

Josh Bendickson is a doctoral student in the Rucks Department of Management at Louisiana State University. His research interests include entrepreneurship education, entrepreneurial ecosystems, and strategic management.

Tanja Bisgaard is the founder of Novitas Innovation, a company that facilitates complex innovation processes for private and public clients. Previously, she was manager of policy analysis at FORA, the Danish Ministry of Economics and Business Affairs where she worked on projects documenting the results of companies' innovation processes. She is now working on projects to understand green business models, and how cities can become more sustainable by becoming "smarter." She holds an MSc in management from the London School of Economics and Political Science, England, and a BSc in business economics from the University of Surrey, England.

Olga Bruyaka is an assistant professor of management at the Pamplin College of Business, Virginia Tech. She got her PhD at EM Lyon (France). Focusing on strategic management, her research interests include determinants of value creation and rent appropriation, strategic complementarity and wealth transfer in alliances and acquisitions, origin and implications of alliance portfolio quality and configuration. Her research has been published in *Strategic Management Journal*, *Strategic Organization*, *Revue Francaise de Gestion* and the *Academy of Management Best Paper Proceedings*. E-mail: o_bruyaka@vt.edu

Nanette Clinch is an attorney and lecturer at San Jose State University. She received her BA (English) from Mount Holyoke College, her PhD (English)

from the University of Toronto and her JD from Rutgers University Law School-Newark, NJ. Her career has included active practice as an attorney with an emphasis on civil and criminal litigation. Her research interests include the law and literature, beauty, bioethics, innovative technologies, international business ethics, religion, and women's rights. E-mail: Nanette.Clinch@sjsu.edu

Avimanyu Datta, is an assistant professor in Illinois State University. He obtained his doctorate in business administration from Washington State University. His research interest revolves around entrepreneurial activities surrounding sourcing and commercialization of radical innovations, especially in the IT and hi-tech sectors. Dr. Datta's research has appeared in numerous peer-reviewed journals: *Information Systems Research (ISR), Communication of Association of Information Systems (CAIS), Technology & Investment, Journal of Management & Strategy, International Journal of Virtual Communities and Social Network, Journal of Cases on Information Technology* and so forth. Dr. Datta has taught courses in strategy, entrepreneurship, technology innovation & electronic commerce. E-mail: adatta@ilstu.edu

Lucy Ford is a member of the management faculty at Saint Joseph's University in Philadelphia. Lucy received her PhD in organizational behavior and human resources from Virginia Commonwealth University. Her industry experience includes human resources practice in the retail goods industry, and consulting on learning and development in numerous industries. At Saint Joseph's University she teaches courses in organizational behavior, managing human capital, leadership, teams, and general management. Lucy's research explores various aspects of leadership and teams, and the impact of collaboration in the workplace, with a particular emphasis on research methods used to examine these phenomena in context. E-mail: lford@sju.edu

Devi R. Gnyawaliis, R. B. Pamplin professor of management at Virginia Tech. His research seeks to understand how firms acquire and develop intangible relational resources and internal resources and how they leverage such resources to create competitive advantages. His research also examines drivers, dynamics, and consequences of competition (simultaneous pursuit of collaboration and competition). His research has been published in prestigious journals, including *Academy of Management Review, Academy of Management Journal, Information Systems Research, Journal of Management, Journal of Management Studies, and Research Policy.* He currently serves on the editorial board of *Academy of Management Review* and *Journal of Management.* E-mail: devi@vt.edu

Carolyn Green joined the School of Business at Texas A&M University-San Antonio in the fall of 2001 while it was a System Center under the auspices of Texas A&M University-Kingsville. She received a BS in mathematics and a PhD in business administration with an emphasis in management information systems from the University of Houston. Dr. Green is currently the director of the Center for Information Technology and Cyber Security and an associate professor in computer information systems. Prior academic appointments include faculty positions at the University of Houston and the University of Texas at Brownsville. E-mail: carolyn.green@tamusa.tamus.edu

Terje Grønning received his PhD in applied sociology from Ritsumeikan University in Japan in 1992, with the thesis *Human Value and "Competitiveness": On the Social Organization of Production at Toyota Motor Corporation and New United Motor Manufacturing, Inc.* His publications on Japanese and Norwegian business and working life include "Biotechnology in Norway: A Marginal Sector or Future Core Activity?" (chapter in *Innovation, Path Dependency and Policy*, edited by J. Fagerberg et al., Oxford University Press, 2009), and he also contributed to the OECD publication *Innovation in Pharmaceutical Biotechnology: Comparing National Innovation Systems at the Sectoral Level* (OECD, 2006). E-mail: terje.gronning@ped.uio.no

Tracy Hurley joined the School of Business at Texas A&M University-San Antonio in the Fall of 2000 while it was a System Center under the auspices of Texas A&M University-Kingsville. She received a BBA in Finance, and MBA, and a PhD in business administration with an emphasis in management and a minor in statistics from the University of Houston. Dr. Hurley is currently the head of the School of Business, an associate professor in management, and the MBA coordinator. She also manages the university's e-book program and is the Chair of the Southwest Teaching & Learning Conference. E-mail: tracy.hurley@tamusa.tamus.edu

Len Jessup, PhD, is the Halle chair in leadership and professor of entrepreneurship and innovation in the Eller College of Management, University of Arizona. Before that Dr. Jessup held numerous positions in Washington State University (WSU): Philip L. Kays distinguished professor in management information systems, dean of the College of Business, vice president of WSU Foundation, and chair of combined department of entrepreneurship and information systems. Dr. Jessup has taught in entrepreneurship, management, and information systems, and has published, presented, and consulted on electronic commerce, computer-supported collaborative work, technology-supported teaching and learning, emerging information technologies, entrepreneurship, leadership, commercialization, technology transfer, and related topics.

Yasuo Kadono received the bachelor's and master's degrees in applied mathematics and physics from Kyoto University, and the PhD degree in business administration from Tsukuba University. He is currently a professor at Tokyo University of Technology and a visiting professor at Tokyo University of Foreign Studies, Japan. He has extensive experience in industry at McKinsey & Company, Accenture, Sumitomo Metal Industries and Management Science Institute. He has also produced important research projects in academic, business, and government circles. His teaching and research interests include management, strategy, and information technology. E-mail: kadono@msi21.co.jp

Kathleen P. King, EdD, is professor and coordinator of the higher education doctoral programs at University of South Florida's College of Education in Tampa, FL. Her major areas of research and expertise include distance learning, transformative learning, faculty development, instructional technology, and diversity. The International Continuing and Adult Education Hall of Fame recognized Dr. King's outstanding contributions to adult and higher education with her 2011 induction. As an award winning author who has published 21 books, she is also a popular keynote and conference speaker, mentor, and professor. You may reach "Kathy" via www.TransformationEd.com or e-mail: KathleenKing@usf.edu

Mette Praest Knudsen is professor of innovation management and research manager of the integrative innovation management (I2M) unit at the University of Southern Denmark. Her research focuses on three topic areas. First, she has investigated open innovation and ways to operationalize it, the dark sides of open innovation adoption, and the effect of negative attitudes on open innovation implementation. Second, her research centers on ecoinnovation and the effect of pursuing ecological aspects on product innovation performance. Third, she studies outsourcing and back shoring of production and research and development activities. Her research has been published in journals such as *Journal of Product Innovation Management, Industrial and Corporate Change*, and *Technovation*. E-mail: mpk@sam.sdu.dk

Eric W. Liguori is an assistant professor of entrepreneurship in the Craig School of Business at California State University, Fresno. His research interests include entrepreneurial self-efficacy, entrepreneurial ecosystems, and entrepreneurship education. E-mail: eliguori@csufresno.edu

Joshua Maurer is a doctoral student in the Rucks Department of Management at Louisiana State University. His research interests include entrepreneurial intentions, entrepreneurial networks, and entrepreneurial self-efficacy.

Asbjorn Osland is a professor of management at San Jose State University. He received his PhD and MBA degrees from Case Western Reserve University, MSW from the University of Washington and BA from the University of Minnesota. He also completed a postbac in accounting. Prior to becoming a professor in 1993, he worked in Latin America and West Africa for 13 years. During the current accreditation period (i.e., since 2006), he has 22 publications, mainly cases. Prior to 2006 he had over 50 publications. His primary interest is developing teaching materials in the form of short cases used in class. E-mail: Asbjorn.Osland@sjsu.edu

Nikolaos Pappas is lecturer in marketing (travel & tourism) at the University of Northampton, England. He holds a PhD in tourism development and a postdoctorate in destination crisis management. In terms of research, he continuously participates in internationally funded research projects since 1998. He has more than 25 publications in international scientific refereed journals and conferences. He is journal reviewer in *Annals of Tourism Research, Tourism Management,* and *Sustainable Tourism,* and book reviewer in Pearson Education. His academic interests concern tourism planning & development, risk and crisis management, e-marketing and e-tourism, destination marketing, and tourism sustainability. E-mail: nikolaos.pappas@northampton.ac.uk

Christina M. Partin, MA is a full-time sociology instructor at University of South Florida, Tampa. She has taught large and small classes online and face-to-face for over 6 years. In this time, she has trained over 25 graduate teaching assistants and taught nearly 10,000 undergraduates. Her research and doctoral studies in curriculum and instruction focus on interdisciplinary applications of instructional technology, higher education and adult learning. E-mail: cmpartin@usf.edu

Gayle Porter, is a member of the management faculty at Rutgers University in Camden, NJ. Her industry experience includes technical work in the oil and gas industry, finance, and accounting with a Fortune 500 company, and consulting on training programs and employee development. Gayle received her PhD in management and human resource from The Ohio State University. At Rutgers she teaches courses in organizational change, social responsibility, international human resource management, and performance improvement/employee development. Gayle's research explores various organizational supports for realization of employees' full potential. Her publications focus on workaholism and work ethic, and issues surrounding collaborative work. E-mail: gporter@camden.rutgers.edu

Damien Power is professor of management in the Department of Management and Marketing at The University of Melbourne. Damien holds a bachelor's degree in manufacturing management, a master's degree (by research) in business, and a PhD focusing on developing strategic models for effective business to business e-commerce implementation. He is a certified fellow of APICS at the level of CFPIM. Damien has research interests that cover supply chain management and business to business e-commerce. Damien has published over 40 articles in refereed international journals including *Journal of Operations Management, Decision Sciences, International Journal of Operations and Production Management, Supply Chain Management, IEEE Transactions on Engineering Management and Internet Research.* He has also published over 50 conference papers, numerous book chapters and coauthored/edited three books. Damien also has extensive management experience gained over a 25 year period across a range of industries including electronics, metering and food, with responsibilities ranging from project management, tender negotiation, technology transfer and facility management. E-mail: damien@unimelb.edu.au

Kheng Boon Quek completed his PhD in organization and management from the University of New South Wales in 2012. His research interest is in industry evolution, competitive advantage, firm capabilities, transaction cost, the theory of the firm, new institutional economics, institutional process, and interorganizational relations. Kheng Boon held a bachelor's of engineering (mechanical) from the University of Sydney and a master's of engineering science (industrial management) from the University of New South Wales before pursuing his doctoral degree. E-mail: kheng.quek@gmail.com

Brendan M. Richard, University of Central Florida, College of Business Administration, United States. Fields of research: networking, coproduction, creativity, entrepreneurship, dynamic capabilities, service innovation. E-mail: brichard@bus.ucf.edu

Juan Pablo Vazquez Sampere is an associate professor at IE Business School. Professor Vazquez' research examines how disruptive innovation increases new venture success rates for both entrepreneurs and established firms. He explores this issue using new research methods that can not only be replicated in a variety of industries but also be helpful to future researchers. These new research methods carefully separate between explanatory and predictive outcomes. His objective is to generate more robust predictive (causal) theories. Professor Vazquez consults regularly for large firms and the European Union on issues related to innovation and has helped cofound three companies. E-mail: jpvazquez@faculty.ie.edu

Manish K. Srivastava is an assistant professor at the School of Business and Economics, Michigan Technological University (Michigan Tech). He received his PhD in strategic management from Virginia Tech. His research has been published in *Academic Management Journal* and *Academy of Management Best Paper Proceedings* and has won awards from the Academy of Management and Strategic Management Society. His current research interests include knowledge structures of firms and strategic alliances, evolution of alliance portfolios and technological innovations. E-mail: mksrivas@mtu.edu

Stoyan Tanev is associate professor in the Institute of Technology and Innovation and member of the Integrative Innovation Management Research Unit at the University of Southern Denmark, Odense, Denmark, and adjunct professor in the Department of Systems and Computer Engineering at Carleton University in Ottawa, Canada. He has an MSc and PhD in physics (jointly by the University of Sofia, Bulgaria, and the University Pierre and Marie Curie, Paris, France), an MEng in Technology Management (Carleton University, Canada), and a MA (University of Sherbrooke, Canada). His main research interests are in the fields of technology innovation management and value cocreation.

Merethe Stjerne Thomsen is PhD candidate at the Institute of Technology and Innovation at the University of Southern Denmark, Odense, Denmark and holds a MSc in engineering with specialization in Industrial Design (Aalborg University, Denmark). She has worked 5 years in R&D at the pump manufacture Grundfos, where she was project manager in a Lead User Study in collaboration with CBS and MIT and developed a Global Design Strategy for the Grundfos Group. Her main interests are in the fields of cocreation and user involvement in new product development and the effect on the innovation performance and management.

Yue Wang received his PhD in international business from the University of Melbourne. His current research interests focus on alliance strategies and internationalization strategies of emerging-market firms. His recent publications appear in journals such as the *Management International Review, Journal of Business Research, Asia Pacific Journal of Management, Journal of International Management, Advances in International Management,* and *Thunderbird International Business Review.* Dr. Wang is the author of the book *Contractual Joint Ventures in China: Formation, Evolution and Performance* and the lead editor of the book *Thirty Years of China's Economic Reform: Institutions, Management Organizations and Foreign Investment*.

K. Mark Weaver is the Ben May chair of entrepreneurship in the Mitchell College of Business at the University of South Alabama. Dr. Weaver is a past president and fellow of both the United States Association of Small Business and Entrepreneurship and the International Council of Small Business. His research interests include strategic alliances, entrepreneurship education, and local business climate, though he is widely published in many related areas. E-mail: markweaver@usouthal.edu

CPSIA information can be obtained at www.ICGtesting.com
Printed in the USA
LVOW070808230113

316871LV00002B/12/P